ISLAM IN THE MODERN WORLD

ALSO BY SEYYED HOSSEIN NASR

A Young Muslim's Guide to the Modern World
An Annotated Bibliography of Islamic Science
An Introduction to Islamic Cosmological Doctrines
Anthology of Philosophy in Persia (ed., with Mehdi Aminrazavi)
Ideals and Realities of Islam
In Search of the Sacred (with Ramin Jahanbegloo)
Islam: Religion, History, and Civilization
Islam and the Plight of Modern Man
Islam, Science, Muslims, and Technology (with Muzaffar Iqbal)
Islamic Art and Spirituality
Islamic Life and Thought
Islamic Philosophy from Its Origin to the Present
Islamic Science: An Illustrated Study
Knowledge and the Sacred
Man and Nature: The Spiritual Crisis of Modern Man
Muhammad: Man of God
Poems of the Way
Religion and the Order of Nature
Science and Civilization in Islam
Sufi Essays
The Islamic Intellectual Tradition in Persia
The Heart of Islam
The Need for a Sacred Science
The Pilgrimage of Life and the Wisdom of Rumi
The Transcendent Theosophy of Ṣadr al-Dīn Shīrāzī
Three Muslim Sages

ISLAM IN THE MODERN WORLD

Challenged by the West, Threatened by Fundamentalism, Keeping Faith with Tradition

SEYYED HOSSEIN NASR

HarperOne
An Imprint of HarperCollins*Publishers*

HarperOne

Grateful acknowledgment goes to Seyyed Hossein Nasr, *The Garden of Truth: The Vision and Promise of Sufism, Islam's Mystical Tradition* (San Francisco: HarperOne, 2007) for permission to reprint the list of transliterations on p. xiii.

HarperCollins books may be purchased for educational, business, or sales promotional use. For information please write: Special Markets Department, HarperCollins Publishers, 10 East 53rd Street, New York, NY 10022.

HarperCollins website: http://www.harpercollins.com

FIRST HARPERCOLLINS PAPERBACK EDITION PUBLISHED IN 2012

Designed by Rosa Chae

Library of Congress Cataloging-in-Publication Data

Nasr, Seyyed Hossein.
Islam in the modern world : challenged by the West, threatened by fundamentalism, keeping faith with tradition / by Seyyed Hossein Nasr. — 1st ed.
p. cm.
ISBN 978–0–06–190581–0
1. Religious awakening—Islam. 2. Islamic renewal—Islamic countries.
3. Globalization—Religious aspects—Islam. 4. Islam—21st century. I. Title.
BP163.N373 2011
297.09'051—dc22 2010040069

12 13 14 15 16 RRD(H) 10 9 8 7 6 5 4 3 2 1

Dedicated to the Memory of Shaykh Abū Bakr Sirāj al-Dīn al-Shādhilī, al-ʻAlawī, al-Maryamī, al-Sirājī

بسم الله الرحمن الرحيم

In the Name of God, the Infinitely Good, the All-Merciful

CONTENTS

III. Tensions Between Tradition, Modernism, and "Fundamentalism"

Education

Philosophy and Science

Art and Architecture

IV. Postscript

Appendices

LIST OF TRANSLITERATIONS

Arabic and transliterated Roman characters

ء	’	ط	ṭ
ب	b	ظ	ẓ
ت	t	ع	‘
ث	th	غ	gh
ج	j	ف	f
ح	ḥ	ق	q
خ	kh	ك	k
د	d	ل	l
ذ	dh	م	m
ر	r	ن	n
ز	z	ه	h
س	s	و	w
ش	sh	ي	y
ص	ṣ	ة	ah; at
ض	ḍ	ال	(article) al- and ’l-

long vowels	
اى	ā
و	ū
ي	ī

Persian letters added to Arabic alphabet	
پ	p
چ	ch
ژ	zh
گ	g

short vowels	
ـَ	a
ـُ	u
ـِ	i

diphthongs	
ـَو	aw
ـَي	ai (ay)
ـِيّ	iyy (final form ī)
ـُوّ	uww (final form ū)

PREFACE TO THE REVISED EDITION

Since this work was first composed over two decades ago and deals not only with the immutable principles of traditional Islam, but also its confrontation and interaction with the ever changing conditions of the modern world, the preparation of this new edition has necessitated extensive revision in both the text and the references. Where necessary, the text has been revised and augmented, and all references have been brought up to date. Moreover, several new chapters and appendices have been added to make the presentation more complete. The truths presented in the original edition have not changed, but everything has been reviewed in light of all that has occurred in recent decades in the domain of traditional Islam, which is faced with unprecedented challenges from the modern world and offers diverse responses to those challenges. The aim of the original edition was primarily intellectual and religious, not political and economic, and this aim has not been revised. The aim and general structure remain the same as in the original edition, but this revised edition, in its consideration of numerous new factors, the incorporation of more recent scholarship, and the addition of much new material, is a new book.

I wish to thank the Radius Foundation, which provided financial support for the preparation of the manuscript, and Abigail Tardiff, whose heroic efforts made possible getting this revised edition ready for publication. I also wish to express my gratitude to Eric Brandt, Suzanne Quist, and the other editors at HarperOne for all their efforts in making the printing and publication of this work possible.

Seyyed Hossein Nasr
Bethesda, Maryland
July, A.D. 2009
Rajab, A.H. 1430

PREFACE TO THE ORIGINAL EDITION

The extensive interest in Islam displayed in recent years in many Western circles, far from simply helping to make the various aspects of Islam better known, has often caused confusion resulting from ignorance, misinformation, and unfortunately sometimes disinformation. Distortions of the teachings of Islam have often resulted from the negative passions that the subject arouses in certain people and from the vested interest that numerous parties have in the kind of treatment that Islam receives.

A few decades ago, Muslims could justly complain of the distortions present in studies by Western orientalists, Islamicists, and missionaries; also of the lack of interest on the part of the general Western public in matters Islamic. Today, thanks to genuine attempts by certain sections of the Islamic world to reassert their Islamic character and to seek to preserve the Islamic tradition, but even more so as a result of the unfortunate use of Islam by all kinds of political forces, some using violent means, apathy toward subjects of an Islamic nature has certainly diminished. A number of new misinterpretations have, however, arisen to supplement those of earlier orientalists and missionaries. There now exists a substantial body of journalistic treatments of Islamic subjects perpetrated in the name of scholarship (or masquerading as scholarship). Until a few years ago there was a leftist and often explicitly Marxist treatment of Islam. These days there is a new so-called resurgent or fundamentalist Islam, which currently produces a quantitatively substantial literature in European languages and plays no small role, in both words and deeds, in forming a distorted image of Islam in the West. And finally there is hate literature by both secularists and religious extremists in the West based on the open vilification of even the most sacred beliefs of Muslims.

As a result of the appearance of these and other contemporary interpretations of Islam, the task of understanding this religion as it has been lived and viewed traditionally over the centuries becomes ever more difficult for those genuinely interested in the subject. One knows who speaks for Western interpretations of Islam, who for the modernists within the Islamic world, and who for that whole spectrum of thought and action usually called "fundamentalism." But, then, who speaks for traditional Islam—the Islam lived for centuries by theologians and jurists, by philosophers and scientists, by artists and poets, by Sufis and simple people of faith throughout the Islamic world during the fourteen centuries of Islamic history—the Islam that is in fact still followed by the vast majority of Muslims from the Atlantic to the Pacific?

It is as a response to the pressing need to expound the teachings of traditional Islam that this and in fact also to a large extent my other works on Islam have been written. Almost every day an issue arises in which the view of Islam is sought, and usually either some modernistic or "fundamentalist" response from quarters bearing Islamic credentials is provided—if not simply a scholarly answer by a Western Islamicist, who may, paradoxically, occasionally provide a more balanced one, precisely because he or she is not personally entangled in the present-day intellectual tensions that beset the Islamic world. Whenever possible, I have sought to make a humble contribution to the knowledge of Islam in the West by presenting the traditional Islamic point of view precisely on such themes as are currently under debate.

In some of my earlier books, especially *Islam and the Plight of Modern Man* and *Islamic Life and Thought,* I have already provided studies of a number of traditional Islamic views that are in confrontation with the modern world. In the present volume, I continue this task by concentrating at the same time more fully upon the contrast between traditional Islam and its "revivalist" and "fundamentalist" manifestations and dealing with issues of particular significance to the Islamic world and to the Western understanding of Islam, beginning with a study of the nature of traditional Islam itself in the Prologue.

The first section then turns to some of the basic facets of the Islamic tradition that are being widely discussed and debated today, beginning with an overall study of Islam in the present-day Islamic world and then turning to the meaning of *jihād,* a term that has now become almost a household word in the West, but is still widely misunderstood and often maliciously misinterpreted. A study is then made of work ethics as described in traditional Islamic sources and found within Islamic society itself; a distinction is made between the two that seeks to bring out the permanent value of traditional Islamic work ethics and its continuing validity despite shortcomings in its application in many sectors of present-day Islamic society. In the next chapter, attention is turned to the critical question of the relationship between the male and the female in both its internal and external (social) aspects. Without simply surrendering to current fads, yet accepting the challenges posed for Islam concerning the role and position of women, I have sought to provide knowledge of the metaphysical and psychological foundations in Islam of the male-female relationship, upon the basis of which all the Islamic social aspects of the relationship must ultimately be founded.

Finally in the last chapter of the first section, Shīʿism is discussed as it developed in Safavid Persia as the state religion, thereby making available the in-depth theological and historical background necessary for an understanding of the role of Shīʿism in present-day Iran, and indeed in the whole of the Middle East, and the current relationship between Shīʿism and Sunnism. One needs to recall here that, after the death of the Prophet of Islam, the Islamic community divided on the question of who should succeed him as leader and what the function of such a person should be. The majority accepted Abū Bakr as the first successor of the Prophet, his vicegerent (caliph), and became known as *ahl al-sunnah wa'l-jamāʿah,* or Sunnis, while those who believed that ʿAlī should have become the leader came to be known as Shīʿites, who have always remained as a minority in the Islamic world. In the (A.H./A.D.) tenth/sixteenth century, however, Persia became majority Shīʿite and remains to this day the most populated Shīʿite country; there are also important Shīʿite populations in some Arab countries, Pakistan, and India. Besides Iran, one must mention Iraq, Azerbaijan, Baḥrayn, and Lebanon, which also have a Shīʿite majority among their Muslim populations, while all other Muslim countries have a Sunni majority.

The second section delves into the subject of Islamic spirituality, its relation to spirituality considered on a global scale, the various domains related to Islamic spirituality, the challenges it faces today, and its prospects in the future. The section concludes with a chapter on an issue that is central to the struggle between various forces within the Islamic world, namely, the understanding of the notion of "development" in the context in which this term is used commonly today, mostly in relation to economic growth and social change considered in their quantitative and not qualitative aspects; this concept is then evaluated in light of Islamic values and norms.

The third and longest section of this work is devoted to the study of the tensions between traditional Islam and modernism in various specific intellectual and cultural contexts. Here the first and foremost topic is education, which is such a central issue in almost every Islamic country. Then philosophy is treated, the study and teaching of which are closely related to education, on the one hand, and to the whole intellectual tension between tradition, modernism, and "fundalmentalism" on the other. This is followed by a discussion of the important subject of the similarities and contrasts between Islamic and modern science. Finally, I turn to art, architecture, and city planning, which again have become major arenas of contention within the Islamic world, arousing much passion and debate and also having a great impact upon the religious and cultural life of the whole community.

The first two appendices of this work include an account of the syllabus of traditional Islamic *madrasahs* (meaning Islamic schools offering courses on levels corresponding to secondary and college education and including all kinds of subjects, not only religious ones in the narrow sense) as well as a survey of the state of philosophy in the Islamic world today. Appendices III and IV not only seek to bring out the value of the works of exceptional academic and non-academic scholars for the understanding of traditional Islam, but also to demonstrate that traditional Islam, in contrast to modernism and "fundamentalism," bases its judgment of Western scholarship on truth and not merely on geography. Although critical of what is distorted in orientalist scholarship, the traditional perspective, as reflected in the works of Traditionalists presented here, does not allow itself to explode into sloganeering and vituperative statements simply because the author of a statement happens to be a Westerner; nor does its praise of any piece of scholarship on Islam simply arise out of an inferiority complex, because that work is produced in a Western language and uses all the paraphernalia of modern scholarship. These sections hope to make clear what Western scholarship on Islam can do and to a large extent has already done toward bringing about a better understanding when it is based upon authentic knowledge, sympathy, and love, without having to compromise either the rigor of scholarship or (of even greater importance) the demands of the truth.

Although the future, according to the Islamic perspective, belongs to God and He alone has knowledge of it, there is today so much interest in the future of the Islamic world and in making projections from present-day trends, that it seemed necessary to give some attention to this burning issue. The final chapter therefore seeks to deal with present religious and intellectual tendencies in the Islamic world and how these trends are likely to develop in the near future. This study is made with full awareness that all human knowledge and science fails to comprehend the exact stages of the unfolding of God's Will in human history and I have therefore been careful to add that in such matters God knows best.

In preparing this manuscript for publication, I wish to express my profound gratitude to Katherine O'Brien, whose aid has been indispensable. I hope that this book will be a humble step toward bringing about better understanding in the West of the views of traditional Islam and also make the teachings of the Islamic tradition more easily accessible to those Muslims whose upbringing and training make this type of exposition more comprehensible to them than truths expressed in older traditional Islamic sources. At the present moment, any step taken toward bringing about better understanding of Islam in the West cannot but be of mutual benefit to both the Islamic world and the West—two worlds whose destinies are interrelated in ways that are not always perceptible, but that embrace spiritual, artistic, and intellectual life as well as activities in the political and economic arenas—or all that constitutes both the tapestry of the inner life and that of human civilization and history as it unfolds in the matrices of time and space.

wa mā ṭāwfiqī illā bi'Llāh

ISLAM IN THE MODERN WORLD

PROLOGUE

What Is Traditional Islam?

> This is the wont [tradition] of God [*sunnat Allāh*] with those who passed before, and you will find no alteration in God's wont.
> *Quran XXXIII: 62*[1]

Two centuries ago, if Westerners, or for that matter Chinese Confucianists or Indian Hindus, were to study Islam, they would have encountered but a single Islamic tradition. Such persons could have detected numerous schools of thought, juridical, theological, and mystical interpretations, and even sects that remained separated from the main body of the community. They would, moreover, have encountered both orthodoxy and heterodoxy in belief as well as in practice. But all that they could have observed, from the esoteric utterances of a Sufi saint to the juridical injunctions of an *'ālim,* or religious scholar, from the strict religious views of a Ḥanbalite doctor of law from Damascus to the unbalanced assertions of an extreme group of Shī'ites, would have belonged in one degree or another to the Islamic tradition; that is, to that single tree of Divine Origin whose roots are the Quran and the traditions of the Prophet of Islam, or *Ḥadīth,* and whose trunk and branches constitute that body of tradition that has grown from those roots over some fourteen centuries in nearly every inhabited quarter of the globe.

Then, some two hundred years ago, the main waves of modernism began to reach the shores of the Abode of Islam (*dār al-islām*) and with the passage of time gradually inundated them. One could detect the influence of modernist ideas and movements as early as the late twelfth/eighteenth and early thirteenth/nineteenth centuries (the figure on the left refers to centuries according to the Islamic calendar, and the one on the right to the Western calendar) in certain fields, such as military science, astronomy, and medicine, in some parts, even if not all, of the Islamic world. Soon there were modernist trends in education, sociopolitical thought, and law and, somewhat later, in philosophy, architecture, and many of the arts, although the influence in painting and design can be seen even in the eleventh/seventeenth century. Finally, such trends came to be seen in certain movements within Islam itself, although during that period their influence on the religion was still quite limited. For anyone who understood the essence of modernism based on and originating in the secularizing and humanistic tendencies of the European Renaissance, it was easy to detect the confrontation that was already taking place between traditional and modern elements in the Islamic world.

Only during the past few decades has a new phenomenon appeared that necessitates distinguishing rigorously between traditional Islam and not only modernism, but also that spectrum of feeling, action, and thought that has come to be identified by Western scholarship and journalism as "fundamentalist," revivalist, or "activist" Islam. There were, needless to say, revivalist movements in the Islamic world in earlier centuries. But this earlier "fundamentalism," associated with, let us say, Salafism in the Arab world or the Deoband school of India, was, to be sure, a more or less truncated form of traditional Islam, opposed to many aspects of the Islamic tradition and highly exoteric, but it was still orthodox, and not a complete departure or deviation from traditional norms. Despite the fact that in the name of reform such movements did much to weaken and impoverish traditional Islam, they could still be understood to some extent in terms of the dichotomy between the traditional and the modern by Western standards, although their importance came to be overemphasized in Western scholarship at the expense of the truly traditional revivers of Islam. There is much more written in European languages on such figures as Jamāl al-Dīn Astrābādī, known as al-Afghānī, or Sir Sayyid Aḥmad Khān, than, let us say, on 'Abd al-Qādir al-Jazā'irī, taking into account his religious and esoteric activities and not simply his political leadership, or Shaykh al-'Alawī.[2]

Today, however, alongside the modernist trend, which stands against traditional Islam, there is a whole series of so-called fundamentalist movements that speak of reviving Islam in opposition to modernism and Western civilization, which for several centuries served as the soil in which modernism grew and was nurtured, but that are also not traditional and in fact stand opposed to traditional Islam in basic ways. It is, therefore, precisely at this moment of history that it is crucial to distinguish these movements that have come to be called the "new fundamentalism," or simply "Islamic fundamentalism," from traditional Islam, with which they are often confused. However, anyone who has read works of a traditional nature on Islam[3] and compared them to those championed by the current "fundamentalists" can immediately discern basic differences between them, not only in content, but also in the whole "climate" in which they breathe. Needless to say, what is branded as "fundamentalism" includes a wide spectrum, parts of which are close to the traditional interpretation of certain aspects of Islam, such as jurisprudence. But the main thrust of that type of politico-religious movement now called "fundamentalism," a term that precisely because of its ambiguity is quite problematic and would have been avoided if possible, is so basically different from traditional Islam as to warrant the sharp distinction drawn between them here, despite the existence of certain areas where some types of "fundamentalism" and certain dimensions of traditional Islam might be in accord.

Before pointing out these basic differences, it is necessary to say a word about the term "tradition" as used here, as in all of my other writings. As used by the Traditionalists, the group that formed around the work of René Guénon that is rooted in the "perennial philosophy," this term implies both the Sacred as revealed to humanity through revelation and the unfolding and development of that sacred message in the history of the particular human community for which it was destined; it implies both horizontal continuity with the Origin and a vertical connection that relates each moment in the development of the life of any single tradition to the metahistorical Transcendent Reality.

Tradition, which needs to be defined universally now precisely because of the onslaught of modernism and more recently the appearance upon the scene of that caricature of tradition called "fundamentalism," is at once *al-dīn,* understood in the widest sense of the word, a sense that embraces all aspects of religion and its ramifications; *al-sunnah,* or that which, based upon sacred models, has become tradition as this word is usually understood; and *al-silsilah,* or the chain that links each period, episode, or stage of life and thought in the traditional world to the Origin, as one sees so clearly in Sufism, which represents most of the esoteric and mystical dimension of Islam. Tradition, therefore, is like a tree, the roots of which are sunk through revelation in the Divine Nature and the trunk and branches of which have grown over the ages. At the heart of the tree of tradition resides religion, and the sap of this tree consists of that grace, or *barakah,* that, originating with the revelation, makes possible the continuity of the life of the tree. Tradition implies the sacred, the eternal, the immutable Truth; the perennial wisdom as well as the continuous application of its immutable principles to various conditions of space and time.[4]

The earthly life of a tradition can come to an end—traditional civilizations can and do decay. But that decay as well as the presence of contending schools of thought, which have always existed in traditional civilizations, is still within the framework of tradition. What is directly opposed to tradition is anti- and countertradition, to which we shall turn later, and of course modernism, which is antitraditional by nature and without whose existence there would in fact be no need for the usage of such a term as "tradition." If traditionalists insist on the complete opposition between tradition and modernism, it is precisely because modernism, understood as a distinct worldview and paradigm, either denies truths of a religious or metaphysical nature or creates in the religious and metaphysical realms a blurred image within which half truths appear as the truth itself, thereby compromising the integrity of all that tradition represents.

The significance of traditional Islam can be understood more clearly in light of its attitude toward various facets of Islam. Traditional Islam accepts, of course, without any ifs, ands, or buts, the Noble Quran in both content and form as the Word of God, as the earthly embodiment of God's Eternal Word, uncreated in its essence and without temporal origin. It also accepts the traditional commentaries on the Quran, ranging from the linguistic and historical to the sapiential and metaphysical. In fact, it interprets the Sacred Text not on the basis of the literal and external meaning of the words alone or by the use of individualistic, linguistic, or historical reasoning, but on the basis of the long tradition of hermeneutics going back to the Blessed Prophet himself and relying upon oral transmission as well as written commentaries. The latter range from the works of Ḥasan al-Baṣrī and Imām Ja'far al- Ṣādiq to those composed by traditional authorities up to the present day.[5]

As for *Ḥadīth,* again the traditional school accepts the orthodox collection of the six *Correct Books,* or *Ṣiḥāḥ,* of the Sunni world and the *Four Books,* or *al-Kutub al-arbaʿah,* of Shīʿism. It is willing to consider the criticism brought forth against spurious *Ḥadīth* by modern critics. But it is not willing to accept unquestioningly the premise upon which modern criticism is based, namely, the denial of the penetration of the Sacred into the temporal order. Traditional Islam believes in divine revelation, the reality of oral transmission, and the possibility of knowledge by the Prophet on the basis of direct access to the Source of all knowledge rather than from purely human agents of transmission. Traditional Islam does not reject *Ḥadīth* because it does not accord with the modern world's conception of historical causality and philosophical historicism and the diluted meaning of revelation that has now penetrated even into modern Western religious thought. It relies upon the critical methods of *Ḥadīth* scholarship as cultivated over the centuries by traditional Muslim scholars of *Ḥadīth,* based as they are on both the historical continuity of the tradition and the *barakah* that protects the truth within a tradition as long as that tradition is alive. Traditional Islamic scholarship is also open to the consideration of all critical appraisals of the *Ḥadīth* corpus, as long as the criticism is not based on the assumption that what has left no traces in written records does not exist. The traditional perspective always remembers the famous principle of Islamic philosophy, that *ʿadam al-wijdān lā yadullu ʿalā ʿadam al-wujūd,* that is, "The nonexistence of awareness of something is not proof of its nonexistence."

Traditional Islam defends completely the *Sharīʿah,* or Divine Law, as it has been understood and interpreted over the centuries and as it has been crystallized in the classical schools (*madhāhib*) of Law and considers following it to be obligatory for all Muslims. Moreover, it accepts the possibility of giving fresh views (*ijtihād*) on the basis of traditional legal principles, which themselves provide the means of applying the Law to newly created situations, but always according to such traditional legal principles as *qiyās* (analogy), *ijmāʿ* (consensus of opinion), *istiḥsān* (judicial preference), and so forth.[6] Moreover, for traditional Islam, all morality is derived from the Quran and *Ḥadīth* and related, in a more concrete manner, to the *Sharīʿah.*

As far as Sufism, or the *Ṭarīqah,* is concerned, traditional Islam considers it the inner dimension or heart of the Islamic revelation, without denying either the state of decadence, in the sense of falling below or deviating from the traditional norms of doctrine and practice, into which certain Sufi orders have fallen over the centuries or the necessity of preserving the truths of Sufism only for those qualified to receive them. The attitude of traditional Islam toward Sufism reflects the view that was current during the centuries prior to the advent of puritanical and modernist movements in the twelfth/eighteenth century, namely, that it is the means for the attainment of sanctity for those wishing to encounter their Creator here and now and not a teaching meant to be followed by all members of the community. Again, the traditional defense of Sufism is based on the acceptance of its reality as manifested in various Sufi orders and on respect for the diversity existing within these orders, not on the identification of Sufism with a particular order or school. Nor does the traditional perspective overlook the disagreement that has existed between certain representatives of the exoteric and esoteric dimensions of Islam over the centuries. In fact, this disagreement is understood as necessary in light of the nature of the Islamic revelation and the condition of the human community to which the revelation has been addressed. The traditional school therefore confirms and reiterates the view of authorities such as Abū Ḥāmid al-Ghazzālī, in the Sunni world, and Shaykh Bahā' al-Dīn al-ʿĀmilī, in the Shīʿite world, recognized religious authorities who have been masters of both the exoteric and esoteric sciences and who have defended both dimensions of Islam while explaining why the esoteric comprehends the exoteric, but the exoteric excludes and does not comprehend the esoteric.[7]

Not every traditional scholar has been a master of all the traditional schools of thought or accepted all their premises and teachings. Even in the traditional world, one school of *kalām* (theology) disagreed with other schools of *kalām,* followers of *kalām* disagreed with those of philosophy, philosophers of one school disagreed with those of another, and some Sufis disagreed with followers of *kalām* or philosophy. But all these various ways of thinking belonged nevertheless to the traditional universe. Traditionalists do not defend only one school at the expense of others, but insist on the value of the whole intellectual tradition of Islam in all of its authentic manifestations with full awareness of different degrees of universality expressed by them, since all of these manifestations have issued from the teachings of the Islamic revelation. Moreover, the various traditional schools of Islamic theology, philosophy, Sufism, and the sciences are evaluated by traditionalists in light of the Islamic worldview. They are in fact seen as diverse keys to the understanding of various aspects of the intellectual universe of Islam, rather than, as in the Western view, as merely stages in the development of this or that school of Western philosophy or science, in other words valued by many Western scholars only because of the contribution they have made to modern Western thought.

As far as traditional Islamic art and architecture are concerned, traditional Islam insists upon their Islamicity and their relation to the inner dimension of the Islamic revelation, as they are crystallizations of the spiritual treasures of the religion in visible or audible form. Traditionalists insist upon the fact that religion possesses not only a truth, but also a presence, and that the *barakah* emanating from Islamic art and architecture is as essential for the survival of the religion as a whole as the *Sharī'ah* itself. Again, traditional Islam recognizes that certain forms of Islamic art and architecture decayed in certain areas and that some types of traditional art are more central and essential than others, but it insists that under no condition can one be indifferent to the power of forms over the human soul. One cannot simply neglect the significance of Islamic art and architecture by insisting only upon the legal and ethical aspects of the religion. From the Quranic revelation there issued not only regulations for how human beings should act, but also the principles according to which they should make things. Islamic art and architecture are directly related to Islamic spirituality,[8] and the Traditionalists remain the staunchest supporters of traditional art and architecture. They are opposed to all the ugliness that is now invading the Islamic world in the form of urban design and architecture, artifacts, dress, and the like, an invasion accepted by both modernists and "fundamentalists" in the name of compassion for human beings, expediency, and concern for the material welfare of society, with total indifference to beauty.

Besides art and architecture, in no domain is the difference between the traditional, on the one hand, and modernist and "fundamentalist" views, on the other, more evident than in the fields of politics, social life, and economics. As far as social life is concerned, the traditional perspective insists upon the preservation of *Sharī'ite* institutions; the importance of units such as the family, the village, the guilds, and local urban quarters; and in general a social fabric based on the bonds created by religion.

In economics, realism is never sacrificed in favor of an unrealizable idealism, nor is it thought possible to inculcate the virtues of hard work, honesty, frugality, and generosity simply by external force or pressure. Economics is always seen as legitimate only if wed to morality within a human situation that preserves personal human contacts and trust between individuals, as one sees in the traditional bazaar, rather than as related to impersonal and excessively large organizations, whose very size precludes the possibility of direct human relationships.[9]

In the political domain, the traditional perspective always insists upon realism based on Islamic norms. In the Sunni world, historically it accepted the classical caliphate and, in its absence, other political institutions, such as the sultanate, which developed over the centuries in light of the teachings of the *Sharī'ah* and the needs of the community. Under no condition, however, does it seek to destroy what remains of traditional Islamic political institutions, which are controlled by traditional restraints, in the hope of installing another Abū Bakr or 'Umar, but meanwhile settling for some form of dictatorship by an army officer. Moreover, such dictatorships are usually outwardly based on the external forms of political institutions derived from the French Revolution and other upheavals of European history, even though they are presented by many as the authentic Islamic form of government. As for the Shī'ite world, the traditional perspective continues to insist that final authority belongs to the Twelfth Imam, in whose absence no form of government can be perfect.

In both worlds, the traditional perspective remains always aware of the fall of the community from its original perfection, the danger of destroying traditional Islamic institutions and substituting those of modern, Western origin, and the necessity of creating a more Islamic order and reviving society from within by strengthening faith in the hearts of men and women rather than simply by external force. The traditional image of sociopolitical revival is that of the "renewer" (*mujaddid*), identified over the centuries with great saints and sages such as 'Abd al-Qādir al-Jīlānī, al-Ghazzālī, Shaykh Abū'l-Ḥasan al-Shādhilī, and Shaykh Aḥmad Sirhindī, rather than the many so-called reformers who have appeared upon the scene since the twelfth/eighteenth century.

To understand traditional Islam better, these views must be compared and contrasted with those of both the so-called fundamentalists and modernists. It is essential to remember that, at this moment in human history, one must distinguish, in all religions and civilizations as well as Islam, not only between the traditional and the modern, but also between authentic tradition and pseudotradition, which is antitraditional and now more and more countertraditional, but which also displays certain characteristics outwardly similar to the traditional. As far as the Islamic world is concerned, these distinctions appear clearly once one is able to distinguish between the traditional, as here defined, and that pseudotraditional perspective that is often identified with one form or another of "fundamentalism." This type of phenomenon, while claiming to restore Islam to its original purity, is in fact creating something very different from the traditional Islam that was brought by the Prophet and that has survived and grown like a living tree during the fourteen centuries since his migration to Medina.[10]

These differences between the traditional and the anti- or countertraditional in Islam become clearer once the traditional is compared to the "fundamentalist" in specific fields.[11] The traditionalist and the "fundamentalist" meet in their acceptance of the Quran and *Ḥadīth* as well as in their emphasis upon the *Sharī'ah,* but even here the differences remain profound as far as interpretations are concerned. As already mentioned, tradition always emphasizes the sapiential commentaries and the long tradition of Quranic hermeneutics in understanding the meaning of the verses of the Sacred Text. So many of the "fundamentalist" movements, however, simply pull out this or that verse from the Quran and give it a meaning in accordance with their goals and aims, often reading into it a meaning alien to the whole tradition of Quranic commentary, or *tafsīr.* As for the *Sharī'ah,* tradition always emphasizes, in contrast to so much of current "fundamentalism," faith, inner attachment to the dicta of the Divine Law, and lenient judgment based upon the imperfections of human society,[12] rather than simply external coercion based on fear of some human authority, some authority other than God.

Outside of this domain, the differences between the traditional and the anti- and countertraditional in Islam are even more blatant. Most of the current "fundamentalist" movements, while denouncing modernism, accept some of the most basic aspects of modernism. This is clearly seen in their complete and open-armed acceptance of modern science and technology. Many of them even seek a Quranic basis for modern man's domination and destruction of nature by referring to the Quranic injunction to the human being to "dominate" (*taskhīr*) the earth, as if the human being addressed in the Quran were not the servant of God (*'abd Allāh*) and God's vicegerent on earth (*khalīfat Allāh*), but rather the modern consumer. They engage in lengthy arguments to demonstrate how Islamic science served as the necessary background for and made possible the creation of Western science despite Christianity, completely disregarding the fact that the nature and character of Islamic science are entirely different from those of modern science.[13] Their attitude toward science and technology is in fact nearly identical with that of the modernists, as seen on the practical plane in the attitude of Muslim countries with modern forms of government compared to those that claim to possess one or another form of Islamic government. There is hardly any difference in the manner in which they both try to blindly adopt modern Western technology, from computers to television, without any thought for the consequences of these inventions upon the minds and souls of Muslims.

This common attitude is in fact to be found in the domain of knowledge in general. The process of the secularization of knowledge that has occurred in the West since the Renaissance, against all traditional Islamic teachings concerning "science" (*al-'ilm*), is not only taken for granted as a sign of progress by the modernists, but is also hardly even noticed by the "fundamentalists." By simply equating modern forms of knowledge with *al-'ilm,* the latter claim to follow the injunctions of Islam in their espousal of modern science, rarely asking themselves what kind of *'ilm* it was that the Blessed Prophet instructed his followers to seek from the cradle to the grave. Nor do they pause to ponder what the real implications are of the famous saying, sometimes attributed to 'Alī ibn Abī Ṭālib, "I become the slave of him who teaches me a single word." Could this "word" possibly be a term pulled out of a chemistry dictionary or one drawn from some computer language?[14] The real nature of much of "fundamentalist" thought in its relation to modernism is made evident in the whole question of the process of the secularization of knowledge in the West and the adoption of the fruit of this process in so many quarters of the contemporary Islamic world, not to speak of some of the solutions being offered to the problem of the Islamization of knowledge by followers of both the modernist and the "fundamentalist" camps.

Another remarkable similarity between the modernist and "fundamentalist" groups that is in complete contrast to the traditionalist position is to be found in their attitudes toward art. As already mentioned, traditional Islamic civilization is marked by its emphasis upon the wedding of beauty with every aspect of human life, from the chanting of the Quran to the making of pots and pans. The traditional Islamic plastic and auditory arts have always been beautiful, for traditional Islam sees beauty as a complement of the Truth. According to the well-known *ḥadīth,* God, who is also the Truth (*al-Ḥaqq*), is beautiful and loves beauty. Moreover, the norms of Islamic art are inwardly related to the Islamic revelation and the spirituality that emanates from it.[15] Beauty represents the aspect of presence in religion, as doctrine represents the truth. Yet the greatest masterpieces of Islamic art appear insignificant to both modernists and "fundamentalists," and their view concerning the spiritual significance of Islamic art seems nearly identical. If one camp now produces mosques that look like factories except for a pseudominaret or dome added superficially merely to signal the building's function, the other is known to have declared that it makes no difference whether Muslims pray in the most beautiful Mogul or Ottoman mosque or a modern factory, as if all Muslims were already saints and not in need of the external support from those traditional forms that act as vehicles for the flow of Muḥammadan *barakah* to the individual and the community. The attitude toward art in its widest sense should in itself be a sufficient criterion to reveal the true nature of revivalist or "fundamentalist" Islam in relation to both modernism and traditional Islam, as it always has been and will continue to be to the end of time.

Nowhere, however, does the veneer of Islamicity that covers so many movements claiming a revival of Islam wear more thinly than in the field of politics. Here, while calls are made to return to the origin of Islam, the pure message of the Quran, and the teachings of the Prophet and to reject all that is modern and Western, one ends up by adopting all the most extreme political ideas that have arisen in Europe since the French Revolution, but always portraying them as the purest and most unadulterated of Islamic ideas. One therefore defends secular revolution and republicanism, ideology and even class struggle in the name of a supposedly pure Islam prior to its early adulteration by the Umayyads, but rarely bothers to inquire whether the Quran or *Ḥadīth* ever used those terms, why a movement that claims Islamicity is so direly in need of such concepts of Western origin, or indeed why the attack against traditional Muslim political institutions coincides so "accidentally" with those of the left in the modern Western world.

The case of "ideology" is very telling as far as the adaptation of modern notions in the name of religion is concerned. Nearly every Muslim language now uses this term, and many Muslims in fact insist that Islam is an ideology. If this is so, then why was there no word to express it in classical Arabic, Persian, and other languages of the Islamic peoples? Is *'aqīdah* or *uṣūl al-'aqā'id,* by which it is sometimes translated, at all related to "ideology"? If Islam is a complete way of life, then why does it have to adopt a nineteenth-century European concept to express its nature, not only to the West, but even to its own adherents? The truth of the matter is in fact that traditional Islam refuses ever to accept Islam as an ideology, and it is only when the traditional order succumbs to the modern world that the understanding of religion as ideology comes to the fore,[16] with momentous consequences for religion itself, not to speak of the society that is ruled in the name of religious ideology rather than according to the dicta of the *Sharī'ah,* as traditionally understood. To fail to distinguish between these two modes is to fail to grasp the most manifest distinction between traditional Islam, on the one hand, and "fundamentalist" and modernist Islam, on the other. In fact, it marks the failure to comprehend the nature of the forces at play in the Islamic world today.

A great deal more could be said concerning traditional Islam in contrast to both the modernist and "fundamentalist" interpretations, although among the latter there are some groups that are closer to the traditional camp, while others are diametrically opposed to it and represent simply the countertraditional. In conclusion, it is sufficient to add that the traditional school opposes the gaining of worldly power and any surrender to worldliness in the name of Islam, never forgetting the Quranic injunction, "The other world is better for you than this world." While accepting the fact that Islam does not separate the religious from the "secular" domain, traditional Islam refuses to sacrifice the means for the end and does not accept as legitimate the use of any and every possible political machination appropriated from completely anti-Islamic sources in order to gain power in the name of Islam. Moreover, traditional Islam does not condone intoxication caused by hatred and anger any more than it does one caused by alcohol; nor does it see such a self-righteous and intoxicating hatred as a legitimate substitute for the need to solve the intellectual, moral, social, economic, and political problems that the Islamic world faces today.

Despite both modernism and this latter-day "fundamentalism," traditional Islam still survives, not only through its past artistic and intellectual movements, but in the present-day lives of those scholars and saintly men and women who continue to follow the path of the Prophet, in the lives of those craftsmen and artists who continue to recreate those visual and audible forms that are vehicles for the grace of the Quranic revelation, and in the everyday lives of that vast majority of pious Muslims whose hearts, minds, and bodies still reverberate in response to the traditional teachings of Islam. One can even say that there has been a certain revival of traditional Islam in the spiritual, intellectual, and artistic domains during the past few decades, a revival that has gone largely unnoticed in the West because of the sensationalism of most of the news media and the lack of in-depth comprehension of many Western scholars concerned with the contemporary Islamic world. Traditional Islam will in fact endure to the end of history, for it is none other than that tree whose roots are sunk in the Quranic revelation and whose trunk and branches have constituted all that Islam has been over the centuries, before the aberrations and deviations of modern times came to cause many to confuse this authentic tradition with not only the antitraditional, but also the countertraditional, whose nature is more difficult to detect precisely because "Satan is the ape of God." But no matter how great the confusion, truth protects itself, because it is none other than reality; on the contrary, whatever apes it while at the same time denying it finally vanishes like the darkness of the early morn before the luminous rays of the rising sun.

Part I

Contentious Issues Debated in Islamic Circles Today

Chapter One

ISLAM IN THE PRESENT-DAY ISLAMIC WORLD

An Overview

Numerous factors, including the revival of Islam within the Islamic world, attempts to reassert the Islamic identity of Muslims, reactions to the political and cultural domination of the Islamic world by the West that take the form of political and even violent challenges to the geopolitical interests of Western powers in Islamic countries, and the spread of Islam in the West itself have all contributed to a greater interest on the part of many people in Europe and America in the Islamic world and the role of Islam in that world.

To discuss Islam in the present-day Islamic world, however, means that a distinction has already been made between Islam as a religious and spiritual reality and the manifestation of this reality in a particular social order or historic context. Such a distinction, although not accepted by all modern interpreters and students of religion, lies at the heart of the traditional perspective, which always distinguishes between levels of reality and between the archetype in relation to its spatio-temporal manifestations. From this point of view, it is therefore not only possible to make such a distinction, but even necessary to do so in order to avoid confusing everything that is called Islamic today by this or that group with the Islamic norm as it has manifested itself over the centuries in accordance with the essential reality of Islam, a norm that has also displayed various modes of development, but always within the possibilities inherent in that reality and according to its principles. It is especially imperative to speak of both Islam as traditionally understood and the present-day Islamic world, precisely because of the bewildering confusion that reigns in this domain, combined with intense interest in the subject in the Western world as a result of factors to which reference has already been made.[1]

As far as Islam is concerned, its meaning is clear from the traditional point of view. Islam is a divinely revealed religion whose roots are contained in the Noble Quran and the traditions of the Blessed Prophet—both written and oral—and whose branches represent fourteen hundred years of a sacred religious history that, in its orthodoxy, has embraced both Sunnism and Shīʿism as well as the esoteric dimension of the tradition, contained mostly in Sufism. It has produced not only the schools of law (*Sharīʿah*), but also theology, philosophy, a whole array of arts and sciences, and a distinct educational system, not to speak of political, economic, social, and family structures and the ethical and moral norms to which those structures are related.

This tree, which has its roots in revelation, has also produced a sacred traditional art, both auditory and visual, ranging from the various methods of chanting the Noble Quran to calligraphy, architecture, and various forms of Islamic literature. Although Islam remains in its essence a transhistorical reality, it has also had this long period of historical development, which links every generation of Muslims through time to the Origin. This direct access to the spiritual world, where the transhistorical reality of Islam is to be found, is made possible by the rites and the *barakah* issuing from the Quranic revelation, which links each Muslim to the Source through a hierarchic "space" that is present and accessible here and now. Islam is at once that inexhaustible transhistorical reality and the whole of the Islamic tradition as reflected in Islamic history. As already mentioned, this is the "tree of Islam," whose roots are sunk in the ground of divine revelation and whose trunk, branches, and fruits symbolize the manifestations of the Islamic reality in various climes and historical epochs.

As for the Islamic world, that term needs some elucidation. In traditional Islamic language the Islamic world is divided into three abodes: *dār al-islām,* the "Abode of Islam," where Islam rules as a majority religion, that is, where the Islamic Divine Law, or *Sharīʿah,* governs human life; *dār al-ṣulḥ,* the "Abode of Peace," where Muslims live as the minority, but are at peace and can practice their religion freely; and finally *dār al-ḥarb,* the "Abode of Conflict or War," where Muslims are a minority, but are in conflict with and struggle against the external social and political environment in order to be able to practice their religion.

Had secularism not intruded into the Islamic world beginning in the nineteenth century, one could have simply defined the "Islamic world" as *dār al-islām*. But today the situation is complicated by the fact that, in many parts of *dār al-islām* itself, non-Islamic forces have gained a footing, sometimes under the name of a foreign ideology or a Western form of nationalism and sometimes even under the name of Islam itself, which, as already noted, has during the last few decades been done more and more in a cunning and sometimes insidious fashion to hide the real nature of some of the forces at work. Moreover, Muslims in both *dār al-ṣulḥ* (such as India and parts of Africa, where they are in fact not always able to live in peace) and what used to be known as *dār al-ḥarb* (such as North America and most of Europe in earlier periods of history, but where they now live for the most part in peace) have now come to play an important role in *dār al-islām* itself, and modern means of communication have linked Muslims in the three "worlds" in a new fashion. It is, therefore, not so easy to define exactly what is meant by the Islamic world on the basis of earlier definitions. For the sake of this discussion, however, let us define it as that part of the world in which there is either an Islamic majority or a substantial Muslim population free to live Islamically, even if the degree of people's attachment to Islam in all these regions is not exactly the same.

This question of the degree and mode of attachment of Muslims to Islam is itself a crucial question in the discussion of the role of Islam in the Islamic world today. Before modern times, the degree of penetration of Islam within a particular region or ethnic group depended mostly on how long the process of Islamization had been going on. For example, in parts of Indonesia or Black Africa, where Islam had penetrated for only a century or two, the process of Islamization had not been as complete as in other areas where this process had commenced, let us say, four centuries earlier, not to speak of a millennium earlier. In parts of the Islamic world where Islam had had time to sink its roots and establish its institutions, the attachment of Muslims to Islamic practices was of such intensity that one could not easily say whether, for example, the Egyptians, Syrians, Persians, or Punjabis were more strongly attached to Islam, although some communities accentuated the formal, legal aspects and others inner attachment and faith, according to the emphasis of the different schools of law and theology that they followed. Wherever orthodox schools of Islam, whether Sunni or Shīʿite, were firmly rooted, the complete practice of Islamic precepts and attachment to the teachings of Islam were taken for granted. Differences existed only in such questions as pietistic attitudes, emphasis upon secondary forms of worship (such as pilgrimage to local shrines or certain supererogatory prayers), theological speculations, expressions of sacred art, and so on, which often demonstrated local variation as a result of differences of language, ethnicity, or culture between various Islamic collectivities. At the same time such differences reflected the positive elements of the ethnic genius of the various groups, elements that Islam did not destroy, but allowed to flower within the matrix of the Islamic universe.

In modern times, however, forces such as Western-style nationalism, revival of tribalism and linguistic affinities, and the different ways in which various parts of the Islamic world have experienced the modern world, encountering such forces as colonialism, secular nationalism, racism, and Western secular humanism, have caused a significant variation in the manner and degree of attachment of many Muslims to Islam. A majority of Muslims never miss their daily prayers and live as much as they can by the *Sharīʿah,* some of whom moreover consider their manner of following Islam to be the only manner. But in contrast to the days of old, there are also others who do not follow all the injunctions of the *Sharīʿah* or even pray regularly, yet also definitely consider themselves Muslims. And there are even others who do not do anything specifically Islamic except follow a vaguely Islamic kind of "humanistic" ethics, yet call themselves Muslims and would protest if called anything else. And again there is another group who perform the Islamic rites meticulously and yet break many of the moral injunctions of the *Sharīʿah* (including, for example, honesty in business), while claiming to be devout. Moreover, another, even more vocal minority has now adopted the most violent forms of modern ideology, which it seeks to present to the world as authentic Islam.

From another point of view, there is the majority for whom Islam is essentially an all-embracing ethical and social code, a way of life embodied in the *Sharīʿah* and, for those who wish to follow the spiritual life, in the *Ṭarīqah.* And there are those for whom Islam is felt more as a culture and now, as a result of Western influence and reactions against it, as an ideology and political force with which to combat other ideologies. There are now in the Islamic world authentic as well as antitraditional and modernistic interpretations along with countertraditional ones, which are not only against tradition but seek to create a counterfeit to replace tradition. There are, as a result, many degrees and modes of attachment to Islam, especially in those parts of that world that have been long exposed to various types of modernistic influences. Those who speak of a "monolithic" Islam or a uniform wave of "fundamentalism" sweeping over the Islamic world, those who try to scare the West by depicting Islam as a violent enemy unified to oppose the rest of the world are all too unaware of the differences and nuances that exist in the perception of Islam and attachment to it by contemporary Muslims. If Islamic history has taught us anything in this domain, it is that, even in traditional times, no part of *dār al-islām* could speak for the whole of it and that the reaction of the whole of the Islamic world to such major events and forces as the introduction of Greco-Hellenistic learning, the Crusades, or the Mongol invasion was never uniform. How much more is this true today when the degree of exposure of a college student in any cosmopolitan center of the Middle East to non-Islamic elements is totally different from the exposure of a villager in the same country to these elements, not to speak of radical differences in the degree and manner of modernization and secularization in, let us say, Senegal and Turkey.

Another point of central importance in the study of Islam in the Islamic world today is the all-embracing nature of Islam itself. This still holds true despite the recent process of secularization or separation from sacred norms in so many domains of Islamic thought, art, and life in general that has influenced the degree and manner of attachment of many Muslims to Islam, especially in the big cities, which are centers of most of the decision making for society. For most Muslims, all of life's relations and concerns are intertwined with their understanding of their religion; religion is a reality inseparable from these other relationships. For example, traditional Muslims have bonds to family, city, nation, business, friends, and so forth, which they do not juxtapose to religion, but see in the context of that totality that for them is, in one way or another, Islam. They do not see Islam only as an ideal, although it is of course an ideal, especially as far as the ethical norms exemplified by the Blessed Prophet and the great figures of the religion are concerned. But for ordinary Muslims it is also a reality with which they live day and night. Therefore, in many cases they make use of religious teachings to solve family problems, to further economic or social goals, or even for the exercise of power. There are, of course, many Muslims who practice their religion only out of the fear and love of God. But it would be a dangerous idealization of Islamic society and denial of human frailty to think that all those who are ostentatious in their attachment to Islam have nothing but the satisfaction of God in mind and that they would continue to perform ostentatious religious acts even if the other areas of their life, work, family, and so forth, would be disrupted or affected negatively by doing so. For many people, all of these forces, bonds, and relationships are intertwined in a manner that can at times cause unexpected social and political upheavals in the name of religion, but can at the same time also cause rapid changes of direction and aim without sacrificing or compromising the religious elements.

Precisely because Islam is still a very powerful force pervading the lives of its believers, the misuse of it to further various personal and group interests is always a possibility. It has, in fact, been and is being made use of for sundry nonreligious goals, not only by some Muslims themselves, but also by many forces originating outside the Islamic world. To better understand this phenomenon, it is sufficient to recall how the term "Islam" is used by diverse forces driven not primarily by religious, but by national, ethnic, tribal, and/or politico-economic interests. Obviously this kind of recourse to religious sentiments and practice is very different from the following of religion for the sake of God alone, a difference that can have, and in fact in some areas is having, devastating effects upon the Islamic world and beyond, whenever there is a manipulation of Islam for non-Islamic ends. Needless to say, one can observe a similar situation in other cases where the religion is still strong, such as Hinduism.

With these general traits of the Islamic world in mind, it is now necessary to turn to the more particular types of reactions that have arisen within that world as a result of its encounter with the modern West, reactions that must be elucidated and fully understood if we are to grasp the nature of Islam in the Islamic world today. During the first twelve centuries of its historic existence, Islam lived with full awareness of the truth and the realization of God's promise to Muslims that they would be victorious if they followed His religion. Such verses as, "There is no victor but God" (*lā ghāliba illa'Llāh*), which adorns the walls of the Alhambra in Granada, also adorned the souls and minds of Muslims. They were victorious in the world, the Crusades and the short conquest of the Islamic world by the Mongols notwithstanding. The grandson of the famous Mongol conqueror Hulagü, Uljaytü, became a Muslim and in fact a patron of Islamic learning and the arts, and the Crusaders were finally defeated and expelled. The authenticity of the Quranic message was borne out by the experience of history, even if there were some exceptions, such as Andalusia and the kingdom of the Tartars, which were lost by Muslims to Christian forces.

Then came the conquest of various parts of the Islamic world by the British, the French, the Dutch, and the Russians, not to speak of the more peripheral conquests by the Portuguese and the Spanish. Although Muslims were at first somewhat indifferent to the long-range significance of these events, the conquest of Egypt by Napoleon caused a shock that made Muslim leaders aware of the dimension and meaning of the Western conquest of the Islamic world. In the early thirteenth/nineteenth century, the Muslim intelligentsia finally came to realize that clearly something had "gone wrong," that, as mentioned by Wilfred Cantwell Smith, among other Western scholars of Islam, a crisis of a cosmic nature had come about.[2] How was it that the Islamic world was being defeated by non-Islamic forces such as the British and the French everywhere from North Africa to India and in such an irreversible fashion? Logically, the answer took the form of three positions:

1. *Messianic Hopes:* Something had gone wrong with the world, as God Himself had mentioned in His Book concerning the end of the world and the Blessed Prophet had described in his traditions. In such a case, the eclipse of Islam was itself proof of the validity of the Islamic message, which, however, also foretold the imminent appearance of the Mahdī, or the savior and messianic figure who Muslims believe will be sent by God before the end of time, and the final eschatological events leading to the end of the world. Needless to say, this view led to the rise of a wave of Mahdiism in several Islamic countries.

2. *Fundamentalist Reaction:* Muslims had ceased to follow Islam properly and should return to the practice of their religion in its pure form and with full vigor so as to defeat the non-Islamic forces and escape the punishment they were receiving from the Hand of God for their negligence in their religion. Such a reaction resulted mostly in the neo-Wahhābī and neo-Salafī movements, movements based on puritanical and outward interpretations of Islam, associated, for example, with some

elements of the Deoband school in India, the Salafiyyah in Egypt and Syria, and the Muḥammadiyyah in Indonesia. But it was also connected with the much less studied inner revivals within Sufi orders and the establishment of new ones, such as the founding of the Darqāwiyyah and Tijāniyyah in Morocco and West Africa, the Sanūsiyyah in Libya and East Africa, the Yashruṭiyyah in the Arab Near East, and the revival of the Naqshbandiyyah in Turkey and the Caucasus, the Ni'matullāhiyyah in Persia, the Chishtiyyah and Qādiriyyah in India, and many others.

3. *Modern Reform Movements:* The Islamic message had to be changed, modified, adapted, or reformed to suit modern conditions; it had to be able to adapt itself to the modern world so that it could succeed overcoming Western domination. Out of this attitude grew all the different types of modernism influenced by the effects of the French Revolution and other elements of European history, by the rationalism of such men as Descartes and Voltaire, the empiricism of Locke, the skepticism of Hume, and later on the idealism of such philosophers as Hegel, Spencer, and Bergson, just to name a few influential currents that came to dominate this or that group of Muslim modernists. So-called Arab liberalism as well as modernistic movements in Turkey and Persia and on the Indian subcontinent were all results of this third possible reaction to the subjugation of the Islamic world by the West.

In some cases elements of these three positions were mixed with each other; here and there one sees Mahdiism, puritanical or "fundamentalist" tendencies, and modern reformist elements coming together in the thoughts and teachings of a single figure or school. Some Sufi figures even had a Mahdiist aspect, as the study of the lives of such figures as the Brelvis in India, Usman dan Fadio in Nigeria, and al-Ḥajj 'Umar of Futa Toro in East Africa reveals. In such cases, Sufism itself undertook the task of reviving the Islamic community as a whole, a task that has not received nearly as much attention from Western scholarship as has the fruit of the efforts of the neo-Wahhābī and modernistic reformers.[3] These reactions continued to animate certain segments of Islamic society for the next century down to World War II, although the wave of Mahdiism gradually died down after giving birth to such diverse phenomena as the Aḥmadiyyah movement in India and Pakistan, the Bābī-Bahā'ī movement in Persia, and the establishment of the Mahdiist state in the Sudan.

After World War II, certain events took place that revived or altered the movements that had grown out of the original reaction of Islam to its domination by the West. First of all, nearly the whole of the Islamic world became politically "independent," but as national states on the model of European states. This apparent freedom brought with it the expectation of greater cultural and social independence, especially as the less Westernized elements of Islamic society began to gain greater political and economic power. Second, the vast wealth from oil pouring into much of the Islamic world, such as Persia and many Arab countries, brought with it the acceleration of the processes of industrialization and modernization and at the same time heightened the tensions already present between Islam and the ethos of modern Western civilization—tensions that had not been resolved either intellectually or socially and that had been mostly glossed over by well-known earlier figures, usually known as "reformers," as well as by most of the *'ulamā',* or religious scholars, who had hardly concerned themselves with them.

These events within the Islamic world were complemented by transformations within the Western world itself that were also to have profound consequences for movements within the Islamic world. From the moment the West conquered the Islamic world until World War II, the Islamic world saw in the West another model or philosophy for human existence, which, although rejected by many in that world, was accepted wholeheartedly by most leaders and many members of the ruling classes belonging to modernizing movements in various Muslim countries.

Few among Muslim modernists, however, doubted the success of this model, at least from the point of view of human life on earth, whatever the consequences might have been for the immortal soul. Before World War II, few Muslims who were aping the West were seriously affected by the ideas of Oswald Spengler expressed in his *Decline of the West,* which in fact had been translated into Arabic and Persian, and fewer still had read the gloomy descriptions of Western civilization given by such literary figures as T. S. Eliot (although this poet has exercised a great influence on certain Arab poets during the past decades). And practically no one, save a small circle in Cairo and Karachi, had read the "prophetic" works of René Guénon, such as *The Crisis of the Modern World* and *The Reign of Quantity and the Signs of the Times,* predicting the collapse of the modern world, although Guénon had moved permanently to Cairo in 1930.[4] It was only after World War II that the Islamic intelligentsia in general became aware that within the Western world itself there were profound criticisms of that civilization and that the Western model that so many Muslims had tried to emulate was itself breaking down and undergoing a major crisis.

The Traditionalist movement in the West, associated with René Guénon and his intellectual followers, which was responsible for the acutest criticism of modernism, was accompanied by an attempt on the part of many to seek their roots once again, to rediscover tradition and to regain access to the Sacred. So, while much of what remained of the Western tradition was floundering and giving way to despair and nihilism, there was also to some extent a reassertion of traditional teachings, a rediscovery of myth and symbols, a positive appreciation of non-Western religions, and even a reappraisal of the medieval Western heritage, which ceased to appear simply as "dark" as its purblind Renaissance and eighteenth-century critics had made it out to be.[5] All these developments were bound to, and in fact did, affect a small but growing number of influential intellectual figures, religious scholars, critics, writers, and other leaders within the Islamic world.

Finally, a change began to appear in the attitude of non-Islamic powers, both Western and Communist, toward the forces within the Islamic world. After World War II, for some time Islam as a religion was belittled as a force to be reckoned with by the outside world, but various nationalistic forces, such as Arab nationalism, which in many cases were in fact combined with religious elements in one way or another, were manipulated in every conceivable way to aid the causes and aims of global powers to the greatest extent possible. The history of the various forms of Arab nationalism, especially those inspired by Nasserism during the past decades, provides a good example of the way these forces were at work. Then, as the situation changed, the same policy of manipulation began to be pursued in the case of religious forces themselves through indirect aid, by the hindrance of a particular religious school or organization, or by the sudden aggrandizement of a particular force or movement and the belittling of others that might not be of immediate political or economic benefit to the interested powers. The case of the creation of the Taliban in Afghanistan at the beginning of this movement is illustrative of this process, as is the support, or lack of it, of various Islamic movements within Pakistan. This external manipulation, although relying on existing movements, tendencies, forces, and personalities within the Islamic world itself, has played and continues to play an important role in the manner in which these forces and processes develop and change and also the degree to which the personalities involved, from leaders of the Muslim Brotherhood (*Ikhwān al-muslimīn*) in Arab countries to those of the Society of Islam (*Jamā'at-i islāmī*) in Pakistan, have been able to exercise influence and political leadership. This manipulation is not the only factor, but is certainly one to be considered seriously, if one wishes to understand the present state of the Islamic world and more specifically Islamic forces at work within that world.

With the earlier reactions of the Islamic world to the West in mind and with full consideration of the new forces and changes brought upon the scene since World War II, it is now possible to describe the present state of forces, movements, and tendencies within Islam as they affect and mold the contemporary Islamic world, from the movement of Badī' al-Zamān Nūrsī in Turkey and Khomeinism in Iran to the Muḥammadiyyah movement in Indonesia.

There are, first of all, a number of forces, differing in many basic features among themselves, that are more or less heir to or related to the earlier type of Wahhābī reactions against the Western world, and others that are of a more antitraditional, although supposedly puritanical and reformist, nature. Yet both are usually termed "fundamentalist," although this term has particular Christian and, more specifically, Protestant connotations that do not apply exactly to the Islamic situation. Despite the basic difference between these two types of forces, however, they share in common a disdain for modern Western culture, a distrust of foreign social mores, in most cases a strong activist tendency, and usually opposition or indifference to the inward aspects of Islam and the civilization and culture that it created, aspects such as Sufism, Islamic philosophy, Islamic art,[6] and so on. They are also outwardly oriented in the sense that they wish to reconstruct Islamic society through the reestablishment of external legal and social norms rather than revive Islam through inner purification and the strengthening of faith and/or by removing the philosophical and intellectual impediments that have been obstacles on the path of many contemporary Muslims. These movements, therefore, have rarely dealt in detail with the intellectual challenges posed by Western science and philosophy, although this trait is not by any means of the same strength among all of them, some being of a more intellectual nature than others. Interestingly enough, despite some differences among them, they also share for the most part unbounded admiration for Western science and technology, a trait that they also have in common with the modernists.

These movements have also shown no uniformity in their political programs either. Some have sought to revive the caliphate; others have supported other traditional forms of government, such as the sultanate or emirate; many speak of establishing an Islamic state without any consensus as to what that term means exactly; and yet others have opted for a Western type of democracy in an Islamic context. Some of the antitraditional yet so-called reformist and puritanical movements, which sometimes appear in the guise of traditional Islam, also possess a violent and revolutionary political nature; and in some of these movements the most fanatical and volcanic elements of Western republicanism and Marxist revolutionary theory and practice have been set in what the followers of these groups consider to be an Islamic context.

There is only one political aim in which nearly all these so-called fundamentalist forces are united, and that is the unification of the Islamic world, or what is called Pan-Islamism. In this sense, they are all heirs to the campaign of Jamāl al-Dīn Astarābādī, known as al-Afghānī, who in the thirteenth/nineteenth century called for the reunification of the Islamic world. But although Pan-Islamism has continued as an ideal espoused by nearly all Islamic leaders and most intellectual figures during the past century and remains encrusted in the traditional Islamic vision of the perfect state to be established by the Mahdī before the end of time, the manner of its execution as part of a practical political program has hardly been agreed upon by the diverse groups who speak of it.

Some preach the reestablishment of a single caliphate or central political authority, as during the time of the four "rightly guided caliphs" (*khulafā' rāshidūn*) in the seventh/thirteenth century. Others speak of a commonwealth of Muslim nations, and yet others, while using Pan-Islamism as a slogan to arouse the religious sentiments of the people, remain deliberately vague as to how it would be carried out in practice. These so-called fundamentalist Islamic forces were manipulated by external powers to achieve ends as diverse as creating a wall of defense against Communism and ensuring that what is commonly termed economic development does not go beyond a certain stage. This was a particularly dangerous policy, because of the ambivalent and vague aspect of the political dimension of these forces, and we are now witnessing some of its worst consequences. The effect of such manipulations upon the Islamic community came out to be very different from what the so-called Western experts who provided the programs for such manipulations envisaged. All one needs to do is to look at the Taliban phenomenon.

Of the "fundamentalist" forces, the oldest are without doubt those that inherited the ideas of the earlier Wahhābī movement and have carried that movement into our own day. These forces are of course centered mostly in Saudi Arabia, which officially follows the Wahhābī interpretation of Islam, and from the beginning they were associated with a group of Islamic scholars in Najd and later Hejaz. But they also include neo-Wahhābīs and Salafīs in Egypt, Syria, Jordan, and other countries of the Arab East, many of whom were influenced by the earlier Salafiyyah movement, whose base was in Egypt and Syria until World War II. Its influence is felt directly in some Muslim seats of learning, but it is less of a directly political, activist force than it was in the thirteenth/nineteenth and early fourteenth/twentieth centuries. The spread of Wahhābism outside of Saudi Arabia into religious schools from Afghanistan to Central Asia during the past few decades has, however, spawned many political movements often of a violent nature.

On the subcontinent of India, this type of "fundamentalist" movement has had many expressions, of which perhaps the most significant today is the *Jamā'at-i islāmī* (literally, "Society of Islam") of Pakistan, founded by Mawlānā Abū'l-'Alā' Mawdūdī in the 1940s. The purpose of this closely knit, semisecret, activist organization is the revival of the Islamic way of life. It has direct political and social goals based on the re-Islamization of society, although it is milder than the violent revolutionary movements, such as the Taliban movement, seen elsewhere but also now in Pakistan itself, and is more interested in promoting consideration of the social and intellectual dimensions of the confrontation between Islam and modernism. There are organizations of a similar nature among Muslims of India itself as well as in Indonesia that have close links to the Pakistani Society of Islam.

An organization with a somewhat longer history, but of more limited political power than Wahhābism at the present moment, is the famous Muslim Brotherhood (*Ikhwān al-muslimīn*), founded in Egypt before World War II by Ḥasan al-Bannā', but later extended to other Muslim countries, especially those in the Persian Gulf region, where many of its members settled after the execution in Egypt of its leader, Sayyid Quṭb, during the rule of Jamāl 'Abd al-Nāṣir. This organization, which had also been involved in earlier political plots of various kinds, but which follows for the most part a peaceful course of political action, has also produced a religious literature and an educational system that has had definite influence among many in the Arab world and even elsewhere. It is important not to confuse the moderate positions of the Ikhwān in Egypt and elsewhere with violent groups, such as *al-Takfīr wa'l-hijrah* (Accusation of Heresy and Migration), that have taken up arms against governments in Egypt and some other lands. Adherents to the philosophy and cause of the Ikhwān are also found in the Arab countries of North Africa, although in smaller numbers, although here again one must not confuse their followers with *jihādist* movements throughout that region, especially in Algeria and Morocco. It is also necessary to mention here that the followers of an organization called the *Fadī'iyān-i islām* (literally, "those who sacrifice themselves for Islam"), founded in Iran in the 1940s and claiming to be based on the model of the Ikhwān, was involved in the elimination of certain political figures such as the Iranian prime minister Ḥasan 'Alī Manṣūr before the Islamic Revolution of 1979.

In Turkey, the appearance of a remarkable politico-religious figure, Sayyid Badī' al-Zamān Nūrsī, during the early decades of the fourteenth/twentieth century at the time of Ataturk and the outward secularization of Turkey, made possible the founding of a semisecret organization, usually known as Nursi, whose aim was the protection of Islam from secularism. The members of this organization grew rapidly in number and represent today a very significant voice in Turkey. Led by Fathullah Gülen, who is now in exile in the United States, they are usually given more to Islamic education and the rejuvenation of the Islamic faith based on the Quranic commentary of their founder than to political activism or direct violence, although they do have their own specific programs for the establishment of an Islamic order. There have been, however, other Islamic movements in Turkey that have been known to use violence in espousing the cause of the reestablishment of the caliphate abolished by Ataturk or some other form of an Islamic state.

Not all Islamic political activism in recent times is necessarily "fundamentalist," as can be seen in the role of the Naqshbandiyyah Sufi

Order during the first Chechnyan war against Russia, in Islamic resistance movements in Central Asia before the fall of the Soviet Union, in Sinkiang in western China today, in the war against the Russian occupation of Afghanistan, in the Balkan wars, and elsewhere. It is noteworthy to recall, however, that in many of these areas neo-Wahhābī movements, usually supported financially by outside sources, particularly of Saudi origin, have sought to replace more traditional forms of Islam, often with opposition from local Muslims, as we see in Bosnia. The most obvious case of this phenomenon is the replacement of the Sufi-inspired movement of Shāh Mas'ūd by that of the Taliban in Afghanistan, resulting in the appearance of al-Qā'idah in that land, the Western conquest of Afghanistan, and the tragic war that continues to this day and has now spread into western Pakistan. To see how different this kind of "fundamentalism" is from traditional Islam, for which it is often mistaken, it is enough to recall that one of the first acts of the Pakistani Taliban when it conquered the Swat Valley was the destruction of the historical Sufi shrines and centers of traditional Islamic religious activity in the region.

As for Iraq, there was little sign of neo-Wahhābī and Salafī tendencies in that land before the second Iraqi war and the fall of the Ba'thist regime. But the ensuing realignment of power between Sunnis and Shī'ites, which has led to horrific sectarian fighting, has brought neo-Wahhābism and even al-Qā'idah, whose ideological roots are to be found in certain extreme interpretations of Wahhābism, upon the scene. When one speaks of "fundamentalism" and Islamic political activism in Iraq, it is important to remember, however, that the supreme leader of Shī'ism, Ayatollah Sīstānī, who resides in Najaf, has continuously opposed religious and political violence, including among certain Shī'ite groups.

The complexity of the notion of "fundamentalism" in the Islamic world becomes particularly evident when one turns to the case of Iran, the largest Shī'ite country in the world. In the West many consider the Islamic Republic of Iran the "fundamentalist" regime par excellence. Yet how different it is from the Afghanistan of the Taliban, the Islamic regime of Sudan, or Saudi Arabia, the home of Wahhābism, which is nonetheless governed by the traditional institution of the monarchy. To understand the Iranian situation, it is necessary to take a step backward in time. Traditionally Twelve-Imam Shī'ism had avoided direct political power, leaving it to the Mahdī to take political power into his hands upon his reappearance on the historical stage, although there have historically been some periods of Shīʿite political activism and some Shīʿite *'ulamā'* played important political roles in the Safavid, Zand, Qajar, and Pahlavi periods. The revolutionary message of Ayatollah Khomeini marks a departure from the "quietist" attitude of many of the Shīʿite authorities before him or even after him, but his movement cannot simply be called "fundamentalist" without any qualification. In the field of Islamic Law and theology he was a strict traditionalist and he was far from being against Islamic intellectuality and spirituality. The reverse is in fact true. Ayatollah Khomeini was an important traditional Islamic philosopher in the line of Mullā Ṣadrā, and a major interpreter and commentator of Ibn 'Arabī, the supreme master of Islamic gnosis,[7] and also a poet who composed poetry in the line of the classical tradition of Persian Sufism.

The Islamic Revolution of 1979 itself took place with the participation of "Islamic Marxists," Communists, and secular Western-oriented so-called intellectuals as well as traditional Islamic elements. Once the dust settled, however, an "Islamic order" was established that cannot simply be called "fundamentalist," although elements that can be called "fundamentalist" have remained strong within it until today. Let us recall a few diverse but important facts. Although Islamic headdress has been imposed upon women, half the students of the medical school of Tehran University, the "mother" institution of higher learning in Iran, are female. Traditional intellectual and artistic life is flowering; and there is more study of Western schools of philosophy, including contemporary ones, in Iranian religious centers of learning, which produce the class of religious scholars, or *'ulamā'*, than in any other Islamic country. Iranian cinema is world famous, and films from Iran continue to win prestigious international awards. Sunnis live side by side with Shīʿites, and there is usually little contention between them (with occasional exceptions, as in Baluchistan), in contrast to the situation in Saudi Arabia or Iraq.

The Islamic Revolution certainly took place to a large extent as a reaction against the encroachment of modernism, which was threatening the Islamic nature of traditional Persian culture and society, but the order that the revolution established cannot simply be called "fundamentalist" as this term is usually understood. Rather, it contains strong traditional elements and paradoxically certain modern ones. The case of Iran, where the most important and consequential religious revolution of the twentieth century took place, reveals fully the complexity of very diverse currents in the Islamic world that are usually clustered together under the heading "fundamentalism." In Iran today there exists a state that stands strongly against Western interests in the Middle East and can in a sense be called "fundamentalist." And yet traditional Islam and its arts and sciences also flourish and are encouraged, while Western science and technology, also strongly supported by the state, are also growing at a remarkable pace.

The types of "fundamentalism" thus far described can also be found in various forms in other Muslim lands, ranging from such countries as Sudan, Somalia, and Nigeria in Africa to Palestine, Lebanon, Pakistan, and Indonesia spread across the Asian continent into the islands of the Pacific Ocean, including even Mindanao in the Philippines. The only part of the Islamic world where such forces had made no headway at all was among Muslims in the Soviet Union and until recent years in China. But with the fall of the Soviet state, the situation also changed in both Central Asia and Caucasia, and "fundamentalist" elements, again usually inspired by neo-Wahhābism, began to appear in such places as Uzbekistan and also the Uighur region of western China.

"Fundamentalist" movements have also been related in many ways to the several international Islamic conferences, organizations, and leagues, such as the Muslim World League and the like, which have their centers in such places as Saudi Arabia, Pakistan, and even Europe and whose main goal is the unity of the Islamic world. Although the political perspectives of these organizations are not always the same, they share the aim of achieving some form of unity and bringing the Islamic peoples closer together. They are therefore often of interest to people who are also attracted to one form or another of the neo-Wahhābī, puritanical, or "fundamentalist" movements, although there is no necessary link between the two, and one can in fact remain a completely traditional Muslim and yet strive for the unity of the Islamic peoples, as is in fact the case in many instances. But there is also no doubt that many of the leaders and administrators of these international Islamic organizations are also the leaders of various kinds of "fundamentalist" movements. This connection is especially evident not only in Saudi Arabia but also in the Indo-Pakistani world and Southeast Asia.

Another reaction to the modern West to which reference was made earlier in this chapter, namely, the espousal of one form or another of modernism, has also led to the creation of powerful forces within the Islamic world today, forces whose nature and degree of Islamicity have, however, been open to debate. Since World War II, the very advent of political independence in many Islamic countries once again brought to the fore the question of the relationship between nationalism and Islam. From this debate have grown several forms of what might be called "Islamic nationalism," that is, a way of thinking that, accepting both Islam and a particular form of nationalism, seeks to wed the two together. Pakistan offers the most outstanding example of such a wedding between the idea of a nation or state in the modern sense and Islam. Because Pakistan was created for the sake of Islam, obviously its nationalism could not be anti-Islamic, as had been the case with certain earlier forms of strong nationalism, like that of Turkey. In fact, many Pakistanis consider this type of coupling of Islam and nationalistic sentiments positive, both from an Islamic point of view and from that of the geopolitical realities of their country. A similar but not necessarily same attitude can be found among many Bangladeshis, Malays, Senegalese, and so forth. In fact, in many Islamic countries, such as Persia, where a sense of nationhood, or at least separate existence as a distinct entity, preceded the intrusion of the modern European concept of nationalism, Islamic and national sentiments developed a modus vivendi that even in earlier centuries allowed Islam to flourish in its authentic, traditional form within the state without being abused for ends beyond itself, although this did also occur from time to time.

As for Arab nationalism, since it is already based not on an actual political entity such as Egypt, Syria, or Iraq, but on the unification of various present-day Arabic-speaking states into a larger and closely knit unit, it is of a unique nature and has created a phenomenon that is different from other types of nationalism within the Islamic world, such as Iranian or Turkish nationalism. But what is interesting from the point of view of this study is that earlier Arab nationalism was essentially a secular movement often led by Christian rather than Muslim Arabs. It has, moreover, left behind still at least one important political expression, that is, the Ba'th party, which survives in Syria. Yet Arab nationalism, whether in the form of Nasser's or Qadhafi's version or any other brand, became more and more mixed with Islamic elements. For most Arabs today, it is impossible to separate their "Arabism" (*'urūbah*) from Islam, and in fact among the general populace, when people use *'urūbah,* the connotation in their minds is almost completely Islamic. Arab nationalism has in a sense nationalized Islam, with all the dangers that such an act implies for the universal teachings of Islam, which are opposed to all forms of parochialism, especially the fanatical and narrow form of nationalism that grew out of the French Revolution in contrast to the natural love of men and women for their nation and country, to which the Prophet of Islam was referring when he said, "The love of one's nation [*waṭan*] comes from faith [in religion]." In any case, this process has caused most Arab nationalistic sentiments and forces to also possess strong Islamic elements, although the secular type of Arab nationalism is of course still also present in both eastern Arab countries and North Africa. Moreover, there are also more local forms of nationalism within the Arab world, such as Egyptian or Algerian nationalism, and within Iraq, Kurdish nationalism.

Another type of movement that grew out of the modernizing quarters within the Islamic world after World War II and that was in vogue among many young Muslims until a couple of decades ago includes "Islamic socialism" and "Islamic Marxism." Many of those who followed these movements were influenced of course by the Soviet and socialist worlds, with their apparent espousal of pro-Arabic and pro-Islamic causes in such matters as the Arab-Israeli question, although such movements tended to overlook the disregard of socialist states for the plight of Muslims within their countries themselves. Many people (such as some Arab socialists in Egypt and the followers of Zolfaqar Ali Bhutto in Pakistan) who after World War II accepted the slogan of "Islamic or Arab socialism," which was also a part of the ideology of many political parties, including the Ba'th, understood by "socialism" not an antireligious and secular ideology, but "social and economic justice"; in their desire to promulgate justice in their own societies they adopted an "Islamic socialist" stance. In certain states such as Libya, this ideological position was directly supported by the state and was made use of by existing political forces more or less sympathetic to the Soviet world. The theoretical constructs upon which this movement was based came, however, mostly out of leftist circles in France, and the movement itself was strongest among Islamic countries that were dominated culturally by the French, such as Algeria. It could also be found in the Arab Near East, where "Islamic socialism" came to replace Arab socialism in many places. There were also proponents of this amalgamation of Islam and socialism in Pakistan, India, and Southeast Asia.

"Islamic Marxism" was a concept of more recent origin with a short life. It became associated with certain extremist groups in the Middle East organized mostly during and after World War II by people who considered themselves nominally Muslims, but who used an almost completely Marxist political ideology and Marxist means of achieving their goals. In fact, the so-called Islamic Marxists interpreted Islam itself as a political revolutionary force in which revolution was understood in the context of the Marxist and post-Marxist schools in European thought. This movement naturally received much attention as well as support from the so-called intellectually Marxist circles in France and other European countries, not to speak of the Communist world itself, and the figures whose works were used by the "Islamic socialist" and "Islamic Marxist" groups were in close contact with leftist circles in the West and in some cases with Communist countries. Today, this type of modernism as an organized movement within the Islamic world is a spent force, but many of those who adhered to such ideologies integrated themselves into other types of political movements, including Islamic ones, and brought many of their ideas with them. There still survives in fact an intellectual movement in Egypt called the "Islamic Left" (*al-yasār al-islāmī*), which is not, however, Marxist in the classical sense, and certain elements of ideas inherited from Marxist ideology survive under different guises in Iran.

Islamic responses to the West on the political and social planes in the form of modernistic interpretations of Islam cannot, however, be limited to nationalism, socialism, and Marxism. There is also the espousal of what one can call Western liberalism, which many in North America consider to be based on democracy and capitalism; in Europe democratic socialism is also identified by many political parties with liberalism. Now, it is true that one does not find any significant movement in the Islamic world that identifies itself with "Islamic capitalism" as such, but there are certainly many movements in Islamic countries that seek to develop what one may call "Islamic democracy" on the basis of the Quranic injunction, "Consult them [the people] in matters of state." As early as 1906, the first constitutional revolution in the Islamic world took place in Iran, leading to the establishment of an elected parliament within a constitutional monarchy on the basis of the promise that all laws passed should be in accordance with the *Sharī'ah*. This was followed by the establishment of regularly elected parliaments in Turkey and then one Islamic country after another. In some places democracy was identified specifically with secularism, as in Turkey, while in other places, such as Malaysia, this has not been the case.

Today in practically every Islamic country there is talk of democracy, and there are "elections" even within countries ruled by one kind of dictatorship or another. An Islamic democratic response to modernism is still a work in progress, and much of the intellectual energy of Islamic society is being devoted to this issue. At the present moment, therefore, many different models are being formulated and implemented. In such conservative monarchies as Kuwait, elected bodies are finally being established. In others, such as Malaysia and more recently Indonesia, democratic institutions are functioning well; they are beginning to do so to some extent also in Iraq. In Pakistan attempts at the practice of democracy have been punctuated by military rule. In the Islamic Republic of Iran, which is governed according to the theory of the "rule of the jurisprudence" (*wilāyat-i faqīh*), there are nevertheless elections for the president and members of the parliament. The present state of the development of an "Islamic democracy" is therefore very complicated and cannot be summarized in simple terms.

What is certain is that the Islamic response to Western liberalism is turning more and more to Islamic solutions rather than simple imitation of Western ideas and institutions; these cannot be simply imported from the West without important modifications. If democracy as currently understood is a Western idea rooted in Western culture and historical experiences particular to Europe and North America, what does it mean in the context of Islamic society? How should Islamic political thought develop in light of authentic Islamic teachings as well as in the context of the challenges posed by the West? These and similar questions are at the center of Islamic intellectual concerns, and influential Muslim thinkers from Morocco to Indonesia are seeking to answer them.[8]

The response of Islam to modernism in the form of what is often called Islamic modernism is not of course confined to the political and social domains. It includes the field of economics as currently understood. There is now a major international movement to Islamicize this field and to develop what has now come to be known as Islamic economics, embracing Islamic banking, finance, and so on. It also encompasses the arts and the humanities including literature and philosophy, and even science and technology. In fact, one of the most important intellectual debates of the past few decades in the Islamic world has been the relation of Islam to science and the meaning of a science based on the Islamic and not the modern worldview, or "Islamic science," which I began to discuss for the first time half a century ago.[9] Many of the chapters that follow will be dealing with these more specific subjects.

The Islamic modernist response has now come to affect to some extent even religion itself. The earlier Islamic modernists going back to such thirteenth/nineteenth-century figures as Sir Sayyid Aḥmad Khān in India and Muḥammad 'Abduh in Egypt were concerned mostly with education, the introduction of some form of rationalism into Islamic theological discourse, the practice of *ijtihād* (the giving of fresh interpretations) in matters of Islamic Law, reform of the educational system, and so forth. The central tenets of the Islamic belief systems concerning such questions as the oneness of God, the finality of the prophetic message brought by the Prophet of Islam, the Quran as the verbatim Word of God, and similar issues were usually not questioned, and when they were, such views had little effect upon the mainstream Islamic community. It is only in recent decades that some Muslim thinkers, including several well-known ones in Iran, have sought to reinterpret the very meaning of revelation and therefore the nature of the Quran in relation to the Prophet. Such thinkers are influenced in many cases by current discussions of Western Christian theologians on the subject of revelation and sacred scripture. This is an extensive subject that cannot be dealt with here, but it is necessary to add that Islamic reformist and modernist movements have had much less religious influence upon the Islamic community as a whole than most Western students of the subject would have us believe. A figure such as al-Ghazzālī, the celebrated theologian and Sufi of the sixth/twelfth century, is still a much more powerful and influential religious authority in the Islamic world than all the so-called reformers taken together.

The cataclysmic events of recent years have also brought back to life the movement of Mahdiism, which had been dormant for over a century since its appearance as a result of the first encounter between Islam and the modern Western world. The fact remains that much of the Islamic world remains today under the cultural and economic domination of non-Islamic forces before whose aggressive power many Muslims feel helpless. Attempts to gain freedom from this domination through industrialization and related processes bring with them, however, a greater destruction of Islamic values, because of the innate opposition of these processes to values taught by Islam. As a result of the spread of modernism, the world as a whole seems to be confronted with so many apparently insoluble problems, such as the environmental crisis, and the forces of destruction have become such that all peoples are threatened with various dangers and even extinction at all times. These conditions have helped to bring back the expectation of the imminent appearance in this world of the Mahdī, the one who will destroy inequity and reestablish the rule of God on earth. The fact that the Blessed Prophet had promised that at the beginning of every century a renewer (*mujaddid*) would come to revive Islam from within only strengthened this feeling of expectation for the Mahdī at the beginning of the fifteenth Islamic century. In the fall of 1979 (corresponding to 1400 of the Islamic calendar), the holiest site in Islam, namely, the House of God in Mecca, was captured temporarily by a number of Saudis in the name of the Mahdī, although the forces at work were far from being simply those of a few pious Muslims helping to bring about the Parousia. During the Iranian Revolution of 1979 many people also believed that the coming of the Mahdī was imminent, and a wave of Mahdiism is to be seen in Iran even today. Without doubt, as the forces of destruction in the world increase, as the order of nature strains ever more under the burden of a technology that is alien to the natural rhythms of the life of the planet, and as movements that speak in the name of Islam itself fail to create the ideal Islamic order that they always promise, this sense of expectation of the imminent coming of the Mahdī and movements associated with it are bound to increase among traditional and devout Muslims. This sense of expectation, or *intiẓār,* among present-day Muslims is certainly a reality to be reckoned with and is bound to continue as a powerful one in the future

Finally, there is a fourth kind of reality in contemporary Islam, not listed above, that must be mentioned, especially since it has received practically no attention so far in Western analyses of the contemporary Islamic world.

This reality is the revival of the Islamic tradition from within by those who have encountered the modern world fully and who, with complete awareness of the nature of that world and all the religious, philosophical, scientific, and social problems it poses, have returned to the heart of the Islamic tradition to find answers and to revive the Islamic world as a spiritual reality amid the chaos and turmoil created throughout the world by what are called modernism/post-modernism and "fundamentalism." The number in this group has of necessity been small, although traditional Islam is still the form of Islam followed by the great majority of Muslims. The theater of action of this group has been not mass meetings or political gatherings, but the hearts and minds of individuals gathered in small circles. For this group, Islam is traditional Islam with its roots sunk in Heaven and its branches spread through a vast world stretching in space from the Atlantic to the Pacific and encompassing a time span of over fourteen centuries.

This group of traditionalists rejects nothing of the Islamic tradition, not its art, sciences, or philosophy, and certainly not Sufism and the inner teachings, which they consider to be the heart of the whole body of Islam, whose limbs, governed by the *Sharī'ah*, are animated by the blood flowing from this heart. For this group, it is Islamic metaphysics that provides answers to problems posed by such modern ideologies and "isms" as rationalism, humanism, materialism, evolutionism, psychologism, and the like. For it, the revival of the Islamic world must come from a revival within Muslims themselves. This group's idea of reform is not that of the modernists or "fundamentalists," which always begins with the outward; the latter always wish to reform the world, but never individual human beings themselves. These traditionalists emphasize inner reform of men and women and through them of Islamic society as a whole. Their attitude toward the world, including the modern one, is not that of passive acceptance. They criticize the modern world in light of immutable principles and view it as a canvas, alluring from afar, but shown to be of an illusory nature when examined from close quarters. They stand at the center of Islamic orthodoxy and consider all violent movements that incorporate the worst elements of Western civilization in order to combat that civilization to be a disservice to Islam and below the dignity of God's last revelation.

This group believes in inner revival (*tajdīd*), which is a traditional

Islamic concept, and not external reform (*iṣlāḥ*) in its modern sense, which has thus become an alien idea grafted upon the body of Islam. The model for this group is an al-Ghazzālī, an 'Abd al-Qādir al-Jīlānī, or a Shaykh Aḥmad Sirhindī, not some thirteenth/nineteenth- or fourteenth/twentieth-century leftist revolutionary who simply bears a Muslim name or some self-righteous puritanical reformer or angry "fundamentalist" who is impervious to the inner and intellectual teachings of religion. This group acts without acting, in the sense that its function is more that of knowledge and spiritual presence than of ordinary activism. But it is from this group that there has flowed and continues to flow some of the most profound and religiously significant Islamic responses to the modern world. And it is this group that in the long run will have the deepest effect upon the Islamic community, as has been the case during most of Islamic history.[10]

Chapter Two

JIHĀD

Its Spiritual Significance

> But those who strive [perform *jihād*] for Our sake, We shall surely guide them in Our ways. Truly God is with the virtuous.
> *Quran XXIX: 69*

> You have returned from the lesser *jihād* to the greater *jihād*.
> *Ḥadīth*

Perhaps today no issue concerning Islam is as sensitive and as often debated in the West as that of *jihād*. Discussed in the mass media as well as in scholarly books, the various meanings given to the term are not only based on the divergent views of Western interpreters, but also reflect the profound differences that exist between the traditionalists and "fundamentalists" in their interpretation of this crucial concept. At the present moment, when the image of Islam in the West depends so much upon the understanding of the meaning of *jihād*, it is of the utmost importance to comprehend the way traditional Islam has envisaged this key idea over the ages and the manner in which it is related to Islamic praxis.

The Arabic term *jihād*, usually translated into European languages incorrectly as "holy war," more on the basis of its juridical usage in limited circumstances than on its much more universal meaning in the Quran, *Ḥadīth*, and Islamic spirituality and ethics, is derived from the root *jhd*, whose primary meaning is "to strive" or "to exert oneself." Its translation as "holy war," combined with the erroneous notion prevalent in the West of Islam as the "religion of the sword," has helped to eclipse its inner, spiritual significance and distort its connotation. Nor has the appearance upon the stage of history during the last century, especially during the past few years, of an array of mostly "fundamentalist" or revolutionary movements within the Islamic world that use the term *jihād* or one of its derivative forms helped to remove the distorted understanding of this key term or to make known to Westerners the full import of its traditional meaning, which alone is of concern to us here. Instead, recent distortions and even a total reversal of the meaning of *jihād* as understood by Muslims over the ages have made it more difficult than ever before to gain insight into this key religious and spiritual concept, and the term has even entered the English language in a caricature form.

To comprehend the spiritual significance of *jihād* and its wide application to nearly every aspect of human life as understood by Islam, it is necessary to remember that Islam bases itself on the idea of establishing equilibrium within human beings, in the human society where they function and fulfill the goals of their earthly life as well as within the environment in which they live. This equilibrium, which is the terrestrial reflection of Divine Justice and the necessary condition for peace in the human domain, is the basis upon which the soul takes flight toward that peace that, to use Christian terms, "passes all understanding." If Christianity sees the aim of the spiritual life and its own morality as based upon the vertical flight toward that perfection and ideal that is embodied in Christ, Islam sees it in first establishing equilibrium, both outward and inward, and then using that equilibrium as a basis from which to undertake the vertical journey. The very stability of Islamic society over the centuries, the immutability of Islamic norms embodied in the *Sharī'ah,* and the timeless character of traditional Islamic civilization, which is the consequence of its permanent and immutable prototype, are all reflections of both the ideal of equilibrium and its realization. This equilibrium, which is so evident in both the teachings of the *Sharī'ah* (or Divine Law) and works of Islamic art, is inseparable from the very name of *islām,* which is related to both *salām,* peace, and *taslīm,* surrender to God.

The preservation of equilibrium in this world, however, does not mean simply a static or inactive passivity, since life by nature implies movement. In the face of the contingencies of the world of change, of the withering effect of time, of the vicissitudes of terrestrial existence, to remain in equilibrium requires continuous exertion. It means carrying out *jihād* at every stage of life. Human nature being what it is, given to forgetfulness and suffering from the conquest of our immortal soul by the carnal soul or passions, the very process of life in both the individual and the human collectivity implies the ever present danger of loss of equilibrium; in fact, of falling into the state of disequilibrium that, if allowed to continue, cannot but lead to disintegration on the individual level and chaos on the scale of community life. To avoid this tragic end and to fulfill the entelechy of the human state, which is the realization of unity (*al-tawḥīd*) or total integration, Muslims both as individuals and as members of Islamic society must carry out *jihād;* that is, they must exert themselves at all moments of life to fight a battle, at once both inward and outward, against those forces that, if not combated, will destroy that necessary equilibrium on the foundation of which normal human life is based. This fact is especially true if society is seen as a collectivity that bears the imprint of the Divine Norm rather than an ant heap of contending and opposing units and forces and the human being is seen as God's vicegerent (*khalīfat Allāh*) on earth rather than a merely terrestrial creature.

Human beings are at the same time both spiritual and corporeal beings; they are a microcosm "complete" unto themselves, if they realize with the help of God all their latent possibilities. Yet they are also members of a society within which alone are certain aspects of their being developed and certain needs fulfilled. They possess at once an intelligence, whose substance is ultimately of a divine character, and sentiments, which can either veil their intelligence or abet their quest for their own Origin. In them are found both love and hatred, generosity and covetousness, compassion and aggression. Moreover, there have existed until now not just one but several "humanities," each with its own distinct religious and moral norms; also national, ethnic, and racial groups with their own bonds of affiliation. As a result, the practice of *jihād,* as applied to the world of multiplicity and the vicissitudes of human existence in the external world, has come to acquire numerous ramifications in the fields of political, economic, and occasionally military activity as well as in social life in general; consequently it has come to partake, on the external level, of the complexity that characterizes the human world.

In its most outward sense, *jihād* came to signify the defense of *dār al-islām,* that is, the Islamic world, from invasion and intrusion by non-Islamic forces. The earliest wars of Islamic history, which threatened the very existence of the young community, came to be known as *jihād* par excellence in this outward sense of "holy war." But it was upon returning from one of these early wars, which was of paramount importance for the survival of the newly established religious community and therefore of cosmic significance, that the Blessed Prophet nevertheless said to his companions that they had returned from the lesser holy war to the greater holy war—the inner battle against all the forces that would prevent humans from living according to the theomorphic norm that is their primordial and God-given nature.

Throughout Islamic history, the call for the lesser holy war has echoed in the Islamic world when parts or the whole of that world have been threatened by forces from without or within. Nearly all Shīʿite religious scholars (*ʿulamāʾ*) and many Sunni ones have in fact insisted that this type of external *jihād* can only be defensive (*difāʿī*) and not aggressive. The call to *jihād* in light of this meaning has been especially persistent since the thirteenth/nineteenth century with the advent of colonialism and the threat that it posed and continues to pose, in one form or another, to the very existence of the Islamic world. It must be remembered, however, that even in cases where the idea of the need to carry out *jihād* has been evoked in certain parts of the Islamic world, it has not usually been a question of religion simply sanctioning war, but rather of the attempt of a society in which religion remains of central concern to protect itself from being conquered either by military and economic forces or by cultural invasions of an alien nature. This does not mean, however, that in some cases, in earlier centuries as well as in recent times, religious sentiments have not been used or misused to intensify or legitimize a conflict. But to say the least, the Islamic world does not have a monopoly on this abuse, as the history of other civilizations, including even those that became secularized, such as the Christian West, demonstrates so amply. Moreover, human nature being what it is, once religion ceases to be of central significance to a particular human collectivity, people then fight and kill each other for issues much less exalted than their heavenly faith, such as economic gain. By including the question of war in its sacred legislation, Islam did not condone, but rather sought to limit war and its consequences, as the history of the traditional Islamic world bears out. In any case, the idea of total war and the actual practice of the extermination of whole civilian populations did not grow out of a civilization whose dominant religion saw *jihād* in a positive light.

On the more external level, the lesser *jihād* also applies in the socioeconomic domain. It implies the reassertion of justice in the external environment of human existence, starting with the individual. To defend one's rights and reputation, to defend the honor of oneself and one's family, is itself a *jihād* and a religious duty. So is the strengthening of all those social bonds, from the family to the whole of the Muslim people (*al-ummah*), which the *Sharī'ah* emphasizes. To seek social justice in accordance with the tenets of the Quran as interpreted traditionally—but not of course in the modern secularist sense—is a way of reestablishing equilibrium in human society (that is, of performing *jihād*), as in the case of constructive economic enterprises, provided the well-being of the whole person and society itself is kept in mind and material welfare does not become an end in itself; provided, in fact, one does not lose sight of the already quoted Quranic verse, "The other world is better for you than this one." To forget the proper relation between the two worlds would itself be instrumental in bringing about disequilibrium and would be a kind of *jihād* in reverse.

All of those external forms of *jihād* would remain incomplete and in fact contribute to an excessive externalization of human beings, if they were not complemented by the greater, or inner, *jihād* that one should carry out continuously within oneself. The nobility of the human state resides in the constant tension between what we appear to be and what we really are, and also in the need to transcend ourselves throughout this journey of earthly life in order to become what we really "are."

From the spiritual point of view, all the "pillars" of Islam can be seen as related to *jihād*. The fundamental witnesses (*shahādah*), "There is no divinity but God," and "Muḥammad is the messenger of God," through whose testimony a person becomes a Muslim, are not only statements about the Truth as seen in the Islamic perspective, but also weapons for the practice of inner *jihād*. The very form of the first letter of the first witness (*lā ilāha illa'Llāh* in Arabic), when written in Arabic calligraphy, is like a bent sword with which all otherness is removed from the Supreme Reality, while all that is positive in manifestation is returned to that Reality. The second witness is the blinding assertion of the powerful and majestic descent of all that in a positive manner constitutes the cosmos, humanity, and revelation from that Supreme Reality. To invoke ritually the two witnesses in the form of the sacred language in which they were revealed is to practice the inner *jihād* and to bring about awareness of who we are, whence we came, and where our ultimate abode is.

The daily prayers (*ṣalāh* or *namāz*), which constitute the heart of the Islamic rites, are again a never ending *jihād* that punctuates human existence in a continuous rhythm in harmony with the rhythm of the cosmos. To perform the prayers with regularity and concentration requires the constant exertion of our will, an unending battle striving against forgetfulness, dissipation, and laziness. In short, it is itself a form of spiritual warfare, to use the title of a classical Orthodox Christian text on spirituality.

Likewise, the fast of Ramaḍān, in which one wears the armor of inner purity and detachment against the passions and temptations of the outside world, requires an asceticism and inner discipline that cannot come about except through an inner *jihād*. Nor is the *ḥajj,* the pilgrimage to the center of the Islamic world in Mecca, possible without long preparation and effort, often suffering and hardship. It requires great effort and exertion, so that the Prophet could say, "The *ḥajj* is the most excellent of all *jihāds*." Like the knight in quest of the Holy Grail, the pilgrim to the house of the Beloved must engage in a spiritual warfare whose end makes all ordinary sacrifice and hardship pale into insignificance; the *ḥajj* to the House of God implies, for the person who practices the inner *jihād,* an encounter with the Master of the House, who also resides at the center of that other Ka'bah that is the heart.

Finally the giving of *zakāh,* or religious tax, is again a form of *jihād,* not only in that in parting with one's wealth one must fight against the covetousness and greed of one's carnal soul, but also in that, through the payment of *zakāh* in its many forms, one contributes to the establishment of economic justice in human society. Although *jihād* is not one of the "pillars of Islam" according to most schools of thought, it in a sense resides within all the other "pillars." From the spiritual point of view, in fact, all of the "pillars" can be seen in the light of the inner *jihād,* which is essential to human life and which does not oppose, but rather complements, contemplation and the attainment of peace that results from the contemplation of the One.[1]

The great stations of perfection in the spiritual life can also be seen in light of the inner *jihād.* To become detached from the impurities of the world in order to repose in the purity of the Divine Presence requires an intense *jihād,* for our soul has its roots sunk deeply in that transient world that, being fallen creatures, we mistake for reality. To overcome with perfect action the lethargy, passivity, and indifference of the soul, characteristics that have become second nature to it as a result of our forgetting who we really are, constitutes likewise a constant *jihād.* To restrain the soul from dissipating itself outwardly as a result of its centrifugal tendencies and to bring it back to the center, wherein reside Divine Peace and all the beauty that the soul seeks in vain in the domain of multiplicity, is again an inner *jihād.* To melt the hardened heart into a flowing stream of love that would embrace the whole of creation by virtue of love for God is to perform the alchemical process of *solve et coagula* (solution and coagulation) inwardly; this "work" is none other than an inner battle against what the soul has become, in order to transform it into what it "is" and has never ceased to be, if only it were to become aware of its own nature. Finally, to realize that only the Absolute is absolute and that only the Self can ultimately utter "I" is to perform the supreme *jihād* of awakening the soul from the dream of forgetfulness and enabling it to gain the highest principal knowledge for the sake of which it was created. Inner *jihād,* or "spiritual warfare," seen esoterically, can be considered therefore at once the key to the understanding of the whole spiritual process and the path to the realization of the One that lies at the heart of the total Islamic message. The Islamic path toward perfection can be conceived in light of the symbolism of the greater *jihād,* to which the Prophet of Islam, who founded this path on earth, himself referred. In no case can *jihād* be simply equated with holy war as understood by either most Westerners or many of the so-called Islamic fundamentalists.

In the same way that with every breath the principle of life, which functions in us irrespective of our will and as long as it is willed by Him who created us, exerts itself through *jihād* to vitalize our whole body, at every moment in our conscious life we should seek to perform *jihād* to establish equilibrium not only in the world about us, but above all within us, so as to awaken us to that Divine Reality that is the very source of our consciousness. For us as spiritual beings, every breath is a reminder that we should continue the inner *jihād* until we awaken fully from all daydreaming and until the very rhythm of our heart echoes that primordial sacred Word or Name by which all things were made and by means of which all beings return to their Origin. The Prophet said, "Man is asleep, and when he dies he awakens." Through inner *jihād,* we die already in this life in order to cease all dreaming, in order to awaken to that Reality that is the origin of all realities, in order to behold that Beauty of which all earthly beauty is but a pale reflection, in order to attain that Peace that we all seek, but that can in fact be found only through the practice of inner *jihād.*

Chapter Three

ISLAMIC WORK ETHICS

Many factors during the past two centuries have combined to bring the issue of work ethics to the fore in debates in the Islamic world, not only among governmental and managerial figures concerned with work and economic activity, but also among religious scholars and academic sociologists and ethicists. This period began with the rapid expansion of Western colonial powers in many regions of the Muslim world, such as North Africa, Egypt, and Muslim India. It also coincided with a degree of passive decadence in traditional Islamic society marked by decreases in energy and efficiency in the workplace. The combination of these factors caused many modernized intellectual and political leaders of Islamic society to admire the work ethics of their colonizers, while criticizing colonialism itself, and to contrast the work ethics of Europeans to those of Muslims. To these elements was added the en masse migration in the Islamic world of many workers from villages into big cities in the fourteenth/twentieth century. Cut off from their traditional social matrix, many of these workers also left behind the norms of Islamic work ethics they had been taught and practiced to one degree or another in the village or small town from which they had hailed. Consequently, the question of honesty in work, responsibility, punctuality, devotion to seeking to do as perfect a job as possible, the correct relation between employee and employer, and many other elements came to be debated in nearly every country. This situation itself necessitated a new discussion of Islamic work ethics, whose resuscitation and application many have considered essential for creating a more efficient and morally upright workforce in various Islamic countries. It is in the context of the interplay of these and other social, political, and economic forces and elements, which one observes from Malaysia to Morocco, that we turn to a study of traditional Islamic work ethics, which remains one of the most important issues in the Islamic world today.

In discussing this question of central concern to present day Muslims it must first of all be remembered that work carried out in accordance with the *Sharīʿah* is a form of *jihād* and is inseparable from the religious and spiritual significance associated with it. Moreover, in order to understand the ethical dimension of work from the traditional Islamic point of view, it is necessary to recall at the outset the fact that the term "work" in Arabic is not distinguished from the word for "action" in its most general sense and is treated by the Divine Law (*al-Sharīʿah*) in the same category. In fact, if one were to look for the translation of the word "work" in an English-Arabic dictionary, one would usually find the two terms, *ʿamal* and *ṣunʿ*, given as its equivalents. The first of these terms means "action" in general as contrasted with "knowledge," and the second, "making" or "producing" something in the artistic or artisanal sense of these words.[1] Human beings perform two types of actions in relation to the world about them. They either act within or upon that world or else make things by molding and remolding materials, forms, and objects drawn from that world.

Work ethics in classical Islamic teachings applies in principle to both categories, to both *ʿamal* and *ṣunʿ*, since the Divine Law covers in one way or another the whole network of human actions. Although the principles of the aesthetic aspect of *ṣunʿ*, or "art," in the original meaning of the word, belong to the inner dimension of the Islamic revelation,[2] the ethical aspect of both *ʿamal* and *ṣunʿ*, or all that human beings do externally, is to be found in the injunctions and teachings of the *Sharīʿah*. It is true that for the purposes of a particular discussion, one may limit the meaning of work to its economic or social aspects, but to understand Islamic work ethics in universal terms it is necessary to remember this wider and more general concept of "work"; "work" is in fact never fully differentiated from human action, including art in general and the ethical considerations contained in the *Sharīʿah* pertaining to the domain of human action as a whole.

The Quran (V: 1) states, "O you who believe! Fulfill your agreements [*ʿuqūd*]." These agreements, or *ʿuqūd*, according to traditional Islamic commentators, include all human relations—to God, self, and world—and are a "commentary of rectitude" for observation of the moral dimension of all human life. As Muhammad Asad states in his commentary on this verse: "The term *'aqd* ("covenant") [translated above as "agreement"] denotes a solemn undertaking or engagement involving more than one party. According to Rāghib [one of the traditional commentators], the covenants referred to in this verse, 'are of three kinds: the covenants between God and man [i.e., man's obligations toward God], between man and his own soul, and between the individual and his fellow men'—thus embracing the entire area of man's moral and social responsibilities."[3]

In the worldview of traditional Muslims, the *'uqūd* to which reference is made in this Quranic verse range from the performance of daily prayers to digging a well or selling merchandise in the bazaar. The moral responsibility placed upon the shoulders of "believers" by this verse extends to work as well as worship and encompasses the whole of human life in accordance with the dicta of the *Sharī'ah,* which concern the dealings of human beings with God as well as with their neighbors and of course with and within themselves. The basis of all work ethics in Islam is to be found in the inescapable moral character of all human action and the responsibility that human beings bear for their actions, not only toward employer or employee, but also in relation to the work itself, which must be executed as well as the "actor," or worker, is capable of doing.

Responsibility for the work exists also and above all before God, who is witness to all human action. This sense of responsibility before God for consequences of all action, and hence work in the more limited economic sense, passes even beyond the grave and concerns humans beings' ultimate end as immortal beings. As in the Judeo-Christian tradition, in Islam human beings remain responsible for the moral consequences of their actions on the Day of Judgment, whose awesomeness and majesty are emphasized with such remarkable eloquence and power throughout the Quran, especially in its final chapters. The unitary perspective of Islam, which refuses to distinguish between the sacred and the profane, goes even farther, refusing to distinguish as far as ethical and eschatological consequences are concerned between religious acts and what are now called secular ones, between prayer and work, or, as Catholics would say, between *orare* and *labore.* The fear of God and the responsibility felt toward Him by traditional Muslims embrace acts of worship as well as work in the usual sense of the word. In fact, according to a well-known *ḥadīth,* God forgives one, upon repentance (*al-tawbah*), what one owes Him, but not what one owes to God's other creatures.

Traditional Muslims who are devout feel a strong sense of responsibility to fulfill the terms of a contract, to complete a task or a piece of work as well as possible, to satisfy the person for whom the work is being done, and to treat the person who does the work well and fairly. Many verses of the Quran and numerous *ḥadīths,* which have also penetrated the literature of the Islamic peoples in the form of poems and parables, continue to remind Muslims of the deeply religious nature of all work that is carried out in accordance with the *Sharī'ah* and the moral responsibility related to work in all its aspects, social and economic as well as artistic and aesthetic. Islamic work ethics is inseparable from the moral character of all that Muslims should accomplish in their earthly journey in accordance with the guidance and injunctions of the Divine Law.

Work is in fact closely associated with prayer and worship in all traditional societies, a link that is preserved and accentuated in Islam. The daily call to prayer (*al-adhān*) in its Shī'ite form repeats this principal relationship five times a day by exclaiming, *ḥayy^{a} 'ala'l-ṣalāh,* "Come unto the prayers"; *ḥayy^{a} 'ala'l-falāḥ,* "Come unto salvation"; and *ḥayy^{a} 'alā khayr al-'amal,* "Come unto good works." From prayer there flows salvation or felicity of soul, and from that state of salvation, correct action and good works; the word *'amal* itself appears once again in this basic assertion. Although the third part of this formula is not repeated in the Sunni form of the *adhān,* there too the rapport between prayer, work, and correct action is always emphasized. Such Quranic verses as, "By the declining day! Truly Man is in a state of ruin, save those who believe [and] perform righteous deeds" (CIII: 1–3), in which it is made clear that righteous deeds[4] follow from faith and attachment to the principles of religion, remind all Muslims, Sunni and Shī'ite alike, of the relation between prayer and work; and also of the prayerful nature of work itself, as long as it is performed in accordance with the *Sharī'ah.*

To understand Islamic work ethics, the intertwining of work, prayer, and even what is known in the modern world as leisure is of great importance. The rhythm of traditional Islamic life has always been such that the hours of work are punctuated by prayer; this is also true of what is considered cultural activity or leisure today. The very architecture of the traditional city is such that spaces for worship, work, education, cultural activities, and rest are harmoniously interrelated and integrated into an organic unity as far as the relation of these spaces and their function to each other are concerned. The very fact that in a traditional Islamic city people move from the space of the mosque to the place of work and to their home in an easy manner and break the hours of work regularly to perform the daily prayers as well as rest colors deeply the meaning of work itself. Both the space and the time within which work take place are transformed by the Islamic prayers, and thereby work itself gains a religious complexion that determines its ethical meaning in the Islamic context.

The first element of Islamic work ethics that must be considered is the *Sharī'ite* injunction that the accomplishment of whatever work is necessary to support oneself and one's family is as worthy, in the eyes of God, as the performance of religious duties classafied as obligatory (*wājib*). All persons capable of doing so must work to support themselves and those who depend upon them for their livelihood and sustenance, including not only those who work under them and the members of their immediate family, but sometimes also female members and old or incapacitated persons belonging to the extended family circle. This duty is usually incumbent upon the man of the family, but the women are also responsible when external necessity dictates their working outside the home, as can be seen very often in the agricultural sector of traditional society. Whatever is necessary for the continuation of human life gains, according to Islamic teachings, a religious sanction as the very result of that necessity.

There is, however, no emphasis in Islam upon the virtue of work for the sake of work, as one finds in certain forms of Protestantism. In the Islamic perspective, work is considered a virtue in light of one's needs and the necessity of establishing equilibrium in one's individual and social life. But this duty toward work, and provision for one's needs and for those of one's family, is always kept in check and prevented from becoming excessive by the emphasis that the Quran places upon the transience of life, the danger of greed and covetousness, and the importance of avoiding the excessive accumulation of wealth.[5]

Work, like everything else in life, must be seen and performed within the framework of the equilibrium that Islam seeks to establish in the life of each individual as well as of Islamic society as a whole. While the earliest Islamic community was still in Mecca, this nucleus of the future society, which consisted of a spiritual élite, was advised to spend much of the night in prayer and vigil; but in Medina, when a complete social order was established, the Prophet emphasized that the members of the new religious community in general should devote a third of their day to work, a third to sleep and rest, and a third to prayer, leisure, and family and social activities.[6] This prophetic example set an ideal for later Islamic society, in which, although the performance of work to support one's family is considered a religious duty, the exaggerated emphasis upon work for its own sake or only for greater material gain is rejected, inasmuch as such an attitude destroys the equilibrium that is the Islamic goal of life. If in many present-day Middle Eastern cities a taxi driver is seen to work much longer hours than is specified by the traditional tripartite division of the day while performing his difficult work as a religious duty to support an often large number of dependents, it is usually economic necessity that dictates such a prolonged working schedule. There is no desire to work as an end in itself. There is no innate religious value connected with work in itself simply as a means of amassing wealth or for any other reason outside of the patterns established by the prophetic *Sunnah* and the *Sharī'ah*.

According to Islamic Law, work itself, considered in its economic aspect, should be carried out following a contract based upon justice and responsibility on the part of both the employer and the employee. Workers are responsible both to the employer and to God to carry out, to the best of their ability, the work they have undertaken to accomplish on terms agreed by the two sides. Only then will the earnings from such a work be *ḥalāl* (that is, religiously speaking, legal and legitimate). The conditions and terms include, on the one hand, the amount of work, whether it be the hours specified, the price to be paid, or the quantity to be produced and, on the other hand, the quality to be achieved. There is a very strong moral element present among traditional Muslims as far as "eating *ḥalāl* bread" is concerned; that is, earning what one deserves for the accomplishment of a legally accepted piece of work according to the conditions of the agreement. If the worker cheats the employer in either the quantity or quality of the work to be accomplished according to their contract, then what is earned is not *ḥalāl,* and the consequences of "eating bread" that is not *ḥalāl* fall upon both the worker and all those who benefit from the worker's earnings. There has developed, in fact, within Islamic society, an elaborate system of giving alms, donations, and the like to make earnings *ḥalāl* and to prevent the negative consequences of eating non-*ḥalāl* "bread," consequences that for believers include the possibility of the wrath of God descending upon them in the form of illness, loss of property, or other calamities.

The *Sharī'ite* concepts of *ḥalāl* and *ḥarām* ("legally legitimate" and "prohibited") also affect the kind of work that Muslims can undertake. Certain types of work, such as the making and selling of wine or pork products, are forbidden by Islamic Law for Muslims (but not for non-Muslims living in Islamic society), while other activities, such as playing music for a public audience, are accepted by most jurists, but not by all, depending upon the type of music involved and the occasion for which it is performed. Of course all work related to acts that themselves are forbidden by the *Sharī'ah,* such as theft, gambling, and prostitution, are likewise *ḥarām* and must be avoided. Other types of work have been particularly encouraged by the *Sunnah* and *Ḥadīth,* among them being crafts and agriculture, which were practiced by many of the companions of the Prophet, including 'Alī,[7] and honest trade, which was the profession of the Prophet himself in his early life.

The responsibility of the worker before the employer and God in the performance of work that is *ḥalāl* and also performed in a *ḥalāl* manner must be reciprocated by the employer, who is also responsible before both God and the employee. The employer must fulfill the terms of the contract just as must the worker. Moreover, the employer must display kindness and generosity toward workers. Also, according to a well-known *ḥadīth,* workers should be paid their wages before the sweat has dried from their forehead.

Altogether the various aspects of work, including the relation between the worker and the employer, are seen by Islam to be at once ethical and economic; the two are never separated in the Islamic perspective. A personal, human relationship has been traditionally emphasized in all economic activity, a relationship that binds not only the two sides to each other, but also stresses that God is aware of all our actions and demands justice in all human relations, including those in this very important domain. The whole question of work and work ethics is in fact never envisaged in traditional Islamic thought from a merely economic point of view; it always includes an ethical component, according to the general Islamic perspective in which economics and ethics are combined. Economic activity divorced from ethical considerations based on justice and general human welfare is considered illegitimate![8]

The qualitative aspect of Islamic work ethics cannot be fully appreciated unless one delves into the kinds of work in which men and women were usually engaged in traditional Islamic society. These types of work involved such activities as agriculture, nomadic pasturing of sheep and other animals, artisanal work, economic transactions associated with the bazaar, domestic work, and employment in the juridical, bureaucratic, and military branches of government. In all these cases, a very human and personal relationship was emphasized in those cases where human beings and their interactions were primarily involved. As for activities such as agricultural and artisanal activities, a science and an art based upon metaphysical and cosmological principles related to the Quranic revelation[9] and a symbolic language inextricably wed to the Islamic religion[10] provided the matrix for work. Hence the very ambience, materials used, actions performed, and relations created took place in a sacralized universe in which everything possessed a religious and an ethical dimension, in which there was no type of work that was "secular" or without religious significance. Islam's success in creating a unified civilization dominated completely by the "idea" and "presence" of the Sacred provided a climate for work within which the ethical could not in fact be divorced from the economic. Islamic society, moreover, developed numerous ways and means whereby the various types of work alluded to above were sacralized, and both the quality of the work and the ethical responsibility of all parties were checked and guaranteed to the extent that the frailties and imperfections of human nature permit in any collectivity.[11]

On the most external level, the ethical requirements of work, including both production and transaction, were traditionally guaranteed by the *muḥtasib* (controller), whose function it was to see to it that, in accordance with the specific teachings of the Quran, the weights and measures used in the purchase and sale of articles were carefully tested, that the quality of the material sold matched the standard claimed by the seller, and so forth. The constant observation of various phases of work by religious authorities and the intermingling of the life of the ateliers and bazaars with that of the mosque also created to some extent an external religious guarantee of the preservation of the ethical conditions required by the *Sharīʿah* for work as both *ʿamal* and *ṣunʿ*. But the most important guarantee in this case was and continues to remain the conscience of individual Muslims and the religious values inculcated in them.

During later Islamic history more specific institutions developed that were directly concerned with the ethical aspects of work, organizations that related specific economic activities with moral and spiritual qualities. These institutions consisted of various guilds (*aṣnāf*), chivalric orders (*futuwwāt*), brotherhoods (*ukhuwwāt*), the *akhī* (my brother) movement, and so forth, which, from the Seljuq period on, spread throughout the cities and towns of the Islamic world on the basis of less formal organizations dating from earlier centuries.[12] These organizations, which still survive to some extent, were directly linked to Sufi orders and considered work itself to be an extension of spiritual discipline. A bond of a religious nature linked the members with each other as well as with the master, who was both the teacher of the craft or trade and a spiritual authority. A spirit of chivalry dominated the guilds, which were in fact connected with and often parts of orders of chivalry (*futuwwah* in Arabic; *jawānmardī* in Persian) both in their morphological and structural resemblance and in their association with Islamic esoteric teachings. The founder of both types of associations is considered traditionally to be 'Alī ibn Abī Ṭālib, whose central role in the dissemination of the esoteric teachings of Islam is only too well known and is reflected in the fact that all Sufi orders except one trace their origin back to him.

A code of honor, strict work ethics, responsibility for and devotion to the quality of work, pride in one's *métier,* generosity to others, aid to members of the guild, and many other ethical and spiritual precepts associated with work developed through such organizations. These guilds and orders were at once the guardians of ethical concern for work and the means by which the ethical character of the work of their members was guaranteed; they also guaranteed their members protection from external pressures and oppression.

In this domain, the particular category of work associated with the making of things, namely, the arts and crafts (which have in fact never been regarded as different forms of activity in Islam), needs to be particularly emphasized. All work that concerns the making of things, or *ṣun'*, possesses religious and spiritual significance when done according to traditional criteria: done with one's own hands and by means of techniques that possess an eminently symbolic, and hence spiritual, significance.[13] The ethical aspect of work in this case embraces also the aesthetic,[14] for to produce a work of beauty and quality requires the love of the maker for that work and brings into play the virtue of love of beauty and goodness. Such a work ennobles the soul of the person who creates it and fulfills deep religious and spiritual needs, while transmitting to the person who obtains the work not only an object that fulfills a certain external need, but also a joy that refreshes the soul and possesses a definite religious significance. It is enough to behold a genuine Persian or Anatolian carpet, woven with love and devotion rather than simply for the sake of economic gain, to realize how important and central is the question of the relation of individuals to their work in any consideration of the ethical dimension of work. A mechanical and impersonal manner of making things destroys a basic dimension of the ethical value of work, no matter how fair the wages or how physically favorable the working conditions.

In Islamic art, objects designed and made traditionally for everyday use, ranging from textiles and carpets to bowls and lamps, testify to the extremely wide range of all those fruits of human labor that reflect not only beauty, but also love, devotion, joy, and peace. These elements are inseparable from the ethical dimension of work in Islam. The traditional guilds, brotherhoods, and orders not only made possible the production of these works and the creation of the material basis of Islamic civilization imbued with beauty and harmony, but also provided a work ethics that embraced aesthetic considerations and related the love of beauty to the moral conditions of work. The moral and spiritual consequences upon the soul of the makers of things, who in creating objects according to the norms of traditional art also remold their own inner being, was always emphasized.[15]

If one were to study work ethics in Muslim society today, one would not discover all the qualities and characteristics that have been mentioned above among all workers—at least not everywhere and not among all types and classes of workers. Until a couple generations ago, many of these qualities could be observed everywhere. But more recently in a number of Islamic lands, many of the moral qualities of workers and the ethical dimension of work have declined or even disappeared, especially in larger urban areas, much of it as a result of the introduction of modern means of production, new labor organizations, dislocation of populations, and destruction of traditional social structures. The thesis presented above represents the traditional Islamic view of work ethics based upon the foundation of the Quran and *Ḥadīth* as well as on centuries of elaboration through *Sharī'ite* institutions, Sufi orders, the guilds, family training, and the general culture of Islamic society. But traditional Islamic society is no longer completely intact, and the attitudes and practices concerning work observable today are not always what they were traditionally. Rather, they represent the partial breakdown of the traditional norm before the onslaught of the various forces of modernism. This partial breakdown can be seen in the severing of the bond between many types of work and ethics; the use of modern technology, which destroys the spiritual and qualitative relationship between the maker of things and objects produced; the destruction of the master–disciple relationship; and the breaking of the spiritual link that used to exist between members of a guild, once guilds were turned into labor unions.

Furthermore, today workers in much of the Islamic world, especially in cities and bigger towns, are often cut off from their family and social matrix. Their relation to the rhythms and norms of nature has become severed. In many cases, modes of production based upon the impersonal machine have replaced traditional modes based upon love and devotion to a craft. Alien laws have partially supplanted the Divine Law and destroyed the homogeneity of the *Sharī'ah* as applied to all facets of life. Traditional institutions, such as the guilds, have declined or ceased to exist, and the all-important human example of a master craftsman who was also a religious and ethical teacher has become rare and, in certain alien forms of industry, nonexistent. All this has happened because the market to which Muslim workers are of necessity related has become increasingly dominated by sheer economic forces, purely quantitative considerations that are concerned only with profitability and blind to ethical and also aesthetic principles.

All of these, as well as other factors and forces, have partially destroyed the traditional fabric within which Islamic work ethics was applied and practiced over the centuries. Nevertheless, neither that work ethics nor the people who are still attached to it have ceased to exist completely. Much of that traditional work ethics survives; even in modernized sectors of society there is great nostalgia among many uprooted workers for that wholeness that characterized the traditional modes of work. Islamic work ethics, therefore, deserves to be better known and further studied, not only because it is still to be found in some segments of Islamic society, but also because it remains the ideal that many Muslim men and women seek to realize today. Despite the havoc caused within the Islamic world by the advent of modernism and reactions against it, devout Muslims, a category that includes most of those who work in one way or another in Islamic society, never forget the content of the *ḥadīth,* "Strange are the ways of a believer, for there is good in every affair of his hand."[16] Men and women of faith know that, if they are really people of faith, they must conform their work to the norms established by God and be able to offer their work to Him by performing it in accordance with spiritual principles, traditional methods, the ethical precepts contained in the sources of the Islamic revelation and the Divine Law promulgated by Islam.

Chapter Four

THE MALE AND THE FEMALE IN THE ISLAMIC PERSPECTIVE

Remembering Certain Basic Principles

> O Mankind! Truly We have created you from a male and a female. . . . Truly the most noble of you before God is the most reverent of you.
>
> *Quran XLIX: 13*

No tradition can pass over in silence the central question of the relationship between man and woman in religious as well as social life. Islam is no exception to this rule. On the contrary, traditional Islam, basing itself on the explicit teachings of the Quran and the guiding principles of the life of the Prophet, has developed intensive teachings concerning the relationship between the male and the female and has formulated the norms according to which the two sexes should live and cooperate in the social order. Today innovations of every sort resulting from emulation of modern Western practices and ideas about marriage, the role of women in society, and dynamics within the fragmented family have destroyed for many Muslims, especially in the big cities, the perennial teachings of Islam concerning the male and female relationship, from its metaphysical and spiritual to its most outward aspects. When to that is added the fact that the question of "women" in Islam has moved to the top of the agenda of the West in its study of and dealings with Islam, it becomes particularly necessary to reinstate the traditional Islamic point of view. And in doing so one must begin with the metaphysical principles that govern human nature and the complementary relationship that exists between the male and the female on the highest level and consequently in everyday life here on earth.

To speak of creation or manifestation is to speak of the manifold, or multiplicity, whose first stage is that primordial polarization between the two contending and complementary principles that are seen throughout the cosmos and that in human life appear as the male and female genders. In relation to the Divine Unity, all multiplicity is a veil, and from the perspective of the Divine Substance everything else is a series of accidents embracing all the reverberations of the One in the mirror of the many, which we call the world; or in fact the many worlds that at once hide and manifest the One. But from the point of view of the human order, the polarization or duality expressed by the differentiation of human beings into male and female is far from simply a biological accident. This differentiation is in fact a reflection of a complementarity within the Divine Attributes and is a most profound feature of what constitutes human nature. That is why in the Quranic verse quoted above, as well as in many other verses, God refers to creating pairs throughout His creation, including of course human beings, whom He made in two different forms, as man and woman. God Himself, and not some biological accident, is the creator of both man and woman, and whatever ensues from the distinction between the two sexes must be related to His Wisdom and Providence. The distinction between the sexes is not a later accident or accretion, but is essential to the meaning of the human state, although this distinction in no way destroys the significance of the androgynic reality (identified in Islam with the Universal or Perfect Man—*al-insān al-kāmil*), which both men and women carry within the depths of their being.[1]

Since God has created human beings in pairs, logically and metaphysically there must exist some element of difference that distinguishes one member of the pair from the other, for if two things were the same in every way, they would be identical. There is, therefore, of necessity a difference between the two sexes. They are not the same, at least if one takes the totality of being of each sex into consideration, although they may be equal under certain aspects and features. From the Islamic point of view, their equality in fact first and foremost involves the entelechy of the human state as such, in which both men and women participate by virtue of belonging to the human species. Both man and woman were created for immortality and spiritual deliverance; both are obliged to follow God's Laws, and both will one day stand before God to be judged by Him for their earthly actions. Below those levels, however, there are differences between the two sexes whose reality cannot be ignored in the name of any form of quantitative egalitarianism.

The difference between the two sexes cannot be only biological and physical because, in the traditional perspective, the corporeal level of existence has its principle in the subtle state, the subtle in the spiritual, and the spiritual in the Divine Reality Itself. The difference between the sexes cannot be reduced to anatomy and biological function. There are also differences of psychology and temperament, of spiritual types and even principles within the Divine Nature that are the sources *in divinis* (within the Divine Order) of the duality represented on the microcosmic level as male and female. God is both Absolute and Infinite. Absoluteness—and Majesty, which is inseparable from it—are manifested most directly in the masculine state; Infinity and Beauty, in the feminine state. The male body itself reflects majesty, power, and absoluteness, and the female body reflects beauty, beatitude, and infinity. But these principles are also reflected in all the intermediate realms of existence that, in each type of microcosm, male and female, separate the corporeal state from the Divine.

But since God is One, and man (*insān*), that is, the human being, whichever sex it might be, is a theomorphic being who reflects God's Names and Qualities,[2] each human being also reflects the One and seeks to return to the One. Hence there is at once complementarity and rivalry between the sexes. There is union and polarization. The female "is" at once Mary, who symbolizes the Divine Mercy in the Abrahamic traditions and the beatitude that issues from this Mercy, and Eve, who entices, seduces, and externalizes the soul of man, leading to its dissipation, although in Islam Eve is not the cause of man's loss of the Edenic state, as she is in traditional Christianity. For the male the female is at once the source of concupiscence and the theater for the contemplation of the Divinity in Its uncreated aspect. Likewise, man is at once the symbol of the Lord and Creator and a being who, having lost sight of his ontological dependence upon the Lord, would seek, as a usurper, to play the role of Lord and Creator while he remains a mortal and perishable being. The veil of cosmic manifestation, the *ḥijāb* of Islamic metaphysics, makes the relation between the sexes an ambivalent one. But the profound metaphysical relationship between the two sexes is such that there is at once the inclination for union with a member of the opposite sex, which means ultimately the need to regain the consciousness of beatific union possessed by the androgynic ancestor of humanity in the paradisal state, and rivalry between the sexes, since each human being is in turn a total image of the primordial *insān*.

Some religions have emphasized the negative aspect of sexuality, but Islam bases itself on its positive aspect as one of the means of perfection of the human state and, on the highest level, a symbol of union with God, sexual relations being of course governed by the injunction of the Divine Law. Addressing itself to the human being in the primordial nature (*al-fiṭrah*), to "man as such,"[3] Islam envisages the love of man and woman as inseparable from the love of God and as leading to God on the highest level.[4] There exists in Islamic spirituality, as a result of this perspective, a hierarchy of love stretching from what is called "metaphorical love" (*al-ʿishq al-majāzī*) to "real love" (*al-ʿishq al-ḥaqīqī*), which is the love of God Himself.[5] The well-known but elliptical *ḥadīth* of the Prophet, that of the things of this world he loved above everything else women, perfume, and prayer, alludes, spiritually speaking, to the positive aspect of sexuality in Islam, to the relation of the spiritual nature of womanhood to prayer, which is the most direct means of access to God for human beings, and to the most subtle of sensual experiences having to do with the olfactory faculty.[6] Moreover, the Quran (XXIV: 26) specifically relates the symbolism of perfume to sexual union.

It is because of the positive role accorded to sexuality in the Islamic perspective that so much erotic poetry, which sees human love as symbol of Divine Love, is to be found in the literature of Islamic spirituality. In much of Islamic spirituality God appears as the Beloved and the female as a precious being symbolizing inwardness and the inner paradise that has become hidden from man as a result of the loss of "the eye of the heart" and the power to perceive beings *in divinis*.[7] The fall of man into the state of separation and forgetfulness has brought about an exteriorization and inversion in that contemplation of female beauty mentioned so often by the mystics of both East and West, the contemplation that can aid man to return to the Center once again and that brings with it the beatitude in whose quest he spends so much of his efforts, knowingly or unknowingly. This power has ceased to operate for most human beings, except in a potential manner. Yet its echo persists; the physical joy of sexual union itself still reflects something of its paradisal archetype, whether one is aware of it or not, and remains proof of the sacred union that is the celestial prototype of all earthly unions between the sexes. It is this reflection that imparts upon the sexual act, despite the ontological hiatus between archetype and earthly reflection as well as the element of inversion that is also present between the symbol and the symbolized, something of the experience of the Infinite and the Absolute.

Ibn 'Arabī goes to the point of describing the contemplation of God in woman as the highest form of contemplation possible. He writes:

> When man contemplates God in woman, his contemplation rests on that which is passive; if he contemplates Him in himself, seeing that woman comes from man, he contemplates Him in that which is active; and when he contemplates Him alone, without the presence of any form whatsoever issued from Him, his contemplation corresponds to a state of passivity with regard to God, without intermediary. Consequently his contemplation of God in woman is the most perfect, for it is then God, in so far as He is at once active and passive, that he contemplates, whereas in the pure interior contemplation, he contemplates Him only in a passive way. So the Prophet—Benediction and Peace be upon him—was to love women because of the perfect contemplation of God in them. One would never be able to contemplate God directly in absence of all (sensible or spiritual) support, for God, in his Absolute Essence, is independent of all worlds. But, as the (Divine) Reality is inaccessible in respect (of the Essence), and there is contemplation (*shahādah*) only in a substance, the contemplation of God in women is the most intense and the most perfect; and the union which is the most intense (in the sensible order, which serves as support for this contemplation) is the conjugal act.[8]

Since religion concerns the final ends of human beings and their perfection, Islam has legislated and provided spiritual and ethical principles that, in conformity with its perspective, make use of this very important aspect of human nature, namely, sexuality, to help perfect human beings and to bring them felicity in both this world and the hereafter. Its perspective on sexuality therefore includes both its biological and spiritual aspects and also its alchemical effect upon the soul. The teachings of Islam on sexuality therefore apply to both the outward and inward dimensions of human life, Islam being the source of a social order as well as a spiritual path, a *Sharīʿah* as well as a *Ṭarīqah,*[9] or spiritual path. Also, as already mentioned, Islam envisages the quest after God, which is the ultimate goal of human existence, as based on the reality of the different aspects of the human state and seeks to establish both social and personal equilibrium. Islamic spirituality is always based on the foundation of an equilibrium that is inseparable from the name of *al-islām,* "peace," an equilibrium that is reflected in a blinding fashion in all authentic manifestations of traditional Islam, especially its sacred art.[10]

To make this equilibrium and the spiritual life based upon it possible, Islam has envisaged a human order in which the sexes are seen in their complementary rather than contending aspects. On the social and family levels, it has legislated for a social order in which there should be a maximum amount of stability, the greatest possible degree of attachment of men and women to a family structure, and emphasis upon marriage as religiously desirable although not obligatory. The reason for Islam's allowing the practice of polygamy under certain conditions must be seen in this light. Marriage is not seen, however, as a sacrament, since from an "alchemical" and metaphysical point of view, which is ultimately that of Islam, the sexual act is already a sacred act; it must of course still be kept within the bounds of the Divine Law in order to govern human passions, but it does not need to be legitimized by marriage as a sacrament in order to become sacralized. Marriage is therefore established as a contract on the basis of the Divine Law, thus remaining a religious institution without being a sacrament as it is in Christianity.

Islamic legislation about marriage and the creation of a social structure based upon its central importance do not, of course, imply the establishment of an order in which everyone could be satisfied in every way, for to speak of manifestation and multiplicity is to speak of separation from the unique source of goodness, and hence to be in the realm of imperfection. What the Islamic social order has always sought to achieve is the creation of the maximum amount of equilibrium possible, upon whose basis human beings can lead a life centered around and pointing to their entelechy and end, to the purpose for which they were created. Otherwise, there is no doubt that some people have been unhappy in a polygamous family situation, as others have been unhappy in a monogamous one—or even as unhappiness is found among totally "free" persons living as atomized beings within an atomized society, where each being is, or at least appears to be, free to act and move about at will. The question for Islam has not been how to make everyone happy, because that is something that is not possible in this world. In fact, the world would not be the world (*al-dunyā* in the language of the Quran) if such a thing were possible. The question has rather been how to create a state in which there would be the maximum amount of stability, harmony, and equilibrium in human life, one that would be most conducive to a person's living as God's vicegerent (*khalīfat Allāh*) on earth with awareness of His Will during this fleeting journey called human life.

Since sexuality, far from being just a biological accident, possesses a profound spiritual and metaphysical significance,[11] it has been possible for Islam to place its perspective on the positive rather than negative aspect of this powerful and profound force within human life.[12] Although both man and woman are *insān,* that is, both are "created in the image of God" and carry the androgynic reality within the depth of their beings, they cannot reach this interior and superior reality through the attainment of a kind of state of least common denominator between the two sexes. Of course, both sexes contain something of both the male and female principles, the *yin* and *yang* of the Far Eastern traditions, within themselves; it is just that in men the male principle is dominant, and in women, the female principle. To attain the perfection of each state, it is necessary to move in the other direction away from reductionism and destruction of the God-given differences between the sexes. Islamic spirituality tends in fact toward a clarification and complete differentiation of the two human types. Its social patterns and art of dress, among other things, help to create masculine types who are very masculine and feminine types who are very feminine. If sexual union symbolizes the androgynic totality that both sexes seek consciously or even unconsciously, this union itself requires the distinction and separation of the two sexes, which can in fact participate in the sacred act precisely because of their very distinctness.

Moreover, each sex symbolizes and reflects in a positive manner a divine aspect. Therefore, not only does sexual deviation or perversion mark a further step away from spiritual perfection; it is an obstacle to it. The loss of masculinity and femininity through movement both psychologically and emotionally toward a neuter and asexual common type and ground implies, from the Islamic perspective, an irreparable loss and further fall from the perfection of the primordial *insān,* who was both male and female. The asexual or "neuter" person in the modern sense of the term is in fact a parody of the primordial human being, who was both Adam and Eve. Islamic teachings have emphasized this point very clearly. In fact, in *ḥadīths* of the Prophet allusions to men dressing and acting like women and vice versa are pointed to as signs of the world coming to an end. In Islam, both the male and the female are seen as directly created by God, each manifesting certain aspects of His Names and Qualities and in their complementary union achieving the equilibrium and perfection that God has ordained for them and made the goal of human existence. It is, however, also possible for each gender to attain perfection in a celibate state, although Islam does not encourage this; nonetheless it is to be found among a number of Islamic spiritual figures and has never been totally absent from traditional Islamic society in general.

The tenets of Islam based upon sexual purity, separation of the sexes in many aspects of external life, the hiding of the beauty of women from strangers, and the division of social and family duties, responsibilities, and the like all derive from the principles stated above. Their specific applications have depended over time on the different cultural and social milieus in which Islam has grown and have therefore been very diverse. For example, the way Malay women hide their female beauty is very different from that of Syrian, Pakistani, or Senegalese women; and even within a single country what is called the veil (*ḥijāb*) has never been the same among nomads, villagers, and city dwellers. Some forms of veil only cover the head; others also include much of the face. Covering the body ranges from the long dress of Arabic villagers to the loose cloak worn in Iran and Afghanistan, from saris in Uttar Pradesh to sarongs in Indonesia, from the pants and long coats of Punjabi women to the female *jallabiyyah* (long traditional one-piece dress) in Morocco and the layers of long skirts of some nomads.

Furthermore the complementary role of the two sexes has not prevented Muslim women from participating in nearly all aspects of life, from running farms or butcher shops to owning major businesses in bazaars and even to ruling countries. Nor has the Islamic world been without eminent female religious and intellectual figures such as Fāṭimah, the daughter of the Prophet, who was a perfect saint and along with the Virgin Mary a prototype of Islamic female spirituality; 'Ā'ishah, the wife of the Prophet, through whom so much of Sunni *Ḥadīth* has been transmitted; Zaynab, the granddaughter of the Prophet, who gave one of the most eloquent discourses in Islamic history before Yazīd after the death of her brother Imām Ḥusayn in Karbalā'; Rābi'ah, one of the most celebrated of Sufi saints; and Sayyidah Nafīsah, who was a renowned authority on *Ḥadīth* and Islamic Law. The existence of these and many other personalities, from antiquity right down to our own day, demonstrates the undeniable fact that learning as well as the fields of commerce, agriculture, and so forth were open to those women who chose to or were allowed to pursue them. But the principle of complementarity, as opposed to uniformity and/or confrontation and competition, has dominated.

This complementarity was rooted in equity rather than equality and sought to base itself on what served best the interests of society as a sacred body and men and women as immortal beings. Although spiritually Islam sees woman as symbolizing the infinitude of God and the aspect of the Divinity above creation (the Sufi poet Jalāl al-Dīn Rūmī refers to woman as "uncreated"), on the cosmic and human levels it recognizes the role of the male as the "immutable" religious pole around which the family is constructed and in whose hands responsibility for the welfare of the women and children as well as protection for God's Law and the social order have been placed. In the Quran man is given "domination" in certain aspects of life over woman, but he has also been charged with responsibility to God as well as to family and society. He is envisaged not only as a two-legged animal acting only on egotistical instincts; rather, he has been entrusted with this task as the *imām* (spiritual leader), representing the authority of God, in the family and His vicegerent, a being whose soul must be surrendered to Him. In a sense, man's soul must be the consort of the Spirit in order for him to be able to play his full spiritual role as husband for his wife and father for his children. The revolt of the female sex against the male in the modern world did not precede, but followed in the wake of the revolt of the male sex against Heaven.

But even the relative predominance given to the male function, which, if seen from the point of view of authentic Islamic teachings, brings with it more responsibility than privilege, has not in any way compromised the view of Islam that both men and women were born for immortality, that the rites of religion are incumbent upon both of them, and that its rewards are accessible to men and women alike. Islamic Law pertains to both sexes, and the *Sharī'ite* rites are meant for all Muslims, male or female. The Quran states explicitly:

> For men who submit and women who submit, men who believe and women who believe, men who obey and women who obey, men who are truthful and women who are truthful, men who are patient and women who are patient, men who are humble and women who are humble, men who are charitable and women who are charitable, men who fast and women who fast, men who guard their private parts and women who guard [them], men who remember God often and women who remember [Him often] God has prepared forgiveness and an immense reward. (XXXIII: 35)[13]

Even in instances where certain rites are reserved for men, such as the prayer for the dead, this does not imply a particular privilege, for though God has not made women responsible for such rites, He still asks them to seek to reach those highest spiritual goals that are the *raison d'être* of all rites. As for the spiritual practices associated with Sufism, they have always been accessible to women, and there have always been many women followers in various Sufi orders, some of whom have attained the level of sanctity and become spiritual guides. There is, in fact, a feminine dimension within Sufism that possesses a distinct perfume of its own.[14]

In conclusion we must remember again the Origin, which, in its Essence, is above the duality of gender and all other dualities, but which yet, in its Majesty and Beauty, contains the roots of what on the plane of cosmic existence appears as the masculine and feminine principles and on the human level as male and female. Individual human beings are born as men and women, not accidentally but according to their destiny. They can fulfill their function in life, reach the perfection that alone can bestow felicity, and even transcend all traces of separative existence and return unto the One only by accepting their destiny and transcending from above the form into which they have been born, not by rebelling against it.

In the Holy Name of God, there is neither male nor female, but no one can penetrate into the inner sanctum of that Name without having fully integrated into his or her own being the positive elements of the gender into which he or she has been born. The Universal Man, who also includes Woman, is inwardly the androgynic being who possesses the perfection of both sexes; human beings, male or female, cannot attain that perfection save by remaining faithful to the norms and conditions that each gender implies. The revolt of the sexes against that equilibrium that results from their complementarity and union is both the result and a concomitant of the revolt of so many modern men and women against Heaven. Human beings cannot reach that peace and harmony that is the foretaste of the paradise they carry at the center of their being, except by bringing to full actualization and realization the possibilities innate in the human state, both male and female. To reject the distinct and distinguishing features of the two sexes and the Sacred Legislation based on this objective cosmic reality is to live below the human level; to be, in fact, only accidentally human. Islam bases itself on the norm and not on departure from the norm without denying that some departures also exist, for example, in the case of homosexuality, which has always existed in certain sectors of Islamic society as it has existed in other societies. To destroy the norm, however, means ultimately to sacrifice and compromise the eternal life of man and woman for an apparent earthly justice based on a uniformity that fails, ultimately even on the purely earthly level, since it does not take into consideration the reality of that which constitutes on the deepest level the human state in both its male and female forms.

Chapter Five

TRADITIONAL TWELVE-IMAM SHĪ'ISM AND THE REALITY OF SHĪ'ISM TODAY

The political and social events of the last few decades, especially the Islamic revolution in Iran, the rise of Shī'ite power in Lebanon, and more recently the formation of a predominantly Shī'ite government in Iraq, have caused so much partisan debate concerning Shī'ism, its tradition, present significance, and relation to Sunnism that few aspects of Islam are as much in need of disinterested and objective study today as Shī'ism in its many dimensions. This is particularly true of Twelve-Imam Shī'ism, the main school of Shī'ism, which is based on belief in twelve imams who are considered the legitimate successors to the Prophet. Twelve-Imam Shī'ism is the school followed in Iran, Iraq, Lebanon, and many other places, including Azerbaijan and among most of the Shī'ites of Pakistan and India. The Ismā'īlīs and Zaydīs (of Yemen) are also Shī'ite, but they constitute a small minority in comparison with Twelve-Imam Shī'ites. Whereas until the 1970s only a small number of works existed on Twelve-Imam Shī'ism in European languages, today there is a sizable collection of books, monographs, and articles on the subject, but still only a few that do not allow present-day events and their political ramifications to color their evaluation and appreciation of traditional Shī'ism. With the interest in the subject intensafied by the political events of the past decades in Iran, Iraq, Lebanon, and elsewhere, there is great need to understand fully the nature of traditional Twelve-Imam Shī'ism as an integral aspect of the Islamic tradition itself.

It must be recalled that a most significant manifestation of this traditional Shī'ism occurred in Safavid Persia, when, for the first time in Islamic history, Twelve-Imam Shī'ism became the official religion of a major Muslim country. Despite the claims of certain recent "Shī'ite revolutionary thinkers," who have sought to dissociate Safavid Shī'ism from "'Alīd Shī'ism," Shī'ism in Safavid Persia represents a very pertinent phase in the historical unfolding of traditional Twelve-Imam Shī'ism and is therefore of much significance today for the understanding of this particular aspect of the Islamic tradition in itself and especially in relation to Iran and its encounter with the modern world. As far as Iran is concerned, no aspect of the religio-political history of the fifteenth/twenty-first century in this country can be fully understood without consideration of the earlier history of Shī'ism, especially Shī'ism in Safavid Persia.

The Safavid period, that is, from the tenth/sixteenth century to the twelfth/eighteenth century, marks a definite turning point in the history of Persia and the beginning of a new phase in the history of Islam in that country as well as in lands nearby. Yet, despite its distinct character and the break it seems to display with respect to the centuries preceding it, there was definitely a long religious and intellectual history that prepared the ground for the sudden establishment of a Shī'ite order in Persia and the transformation of the country into a predominantly Shī'ite area.[1] Several centuries of growth in Shī'ite theology and jurisprudence, the development of Sufi orders with Shī'ite tendencies, and the establishment of Shī'ite political power—albeit of a transient character—in Persia and Iraq all preceded the Safavid period.

As far as Shī'ite thought is concerned, the advent of the Mongols and the destruction of the major centers of Sunni political power in western Asia in the seventh/thirteenth century enabled Shī'ism to flower in Persia more than ever before, culminating in the establishment of Shī'ism as the state religion for a brief period under Sultan Muḥammad Khudābandah, the Īl-Khānid Mongol ruler of Persia in the seventh/thirteenth century who converted to Twelve-Imam Shī'ism. But the most significant aspect of the post-Mongol period as far as Twelve-Imam Shī'ism is concerned was the appearance of Shī'ite intellectual figures of outstanding merit, such as Khwājah Naṣīr al-Dīn Ṭūsī, the founder of Twelve-Imam Shī'ite theology as well as a major philosopher, and his student 'Allāmah al-Ḥillī. Shī'ite theology became definitely established as an intellectual discipline with the *Tajrīd* ("Catharsis") of Ṭūsī, as commented upon by Ḥillī. Other outstanding Shī'ite theologians followed, such as Ibn Makkī al-'Āmilī, known as al-Shahīd al-Awwal, author of the well-known *al-Lum'at al-*

dimashqiyyah ("Damascene Spark"), followed by Zayn al-Dīn al-'Āmilī, al-Shahīd al-Thānī, whose commentary on this work, *Sharḥ al-lum'ah* ("Commentary on the Spark"),[2] is widely read to this day. The works of these and earlier figures, such as Shaykh Muḥammad al-Ṭūsī, al-Kulaynī, and Shaykh al-Mufīd, who were foundational figures in the Shī'ite sciences, were the intellectual props of Shī'ism at the outset of the Safavid period; in fact, they are of such importance that the history of Shī'ism during the Safavid and subsequent periods would be incomprehensible without them.

Parallel to this development in the religious sciences, one can observe a remarkable spread of activity in post-Mongol Persia in the domain of philosophy and in that combination of Peripatetic philosophy, Illuminationist doctrines, and gnosis that came to be known later as *al-ḥikmat al-ilāhiyyah* (*ḥikmat-i ilāhī*), or theosophy and metaphysics, and that gradually moved into the orbit of Shī'ism.[3] Such famous philosophers, theologians, and gnostics as Ibn Abī Jumhūr, Ibn Turkah, Rajab Bursī, and especially Sayyid Ḥaydar Āmulī, who sought to harmonize and in fact identify the Sufism of Ibn 'Arabī with esoteric Shī'ite doctrines,[4] are among the notable intellectual ancestors of the most famous Safavid sages and philosophers, such as Mīr Dāmād and Mullā Ṣadrā.

As for Sufism, the period between the Mongols and the Safavids was witness not only to a remarkable flowering of Sufism as exemplified by the appearance of such great spiritual pivotal figures or poles of sanctity and wisdom as Mawlānā Jalāl al-Dīn Rūmī, Najm al-Dīn Kubrā, Ṣadr al-Dīn Qunyawī, and the like, but it was also the period during which Sufism became a bridge between Sunnism and Shī'ism and in many instances prepared the ground for the spread of Shī'ism.[5] The role of the Kubrawiyyah,[6] the Nūrbakhshiyyah, and the Ni'matallāhiyyah Orders, all important Sufi orders that had spread widely throughout Persia and Central Asia, bears close study in light of their relation to the later spread of Shī'ism in Persia established by a dynasty of Sufi origin. This takes us in turn to the Ṣafawī Sufi Order itself, to the two and a half centuries that separate Shaykh Ṣafī al-Dīn of Ardabil from Shah Ismā'īl, to the transformation of a simple Sufi order organized around a saint and ascetic to a militant political movement with extreme Shī'ite tendencies under Sultan Junayd and Ḥaydar, and finally to the establishment of the military basis that made the Safavid conquest of Persia possible.[7]

Finally, as far as political aspects of religion are concerned, the brief rule of Shīʿism under Sultan Muḥammad Khudābandah as well as such small Shīʿite dynasties as the Sarbadārān in Khurasan, the Mushaʿshaʿah in Iraq, and the leaders and spiritual masters or shaykhs of the Safavid Sufi Order itself preceding Shah Ismāʿīl all present historical antecedents of great importance.[8] They point to political and social transformations of a religious nature that are directly related to the whole question of religion in Safavid Persia and the transformation of Persia into a Twelve-Imam Shīʿite state.

In reality, the discussion of religion in its widest sense as tradition (*al-dīn*) in the Safavid period must of necessity include every facet of life in Safavid society, inasmuch as we are dealing with a traditional world in which all activity is related to a transcendent norm. Whether it is literature, as reflected in the poetry of Ṣāʾib-i Tabrīzī and Muḥtashim-i Kāshānī, architecture and city planning, as seen in the central region of the city of Isfahan,[9] or even sports, as in the case of the *Zūrkhānah* (house of strength), a traditional form of exercise that combines bodily exercises with religious music and poetry, we are in fact dealing with something that is directly related to religion itself. Even the natural elements, the water that flowed in geometrically shaped gardens and the earth from which the mud walls of structures were made, possess a religious significance if seen from the point of view of those who lived and breathed in the traditional Islamic world, whether it was Abbasid, Seljuq, or Safavid. Here, however, it is only with religion and religious thought in the strict sense of the word that we shall deal, leaving the ramifications of religion in the arts, the sciences, and society in general out of consideration.

The most noteworthy feature of religion in Safavid Persia is, first of all, the rapid process by which Persia became Twelve-Imam Shīʿite. Although, as already mentioned, the ground for this transformation had been prepared by subtle religious changes during the Īl-Khānid period, which followed the Mongol conquest of western Asia and lasted from the seventh/thirteenth to the eighth/fourteenth century, when Shah Ismāʿīl was crowned, probably the majority of Persians were still Sunnis. Certainly the city of Tabriz, where the crowning took place in 1499, was about two-thirds Sunni at that time, although the Shīʿite element was at that moment the strongest religious element among the Āzarī-speaking segments of the population (Āzarī is a Turkic language related to Turkish that also contains many Persian words; it is spoken to this day in the Iranian province of Azerbaijan and is the official language of the Republic of Azerbaijan). It was the policy, ardently followed by the Safavids, to establish Shī'ism as the state religion that led to the rapid change.

To make the process of transforming Iran into a Shī'ite land possible, many outstanding Shī'ite scholars were invited to Persia from the Arab world, especially Ḥillah in Iraq, what was known traditionally as Baḥrayn in the eastern region of the Persian Gulf, and the Jabal 'Āmil in present-day Lebanon, all of which had been for some time seats of Shī'ite learning. In fact, so many scholars from these regions came to Persia that two works, the *Lu'lu'at al-baḥrayn* ("The Pearls of Baḥrayn") and *Amal al-āmil* ("Expectation of the Expector"), are entirely devoted to their biographies. These scholars ranged from simple *mullās* (lower-level clerics) who fulfilled small religious functions, to men such as Shaykh Bahā' al-Dīn al-'Āmilī and Sayyid Ni'mat Allāh al-Jazā'irī, both of whom came to Persia at a very young age, but soon developed into leading religious authorities.

Few modern Western scholars have examined the effect of the presence of all of these Arabic-speaking scholars on the role of Arabic in Persian intellectual circles at this time. Many present-day traditional authorities[10] in Persia, however, believe that, because of the great power and prestige of these men, some of whom, like Sulṭān al-'Ulamā', hardly knew Persian, there came into being a new emphasis upon Arabic among the religious authorities, and it even became fashionable to use Arabic in situations where during the centuries immediately preceding the Safavid period Persian had commonly been used. Certainly the dearth of Persian prose writings in the religious field at this time in comparison with either the preceding Seljuq and Mongol or the later Qajar periods bears out this truth.[11] More Persian religious works were written in Persian on the Indian subcontinent during this period than in Persia itself. The migration to Persia of this class of Arabic-speaking scholars, who became rapidly Persianized and absorbed within the matrix of Persian society, had, therefore, an effect upon both the religious life of the country and the type of religious language employed.

The result of the spread of Shī'ism, which, as already mentioned, did not completely replace Sunnism but became the most dominant form of Islam in Persia,[12] implied the establishment of typically Shī'ite institutions. These included, in addition to the daily prayers, the pilgrimage, and fasting, the religious sermons depicting mostly the tragedy of Karbalā', or *rawḍah-khānī,*[13] held especially during the month of Muḥarram; the *ta'ziyah,* or passion play, which is the most elaborate form of theater in the Islamic world and again involves mostly the tragedy of Karbalā'; the religious feast, or *sufrah,* where a meal is prepared and laid out, prayers are offered, and most of the food is then given to the poor; religious processions; and visits to tombs of holy men, or *imāmzādahs*—all of which still comprise the main day-to-day religious activity of Persian Shī'ites as well as Shī'ites elsewhere. Of course the rites of daily prayers, fasting, and pilgrimage are shared by Sunnis and Shī'ites alike.[14] Moreover, as far as the ritual and practical aspects of religion in the Safavid period are concerned, the situation was nearly the same then as what can be observed today in Iran.

The role and function of other aspects of religion in Safavid Persia after the early period of transformation can perhaps be best understood by studying such questions as classes of religious scholars, the various religious functions in society, the types of religious thought of the period, and finally the position of Sufism and of the guilds, which played a paramount role in the religious life of the Persians at that time. As far as the classes of religious scholars are concerned, it is important to note that during the Safavid period, as in most other periods of Islamic history, and even more so because of the particular politico-religious structure of Shī'ism, there were two classes of religious scholars, or *'ulamā';* one class was supported and appointed by the Safavid kings and their representatives, and the other remained completely aloof from central political power and gained its authority from the support of the populace.[15]

As far as the first group is concerned, its members were chosen from the class of *'ulamā'* and were then appointed to a hierarchy of functions that, in a sense, paralleled the administrative structure of the Safavid state. There was, first of all, a learned person of high repute called the *mullā bāshī,* whom many Safavid kings chose as a close companion to counsel them on religious matters and read prayers for them on different occasions.[16] Then there was the position of the *ṣadr,* the highest religious office of the land, whose incumbent was chosen directly by the king and who rivaled the grand *mufti* of the Ottomans. The *ṣadr* was responsible for all the official religious duties of the country, especially the supervision of the endowments (*awqāf*), which he administered with the help of such officials as *mustawfīs, mutaṣaddīs,* and *wazīrs.* Sometimes the function of the *ṣadr* was in fact divided into two parts: the *ṣadr-i mamālik* concerned the supervision of the general endowments, and the *ṣadr-i khāṣṣah* was related to the royal endowments. The *ṣadr* also appointed judges (*qāḍīs*) and the chief official religious dignitaries (*shaykh al-islām*) of the bigger cities with the consent of the king.[17]

As for the class of *ʿulamāʾ* who stood aloof from the central political power, at their head were the *mujtahids,* literally those who could practice *ijtihād* (that is, give fresh opinions on questions of Divine Law): men who were and still are highly revered by Iranian society because of their knowledge and piety, and because it is they whom the Shīʿites have traditionally considered the guardians and interpreters of the Divine Law and representatives of the Hidden Imam.[18] From among them was chosen the person who was emulated according to Shīʿite doctrine (*marjaʿ-i taqlīd*)[19] and who at times gained a power rivaling that of the king himself. The *mujtahids* usually supported the Safavid monarchy, but also often acted as protection for the people against the tyranny of some local government officials and fulfilled a major function of both a religious and social nature. The aloofness of these scholars from centers of political power must not, however, be taken to mean they were opposed to the political system itself.

One cannot mention the *mujtahids* of this period without recalling the *akhbārī-uṣūlī* debate that took place at that time. The *uṣūlīs* were a group who derived rulings from the Quran and *Ḥadīth* on the basis of *ijtihād,* or giving fresh opinion on the basis of the revealed sources of Islam. The *akhbārīs* were those who insisted that only the text of the Quran and *Ḥadīth* (which for Twelve-Imam Shīʿism includes the sayings of the Twelve Imams) must be used; they were opposed to the *ijtihād* of the *uṣūlīs.* The *akhbārīs* have usually held, therefore, a more anti-intellectual position. In the end they lost the battle to the *uṣūlīs,* but they nevertheless played no small role in the religious and intellectual life of Safavid Persia and even later.

To come back to the *mujtahids,* it must be mentioned that there were other religious scholars of lower rank whose authority also relied upon the people, for whom they fulfilled daily needs. Foremost among these were the leaders of prayers (*imāms*) of various mosques. One can in fact see a clear hierarchy among nonpolitical *'ulamā'* that can be summarized as follows. At the top is the *mujtahid* who is the source of emulation (*marja'-i taqlīd*). Then come the other major *mujtahids* who later gained the title of grand ayatollah, then other ayatollahs, then accomplished religious scholars of lower rank called *ḥujjat al-islām* (literally, "proof of Islam"), some of whom were and still are imams of Friday prayers (*imām juma'ah*) or simple imams of various mosques, and finally ordinary *mullās.* Many of the religious offices of a "political" nature, such as that of the *ṣadr,* were discontinued after the Safavid period. In any case, because of the stringent ethical conditions set in Shī'ism for those who lead the daily prayers, these men, whom people accepted as their prayer leader and who also catered to other religious needs of the populace, were not appointed by any government authorities. Rather, they were freely chosen by the members of the religious community itself. Of course, occasionally such functions were fulfilled by men who also held state-appointed offices, and sometimes this reached the highest level when a leading *mujtahid* also became an official religious dignitary, but this was an exception that nevertheless did not invalidate the basic separation between the two types of religious authority just mentioned.

From the point of view of religious thought, however, all these classes of *'ulamā'* belonged to the single category of specialists in jurisprudence and other Islamic legal sciences. They were *faqīhs,* or jurisprudents, first and foremost. But there developed in the Safavid period, upon the basis of earlier examples, another type of religious scholar who, rather than being a specialist in law and jurisprudence, was a master of Islamic metaphysics and theosophy. The *ḥakīm-i ilāhī,* literally, "theosopher," who came to the fore during this period, was the successor to earlier Muslim philosophers from al-Fārābī and Ibn Sīnā, through Suhrawardī and Naṣīr al-Dīn Ṭūsī, to Ibn Turkah, Sayyid Ḥaydar Āmulī, and the Dashtakī family, who were the immediate predecessors of the Safavid sages. During the Safavid period the attempt begun by Suhrawardī and later Ibn Turkah and others to harmonize rational philosophy, intellectual intuition, and revealed religion[20] reached its apogee, and *ḥikmat-i ilāhī* , theosophy, became a most important, if not the central, expression of religious thought in its most intellectual aspect.[21] Therefore, the *ḥakīm-i ilāhī* also became a much more central figure in the religious life of the community than before.

The founder of this remarkable period of Islamic philosophy, which has come to be known as the School of Isfahan, is Mīr Dāmād, himself the son-in-law of one of the most influential of the early Safavid *'ulamā'*, Muḥaqqiq-i Karakī. Mīr Dāmād was also an authority in the "transmitted sciences" (*al-'ulūm al-naqliyyah*), including jurisprudence, but he was above all a *ḥakīm*, or philosopher, who opened up new horizons for Islamic philosophy and who was responsible for the rapid spread of *ḥikmat-i ilāhī* through his numerous writings and his many students. Among his disciples, Ṣadr al-Dīn Shīrāzī (Mullā Ṣadrā), the greatest metaphysician of the age and perhaps the foremost *ḥakīm* in Islamic history in the domain of metaphysics, stands out particularly. Mullā Ṣadrā built primarily upon the foundations laid by Mīr Dāmād, but went farther by making a grand synthesis of all the major intellectual perspectives of the nearly thousand years of Islamic intellectual life that went before him in a new school of philosophy/theosophy known as "the transcendent theosophy" (*al-ḥikmat al-muta'āliyah*). No other figure of the Safavid period characterizes as well as Mullā Ṣadrā the special genius of this age for intellectual synthesis and the expression of unity in multiplicity, which is also so evident in the extremely rich art of the age.

Mullā Ṣadrā himself was practically an inexhaustible source for the doctrines of *ḥikmat-i ilāhī;* he was responsible for the spread of its teachings, and he continues to dominate traditional philosophical thought in Persia to this day. He was at once a prolific writer[22] and a peerless teacher; his foremost students, Mullā Muḥsin Fayḍ Kāshānī and 'Abd al-Razzāq Lāhījī, are themselves among the most outstanding intellectual figures of Persia.[23]

It is characteristic of the religious life of Safavid Persia that a dynasty that began as a Sufi order moved so much in the direction of legalism and exoterism that Mullā Muḥammad Bāqir Majlisī, the most powerful *'alim* (religious scholar) of the later Safavid period and the author of a monumental encyclopedia, *Biḥār al-anwār* ("Oceans of Light"), repudiated the Sufism of his father, Mullā Muḥammad Taqī, and forced the last great *ḥakīm* of the Safavid period in Isfahan, the saintly Mullā Ṣādiq Ardistānī, into exile. It is an irony that both Sufism and *ḥikmat-i ilāhī,* which also possesses an esoteric character, were finally forced into a kind of marginal existence at the end of the reign of the Safavids, a dynasty of Sufi origin.

Some Sufi orders, however, survived. The Dhahabiyyah Order, which is still strong in Persia today, was also active at that time. Some of the great Sufis of this age, such as Pīr-i Pālāndūz (Muḥammad Karāndihī), Shaykh

Ḥātam Harāwandī, and Shaykh Muḥammad ʿAlī Sabziwārī Khurāsānī, the author of the well-known *al-Tuḥfat al-ʿabbāsiyyah* ("The ʿAbbāsid Gift"),[24] are considered by later Dhahabīs to be spiritual poles of their order. But although the Dhahabīs continued their life into the Zand and later periods, they too became less visible toward the end of the Safavid era.

Other orders mentioned by various sources, both Persian and European, as being active during the Safavid period include the Qādiriyyah, Baktāshiyyah, Khāksār, Mawlawiyyah, and Niʿmatallāhiyyah.[25] The case of the Khāksār and the Niʿmatallāhiyyah Orders, which are still very much alive today in Persia, in contrast to the Baktāshiyyah and Mawlawiyyah, which no longer have any following in that country, is of particular interest. The Khāksārs somehow fell out of favor at the time of Shah ʿAbbās, and some of their leaders retired to cities far away in the south of the country. As for the Niʿmatallāhiyyah, some of their leaders were closely associated with the court and held positions of great eminence at the beginning of the Safavid period, and the order itself had a wide following. But soon they too fell out of favor and were persecuted so severely that their outward organization in Persia disappeared completely. Their masters and many disciples retired to the Deccan in India, and their very history in Persia was interrupted. It was in fact from the Deccan that the order was reestablished in Persia during the early Qajar period.[26]

The reason for this rather violent opposition to Sufism and even *ḥikmat-i ilāhī* in the late Safavid period lies partially in the fact that the Ṣafawī Order, because it had become a ruling dynasty, tended to lose some of its spiritual discipline as a Sufi order and became diluted through the intrusion of worldly elements into its very structure. This fact in turn caused the resentment of other Sufi orders, which were eventually suppressed by the Safavids, as well as by the exoteric religious authorities. In the second case, it was not possible for the state to suppress them, for the very power of the Safavids lay in the support of Shīʿism. Henceforth the Safavid kings, if not all the members of the order, tended to become ever more detached from their Sufi background and to support exoteric authorities in their opposition to Sufism. As a result, if before the rise of the Safavids a figure such as Sayyid Ḥaydar Āmulī could say, "True Sufism is Shīʿism and true Shīʿism is Sufism," at the end of the Safavid period the opposition between Shīʿism and the organized Sufi orders had become so great that, even in later periods of Persian history, Sufism could return to the centers of Shīʿite learning only under the name of *ʿirfān* (gnosis) or in the guise of *ḥikmat-i ilāhī* (theosophy and metaphysics). This situation that prevails in such centers as Najaf and Qom to this day is inherited from the complete polarity and opposition between the most powerful Shīʿite *ʿulamāʾ* and organized Sufism during the latter part of the Safavid period.[27]

Finally, a word must be said about the guilds and forms of craft initiation that were widespread in the Safavid period and that bridged the gap between the most inward principles of the tradition and various aspects of everyday life, from making and selling merchandise in the bazaar to constructing mosques. The tradition of "chivalry" (*futuwwah or jawānmardī*) as related to various social and artistic activities was already strong in the pre-Safavid period and continued on into this period itself.[28] Those remarkable architects who designed the various mosques, palaces, and caravanserais of this era, the rug weavers who created some of the most remarkable color harmonies of any school of art, and the masters of plaster and tile design were mostly members of guilds with a spiritual discipline related to various Sufi orders, especially the Khāksār. In fact, what has survived in Iran of the techniques of the traditional arts is to this day of an oral nature, preserved within the still existing guilds and transmitted by way of a master–disciple relationship, as can be observed in some cities and towns today, is a remnant of the fully active guilds of the Safavid period. What remains of traditional Persian art, even those forms that are not, strictly speaking, religious according to Western categories, such as carpet weaving, tile work, and vernacular architecture, but are nevertheless traditional art, is related in the profoundest way to the artistic and religious life of the Safavids. No account of religion in Safavid Persia would be complete without taking the role of the guilds and the deep religious nature of their activity into account.

Religion in the Safavid period is not only the key to the understanding of the Safavid period itself; it also represents a new chapter in Islamic history and a new crystallization of the possibilities inherent within the Islamic tradition. Moreover, the study of the very complex and rich pattern of religious life in Safavid Persia—a study that still needs to a large extent to be continued—is necessary for an understanding of life not only in Persia but also in adjacent lands at a time when the central region of the Islamic world became divided into three major empires: the Mughal, the Safavid, and the Ottoman. Also, such a study is necessary for an understanding of the subsequent religious history of Persia itself to this day (modern-day Iran), for the basic religious institutions, practices, and forms of thought established during the Safavid period have comprised the foundation of the religious and intellectual life of Persia and much of the rest of the Twelve-Imam Shī'ite world down to the contemporary period; they also represent their link with the classical tradition of Islam dominant in Persia before its particular crystallization in the Safavid period in the form of a religious order dominated by Shī'ism.

It is important to emphasize the fact that the reality of Shī'ism today is still deeply affected by what took place five centuries ago with the establishment of the Safavid Empire and Twelve-Imam Shī'ism as its "state religion." Such countries as Iraq, Baḥrayn, Afghanistan, and the Republic of Azerbaijan are no longer directly linked politically with what remains of the Safavid Empire in modern-day Iran as they were in the tenth/sixteenth, eleventh/seventeenth, and twelfth/eighteenth centuries, but their religious, social, and intellectual life is still deeply rooted in the Safavid past. Furthermore, the links created between Persia, Iraq, and what later became Lebanon as well as the cultural and intellectual relations created between Persia and the Indo-Pakistani subcontinent involving various currents of Shī'ism in that land have never been severed. During the Safavid period many families of religious scholars gained prominence in Jabal 'Āmil, Baḥrayn, Iraq, the countries of the Indian subcontinent, and Persia itself, a reality that has continued to this day. One needs only to recall as an example the Ṣadr family, which during the past half century alone has produced such figures as Imam Mūsā al- Ṣadr, the leader of Lebanese Shī'ites, who had studied in Tehran and Qom; Muḥammad Bāqir al- Ṣadr, the eminent Iraqi religious leader and thinker who was martyred in the prime of his intellectual life in Iraq; and the many other well-known ayatollahs and political figures in Iraq, Lebanon, and Iran who belong to the same family.

In recent years, in a manner that could hardly have been imagined a few decades ago, the reality of the heritage of the Safavid period has struck the center of the arena of Middle Eastern politics like a bolt of lightning. The Iranian Islamic Revolution of 1979; the rise of the Amal and Hezbollah movements in Lebanon; the destruction of the Baʿthist regime through the American conquest of Iraq and the subsequent establishment of a predominantly Shīʿite regime in that country; the spread of the influence of Iran in a Syria governed by the ʿAlawīs, who consider themselves to be a branch of Shīʿism; the revival of Shīʿism in the Republic of Azerbaijan after the downfall of the Soviet Union; and certain other events have come together to make Shīʿism a major political reality in an arc stretching from the Mediterranean to Pakistan and India. Moreover, all these transformations have been concurrent with the spread of Wahhābism, the dominant form of Islam in Saudi Arabia and a movement that has been since its founding strongly anti-Shīʿite; beyond its old borders in the Arabian Peninsula it takes the form of neo-Wahhābism and has resulted in fierce struggles between Sunnism and Shīʿism in many areas. These confrontations, which have become ever more bloody in certain places, are often interpreted by Western commentators as the continuation of centuries-old rivalries, but this is far from the truth. Rather, the tragic sectarian struggles of the past few decades and the present day are to a large degree the result of consequences of the confrontation between traditional Islam, "fundamentalism," and modernism, an event that is also to a large extent related to the spread in recent years of neo-Wahhābī "fundamentalism" beyond the borders of Arabia. In this new context the old rivalries have come to gain another meaning and a new intensity, lighting a dangerous fire that is often abetted by external forces bent on following the policy of divide and conquer.

Since my concern in this book is primarily traditional Islam in its confrontation with modernism and "fundamentalism" and not the present-day political situation in the Islamic world, I do not wish to dwell on the political aspect of the reality of Shīʿism today.[29] But there is one point that nevertheless needs to be mentioned. One of the important consequences of the spread of modernism into the traditional Islamic world from the twelfth/eighteenth century on was of course the rise of nationalism. Iranian and Turkish nationalism followed different paths, but were both based on the primacy of cultural and ethnic identity, not Islam. Arab nationalism, however, sought to nationalize Islam itself, considering Islam and its civilization to be primarily the fruit of what some Arab theoreticians of Arab nationalism have called "the Arab genius" (*ʿabqariyyat al-ʿarab*). As this way of thinking grew, many

Arabs came to identify "Arab identity" not with the whole of Islam, now nationalized, but with Sunnism. The Arab Shīʿites, whether in Iraq, Lebanon, the Yemen, the Persian Gulf, or Saudi Arabia itself, were more or less marginalized, especially politically. The reassertion of the reality of Shīʿism outside of Iran and within the Arab world itself has in a sense posed an existential challenge to the modern "Arab self-identity" forged to some extent by Arab nationalism. And this phenomenon is having an effect not only on the negative attitude of some Arab countries concerning political expressions of Shīʿism, but also upon the ideology of Arab nationalism itself and the modes of encounter of traditional Islam with modernism in the Arab world.

The reality of Shīʿism today is not of course only political. There is much Shīʿite intellectual activity of importance going on, especially in Iran today, and this activity is bound to have also an important effect upon religious thought in the Sunni world from Indonesia to the Arab world and Muslim Black Africa. One can observe such interactions already from Jakarta to Cairo to Dakar. Moreover, this current situation has set in motion a new spate of activity to carry out intrareligious dialogue within the Islamic world and to create modes of mutual understanding between Sunnism and Shīʿism that are bound to affect in many ways the life of Muslims in the Islamic heartland, the rest of the Islamic world, and even beyond the borders of the "Abode of Islam" (*dār al-islām*).

Part II

Traditional Islam and Modernism

Chapter Six

ISLAMIC SPIRITUALITY

Reflections on Conditions Today and Prospects for Tomorrow

During the past few decades, amid all the materialism, skepticism, and nihilism so characteristic of the modern world, there has been a remarkable increase in interest in what is called, often ambiguously, "spirituality," so much so that the leading American scholar of world religions, Huston Smith, once told us, "Here in California religion is out and spirituality is in." One cannot, therefore, discuss Islam and modernism without turning to the question of Islamic spirituality in the context of contemporary Islam as well as in the context of increased worldwide interest in spirituality. But before dealing with this vast and momentous subject, it is essential to define exactly how this term is understood.

This precision is needed despite the extensive debate that took place over the years during the process of writing and editing the various volumes of *World Spirituality: An Encyclopedic History of the Religious Quest* and precisely because of the differences of view that emerged from these discussions among the editors. In the introduction to volumes 19 and 20 of that series, which I edited, I sought to provide a definition of what is meant by "spirituality" in the context of the Islamic tradition.[1] Here, it is necessary to summarize in a few words the above treatment of the subject in the Islamic context as well as to mention what is understood by "spirituality" considered globally.

WHAT DO WE MEAN BY SPIRITUALITY?

In major Islamic languages such as Arabic, Persian, and Turkish the term "spirituality," which is itself fairly new to the Christian world, originating with the use of the term *spiritualité* by some French theologians in the nineteenth century, would be rendered as *rūḥāniyyah, ma'nawiyyat,* or terms related to them. The first of these terms is derived from the word *rūḥ,* which is equivalent to *pneuma* or *spiritus* with the precision that these terms have in Greek and Latin in contrast to the more nebulous and ambiguous term "spirit" in English, which conveys a number of meanings. The second term is derived from the word *ma'nā,* or "meaning," in the metaphysical sense of the term, implying what is inward in contrast to form (*ṣūrat*), the reality to which the outward form alludes and to which it points through its very existence as well as the symbolic significance of its outward reality.[2] Based simply on this linguistic consideration and the etymological significance of the Islamic terms corresponding to "spirituality," one could say that spiritual is that which is related to the world of the *spiritus,* or Spirit, as traditionally understood or to the inward reality or meaning to which the outward aspects of things point.

This definition is based on the rigorous distinction between the spiritual and the psychic, which are often confused in the modern understanding of the term "spirituality," and is rooted in the conception of reality as multi-layered and consisting of both an outward and inward aspect or dimension, the latter in turn consisting of many levels until one reaches the innermost essence of a thing. What is beyond the physical is not necessarily spiritual, but could simply be the psychic world, as is in fact the case in much that is considered "spiritual" in the modern and the so-called postmodern worlds. Moreover, the manifestation of the Spirit and access to It take place within the sacred universes that are called "traditional" as already defined earlier in this book.

It is, however, necessary to recall what the term "tradition" signifies in order to make clear what is meant by the assertion that there is no authentic spirituality possible outside tradition; there are of course exceptions that only prove the rule, reminding us that "the Spirit bloweth where it listeth." In light of a universalist understanding of the term "tradition," it is possible to expand the specifically Islamic understanding of the term "spirituality" given above to other traditions in order to be able to discuss spirituality in a global context. One could then speak of, let us say, Christian, Hindu, or Navajo spirituality in the context of these traditions and the corresponding concepts of *spiritus* and inwardness as understood in them. The remarkable unanimity of truth on the highest level and correspondences between the grades of the sacred cosmos, that is, the various levels of existence above the terrestrial in the universe in which people of various traditions live, makes the discussion of spirituality on a global scale much easier from the traditional point of view, than if one were to deny the doctrine of universality of the truth and its manifestations in various worlds of sacred form. In any case, throughout, our perspective remains based on tradition and the ultimate oneness of that Reality or Truth that all authentic spirituality seeks to realize, whether this realization aims for the Truth in itself or in its manifestations, reflections, and theophanies in the cosmic and human orders.

SPIRITUALITY IN THE WEST TODAY

To discuss the situation of spirituality thus understood globally, we shall first of all turn to the Western world, where the traditional structures have been more modified or even eliminated than elsewhere as a result of the fact that the rise and early growth of modernism was confined to that part of the globe. Then we shall turn to the Islamic world and finally to the future of Islamic spirituality. Although the human condition has certain characteristics that are global, there still exist immense differences between places where tradition still survives to an appreciable degree and places where religion, including its inner or spiritual dimension, has become marginalized or eclipsed, and the quest for spirituality often takes place in a religiously amorphous ambience.

As far as the situation of spirituality in the West is concerned, it must be said at the outset that the contemporary scene is witness to a number of currents flowing in different directions, some of which are in fact directly opposed to each other. There is first of all the widely occurring weakening and destruction of what remains of traditional religion, especially its inward and contemplative aspects. During the past few decades the contemplative Christian orders have in general diminished in number, although one does observe a revival here and there as witnessed by the popularity of a figure such as Thomas Merton; also formally diminished in many places have been those practices of Christianity connected directly to the life of prayer and spirituality. The very forces unleashed by the *aggiornamento* within the Catholic Church have worked for the most part against the traditional forms of spirituality, which, however, still continue to survive here and there, and in a few places there is even renewed interest in monasticism. Even attendance in traditional churches, both Catholic and mainstream Protestant, has diminished, while new religious movements, such as many of the evangelical ones, most of which are more activist and socially oriented and less given to contemplation, meditation, and the mystical teachings of Christianity, are on the rise. No matter how one defines spirituality, there is little doubt that one of the notable contemporary trends in the West is the continuous weakening of traditional forms of Christian spirituality associated with contemplative orders, inner spiritual exercises, the life of prayer, and mysticism.

The eclipse of traditional Catholicism, as it existed until Vatican II, itself marks the eclipse and near disappearance of a distinct world of contemplative spirituality that had produced so many great saints and mystics over the ages. Whatever the spiritual significance of this eclipse might be, there can be little doubt that that universe was the continuation of the main spiritual tradition of Western Christianity and that it has weakened in its classical form during the past few decades. In speaking here of Catholicism, I do not want in any way to dismiss the spiritual significance of Lutheranism and certain other forms of Protestantism whose spiritual dimensions have also suffered to some degree.

In any case, this eclipsing of traditional forms of spirituality in the West has been combined with the ever greater marginalization of traditional religion itself and ever greater desacralization of human life. Interest in religion is itself on the rise globally, but it is often of the "fundamentalist"—not traditional—kind. This trend in the weakening of traditional religion especially in the West can be seen not only in the decrease of participation in sacred rites that sanctify the rhythm of everyday life, but even in the weakening of the Christian roots of morality and the attempt by many to substitute a purely secularist ethics for one that has its roots in Christian and also Jewish teachings. One can hardly neglect the spiritual implications of this transformation, which is now manifesting itself to a greater degree than before on both the intellectual and the social planes and is often combined with great passion and aggressiveness, as can be seen in the current increase in the number of books written on atheism and violent attacks against religion as such.

A word also needs to be said concerning Judaism in the West. Although Judaism has interacted more closely with Christianity since the nineteenth century than it had done before and such forms as Reformed

Judaism have developed to a large extent in response to both Protestant Christianity and modernism, the traditional and orthodox forms of Judaism have remained more intact and less affected by the winds of rapid change than most forms of Western Christianity. Even traditional mystical forms of Judaism such as Kabbalistic teachings and Hassidism seem to have been able to remain more intact and accessible than their Christian counterparts, which is not to claim that comparable elements in Western Christianity have become totally inaccessible. As for the ever greater secularization of everyday life, Judaism, like Christianity, faces challenges and obstacles to the leading of an intensely spiritual life amid the stream of modern and postmodern life that are difficult to surmount.

Parallel with this process of weakening of traditional spiritual forms and practices, one can observe the opposite movement toward the rediscovery of spirituality in the West. The human soul, having issued from the world of the Spirit, yearns forever for return to the state of that eternal wedding with the Spirit, the apparent separation from which involves only the outward dimension of the soul and cannot reach its inner center, which continues to remain in that blissful union. Therefore, whatever the outward circumstances, the soul's yearning for the world of the Spirit continues and, externalized and turned to the world of multiplicity, manifests itself in whatever external situation human beings find themselves. Consequently, the very eclipsing of traditional spiritual life in the West has been combined with a deep yearning on the part of many for spirituality. This yearning characterizes the life of many present-day Westerners and is the basic cause for the rapid proliferation of all kinds of religious teachings from beyond the borders of the West within the West itself. Moreover, most of the new religious movements that have attracted attention in the West have had a "mystical" or "esoteric" character, and most of those interested in them have identified them as spirituality rather than religion in the ordinary sense, as the case of various forms of Hinduism in the West such as Advaita Vedanta exemplifies clearly.

Wherever traditional Western religious practices have been strong, such as in Ireland and pre-Franco Spain, interest in foreign forms of spirituality has been less evident, needless to say, because the spiritual needs of those in quest of spirituality have been fulfilled satisfactorily by existing local institutions, persons, and practices. The reverse is also clearly true, as seen in the case of California and other New Age centers of more recent origin in the United States (such as Oregon and New Mexico), where the relatively weak presence of traditional forms of Western religion and spirituality as integrated into the texture of society has contributed to the creation of a spiritual vacuum, which, like a physical vacuum, attracts all kinds of sundry elements to itself.

The case of Spain is particularly telling. Until the 1970s the country was solidly Catholic and the piety of most of the people intense. With the weakening of traditional Catholicism combined with the politically open society ushered in after Franco, one can observe not only the rapid secularization of life, but the influx into the country of foreign forms of "spirituality" as well as occultism, with which it is often confused. Who would have ever imagined in the early 1970s that in a few years there would be a Hindu ashram outside of Madrid, complete with a temple and statues of Hindu gods, catering to the needs of Spaniards coming to visit it in quest of "spirituality"?

The yearning for the rediscovery of spirituality in the West has taken and continues to take many different forms, some of the more important of which we need to delve into, albeit briefly. There is first of all intense interest in what has generally been called Oriental spirituality, which refers to the currents issuing from India, the Far East, and the Islamic world and including of course the Vedanta, Taoism, Zen and Tibetan Buddhism, and Sufism, among others. Interest in "Oriental spirituality" in the West did not begin just since World War II. Putting the contacts that medieval Christians and Western Jews made with Islamic esoterism aside,[3] in modern times such major nineteenth-century figures as Goethe, Blake, and Emerson showed serious interest in Sufism and/or Hinduism and some have even referred to an "Oriental Renaissance" at the time. During the twentieth century, however, this interest intensified to the extent that in the past few decades Oriental spirituality, of both an authentic and dubious nature, has become part of the Western landscape. It is in this context that one must view the great interest in Sufism in the West today.

The distortions of Oriental teachings by a whole army of orientalists, social scientists, New Age gurus, and the like are too extensive for me to be able to discuss here. What is of much greater significance is the authentic presentation of Oriental teachings that began in the early decades of the twentieth century with such figures as René Guénon,

D. T. Suzuki, and Ananda K. Coomaraswamy and that continues to this day. In the presentation of genuine Oriental doctrines and practices to the West, the works of the Traditionalist School identified with Guénon, Coomaraswamy, Frithjof Schuon, Marco Pallis, Titus Burckhardt, Martin Lings, and others is of the utmost significance,[4] for those figures have not only sought to present Oriental teachings in an authentic manner that is confirmed by the authorities of the various traditions. They also have appealed to the Western tradition, which they have defended and sought to revive wherever and whenever possible. In addition to the work of these Traditionalists in the process of the rediscovery of spirituality in the West, the contributions of notable Western scholars with sympathy for their subject, such figures as Louis Massignon, Henry Corbin, Heinrich Zimmer, Mircea Eliade, Arthur Waley, Annemarie Schimmel, and many others, must also be remembered. Such scholars have contributed much to the contemporary Western scene as far as the presentation of non-Western spirituality is concerned through their translations of major works of Oriental spirituality and their explanation of their content, even if their aim, at the beginning at least, was meant to be "academic." The use made of this vast treasury of Oriental spirituality available in the West has of course depended on the seriousness of the seekers and ranges from harmless distortions to demonic perversion to authentic understanding leading to either participation in one of the Oriental spiritual paths or, with the help of such teachings, a return to Western spirituality.

One of the major consequences of this yearning for spirituality in the West has actually been the attempt to revive Christian spirituality itself in the face of all the forces in the modern West that are opposed to religion in general and to its spiritual dimension in particular. One can observe a number of Westerners, disillusioned with the modern world, turning to Christian contemplative practices; some have entered or reentered the Orthodox church and follow the discipline and technique of the prayer of the heart as practiced in Hesychasm, which has been preserved in that tradition.[5] Moreover, the writings and lives of such figures as Charles de Foucault and Thomas Merton have become the subject of widespread interest precisely because of their devotion to the contemplative life. Likewise, there has been a general spread of the writings of such masters of Christian spirituality as Meister Eckhart, and a project such as the *World Spirituality* series, especially the part devoted to the classics of Western spirituality, has been successful beyond all expectation. The ever increasing activity in the translation, editing, and exposition of works on Christian spirituality points to the great interest in the West in the rediscovery of spirituality within the Western tradition itself, despite the ever more extensive destruction of what remains of traditional spiritual disciplines and norms.

Some of this revival of Western spirituality is, interestingly enough, related to the discovery of authentic Oriental intellectuality and spirituality, especially unadulterated metaphysics and techniques of spiritual practice. There are now numerous Christians who are seeking to revive the spiritual practices of their religion with the help of Zen or Yoga[6] while others have benefited from various currents of Islamic spirituality in their study and revival of Christian and Jewish esoterism and spirituality.[7] It can be stated once again that in general the role of Oriental teachings in the revival of Christian spirituality has been primarily in the domains of sapience and traditional metaphysics, on the one hand, and techniques and methods of spiritual practice, on the other. The writings of the Traditionalists, especially Frithjof Schuon, who has had greater influence in Christian circles than other expositors of Tradition and the *Sophia Perennis,* bear testimony to the truth of this assertion.[8]

An important element in the revival of the Western spiritual tradition is the recent serious interest in the study of esoterism. Banished to the margin of the intellectual and religious life of the West for several centuries and reduced for the most part to "occultism," esoterism was reestablished as a most serious subject of study by the Traditionalists, who have sought to revive it in the West and who consider esoterism the heart of religion, synonymous with that inwardness toward which all authentic spirituality aspires.[9] Through their efforts and in recent decades the work of a number of scholars[10] who have sought to rescue it from the lowly status it has had in both academic and religious circles as superstition or dangerous occultism, Western esoterism is now becoming much better known and respected and plays a crucial role in the revival of spirituality in the West, especially in its sapiential dimension. The explosion of writings during the past few decades, especially in France and Germany, devoted, for example, to Hermeticism, far from being of simple academic interest, signifies a transformation in certain circles that is at once intellectual and spiritual, despite the many distortions and misunderstandings that the study of esoterism still entails.

Yet side by side with the introduction of authentic Oriental doctrines and practices and the revival of the spiritual and esoteric dimensions of the Western tradition, one can observe in the West today numerous currents that have a claim on spirituality, but that cannot be considered authentic from the point of view of tradition and the definition of spirituality given above. One of these currents is an eclecticism that is often combined with novelty, that is, the amassing of elements of various traditions by individuals claiming to be masters or spiritual authorities who, however, do not accept the authority of any single tradition and in fact claim to have either created a new synthesis or invented something utterly new. Usually avid supporters of the evolutionary theory, they claim to have evolved beyond the teachings of the existing traditions, for which they hold little respect, but which they consider repositories from which they can extract certain ideas, techniques, or forms at will. Such eclecticisms and novelties usually end up as cults and are characterized by their claim to possess spiritual teachings or esoteric knowledge preserved only for their members. They are in fact parodies of traditional esoteric and initiatic organizations, which always function within the matrix of a living tradition.

Another current that is part of the present-day landscape and closely akin to eclectic and novel movements is "uprooted" Oriental teachings, by which is meant teachings of an Oriental origin that are cut off from their foundations and roots and usually presented to the Western audience in a diluted, but also often distorted and even perverted manner. Among these types of movements it was pseudo-Vedanta that appeared first on the scene early in the twentieth century, becoming further strengthened after World War II, which marks the beginning of a new chapter in the history of such movements in North America. The distorted treatment of the Vedanta was followed by distorted presentations of Zen and then Sufism, which was spared such profanation for a while longer.[11] Such uprooted forms of Oriental spirituality, usually divorced from both strict moral laws and sacred rites, have been perpetuated by both native Orientals and Westerners and have even led to many clashes with Western institutions and laws. For the most part they have now become part and parcel of the religious landscape of the West, often being mistaken for the authentic Oriental teachings, whose presence has also been growing steadily in the Western world during the past few decades, as witnessed by the spread of various Sufi orders and Tibetan Buddhism.[12]

Both eclectic movements and uprooted forms of Oriental spirituality are related to a more general phenomenon that is often called "New Age spirituality." This phenomenon is characterized by the usual disdain for orthodox and traditional forms of religion; interest in the residues of traditional sciences, such as astrology, that have survived as "occult" sciences during the past few centuries; a marked individualism, usually combined with sentimentalism and opposition to theology and intellectuality, which are made to appear as restraining dogma; a vision of the most recent developments of modern science as support for spirituality; a decidedly non-Christian attitude toward sexuality, which is seen as a means of spiritual fulfillment even outside traditional moral norms; a love of nature and natural foods, the latter of which has an almost spiritual significance in the eyes of followers of such movements; and a general inclination to seek to discover and emphasize the spiritual significance of the body. Many of the tendencies within the so-called New Age movement represent reactions to the most negative aspects of modern civilization, such as strong opposition to the pollution of the environment or neglect of the spiritual significance of the body, which has been reduced to pure matter or a machine in the dualistic worldview that has ruled over the West since Descartes. But most of what is called New Age spirituality is in reality involved with the psyche rather than the Spirit, the lack of distinction between which is one of the marks of the New Age phenomenon. In any case this type of phenomenon has been part of the current scene for several decades, so that no account of spirituality in the West today could remain silent about it. In fact, some would claim that the so-called New Age spirituality embraces nearly all the different movements of a supposedly spiritual nature today that are not included in traditional spiritual norms and practices.

A phenomenon related to the New Age movement, but distinct in its own right, is the rise in the West of interest in the magical and the demonic as substitute for the spiritual. The increase in the practice of witchcraft particularly in England and North America in the 1980s, the appearance of cults in which demonic forces are consciously worshiped, interest in demonic phenomena such as possession by evil spirits and the like, along with renewed interest in exorcism are all indicative of this type of phenomenon, which seeks to substitute the demonic for the angelic in what could only be called a perversion of traditional spirituality; Guénon refers to this as the countertradition.[13] If, on the one hand, such movements represent the breakup of the paradigm of modernism, from which both the angels and the demons have been banished, they mark, on the other hand, the penetration of dark forces into the modern world from below rather than above, forces that are falsely seen by many as spiritual in a world in which the sense of discernment between the spiritual and the psychic, the angelic and the demonic has to a great degree been lost.

Before concluding this survey of the Western world, it is necessary to say a few words concerning the ever growing interest in much of the West in sacred art and the sacred meaning of nature, both of which are closely connected to the revival or at least quest for spirituality. One of the remarkable events of the past few decades is the increased interest in the sacred art of the West, not to speak of that of other traditions, and the ever greater availability of this art. Parallel with the destruction of forms in the main currents of modern art, one observes renewed interest in Christian icons, their reproduction and theological and spiritual explanation, as well as in medieval Western art from architecture to painting. The same phenomenon can be observed in the field of music. Half a century ago only a few connoisseurs were acquainted with Gregorian chant or the masses of Palestrina and Vittoria, whereas today the whole tradition of Western classical music up to and including Bach, a tradition that has created some of the most spiritually fecund works of Western art, has a notable following. Who would have ever imagined a few decades ago being able to purchase the music of the thirteenth-century German mystic Hildegard of Bingen in practically any serious music store in the United States? Interest in arts impregnated with a spiritual message is a notable element in the contemporary spiritual scene, compensating, for some, for the singularly ugly ambience of the modern world dominated by the shapes and noises of the machine.

Likewise, the love for nature as God's creation and a sacred reality complementing sacred art is of profound spiritual significance, even if some of those who valiantly seek to defend the natural environment against rape and desecration by the application of modern technology may not be always aware of this connection and consider themselves secularists. Recently, parallel with the development of new theologies of ecology and the environment, which usually repudiate the formulations of Christian theology made during the past few centuries, a number of Christians, deeply involved in the spiritual dimension of their religion, have realized the existence of the strong connection between the destruction of the environment and the inner spiritual plight of modern humankind. They have sought to reestablish the profound relationship that must of necessity exist between spirituality and love of nature and to protect it from the follies of modern human beings blind to their own spiritual nature.[14] In any case those with deeper concern about the environment are part and parcel of that segment of the contemporary world seeking to rediscover the roots of human existence in its essential reality and in its relation to both nature and the Author of nature; they must therefore be considered in the study of spirituality in the contemporary world.

One should add here that in North America the rise of attention to the spirituality of the Native American traditions is to a large extent connected with their message based upon the sacred quality of natural forms and phenomena. The great interest shown in these traditions by many in the white population, albeit sometimes in a distorted manner (for example, ending up with weekend workshops on Shamanism), is of much significance for the understanding of a certain dimension of spiritual activity among the dominant American culture, while the continued presence of the Native North American traditions with their archaic and primal spiritual vision is itself remarkable and constitutes a precious component of contemporary spiritual life in North America.[15]

When we think of Islamic spirituality in its encounter with the modern world, the complex panorama depicted in general outlines here must be considered. Both the study and spread of this dimension of Islam in the modern West are related to the various spiritual currents and movements as well as distorted forms of spirituality described briefly above.

THE ISLAMIC WORLD

Having provided this survey of the state of spirituality in the West, from which modernism originated, it is now necessary to turn to the Islamic world itself and view the situation from the point of view of Islamic spirituality. As already mentioned, the Islamic world is itself beset with many problems issuing from the advent of modernism and secularism, which are also affecting other regions of the world. Yet the condition of spirituality in the Islamic world is quite different from what one finds not only in the West, but also in the former Communist world, in such areas as China and South America, and to a lesser extent in the Buddhist and Hindu worlds. Although the advent of modernism has caused a number of people to turn away from the everyday practice of religion and has diluted faith and piety in certain climes, the vast majority of Muslims continue to remain strongly attached to the practice of their faith. The small numbers of secularized and nonpracticing Muslims are generally to be found in the larger urban areas. But their percentage is much lower than what one finds in either the partially Christian West or Shinto or Buddhist Japan, not to speak of postcommunist Russia or Communist China.

The spirituality connected with intense piety and faith continues to be manifested throughout the Islamic world in daily prayers and fasting, pilgrimage and psalmody of the Quran, the performance of supererogatory prayers and litanies, and in many other ways. There is a great deal of political and social confusion and in certain areas upheaval, which tends to destroy the peace and tranquility and diminish the spiritual quality of traditional Islamic life; nevertheless faith continues to be strong, as does the traditional Islamic view of God and His creation. Although endless debate takes place concerning the relation between religion and politics, Western and Islamic education, the application of Divine Law (*al-Sharī'ah*) and that of secular law, and other important issues of that nature, the Islamic world does not experience the same theological malaise and turmoil that one observes in the West. God still sits firmly upon His Throne (*al-'arsh*), to use the Quranic image, and His Transcendence as well as Immanence, Beauty as well as Majesty are not challenged, as one sees in the West. In the 1980s and 1990s in the West some questioned and debated even the gender of the Divine, and others reduced the Divinity itself to a process, a way of thinking associated especially with the philosophy of Alfred North Whitehead, which still has followers today. The traditional language of the Islamic revelation is still fully coherent for the faithful.

Consequently, although in recent decades Muslims have been witness to painful upheavals, wars, and the killing of many of their number from Bosnia and Chechnya to Palestine, Iraq, Afghanistan, and Kashmir, the traditional theological and legal structures in whose matrix the life of piety and faith has functioned over the centuries still continue, and one can observe easily something of the spiritual quality emanating from a life based on intense awareness of the Transcendent Dimension of reality in most areas of the Islamic world, even amid very difficult economic and political conditions. This fact is most evident in the case of the sacred rites such as the daily prayers and pilgrimage, which continue to be performed regularly on a very wide scale.

The most intense form of Islamic spirituality as related to the world of the Spirit and the dimension of inwardness is of course to be found in the inner or esoteric dimension of Islam, which became crystallized primarily in Sufism and certain aspects of Shīʻism. A survey of the condition of spirituality in the Islamic world today must, therefore, turn most of all to a study of Sufism and its ramifications and manifestations, without disregarding either the spirituality related to the life of piety and faith among ordinary believers or the inner life of Shīʻism.

Opposed by both the forces of modernism and puritanical reform movements in the thirteenth/nineteenth century, the influence of Sufism receded in many areas of the Islamic world despite the revival of certain of the Sufi orders, such as the Shādhiliyyah, or the establishment of new ones, such as the Sanūsiyyah and Tijāniyyah in modern times.[16] In the twentieth century this opposition increased at the same time that a revival of interest also took place among certain sectors of Islamic society, as mentioned elsewhere in this book. In the lands conquered by Communism, Sufism became completely banned by the avowedly atheistic regime; even in such independent areas of the Islamic world as Turkey all public manifestations of Sufism were prohibited after the rise to power of Ataturk in the third decade of the fourteenth/twentieth century, and most Sufi centers were closed. The same situation could be found in Saudi Arabia, but for very different reasons; here the opposition came not from secular modernism, but from Wahhābism.

During the past few decades, however, the situation of the Sufi orders has somewhat improved in many areas, although there is no doubt that one cannot find great spiritual masters in every city and town as one did in days of old. Even the outstanding masters of the early part of this century, such as Shaykh Muḥammad al-Tādilī of Morocco, Shaykh al-ʻAlawī of Algeria, Sidi Salāmah al-Raḍī of Egypt, and Shams al-ʻUrafā' of Persia, did not always leave successors who could match their spiritual eminence. Yet the Sufi orders continue to flourish openly in much of Black Africa and North Africa, especially the Sudan, Senegal, Algeria, and Morocco;

in Egypt, where the spiritual presence of Sufism is palpable even on the more external plane; and in Persia, Pakistan, Muslim India, and Southeast Asia. Having survived the repressions of the Communist regime, Sufism is still alive to some extent in Albania, Bosnia, and Macedonia as well as in Central Asia and Caucasia, where, as already mentioned, the role of the Naqshbandiyyah Order, founded originally in Central Asia in the eighth/fourteenth century but later spreading widely throughout most of the Islamic world, has been central in the presentation of the religion itself. As for Turkey, some seventy years after being banned, Sufism is again quite active there, with a number of important masters and centers in both the big cities and the countryside. Amid all this activity, however, the number of great masters has decreased, as already mentioned, and those orders emphasizing the purely sapiential and gnostic teachings of Islam have diminished in number.

One can experience even on a more external level something of the perfume of Sufi spirituality in the public performances of Sufi prayers, litanies, and spiritual concerts (*samāʿ*) held in such places as the Ra's al-Ḥusayn in Cairo; the many tombs of Sufi saints in Lahore, Delhi, Ajmer, and other cities of the Indian subcontinent; and on the anniversary of the death of Jalāl al-Dīn Rūmī in Konya, just to cite a few examples. The vast majority of the activities of the Sufi orders remain, however, hidden from public sight, although this hidden spiritual spring affects the whole body of Islamic society much like the heart, which, although hidden, governs the rhythm of life of all the organs of the body.

Parallel with the continuous activities of Sufi orders, both hidden and manifest, the last few decades have been witness to an outpouring of Sufi writings for the wider public in nearly all Islamic languages. For the first time many Sufi treatises have been made available in print, and some of the major works, such as the *Futūḥāt al-makkiyyah* ("Meccan Illuminations") of Ibn ʿArabī and the *Mathnawī* of Jalāl al-Dīn Rūmī, have been or are in the process of being reprinted in new, critical editions. Altogether this period has been very rich in both the writing of new and the dissemination of older Sufi works. Many educated Muslims are greatly drawn to Sufi literature, not only because these writings contain the greatest literary masterpieces in Islamic languages, but also because they provide answers to questions posed by the challenges of the modern world. Both classical Sufi literary works, especially poetry, and traditional didactic and metaphysical expositions, usually in prose, have been and continue to be widely distributed and read, some of them becoming what one would call "best sellers" in the West.

It is interesting to note in this context that during this period English and French have also become important vehicles for the expression of the authentic teachings of Sufism. Works in these languages, written by both Western followers of Islam and Sufism and native Muslims as well as by at least some Western Islamicists, are read not only in the West, but also by a large number of Muslims within the Islamic world itself. Consequently any discussion of the remarkable increase in the printing of works on Sufism in recent decades must include works in European languages, which, in cases where they are authentic, usually have a wide-ranging audience within the Islamic world itself from Malaysia to Morocco, including especially such countries as Turkey and Pakistan.

Metaphysical and doctrinal works, which represent the intellectual dimension of the Islamic tradition and which are inseparable from Islamic spirituality in its sapiential dimension, continue to appear in various Islamic languages, especially Arabic and Persian. This is particularly true in Persia, where not only Sufi metaphysics but also the "mystical" philosophy associated with the name of such masters as Suhrawardī and Mullā Ṣadrā are very much alive and have in fact been witness to a major revival during the past few decades.[17] This type of philosophy, which resembles in many ways mystical theology and esoteric philosophy in the West, is needless to say of great spiritual significance, and its recent revival not only in Persia, but also elsewhere in the Islamic world, must be considered in any survey of the conditions of spirituality in that world today.

In contrast to Sufi metaphysical doctrine, newly composed Sufi poetry has been eclipsed during the last half century, because most of the best-known Arabic, Persian, Turkish, or Urdu poets are no longer concerned with either classical Sufi poetry or spirituality in general, except insofar as it is related to the social themes to which these poets have turned their attention. Influenced by European and American literature and leftist ideologies, most of the well-known figures have parted ways with the domain of traditional Sufi poetry. That does not mean, however, that wide appreciation of Sufi poetry does not continue, as one observes in the incredible popularity of Ibn al-Fāriḍ in Egypt, Yūnus Emre in Turkey, or Rūmī in

Persia, Afghanistan, Pakistan, and again Turkey. Nor does it mean that Sufi poetry does not continue to be composed. On the contrary, in many of the orders the poems of contemporary masters are sung,[18] and a few of the well-known poets are devoted to the treatment of the deepest spiritual themes with which Sufi literature has been engaged over the ages, even if they do not follow the traditional canons of Sufi poetry in the classical sense.[19]

The field of music presents a very different picture. Classical music of the Islamic peoples, whether Arabic, Persian, Turkish, or North Indian, was cultivated over the ages mostly by the Sufis and is impregnated with the deepest spiritual message of Sufism. These musical traditions survive and have in fact been renewed in the past decades. They are performed in the gatherings of certain Sufi orders as well as in public, and many of their performers, especially in such countries as Turkey, Egypt, Morocco, and Muslim India, belong to Sufi orders. In any case, the continuation of this art form represents one of the most powerful means for the preservation of the presence of Sufi spirituality in Islamic society, and its impact cannot be overestimated.

Space does not allow a survey of all the Islamic arts that over the ages have been a vehicle for the transmission of the message of Islamic spirituality as well as a doorway to the world of the Spirit.[20] Suffice it to say that some of these traditional arts, such as architecture and garden landscaping, continue here and there, despite the ravages brought upon the traditional Islamic cities during the past century and in fact have been renewed in some places. Others, like calligraphy, have preserved their tradition strongly to this day. The survival of all these arts is of great importance for the survival of Islamic spirituality precisely because of their connection over the ages to the spiritual and inward message of Islam and more specifically to Sufism.

It must be mentioned that, during the past few years, interest in Sufism has increased greatly among the well-educated classes in many parts of the Islamic world. Whereas from the thirteenth/nineteenth century on, when modern education was introduced into that world or Muslims were sent to Europe to study, those so educated usually turned away immediately from Sufism, in recent years some of the most intelligent among this class of Islamic society have returned to its bosom. A number have formally entered Sufi orders, while many others read Sufi literature avidly. A study of the Sufi orders in Egypt, Turkey, Pakistan, and many other important centers of Islamic culture reveals this fact clearly.

In a sense this return to Sufism by many modern, educated Muslims reflects, *mutatis mutandis,* the thirst for spirituality visible in the contemporary West. In the Islamic world, however, nearly all of those stricken with this thirst have sought the fountains of traditional Islamic spirituality and particularly Sufism, although a very small minority have sought the satisfaction of this need in modern cults and movements of various kinds outside of Islam, usually originating in the West. A tiny few have even tried to attach themselves to authentic spiritual currents of Oriental origin such as Zen. In a country such as Turkey, which has experienced a greater degree of secularism than other Islamic countries, the number of such seekers of either Oriental teachings, Western interpretations thereof, or other forms of twentieth-century eclecticism and "New Age spirituality" is relatively greater than elsewhere in the Islamic world. Altogether, however, this type of phenomenon is very minor and secondary in Islamic countries not only in comparison with the West, but also with Japan and India. Nearly all of those Muslims who, having experienced the spiritual nihilism resulting from secularism, have sought to rediscover spirituality have returned to the bosom of Islamic spirituality, especially Sufism in either its operative or cultural aspect or both.

As for Islamic spirituality as it has manifested itself in Shīʿism, it also continues as a living reality despite the politicization of religious symbols and even rites during the past few decades in much of the Shīʿite world, a phenomenon to which we shall turn shortly. The participation, each month of Muḥarram, in the suffering of Imam Ḥusayn during the mourning of his martyrdom at the hands of the army of Yazīd in Iraq in the first/seventh century and in the redemptive quality of this suffering continues unabated in Persia, Pakistan, India, Lebanon, the Persian Gulf states, and since the fall of Saddam Ḥusayn in Iraq.[21] Men and women continue to make pilgrimages to the tombs of the Imams and to recite the prayers related to them, most of which possess an esoteric character.[22] Likewise, the esoteric knowledge flowing from their teachings continues to be studied even in official religious schools often dominated in some areas by immediate political considerations. And the vast majority of Shīʿites still await the appearance of the Twelfth Imam, who, as the Mahdī, will commence the era of the Parousia and inaugurate the eschatological events that will terminate with the return of Christ to earth.[23] The spirituality of expectation (*intiẓār*) is very much alive especially in these days, when a wave of Mahdiism or millennialism is sweeping throughout the Islamic world with its own particular characteristics, a current that is combined with what we could call eschatological spirituality, which will be discussed in a more global context later. Despite its specifically Islamic and in certain areas especially Shīʿite character, this Islamic eschatological spirituality has certain similarities to the eschatological spirituality of some medieval Christian mystics, such as Joachim of Flora, although there are also major differences in the perspectives of the two groups.

Before concluding the discussion of the situation of spirituality in the Islamic world, it is necessary to say a few words about that set of movements and phenomena assembled and categorized as "Islamic fundamentalism" in their relation to the subject. It needs to be emphasized again that what is called "Islamic fundamentalism" is comprised of many disparate elements. There are those who wish to return to the practice of Islam and to live within Islamic culture, rather than being drowned in the world dominated by an alien worldview and set of laws, for example, those who follow the Tablīghī Jamāʿat (Society for Propagation [of Religion]) movement of Pakistan and India, members of some of the more Salafī inclined Sufi orders in the Arab world and Islamic Black Africa, and many followers of the Muslim Brotherhood (*Ikhwān al-muslimīn*). In a sense they wish to complete the process of decolonization that took place half a century ago politically, but not culturally and socially. Others react in the name of Islam against modernism by having recourse to the very isms and ideologies they claim to oppose; they represent, as already mentioned, the other side of the coin of modernism. This includes groups within Iran, Pakistan, Bangladesh, and certain other Muslim countries for whom Islam itself is considered an ideology. And yet other groups are really exoterists, insisting upon the external aspects of Islam alone to the detriment of the inward ones, as we find in neo-Wahhābism and many Salafī movements. Also in some cases more than one of these elements are to be found within a single movement.

Obviously the spiritual significance of these and other movements called "fundamentalism" varies a great deal; some are highly antispiritual, and others are not. Those who, through anger, participate in political actions that take recourse to violence certainly do not contribute to the peace and beauty of the ambience that has always characterized Islamic spirituality. Nor is their anger to be mistaken in most cases for the holy anger of the saints, which is certainly a viable possibility in any total spiritual universe. It is important, however, to mention that judging politicized action tinged with religious color or making use of religious symbolism through the lens of the usual Christian understanding of spirituality as based on withdrawal from the world of external struggle and contention may not always be correct. One cannot neglect the spirituality connected with chivalry in Christian history itself nor of course the spiritual dimension of *jihād,* which has already been discussed (see chapter 2). The relation between combativeness and spirituality is a very complicated one. Let us remember that, as recorded in the *Bhagavad Gita,* the highest spiritual truths of Hinduism were taught by Krishna in the midst of battle, and Japanese samurai combined combativeness with self-sacrifice and spirituality.

In Islam similar situations are to be found. Whereas most "fundamentalism" is opposed to authentic Islamic spirituality, there have been some military actions associated with Islam that still preserved something of the wedding between chivalry and spirituality. For example, in the war in Afghanistan against the Soviet army, whole Sufi orders composed of many men of great spiritual attainment participated in the struggle, which involved the issue of the survival of the traditional life of a whole people and which was a *jihād* in the external sense of the term. Yet it also possessed a spiritual significance and many of those who were killed are considered martyrs. The same can be said of the first Chechnyan war. It is enough to compare the phases of the Chechnyan and Afghan wars to see the difference between the traditional forms of military action and the "fundamentalist" ones in relation to spirituality exemplified by the Taliban of Afghanistan and the neo-Wahhābīs of Chechnya. It must be remembered that the first Chechnyan war was fought by the traditional Muslim population of Chechnya, led by the Naqshbandīs. Soon thereafter, with the help of the Saudis, neo-Wahhābism spread in the devastated lands of Chechnya, and the second war was spearheaded to a large extent by neo-Wahhābīs, whose interpretation of Islam was itself to a large extent alien to the traditional understanding of Islamic norms and teachings in that land. A similar situation can be observed mutatis mutandis in Afghanistan.

In contrast to earlier forms of resistance based on the principles of Islamic Law, there have appeared more recently other movements and actions also claiming an Islamic character, but they have been opposed to all the contemplative dimensions of the religion and in violation of explicit dicta of Islamic Law, such as the prohibition against killing the innocent, even in war. By and large one can determine to an appreciable degree the character of a so-called fundamentalist movement by studying its attitude toward the millennial intellectual and spiritual traditions of Islam, including of course Sufism as well as Islamic art and intellectuality in all their forms, which have always been part of the authentic manifestations of Islamic spirituality.

One might say, by way of summary, that the peaceful forms of revivalism often included in the category of "Islamic fundamentalism" have brought a number of people back to the fold of Islam as practicing Muslims and thereby have assisted in that aspect of spirituality that is related to intense piety and faith. But they have at the same time weakened spiritual forces by opposing the dimension of inwardness, remaining satisfied with only the outward interpretation of religion, and being impervious or even opposed to traditional Islamic intellectuality. As for those movements that have taken a violent turn and are based on anger that claims for itself righteousness, but is devoid of that peace that lies at the heart of the Islamic message, there is no doubt that they have contributed to the creation of an atmosphere of tension and dislocation in which the practice of spirituality becomes ever more difficult.

To see, however, how complicated these considerations are, one needs only to turn to the case of Persia, in which one of the major upheavals closely associated with the very concept of "Islamic fundamentalism" took place in the late 1970s. There is no doubt that, on the one hand, there occurred a major political and social upheaval followed by a long war with Iraq, with its consequent social and economic difficulties, which continue on many fronts to this day, and that many of the traditional centers of religion became politically activated, with all that this activism implies spiritually. There is also no doubt that these events have affected the structure of Shīʿism itself and created problems of a religious nature for many Persians within the country, not to speak of those in exile. Yet, on the other side, one sees the continuation in Persia of much of the traditional Shīʿite piety alluded to above and the survival of some of the Sufi orders, although the activity of certain others has been curtailed. Most telling is the intense interest in the spiritual aspects of Islam, as manifested in the publication of numerous works on Sufi doctrine, practice, and history as well as continuous printing and reprinting of the classical Sufi works of such figures as 'Aṭṭār, Rūmī, and Jāmī. Even classical Persian music, so deeply pervaded by the ethos of Sufism and of a highly spiritual character, has been revived after a period of early opposition by the revolutionary authorities. There is perhaps no other Islamic country, with the possible exception of Egypt, in which so many works concerned with Islamic spirituality have appeared during the past decade. This example should demonstrate the complexity of the relation between "Islamic fundamentalism" and Islamic spirituality.

One might conclude by saying that, in most of the Islamic world, spiritual currents are faced with two challenges: one from modernism and secularism and the other from those movements that have now become known as "Islamic fundamentalism." These spiritual currents have suffered as a result, but remain nevertheless alive and vibrant in many places. In the same way that these currents survived seventy years of Communist repression in Russia, southern Europe, Caucasia, and Central Asia and secularist opposition in such places as Turkey, they have also survived even those types of Islamic activism or "fundamentalism" that have become violent and in fact play a moderating influence upon such types of activism. The constant attention paid in the media to "Islamic fundamentalism" and the disturbing images that hardly remind one of spirituality should not cause one to forget the continuous survival, throughout the Islamic world and even amid situations affected by Islamic activism, of authentic Islamic spirituality in its various forms, especially paths that are able to guide men and women from the world of outwardness to the inward abode at the center of which resides the Spirit, paths that lead finally to God.

FUTURE PROSPECTS FOR SPIRITUALITY IN THE WEST

There are those more qualified to comment upon the future of spirituality in the West, but since this chapter seeks to discuss the situation of Islamic spirituality in a more global context, it is necessary to say a few words on this most difficult subject. It is difficult because the Spirit "doth" in reality blow where it "listeth," and there are imponderable factors known only to God that make any claim to speak definitively of the future seem like a description of a landscape by one deprived of eyesight. It is, therefore, with the utmost humility and full awareness of the presence of the Vertical Dimension at all moments of human history and at every point in the chain of horizontal causality that these observations are offered about the West as well as the Islamic world.

Most of the trends in the West mentioned at the beginning of this chapter seem likely to continue in the near future, including the further erosion of traditional spirituality. But at the same time the process of revival and return in some circles to the traditional sources and practices of Christian spirituality and deeper concern for the spiritual dimension of the natural environment will also most likely continue. "Oriental spirituality" will also continue to grow in the West, especially Islamic spirituality, and that primarily in the form of Sufism. Already several authentic Sufi orders, such as the Shādhiliyyah, Qādiriyyah, Naqshbandiyyah, and Ni'matallāhiyyah, have sunk their roots in the West and are growing rapidly. One observes a dilution or sometimes distortion in their teaching in some places, such as California, but by and large they have preserved and are most likely to preserve in the future their authentic doctrines and methods. There is also the continuous translation and exposition of Sufi works, which are slowly transforming the larger intellectual and spiritual landscape beyond the circle of scholars of Islam or Western practitioners of Sufism. This trend is also likely to continue, so that in a few years many of the important works of Islamic spirituality, often interpreted by those knowledgeable in the subject in more than an academic way, will be available in European languages, especially English and French, and are bound to have a greater effect than at present upon both the intellectual and spiritual scenes in the West.

Besides Islam, Buddhism, especially in its Tibetan form, is also likely to continue to grow through the establishment of centers with qualified teachers as well as the dissemination of texts dealing with meditation, rites, cosmology, sacred psychology, and other related subjects. The spread of authentic Hinduism seems somewhat more problematic, seeing that its orthodox practice implies belonging to the caste system. But Hindu spirituality is also bound to continue to attract great attention, as it has done during the past century, and its classics, such as the *Bhagavad Gita,* are likely to become increasingly part and parcel of the Western spiritual landscape. Whether Taoism and other spiritual currents emanating from the Chinese traditions will also grow in the West outside of the circle of Far Eastern peoples now living there is difficult to predict. But here also one can say with near certitude that such texts as the *Tao Te Ching,* already enjoying universal popularity, will become even more than at present a part of the intellectual and spiritual universe of Western people.

This growth of authentic Oriental traditions in the West is bound to create a greater sense of discernment vis-à-vis parodies of Oriental teachings that have invaded the West during the past few decades. It might be more difficult to disseminate counterfeit Oriental doctrines and practices in a world in which the authentic teachings are more readily accessible, providing the criteria for a greater sense of discernment in these matters, at least for those who possess a general sense of discernment within themselves.

This possible decrease in infatuation with pseudo-Oriental doctrines does not mean that pseudospirituality in general will diminish in the West. On the contrary, the false prophets, to whom Christ referred, cannot but manifest themselves in a world surrounded by ever more spiritual darkness and the eclipse of sacred forms and authentic rites and practices. These "prophets" almost always stake their claims on the esoteric and spiritual dimension of religion or in certain cases on eschatological considerations, to which we shall now turn. But in any case amid the chaos of the world of so-called postmodernism, in which the very notion of truth is challenged as not having any ultimate significance, counterfeit spirituality, perversions of authentic teachings, and demonic phenomena posing as the spiritual are bound to flourish, even if the presence of authentic Oriental teachings will make the spread of pseudo-Oriental spirituality more difficult among people with some discernment.

It is precisely in a world falling apart at the seams that eschatological expectations increase and give birth to forces that are spiritually significant in both a positive and negative manner. One can in fact assert with confidence that the rapport between spirituality and eschatology, already noted in the case of the Islamic world, will increase worldwide, especially in the West, as the modern world approaches closer to its end.

Of course such conditions also give rise to exclusivist eschatologies with dangerous consequences, as we see in certain Protestant circles and also in certain forms of messianic Judaism. Let us remember that most authentic spiritual paths that function within a traditional matrix today operate in a climate influenced by eschatological considerations, or what Hindus associate with the terminal phase of the Kali-Yuga, or Age of Darkness. Awareness that the end of this chaotic world as we know it cannot be far away has of course the deepest effect upon one's spiritual life and makes it easier to detach oneself from the world, which in times gone by at least carried some nobility and beauty with it, but which today has none of those connotations for anyone with a contemplative nature. Spirituality is, therefore, for the most part, not divorced under the conditions of this age from eschatology for individuals of spiritual discernment who are at the same time aware of the ravages brought about by the advent of modernism, whether they are Hindus and speak of the end of the Kali-Yuga, Navajos awaiting Purification Day, Muslims expecting the advent of the Mahdī, or Christians expecting the second coming of Christ. And this rapport is bound to continue and in fact become stronger in the future, as the ambience becomes marked by the ever greater presence of millennialist movements and the natural environment that is our home here below becomes threatened to an even greater degree by the follies of a humanity cut off from its spiritual traditions.

In the West, especially in North America more than elsewhere, however, there exists the possibility of a special kind of subversion of the normal relationship between spirituality and eschatology, one that has already been observed in the tragedy of Waco, Texas, in 1993 and is likely to grow in the future. The recurrence of the majestic images contained in the *Book of Revelation* of John—the vivid descriptions of the four beasts of the Apocalypse, the coming of the Anti-Christ, the return of Christ, and the end of human history—are bound to play not only the positive spiritual role for which they were meant, but also to become distorted and used as basis for cultic teachings. Such cultic teachings are likely to flower with ever greater frequency in a world that has lost its spiritual bearing and in which eschatological realities loom ever larger and more vividly upon the horizon. The vision of St. Malachy concerning the papacy and leading to the end of time ends with the description of the few faithful who remain assembled around the last representative of St. Peter. But before that event, there are likely to be many other figures who will claim to save the few real believers before the onslaught by the forces of darkness. Distortions of eschatological spirituality are also bound to occur elsewhere in the world and have done so already, as we shall see in the case of Islam. But in the West they are bound to be specifically Christian in outer color if not in depth, causing more frequent occurrences of tragic phenomena of which the West has already had a foretaste. For such movements in the West the Arab-Israeli world and especially Jerusalem are likely to continue to be central; these movements are likely to cause even more human tragedies and suffering than they already have.

THE FUTURE OF ISLAMIC SPIRITUALITY

As far as the Islamic world is concerned, the piety associated with the fervent practice of the rites promulgated by the Divine Law (*al-Sharī'ah*) is likely to continue. The Quran itself refers to there being many of those who have faith and follow the formal religious practices at the beginning and many at the end.[24] This is one of the features that distinguishes sharply the religious scene in the Islamic world from that in the West, especially Europe, where the formal and ritual practices associated with religion become less and less common in a world characterized by ever greater secularism and amorphousness as far as traditional religious structures and norms are concerned. In the Islamic world, the intensity of the daily prayers and all the piety and spiritual fervor associated with them are likely to persist, along with the psalmody of the Quran, the writing of its text in beautiful calligraphy, pilgrimage, fasting, and the like. To the extent that these rites and the general symbols of religion become politicized, the serenity and peace connected with and issuing from them will be disturbed and diminished. We see this with politicization of the powerful religious concept of martyrdom and the sermon in Friday prayers in certain Islamic countries, but it is unlikely that these spiritual practices will be totally eclipsed even in those areas of the Islamic world faced with political movements of an overtly religious color.

It is also necessary to repeat that interpretations of Islam combined with political upheavals and associated with "Islamic fundamentalism" have not and are not likely to replace completely traditional Islam, which is still dominant even in lands particularly marked by such upheavals. And within this traditional ambience, the efficacy of the rites, their beauty, and the spirituality that flows from them are bound to continue in both the Sunni and Shī'ite worlds.

As for Sufism, in certain areas where neo-Wahhābism and Salafism are on the rise, its outward practice is bound to become curtailed with the triumph of those politico-religious forces opposed to Sufism, as has happened in such a country as Saudi Arabia since its foundation. But even in such areas, most likely the inner activity will continue in the manner that one observes in Saudi Arabia today. In countries that have been great centers of Sufism over the ages, such as Persia, Egypt, or Turkey, most likely the intense presence of Sufism will persist, no matter what outward changes are brought about, as in fact the Islamic revolution in Persia, the Ataturk secularization of Turkey and the Nasserite revolution in Egypt, three major political transformations of very different natures, demonstrate. The transmission of the inner teachings, inward prayer, and the grace, or *barakah,* flowing from Sufism, which is itself inseparable from Muḥammadan grace (*al-barakat al-muḥammadiyyah*), are likely to persist, no matter what the external circumstances.

What is most likely to become somewhat further destroyed is the general spiritual ambience that one still experiences in what remains of traditional Islamic cities from Lahore to Isfahan, to San'a, to certain quarters of Cairo, to Fez and Timbuktu. That ambience, dominated by the serenity of Islamic art and the peace that issues from inner surrender to the Divine Will as the soul gains the station of contentment, is likely to further diminish in both size and intensity, as it has during the past few decades. The very ugliness of the modern world, as it spreads ever farther into the Islamic world and elsewhere, is a powerful instrument for the destruction of such a spiritual ambience. So are more local factors, such as the rapid increase in population and urbanization and the indifference of many of the so-called Islamic fundamentalist movements and so-called Islamic governments to Islamic art and the creation and maintenance of an atmosphere that reflects Islamic spirituality, as was prevalent in the Islamic cities and towns of old over the ages.

In the intellectual realm, various "fundamentalist" and modernist groups remain strongly opposed to Sufism and the intellectual dimension of Islam in general. But with the intellectual shallowness of the modernists, demonstrated in the quality of their thought as well as the innate weakness of the ever changing Western models they seek to emulate, along with the inability of the "fundamentalists" to provide Islamic answers to the intellectual challenges the modern world poses for Islam, more interest is now being taken in the Islamic intellectual tradition throughout the Islamic world, a tradition that is inseparable from Islamic spirituality. Works of Ibn 'Arabī and his school as well as of Suhrawardī, Mullā Ṣadrā, and similar figures are much more a part of the world of the younger generation of "intellectuals" than of their fathers (we shall return to this issue later in the book). This trend is also likely to continue. Traditional Islamic metaphysics, cosmology, psychology, aesthetics, and other disciplines, many of them connected with Sufism, remain alive and are bound to continue to receive new interpretations and be expressed in fresh formulations in the future, as they have in the recent past.

An element of great significance as far as the future of spirituality in the Islamic world is concerned is Mahdiism, which corresponds, within the context of the Islamic tradition and therefore with its own characteristics, to millennialism and messianism in Judaism, Christianity, and elsewhere. Belief in the coming of the Mahdī to inaugurate the events of the Last Days is widely held among all Muslims; in addition, Shī'ites believe that they know his exact identity as the Twelfth Imam, now in occultation (*ghaybah*), concealed from the gaze of the outward world.[25] In any case in both the Sunni and Shī'ite cases, there is the expectation of his appearance soon, as the catastrophic events of the modern and postmodern worlds, including the destruction of the environment, loss of the harmony of Muslim life from Bosnia to Indonesia, destruction of the quality of life within Islamic cities, the rebellion of the young and their alternative lifestyles in the West with their ever greater spillover into the Islamic world, and other chaotic events increase. The Islamic world, like certain Christian circles in the West, is also living to some extent in a millennialist atmosphere. This climate has already produced the takeover of the Mecca mosque and violent movements in Nigeria in the name of the Mahdī. Furthermore, the Iranian Revolution itself had a Mahdiist dimension.

In the future this type of phenomenon is likely to grow rather than diminish. But Mahdiism does not always manifest itself only in sociopolitical movements. It also has a distinct spiritual significance of an inner nature, not only in relation to and within such movements, but also independent of them. One cannot conceive of the future of spirituality in the Islamic world without meditating upon the ever greater significance, even on the outward plane, of the esoteric function of the Mahdī, his relation to the "invisible men" (*rijāl al-ghayb*), that is, spiritual beings who are not ordinary men but creatures of the spiritual world who can and do act in the arena of earthly life, and the invisible hierarchy that, according to traditional Islamic teachings, governs through the Divine Will the spiritual life of each generation. But these are matters about which nothing definite can be asserted outwardly, as emphasized in the saying of the Prophet according to which all those who predict the Hour are liars. But with full consideration of the mysteries known only to God and the selected few He has chosen, it can still be asserted with certainty that Mahdiism is bound to play an ever greater role in the future of Islamic spirituality, not to speak of social and political life, until that tomorrow that Muslim authorities identify with the *eschaton* (end times) itself.[26]

CONCLUDING REMARKS

The modern world is like a flower whose petals and husk are withering away and falling apart, while its golden kernel is becoming ever more manifest, recalling the perfection of that flower as it existed primordially and as it will be in the dawn that is to come.[27] As the modern world dissolves and disintegrates, pseudospirituality is bound to make an important contribution to the process of its dissolution, as the earlier repudiation of spirituality had contributed to its coagulation. But authentic spirituality is also bound not only to survive, but also to become ever more intense as that golden center that will integrate all that is positive in the life of the cycle of the world that is about to come to an end.

In the Abrahamic tradition there exists the esoteric teaching concerning the "Eliatic function" in reference to Elias (Elijah), identified in Islam with Ilyās and Khaḍir and even associated with the Mahdī, the ever present spiritual current that does not wither away and will last until the end of time. In fact, according to Jewish sources, at the end of time Elias will raise his voice until it is heard from one end of the earth to the other announcing the oneness of God and proclaiming peace. "On that day God will be one and His Name will be one" (Zechariah 14:9).[28] One might say that this "Eliatic function" is related to the ever present current of authentic spirituality, which will survive to the end of time and whose final manifestation will concern the whole of humanity rather than simply the Judeo-Christian-Islamic worlds.[29]

Despite the many differences in the condition of spirituality between the West and the Islamic as well as other non-Western worlds, there is bound to be a profound interconnection between these various worlds in the future, reflecting not only the profound unity of the human species, but also the fact that the "Age of Darkness," or what Hindus call the Kali-Yuga, is not confined to one group alone, but concerns the whole of humanity. That is why when, according to Islamic sources, the Mahdī appears and leans against the wall of the Ka'bah, calling upon his helpers to aid him in restoring peace and order based upon God's laws and the predominance of the spiritual over the mundane, his voice will be heard all over the globe from east to west. Meanwhile, authentic spirituality is bound to survive protected more by religious forms in the non-Western world, providentially especially Islam, than in the West; it will have to confront the challenge of not only its denial, but also its false imitation through inversion and ultimately perversion, for as was said in days of old, "Satan is the ape of God." The final act, however, is bound to be witness to the triumph of the Spirit, and the final word will be that of the Truth, which has been and will always remain the goal of all authentic spirituality, whether in the East or the West.

Chapter Seven

"DEVELOPMENT" IN THE CONTEMPORARY ISLAMIC WORLD

Since the late thirteenth/nineteenth century, when Western ideas became prevalent among a notable section of the ruling classes of the Islamic world, the ideas of "progress" and "development" in the material realm and not understood only spiritually became widely accepted, and for some time they were considered the normal consequence of the flow of historic time. Rarely were these notions analyzed objectively and in light of both the "values" they imply and the Islamic ideas and norms they threaten with destruction. In the earlier days of contact with the West, philosophical definitions of progress did encounter intellectual rebuttal from the traditional Islamic intelligentsia, but once the general notion of development became prevalent in the fourteenth/twentieth century, there was for some time even less inquiry than before concerning the implication of what is usually understood by development for the "value system" existing within the Islamic world.

It has only been during the past few decades, thanks to the crisis of modern civilization and some of the bitter fruits of what has been taken for granted as the "natural" course of human societies as a result of the process of development, that some of the more perceptive people in the Islamic world have begun to question the nature and meaning of development as understood in the modern West and its implications for the Islamic system of "values." During this period at least some, along with a number of Western thinkers, have begun to ask such questions as, "What is development?" and "Development toward what goal?" In fact one of the most significant developments during the past few decades in the Islamic world is the reexamination of development itself as it had been understood in the West and by Westernized Muslims for so many years.

In this short discourse, at least some of the more important issues that development as usually understood poses for Islamic values will be discussed. One of the most basic of these values concerns the nature of time and the historical process itself. The Western idea of continuous development and progress grew out of a utopianism that is itself a parody of the traditional doctrine that time will end when God intervenes in history to reestablish the primordial harmony of the Edenic state. It is significant to note how difficult it actually is to translate the modern idea of utopia into Arabic and Persian. How different is in fact the meaning of that "ideal city," or *nā kujā ābād,* of Suhrawardī in the eighth clime beyond our ordinary experience of space and "utopia" as currently understood, despite the fact that the term used by Suhrawardī means, literally, *u-topia,* that is, land of nowhere. The Islamic conception of time is based essentially on the cyclic rejuvenation of human history through the appearance of various prophets, which ends finally in the eschatological events identified with the appearance of the Mahdī. This event reestablishes harmony and peace in the world through direct Divine intervention and not through the secular changes brought about by means of mere human agency. The first challenge of the modern Western theory of development to the Islamic world concerns the very nature and meaning of history and the final end of human action, which is usually seen by modernists as bound solely to historical time. Between traditional Islamic eschatological doctrines and Western philosophical utopianism, there is a chasm that cannot be bridged in any way, a chasm that has also created a profound tension within the minds and souls of those Muslims who are caught between the teachings of traditional Islamic culture and modern Western utopian ideas.

Development implies activity directed toward a particular goal. In Islam all human activity must be carried out in accordance with God's Will as embodied in the Divine Law (*Sharī'ah*) and, as far as the making of things is concerned, in accordance with the norms and principles of Islamic art, which are also derived from the Islamic revelation. Human action must be pleasing and acceptable in God's eyes. Obviously the aspect of development in its modern sense that deals with human welfare, with such problems as providing food and housing, can be easily justified and in fact supported from the religious point of view. But such is not the case with the goal of development as indefinite material growth for human beings considered merely as earthly creatures, purely economic animals. Islam, like other religions, sees the end of human beings in the perfection of their spiritual possibilities and defines them as creatures born for transcendence, for going beyond themselves. Obviously an understanding of development that concentrates solely on the material and the worldly cannot but destroy the Islamic conception of the meaning of human life and activity. It is true that in Islam the gaining of a livelihood and the provision of material needs are stressed and are in fact basic to the *Sharīʿah,* but even these worldly activities (those of *al-dunyā*) are judged praiseworthy only in relation to human beings' final end or the other world (*al-ākhirah*). As the Quran states in clear terms in the verse "For those who are virtuous in this world, there shall be good, and the abode of the Hereafter [*al-ākhirah*] is better" (XVI: 30). The modern idea of development, therefore, which has been until recently purely materialistic and economic, disrupts the Islamic balance between the spiritual and material aspects of human life, the need to live and be active in the world with some degree of detachment from it and full awareness of humanity's final end.

Islamic society is one in which individuals are related to an organic social whole within which they find meaning and support. Islamic society is based neither upon individualism, as a result of which society is pulverized into atomic units, nor upon the ant heap, in which individuals lose inner freedom and are faced with the danger of the stultification of their creative powers through regimentation and uniformity. Modern development, especially since it has implied until now indiscriminate and blind industrialization, has also tended to destroy the very basis of the organic structure of traditional Islamic society, in which the individual is related to a greater whole through the extended family, local bonds, guilds, and—on a more inward plane—through Sufi orders. The value system of such a society is obviously challenged by any force that would destroy or disrupt such relationships. Development in the modern sense has certainly strained these relationships in the Islamic world, although it has not as yet been able to break them completely.

Development, as it has been conceived by modernized Muslims and their governments and as it has taken place in the Islamic world during past decades, affects the relationships between human beings and society, human beings and nature, and finally human beings and God. It tends to create an anthropomorphic philosophy of life based solely on terrestrial humanity and its earthly well-being, a philosophy that stands opposed to the theomorphic conception of Islam. Those affected by this view tend to regard society not as the *ummah,* or religious community governed by God's laws, but as an aggregate of atomized units bent on producing and consuming at an ever greater speed. Such persons tend to see nature not as God's handiwork to be contemplated and lived with in harmony, but as a warehouse of raw materials and sources of energy to be plundered and exploited as rapidly as possible. Finally, they see God not as the all-powerful Presence who dominates every moment of human life and before whom men and women are responsible for their every deed and action, but at best as a Being watching His creation from afar, if He is not disavowed altogether.

These tendencies are prevalent, but have not as yet destroyed completely the Islamic "system of values." In fact, these "values" are strong enough to have caused a reaction in many spheres against the stresses caused by the notions of development that have been dominant until recently. Furthermore, attempts are now being made in the Islamic world to redefine the process of development itself in light of "Islamic values," at a moment when many perspicacious observers of the human condition in the West itself are reexamining the modern notions of development based on secular humanism, utopianism or historical determinism, and consumerism, which are destroying the natural environment so rapidly. The more perceptive are increasingly realizing that it is impossible to have indefinite economic growth on a finite planet with limited resources and a delicate ecological balance upon which human life itself depends. An ever growing number of Muslims are also coming to realize that even with the rapid growth of the population in many Islamic countries, which seems to require more and more material development, there has to be another understanding of "development," not only because of the limitations of natural resources and the dangers of the environmental crisis for all of humanity, including Muslims, but also because of the necessity to preserve Islamic values and the understanding of who human beings are in their total reality with their spiritual as well as material needs.

Even when governments and various international organizations keep clamoring for more development and growth, many in the Islamic world, along with so many voices in the West, are becoming to an even greater degree aware that there *is* actually a limit to growth[1] and that the sanest philosophy is to aim for zero growth in a society living in equilibrium within itself and with the natural environment. A number of Muslim thinkers are therefore calling for the formulation of a truly Islamic philosophy of development itself. Whatever the future may hold as far as the "development" of the Islamic world is concerned, there is no doubt that, from the Islamic point of view, true development has a spiritual character and cannot but mean the realization by men and women of all that they can become and all that they actually are here and now, even if many today remain unaware of their own nature considered in its totality and of all their God-given possibilities.

Part III

Tensions Between Tradition, Modernism, and "Fundamentalism"

Education

Chapter Eight

ISLAMIC EDUCATION, PHILOSOPHY, AND SCIENCE

A Survey in Light of Present-Day Challenges

If in the previous section the aim was to examine the tension between traditional, modern, and "fundamentalist" Islam and some of the most debated issues this context, in this section the goal is rather to turn to more cultural and intellectual aspects of the subject at hand. It is to present the traditional teachings of Islam as they encounter various forces within the modern world in such fields as education, science, philosophy, art, and architecture. To bring out these tensions, however, it is necessary first to present some of the traditional teachings themselves as they apply in each specific domain under discussion, teachings with which not everyone concerned with the confrontation of traditional Islam and the modern world is fully acquainted.

As far as Islamic education and science are concerned, they both cover such a vast expanse of intellectual space and historical time that it is hardly possible to do justice to them in this appraisal, except by pointing out some of the chief principles and salient features that have always characterized them as authentic manifestations of traditional Islam and notable aspects of Islamic civilization. If some of the achievements of Muslims in these domains are mentioned, it is with the purpose of providing necessary examples to elucidate those principles and features, not in order to enumerate the achievements of Muslims in these fields in an exhaustive manner. Needless to say, even a cataloguing of what Muslims have accomplished in these fields would require volumes.[1]

Both the educational philosophy and the sciences that developed in Islamic civilization over the centuries are essentially Islamic in character, whatever their historical origin may have been. The living organism that is Islamic civilization digested various types of knowledge from many different sources, ranging from China to Alexandria to Athens; but whatever survived and flourished within this organism was assimilated and made to grow within the living body of Islam. Whatever the origin may have been of the "matter" or *materia* for education and the sciences, the form in the traditional sense of *forma* or *morphos* and the framework were always Islamic. Both Islamic education and the Islamic sciences are in fact related in the most intimate manner to the principles of the Islamic revelation and the spirit of the Quran.

The Quran contains, according to the traditional Islamic perspective, the roots of all knowledge, but not of course its details, as is contended by certain apologists who would make the Sacred Book a textbook of science in the modern sense of the word and write "scientific commentaries" (*al-tafsīr al-'ilmī*) on it. The word "Quran" comes from the Arabic *al-qur'ān,* which, in addition to the meaning "recitation," is also understood by some commentators to mean "the gathering," namely, the treasury in which are gathered the pearls of wisdom and the principles of all authentic knowledge as well as correct action. The Sacred Book is also called *al-furqān,* "discernment," for it is the supreme instrument of knowledge whereby truth is distinguished from falsehood. It is, furthermore, the *umm al-kitāb,* "the mother of all books," for all authentic knowledge contained in "all books" is ultimately contained in its bosom. It is *al-hudā,* "the guidance," for in it is contained not only moral guidance, but also educational guidance, the *hidāyah,* or guidance that educates the whole human being in the most profound and complete sense.[2] No wonder, then, that the Quran, the Word of God, has always been the alpha and omega of all Islamic education and science, being at once their ultimate source, inspiration, and guide.

Wrapped in the perpetual presence of the Quran, the life of traditional Muslims was witness to a continuous process of education based on the form and spirit of the Quranic revelation as contained in the Sacred Book and reflected in the words and deeds and in fact the very substance and being of the Prophet. From the *shahādah* uttered into the ear of the newborn child until the moment of death, the words of the Book and the sayings of the Prophet molded the mind and soul of traditional Muslims, providing the primary content as well as the ambience of their education and the principles of the sciences. The quest for knowledge and its veritable celebration in traditional Islamic society[3] were dominated from beginning to end by its sacred quality and nature. In Islam, knowledge was never divorced from the sacred,[4] and both the whole educational system and the sciences that it made possible breathed in a universe of sacred presence. Whatever was known possessed a profoundly religious character, not only because the object of every type of knowledge was either God Himself or what has been created by Him, but most of all because the intelligence by means of which human beings *know* is itself sacred and a Divine gift, a supernaturally natural faculty of the human microcosm, in which even the categories of logic are seen as reflections of the Divine Intellect upon the plane of the human mind.[5]

Being related to holiness, hence wholeness, Islamic education had to be concerned with the whole being of the men and women it sought to educate through the process of imparting knowledge combined with integration of the mind and soul of the student. Its goal was not only the training of the mind, but that of the whole being of the person. That is why it implied not only instruction or transmission of knowledge (*ta'līm*), but also training of the whole person of the student (*tarbiyah*).[6] The teacher was not only a *mu'allim,* a "transmitter of knowledge," but also a *murabbī,* a "trainer of souls and characters." This was true to such an extent that the term *mu'allim* (or *mullā*) came to gain the meaning of *murabbī* as well; that is, it came to be imbued with ethical connotations that in the modern world have become nearly totally divorced from the question of teaching and the transmission of knowledge, especially at higher levels of education. The Islamic educational system never divorced the training of the mind from that of the soul and in fact the whole being of the student. It never considered the transmission of knowledge or its possession to be legitimate without the possession of appropriate moral and spiritual qualities. In fact, the possession of knowledge without these qualities was considered dangerous. The Persian poet Sanā'ī calls a person who possesses knowledge without moral and spiritual character a virtual thief more dangerous than an ordinary robber: "If a thief comes with a lamp, he will be able to steal more precious goods."[7]

The intrusion of modern systems of education into the Islamic world from the nineteenth century onward destroyed much of the Islamic educational system but the system has nevertheless survived in part or as a whole in some places and so I use the present tense in decribing it. Although Islamic education encompasses ideally the whole life of traditional Muslims, there are distinct phases and periods to be detected in this organic whole. First of all, in the primary period of early family education, the father and mother both play the role of teacher and educator in religious matters as well as in matters relating to language, culture, social customs, and so on.[8] After this period, which is usually longer than the prekindergarten phase in the West today, growing children go to one of the Quranic schools, which corresponds more or less to elementary and early high school, and then to the *madrasah*. *Madrasah* is a technical term in Islamic education that means more than "school" in general; it corresponds to secondary school and undergraduate college. Finally students go to the *jāmi'ah,* or place of the highest formal education. Moreover, in many parts of the Islamic world, the *madrasah* has incorporated the *jāmi'ah* and now provides what would at once correspond to secondary, college, and graduate university education.

The Quranic school not only acquaints children with the religious foundation of their life, society, and civilization, but also serves as an introduction to the mastery of language. Although, of course, the situation for Arab children differs from non-Arab Muslims, because Arab children do not have to study Arabic as a foreign language, as do non-Arabs, there is no doubt that in both cases literacy becomes impregnated with religious meaning and the very process of reading and writing is seen as a religious activity. The word "pen" (*al-qalam*) signifies not only the implement with which children write their first words, but also the instrument of revelation by which God has even sworn in the Quran. Likewise, "book" (*kitāb*) is understood first of all to be *the* Book, namely, the Quran, with all that the term implies in the Islamic context. The respect shown by illiterate traditional Muslims for any piece of printed material when printing first came to the Islamic world was based on this identification of the written with the sacred. Outside the Arab world children are of course taught their own language, but since both the alphabet[9] and much of the basic vocabulary dealing with both religious and moral ideas have been drawn from Quranic Arabic in various Islamic languages, the two types of training complement rather than oppose each other. Many children are also taught at home rather than at a school located physically in a mosque. This used to be particularly true of girls, although in many places such as certain cities in Persia girls do also attend formal schools outside the home and even study in *madrasahs.*[10] Also, many children receive a high-quality oral education based upon the Quran and traditional literature, so that literacy is not at all synonymous with formal education. The remarkable literary knowledge of certain "illiterate" Muslims even today testifies to the strength of the less formal, oral education, which usually starts at an early age.[11]

The spread of "fundamentalist" ideas in Islamic schools in an arc extending from Afghanistan to Central Asia and India, thanks to foreign (in fact, mostly Saudi) financial support, has created in the West a false image of the institution of the *madrasah*. Although the *madrasah* is in many ways like a Jewish yeshiva or Christian seminary, the widespread current misconception of this major Islamic educational institution makes it necessary to elucidate its real historical significance. The *madrasah* became a formal educational institution early in Islamic history and developed into a full-fledged college and university system by the fourth/tenth century. The radiance and significance of such institutions were so great that they soon began to become a noticeable element throughout practically the whole of the Islamic world; in fact, they played a fundamental role in the foundation of the European centers of higher education, a role that is only now becoming fully recognized.[12]

The *madrasahs* range from fairly modest schools with one or two hundred students to major universities, such as the Qarawiyyīn in Fez, Morocco, which is over eleven hundred years old; the al-Azhar,[13] founded over a millennium ago in Cairo and still the greatest seat of Sunni learning; and the Shīʿite *madrasah* of Najaf,[14] established some nine hundred years ago. Some *madrasahs* even developed into university systems with several campuses and sites, as in the case of the Niẓāmiyyah, established in Baghdad as well as in Khurasan by the Seljuq *wazīr* (prime minister) Khwājah Niẓām al-Mulk. The *madrasahs,* which were endowed and extended to students free room and board as well as compensation for other expenses, were almost always constructed with great care in beautiful settings. To this day in most Islamic cities, after the mosques, the *madrasahs,* which in fact were usually related geographically to mosques, are the most notable architectural masterpieces to be found in the Islamic world, and some of them, like the Qarawiyyīn, the Mustanṣariyyah of Baghdad, and the Chahār Bāgh of Isfahan, are among the greatest achievements of Islamic architecture. Since in Islam knowledge has never been divorced from the sacred and Islam sees in the sacred, especially in its numinous and inward aspects, the aura of Divine Beauty, Islamic education has always been imparted in an ambience of beauty.[15] Great care was taken to create an atmosphere in which the sacred quality of knowledge and the religious nature of all educational pursuits in the traditional context, including what are now called secular subjects, were confirmed rather than denied.

The main activity of the *madrasahs* is instruction in the religious sciences, especially Divine Law (*al-Sharī'ah*), its principles (*al-uṣūl*), jurisprudence (*al-fiqh*), and so on, although in earlier days other disciplines were also taught in many *madrasahs*. The study of the Law is itself based on the careful study of the Quran and its commentaries (*tafsīr* and *ta'wīl*), the traditions of the Prophet (*Ḥadīth*), and the sacred history of Islam, which is related to both the Quran and *Ḥadīth*. These studies in turn require complete mastery of Arabic and all the literary disciplines connected with it. They also led in many places to the study of theology (*kalām*) in its manifold schools, which developed beginning in the first Islamic century and reached a period of intense activity in Baghdad during the third/ninth and fourth/tenth centuries. These disciplines together were referred to as the transmitted (*naqlī*) sciences, and they dominated the educational activity of most *madrasahs*.

There were, however, a series of other disciplines, including logic, mathematics, the natural sciences, and philosophy, that, according to Muslim thinkers, could be arrived at by human intelligence and were not transmitted in the same way as the religious, linguistic, and historical sciences. Hence they were called the "intellectual sciences" (*'aqlī*) in contrast to and as complement of the *naqlī* sciences. This division of the sciences became reflected in the curriculum of the *madrasahs*,[16] many of which taught at least some of the *'aqlī* as well as the *naqlī* sciences until a few centuries ago. In certain parts of the Arab world, most of the *'aqlī* sciences ceased to be taught after the eighth/fourteenth century, while in Persia and such Turkish centers as Istanbul as well as on the Indian subcontinent, they were taught until much later. Islamic philosophy continues to be taught seriously in *madrasahs* in Persia to the present day. But there is no doubt that, when the modern Western educational system was brought to the Islamic world in the nineteenth century, there was practically no *madrasah* that had preserved its former vitality in the different fields of knowledge, especially in mathematics and the natural and medical sciences.[17]

Moreover, even during the height of activity in the Islamic sciences, there is little doubt that in the domain of the *'aqlī* sciences, except for logic and philosophy, the natural and mathematical sciences were often taught outside of the *madrasahs*. This seems at least to be the conclusion when one reflects upon the curricula that have survived from the earlier periods. One can therefore state with some assurance that, as far as the *'aqlī* sciences are concerned, the activity of the *madrasah* in traditional Islamic society was complemented and augmented by two other types of centers: specifically scientific institutions and private circles.

Islam developed many scientific institutions, such as teaching and research hospitals and observatories, in both of which instruction for a professional cadre was carried out extensively. For example, from the hospital of Baghdad, which dates from the third/ninth century, where the famous Persian physician Muḥammad ibn Zakariyyā' al-Rāzī (the Latin Rhazes) treated patients and taught, there are records of how medical students were trained both theoretically and practically, how they had to undergo a period of internship, and how they were finally examined and given the professional status of a physician.[18] Likewise, in the major observatories that were established in Islamic countries and that must be accounted as the first scientific institutions of this kind in the general history of science, instruction in mathematics and astronomy as well as in related disciplines such as logic and philosophy was given, as we see in the first of these major observatories in Maraghah, which was directed by Khwājah Naṣīr al-Dīn Ṭūsī.[19]

Private circles, which exist to this day in Persia and are referred to as "outside instruction or lessons" (*dars-i khārij*), had always existed as a means of teaching less common disciplines to groups of chosen students, both in order to avoid the anathema of those religious scholars who might object to such subjects being taught in *madrasahs* and to have a more intimate ambience for the transmission of certain of the *'aqlī* sciences. This type of instruction has been especially important in the teaching of Islamic philosophy and must be considered in any serious study of the traditional Islamic educational system.

Another institution, whose impact upon Islamic education has been immense in certain periods of Islamic history, is the Sufi center, called *zāwiyah* in the Arab world and *khānqāh* in the Persian, Indian, and Turkish worlds (the term *tekkye* was also used for certain types of Sufi centers in the Ottoman Empire). In such centers, whose function is to provide a place for the transmission of the highest form of knowledge, namely, Divine Knowledge (*al-ma'rifah* or *'irfān*) or what could be called *scientia sacra* ("sacred science"),[20] there has always been educational activity of a most intense nature. Sufism has always been concerned first and foremost with the training of the human soul, so that it may become a worthy receptacle of Divine Presence.[21] It has therefore been concerned with education as *tarbiyah* on the highest level. But Sufism is also concerned with knowledge of the world of contingency in light of knowledge of the Divine, a knowledge that is imparted to the disciple by the master or, more exactly, that is caused to be born from within the depth of being of the disciple with the help of the master. This knowledge, although in essence inseparable from metaphysics, also possesses cosmological and psychological dimensions. Moreover, since Sufism has usually expressed its teachings in the form of literature and music of the highest order, the Sufi centers have been also places for artistic education. Finally, it must be remembered that in such periods of Islamic history as after the Mongol invasion, when the formal educational system was destroyed in many of the eastern regions of the Islamic world, Sufi centers also took the task of formal education upon themselves, and in some areas for long periods of time they were the sole educational institutions still functioning. Altogether, Sufi centers must be considered among the most basic institutions of Islamic education, in addition to being the place of assembly of the friends of God, where the ecstasy of Divine intimacy is experienced and celebrated.

No discussion of Islamic education would be complete without mention of the practical education connected with the arts and crafts.[22] Within the guilds (*aṣnāf, futuwwāt*) as well as through individual instruction in homes or ateliers of master craftsmen, not only were the techniques for the production of objects of art ranging from carpet weaving to tile making and the creation of architecture transmitted to students, but a "sacred" science was also taught that had both a microcosmic and macrocosmic significance. It concerned the mind as well as the soul of the individual students, who, while making an object of traditional art, were also molding their own souls. Students also received instruction concerning the nature of the object at hand and in the symbolism involved in making it. Islamic art is a science, as Islamic science is an art.[23]

Not all those who learned to weave carpets or make tiles were consciously aware of the profound metaphysical and cosmological significance of the symbolism of geometric patterns, forms, and colors with which they were dealing. Nevertheless, something of the science involved was transmitted from the beginning, and the knowledge became more explicitly elucidated as students advanced in the mastery of their craft and came to gain a more immediate awareness of the nature of the materials with which they were working and the principles by which their art was ennobling the material they were molding. There is no doubt that a vast oral tradition was transmitted over the centuries that enabled architects to construct domes of incredible beauty and durability or to create gardens with perfect harmonic ratios. A science of a high order was somehow preserved and transmitted as long as the traditional arts survived and in fact to the extent that they survive today. This process could not be called anything else but educational, and this type of teaching, which concerned technological and scientific knowledge within the context of Islamic cosmological and artistic spheres, cannot but be considered a major component of the traditional Islamic educational system.

As far as the *ʿaqlī* sciences that the Islamic world fostered through this educational system are concerned, their development constitutes both an important chapter in the history of science and philosophy in general and a dazzling achievement of Islamic civilization, of which it was an integral part. The rapid geographical expansion of Islam from the vast plains of western China to the snow-covered mountain peaks of southern France made it heir to most of the sciences and philosophies of antiquity. As early as the first century of its existence, when it was building the very foundations of classical Islamic civilization, Islam was confronted with the learning of the Greco-Alexandrian world as it had been cultivated not only in the school of Athens, but especially in Alexandria and its offshoots in Pergamon, Antioch, Edessa, and other cities of the Near East.[24] Islam also inherited the sciences of the Persians and, to a large extent, those of the Indians through the university center of Jundishapur, where the disciplines of both Persian and Indian sciences, including astronomy and medicine, had been taught extensively before the rise of Islam. This center in fact continued to flourish until the founding of Baghdad by the Abbasids, when its activities were for the most part finally transferred to the new capital.[25] Islamic civilization also received some of the Babylonian and the more esoteric elements of the Hellenic and Hellenistic sciences dealing with what came to be known later in the West as the "hidden or occult sciences" through the Sabaeans of Harran.[26] Moreover, it had much contact with China, and traces of Chinese alchemy, which has some of its own distinct characteristics, such as its relation to Taoist cosmology and numerology, had begun to appear in Islamic sources as early as the second/eighth century. As the last religion of this cycle of human history, Islam led to the founding of a civilization that became heir to nearly all the sciences of the ancient world. Thus Islamic civilization created a number of sciences and schools of philsophy that, while being profoundly Islamic,[27] at the same time integrated in an unprecedented manner the intellectual and scientific heritage of many different civilizations that had gone before it.

The mere physical presence in *dār al-islām* of centers of learning related to ancient civilizations could not, however, have been sufficient to generate a major movement within the Islamic world intent upon transmitting these pre-Islamic, or *awā'il,* sciences to Muslims and translating their sources into Arabic. Muslims had no military, economic, or political compulsion to study Aristotle or Indian astronomy. They already possessed perhaps the most powerful empire on earth. Nor could turning to these sciences have been merely utilitarian. The reason for the great interest of Muslims in them was primarily intellectual and religious and directly related to the nature of Islam as a revelation based upon the primacy of knowledge. As a way of knowing the truth, Islam could not remain indifferent to other ways of knowing, to philosophies and sciences that also claimed to explain the nature of things. Moreover, since Islam accepted the religions that went before it as having come from the same Source as itself, a principle that was particularly emphasized in the case of Judaism and Christianity but also accepted for Zoroastrianism and even to some extent for the eclectic religions of the Sabaeans of Harran, which contained elements drawn from ancient Mesopotamian religions as well as Greek gnostic ideas and later Hinduism and Buddhism, Muslims could not but engage in theological and philosophical debates with followers of these religions, all of whom had already developed their own theologies and philosophies. Muslims, therefore, had to confront the challenge of modes of knowing related to both the sciences of antiquity and the philosophies and theologies of religious communities that lived in their midst and that had already confronted and in certain cases integrated some of those philosophies and sciences into their theologies and religious philosophies.

Muslims' answer to this challenge was a concerted effort to translate philosophical and scientific works from Greek, Syriac, Sanskrit, and Pahlavi into Arabic. Once they had determined to carry out this task, they had at their disposal a whole group of excellent translators belonging to various minority religious communities, especially Arab Christians, some of whom, like Ḥunayn Ibn Isḥāq, were accomplished Christian scholars who knew Greek and Syriac as well as their native Arabic. Schools and centers of translation were established, often supported by public funds, the supreme example of which is the *Bayt al-ḥikmah,* or House of Wisdom, in Baghdad. As a result, in a period of less than two centuries ranging from the end of the second/eighth to the fourth/tenth century, an immense corpus of learning was translated into Arabic, making the Arabic language the most important scientific language in the world for several centuries and a major depository for the sciences of antiquity to this day. There are many Greek works, especially of the Hellenistic period, which can be found only in Arabic, because the originals have been lost.[28] Altogether, the transmission of the sciences of antiquity to Islam is a cultural phenomenon that, from the point of view of quantity and quality as well as its later impact upon the world at large, must be considered one of truly global significance.[29]

At the pinnacle of the Islamic intellectual sciences stands philosophy, or "divine wisdom" (*al-falsafah,* or *al-ḥikmat al-ilāhiyyah*). Islam brought into being one of the richest philosophical traditions, one that has survived as a continuous tradition until now and possesses to this day great intellectual and spiritual significance for the Islamic world itself.[30] Heir to Pythagoreanism, Platonism, Aristotelianism, Neopythagoreanism, Hermeticism, and Neoplatonism and aware of many branches of Stoicism and the later schools of Hellenistic thought as well as elements of Indian and pre-Islamic Persian thought, Islam created a powerful and original philosophy within the intellectual universe of Abrahamic monotheism and the Quranic revelation, while incorporating into its intellectual tradition those elements of Greek philosophy that conformed to the Islamic unitarian perspective. The origin of what is known as medieval philosophy, whether Jewish or Christian, is to be found to a large extent in Islamic philosophy.

As a traditional philosophy based on the supraindividual intellect rather than on individualistic reason and opinion, Islamic philosophy developed schools and perspectives that were to last over the centuries, rather than changing with each philosopher who came in and went out of fashion. As early as the third/ninth century, Islamic Peripatetic (*mashshā'ī*) philosophy, which itself represented a synthesis of Plato, Aristotle, and Plotinus in the context of the Islamic worldview, was begun by al-Kindī, further developed by al-Fārābī, pursued in the fourth/tenth century by al-'Āmirī and Abū Ya'qūb al-Sijistānī, and reached its peak with Ibn Sīnā (in Latin, Avicenna), who became the prototype of the philosopher-scientist for all later Islamic history.[31] Criticized by such theologians as al-Ghazzālī, al-Shahrastānī, and Fakhr al-Dīn al-Rāzī, this school, which was the most important of the early schools of Islamic philosophy, was temporarily eclipsed in the eastern lands of Islam, but enjoyed a period of intense activity in Spain with Ibn Bājjah, Ibn Ṭufayl, and Ibn Rushd (or Averroës), the foremost expositor of this school in the Islamic West (al-Maghrib). As for the East, the school of Ibn Sīnā was resuscitated by Naṣīr al-Dīn Ṭūsī in the seventh/thirteenth century and continued as an important intellectual tradition during the centuries that followed.[32]

Parallel with the genesis of Peripatetic philosophy, there developed an Ismā'īlī philosophy that was closer to the Hermetico-Neoplatonic tradition than the Peripatetic, but that itself developed into a distinct philosophy of great variety and richness. Growing out of the enigmatic work *Umm al-kitāb* ("The Archetypal Book"), this philosophy produced in the figures of such men as Abū Ḥātim al-Rāzī, Abū Sulaymān al-Sijistānī, Ḥamīd al-Dīn al-Kirmānī, and Nāṣir-i Khusraw, many of whom wrote in Persian as well as in Arabic, a philosophy that vied with the better-known Peripatetic School. The *Rasā'il* ("Epistles") of the Ikhwān al-Ṣafā', a collection that appeared in Iraq in the fourth/tenth century and that possesses a strong Pythagorean tendency, is also related to this important school. Ismā'īlī philosophy continued even after the eclipse of the Fāṭimids, producing works of significance in Persia and Yemen and finally India, where Ismā'īlism, this important branch of Shī'ite Islam, found its final intellectual home.[33]

In the sixth/twelfth century, while Avicennan philosophy was being criticized by the theologians, a new intellectual perspective was being established by Shaykh al-Ishrāq Shihāb al-Dīn Suhrawardī, whose work, because it was not directly translated into Latin, is not well known in the West. Suhrawardī, who claimed to be the resurrector of the perennial philosophy (*al-ḥikmat al-khālidah*) that had existed in both ancient Greece and Persia, established the School of Illumination (*al-ishrāq*), which holds that knowledge is derived from light and indeed the very substance of the universe is ultimately composed of degrees of light and shadow.[34] This school, elucidated and elaborated a generation after him by Muḥammad Shams al-Dīn Shahrazūrī and Quṭb al-Dīn Shīrāzī in the seventh/thirteenth century, has also had many exponents and followers during later centuries, especially in Persia, but also among Muslims of the Indian subcontinent and in the Ottoman world.

During later centuries, in most of the Arab world philosophy as a distinct discipline became integrated into either Sufism in its intellectual aspect or philosophical theology (*kalām*), but in Persia and the adjacent areas, including India, Iraq, and Turkey, various schools of philosophy continued to flourish. At the same time, the different intellectual disciplines, such as Peripatetic philosophy, the School of Illumination, theology, and Sufi metaphysics, were drawing closer together. The ground was thus prepared for the already mentioned revival of Islamic philosophy in the Safavid period in Persia with Mīr Dāmād, the founder of the "School of Isfahan," and especially Ṣadr al-Dīn Shīrāzī, his student, who is perhaps the greatest of the later Islamic philosophers.[35] Even through the gradual decline of the teaching of the "intellectual sciences" in the *madrasahs,* these later schools associated with the name of Ṣadr al-Dīn Shīrāzī as well as those of Ibn Sīnā, Suhrawardī, Ibn 'Arabī, and their commentators have continued to be taught and have produced noteworthy figures, some of whom are still teaching today.[36]

The Islamic philosophical tradition, although of great diversity and richness, is characterized by certain commonly shared features that are of special significance both for the deeper understanding of this philosophy and for an appraisal of its import for the world at large as well as for its central role in the confrontation of Islam with modern thought. This philosophy lives in a religious universe in which a revealed book and prophecy understood as sources of knowledge dominate the horizon. It can, therefore, be considered "prophetic philosophy," whatever its subject might be. Moreover, it is a philosophy that, in conformity with the Islamic perspective, is based upon the intellect as a supernaturally natural faculty within human beings that is a sacrament and that, if used correctly, leads to the same truths as those revealed through prophecy. Islamic philosophy is therefore concerned above all with the doctrine of unity (*al-tawḥīd*), which dominates the whole message of Islam.[37] This philosophy is also concerned with the basic issues of the harmony between reason and revelation and providing, within the context of a religious universe dominated by monotheism, a metaphysics centered around the supreme doctrine of the One. It is also concerned with providing keys for the understanding of the manifold in relation to the One. It is therefore rich not only in religious and ethical philosophy, but also in cosmology and the philosophy of nature and mathematics as well as of art. In fact, the Islamic sciences were cultivated in the bosom of the Islamic philosophical universe very often by men who were not only scientists, but also philosophers.

Islamic philosophical texts provide not only a study of metaphysics and logic, but an elaborate philosophy of nature that provides the key for the understanding of both physical nature and the soul. Although the Peripatetics treat the soul as a part of natural philosophy, as seen in Ibn Sīnā's *Kitāb al-shifā'* ("The Book of Healing"), and the Illuminationists as part of metaphysics (*ilāhiyyāt* rather than natural philosophy, *ṭabī'iyyāt*), there is no doubt that both schools as well as those of the Ismā'īlīs and of Mīr Dāmād, Ṣadr al-Dīn Shīrāzī and their followers all provide a general matrix wherein individual sciences pertaining to both the world of nature without and the world of the soul within can be studied in light of the principles that belong to metaphysics, as traditionally understood, and that relate the many to the One; that is to say, the points on the periphery of the circle of cosmic existence to the Divine Center.

A science that found special favor with Muslims and that accorded well with the unitarian, aniconic, and "abstract" character of Islamic thought was mathematics, in which the accomplishments of the Islamic sciences were many.[38] Muslims integrated Greek and Indian mathematics and on that basis continued the development of geometry, formulated algebra, and developed plain and spherical trigonometry and number theory, expanding the definition of numbers to include irrationals. They received the Sanskrit numerals and developed them into the form that we now know as Arabic numerals. The transmission of the Arabic numerals to medieval Europe revolutionized reckoning in the West. (The Sanskrit numerals are of Indian origin and are still used in the eastern lands of Islam, from east of Libya to Morocco.)

The last name of the mathematician Muḥammad ibn Mūsā al-Khwārazmī, whose work on arithmetic first introduced these numerals into the West, entered into European tongues as "algorism," while the treatise on algebra by Khayyām along with several other Arabic works on the subject made this science, which still preserves its Arabic name, known to the West in a highly developed form. The trigonometric functions also still bear in their very names the traces of their Arabic origin. Furthermore, Muslims developed computation theory and even made computation machines, as seen in the work of Ghiyāth al-Dīn Jamshīd Kāshānī, who also discovered decimal fractions. Muslim mathematicians were, moreover, interested in problems that concerned the foundations of mathematics, as seen in their study of the theory of symmetry and of parallel lines that concern the hypotheses underlying Euclidian geometry.

In astronomy, Muslims began their activities early, encouraged by a practical concern to locate the direction of the *qiblah,* calculate the time for the daily prayers, and devise calendars as well as by more "theoretical" and philosophical considerations. They first mastered the Indian and Persian works of astronomy before becoming acquainted with Ptolemy, whose *Almagest* still bears, in the very name by which it is known in Western languages, the stamp of the influence of Islamic astronomy upon the West. Muslim astronomers synthesized these schools on the basis of which they established Islamic astronomy, whose distinct features can be seen as early as the third/ninth century. By the time al-Bīrūnī wrote his *al-Qānūn al-mas'ūdī* ("The Mas'ūdic Canon") a century later, Islamic astronomy was the most complete and perfected astronomical science known anywhere in the world at that time.

Muslims were interested in both observational and mathematical astronomy. They compiled numerous tables, called *zīj,* based on their observations and discovered new stars, some of which still bear Arabic names. They founded the first full-fledged observatory in history in Maraghah and made numerous instruments for observation, of which the astrolabe, that remarkable synthesis of science and art, is perhaps the one best known in the West. Parallel with observation of the heavens, they also refined mathematical astronomy, beginning a criticism of Ptolemaic astronomy in Persia, Syria, and Spain. While the anti-Ptolemaic astronomy of Spain was mostly philosophical, those of Syria and Persia, associated mostly with the school of Maraghah and the figures of Naṣīr al-Dīn Ṭūsī and Quṭb al-Dīn Shīrāzī, were combined with a mathematical study of the motion of two vectors (to use the modern terminology)[39] and led to new planetary models for Mercury and the moon, which somehow reached the Poland of Copernicus and were most likely known by him.

In physics, the Muslim contribution can be seen especially in three distinct domains of study: the nature of matter, projectile motion, and optics. For over a millennium, Muslim scientists, philosophers, theologians, and even Sufis studied and discussed the nature of matter, time, space, and motion. They developed numerous "philosophies of nature," ranging from the atomism of the theologians (*mutakallimūn*) and Muḥammad ibn Zakariyyā' al-Rāzī[40] to the physics of light of Suhrawardī and the School of Illumination. In the study of motion, such figures as Ibn Sīnā, al-Bīrūnī, Abū'l-Barakāt al-Baghdādī, and Ibn Bājjah criticized prevalent Aristotelian concepts and developed ideas in mechanics and dynamics, such as the concept of momentum, that are of much importance for the history of physics in general; their effect is to be seen not only in the physics developed by Latin Scholastics, but in the early work of Galileo and in some cases in classical physics.[41] As for optics, perhaps the greatest Islamic physicist, Ibn al-Haytham, placed this discipline on a new foundation in his *Kitāb al-manāẓir* ("Optics"), in which he used the experimental method in its contemporary sense to study the problem of vision, the camera obscura, and reflection and refraction through lenses and by means of mirrors, and made many basic discoveries in the field of the study of light. On the basis of his work, some two centuries later Quṭb al-Dīn Shīrāzī and Kamāl al-Dīn Fārsī provided the first correct explanation of the phenomenon of the rainbow as a combination of reflection and refraction, solving a problem that had preoccupied men of science since antiquity.

Muslims also showed interest in mechanical devices, which they treated as a branch of applied mathematics involving engineering. In fact, most of the early masters of the subject, such as the Banū Mūsā and Ibn al-Haytham, were mathematicians. In works on this subject, of which the most elaborate is the "Treatise on Automata" of Ismā'īl al-Jazarī,[42] many machines are described, some of which are quite complicated. Though complicated and of quite a refined nature, they were, however, always closely related to the forces and rhythms of nature. It is important to realize, however, that although Muslims devised these complicated machines, such as automata, which among the artifacts of Islamic civilizations most resemble products of modern technology, they did so mostly for amusement and play rather than for economic production, although some of these technologies did also have practical use.

As far as medicine and pharmacology are concerned, in these and related fields the achievements of Islamic science were no less startling than in mathematics and astronomy. Again making use of Greek as well as Iranian and Indian sources, Muslims integrated the Hippocratic and Galenic traditions with Iranian and Indian elements to create a distinct school of medicine that survives as a living school to this day in certain parts of Asia. They also developed in parallel a medicine based on prophetic sayings (*aḥādīth*) and known as prophetic medicine (*al-ṭibb al-nabawī*). The early masters of Islamic medicine, such as Rāzī, became as well known in Europe and Hindu India as in the Islamic world itself, while Ibn Sīnā, the author of *al-Qanūn fi'l-ṭibb* ("The Canon of Medicine"),[43] became known as the "Prince of Physicians" in the West and in certain areas has given his name in its common Persian form of Bū 'Alī to Islamic medicine itself.[44] Islamic medicine combined a philosophical approach based on the application of cosmological principles that govern the human body considered as microcosm with the clinical and observational approaches based on the study of concrete cases of illness, bodily symptoms, and so on. Muslim physicians emphasized preventive medicine, especially diet, and made an extensive study of the relationship between psychological and physical health. But they also developed surgery, as seen in the works of the Spanish master Abū Marwān ibn Zuhr, and perfected many surgical instruments. Besides discovering the causes and distinguishing many diseases, such as measles, meningitis, and whooping cough, Muslim physicians also dealt with physiology and anatomy; 'Alā' al-Dīn ibn Nafīs discovered the minor circulation of the blood long before Michael Servetus and William Harvey.

The cultivation of Islamic medicine was inseparable from that of pharmacology, which was usually studied by the same figures who studied medicine. Upon the basis of Dioscorides and the extensive pharmacological knowledge of the Iranians and Indians, Muslims developed pharmacopoeias that reflected extensive knowledge of both mineral and herbal drugs. Herbs were studied from the more botanical point of view, especially in Spain, where the study of the plant world reached its peak with Abū Ja'far al-Ghāfiqī and Ḍiā' al-Dīn ibn al-Bayṭār. The study of plants, especially in relation to their medicinal properties, was one of the fields, along with certain branches of medicine, in which notable work continued in Persia, the Ottoman world, and Muslim India after the period of gradual decline of activity in the other Islamic sciences.

The study of botany by Muslims was also carried out in the context of their study of natural history and geography, which were deeply permeated by the Quranic idea of studying the wonders of creation (*'ajā'ib al-makhlūqāt*) as signs (*āyāt*) of God and His wisdom. As a result of the possibilities of travel and the exchange of ideas throughout the Islamic world, to which the annual pilgrimage to Mecca contributed greatly, Muslim natural historians and geographers were able to assemble knowledge of a very wide range of flora and fauna, from those native to China to those of western Europe. Abū'l-Ḥasan al-Mas'ūdī, often called the "Arab Pliny" in the West, composed works on natural history that were related to those of the Greeks, but were of a more comprehensive nature. Moreover, they were deeply integrated into the religious worldview of Islam. As for geography, Muslims, such as Abū 'Abd Allāh al-Idrīsī, produced the first medieval maps of remarkable accuracy, and Muslims succeeded in gaining detailed geographical knowledge of such areas as the Indian Ocean. Paradoxically enough, it was Muslim geographers and sailors who led Europeans around the Cape of Good Hope to India, which in turn facilitated the destruction by Portuguese and later other European navigators of the trade routes that had been dominated by Muslims until the sixteenth century. This in turn prepared the ground for the colonization of much of the Islamic world in the centuries that followed.

No account of the Islamic sciences would be complete without reference to what Muslims called "the hidden sciences"[45] (*al-'ulūm al-gharībah*), comprising such subjects as astrology, alchemy, physiognomy, geomancy, and other disciplines. These subjects have now become relegated to the category of pseudoscience as a result of the fact that their symbolic language and the cosmological principles underlying them have become forgotten. As far as Islamic alchemy is concerned, it reached its peak early in Islamic history with Jābir ibn Ḥayyān in the second/eighth century and continued as a long tradition embracing a range of meanings related to spiritual psychology and cosmology, medicine and a symbolic science of materials. From the cadaver of spiritual alchemy was also born that science of material substances called chemistry today.[46] The word "alchemy" itself and the spread of alchemical ideas from Arabic sources in the Occident attest to the great influence and significance of the Islamic alchemical tradition in Europe in addition to its presence in the Islamic world itself. Many of the instruments still used in the modern chemistry laboratory, such as test tubes and alembics, are the descendants of instruments of old and bear witness to the roots of modern chemistry in that aspect of medieval alchemy that had relinquished the internal task of transmuting the lead of the soul into the gold of the Spirit in favor of an external project for manufacturing physical gold.

From the point of view of the global history of science, the Islamic sciences stood for some seven centuries as the most developed among the sciences cultivated in different civilizations. Islamic sciences influenced the sciences of Hindu India and China as well as those of the West. They were only eclipsed in the West with the advent of the Renaissance and the Scientific Revolution, which made use of the material of Islamic science but within a worldview diametrically opposed to that of Islam. The important question to ask is not why Islam did not continue to devote its intellectual energies to the cultivation of an ever changing science of nature divorced from higher orders of knowledge, as has happened in the West since the seventeenth century,[47] a question often asked by both Muslims and Westerners as a result of the spread of the modern understanding of science and its history. The basic question to pose is how it was that Islam was able to create an educational system and a scientific tradition that produced knowledge of the world of nature and of mathematics of the highest order for many centuries, but within a worldview dominated by the Transcendent and imbued with the fragrance of the Divine Presence as contained in the Quranic revelation. In a world on the verge of destruction as a result of the application of a science that is both divorced from knowledge of a higher order and blind to the unity that pervades not only nature, but all orders of reality leading to the One, Islamic science possesses a message that is of more than historical interest. This science is a reminder to contemporary human beings, whether Muslim or non-Muslim, that besides modern science, which is legitimate only if kept within the confines of its own limitations, there are other sciences of nature that unveil dimensions and aspects of nature and of human beings that have become hidden in the modern world, but for which contemporary men and women yearn because of what by their essential nature they always truly *are,* no matter where or when they happen to live and what they *appear* to be.

The nature of this inner reality, which humans bear in their essence, is elucidated by traditional Islamic philosophy, which is wedded at once to the intellect and revelation and brings out the relation between humankind and God, the cosmos and human society. Islamic philosophy is one of the richest treasures of traditional wisdom that have survived to this day, and it stands at the center of the battle that traditional Islam must wage on the intellectual front in the modern world. Likewise, the educational system, which over the centuries produced all those philosophers and scientists as well as jurists, men of letters, and experts in other fields of knowledge, must remain the basis upon which all attempts made in the field of education to accommodate conditions created by the encounter of Islam with the modern world should be carried out. The traditional educational institutions as well as traditional Islamic philosophy and science, in addition to being glories of classical Islamic civilization, are of the utmost significance in the whole question of the encounter of traditional Islam with modernism.

It must be remembered that in them are embedded those perennial values and doctrinal truths that alone can aid contemporary Muslims in preserving their Islamicity in the face of the unprecedented challenges posed by a world whose general worldview, with regard to both philosophy and science, is based on disregard for and forgetfulness of the One as well as denial of the relevance of the Transcendent.

Chapter Nine

ISLAMIC PHILOSOPHERS' VIEWS ON EDUCATION

> Whoever wishes to perfect himself as a human being [*insāniyyah*] and reach the rank [*amr*] which is meant by "human nature" in order to integrate his self [*li-yatimma ḍātahu*] and have the same preferences and intentions as those of the philosophers, let him acquire these two arts [*ṣinā'atain*]. I mean the theoretical and practical parts of philosophy; as a result, there will accrue to him the essential natures of things [*ḥaqā'iq al-umūr*] by means of the theoretical part, and good deeds by means of the practical part.
> *Ibn Miskawayh, Tartīb al-sa'ādah*[1]

The crisis in the contemporary Islamic world resulting from the onslaught of modernism has naturally turned many Muslim scholars to the question of education and initiated a reexamination of the traditional Islamic educational system, which has been neglected to a large extent during the past century in so many Islamic countries. The principles underlying Islamic education in turn cannot be fully understood without an appreciation of the views of Islamic philosophers concerning all aspects of education, ranging from its goal and content to its curriculum and method. In recent years, however, the significance of Islamic philosophy, especially in this domain, has often been neglected and even its Islamic character denied, not only by many Western scholars, but also by many of those "fundamentalists" who, in the name of an externally interpreted Islam, oppose things Western yet at the same time allow many modern ideas to fill the vacuum created in their minds and souls as a result of the rejection of the Islamic intellectual tradition.

These days a form of scientism has crept into the worldview of not only Muslim modernists, as would be expected, but also of many "fundamentalists" and "revivalists" who voice their opposition to things Western;[2] they praise Islamic science and the men of learning who produced it, but, ironically, attack the philosophers who formulated the worldview upon which the much-praised Islamic science is based. It must therefore be stated at the outset that Islamic philosophy as it developed over the centuries is Islamic in character and is an integral part of the Islamic intellectual tradition.[3] Moreover, the educational system that trained the Islamic philosophers also produced the Islamic scientists; there existed a single educational system that made possible the appearance of the Muslim philosopher-scientists over the ages, of men who were at once philosophers and masters of some field of science.[4] Finally, the views of these philosopher-scientists concerning education are essential in making possible today the reestablishment of an educational system that would be at once Islamic and of a veritable intellectual character. If there is to be once again an educational system to produce an al-Bīrūnī or an Ibn Sīnā, it must at least take seriously the views that they and others like them held concerning education. For centuries Islam produced men who were at once devout Muslims and the foremost thinkers of their day in various intellectual disciplines, including both philosophy and the sciences. Present-day Muslims seeking to recreate an authentic Islamic educational system cannot but take into consideration the views of such men concerning the philosophy, content, goal, methods, and meaning of education.

As has already been stated, Islamic philosophy is not of course confined to a single school, nor is it simply the sum of the views of individual philosophers with different and often opposing views following one after another, as one finds in postmedieval European philosophy. Although certain individuals stand out as solitary figures in the history of Islamic thought, Islamic philosophy consists essentially of perspectives or schools that have survived over the ages. To grasp in a synoptic fashion the views of the Islamic philosophers concerning education, it is thus sufficient for our purposes here to turn to outstanding representatives of each school or perspective, rather than try to cover all the major philosophers of each particular school,[5] while to survey the field completely would require the examination of each school and various interpretations with it as it has developed over the centuries. For the purpose of the present chapter, therefore, I have chosen the Ikhwān al-Ṣafā', Ibn Sīnā, Suhrawardī, and Mullā Ṣadrā, representing the Ismā'īlī and Hermetic-Pythagorean, Peripatetic (*mashshā'ī*), Illuminationist (*ishrāqī*), and the "transcendent theosophy" (*al-ḥikmat al-muta'āliyah)* schools, respectively.

Although the Ikhwān al-Ṣafā' came to be associated later with Shī'ism in general and Ismā'īlism in particular,[6] their *Rasā'il* came to be read by a wide circle of Islamic scholars and thinkers, both Shī'ite and Sunni, including the celebrated Sunni theologian al-Ghazzālī, who was influenced by them even though he wrote disparaging words against Ismā'īlism. Although the *Rasā'il* are a synthesis of Shī'ite learning presented in more "popular" and encyclopedic fashion than other major works of Islamic philosophy, they had an educational impact that went beyond the confines of a particular school to touch the whole of the Islamic community. Likewise, although the perspective of this work, in which Neoplatonic, Hermetic and Neopythagorean elements were integrated into Islamic and more particularly Shī'ite teachings, remained closely wedded to Ismā'īlī philosophy, its philosophical influence was felt widely among many different figures in later periods of Islamic history. It is enough to read the pages of the *Asfār* of Mullā Ṣadrā to realize how powerful indeed were the echoes of the *Rasā'il* some seven centuries later.

The purpose of the Ikhwān al-Ṣafā' in composing the *Rasā'il* was itself educational, and the issues of education, its goal, stages, content, methods, and other elements, are to be found throughout the fifty-one treatises that comprise this work.[7] It is, however, especially in the seventh treatise of the first volume, entitled *Fi'l-ṣanā'i' al-'ilmiyyah* (On the Intellectual Discipline) (more specifically, the second section titled *Fi'l-'ilm wa'l-ma'lūm wa'l-ta'allum wa'l-ta'līm,* "On Knowledge, the Known, Teaching, and Learning"), that they deal with education, while in the ninth treatise, called *Fī bayān al-akhlāq wa asbāb ikhtilāfihā* . . . ("Concerning the Description of Ethics and the Cause of Differences Among Its Schools . . ."), they deal with the influence of the environment, the home, the school, professors, and other pertinent factors bearing upon the education of students.[8] According to the Ikhwān, the soul is a "spiritual, celestial, luminous, living and knowing substance potentially and active by nature."[9] The goal of education is to enable the soul to actualize these potential possibilities, thereby perfecting it and preparing it for eternal life.[10] Knowledge acquired through education is in fact the ultimate nourishment that sustains the immortal soul, while actualization of what is potential in the soul is of existence (*wujūd*) itself, the mode of human existence that does not perish with death.

This process of actualization is composed of stages, of which the most important are *tahdhīb* (refinement), *taṭhīr* (purification), *tatmīm* (completion), and *takmīl* (perfection).[11] These stages are moral as well as propaedeutic and mental; in fact, these elements are never separated in the view of the Ikhwān, who reassert the universal Islamic principle, stated in so many *ḥadīths,* that the gaining of theoretical knowledge and the purification of the soul have to be combined in order for "science," or *'ilm,* to become rooted in the soul, to transform its substance, and to embellish it in such a way that it will be worthy of eternal life in the Divine Presence.

The Ikhwān also consider the stages of life in which education has to be imparted to body, mind, and soul. From birth to the age of four, the senses and instincts are to be strengthened. From the age of four through fifteen, the basic skills of reading, writing, mathematics, and so on, are to be mastered in "lower" school (*maktab*) with the help of a teacher (*mu'allim*) through the process of dictation (*imlā'*). After this age, the mental powers become more mature and the student begins to learn, usually in a *madrasah,* or college, from a master (*ustād*) through the use of the intellect (*'aql*) by means of demonstration (*burhān*) and inspiration (*ilhām*).

There is a hierarchy of knowledge, as there is a hierarchy of teachers. Education is based on a hierarchy that leads from the exoteric sciences to the esoteric through the instruction imparted by teachers, who themselves stand in a hierarchy ranging from the *mustajīb* to the *ḥujjah* to the *imām,* the last possessing perfect knowledge of both the exoteric and the esoteric orders.[12] The goal of education is to perfect and actualize all the possibilities of the human soul, leading finally to that supreme knowledge of the Divinity that is the goal of human life. Although education prepares people for felicity in this life, its ultimate goal is the abode of permanence, and all education points to the permanent world of eternity (*al-ākhirah*) beyond the transient vacillations of this world of change. According to the Ikhwān, the ultimate goal of education, even while one is mastering the sciences of nature, is not to dominate the world and gain external power, but to dominate oneself in such a manner as to be able to go beyond the world of change into the abode of eternity, and to do so embellished with the ornament of knowledge combined with virtue, which alone are worthy of the world into which the soul of the faithful hopes to enter at the end of this earthly journey.

Having considered these general principles and ideas, let us now turn to the specific teachings of Islamic philosophers. Among the well-known Islamic philosophers, the first to have treated the question of education in a substantial manner was Ibn Sīnā, the foremost among the Muslim philosopher-scientists, who is the source and origin of so many basic aspects of traditional Islamic thought.[13] He deals specifically with the question of education in his *Tadbīr al-manāzil* (literally, "Management of the Household," or "Economics" in its original Greek sense)and refers to this subject in several passages in the *Shifā'* ("Healing"), *Risālat al-siyāsah* ("Treatise on Politics"), and *al-Qānūn* ("The Canon of Medicine"). Of course, his discussion of the nature of human beings and their entelechy in several of his philosophical works should also be considered related to the subject of education in the most general sense of the term, for, whenever Ibn Sīnā deals with human beings, he also concerns himself with their final end and the means whereby men and women can attain perfection, and the process of the attainment of this perfection is nothing other than education in its most universal sense.

For Ibn Sīnā, education begins even before birth—at the moment a man chooses a mate, because that mate's moral and intellectual character will deeply affect the child who is yet to be born. He also emphasizes the role of the wife and mother in the bringing up of children and her share in their earliest education. Children are to be given discipline from the time of breast-feeding, and in fact their first lessons in manners and morals as well as the building of character (*ta'dīb*) are to be given in this earliest stage of human life. The teaching of the sciences, on the other hand, should begin when children's bodies begin to form fully, when the joints are becoming firm and the ears and tongue are functioning properly. Ibn Sīnā insists, moreover, that each child should be given individual attention and brought up according to his or her particular makeup. In no case should there be a quantitative egalitarianism imposed upon everyone, for this would be counter to the qualitative differences that are ingrained in the very substance of human nature and that must be nurtured and protected with the greatest care. He in fact goes so far as to assert that the consideration of human beings solely on the basis of quantitative equality leads to their destruction and perdition.[14]

In the *Canon,* Ibn Sīnā specifies the regimen from infancy to adolescence, which has both an educational and a medical goal in mind: "The great principle here is the inculcation of control of the emotions. One should take care that children do not give way to anger and fear, or be opposed by despondency, or suffer from sleeplessness. They should therefore be allowed that which is pleasing and appetizing, and one should avoid giving them anything arousing disgust."[15] As a result, the mind becomes accustomed to positive emotions from the beginning and develops good habits, which are also of benefit to the body.

Meanwhile, children grow to an age when, in addition to the parents and family, who have been their sole teachers until now, a suitable teacher from the outside must be sought for them. "At the age of six, he may be given tuition by a master [who is of mild and benevolent disposition], who will teach him step by step and in order [cheerfully, without constraint]. He should not be compelled to stay continuously in school. [Relaxation of the mind contributes to the growth of the body.] At this age, bathing and rest should be less frequent, and the exercise before meals should be increased."[16] Ibn Sīnā advises that this program be continued until the age of thirteen, insisting that light exercise should be encouraged, while anything that entails toil and hardship should be avoided at this stage. Meanwhile, grammar should be taught to the student, followed at the age of fourteen and older by mathematics and then philosophy.

Ibn Sīnā distinguishes clearly between the first stage of education carried out in the home and the second carried out at school (*maktab*) under the care of a teacher (*mu'allim*). At this stage, school and home begin to complement each other in promoting the goals of early education, which are the strengthening of faith, the building of good character and health, and the teaching of literacy and the rudiments of correct thinking and learning a craft. The teacher should be carefully chosen, for, at this stage, the teacher's influence upon the pupil's character is as great as upon the pupil's mind. Therefore, the teacher should be pious, have firm moral principles, and be of gentle disposition as well as being knowledgeable. The teacher must possess wisdom (*ḥikmah, khirad*), have insight into the character of pupils, and even judge their aptitude for pursuing different fields of knowledge, so as to be able to advise them which subjects to pursue in later stages of life.

As for school, it is necessary, because not only does it make possible the transmission of knowledge, but it also provides a social ambience in which students can learn from each other and live with one another. Ibn Sīnā emphasizes the importance of healthy rivalry and competition; students are to be encouraged to attain educational goals while competing with other students. Moreover, the presence of other students makes possible discourse and disputation, which increase understanding, and friendship, which helps to purify character and strengthen certain virtues.[17]

The eight-year program of the *maktab,* which is to be followed by those qualified in the more advanced *madrasah,* begins with the teaching of the Quran, religious instruction, and language. This is naturally followed by the teaching of ethics and then of some kind of art or craft, in light of the students' capabilities and interests, that will enable them to earn a living. Sport should also be taught, and students should spend certain hours of the day participating in some form of it. At this stage, most students should begin some kind of livelihood, while those who have the appropriate mental constitution and intellectual ability should continue their education and enter such fields as medicine or the other sciences.

As far as the method of instruction is concerned, Ibn Sīnā emphasizes moderation in dealing with students. Teachers should be neither excessively lenient nor overly harsh—not simply cruel and capricious, which is the current Western notion of *madrasah* teachers. They should choose a manner of instruction (mental training, imitation, repetition, logical analysis, and so on) that fits the nature of the student. Likewise, in the choice of the particular field of the arts in which the student should specialize, the capabilities and interests of the student should be taken fully into consideration.[18]

No discussion of Ibn Sīnā's views on education would be complete without mention of his doctrine of the intellect, the faculties of the soul, the hierarchy that determines the different levels of human intellectual faculties, and the process whereby one can attain to the highest level of intellectual perfection. Education on the higher level is in fact nothing other than the process of actualization and perfection of the faculties of the theoretical and practical intellect (*al-ʿaql al-naẓarī* and *al-ʿaql al-ʿamalī*).

Ibn Sīnā deals with this subject in several of his works, especially book six of the *Ṭabīʿiyyāt* ("Natural Philosophy") of the *Shifāʾ,* where he considers the soul and its faculties and powers.[19] A full discussion of this theory of the intellect (*ʿaql*) would require a separate study; in fact, there have already been several works devoted to this very subject,[20] but its brief mention is nevertheless necessary here because of its crucial educational significance.

According to this theory, human beings "possess" both a theoretical and a practical intellect, the faculties of which they must strengthen, moderate, and perfect as the case may be. Education of the mind is essentially that of the theoretical intellect,[21] while that of character involves both the theoretical and practical intellects. The practical intellect includes all the vegetative and animal faculties (*al-quwwat'l-nabātiyyah* and *al-quwwa'l-ḥayawāniyyah*), including the power of growth (*numuaw*) for the vegetative, and apprehension (*wahm*), imagination (*khayāl*), and fantasy (*fantasiyyah*) for the animal; the theoretical intellect encompasses the levels of material intellect (or intelligence; *al-ʿaql al-hayūlānī*), intellect *in habitus* (*al-ʿaql bi'l-malakah*), intellect in act (*al-ʿaql bi'l-fiʿl*), and finally sacred or acquired intellect (*al-ʿaql al-qudsī* or *al-ʿaql al-mustafād*). The process of learning implies the actualization of the potentialities of the intellect through the effusion of the light of the Active Intellect. It is this separate Intellect, identified with the angelic substances, that is the real teacher of seekers of knowledge on higher levels of intellectual attainment. The hierarchy of Intelligences are the instruments for the actualization and illumination of the human intellect, and this transformation lies at the heart of the whole process of attaining knowledge, the highest level of which is intuitive knowledge (*al-maʿrifat al-ḥadsiyyah*) attained directly from the Active Intellect.

The *Visionary Recitals* of Ibn Sīnā, in which his "Oriental Philosophy" (*al-ḥikmat al-mashriqiyyah*) is expounded in a symbolic fashion,[22] can also be studied as a source for his philosophy of education at the highest level. In these treatises the doctrine of the intellect becomes depicted concretely in the form of angels and celestial guides who lead human beings to the highest degrees of Divine Knowledge. The guide in *Ḥayy ibn Yaqẓān* ("The Living Son of the Awake") is the teacher par excellence, and Avicennan angelology is a key for the understanding of the master's educational philosophy.[23] In his vast philosophical synthesis, Ibn Sīnā begins the process of education with the role of the parents as the first teachers of the child and concludes with the angel who, in illuminating the soul, enables it to experience the vision of God and fulfill the ultimate goal of all education and in fact of human existence itself.

It is this last strand of Ibn Sīnā's philosophy that is fully elaborated and developed by the Master of Illumination, Shaykh al-Ishrāq Shihāb al-Dīn Suhrawardī.[24] The founder of the School of Illumination, or *ishrāq,* emphasizes the necessity of the education of the whole person as the goal of philosophy. For him all of life should be oriented toward the attainment of knowledge through a process that is none other than educational in the universal sense of the term. The beginning of this process is marked by the thirst for knowledge, when the "student" experiences the need to seek knowledge. This yearning or searching is called *ṭalab* (literally, "seeking"); hence, the person at this first stage of the educational process is called *ṭālib* ("seeker").[25] The process continues with the development of the mental faculties, or those of reason; here the student is called *ṭālib al-baḥth,* "seeker of discursive thought." This stage is followed by one in which the passions are disciplined and the soul purified, for, according to Suhrawardī, true knowledge and philosophy can be attained only if the discursive faculties are perfected and at the same time the soul is purified of its defilements and imperfections, so that it can attain illumination. At this stage the seeker is called *ṭālib al-ta'alluh,* "seeker of 'theosis,'" the state of becoming godlike. At a still higher stage, the student becomes a seeker of both discursive knowledge and theosis, while gradually developing into a philosopher *(ḥakīm)*, well versed first in discursive thought, then in theosis, and therefore finally in both. At last the seeker becomes a theosopher (*al-ḥakīm al-ilāhī*), master first of *baḥth,* then of *ta'alluh,* and finally of both. Above those human stages of perfection, which are traversed by means of education understood in its *ishrāqī* sense, stands the Imam, who possesses on the highest level both moral perfection and full knowledge of metaphysical, cosmological, and eschatological realities and who is both the prototype of the human state and the exemplar of the perfection that is possible for human beings.[26] The final goal of education is, therefore, the attainment of illumination, which in turn requires the perfection of all the faculties, both mental and psychological, involving both the rational element of the mind and the soul in all of its aspects and dimensions.

In this educational process, the angel plays a particularly central role; and in many of his treatises, such as *Qiṣṣat al-ghurbat al-gharbiyyah* ("The Story of the Occidental Exile")[27] and *Rūzī bā jamā'at-i ṣūfiyān* ("A Day with the Community of Sufis"),[28] Suhrawardī identifies the angel with the Archangel Gabriel, who, as the instrument of the Quranic revelation, "taught" the Prophet the Word of God. The angel is also identified with the Holy Spirit and is considered to be represented by the spiritual master (*murshid*), who is the veritable teacher in the process of authentic education that constitutes the heart of both *ishrāqī* theosophy and Sufism.

As Suhrawardī writes at the beginning of his *al-Risālah fī ḥālat al-ṭifūliyyah* ("Epistle on the State of Childhood"):

> When I was a child I used to play, as children do, at the edge of the village. One day, I saw some children walking along together whose meditative appearance surprised me. I went up to them and asked: "Where are you going?"
>
> "We are going to school to acquire Knowledge," they told me.
>
> "What is Knowledge?" I asked.
>
> "We do not know how to answer that," they said to me. "You must ask our teacher." And with that, they went on their way.
>
> Some time later, I said to myself, "Now, what is Knowledge? Why shouldn't I go with them to their teacher and learn from him what Knowledge is?" I started looking for them and could not find them; but I saw the shaikh standing alone in the deserted countryside. I approached and greeted him, and he returned my greeting, his whole manner toward me exhibiting the most courteous affability.
>
> SELF: "I saw a group of children on their way to school, and I asked them: 'What is the point of going to school?' They told me that I should ask their teacher that question. I was not interested at the time, so they left me. But after they had gone I felt the wish to find them again, and I started looking but couldn't find them. I am still looking for traces of them. If you can't tell me anything about them, tell me at least who their teacher is."
>
> SHAIKH: "I am their teacher."
>
> SELF: "You must teach me something about Knowledge."
>
> The shaikh took up a tablet on which he had written *alif, ba, ta* . . . (a, b, c . . .) and proceeded to teach me.
>
> SHAIKH: "Stop there for today. Tomorrow I will teach you something else, and every day a little more, until you become a Knower."
>
> I returned home, and until next day I kept repeating, *alif, ba, ta* . . . The two following days I went back to the shaikh for another lesson, and I assimilated these new lessons as well. It went so well that I ended up going to the shaikh ten times a day, and each time I learned something new. Finally, I never left his presence for a single moment, and acquired a great deal of Knowledge.[29]

Education for Suhrawardī is inseparable from the spiritual life, from the illumination of the soul by the angel and the guidance provided for the human soul and mind by the angelic beings who, being themselves light, illuminate the soul with veritable knowledge that is itself light, according to the *ḥadīth,* "Knowledge is light" (*al-'ilm*[u] *nūr*[un]), and that enables the soul to finally experience God, who is the Light of lights (*Nūr al-anwār*).

In the field of education, as in so many other domains, the most extensive elaboration in the annals of Islamic philosophy is to be found in Mullā Ṣadrā, whose synthesis of philosophy, Sufism, *kalām,* and the *Sharī'ite* sciences is fully reflected in his doctrine of the growth and development of the soul, which underlies the whole question of education.[30] For Mullā Ṣadrā, the genesis, growth, and perfection of the human soul, a subject that he usually identifies as a whole as *istikmāl al-nafs,* or perfection of the soul, occupies a central position, and he deals with it in many of his works. The most complete treatment is to be found in the fourth journey of his magnum opus, *al-Asfār al-arba'ah* ("The Four Journeys");[31] other of his major works, such as *al-Mabda' wa'l-ma'ād* ("The Origin and the End") and *al-Shawāhid al-rubūbiyyah* ("Divine Witnesses"), also deal extensively with the subject. Moreover, Mullā Ṣadrā returns to this theme in his commentaries of and works on the Quran, including his commentary on the Light Verse (*āyat al-nūr*)[32] and his *Asrār al-āyāt* ("The Secrets of Quranic Verses"),[33] which contains the synthesis of his doctrine of the nature of the human state.

Mullā Ṣadrā depicts upon a vast canvas the human journey from the embryonic stage to the meeting with God and combines the trajectory of life in this world with that in the world to come, treating these phases as parts of a single "course of life" stretching from the Origin (*al-mabda'*) to the End (*al-ma'ād*). For him there is an organic relation between this life and the life to come, and all moments and stages of life exist in light of that final goal, which is the encounter with God. He describes the nature, faculties, and powers of human beings and the purpose and entelechy of their existence. This entelechy is perfect knowledge of God and the happiness that results from it. For Mullā Ṣadrā, knowledge transforms the being of the knowers, so that the whole process of education is the means whereby human beings ascend in the scale of being and move toward the state of perfection for which they were created.[34]

According to the principle of transubstantial motion (*al-ḥarakat al-jawhariyyah*), the very substance of all beings in the world of generation and corruption is being continuously transformed; motion or change is not only in the categories of accidents, but in the very substance of beings. In the case of human beings, this process is most noticeable and "radical"; the human state is central in the terrestrial domain, where the human being stands at the foot of the vertical axis that relates all levels of being. Men and women are transformed through transubstantial motion, which must not, however, be confused under any condition with evolution in the modern sense,[35] from the mineral state to the plant, from plant to animal, from animal to the ordinary human state, from this stage to the angelic, and finally beyond the angelic to the domain of Divine Proximity, or, to use the Quranic image, "the length of two bows."[36]

Up to the stage of the "ordinary" human state, the process is carried out by both the angels and the forces of nature as God's agents in this world. But from this stage on, it is by means of the actualization of the potentialities of the soul and its faculties through education that the process is carried out. Since human beings have free will, this stage of the process does not take place "naturally" and automatically, as with the earlier stages. Since the knower becomes united with the known at the moment of intellection (*ta'aqqul*), the very mode of human existence is changed through the process of knowledge. For Mullā Ṣadrā, the process of knowing is the key to the future of the mode of being of human beings and hence lies at the heart of the concerns of religion.

Human perfection resides in the perfection of the soul, for which Mullā Ṣadrā uses the traditional philosophical term *al-nafs al-nāṭiqah,* or "rational soul." But the term *nāṭiqah* must not be reduced to the modern understanding of the term "rational." This word in Arabic still contains connotations related to such terms as *nous, intellectus,* and *verbum* in classical Western sources and even to the meaning that *ratio* possessed before Cartesianism and empiricism deprived reason of its connection with the intellect and reduced it for the most part to its rapport with the outer senses. For Mullā Ṣadrā the *al-nafs al-nāṭiqah,* which is the first perfection of the body and the faculty capable of intellection,[37] possesses in turn two basic faculties: accepting that which descends from above (*al-quwwat al-'ālimah*) and acting upon that which is below it (*al-quwwat al-'āmilah*). The second faculty, which is the practical, is helped by and depends upon the first, which is the intellectual. The goal of education is the actualization and perfection of these faculties, with the aim of fulfilling the purpose for which human beings were created, that is, the knowledge of God (*ma'rifat Allāh*).[38]

The intellectual faculty consists of stages, as mentioned above, ranging from the "material intellect" (*al-'aql al-hayūlānī*), to the intellect *in habitus* (*al-'aql bi'l-malakah*), to the intellect in act (*al-'aql bi'l-fi'l*), which represents the perfection of the intellectual faculty on the human level. As for the perfection of the practical faculty, it resides in following faithfully the Islamic Divine Law (*al-sharī'at al-muḥammadiyyah*). The very process of learning (*ta'līm*) transforms the soul and enables it to undergo the process of going from a state of potentiality to one of actuality. Education, therefore, lies at the heart of religion and is the basic concern of Islam; in its totality, embracing both the *Sharī'ah* and the inner way, or *Ṭarīqah,* the religion of Islam itself may be said to consist of a vast program of education for all aspects of the human being, from the corporeal to the highest faculties of the soul.

The most elevated form of knowledge is the perception (*idrāk*) of God, a knowledge that, however, cannot be attained save through the possession of faith (*īmān*).[39] The strengthening of faith is therefore a prerequisite of any educational system that seeks to possess an Islamic character, while this strengthening is itself not possible without moral education and the acquisition of the virtues of purity and reverential fear of God (*taqwā*). Human beings are able to attain to this supreme knowledge, because their archetype (*al-insān al-kāmil*), which they bear within the depth of their being, is the mirror in which is reflected the Supreme Name, *Allāh,* and hence the essential reality that is also reflected in the whole world of manifestation.[40] Men and women are created in such a way that the Active Intellect appears at once, before their *nafs* and can be attained as the fruit of the perfection of the *nafs.* Through the process of education, which results in this perfection, they realize that they are the complete book containing all the signs (*āyāt*) of God manifested in His creation.[41] All learning and every step in the process of education is legitimate if it enables human beings to read this "book" that they carry within themselves. Moreover, to read this "book" is to fulfill the goal of life and to attain the end for which humankind was created. It is the ultimate goal of Islamic education.

In present-day discussions of Islamic education, far too little attention has been paid to the views of these and other Islamic philosophers and sages who, over the centuries, have meditated upon the meaning of education in light of such fundamental questions as: "Who are we?" "What is our nature?" "Where do we come from?" "Where are we going?" They have formulated an elaborate educational philosophy that, while remaining faithful to the nature of human beings and their entelechy, serves as framework for the creation of not only Islamic philosophy, but also the Islamic sciences. The Islamic philosophers' views on education represent an important branch of that tree of the Islamic intellectual tradition whose roots are sunk in the teachings of the Quran and *Ḥadīth*. No serious concern with Islamic education today, confronted with a crisis resulting from the advent of modernism and also "fundamentalism," can afford to remain oblivious to this millennial heritage. Nor can any account of Islamic education be considered complete without taking into account the remarkable depth, amplitude, universality, and also practical significance of the Islamic philosophers' educational concepts and views.

Philosophy and Science

Chapter Ten

TEACHING PHILOSOPHY IN LIGHT OF THE ISLAMIC EDUCATIONAL ETHOS

As a result of the penetration of very diverse philosophical currents and ideas into the Islamic world, one is confronted with a complex and bewildering philosophical situation in that world today (see Appendix II). It is precisely in such a situation that the question of teaching philosophy in the Islamic world looms large upon the horizon. Before discussing how philosophy should be taught, however, it is important to deal with the question of whether it should be taught at all, because there are many within the Islamic world, even in positions of educational responsibility, who doubt the usefulness of teaching such a subject—or who even oppose it completely. If by "philosophy" we mean modern, Western philosophy, then it is of course very much open to debate whether this subject should be taught at all to those Muslim students who have had no grounding in the Islamic philosophical tradition. But remembering that "philosophy" is a polysemic term (a word with many meanings), it can be confidently asserted that it is impossible to have an educational system without teaching some kind of philosophy, even if the subject is never mentioned as such by name. One cannot teach modern physics or chemistry without accepting certain assumptions concerning the nature of reality that are intimately related to seventeenth-century European philosophy, or biology without teaching at the same time certain very hypothetical ideas about change, process, and so-called evolution, which have all issued from nineteenth-century European thought. Nor can one study even classical Islamic theology without a basic knowledge of logic.

In fact, even in classical Islamic education, all students were taught some kind of philosophy, understood here in the sense both of worldview and of a method of thinking applicable to various sciences, including jurisprudence (*fiqh*). It must, therefore, be accepted that one cannot impart knowledge in a formal educational system without having some kind of philosophy, without some kind of worldview and notion of what constitutes the correct method of thinking. The question, therefore, is not whether one should teach philosophy to Muslim students, but rather *what kind or kinds* of philosophy should be taught and how the subject should be approached. Lack of attention to this crucial question has caused innumerable problems in modern educational institutions throughout the Islamic world. It has been one of the main causes for the inability of contemporary Islam to create a fully Islamic educational system that would not shun the philosophical questions that the modern world poses for Muslims or remain indifferent to the philosophical underpinning of the Western natural and social sciences taught in educational institutions in the Islamic world.

If philosophy is to be taught, then one must first decide what is meant by "philosophy" and what kind of philosophy or philosophies one should teach. For most modernized and Western-educated Muslims the term simply implies Western philosophy, especially its main current from Descartes, Leibniz, and Malebranche through Locke, Hume, Kant, and Hegel to the various modern schools of existentialism, positivism, structuralism, and deconstructionism. Most Western-educated Muslims have also heard of al-Fārābī and Ibn Sīnā, but without knowing exactly what they really said. For many traditional Muslims not yet touched by modern education, the term "philosophy" still implies wisdom, *al-ḥikmah,* which they associate with the prophets as well as with the Muslim saints and sages. As for the learned among the traditional segment of Islamic society, those not influenced by the rationalizing movements of the twelfth/eighteenth and thirteenth/nineteenth centuries associated with the name of 'Abd al-Wahhāb and others, philosophy is simply associated with the traditional *falsafah,* toward which they have the same traditional attitude as in older days. But few are aware of the fact that, in the context of present-day education and the current understanding of philosophy, not only is *falsafah* truly philosophy, but that there is also "philosophy" in many other Islamic sciences, such as *tafsīr, Ḥadīth, kalām, uṣūl, al-fiqh,* and *taṣawwuf,* as well as of course in the Islamic natural and mathematical sciences, all of which are rooted in principle in the Quran, which is of course the fountain of *ḥikmah,* or wisdom, for Muslims.

In order to define what is meant by "philosophy" in the present context, it is necessary to go beyond this polarization. One cannot consider philosophy as simply modern Western philosophy or completely accept the appraisal of even the most knowledgeable of Muslim "reformers" in philosophical matters, for example, Muḥammad Iqbāl, who took certain strands of European philosophy so seriously that in his *Jāwīd-nāmah,* as Rūmī is guiding him in Paradise, he comes upon Nietzsche and asserts:

> I said to Rūmī, "Who is this madman?"
> He said, "This is the Wise Man of Germany."

Nor can one be completely successful and honest, intellectually speaking, by simply rejecting philosophy as *kufr* (infidelity) and refusing to understand it, although most of modern philosophy is in fact *kufr* from the Islamic point of view. This cannot be done because Western philosophical ideas will simply creep in through the back door in a thousand different ways, and students will then be much less prepared to confront them, since they will not have been properly inoculated against them through a vigorous study and intellectual refutation of their false theses. What must be done, therefore, is to define philosophy itself as the framework of an authentic Islamic educational system and then to reappraise the current meaning or meanings of philosophy in light of the Islamic perspective.

It is true that the Islamic intellectual tradition is too rich and diversafied to provide just one meaning for the Quranic term *al-ḥikmah,* but it is also true that the several enduring intellectual perspectives that have been cultivated in the Islamic world all conform to the doctrine of unity (*al-tawḥīd*). One can thus come to understand the term "philosophy" as implying knowledge of the nature of things based upon and leading to *al-tawḥīd;* this form of knowledge is therefore profoundly Islamic even if issuing originally from non-Islamic sources. The view of traditional Islamic philosophers that "philosophy originates from the lamp of prophecy"[1] derives directly from their using *al-tawḥīd* as the criterion for the Islamicity of a particular teaching. In any case, "philosophy" could be redefined according to Islamic standards to preserve its intellectual vigor, but at the same time remain attached to the revelation and its central doctrine, which is none other than unity.[2] From the very beginning, the currently prevailing idea of philosophy as skepticism and doubt, as an individualistic activity of human beings who have rebelled against God, and as the objectification of the limitations of the particular kind of man or woman called "philosopher" should be dispelled from the minds of students. It should be replaced by the idea of wisdom; the universality, certitude, and the supra-individual character of the intellect; and the Truth as such and its major traditional formulations and crystallizations, so that philosophy becomes identified with an enduring intellectual perspective, as it has always been in the traditional East, rather than with an individualistic interpretation of reality, as has been the case in Western philosophy since Descartes.

The teaching of philosophy to Muslim students should begin not only with an Islamic understanding of the meaning of philosophy, but also with a thorough study of the whole of the Islamic intellectual tradition. Before students are exposed to Descartes and Kant or even Plato and Aristotle as seen through the eyes of modern Western philosophy, they should receive a thorough grounding in Islamic philosophy and other related disciplines. Those devising curricula should possess as wide a perspective as possible and go beyond the debilitating attacks of the past century upon the Islamic tradition itself, which would reduce the great wealth of the tapestry that is the intellectual life of Islam to simply one of its strands or imply that this intellectual tradition is simply the result of borrowing from alien sources. Whether the planners or teachers sympathize with the jurisprudents or theologians, the philosophers in the technical sense of *falāsifah,* or the Sufis, with critics of logical discourse or its supporters is really beside the point. If there is to be a successful program of philosophy enabling Muslim students to confront modern philosophical disciplines, ideologies, and points of view without losing their intellectual and spiritual orientation, then the full force of the Islamic intellectual tradition must be brought into play and a narrowing of perspective carefully avoided.

Even great debates between various Islamic schools of philosophy and thought in general, such as those between Ibn Sīnā and al-Bīrūnī,[3] al-Ghazzālī and Ibn Rushd,[4] Naṣīr al-Dīn Ṭūsī and Ṣadr al-Dīn al-Qunyawī,[5] and many others, must be made known and their significance fully brought out. After all, during the periods of Islamic history when Muslims produced world-famous scientists and thinkers, such as al-Fārābī, Ibn Sīnā, and al-Bīrūnī, the debates held between various perspectives did not "harm"

Islam in any way, since they were all carried out within the context of the worldview of the Islamic tradition. Students should be encouraged to know something of this rich intellectual background and not be presented with a picture of the Islamic intellectual tradition as a monolithic structure amenable only to one level of interpretation. Such a perspective only deadens the mind and creates a passivity that makes the penetration of foreign ideas into the Islamic world so much easier.

The Islamic intellectual tradition should also be taught in its fullness and as it developed throughout Islamic history. Nothing has been more detrimental to an authentic revival of Islamic thought than the fallacious notion that it decayed at the end of the Abbasid period. This interpretation of Islamic history was originally the work of orientalists who could accept the historic importance of Islamic civilization only as a phase in the development of their own civilization. The adoption of this Western view by certain Muslims, abetted in certain circles by the Ash'arite opposition to *falsafah,* is, therefore, even more surprising, since it does so much injustice to the grandeur of Islamic civilization and, even more important, is manifestly false. It was adopted in certain Islamic circles for nationalistic reasons or for political opportunism, but surely cannot be entertained seriously today.[6] How can a civilization that created the Sultan Aḥmad Mosque, the Shaykh Luṭf Allāh Mosque, or the Taj Mahal be decadent? Or, on the intellectual plane, can one call Mīr Dāmād or Mullā Ṣadrā a less serious metaphysician than any of their contemporaries anywhere else in the world? The presentation of the Islamic intellectual tradition should definitely cover the period up to the present day, categorically dismissing this false notion of decadence in Islamic thought derived from European historical studies of the nineteenth and early twentieth centuries.

This presentation *should,* however, also include discussions of periods when there was a lack or lessening of intellectual activity, if such indeed was really the case. Those parts of the Islamic world where Muslims were actually "sleeping over treasures," to quote Frithjof Schuon, a contemporary metaphysician and master of Islamic intellectuality, should be mentioned. But so also should such figures as Shaykh al-Darqāwī, Ḥājjī Mullā Ḥādī Sabziwārī, the philosophers of Farangī Maḥall, and Mawlānā 'Alī Thanwī, all of whom rekindled various schools of traditional Islamic intellectuality in different parts of the Islamic world during the past two centuries. In fact, the so-called Muslim reformers, about whom so much has been written, should be reappraised in light of full knowledge of the Islamic intellectual tradition.

Having gained a thorough grounding in the complete Islamic intellectual tradition in its general features, if not in its details, Muslim students should then be introduced to other schools of philosophy, not only Western, but also non-Islamic Oriental ones. Besides Islamic thought itself, no better antidote can be found for the skepticism inherent in much of modern Western philosophy than the traditional doctrines of the Orient, such as those of India and China, which, like Islamic philosophy itself, are philosophy in the sense of *wisdom,* because they all are based upon the Absolute (or the Void in the metaphysical sense) and the means of attaining the Absolute. They are, in a sense, various forms of commentary on the Quranic verse, "Truly we are God's and unto Him we return" (XI: 156). Muslim students should in fact be made aware that, in addition to the Islamic world and the all-powerful Western philosophies and ideologies, there are other civilizations with their own profound intellectual traditions.

Besides those of the Orient, ancient Greek philosophy and its antecedents in Egypt and Mesopotamia should be taught, not as a part of Western thought, but independent of their influence on the West, as traditional Muslim thinkers have always considered them. It is strange that most Islamic modernists have seen Greek philosophy almost completely through the eyes of its modern Western interpreters.[7] When Iqbāl calls Plato "one of the sheep," he is following Nietzsche's interpretation of Platonism rather than that of those Islamic philosophers who saw the teachings of Pythagoras, Empedocles, Parmenides, Plato, and Aristotle as confirmations of the Islamic doctrine of *al-tawḥīd.* The study of Greek thought according to the Islamic intellectual tradition and independent of its Western interpretation is in fact crucial for the Islamic confrontation with modern Western philosophy itself, whether it be the thought of those like Karl Jaspers and Martin Heidegger, who have dealt extensively with the Greeks, or positivists who do not consider anything before Kant or Hume to be philosophy at all.

The study of non-Islamic schools of thought should also emphasize Christian and Jewish philosophy in the European Middle Ages and their later continuation. Muslim students should be introduced to such medieval figures as St. Bonaventure, St. Thomas, Duns Scotus, Ibn Gabirol, and Maimonides, who were also very close to Islamic thought. But instead of just relegating the Christian and Jewish philosophy to the medieval period and following it immediately with secularized modern philosophy, as is the case today, more emphasis should be placed on the continuation of these schools, not only through Francisco Suarez and Baruch Spinoza, but into the twentieth century with such figures as Franz Brentano, Étienne Gilson, Jacques Maritain, Henry A. Wolfson, Émil Fackenheim, and David Hartman.[8] The purpose of this exercise is to demonstrate to Muslim students, who might get carried away as a result of their encounter with modern Western philosophy, how, despite the weakening of religion in the West, religious or "prophetic" philosophy in many ways similar to the Islamic kind, based upon God and revelation, has continued in certain circles to this day. Of course in such an enterprise thoroughly anti-traditional but outwardly "Christian" philosophies, such as Teilhardism, should also be exposed for what they are.

Finally, as far as the development of Western philosophy is concerned, some emphasis should be placed upon what has been called by the Islamicist Henry Corbin the "anti-history of anti-philosophy," namely, those more traditional schools of philosophy that remained on the margin of European thought and that are not usually discussed in standard texts on the history of Western philosophy employed in both Western universities and those of the Islamic world. The research of the past few decades has revealed that certain forms of nonrationalistic philosophy, such as Hermeticism, survived to a greater extent during the Renaissance and the seventeenth and eighteenth centuries than had been thought before, and that such schools as Kabbalah, the Rosicrucian movement, Hermeticism, and the like were even influential in the rise of experimental science to a degree hitherto unsuspected.[9] Giordano Bruno, Paracelsus, Basil Valentine, Robert Fludd, and many similar figures are seen to be of much greater significance, even from the point of view of science, than the rationalistic interpretations of earlier days had led everyone to believe. It is important to make Muslim students aware of these elements, since such philosophies are both akin in structure and related through historical sources to various schools of Islamic thought.

As for later centuries, more should be said about such figures as Jacob Böhme, Johann Wolfgang Goethe as a philosopher, Friedrich Wilhelm Schelling, Franz von Baader, Louis Claude de St. Martin, Karl von

Eckartshausen, and many other similar figures. They are also attracting much attention in the contemporary West itself as part of the quest for that lost *sophia* or *sapientia* that much of its own so-called philosophy denies or abhors.[10]

Since it is primarily modern Western thought that is the source of doubt and skepticism for educated Muslims, it is essential to acquaint Muslim students fully not only with this thought but also with the criticisms made against it in the West itself. It has always been said that the cure for a snake bite is the poison of the snake itself. In the same way, the best antidote for the errors that constitute the essence—though not necessarily all of the accidents—of what is characteristically modern, in contrast to contemporary, thought, can be found in the criticisms made in the West itself. To be sure, certain profound criticisms have come from the East, but for the most part Orientals have been either too enfeebled as a result of the process of Westernization itself to stand totally on their own ground or unable to get to the heart of the problem involved as a result of a lack of knowledge of the inner workings of Western thought. The few profound criticisms from the East, such as those of the incomparable Indian metaphysicians and scholars Ananda K. Coomaraswamy and A. K. Saran, have been the exception rather than the rule.[11]

From the West, however, has come a complete and thoroughgoing critique of the very structure of modern thought. Its criticisms include magisterial expositions based on traditional authority and grounded in thorough knowledge of traditional metaphysics and philosophy, such as the *Oriental Metaphysics* of René Guénon and the *Logic and Transcendence* of Frithjof Schuon,[12] as well as a description of the "malaise" inherent in modern philosophy and thought by a large number of notable thinkers seeking to rediscover the Truth, a task from which many critics believe the mainstream of European philosophy has departed since the Renaissance. These include philosophers as well as scientists and literary figures: figures such as Julius Evola and Élemire Zolla in Italy; Henry Corbin, Gilbert Durand, and Antoine Faivre in France; Leopold Ziegler in Germany; Tag Lindbom in Sweden; Huston Smith and Theodore Roszak in the United States, and many others. They also include those, such as Étienne Gilson, who have written histories of Western philosophy from the point of view of Thomist ontology and epistemology and who have detected in the history of Western thought a gradual erosion in the role of philosophy, which changed from being the study of Being Itself or of the One who alone *is,* in the absolute sense, to the study of logic alone.[13] Muslim students should be presented with these criticisms when they are studying the history of Western thought, so that they acquire certain intellectual concepts necessary to protect themselves from the withering effects of the agnosticism and doubt associated with so much of modern philosophy.

In teaching philosophy, then, traditional Islamic philosophy should be made central and other schools of philosophy taught in relation to it. It must be remembered, however, that "Islamic philosophy" does not mean only its history. The method of reducing philosophy to the history of philosophy is itself something completely modern and non-Islamic. Nor in fact does this method conform to the perspective of any of the other major traditional civilizations. In such civilizations, philosophy is not identified with an individual who gives his name to a particular philosophical mode of thought, which is then called, for example, Cartesianism or Hegelianism, but which is almost immediately criticized and rejected by a subsequent philosopher. Rather, philosophy is identified with an intellectual perspective that lasts over the centuries, even if given the name of its providential founder, as we see in the case of Platonism and the like, and that, far from being a barrier to creativity, remains a viable means of access to the Truth within the particular tradition in question. Men who give their names to traditional schools of thought are seen more as "intellectual functions" than mere individuals. Such a situation was also found in the West when it was Christian; for centuries, people followed the Augustinian, Thomistic, or Palamite schools of theology and philosophy, and these schools were seen, and still continue to be seen to the extent that Christian philosophy is alive, as intellectual perspectives transcending the individualistic order. In traditional India and China, the situation has of course always been of this kind; namely, wisdom or philosophy has been identified with the name of a great sage, whether he was a historical or a mythical figure, who opened up an intellectual perspective of a supra-individualistic order that survived over the centuries, far beyond the life span of the founder himself or his immediate disciples.

In contrast, Islamic philosophy should be taught in a morphological manner, as schools rather than as a continuous history of individual philosophers and their philosophies, as has been the case even in many books written by modernized Muslims emulating Western models.

Islamic intellectual life should be divided into its traditional schools of *uṣūl* (principles of faith and jurisprudence), *kalām* (theology), *mashshā'ī* (Peripatetic) philosophy, Ismā'īlī philosophy, *ishrāq* (the School of Illumination), *ma'rifah* or *'irfān* (theoretical or doctrinal Sufism) and, finally, the later school of *al-ḥikmat al-muta'āliyah* (the transcendent theosophy) associated with the name of Ṣadr al-Dīn Shīrāzī, just to cite some major examples without being exhaustive. Then each of these schools should be subdivided according to their traditional divisions, such as Sunni and Shī'ite *uṣūl,* Mu'tazilite, Ash'arite, Ithnā 'Asharī and Ismā'īlī *kalām,* eastern and western schools of *mashshā'ī* philosophy, and so forth.

Also each school should be taught according to its own traditional methods, that is, beginning with principles related to the Quran and *Ḥadīth* and intellectual principles, then followed by the application and development of these principles. Only after the intellectual structure is introduced should a historical account be given of each school, a historical account—or we could say "historial" to avoid the danger of historicism—that should come up to the present day, if a school has survived until now, which is in fact the case for nearly all the major Islamic intellectual disciplines, provided the whole of the Islamic world is considered and not only its central lands. For example, once the doctrinal and philosophical aspects of the Mu'tazilite school are presented, the discussion of its historical unfolding should be taught, not ending with Qāḍī 'Abd al-Jabbār in the fifth/eleventh century, but also including the whole later development of this school among the Zaydīs of the Yemen up to modern times and, finally, its revival among certain of the theologians of al-Azhar during the twentieth century.

In the same manner, the development of *mashshā'ī* philosophy should not stop with Ibn Rushd, as is usually the case following Western sources, but include the later Turkish criticisms of his *Tahāfut al-tahāfut* ("Incoherence of the Incoherence") during the Ottoman period, the revival of *mashshā'ī* philosophy in the East by Naṣīr al-Dīn Ṭūsī and Quṭb al-Dīn Shīrāzī, and the continuation of the school of Ibn Sīnā up to our own times, when major philosophical commentaries and analyses of his work continue to appear in Persia, Pakistan, India, the Arab world, and Turkey. The same could be said of the other schools.

Of course, this task is not an easy one, because of the state of present-day knowledge of Islamic intellectual life in its totality. The detailed development of every one of these schools remains unknown in certain areas of the Islamic world. There may be Malay scholars who know how *kalām* developed in their part of the Islamic world, as there may still be scholars in Morocco who are familiar with the development of the metaphysics of the school of Ibn 'Arabī in that region. But there is no single work or any one center of research where all of this knowledge has been brought together. Yet once it is realized how important it is to provide a total and complete map of Islamic intellectual life in both space and time for current Muslim students, it would not be difficult to provide the means to carry out the task of studying these schools, beginning with the traditional method of presenting first their principles, then their branches and various other details, and only later their development in history. This method helps to avoid the relativization of the truth and the reduction of all permanence to becoming, which are inevitably implied by the methods used when the history of philosophy is studied and taught in the West. Of course, even here the anti-historicism of certain current Western thinkers can be of help in preventing Muslims from falling into the trap of historicism without at the same time being in any way against historical facts. After all, al-Bīrūnī and Ibn Khaldūn were able to be very keen historians without reducing all truths to their history and all permanence to becoming.

The traditional conflicts between the various schools of Islamic thought should also be taught as contentions between many different perspectives converging upon the Truth, contentions that are of a very different nature from those found between conflicting philosophical schools in the modern world. In the first case, there are always the transcendent principles of the Islamic tradition that ultimately unify, whereas, in the second case, such unifying principles are missing. It is true that the Ash'arites opposed the Mu'tazilites, that the *mutakallimūn* in general were against the *mashshā'ī* philosophers, that Suhrawardī, the founder of the School of *ishrāq*, criticized Peripatetic logic and metaphysics, that Ibn Taymiyyah wrote against formal logic, Ibn 'Arabī and Sufism, and so on. But had these oppositions been like those of modern thought, the Islamic tradition would not have survived. There was, however, always the unifying principle of *al-tawḥīd* and a sense of hierarchy within the Islamic tradition itself, which allowed intellectual figures to appear from time to time who were at once *mutakallimūn*, philosophers, and metaphysicians of the gnostic school (*al-ma'rifah*), men who realized the inner unity of these perspectives within their own being and did not present self-contradictory worldviews.

The fact that there were many and not just one school of thought should not therefore be taught to students as a sign of either chaos or weakness, but as the result of the richness of the Islamic tradition, which was able to cater to the needs of different intellectual types and therefore to keep within its fold so many human beings of differing backgrounds and intellectual abilities. The diversity should be taught as the consequence of many diverse applications of the teachings of Islam, some more partial and some more complete, yet all formulated to prevent those with different mental abilities and attitudes from quenching their thirst for knowledge outside the structure of the Islamic tradition itself, as happened in the Christian West during the Renaissance. This profusion and diversity of schools in Islam, which, although different, all drew from the fountainhead of the Quranic revelation and *al-tawḥīd,* was the means whereby Islam succeeded in preserving the sacred character of knowledge, while at the same time creating a vast civilization in which the development of various modes of knowledge and different sciences was not only possible, but also necessary.

The study of Islamic philosophy in this manner should be complemented by the study of the different philosophical questions and themes with which contemporary students are usually faced. For example, for students of different professional disciplines, such as law, medicine, engineering, and the like, questions such as the nature of the world, causality, the origin of "laws of nature," the nature of life, the relation between creation and God, and so on, could be fitted into a general program for the study of a philosophy within whose matrix the different disciplines cited above would be taught. But for those who study philosophy itself, the religious sciences, or certain other sciences, such as physics, it would be very helpful and perhaps even necessary to deal with philosophical subjects separately and morphologically. Even in the Western philosophical syllabus, students study logic, aesthetics, ethics, social and political philosophy, and, in many places, metaphysics, cosmology, and philosophical psychology.

From a pedagogical point of view, it is important to deal separately with these disciplines for particular groups of students concerned with the subjects mentioned above in combination with general courses on Islamic intellectual life along the lines described already. It is also obviously essential to teach Islamic political philosophy in a more fully developed and thorough manner to students of political science, the philosophy of art and aesthetics to students of art and architecture, the Islamic philosophy of science to students of all the different natural and mathematic sciences, and so on. In such cases, each discipline should be taught from the Islamic point of view; then the views of Western or non-Islamic Eastern schools should be presented and, when in contradiction to Islamic teachings, critiqued and explained.

In nearly every branch of philosophy, the Islamic tradition is rich beyond belief, if only its sources were made known. This is especially true of metaphysics. Islamic metaphysics should be presented as what it is, that is, the science of Ultimate Reality, which is the One (*al-Aḥad*) or Allah, who has revealed Himself in the Quran, and not as a discredited branch of rationalistic philosophy. There has been no Islamic school whose teachings are not based on the doctrine of the One, who is both Absolute and Infinite. In the study of this Sublime Principle, Muslim sages developed several languages of discourse, some based on the consideration of the One as Pure Being with an ensuing ontology conforming to that view, but always seeing Pure Being not as the first link in the "great chain of being," but as the Source that transcends existence altogether. Others saw the One as Light (*al-Nūr*), according to the Quranic verse, "God is the Light of the Heavens and the earth" (XXIV: 35); and yet others as the Truth (*al-Ḥaqq*), which transcends even Pure Being, as the supraontological Principle whose first determination or act is in fact Being, for God said according to the Quran: "Be (*kun*) and there was!" (XXXVI: 82). It is Western scholars of Islamic philosophy who have called Ibn Sīnā "the first philosopher of being"; and without any exaggeration or chauvinism, one could say that, in a sense, the development of ontology in the West is a commentary or footnote to Ibn Sīnā, but one that moves toward an ever more limited understanding of Being, until finally it results in either the neglect of ontology or a parody of it. Even the present-day *Existenz Philosophie,* identified with philosophers such as Heidegger, seems like a rudimentary discussion of love by someone who has never experienced it when compared to the philosophy of Being of a figure such as Ṣadr al-Dīn Shīrāzī, who writes about Being only after having drowned in the Ocean of Pure Being and who, after purification, has been endowed with the sanctified intellect that alone can speak of this Ocean.

In other philosophical subjects also, such as logic and epistemology, the Islamic tradition presents an immense richness that should be first resuscitated in a contemporary language and then taught to students. Only then should the various modern schools of logic and discussions of the questions of epistemology be presented. There are, of course, certain problems of contemporary concern that have no antecedents in Islamic thought, and it would be a falsafication of the truth, in fact a betrayal of the Islamic tradition, to read contemporary questions and their solutions back into the Islamic sources and find there, let us say, allusions to cybernetics, Riemannian space, or modern information theory, when in actuality they do not exist. But even in these cases, a mind disciplined in the Islamic sciences would be able to approach such subjects from the point of view of Islamic thought rather than as a *tabula rasa*. There are, of course, other concerns of a particularly modern nature, such as semantics and the question of causality, in which the Islamic tradition is remarkably rich. In such instances, the Islamic teachings could be presented first, and only then the current—and of course ever changing—modern theories and views taught to students who have to be concerned with such fields.

The modern world does not possess a cosmology in the real sense of the term, but there are many theories about the universe based on the generalizations of contemporary physics. In Islamic civilization, however, several forms of cosmology were developed, all related to the basic teachings of the Quran concerning the creation of the world by God, the higher planes of being associated with *malakūt* in the Quran, and so forth.[14] These cosmologies, which are of an eminently symbolic character and cannot be negated by any form of modern physics and astronomy, should first be taught to the students along with their full metaphysical and religious significance, which would also explain such otherwise inexplicable events as the nocturnal ascension (*al-mi'rāj*) of the Blessed Prophet.[15] Only after students have acquired a "feeling" for and an intellectual appreciation of the Islamic universe, should they be exposed to various modern forms of so-called cosmology, all of which should be presented for exactly what they are, namely, theories based upon certain questionable, far-fetched extrapolations and usually empirically unprovable assumptions.

Students should also be taught about the various schools of the Islamic "philosophy of nature," which is closely related to cosmology. These schools have views concerning time, space, substance and matter, change, cause and effect, and many other subjects that form the basis of all natural sciences and that in fact have attracted the attention of several important contemporary Western scientists and philosophers of science. With modern physics being in quest of a new "philosophy of nature," the Islamic teachings on this subject are of the utmost importance for Muslim students of the sciences and perhaps even for the development in general of a new type of physics or science of nature sought by many perceptive minds today. The same could be said of Islamic works on the philosophy of mathematics, which have rarely been studied in modern times.[16]

Likewise, in philosophical psychology, the Islamic sources are replete with teachings that are of great value in the investigation of questions posed in psychology today. In this field, material can be drawn all the way from Quranic commentaries and *Ḥadīth* to Sufi ethical and psychological tracts, not to speak of the philosophical psychology of the philosophers themselves, such as Ibn Sīnā and Mullā Ṣadrā, and works of Islamic medicine.

In the philosophy of art or aesthetics, the teaching of the Islamic perspective is important not only from the educational point of view, but also because of the effect that the training of Muslim students of art and architecture in Western ways has had upon the destruction of the Islamic character of cities and the way of life of the people within the Islamic world. Islamic art is not accidentally Islamic; rather, it is a direct crystallization of the spirit and form of the Islamic revelation complementing the *Sharīʿah*. One provides the Islamic mode of conduct and action and the other principles for the creation of an environment in which the spirit of Islam breathes and which provides the necessary background and support for the Islamic way of life. If Islamic art were only accidentally related to Islam, one could not observe and perceive the unmistakable fragrance of the Islamic revelation in the mosques or handicrafts of lands as far apart as China, Bangladesh, and Senegal.

Until recently oral traditions and the homogeneity of the Islamic environment did not necessitate an explicit formulation of the Islamic philosophy of art. But now, along with the teaching of the techniques of Islamic art, it is essential to formulate and teach the principles of the philosophy or wisdom (*al-ḥikmah*)[17] that underlies Islamic art, remembering that this form of art is the fruit of the marriage between technique (*al-fann*) and wisdom (*al-ḥikmah*). This is especially necessary today, since modern theories of art and aesthetics and works based upon them have engulfed much of the Islamic world, corroding the soul and weakening the faith of Muslims in a direct manner that is often more insidious and pervasive than the effect of antireligious ideologies. Many Muslims are in fact painfully unaware of the religious danger of antitraditional art forms and therefore display a remarkable passivity toward them.[18]

In the practical aspects of philosophy, such as the social, political, and economic ones and ethics in general, Islamic sources once again possess an immense richness. Here, as before, the various schools of Islamic thought should be presented as so many elaborations upon the themes of the Quran and the *Ḥadīth*. For example, Islamic ethics is of course itself based upon these twin sources of Islamic revelation; but there are elaborations of ethics as a "moral science" or as a branch of philosophy in works as different as *al-Risālat al-qushayriyyah* ("The Treatise of Qushayrī") of Imam Abū'l-Qāsim al-Qushayrī and sections of *al-Mughnī* ("[The Book] that Makes Others Superfluous") of Qāḍī 'Abd al-Jabbār. To those may be added the many works of Islamic literature, such as the *Kalīlah wa Dimnah* ("Kalīlah and Dimnah") translated originally from Sanskrit into Arabic and later Persian, and the *Gulistān* ("The Rose Garden") of Sa'dī, the *Iḥyā' 'ulūm al-dīn* ("Revivification of the Sciences of Religion") of al-Ghazzālī, and the *Akhlāq-i nāṣirī* ("Naṣīrean Ethics") of Naṣīr al-Dīn Ṭūsī and similar works of *akhlāq* literature. All of these works aim to inculcate within the human soul the virtues taught by Islam, but each provides a different type of ethical theory and method and emphasizes different aspects of ethics. In a domain such as this, it is even easier than in the other fields mentioned above to teach first the ideas of the different schools of Islamic ethics and only then the current ethical theories of Western philosophers and theologians or even Confucian, Buddhist, and Christian ethical ideas, for that matter, all of which should also be definitely taught in a more advanced stage after the students are well-grounded in Islamic ethics.

As for social, political, and economic philosophies, there too the Islamic sources are very diverse, embracing not only books of philosophy in the strict sense of the term, but also those dealing with history and literature as well as of course works of jurisprudence (*fiqh*) and the different branches of the Law. In these fields, a certain amount of work has already been done toward presenting students with the views of the various Islamic schools before embarking upon the teaching of Western theories. Unfortunately, however, in many cases, instead of presenting the different Islamic schools objectively in all their diversity and richness, local political conditions have often dictated the criteria for choosing the genuinely Islamic schools that should be taught; and among Western ideologies, the only ones studied are those closest to the political stance of the local Muslim state. In fact, all the different Western schools of political and social philosophy that have been or are still of any consequence should be studied, evaluated, and criticized from the stance of the Islamic tradition. In this way, students will feel secure within their own tradition, no matter which type of modern philosophy they confront. For example, if the *laissez-faire* type of social, political, and economic philosophy is studied and rejected from the Islamic point of view, but the Marxist and socialist passed over in silence, Muslim students may be completely unequipped intellectually when confronted with them and consequently unable to defend their position against their arguments or the arguments of those pseudosyntheses that try to combine the Islamic and Marxist and socialist views, as if ice and fire could be made to exist harmoniously side by side.

The implementation of the program outlined above requires educational planning, the training of qualified individuals as both teachers and research scholars, the collection of manuscripts, and the composition of books and monographs on various levels. As far as educational planning is concerned, it must be said at the outset that obviously Islamic philosophy should be taught to students who have already studied the principles of Islam, the Quran, *Ḥadīth,* the sacred history of Islam, and at least some aspects of *fiqh* and *uṣūl al-fiqh,* even if only in rudimentary fashion. In this way, the minds of students would be impregnated with Islamic values, norms, and methods of reasoning, and they could confront alien ideas and ideologies accordingly. But if philosophy is taught in the manner outlined above, this function will also be performed by the various schools of Islamic philosophy themselves. Ibn Sīnā was already thoroughly educated in the purely Islamic disciplines before confronting Aristotelian and Neoplatonic metaphysics; therefore, his works can help Muslim students and strengthen their Islamic intellectual formation before they face the works of a Hegel or a Heidegger, with which classical Islamic philosophy was of course obviously not concerned. But if the Islamic intellectual tradition is put aside and students are presented with only the Quran and *Ḥadīth,* from which they are expected to deduce their own "philosophy of Islam," then such an enterprise can never succeed in face of modern philosophical challenges. Students thus educated would, at best, shy away from problems posed by modern thought in order to protect their faith and, at worst, be overcome by what, for the untrained, is an overwhelming challenge. As a result, they would either lose their faith, develop an anti-intellectual attitude, which would substitute intoxicating fury for intellectual response, or end up with some kind of a pseudosynthesis of Islam and different modern ideologies, which is often more insidious and dangerous in the long run than complete loss of faith.

As far as educational programming for the teaching of Islamic philosophy is concerned, it must begin on the secondary—or even in a simple language on the elementary—level and not be limited solely to the university. From the earliest grades, references in the textbooks of Muslim children should be primarily to learned Muslims. Biographies of great sages and thinkers, such as al-Ghazzālī, 'Abd al-Qādir al-Jīlānī, al-Fārābī, Ibn Sīnā, al-Bīrūnī, Ibn Khaldūn, and so on, should be liberally used in the history and cultural programs established for the earlier years of education, following directly upon the study of the life of the Prophet, the Companions, the imams of the *madhāhib,* and, for Shī'ism, the Shī'ite Imams. Moreover, the popular literature of an authentic nature concerning many Islamic intellectual figures should be adapted and couched in the appropriate language for the level of education in question.

In secondary education, the names of the major books of Islamic thought and a few of the basic ideas and debates, such as those mentioned above, should be added. Finally, for the last two years, programs comprising metaphysics, ethics, and a brief intellectual history of the various schools should be devised along thoroughly Islamic lines, as, for example, the French and German educational systems have done for the *lycée* and the *Gymnasium,* though there based on purely European lines. Only then should something be mentioned in the program for Muslim students about Western and possibly Indian and Far Eastern philosophies. But the treatment of Western thought, although very elementary at this stage, should still be critical and neither apologetic nor defensive.

As for university education, there must be several types of programs: one for those majoring in philosophy; one for those whose field is close to philosophy, such as theology, Islamic Law, comparative religion, or one of the other religious disciplines; one for those majoring in the theoretical sciences, such as physics and mathematics; one for those majoring in one of the descriptive sciences, such as biology, ecology, or geology; one for students of the social sciences and psychology; another for the arts and architecture; and so on. The details of such programs need careful study and cannot be provided in this chapter, but it can be emphasized that the general aim of the educational system should be to make its intellectual perspective and worldview totally Islamic. This principle must be emphasized even before one undertakes the creation and implementation of the actual details of such a program, including syllabi.

The training of personnel for such a program poses a major problem at the present moment, but not an insurmountable one. Today, only a handful of the traditional masters of Islamic philosophy who connect the present generation to the days of Suhrawardī and Ibn Sīnā survive. The knowledge of the oral traditions that they still possess and that complements the written texts is a most precious treasure of Islamic intellectual life. Before such people disappear from the face of the earth altogether, it is essential to choose a number of gifted students and provide the means for both teachers and students to make this vital training and transmission possible.[19] Furthermore, scholars with more contemporary training but also expert in the Islamic intellectual disciplines are limited in number. There are not enough teachers to staff even the major universities of the Islamic world. Therefore, every effort should be made to create several institutes or academic societies that would bring such experts together with qualified students. To train such students, it is necessary to both create the atmosphere and acquire the minimum number of qualified teachers who would in fact attract good students through their own presence. Efforts by the writer of these lines in this direction have produced satisfactory results in the past. With all the funds available in the Islamic world today, it should not be difficult to finance a few such centers, whose students could later become professors at the university level, training men and women who would in turn later teach on both the secondary and elementary levels.[20]

An urgent and highly important task for promoting a fuller understanding of the various dimensions and the immense richness of Islamic thought is the collection and preservation of manuscripts relating to Islamic philosophy, metaphysics, and other intellectual subjects. Most of these manuscripts are in Arabic, but a large number are also in Persian and a few in other Islamic languages, such as Turkish, Urdu, and Malay. Despite the laudable efforts of various public and semipublic libraries, especially in Turkey and Iran, as well as the Arab League Center for Arabic Manuscripts in Cairo, the al-Furqān Foundation in England, and the collection on Islamic medicine and related sciences being assembled by the Hamdard Foundations in Delhi, Karachi, and independently in Kuwait, a great deal more needs to be accomplished in collecting and cataloguing manuscripts still in private collections, many of which are in danger of being lost or destroyed. This is especially a problem in India and Pakistan, which are extremely rich in Islamic manuscripts, but also have a warm and humid climate that causes manuscripts to decay and fall apart very rapidly if they are not well stored and cared for. Parallel with this effort, copies should be made of manuscripts dealing with Islamic philosophy and related subjects and collected in the few centers created for the advanced study of Islamic philosophy and thought in general.

As far as books and monographs are concerned, so much needs to be done that a separate study would be required to even outline the work involved. Here it suffices to point out some of the major projects that need to be undertaken. First of all, the work of the combined group of Muslim and Western scholars who have performed the thankless task of editing the actual texts of Islamic thought must be continued in force, so that within a few years complete critical editions, or *opera omnia,* of at least the major Islamic intellectual figures, such as al-Fārābī, Ibn Sīnā, al-Bīrūnī, al-Ghazzālī, and Ibn Khaldūn, will be available. Islamic civilization lags behind others, like those of Japan and India, not to speak of the West, in this respect, and even today there is not a single major Islamic intellectual figure all of whose writings can be found in a critical edition.

Parallel with this effort, dictionaries must be compiled of philosophical and scientific terminology in Islamic languages. To this end, there must be greater cooperation between the scholars of these languages than has been the case until now. Some activity in this field has taken place under the auspices of the Arab Academy and several Iranian organizations as well as in Turkey, but much remains to be accomplished before philosophy, including Western thought, can be taught to Muslim students in their own languages in a way that would remain faithful to the genius of those languages and their traditional roots. The secularization of thought is always closely related to the secularization of language.

The question of language is so essential that it is necessary in some cases to rewrite classical works in a contemporary medium, especially for students, while preserving the classical technical vocabulary to the greatest extent possible. Not only is there an urgent need to translate the major masterpieces of Islamic metaphysics and philosophy, such as the *Kitāb al-ḥurūf* ("The Book of Letters") of al-Fārābī, *al-Najāh* ("The Salvation") and *al-Shifā'* ("The Healing") of Ibn Sīnā, *Tahāfut al-falāsifah* ("Incoherence of the Philosophers") of al-Ghazzālī, *Ḥikmat al-ishrāq* ("The Theosophy of the Orient of Light") of Suhrawardī, *Fuṣūṣ al-ḥikam* ("Bezels of Wisdom") of Ibn 'Arabī, *al-Insān al-kāmil* ("The Universe of Man") of 'Abd al- Karīm al-Jīlī, and *al-Shawāhid al-rubūbiyyah* ("Divine Witnesses") and *al-Asfār al-arba'ah* ("The Four Journeys") of Ṣadr al-Dīn Shīrāzī, from Arabic into various Islamic languages (some of this task has already been accomplished with varying degrees of success), but such works should also be "rewritten" or paraphrased in recensions in contemporary Arabic in such a way as to preserve their original technical vocabulary and at the same time make their content more accessible to less advanced contemporary Arab students. Many classical recensions in fact performed the same task for people who lived in days of old.

The teaching of philosophy also requires that works be written on the basis of these traditional sources, but dealing with more specific subjects, such as metaphysics, cosmology, natural philosophy, ethics, aesthetics, and so on. Such treatises, written from the Islamic point of view, are rare indeed, although a few fine examples may be found in Arabic, Persian, Turkish, and even Urdu. Treatises of this kind must be written on different levels, so as to reach the whole spectrum of students, from those undergoing the higher stage of secondary education to the most advanced. In the more advanced works of this kind, comparisons can also be made with non-Islamic thought, although separate works on "comparative philosophy" remain essential.

Muslims have been somewhat more successful in writing histories of philosophy, if one judges by numbers. Such works, many but not all emulating Western models, range from the large two-volume history edited by M. M. Sharif[21] and sponsored by the Pakistani government and the two-volume work on the history of Islamic philosophy edited by S. H. Nasr and Oliver Leaman to individual efforts, some of much more modest dimensions. Still, the Islamic world has not been able to produce such definitive and thorough works on the history of Islamic thought as those produced on their own traditions by Indian, Chinese, and Japanese scholars, not to speak of Western ones. What is needed in the case of Islamic thought is many more monographic studies, which would make known so many areas of learning that remain still *terra incognita.* A few decades ago one could hardly have imagined that the anthology prepared by Henry Corbin and Sayyid Jalāl al-Dīn Āshtiyānī dealing with Islamic philosophy in Persia alone and only since the Safavid period would have run into some seven weighty volumes. Even so, many basic selections had to be left out because of the unmanageable size of each volume.[22]

Finally, the teaching of Islamic philosophy requires the preparation of encyclopedias and philosophical dictionaries, based on traditional technical vocabulary of Islamic philosophy,[23] similar to those available for not only Western but also the Indian, Chinese, and Japanese traditions. At the present moment, knowledge about many facets of Islamic thought is not easily accessible and certainly beyond the means of most students even if they are advanced. Considering that Muslims were accustomed to composing encyclopedias dealing with various subjects, such as the Mu'tazlilite encyclopedia *al-Mughnī* of Qāḍī 'Abd al-Jabbār, the *Shifā'* of Ibn Sīnā on Peripatetic philosophy, and the *Biḥār al-anwār* ("Ocean of Light") of Mullā Muḥammad Bāqir Majlisī on Shī'ism, it is even more difficult to understand why this tradition has been rarely pursued in our own day. In various fields of intellectual life, certainly, such encyclopedias, presented in a contemporary manner and in such a way as to be easily accessible, are badly needed.

Of course, the Islamic world cannot wait until all these tasks are accomplished before its philosophy is taught seriously in its educational system. Time is in fact a most important factor because the withering influence of secularizing ideologies and false philosophies continues to erode the foundations of the Islamic intellectual tradition before our very eyes. Every effort should therefore be made to do what is possible here and now. It must always be remembered that the greatest obligation of Muslims is to the Truth (*al-Ḥaqq*), which is another name of Allah. From this Truth, or *al-Ḥaqīqah,* has issued, not only a Divine Law whose obedience guarantees human felicity on the plane of action and a path to reach God, but also a wisdom that alone is the guarantee of authentic knowledge in which is also the royal path to the Divine. The loss of this wisdom cannot but affect the understanding and mode of the attachment of many to Islam itself and to its Divine Law. The teaching of Islamic philosophy as *ḥikmah,* or wisdom, and in the sense defined above is the means for attaining the Truth and protecting it, providing ways for repelling the attacks that are made against it from all sides, thereby protecting the citadel of faith, or *īmān*. Its teaching in the correct manner is, therefore, in a sense a religious duty, for any step taken in the understanding of *al-Ḥaqīqah* as well as in providing means to protect it from profanation, distortion, and obliteration lies at the heart of the concerns of Islam as the message and the embodiment of the Truth, for whose sake alone human beings were created and placed as vicegerents of God on earth.

Chapter Eleven

TRADITIONAL ISLAMIC SCIENCE AND WESTERN SCIENCE

Common Heritage, Diverse Destinies

It goes without saying that at the heart of the problems posed by the confrontation of traditional Islam and the modern world stands the question of modern science and its applications in the form of modern technology, which, however, pose their own problems that are not always the same as those of modern science.[1] Is modern science simply the continuation of Islamic science? Is the unquestioned and blind acceptance of modern science by most Muslims today simply the reclaiming of their own heritage? Is there in fact such a thing as Islamic science, as I and now many others have been claiming for the past half century? In view of the fact that modern science and technology are spreading rapidly throughout the Islamic world, supported by every form of government from conservative to liberal, from "fundamentalist" to "secular," and the problems created by this process are increasing from day to day, those and similar questions remain some of the main concerns of the Muslim intelligentsia; numerous responses have been given to them during the past two centuries and continue to be given today.[2]

From my earliest works written in the 1950s and 1960s, I have claimed that there is such a thing as Islamic science with a twelve-hundred-year tradition of its own and that this science is Islamic not only because it was cultivated by Muslims, but because it is based on a worldview and a cosmology rooted in the Islamic revelation.[3] This is in fact true *mutatis mutandis* of other traditional sciences, whether they are Babylonian, Egyptian, Chinese, Hindu, Buddhist, or otherwise.[4] To bring out the problems that modern science poses for traditional Islamic thought and civilization, it is of some value to compare and contrast Islamic science and Western science, which in fact shared to a large extent the same heritage of antiquity; Islamic science then exercised deep influence upon Western science, and yet the two followed very divergent destinies.

To understand all that separates the traditional sciences in general in their worldviews, methodologies, goals, and significance from modern science, no comparison is as revealing as that of Islamic and Western science, precisely because of their common heritage and the influence of Islamic science in the West. There are many different forms and schools of traditional science, but either they were cultivated in areas far away from Europe and remained completely removed from the stages of the development of Western science or they preceded it by many centuries and, therefore, are seen more as the historical background of Western science or distant developments of a completely foreign nature rather than a parallel tradition to be noted for its contrast with and similarities to what was to take place over the centuries in the West.

Islamic science is one of the most important schools of traditional science because of both the wealth of its achievements and the survival of its teaching. It is a major scientific tradition that shared more or less with the West the common heritage of antiquity and a similar religious and philosophical universe, but that, in contrast to what occurred in the West from the seventeenth century on, remained faithful to the traditional point of view. Moreover, this tradition was itself influential in the rise of medieval and Renaissance science in the West, which still possessed a traditional character before the Scientific Revolution. Yet Islamic science did not share in any way in those upheavals that transformed the science cultivated by Robert Grosseteste in his treatise *On Light* to the physics of Galileo's *Discorsi* and Newton's *Principia*.

It is true that Islam inherited certain aspects of the scientific heritage of the Mediterranean world that were not known to the West, not to speak of the sciences of India and ancient Persia, which never reached the Occident save through Islamic science itself. Islam inherited nearly the whole corpus of Aristotelian science, including the works of his Alexandrian commentators, Platonic cosmology, most of the important scientific achievements of Alexandria and its satellites in Pergamon, and similar centers, and the more esoteric strands of Greek science associated with both Pythagoreanism and Hermeticism.[5] Muslim scientists also became acquainted early in the history of Islam with Sassanid astronomy and pharmacology and the Indian sciences, especially medicine, astronomy, and mathematics. They also gained knowledge of certain aspects of Babylonian science that were not even transmitted to the Greeks as well as some elements of Chinese science, particularly in the field of alchemy.

Not all of these strands of the sciences of antiquity, even the Greek and Alexandrian, reached the Christian West directly. Much of the Aristotelian heritage, Hermeticism and Pythagoreanism, remained unknown in Europe until the second millennium of the Christian era and then became known mostly through Islamic sources. It might be argued that the heritage of Western science and Islamic science were therefore not the same. But the fact remains that both were heirs to the sciences of the Mediterranean world, and their knowledge of the natural order, concept of law, causality, and general cosmology drew much from the same sources, although each developed these inherited concepts differently. Moreover, even if this difference of early heritage is accepted, the West itself became heir to early Islamic science and, through this science, to the sources that Islam had inherited and itself developed for several centuries before the translations made in Toledo in the eleventh century began to make much of Islamic science available in Latin. Also even if one leaves aside the earlier history of science in the West, which points to the much richer development of Islamic science from the eighth to the eleventh century than anything to be seen in Christian Europe at this time, the fact remains that by the thirteenth century medieval European science was developing along lines parallel to and usually based upon Islamic science. These two traditions were much closer to each other than, let us say, medieval Latin science and Chinese science or even Indian and Chinese science.

Considering the fact that Christianity and Islam belong to the same family of Abrahamic religions and that the philosophical schools of Islam soon came to find their counterparts in both Western Judaism and Christianity, one might have expected science to "develop"[6] in the Christian West along lines similar to those that one observes in traditional Islamic civilization. This parallelism would seem to be especially dictated by similarity of methods, cosmological and philosophical ideas concerning matter, motion, and so on, and the goal and end of the sciences of nature as means of discovering the wisdom of God found in both Islamic and medieval and Renaissance Western science. The School of Chartres,

Albertus Magnus, Robert Grosseteste, Roger Bacon, Raymond Lull, and many others were cultivating sciences very similar in nature, method, and scope to those of the Muslims from whom they had learned so much.

Yet in the West by the fourteenth century nominalism was already gaining the upper hand in theological circles, while Christian philosophy was gradually becoming eclipsed. While during what is called the Renaissance, science in the West was still of a basically traditional character, philosophical ideas based on rationalism and humanism were becoming dominant and preparing the ground for that scientific revolution that was brought about primarily by Descartes, Galileo, Kepler, and finally Newton. Between Robert Grosseteste and Newton, at least the Newton of the *Principia,* or Roger Bacon and Francis Bacon a transformation took place in the West in the understanding of the very goal, meaning, and methodology of science that was not at all either emulated or repeated until much later in the Islamic world on the basis of what had occurred in the West. The modern astronomy and physics of Galileo and Newton were based on an already secularized view of the cosmos, the reduction of nature to pure quantity, which could then be treated mathematically, and a complete separation between the knowing subject and the object to be known based on Cartesian dualism.[7] A new science was indeed born, one that discovered much in the realm of quantity, but at the price of losing the traditional worldview and neglecting the spiritual dimension and qualitative aspect of nature—a tradeoff the bitter fruits of which are only now being fully tasted through the consequences of the environmental crisis.

In contrast to these transformations in the West, in the Islamic world the sacred character of God's creation continued to dominate the intellectual horizons. The symbolic sciences of nature as expounded during earlier centuries of Islamic history from the time of Jābir ibn Ḥayyān to that of Suhrawardī continued to be cultivated, while mathematical and physical sciences continued to be studied in the bosom of the symbolic sciences and in light of the metaphysical and cosmological principles derived from the Quranic revelation.[8] On the philosophical level such figures as Ṣadr al-Dīn Shīrāzī, the contemporary of Descartes, added a significant new chapter to the Islamic philosophy of nature, but in the sciences themselves innovation decreased; however, knowledge of the traditional sciences and its expansion in certain fields continued to some extent, as can be seen in development of fivefold symmetry and the application of these sciences in such domains as architecture and the making of tiles and dyes. A civilization that created the Shah Mosque of Isfahan or the Taj Mahal in India could not be simply dismissed as of no significance in the realm of sciences and technology, nor could the existing traditional sciences be considered insignificant simply because they did not change and develop in the manner of Western science.

Muslims continued to create and/or to preserve glories of art, thought, and traditional technology and science within their own traditional worldview based on the harmony with nature and awareness of the spiritual significance of nature in human life, while the West was rapidly developing a science based on considering nature a "thing" or an "it" to be quantitatively studied, conquered, controlled, manipulated, and, finally, despite the opposition of many scientists, raped with such ferocity that the results now threaten human existence itself. This process continued until the applications of that science based on power rather than contemplative wisdom provided such military advantage to the West that it was able to colonize most of the Islamic world and finally destroy, if not completely, at least to a large extent the homogeneous Islamic civilization that had developed parallel to that of the West for so many centuries.

For several centuries, as the Eurocentric conception of history was taken for granted even in the intellectually colonized East, the development of science in the West was considered the crowning achievement of the whole history of science of humanity. Modern science came to be considered globally as the only valid science of nature, and the question of the parallel development of science in another civilization was rarely posed. It is only now, when the horrors of modern war and the environmental disasters brought about by the application of modern science along with the unprecedented alienation of human beings from God, nature, and themselves have become manifest to everyone, that one may even ask about parallel developments of science elsewhere. Finally, one can at last ask not only why Islam and China, with their long and rich scientific traditions, did not produce a Descartes or a Galileo, but rather why Europe did. To understand the roots of the crisis of present-day humanity, it is necessary to address this last question and especially to inquire into the factors that caused the destinies of science in the West and the Islamic world to become separated and the two civilizations to part ways so drastically. Considering the incomparable value of what was lost of traditional knowledge in comparison to what was gained in the quantitative and empirical knowledge of the physical world, it is most important to delve into the factors of a negative nature that destroyed the vision of the traditional cosmos in the West and blinded Westerners to the comparative value of what was lost and what was gained in that process, a process that transformed Europe from the land of traditional Christian civilization to the citadel of the first civilization in historic times based on the negation of the traditional worldview.

Many factors led to the development of science in the West in such a manner that the science cultivated in the School of Chartres and the Oxford School of the thirteenth century and that cultivated in Paris and Oxford four centuries later seem to belong to two different universes rather than to a single civilization. The main factors, however, can be summarized and enumerated under several headings. The most central of these factors, which was most responsible for the difference between the destinies of science in Islam and science in the West, is the eclipse of the sapiential aspect of Christianity toward the end of the Middle Ages; in contrast, the sapiential tradition of Islam has continued to this day. The gnostic and sapiential modes of Christianity were flowering in the teachings of such figures as Dante, Meister Eckhart, and even Nicholas of Cusa, when Christian civilization was mutilated by the intrusion of the paganism of antiquity in the form of Renaissance humanism; as a result, this civilization and its sapiential dimension could not bear their fruits completely.

Every science of nature relies upon a worldview concerning the nature of reality. Medieval Christianity shared with Islam a worldview based at once upon revelation and metaphysical knowledge drawn from the sapiential dimension of the tradition, although, as far as the metaphysical significance of nature was concerned, this knowledge was not as fully integrated into the mainstream of Christian thought as it was into that of Islam. Once this knowledge was eclipsed and for all practical purposes lost to the mainstream of modern Western thought, there was no means whereby a science based on metaphysical principles could be cultivated or even understood.[9] Without such knowledge the traditional sciences became opaque and even meaningless. Soon they ceased to satisfy the human need for causality. A vacuum was created that men sought to fill by means of a rationalistic philosophy grounded outside of the Christian tradition and a science of a purely earthly nature, which was, however, satisfactory from the point of view of rationalism and empiricism.

Having lost the vision of Heaven, the newly formed Western "intelligentsia" discovered a new earth, whose discovery they considered ample compensation for the infinitely superior Heaven, whose very reality they cast into doubt fairly rapidly.[10] Without metaphysical knowledge, the traditional sciences could not survive. First, they reappeared as occult sciences shorn of their metaphysical significance, and finally their residue survived as mere superstition in the eyes of those for whom any science pointing to metaphysical principles beyond themselves and to realms of reality beyond the physical can be nothing but superstition. All that had been considered the highest form of knowledge became subverted to mere conjecture and shorn of the dignity of being called science, while all that was accepted as science was accepted as such on condition that this form of knowledge had no relation to any knowledge of a higher order. No single factor was as significant in the parting of ways of the West not only from Islam, but from all other traditions, than the loss in the West of gnosis or sapience and the ever increasing eclipse of the metaphysical dimension of Christianity from the thirteenth century on.

A closely related factor was the rise of nominalism in the fourteenth century. By depriving intelligence of the possibility of knowing the Platonic archetypes, or ideas of things, and in fact denying that universals possessed reality beyond that of names, nominalism affected profoundly not only theology, but also philosophy. Nominalism, by basing religious truth upon faith rather than upon both faith and knowledge, had no small role in secularizing knowledge and preparing the ground for the rise of modern science. The destruction of medieval Christian philosophy based on ontology could not but lead, after a period of uncertainty and groping, to the rationalistic philosophy associated with Cartesianism that served as the necessary basis for the seventeenth-century Scientific Revolution.[11] Without the withering criticism by nominalism, medieval Christian philosophy and theology would not have relinquished their claim to the role of knowledge in discovering the nature of things in light of higher principles; instead, it caused them to leave the field of battle without any defense before the onslaught of secularism, rationalism, and empiricism, which were, as a result, able to gain a remarkably easy victory.

The domination of nominalism combined with a tendency to substitute logic for philosophy was both a result of the loss of the symbolic science[12] of nature, that is, a science that concerns itself with natural phenomena as symbols and not only facts, and a cause in the destruction of such a science, which is always wed to metaphysics. Medieval Europeans still understood the language of symbolism that dominated their art and science as well as nearly every level of expression of their religion. A medieval cathedral is an expression of a symbolic and sacred science of the cosmos and in turn enables people to gain access to the realities to which such a science leads, provided they still possess that "symbolist spirit" that Western medievals shared to a large extent with the rest of humanity, a "spirit" that perceives cosmic and natural phenomena as symbols and not simply events or facts without a higher level of meaning.

As early as the late Middle Ages there appeared a rationalistic tendency that had lost sight of the symbolic content of the traditional sciences of nature. Although the life of the symbolic sciences of nature did not cease completely, as seen in Hermeticism and to a certain extent Pythagoreanism, which continued to be cultivated in certain circles, the center of the intellectual arena of western Europe became ever more occupied by a type of thought that was impervious and even blind to the language of symbolism. This type of thinking helped further destroy the influence of symbolic modes of thought, while the domination of a mentality blind to the symbolic significance of nature as well as of Sacred Scripture only helped to strengthen nominalism and rationalism and make possible their victory. Soon, symbols became reduced to signs and facts; both the book of nature and the book of revelation became opaque and reduced to their literal and external level of meaning.

Parallel with the loss of the symbolic sciences of nature, there occurred a marked decrease of interest in sapiential commentaries on Sacred Scripture. Blindness to the inner dimension of the "book" of nature was accompanied by the neglect of the inner meaning of revealed scripture. Although the symbolic sciences of both nature and Sacred Scripture survived to some extent on the edges of the main currents of development of European thought, the mainstream was left bereft of these sciences. What remained was a literal and external interpretation of religion left face-to-face with a science of the literal, quantitative, and factual aspects of nature, which saw nothing in nature but brute facts to be gathered solely empirically and understood only rationally and mathematically; this science no longer had any intellectual relation with the existing religion except one of confrontation or indifference. As the *vestigia Dei* (vestiges of God) became reduced to quantifiably veritable facts, science developed in a direction in which it could no longer concern itself with whatever those facts or laws established by it could possibly signify beyond the realm of facts.[13] A Jacob Böhme could still cultivate a symbolic science of nature in the seventeenth century; but by then he was no longer at the center of the arena of scientific activity in Europe and not even in the mainstream of the religious and theological thought of his day.

Parallel with this loss of a symbolic science of nature one can observe the rapid process of the desacralization of the cosmos in medieval Christian thought. In the Bible the cosmos still possesses a sacred aspect, and certain verses, such as, "The invisible things of Him from the creation of the world are clearly seen, being understood by the things that are made, *even* His eternal power and Godhead,"[14] indicate the significance of this theme in Christian Sacred Scripture. Early Christianity, faced with the danger of naturalism in the Greco-Roman world and seeking to prevent at all costs the danger of cosmolatry (worship of the cosmos),[15] did not emphasize the spiritual significance of nature, drawing a rigid line between nature and supernature. Yet in the early Middle Ages the religious significance of nature was not forgotten, at least in the writings of such men and women as Erigena, Hugo of St. Victor, and Hildegard of Bingen, while the traditional Christian cosmos continued to be populated by angels and spirits. By the thirteenth century, however, the more dominant schools of Scholasticism began the philosophical and theological process of desacralizing the cosmos and thereby making it, despite their wish, a suitable object of study for a purely quantitative science of nature.

The reception given to Ibn Sīnā in the Latin West in comparison to that given to Ibn Rushd is indicative of this trend. Avicennan cosmology emphasizes the significance of angels who carry out the commands of God in the cosmos and make possible its life and order. For Ibn Sīnā cosmology is inseparable from angelology.[16] For Ibn Rushd, however, the "souls of the spheres," which are identified with angelic substances, are dispensed with in favor of the intelligences. The fact that the Latin West was more influenced by Averroism than by Avicennism and that even those deeply influenced by Ibn Sīnā tried to brush aside the central role he accorded to angels in both his cosmology and epistemology points to an important tendency taking place at that time. This tendency refused to accept the angels of the traditional Christian cosmos as essential and necessary to the governance and functioning of the cosmic and the natural order. The traditional cosmos became thus philosophically and theologically prepared to be treated as that great mechanical clock whose laws would be discovered by a Galileo, a Newton, and others by means of a mechanical science born during the seventeenth-century Scientific Revolution.

The fascination with mechanical clocks was already present in Europe long before Galileo wrote his *Discorsi*. Likewise, the angels had ceased to be considered metaphysically necessary to the running of the cosmos long before the advent of the seventeenth century philosophers and scientists even if ordinary men and women continued to believe in them and revere them into later centuries. It seems as if the vision of nature in the minds of European thinkers had already gained a strong mechanical component before an actual science based on the mechanistic point of view developed. Moreover, this science in turn helped to generalize and expand the mechanistic philosophy to such an extent that, by the eighteenth century, it had become part and parcel of the worldview of Europeans, going beyond the confines of the sciences of nature to embrace the whole philosophical *Weltanschauung* of mainstream Western thought.

The desacralization of nature and the cosmos was also abetted by a factor of practical import, namely, the quest for gaining power over nature. The traditional sciences of nature sought to lead one to wisdom and enable one to perfect the soul through the contemplation of Divine Wisdom in God's handiworks. Even in alchemy, where there was an attempt to accelerate the natural processes of "giving birth" to gold,[17] in a way an attempt to gain power over nature, the whole process was contained within the matrix of tradition and protected by the presence of the sacred. The ultimate goal of true alchemists was not in fact to gain power and control over the external world, but rather over their own soul; alchemy was based on the correspondence between the microcosm and the macrocosm, and the spiritual goal was to transmute the base metal of the soul into the gold of sanctity, not simply to manipulate substances in order to gain wealth.[18]

Gradually, with the rise of mercantilism and the rebellion of modern Westerners against the traditional Christian image of human beings as fallen beings alien to this world, there grew the desire not only to explore the world, but also to dominate it. The age of exploration was also the age of exploitation, domination, and exercise of power over nature with the aim of tearing her riches from her bosom. Western science since the Scientific Revolution has become increasingly associated, although not completely, with power and control. The goal of science in the minds of many, if not all, of its practitioners has become the control and manipulation of nature, not its contemplation. In direct contrast to the Islamic world, where science has always been related to wisdom and even its utility has been envisaged in the light of human needs as immortal beings, science in the modern West became wed to the quest for power, control, and to a large extent wealth, and the utility of science became confined to the welfare of human beings seen as purely earthly creatures with no needs beyond those of animals with certain mental powers. Many notable scientists in the West were and remain to this day opposed to the wedding between science and power, but there is no doubt that one of the factors that caused the destinies of Islamic science and Western science to follow such diverse paths despite so many common factors is this relation of science to worldly power, a relation that remained totally alien to traditional Islamic science. It is only modernist and so-called fundamentalist Muslims today who claim otherwise and who seek to master Western science at any cost because of its relation to the power they seek to gain.

If one were to ask what element or elements within Western Christian thought were responsible for this turn of events in Europe as far as the development of the sciences of nature are concerned, one could point most of all to the type of theology that developed in the Occident. In order to avoid the danger of naturalism, Christianity as formulated by the Latin Fathers drew too strong a distinction between the supernatural and the natural orders, did not emphasize sufficiently the cosmic function of the "Word become flesh," and did not consider central the spiritual message of nature. Despite the songs dedicated to nature by early Irish monks, the development of a Celtic theology of nature, and even the development of Christian Hermeticism, which Christianized a whole traditional science of nature, the mainstream of Catholic theology did not concern itself as much with nature as did Islam, or even Judaism, which interacted with both Christianity and Islam.

The voice of St. Francis of Assisi singing the canticle of the sun was not typical of the Christian spirituality of the Occident any more than were the cosmic visions of Hildegard of Bingen. The discovery of nature by Renaissance art and science appeared, therefore, almost as a "revelation" but outside the mainstream of the Christian tradition, while the whole realm of nature was soon surrendered by Christianity to science to be dealt with irrespective of the religious and spiritual consequences of the development of a purely quantitative science. The abdication of religion in the West from the realm of nature, especially after Galileo, did not appear at that time as a great defeat for the religious worldview, because the rule of religion over this realm had already been a half-hearted one, since the integration of a complete theology and metaphysics of nature into the main current of Christian theological thought had never been fully achieved. As a result, despite St. Francis or Albertus Magnus, who was at once a theologian and a scientist, and despite the later religious reactions of German mystics and the Romantic movement against the total dominance of a purely mechanical science of nature, the ground was left clear for such a science to develop without constraint or opposition of a serious kind and to claim for itself completely monopoly of knowledge of the natural realm. Any spiritual view of nature was relegated to the category of "nature mysticism" or other categories irrelevant to serious science, while, as already mentioned, what remained of the traditional sciences of nature in the West became reduced to the category of the occult or even superstition, to survive solely in the margin of Western intellectual life.

Finally, it must be remembered that what distinguishes the destinies of science in the West and the Islamic world are not only the presence of the metaphysical and cosmological doctrines of Suhrawardī, Ibn 'Arabī, Ṣadr al-Dīn Shīrāzī, and the like at the heart of the Islamic intellectual tradition and the eclipse, after the Middle Ages, of doctrines of such nature in the West and their relegation to the periphery of the intellectual life of Westerners. One must also consider in a more inward sense the continuous presence in Islam of contemplatives of a sapiential nature and gnostics, despite the relative decrease of their number during the next few centuries in contrast to their almost complete disappearance in the West during the modern period. Contemplatives who are of a gnostic bent are channels of grace for nature. They hear the invocation of nature in the solitude of high mountains and deserts, along the shore of the sea and in the heart of forests. They pray with nature and act as her protector and intermediary vis-à-vis the Divine Presence. The minds of such sages are indeed a mirror that reflects the light shining in their hearts. Their speculation is a reflection of the knowledge of the heart upon the plane of the mind, according to the literal meaning of the term *speculum,* which means nothing other than reflection in a mirror. From the heart a light is reflected upon the mirror of the mind, which in turn provides a doctrine concerning nature that cannot but reflect in conceptual terms that intimacy and inner *sympatheia* that contemplative gnostics share with the inner reality of nature.

Once that light ceases to reflect upon the mind, the fundamental connection between humanity and the inner significance of nature becomes severed. Not only do the metaphysical and cosmological doctrines concerning nature become opaque and meaningless, but people lose the capacity to hear the prayer of nature and pray with her. The rustling of the wind in the forest, the sound of the brooks rushing down the mountainside, and the chant of the birds celebrating the rising of the sun can no longer be heard as the invocation (*dhikr*) of God's Blessed Names and as His Praise according to the Quranic verse, "All things hymn the praise of God." Rather, they become meaningless noise, at best pleasant but devoid of a spiritual message to be heard and understood. Nature, rather than aiding such types who have now become deaf and blind to the world of the Spirit, hides her inner reality from them, seeming outwardly to confirm the view of that science that would deny the existence of this inner reality.

But nature's "turning away" from an avaricious and irresponsible humanity bent on the rape of nature with the tools of a quantitative science and in the name of human progress and welfare based on a purely earthly and animal conception of human beings must not be considered proof of the complete surrender of nature and the final victory of modern science and technology. Nor must the remarkable success of Western science to make known the quantitative aspects of the natural order be seen as proof of either its claim to the monopoly of all knowledge concerning nature or of the lack of validity of the traditional sciences developed by Islam and other traditions. Already the havoc wrought by modern science has made many a thinking person pause and ask about the wisdom of accepting modern science as the only possible science of nature and to seek, for the first time since the rise of modern science, to understand seriously the significance and the worldview of the traditional sciences. It is also for Muslims to ponder over these questions and to understand how important it is for Islam itself as well as for its culture and civilization to preserve its own scientific tradition and to understand, amid its confrontation with the modern world, what modern science really is and what it is not.

As the world of creation continues to suffer as a result of the applications of modern science, the prayer of nature and her creatures, which have always accompanied contemplatives who seek refuge from the noise and fury of the world in her bosom, has meanwhile turned to a prayer to the Creator for protection against the ever greater modern ravaging of the natural order. And despite appearances and despite what seems to be the complete victory of Promethean humanity over nature, the prayer of nature and the creatures of the natural order will not go unheeded. It is nature that will have the final victory, for her victory is that of the Truth over falsehood and of the Spirit over every form of materialism, scientific or otherwise, that would deny its reality. To know nature in her intimate reality and according to the norms of the traditional sciences of nature, so richly cultivated in Islam, is to gain a knowledge that is permanent, that satisfies the mind while nourishing the soul. It is also to gain a knowledge that no form of quantitative science can replace, a knowledge without which human beings cannot ultimately survive on earth, but with the aid of which they can live in harmony with themselves and with nature, because they live in harmony with that Reality that is at once the origin of themselves and of the natural order.

Art and Architecture

Jāmiʿ Mosque, Isfahan, Iran. From the fifth/eleventh to the tenth/sixteenth centuries.

Chapter Twelve

ISLAMIC ART AND ITS SPIRITUAL SIGNIFICANCE IN THE CONTEMPORARY WORLD

Without doubt one of the most important domains of tension created by the cultural invasion of the traditional Islamic world by modernism is that of art, understood in its most universal sense, including architecture. In contrast to days of old, today in many parts of that world, especially in cities and towns, nearly everything, from the spaces in which Muslims live, to the objects with which they surround themselves, to the clothing that they wear, to the sounds they hear, is affected by the penetration of an art and architecture coming from the modern West. This foreign import is grounded in an understanding of human beings and their art that is diametrically opposed to the Islamic conception of who man is and what constitutes the meaning and purpose of the art that human beings create. Throughout this book reference has been made in passing to this all-important subject. It is now necessary to turn more fully to it by elucidating some of the principles of Islamic art, or one might say the philosophy of Islamic art.

When Muslims lived in a world completely determined by the spirit and concrete teachings of traditional Islam, there was no need for written formulations of the Islamic philosophy of art. The wisdom (*ḥikmah*) underlying this art and the techniques and methods (*fann*) necessary to create Islamic art and architecture were transmitted orally from masters to apprentices, and where there were written texts, they were often kept secret and not divulged publicly. That is why there are no sections on art per se in Islamic works of philosophy such as those of Ibn Sīnā or Mullā

Ṣadrā. Those who did write about the science of forms and theories of beauty, subjects central to the Islamic philosophy of art, did so within the context of more general considerations. For example, one has to go through the thousands of verses of the *Mathnawī* of Rūmī to bring out the science of forms that he expounds here and there within the vast ocean of gnosis that is the *Mathnawī*.

It was the inundation of the Islamic world, from the nineteenth century on, by modern Western art and architecture and the stark contrast between the Islamic and the modern in matters ranging from architecture and urban design to dress that has now necessitated the formulation, in a contemporary language, of the traditional Islamic understanding of this matter. And so let us turn to Islamic art and its spiritual significance for contemporary Muslims.[1]

When it comes to discussing the subject of Islamic art in the West, it is necessary, strangely enough, to demonstrate, first of all, that there is such a thing as Islamic art and that this art is Islamic not because it was created by Muslims, but because it draws its principles from the Islamic revelation and is one of the most important manifestations of the spirit and form of that revelation. When the history of art began as an academic discipline in Europe in the nineteenth century, many turned their attention to the domain of Islamic art, which they, however, treated not as Islamic art as such, but only historically and on the basis of ethnic and geographically defined cultural zones. And so there appeared works on Persian, Egyptian, Turkish, or Muslim Indian art, just to cite a few examples, but rarely any on Islamic art per se. Also major Western museums from the Louvre to the Victoria and Albert to the Metropolitan created galleries and sections devoted to Persian art, Ottoman art, and so forth, but there was no distinct section devoted to Islamic art. This model was even followed in Islamic countries that established museums on the basis of Western models. Before World War II the only Islamic city to have a major museum of Islamic art was Cairo. The same situation also existed in Western museums for other types of Oriental art, such as those of India and Japan.

The pioneering works of Ananda K. Coomaraswamy in the early twentieth century, followed by those of such scholars as Heinrich Zimmer and Stella Kramrich, who were deeply influenced by him, made it clear that there was such a thing as Hindu and Buddhist art and that these arts

View of the Mosque of the Prophet in Medina. Begun in the first/seventh century, with most recent renovations in the fourteenth/twentieth century.

were profoundly related to these religions in their meaning, symbolic language, and spiritual significance. It was not until after World War II, however, that this truth was also made evident for Islamic art, thanks mostly to the efforts of Burckhardt and his collaborator and friend Jean-Louis Michon, but also to the work of a few academic historians of art such as Richard Ettinghausen. After the two Festivals of the World of Islam held in London in the 1970s, the reality of Islamic art became widely accepted in the West. One major museum after another, whether in Europe or North America, organized galleries devoted to Islamic art. Universities such as Harvard began to establish chairs of Islamic art, and works began to appear in Western languages concerned with Islamic art as such. The truth that an art can be at the same time Islamic and Persian or Egyptian, for example, in the same way that an art can be Japanese and yet Buddhist or a thirteenth-century French cathedral is French but even more importantly Christian architecture became well established. And yet even among the many academic scholars who now accept the category of Islamic art, few have delved into why and in what way this art is Islamic.[2]

The interior of the Mezquita, Cordoba, Spain, second/eighth century.

This brief history has been mentioned to bring to light how recent the acceptance of the very category of Islamic art has been in the West. As for the Islamic world itself, attention to Islamic art has also been recent, but for different reasons. Until the onslaught of the West during the colonial period, Muslims lived in an, artistically speaking, homogeneous world where everything created by human beings, from objects seen to sounds heard, was related in one way or another to Islamic art and *was* in fact for the most part Islamic art. It was the increasingly rapid destruction of this homogeneous world with all its diversity and yet inner unity that necessitated in the fourteenth/twentieth century the rise of consciousness among a number of Muslim thinkers, artists, and architects of the significance of Islamic art as such and its spiritual significance for the life of Muslims in all its different dimensions.

Like Buddhism and Christianity, Islam developed its art and created an ambience within which its religious and spiritual realities were reflected in a concrete manner before it developed its great theological and philosophical syntheses. Islamic art, whose earliest examples in the form of calligraphy, geometric design, and architecture go back to the first and second Islamic centuries, came into being as a result of the spirit and form of the Quranic revelation and more specifically the *ḥaqīqah* at the heart of the Quran and in the hands of men and women whose inner being, mental landscape, and general worldview were completely transformed by the Islamic revelation and the grace, or *barakah,* emanating from it. Like all sacred and traditional art, Islamic art was based on heavenly inspiration and not only human invention and artistic creativity.

As certain authorities on traditional art such as Burckhardt have pointed out, the role of this "heavenly inspiration," which includes both a purely spiritual element and specific sacred forms, in the creation of the art of traditional civilizations can be better understood by appealing to the Aristotelian theory of form and matter. According to this theory any object, whether natural or constructed, is composed of form and matter, those terms being understood as *forma* and *materia* in classical Western works and not in the modern sense, although the modern understanding of these terms still bears a relation to the earlier defined concepts of *forma* and *materia.* A wooden chair is made by imposing the form of chair upon the matter or material of wood; a snowflake consists of a particular geometric form imposed upon frozen water under specific conditions.

Now, if we apply this idea to Islamic art, we can say that the form of this art derives from the spirit and form of the Islamic revelation and the matter, in the first instance, from the psychological and mental substance of the people to whom it was revealed and those who were later transformed by it. On a second level, the "matter" of this art can be considered the artistic heritage that Muslims received and that they turned into Islamic art through the transformations they brought about in what they had inherited by means of the applications of the Islamic form and principles related to it. At the heart of the Islamic revelation stands the doctrine of unity (*al-tawḥīd*), which also means integration and wholeness. Islam is a religion based upon the One, the Reality that is the Absolute and the Infinite and not on a particular manifestation of the One in the form of an incarnation, or what Hindus would call avataric descent.

The psychological and mental substance of the first recipients of the Islamic revelation were the Arabs who belonged to the nomadic branch of the Semitic people. Islam spiritualized certain traits of this nomadic Semitic mentality, and this in turn played a major role in the creation of Islamic art in ways that shall be discussed below. As to the heritage of the arts and architecture of the earlier civilizations that Islam encountered, it consisted in the first instance of works of the Persian Sassanid and Byzantine civilizations, some forms of art of the pre-Islamic Arabs, and in a few instances those of the Romans. Later, as Islam spread, it encountered other forms of art, such as the Indian, Chinese, Malay, and Black African, which it also transformed into distinct Islamic art forms. This transformation always occurred with full consideration of natural and climatic diversity and the artistic genius of the various non-Arab and non-Persian ethnic groups who created the art and architecture of various areas in the Islamic world outside of the heartland, whose art was first created by Arabs and Persians. In any case everywhere in the world one can observe both unity and remarkable diversity in Islamic art, which nevertheless reflects in different ways those traits that were marked by unity and the spiritualized nomadic Semitic mentality that persisted from the beginning of the earthly life of Islam.

Some of the traits of this mentality are vivid awareness of the transience of the world, opposition to overconcentration and fixation in a particular point of space, which is anathema to the nomadic mentality, closeness to the rhythms of nature, and the creation of living spaces that are not cut off from the natural order. This can be seen even in traditional Islamic architecture and urban design that belong by definition to the arts of sedentary people and not to nomadic arts. The pre-Islamic Arabs had no architecture of any significance, although the Ka'bah itself can be considered in an esoteric manner the prototype of the Islamic architecture that developed later. And yet Islamic architecture and urban design nearly everywhere reflect these traits in numerous ways, for example, mosques open to natural space and houses built to reflect the idea that one is not going to live in this world "forever." The building of private houses out of mud and brick rather than stone in a country such as Persia, where so much stone is available, was not for economic reasons, but for a religious and philosophical one. When modern concrete came to Iran and some began to use it for building houses, an old man who still lived within the traditional Islamic worldview once asked me, "Why are these people using concrete for their houses? Do they think they are going to live a thousand years? Each generation should build its house anew." This attitude is a reflection of the traits of a spiritualized nomadism, even within a civilization that created some of the greatest architectural masterpieces in human history; much more enduring edifices were constructed, however, where buildings that had a public and

Imam (Shah) Mosque, Isfahan, Iran, tenth/sixteenth century.

not only a private function, such as mosques, palaces, bazaars, schools, hospitals, and forts.

To come back to the form of Islamic art, as has been already mentioned, at its heart lies the doctrine of Unity, which is reflected in the creation of this art. Being based on the One, the Absolute, the sacred art of Islam was and remains aniconic in contrast to, let us say, the art of Hinduism, Buddhism, or Christianity, where the iconic representation of the gods or the founder of the religion plays a central role. Islamic sacred art is more like the art of Judaism, which, being also based on the centrality of God as the One, does not have iconic art. But since we live in the world of multiplicity, Islam had nevertheless to create an art that could reflect Unity in multiplicity. It had to create an ambience in which its followers could experience unity in multiplicity and multiplicity in unity, or what is called in Arabic *waḥdah* in *kathrah* and *kathrah* in *waḥdah*. To achieve this end the use of geometry and empty space was made central. Now, sacred geometry, that is, geometry considered in its symbolic significance, is to be found in nearly all sacred art, from Hindu temples to Egyptian temple paintings, from Christian icons to medieval cathedrals. But there is no sacred art in which sacred geometry is so evident and

Burūjirdī House, Kashan, Iran, thirteenth/nineteenth century.

visible as Islamic art.[3] That is why many in the West refer to this art as abstract art. But the use of "abstract" in this context is misleading, since it is usually juxtaposed to "concrete," which is then identified with the "real." Metaphysically, however, it can be said that it is God who alone is concrete Reality in the absolute sense and who is Ultimate Reality compared to which everything else is an "abstraction."

In any case geometric patterns and arabesques, which are themselves based on geometry, are for the Muslim mind, as for Plato, related to the intelligible world. They are more concrete realities than physical objects, not simply mental abstractions. Furthermore, geometric patterns in the form of often intertwined polygons represent the masculine and arabesques the feminine cosmic principle; their rhythmic repetition in Islamic art represents the principle of the rhythms of life itself. These forms are therefore symbolic of spiritual realities and are by no means simply accidental or merely decorative.

The void, or empty space, also plays a central role in Islamic art different from what one finds in Christian art. To Muslim sensibility the void is not simply nothing. It is not a thing, but it does represent, because of this very absence of things or visible forms, the "presence" of the "absent," or the invisible world (*'ālam al-ghayb*), which for Muslims connotes the spiritual world. That is why the space of the mosque is empty and why there is an "emptiness" even in traditional Muslim living spaces that are uncluttered by furniture, not to speak of statues, paintings, and the like. Something of the emptiness of the space of the desert is reflected in the spaces of Islamic art and architecture. Even the space of traditional urban areas is not defined by the outer surfaces of buildings, monuments, and the like, but by interiorized spaces defined by inner surfaces of walls, which some have called negative space.[4]

Many in the West and some contemporary Muslims, both modern and "fundamentalist," have claimed that there is no symbolism in Islamic art. This is a totally false assertion that mistakes symbol for sacred image. Of course Islamic art is not based on a sacred iconography, as are, let us say, Buddhist and Christian art, but that does not mean that Islamic art is not symbolic, if symbol is understood in its original sense of something that binds a lower level of reality to a higher one. Even the forms of letters of the Arabic alphabet used in Islamic calligraphy have a symbolic meaning, as do the colors used in Islamic art, from miniatures to cupolas, from the color white of early mosques and the traditional villages and towns of the Maghrib to the earthen color of places of habitation in Syria, Persia, and Afghanistan. In architecture light and water (for example, in the Alhambra) are used in a highly symbolic fashion, the symbolic significance of both of which is described eloquently in the Quran itself. And then there is the symbolism of geometric forms themselves, used in both architectural components and the decoration of surfaces. For example, the spherical cupola symbolizes Heaven; the square base, the earth; and the octagonal transition from square to circle, the angelic realm. In mosque architecture of the eastern lands of the Islamic world from Egypt to Bengal there are both domes and minarets; the first symbolizes the feminine principle or Divine Beauty and the second, the masculine principle or Divine Majesty.

Although, like all traditional art, Islamic art is symbolic, it is also realist, but not in the modern naturalistic sense that identifies reality with only the external aspects of the natural world. The "Islamic form" itself, which, along with certain principles, is responsible for the creation of Islamic art, is realist, not idealist, in the sense that it is created in accordance with the nature of reality not only on the physical level, but on its many levels, including the reality of the human state with all its strengths and weaknesses. Islam addresses men and women as such and does not idealize them as potential saints without of course neglecting that possibility. It caters to all human needs both spiritual and worldly, not only to spiritual needs. In fact, it makes no distinction between the sacred and profane, or secular, in human life.

This realism is reflected directly in diverse types of Islamic art. The space of the mosque rests in peace upon itself; heavy brick and stone are not fashioned to appear as if they were moving against the force of gravity upward, as one sees in Gothic cathedrals, which are based on another set of principles. In Islamic art materials are used in a way that reflects their natural reality. Clay is used according to the nature of clay, and the two-dimensional surface of a wall, a canvas, or a piece of paper is not presented as if it were three-dimensional. That is why, although Muslims possessed the geometric knowledge, they did not try to create the three-dimensional perspective we see in postmedieval Western art. Miniature painting, before its decadence resulting from the influence of Renaissance and seventeenth-century Western art, was always two-dimensional and remained faithful to the nature of the two-dimensional space on which the artists painted. In general there was great sensitivity to the nature of the materials used by artists and craftsmen, to the reality of these materials as God originally created them.

It might at first appear as paradoxical that despite this "realism," Islamic art has always avoided naturalism, that is, simply copying the external forms of nature, as we find in seventeenth- and eighteenth-century

Bādshāhi Mosque, Lahore, Pakistan, eleventh/seventeenth century.

European art. Traditional Muslims have always considered creating an animal or human form in painting or sculpture tantamount to attempting to copy the Divine creative act without, however, being able to breathe life into it, which is a sacrilegious act, based on a prophetic *ḥadīth* that confirms the validity of this attitude. Islamic art is in fact close to nature and her rhythms without being naturalistic. It is concerned with the modes of operation of nature in both her outward and inward aspects rather than simple emulation of its external forms. The fact that Islamic civilization, in contrast to the two great civilizations situated east and west of it, that is, Hindu and Buddhist India in the east and the Christian West, did not develop the art of sculpture to any appreciable extent has everything to do with the spiritual and intellectual principles of its worldview.

Having created a major world civilization, Islam did, however, create many other forms of art of the highest order, from calligraphy and architecture to arts associated with everyday life such as carpet weaving and the art of the dress. Moreover, it permitted remarkable diversity based on ethnic genius, climatic conditions, available techniques and materials, and many other local factors, a diversity that, however, reflects strongly the unitary principles of Islam. There are wooden mosques in Java, brick ones

Sultan Aḥmad Mosque, Istanbul, Turkey, eleventh/seventeenth century.

in Persia and Central Asia, stone ones in Turkey, Syria, and Egypt, and mud ones in Yemen and Mali, and they do not look the same, if viewed only outwardly. Yet they possess a remarkable inner unity that can be experienced by any perceptive observer. They all reflect on a deeper level the same principles.

On the basis of all the principles and factors mentioned above, Islamic civilization developed a hierarchy of the arts the knowledge of which is essential for the understanding of Islamic art.[5] Let us first turn to the plastic arts and architecture. At the top of this hierarchy stand Quranic calligraphy and mosque architecture,[6] both of which are related to what for Muslims is the Word of God, that is, the Quran. One depicts the Word in written form and the other creates spaces in which the Word is recited and reverberates. Moreover, the centrality of these sacred arts is reflected in the important role of calligraphy in general in Islamic civilization and the development in traditional Islamic towns of vernacular architecture whose spaces are in a sense the extension of the sacred space of the mosque. Moreover, the exalted role of architecture in the hierarchy of the arts is reflected not only in individual buildings, but also in a profound way in urban design. It also embraces the creation of courtyards with their sense of interiority and gardens that reflect the Garden of Paradise. In the Quran Paradise itself is often called the Garden, *al-firdaws,* which in fact is the Arabic form of the Middle Persian word *pardīs,* which means "garden." This word is likewise the origin of the English word "paradise."[7]

After calligraphy (along with the art of Quranic illumination) and architecture, which are the sacred arts at the heart of traditional plastic art of Islam and at the top of the hierarchy of that art, the most important arts are those that concern the daily life of human beings and therefore have a profound effect upon the human soul. They include carpet weaving, into which so much of the artistic creativity of Muslims has gone over the ages, inasmuch as carpets play a central role in the spaces of everyday living. There are also the arts associated with the creation of objects made for everyday use, from textiles, to utensils, to lamps, and so on. Then follows the art of the dress, both male and female, with all its diversity and yet unity in its effect upon the human soul; dress is the closest object to the soul after the body. In this art, as in architecture and urban design, there are certain conditions set by Divine Law, or *Sharī'ah.* In the case of dress, these conditions involve modesty and ease in the performance of the Islamic rites of ablution and the canonical prayers that involve various movements of the body, but the art itself issues from the inner truth, or *ḥaqīqah,* of the Quran and not from the Law. Female Islamic dress stresses femininity and male dress masculinity, and both highlight the dignity of the human body and bring out the role of human beings as God's vicegerents on earth.

Such arts dealing with objects of everyday life are usually referred to as minor arts in the West (the major arts are usually identified with painting and sculpture), but this kind of division into minor and major arts does not exist at all in Islamic art, which is based on the fact that the soul is much more affected by what it experiences every day than by a painting that one might see on a Sunday in a museum or a church. These so-called minor arts are therefore seen as major arts in the Islamic hierarchy of the arts. It might also be added that in traditional Islamic art there was also no category of fine arts, or *beaux-arts* in French, which developed as a result of the Industrial Revolution when most objects came to be made by machines, not human hands. It was this transformation in human life that created the new meaning of "art" as a particular *kind* of making things, rather than *ars,* which in Latin means simply "to make" or "to create." And it was the influence of the modern West upon the Islamic world that caused such languages as Arabic and Persian to coin such terms as *al-ṣanāʾiʿ al-mustaẓrafah* and *al-funūn al-jamīlah* (in Arabic) and *hunarhā-yi zībā* (in Persian), all of which are translations of "fine arts" or *beaux-arts.*

Although painting and sculpture do not figure prominently in the Islamic hierarchy of the arts, a word must be said about them. For reasons already mentioned, sculpture played a minor role in Islamic civilization; this civilization did not produce significant works of sculpture like those seen in the Christian, Hindu, and Buddhist worlds or in certain primal cultures such as those of Black Africa. But the case of painting is different. Several Islamic cultures have produced notable paintings, especially the Persian, Turkish, and Mogul; among Persian miniatures are some of the greatest masterpieces of the art of painting in the world. But this art form originated in connection with the arts of the book and was experienced mostly by those who read illustrated books. A certain number of popular paintings were, however, produced that adorned the walls of public places, such as bathhouses and inns, but they were for the most part folk art and were not as sophisticated as the examples of this art produced by other Muslim artists. And yet from the tenth/sixteenth century on some notable wall paintings began to appear in palaces; some representative examples are to be found in Safavid Isfahan.

Before leaving the subject of the plastic arts, it is important to mention the art of ornamentation and design, which relates to so many of the arts mentioned above. This art essentially involves geometric designs and arabesques, but also makes use of various colors (such as in the frontispieces of Mamlūk Qurans and in the blue and cobalt domes of Isfahan and Samarqand) and can be seen in the textile masterpieces produced in the ateliers of Isfahan, Delhi, and elsewhere as well as in the tile work of the mosques in Fez and Istanbul, not to speak of the lamps made in Damascus. The art of geometric design and ornamentation is ubiquitous in Islamic art and is one of its most notable features.

Art, however, is not only plastic. There is also the whole domain of the auditory arts that include not only music, but also poetry, which most Muslims over the ages have experienced primarily orally, not visually through individual reading. The highest form of music in the hierarchy of the acoustic arts is the chanting of the Quran in Arabic, although

The tomb of a saint in Kashan in Iran, thirteenth/nineteenth century

technically this chanting is not called *mūsīqā,* or music. Nevertheless, the psalmody of the Sacred Text, which surrounds the life of Muslims from birth to death and which can be heard even in modern cities inundated with noise and cacophony, is music of the highest order. This is followed by the chanting of religious songs, especially those associated with the praise of the Prophet and Sufi songs that are concerned with the love of God and the Prophet as well as with the realities of the spiritual life. Below these categories stands the classical music of various Islamic cultures, such as Persian, Arabic, Turkish, and northern Indian music and the Sundanese music of Java. Most of this classical musical tradition has been propagated and performed by the Sufis over the ages, as we see in the efforts of the members of the Mawlawiyyah Order in the Ottoman world in the creation and preservation of classical Turkish music. That is the reason why the various schools of classical music in the Islamic world have such spiritual depth and why much of this music is accompanied by Sufi or Sufi-inspired poetry, from *qawwālī* in India and Pakistan to traditional music in Morocco.

Below this level stands music related to specific vocations, such as military music or music played while weavers make a carpet or masons construct

Miḥrāb (prayer niche) of the Jāmi' Mosque, Isfahan, eighth/fourteenth century.

a building. And then there are the various forms of folk music that are widespread in villages concerned with agriculture or among nomads. All of these types of music still belong to traditional Islamic art and are imbued with its principles and values. Some among the exoteric interpreters of the religion in the Islamic world claim that Islam is against music, and this view is adopted by many "fundamentalists" today. But this view is patently false.

What Islam opposes is the type of music that leads to lasciviousness and the arousal of the fires of the lower passions, not music as such. Otherwise Islamic civilization could not have produced such a rich musical tradition. Even the Prophet enjoyed and permitted certain kinds of music, such as wedding music and caravan songs.

A few words must also be said about the art of poetry, although it is such a vast subject that its more detailed discussion would take us too far away from this summary presentation. It must, however, be mentioned that poetry is a central reality of the life of Muslims and lies at the heart of nearly all Islamic cultures. In its mystical and religious forms, it stands very high in the hierarchy of Islamic art, although it is not considered sacred art, strictly speaking. Poetry as sacred art belongs to the language of the Quran itself, although, like the term "music" (*al-mūsīqā*), which is not applied to the chanting of the Sacred Text, the term "poetry" (*al-shi'r*) is not usually applied to its verses and phrases. The reason for this "prohibition" is that pre-Islamic Arabs had developed a very high art of poetry, which, however, was divorced from truth, on the one hand, and was concerned to a large extent with telling the future, on the other. Poets are therefore castigated in the Quran, which distinguishes itself from the category of poetry, as the term was understood by the Arabs to whom it was revealed. It was precisely because of their highly developed poetry that early Arabs came to appreciate the eloquence of the Quran, as did Muslims of later generations, and the Divine Art of Quranic eloquence (*al-balāghah*) came to be easily accepted as a miracle.

The Quran is in fact a work of the highest eloquence and the supreme "poetry" of the Arabic language, which no human poet has been able to equal, although many have tried. Consequently, wherever Islam went, the art of poetry became central, as we see not only in Arabic, but also in other Islamic languages such as Persian, Turkish, Sindhi, Punjabi, Bengali, Urdu, and African languages such as Swahili. The ethos of Islamic culture and thought found some of its most remarkable expressions in poetry, and much of the teaching of the religion, from ethics to theology and metaphysics, was carried out through poetry, although of course prose was also used. Moreover, nearly all kinds of poetry, from elegies to lullabies, from didactic to lyrical and epic poetry, possessed religious significance. The most universal poetry of the Islamic peoples, however, is Sufi poetry, a genre around which Persian Sufi poets in fact formed several schools of literature in Asia and a genre that played a major role in the spread of Islam itself in much of Asia, especially among Turkic peoples and on the Indian subcontinent.

The tradition of Persian Sufi poetry produced such figures as Rūmī and Ḥāfiẓ. The translations of Rūmī into English are now the most widely sold works of any poet in North America, precisely because of the universality of his message and the timeliness of his thought, which is so timely precisely because it is timeless. As for Ḥāfiẓ, it has been said that in the world influenced by Persian culture, including not only Iran, Afghanistan, and Tajikistan, where Persian is the spoken tongue, but until the nineteenth century also in the Ottoman world and Muslim India, where Persian was understood by educated people, his *Dīwān* was the most commonly found book in Muslim homes after the Quran. One cannot overemphasize the spiritual significance of Sufi poetry when speaking of Islamic art in the wider sense of the word.

Finally, before leaving this discussion of traditional Islamic art, a word must also be said about the performing arts, which do not figure as prominently in the hierarchy of Islamic art as they do in some other traditions, such as Hinduism. Nevertheless Islamic civilization did produce both dance and theater of religious and spiritual significance. It is true that there is nothing in Islam to correspond to the Hindu goddess Nataraja and the sacred temple dance Bharat Natyam, which is central to Hinduism. But there did develop in the Islamic world the sacred dance of the Sufis, which along with the spiritual concert that accompanies it is called "audition," or *samāʿ*. In most cases such performances are closed to the public and are meant only for members of the particular Sufi order, but in the case of the Mawlawiyyah the dance, instituted through Divine inspiration, became highly elaborate, stylized, and known to the public at large. The Europeans who were able to observe it came to call the Mawlawī Sufis whirling dervishes, because of the centrality of whirling in this highly spiritual and cosmic dance whose purpose is drawing the soul closer to God.

As for theater, it is known that since Islam is not based on the drama between human beings and the gods, it did not develop the same kind of religious theater as one finds, for example, in ancient Greece or India. In fact, despite so much translation from Greek into Arabic in the second/eighth to the fourth/tenth centuries little attention was paid by Muslims

Contemporary mosque in traditional style: Qubā Mosque near Medina designed by Abdel-Wahid El-Wakil, fourteenth/twentieth century.

to this important aspect of Greek culture and religion. Even the use of the word "tragedy" in Arabic and Persian today is based on modern influences. Nevertheless, there did develop among Shīʿite Muslims a form of theater of religious significance based on the martyrdom of the grandson of the Prophet, Ḥusayn, in Karbala' and related events of Islamic sacred history. Called in English "passion plays" (*al-taʿziyah*) because of their similarities to Christian passion plays based on the life and death of Christ, these Islamic passion plays became more and more elaborate over the ages, especially in Persia and Muslim India, and remain to this day among the most notable religious spectacles in the Shīʿite world.

It should be clear from what has been stated that Islamic art was ubiquitous in traditional Islamic civilization, where no distinction was made between sacred and profane, between religious and secular art, or between arts and crafts, as we find in the West. The word used for "art" as "technique" in Arabic is *al-fann,* and traditionally everything is considered to have its own *fann*. In the deepest sense everything that one does or says in life should be done according to its appropriate art, or *fann*. The great Sinhalese metaphysician of art A. K. Coomaraswamy once said, concerning traditional in contrast to modern society, that in modern society an artist is a special kind of man, whereas in traditional societies every man was a special kind of artist. This profound observation certainly held true for traditional Islamic society and the civilization created by Islam.

Before the onslaught of modernism, which commenced with the rise of European colonization of the Islamic world, beginning as early as the eleventh/seventeenth century for some outlying Islamic areas, Muslims lived and breathed in an atmosphere in which the spiritual message of Islamic art was everywhere. The spaces in which they lived and moved were replete with the echoes of the chanting of the Quran, which in the deepest sense defined these spaces. The urban settings they inhabited were defined by an architecture and an urban design that were organically linked to the Quranic spirit and message. The objects with which they surrounded themselves constantly provided them with opportunities for the recollection of God's Presence. The dress that Muslim men and women wore had a spiritual impact upon them. The music Muslims heard was infused with spiritual values, and the poetry they recited and often memorized usually drew their attention to God and spiritual realities. Even the sports in which Muslims participated, from horse racing to wrestling, were combined with an art of religious significance.

The advent of modernism destroyed much, if not all, of this spiritual ambience. Paintings became ever more naturalistic, and gradually many Muslim artists began to simply emulate various styles of Western painting. The architecture and urban design, especially in most big cities, began to resemble Western models, leading to the ugly urban growth, so divorced from the Islamic norm, that we see in so many Muslim cities today. Western music, much of which is far from being of a spiritual nature, to say the least, began to marginalize classical and folk schools of Islamic music for many modernized people. Some Muslim poets began to compose poetry in Western styles, even breaking the laws of traditional prosody in what is called "free poetry" (*al-shi'r al-ḥurr*) in Arabic and "new poetry" (*shi'r-i naw*) in Persian. Even the dress that traditional Muslims wore was changed for modern Western dress in many areas, resulting in the loss of the Islamic values and "ambience" connected with the traditional dress. One could go on and on, but enough has been said to demonstrate the extent of loss of the spiritual message of traditional Islamic art for Muslims as a result of the process of modernization, which means Westernization.

The loss of this aspect of Islamic culture and civilization is as important as the curtailment of many aspects of Islamic Law and the secularization of thought, with which so many contemporary Muslim thinkers are concerned today. Both the modernists and the so-called fundamentalists have been more or less oblivious to the central importance of the heritage of Islamic art and its spiritual message. During the past few decades there have been some signs of hope and attempts here and there to preserve and even revive Islamic art in its many forms, especially in the domains of calligraphy and architecture, but much remains to be done and done rapidly in light of the speed of the destructive forces. It is, however, only traditional Islam that is able to achieve this task, that is able to reformulate the principles of Islamic art and provide once again an ambience of an Islamic character that can bring the spiritual message of Islam into various facets of the everyday life of Muslims.

Beni Isquen and Ghardaia Oasis, Algeria.

Chapter Thirteen

THE ARCHITECTURAL TRANSFORMATION OF THE URBAN ENVIRONMENT IN THE ISLAMIC WORLD

The same tensions and conflicts observed in the domain of ideas and treated in earlier chapters can also be seen displayed in the most tangible and visible manner in the arts, to which brief reference was made in the last chapter. But nowhere is this tension more evident than in the architecture of the urban environment that surrounds Muslims living in the modernized parts of the Islamic world. If in the intellectual field, German, French, and English philosophies have been contending with traditional Islamic thought, in the field of architecture one observes modern German, French, or English styles in one region, American ones in another, and Italian in yet a third area. These foreign imports vie with traditional Islamic architecture for nearly every foot of available space in various Muslim urban centers in a struggle that, from the early twentieth century until quite recently, nearly always went in favor of the foreign styles. The result has been the creation of the very tangible disorder and chaos in the urban setting of so many cities in the Islamic world, a chaos that reflects directly the tensions and confusions created in the minds and souls of so many Muslims as a result of the confrontation between traditional Islam and modernism.

Surely one can hardly deny the fact that today the major modern urban environments of the Islamic world are suffering from a crisis that is most directly reflected in their ugliness. The ambience of modern parts of Islamic cities stands in stark contrast to the serene and beautiful atmosphere of the traditional Islamic city.[1] Islamic architecture has in fact been eclipsed by a conglomeration of often hideous styles, or at best bland ones, that imitate foreign models, with pretention of the universality and worldwide applicability of modern architecture. The crisis within Islamic architecture and modern Islamic cities hardly needs to be underlined. Nor is it necessary to elaborate here the principles and values of traditional Islamic architecture and city planning, the loss of which has brought the present crisis into being.[2] Our task here is to study the transformations that have taken place within the minds and souls of contemporary Muslims resulting in that inner chaos whose externalization is to be seen in the architectural creations and urban design of much of the contemporary Islamic world. The external environment that people create for themselves is no more than an externalization of their inner state. As the saying goes, "As within, so without."

What transformations have overcome contemporary Muslims, and who is responsible for the prevailing architectural and urban crises within the Islamic world? Perhaps, such questions should not be directed to all contemporary Muslims, but only to the members of the small Westernized minority who possess economic and social influence far exceeding their numbers, a minority that represents in fact an elite (*khawāṣṣ*) in reverse. One must remember the Latin proverb *corruptio optimi pessima* ("Corruption of the best is the worst") and the well-known Arabic and Persian proverb that states that the fish begins to stink from its head.[3] The changes that have affected this small yet very influential Westernized minority as far as architecture and city planning are concerned have nevertheless had an effect upon the intellectual, emotional, and artistic aspects of the life of the majority. The architecture and urban design created by them have an impact on the intelligence as well as the imagination and sensitivity of the Islamic community, not to speak of their negative effect upon many aspects of the practice of Islam and the social and family bonds promulgated by the religion.

To understand this process of change and transformation fully, it is necessary to review, besides obvious demographic and economic factors, the two major effects of Westernization upon Muslims. The first is the spread of secularization, or more precisely the desacralization of life, thought, and art; and the second, related to both internal and external factors, is the narrowing of the tradition (*al-dīn*) to include only the principles of human action as embodied in the *Sharī'ah,* not the principles of wisdom

General view of the town and mausoleum of Moulay Idrīs, Morocco, twelfth/eighteenth century.

(*ḥikmah*) and the traditional norms of making things that constitute the principles and methods of Islamic art and architecture.

As far as secularization or desacralization is concerned, the effect of Westernization has been to reduce the Islamic conception of *'ilm,* according to which all knowledge, including mathematics, is considered sacred, to the conception of science as a purely profane form of knowledge. The traditional architect, who is entitled *mi'mār* ("he who builds," *'umrān,* in the traditional sense) or *muhandis* ("he who is a geometer," again according to the traditional conception of geometry similar to that found in the Pythagorean and Platonic tradition), becomes transformed into the modern architect with fancy offices filled with the latest gadgets, a person who now deals with profane mathematics and engineering techniques divorced from both wisdom and craftsmanship and who usually has no knowledge at all of traditional Islamic sciences and cosmology. Often, notable exceptions notwithstanding, the change also implies a loss of humility and dignity that one sees so commonly among traditional architects and in contrast the rise of a sense of egotism and worldliness among many modern Muslim architects that is usually associated with the "in-

General view of the city of San'a in Yemen.

ternational" architect and businessman. The changes responsible for the creation of modern buildings and urban design also imply in many cases a weakening of moral fiber and possibly even a divorce from the ethical considerations normally associated with one's professional work. All of this change among so many Muslim architects is of course abetted by the transformation that has taken place today among so many patrons and clients of architecture, who are often driven by economic factors based so often on crass materialism and greed and who are indifferent to the spiritual significance of art and architecture. This assertion is not of course meant to deny demographic and economic realities, which can, however, be faced without creating slums in the name of building for the poor. One need only recall master traditional architect Hasan Fathy's famous book *Building for the Poor* and his actual architectural creations in Egypt.

These intellectual and mental changes have also been depleting, in the minds of modernized Muslims, the sacred content of such fundamental realities and concepts as space, light, rhythm, form, and matter. Such realities are transformed into post-Cartesian Western ones but bearing the same name as Islamic realities, which are now experienced on only a limited material level. Space is then no longer the symbol of Divine Presence,

View of old and new Cairo from the Citadel.

nor light a reflection of the Light of the Divine Intellect. Architectural rhythms that reintegrate multiplicity into Unity are forgotten. Form loses its symbolic value, and material substance becomes simply the dead, inert matter of Newtonian physics, far removed from the concept and experience of "matter" entertained in traditional Islamic cosmology.[4]

Moreover, these changes that are taking place within the minds not only of most of the modern-trained Muslim architects, but also of most of their major clients, who are drawn from either the ranks of the rich or government authorities and who pay for most of the new modern architecture and urban planning in the Islamic world, complement each other. In fact, in many places the transformation has been so rapid and abrupt that most people who are responsible for the modern-built environment do not even realize that the vast majority of the Muslims for whom they are building still entertain different notions of space, light, form, and matter from those that the modernized classes have learned from modern sources and/or in modern universities, whether these schools are located geographically in the Occident or in the Islamic world itself. It is of much interest to note that, although knowledge of traditional Islamic architecture still survives in

General view of the Kazimiyyah area of Baghdad, Iraq.

the craft guilds and "in the breast" (*ṣadr*) of certain individuals, until quite recently there has not been a single school of architecture in the universities of the Islamic world where this traditional Islamic architecture and its principles are taught in a serious manner.[5]

A nearly identical process of desacralization is to be observed in relation to the imagination. The imagination of traditional Muslims is conditioned by forms and symbols drawn mostly from the Noble Quran, *Ḥadīth,* and traditional Islamic culture. Their soul consists essentially of the intertwining of the meaning of certain basic formulas of the Holy Book, which imbue their inner being with fundamental attitudes vis-à-vis God and His creation.[6] In Islamic cosmology, the world of imagination occupies an intermediate region in the hierarchy of cosmic existence between the material and purely spiritual worlds. Its forms, sounds, and colors have an objective reality, and its ontological reality serves to give

General view of the city of Yazd, Iran.

human imagination a function above and beyond profane imagination as understood in the modern world. It is this imagination that Ibn 'Arabī refers to so often in his work, speaking of its creative power,[7] and that has been translated as *mundus imaginalis* (imaginal world) to prevent its being confused with the profane use of the term "imagination" in modern parlance.[8] The imagination of traditional Muslim artists was constantly nourished by the Islamicized cosmic sector of the universe, and of course more directly by the central theophany of the Islamic revelation, which is the Quran. Modern Muslims have, on the contrary, been deprived of this celestial sustenance, so that even where there is a degree of creativity on the part of some modernized Muslim architects, the fruit of this creativity has hardly anything to do with Islamic art and architecture. There are of course exceptions, but this holds for the majority, not isolated cases.

Finally, it needs to be mentioned that the sensibility of those Muslims

Cairo minarets, many from the Mamlūk period, with TV dishes in foreground.

affected by the withering influence of Westernization has been deeply changed. In fact, in this domain, even those Muslims who still live within the traditional Islamic world suffer from the same problem when it comes to the judgment of art forms outside their own traditional world. In Islamic art, beauty is considered a reflection of the Divine Beauty, as the famous prophetic *ḥadīth* asserts, "God is beautiful and loves beauty."[9] Moreover, beauty is an intrinsic dimension of the Truth and its manifestations, and it is therefore a necessary component of every legitimate artistic creation. Islam never separates beauty from utility, or art from the making of useful objects, as was the case in the traditional West when art meant *ars* and technology was still related to *techne.* The change of sensibility due to modernization has caused many Muslims to lose this inner sense of beauty, dignity, harmony, and nobility, which characterize Islamic art, as indeed do other authentic manifestations of the Islamic spirit. It is hard to see most modernized Muslims as the descendants of those who built the Sultan Ḥasan Mosque in Cairo or the Maydān-i Naqsh-i Jahān in Isfahan.

Likewise, traditional Islamic sensibility saw the world in its transient aspect; it was aware of the negation, or *lā,* of the *shahādah* (*Lā ilāha illa'Llāh,* "There is no divinity but God"), which reduces everything to nothingness before the Immutable Majesty of Allah. Hence, architecture sought to avoid the glittery and the worldly even in public buildings made to endure longer than private domiciles; it aimed to preserve and substantiate the basic intuition about the ephemerality of the world that the spiritualized form of Semitic nomadism, as already mentioned, accentuated and strengthened. Traditional Muslims looked at the houses in the city with full awareness of their passing, transient quality with respect both to God Himself and to virgin nature, the handiwork of God. Moreover, they saw the city as the extension of the natural environment, in harmony rather than in discord with it.

Islamic architecture remained faithful to simple building materials and employed the elemental forces of nature such as light and wind for its sources of energy. It brought nature into the city by recreating the calmness, harmony, and peace of virgin nature within the courtyards of the mosque and the home. Modernized Muslims, whose spiritual sense has become dulled by the forces of secularization, have forgotten the ephemeral quality of human life on earth and the peace and harmony pervading nature. Like modern Westerners, whom they emulate, they want to build homes as if they were going to live forever and construct cities whose very existence is based upon defiance of nature, the violation of her rhythms, and the depletion of her resources. One need only look at the glittering palaces built in the middle of the Arabian desert or the skyscrapers of the Persian Gulf to find clear examples of this assertion. Modern people, including secularized Muslims, want to create an ambience in which God is forgotten. This means creating an urban environment in total disequilibrium with that natural environment, which is created by God and which, being itself a reminder of the Divine, gives the lie to the very notion of secularism and desacralization.

In addition to the transformations brought about on the levels of intelligence, imagination, and sensibility in modernized Muslims, there is also a general loss of the sense of unity and integration of life that directly affects architecture and city planning. As has already been stated, Islam is based on Unity (*al-tawḥīd*) and is the means toward the integration of human life, and in fact of all multiplicity, into Unity.[10] Every authentic manifestation of the Islamic spirit reflects the doctrine of *al-tawḥīd.* This doctrine is the principle of all the Islamic arts and sciences as well as of the *Sharī'ah,* which integrates all human action and prepares people to return to the One in the mold of the perfection that is found on the highest level in the Blessed Prophet, in the mold that could be called "The Muḥammadan Perfection," that is, the *uswah,* the model, that Muslims are instructed by the Quran to emulate.

The traditional Islamic city reflected this unity directly. Since there is no distinction in Islam between the sacred and profane, a unity pervaded the architecture of the traditional city that related the architecture of the home, of the bazaar and even of the palace and other municipal buildings to that of the mosque. This unity made the space within the Muslim home an extension of the space within the mosque, which in fact it is from a ritual as well as an artistic point of view. The all-embracing nature of the *Sharī'ah,* which includes worship (*'ibādāt*) as well as transactions (*mu'āmalāt*), made possible the integration of all forms of activity. In the heart of the Islamic city, spaces designed for worship became interconnected with those designed for education, the making of things, and business transactions as well as for private living and cultural activity. The heart of many traditional Islamic cities today still displays, despite the ravages of time and long periods of neglect, this remarkable unity of space and integration of spatial functions within the mosque, *madrasah,* bazaar, private homes, and the like. Needless to say, secularism destroys this vision of unity and the integration of all human activity within a Divine norm and pattern. The loss of this unity, at least on a more external level,[11] is one of the primary factors responsible for the plight of the modern city within the Islamic world. This fact becomes even more disturbing if we consider that the vast majority of Muslims still live inwardly within a unified worldview and cannot bear the compartmentalized form of life imposed upon them by the mind and will of the minority, who build for them according to models of architecture and city planning based not on unity, but on the segmentation and separation of the various domains of human activity.

Another effect of contact with the modern world has been, by way of reaction, the narrowing of the concerns of religion among some Muslims to only the laws pertaining to human action. The current understanding of the applications of the *Sharī'ah* includes a series of complex factors, some of which are related to forces within Islamic society and some to contact with and response to the West. It is not possible to elaborate more than has already been done in this book on the how and why of the

View of present-day Tehran.

spread of puritanical, rationalistic movements, such as various forms of neo-Wahhābism and different so-called reformist movements associated with groups such as the Salafiyyah, the Ikhwān al-Muslimīn, aspects of the Deoband movement, the Jamā'at-i Islāmī, and the like, and the reason for their more or less indifference to Islamic art. What is important for the present discussion is that these movements, in their attempt to revive the *Sharī'ah* and the Islamic practices associated with daily life, have for the most part neglected Islamic art and architecture and the metaphysical and philosophical principles underlying them. Moreover, they have made possible the appearance of later forms of violent "fundamentalism" which, as mentioned at the beginning of this book, are as indifferent and even opposed to traditional Islamic art as are the partisans of modernism.

When this type of religiosity is combined with modernistic tendencies, it creates an atmosphere in which the only thing that matters is the juridical aspect of the religion, whether interpreted traditionally or in a modernist fashion, and not its artistic dimension. At best, God is remembered as Truth, at least on a certain level, but He is forgotten as Presence. Hence, beauty becomes incidental, and the Islamic character of architecture and city planning is of total inconsequence. What matters is that the

Present-day Dubai skyline.

new city development has a mosque or two somewhere; however, even the mosques themselves are not built according to Islamic principles. It matters little if the rest of the city is a copy and usually a poor one of the secularized and inhuman urban growth of many modern Western cities or their suburbs, where to a large extent either inhuman regimentation or a rugged individualism dominates. In such places, the only question that is never considered is the wholeness of life, the spiritual significance of beauty, and the integration of human society.

Despite the religious character of this type of reform movement and its reactions to many Western elements on the level of ideas and laws, the transformations it brings about in the minds and souls of contemporary Muslims fortify the secularizing tendencies in the Islamic world especially as they affect art, architectures and city planning. These factors alienate Muslims from those aspects of the Islamic tradition that bear most directly upon art and architecture; that is, the wisdom (*ḥikmah*), or *sapientia,* always associated with Islamic esoterism, the cosmology that issues from it, and the principles governing Islamic art itself. This secularizing tendency causes certain Muslims to become completely indifferent to their own religion, whether reflected in the *Sharī'ah* itself or in its sapiential teachings. The reformists try to combat this effect and to resuscitate religion, but they reduce it for the most part to just its juridical and political aspects. Through the belittling of and even disdain for wisdom (*ḥikmah*), they accept the secularization of both art and nature and make inaccessible those very elements of the Islamic tradition of which Muslims are most direly in need in order to recreate an authentic Islamic ambience. The atrocious destruction of so much Islamic architecture and even of sanctuaries and holy cities by apparently devout Muslims is proof, if proof is necessary, of the significance of the loss of that Divine wisdom that contains the principles of Islamic art. This is true whether the loss comes from a lack of interest in religion as such caused by secularism or by means of the narrowing of religion to only one of its dimensions and the consequent loss of the sacramental character of traditional Islamic art as an integral aspect of the manifestations of the Islamic revelation.

Of course, besides these spiritual and intellectual factors, there are important social, political, and economic elements with which the present chapter is not concerned, but whose significance it does not wish to deny. But one cannot avoid at least mentioning that today most nations of the Islamic world suffer from an inferiority complex vis-à-vis the West. They seek to create Western forms of architecture, often as prestige projects, in order to become acceptable, even if, for example, it is not economically or environmentally feasible to manage a high-rise building covered with glass in the middle of a desert. Likewise, the great wealth of some Islamic countries provides just the right conditions for satiation of the greed of many Western contractors and planners, who operate with the help of their Muslim counterparts to present plans and projects that often manage to be most costly and yet not create what is most Islamic. Of course, a few arches are usually added to give the impression of conformity with the local culture, but the real intentions remain hidden only from those who are unaware of the nature of Islamic art and architecture. However, the people who are in favor of a few arches without respect for the principles of Islamic art are, unfortunately, often the very persons asked to judge the validity of these projects. One wonders what will happen to many of the new urban developments within the Islamic world if architects continue to build as if the energy crisis did not exist and as if the environmental crisis were just a fiction to scare the gullible. There is certainly no excuse for Muslim countries to repeat the errors of Western urban development. The fact that an error may gain worldwide acceptance for a short time does not turn it into a truth.

To remedy this serious situation, one cannot suggest a more obvious first step than the training of Islamic architects, men and women who are committed to specifically Islamic architecture, rather than those who practice Western architecture with the claim that it is international and who happen to be named Muḥammad, Aḥmad, or ʿAlī. To train Islamic architects, in turn, requires certain essential resources for education in this field. Fortunately, traditional Islamic architecture is still alive in the villages and smaller towns of many Islamic countries, and secret documents are still preserved in some of the guilds. Where modern architects and their imitators do not interfere, the architecture in many villages continues to be at once beautiful and functional. Moreover, the vast majority of the Islamic people are still drawn to the authentic expressions of their architecture. Advantage can be taken of these factors to create schools of Islamic architecture to train architects and city planners who can build in the future in an authentic Islamic manner the cities, public monuments, housing projects, and other major developments that have been necessitated by the population explosion, migration to cities, changes in ways of production, and other factors. These projects are now usually carried out by people trained in Western architecture, whether they happen to be citizens of Western or Islamic countries.

The establishment of such schools and institutions[12] requires the revival of the Islamic arts and sciences, which has already been alluded to in a more general context, and the rediscovery of their spiritual and metaphysical principles. This means that, ultimately, Islamic architecture cannot be revived unless the contemporary Muslim is reborn and the shackles of Western cultural and philosophical domination overthrown. The external world made by human beings cannot be adorned with beauty, which is the theophany of the Divine Beauty, unless the inner person is adorned with those virtues (*faḍāʾil* and *iḥsān*) and forms of wisdom that have always characterized creative scholars and artists within Islamic civilization. The task remains a vast one, but one can always begin with the training of a few.[13] One can hope and pray that their personal example and the beauty of works they create according to Islamic principles, of which we can already observe a few rare examples here and there, as in the villages and individual houses built by Hasan Fathy in Egypt, the mosques built by 'Abd al-Wāḥid al-Wakīl in Saudi Arabia, and certain town quarters and buildings designed by Kāmil Khan Mumtāz in Pakistan, will serve as a light that will transform the present darkness. With the help of authentic Islamic art and architecture, it is still possible to transform the chaos, disorder, and ugliness that pervade much of the urban environment of the Islamic world into that harmony of light, space, and form that has always characterized the traditional Islamic city and town.

Chapter Fourteen

THE PRINCIPLES OF ISLAMIC ARCHITECTURE AND URBAN DESIGN, AND CONTEMPORARY URBAN PROBLEMS

Many people today claim that contemporary urban problems are so overwhelming that the principles of traditional Islamic architecture and urban design are no longer relevant, but this is a fatalistic view that would deny the possibility of principle-based human creativity and human freedom itself as they are related to the creation of living spaces. Needless to say, I do not accept this fatalistic view and believe that the principles of Islamic architecture and urban design are still very much relevant and their applications of the utmost importance for the preservation of the Islamic character of societies whose members are still Muslim. To be sure, many external conditions have changed from the days of old, and there are now daunting new problems at once sociological, political, economic, technological, and environmental facing Islamic society, as they do most other societies. Let us just consider the question of population and urban growth in the Islamic world in comparison to the West, a growth that is itself one of the consequences of the advent of modernism.

In 1900 the population of Karachi was about 136,000, Cairo 600,000, and Tehran 200,000. Now they are about 15, 13, and 12 million, respectively. The population of Egypt was about 8 million; that of Persia, 7 million; and that of Turkey proper, also about 7 million. Today in all three countries the population is over 70 million. To see how vast this growth is, it is instructive to compare it to figures related to Western countries. The population of Paris in 1900 was about 3.3 million; today it is about

10.4 million; that of London in 1900 was about 6.5 million, and today it is about 12.4 million. As for Western countries, in 1900 the population of France was approximately 38 million; today it is 65 million. Germany's was 56 million and today 82 million. As for the United Kingdom, it was 38 million and is now 62 million. Even in the United States, which has witnessed greater population growth than Europe since 1900, the population was about 76 million then, and today it is about 310 million. The urban population of the world has grown from about 14 percent in 1900 to about 50 percent today. Even now the urban percentage of the population is greater in nearly all Western countries than in most of the Islamic world, but the migration from farm communities and small towns to big cities in the West took place much more slowly and at a much more orderly pace than in most of the Islamic world, where one observes during the last century, especially during the past few decades, such rapid migration to cities from the countryside along with the permanent sedentary settlement of much of the nomadic population.

A study of these figures alone, not to speak of many political and cultural factors, reveals how immense the urban problems are that the Islamic world is now facing. Some will doubtless say that these problems are not unique to Muslims and that it is enough to compare the populations of such present-day megacities as Tokyo, Delhi, and Rio with their population in 1900 to realize the global nature of urban problems. The answer is that, first of all, the immensity of the problem does not mean that Muslims should shy away from finding Islamic solutions to it rather than simply seeking to emulate foreign models; and second, the fact that urban areas in other parts of the non-Western and non-Islamic world also face daunting urban problems, as do even many Western cities, is no excuse for Muslims to remain passive and not seek to build in accordance with the principles of their own architecture and urban design. This field is yet another in which traditional Islam must face the challenges of modernism and seek to apply to the creation of living spaces under new conditions the principles of its own tradition of architecture and urban design.

Let us then turn again to the principles that govern Islamic art, architecture, and city planning, principles that, as already mentioned, are related to the spirit and form of the Islamic revelation. This connection exists in two different ways: one direct and the other indirect. These principles derive directly from the inner dimension of the Quranic revelation and the sacred sciences contained therein. They derive from the Divine Word as contained in the Quran and echoing in the hearts of Muslim men and women and in diverse forms throughout the traditional Islamic city, determining the spaces and forms in which they live and function. These principles derive also from an aspect of the soul of the Prophet, the recipient of the Word, from a prophetic presence that embraces and, one might say, envelopes the traditional Islamic city in a kind of beatific purity of spiritual death within whose bosom is to be found the fountain of spiritual life.

Indirectly, Islamic architecture and city planning are related to and influenced by the Divine Law, or *Sharī'ah,* which molds the life of the individual Muslim as well as that of the Islamic community and society as a whole. The Divine Law itself issues from the Islamic revelation and, although it does not create art, architecture, or city planning, it does provide the social conditions and the human matrix and background for that art, architecture and urban design, the origin of whose sacred form is suprahuman. Let us confine ourselves to only Islamic architecture and city planning in their traditional form. They were created, molded, and influenced by the Islamic religion in their inner principles, symbolic language, and intellectual basis as well as through the human and social setting and relations for which they serve as the external framework.

It might of course be asked what pertinence such an architecture or city planning has for the modern world as a whole and the present-day urban crisis that modern or modernized civilizations face everywhere, not only in the West, which gave rise to modernism, but wherever modernism has spread, whether in Asia, Africa, South America, or of course the Islamic world itself. One can reply that Muslims, many of whose present-day cities are not at all traditional Islamic cities, can make use of the principles of their architecture and urban design to overcome the terrible urban problems they now encounter. One can assert that, at least theoretically and in principle, they possess this ability, because they still have access to these principles and also still live within a society in which the *Sharī'ah* is functioning, albeit partially, and in which it can be revived and strengthened, because faith in Islam is still strong in the hearts of men and women.[1]

It is also of interest to ask how these principles can be of significance or possibly help to solve problems relating to architecture and urban set-

Modern style mosque: Istiqlāl Mosque in Jakarta, Indonesia, fourteenth/twentieth century.

tings in general, even perhaps in the West itself where the vast majority of the population is non-Muslim and in many cases even disinterested in any form of religion. The answer is that, first of all, there are certain universal elements within human beings and in their relation to the natural environment. These elements make possible the introduction of such principles even in settings that are alien to the particular religious world from which those principles issued in the first place. Second, the dominant religion of the West, namely, Christianity, which gave birth to European civilization, belongs to the same religious family as Islam, and certain principles, norms, and ideas drawn from Islam can always evoke a sympathetic response in the minds and souls of Europeans or North Americans, the very strands of whose being are woven by centuries of experience of Christian religion and culture, even if many now consciously reject this tradition.[2] Third, Islam is in a sense a return to the primordial religion of Divine Unity and possesses a message at once simple and universal that can appeal to that primordial nature that lies, often hidden and only in a latent state, in the heart and indeed the very substance of all human beings.[3] Its principles and teachings, even when pertaining to the domain of architecture and city planning, can therefore be of significance and interest even in a world where its tenets are not practiced. In light of these considerations, it is perhaps of some value to discuss certain of the principles of Islamic architecture and then see how they can be applied to contemporary urban problems everywhere in the modern world, whether in the West, the Islamic world, or elsewhere.

We have already mentioned that, as in other aspects of Islam, in architecture and urban design the principle of Unity (*al-tawḥīd*) is of central importance. In the domains of metaphysics and religion, this principle implies the unity of the Divine Principle, the interrelation of all things, the integration of multiplicity into unity, and the utter ontological dependence of all beings upon the One as well as the total dedication of the individual to the Will of the One. In architecture and urban design unity implies the integration of the elements of architecture, the interrelation of the functions and purposes of space, and the ubiquitous presence of the sacred in all forms of architecture in such a way as to remove the very notion of the secular as a category in opposition to the sacred. It implies realization of the theophanies of the One in the buildings created by human hands in the same way that virgin nature reflects its Unique Creator through the harmony, equilibrium, and interrelation that characterize its manifold forms and phenomena. Since *al-tawḥīd* in Arabic means both "oneness" and "making one" (or "integration"), the principle of unity in architecture and urban design implies at once the state of oneness reflected through the peace, tranquility, and harmony of Islamic architecture and the act of making one, or integration, that interconnects the functions of human living space, starting from a single edifice and extending to a whole village or urban setting, creating ever greater degrees of unity leading to Unity as such.[4] One could in fact say that in the same way that an Arabic treatise is in reality one long sentence, the Islamic town or city is one single edifice that integrates all its parts into a whole that transcends those parts, a whole that comes before the parts in both conception and execution and bestows upon them sense and order. Likewise on a smaller scale, the whole of a single edifice precedes its parts, as unity always predominates over multiplicity and the whole is greater than the sum of its parts.[5]

Turning more specifically to the Islamic world, one can assert that this principle of unity is observable in the interrelation of various types of architecture within an organic urban design. In traditional Islam, religious and secular architecture do not exist as two distinct and opposing realities; rather, Islamic architecture in a sense grows as a whole out of the mosque and is its extension. Any action or rite performed in the mosque can also be accomplished in the home or the bazaar, whose spaces are in this sense the extensions of the space of the mosque. Something of the grace of the Quran and the soul of the Prophet spreads over the whole ambience of the Islamic city, much as the call to prayers penetrates into every architectural space or the rain of mercy from Heaven falls upon the roof of every building, whether private house, mosque, or school. The same techniques, architectural symbols, and use of light, space, and forms found in the mosque are also to be found in the palace, bazaar, or private house, except of course such distinct architectural features as the minaret or prayer niche (*miḥrāb*), which belong solely to the mosque.

The mosque, palace, bazaar, school, and home are intertwined in a concrete manner that is palpable by virtue of that very organic unity that links their architectural space. In a traditional Islamic city such as Fez[6] or Isfahan, the mosque is not only itself the community center as well as the locus of religious activity, but opens to the area of economic activity, private homes, schools, and palaces in such a way as to link them all together. The spaces of all these activities are related to each other and form an organic whole. The architecture and city planning thus reflect the unity of traditional Islamic life, while themselves facilitating the living of an integrated life based on and also resulting in the interconnection between the religious, educational, cultural, social, economic, political, and other facets of human life.

The principle of unity is also to be seen in the manner in which Islamic architecture treats the outside of an edifice, the inside spaces, and the landscaping. In modern architecture, these three features are distinguished and in fact handled by different persons, who are usually trained as specialists in the construction of each. A modern architect usually leaves the interior decoration of a building to a decorator and the area surrounding it to a landscape architect. In Islamic architecture, on the contrary, these three components are three facets of a single reality usually conceived and executed by the same master craftsman or his group. When one contemplates the Court of Lions in the Alhambra or the garden pavilions of the Fīn Garden in Kashan or the Shālīmār in Lahore, one realizes that all these facets of architecture comprise the same reality and possess a unity

Modern style mosque: Faisal Mosque in Islamabad, Pakistan, fourteenth/twentieth century.

that enables them to become organically integrated into a single experience embracing the interior spaces, the structure itself, and the landscape surrounding the edifice.

One can also see the principle of unity in the multiple functions that the spaces of traditional Islamic architecture, especially those of the home, usually serve. In modern architecture, functions for various spaces are first defined and then a building created that sees the whole as the aggregation of those well-defined component parts. In contrast, in Islamic architecture the different components of the space created are born from the conception of the structure as a whole and possess a plasticity of usage derived from the multiple functions that most spaces serve. A room in the traditional Muslim home can serve during a single day as bedroom, dining room, guest room, or place of worship, and the lack of fixed furniture in the modern sense aids greatly in facilitating such multiple usage. In older days, one hardly ever ordered a three- or four-bedroom house. The traditional architecture would create a whole out of which the spaces necessary for everyday life would grow in such a way that wholeness always dominated over the living space of the family or families, in much the same way as the town or city possessed a wholeness that predominated over its parts. There were, to be sure, distinct components, elements, and features, ranging from a single house to a quarter of the city, but unity always predominated over multiplicity and prevented the parts from becoming realities independent of the whole. In the same way that all the living spaces of the traditional Islamic city seem to have but a single roof, unity in both a metaphysical and architectural sense has always dominated over the parts, allowing the growth of the parts, but always in relation to and in harmony with the whole.

It is also important to mention the direct relation of the principle of unity to the combining of beauty and function, or utility, so characteristic of all Islamic art, especially architecture and urban design. Islam emphasizes the importance of beauty as the aura of the truth, for, as the already quoted *ḥadīth* states, "God is beautiful [in Himself] and loves beauty." Furthermore, to quote another *ḥadīth*, "God has 'inscribed' the mark of beauty upon all things." The need for beauty is innate to human nature and as necessary for human beings' ultimate survival as the air they breathe. Far from being a luxury, beauty is a human necessity. From the Islamic point of view and in direct opposition to the claims of most modern theoreticians of art, to be beautiful is to be "useful" in the deepest sense of the word, that is, in the sense of fulfilling a basic human need. Functionality and utility are therefore not juxtaposed to beauty, but complement it.

To have a holistic image of the human person as at once a body, soul, and spirit, at once a creature of this earth and yet created for immortality and eternal life, is to realize that no authentic functionality or utility can be divorced from beauty, for what is ugly is ultimately "useless"—it is false and finally goes against the deepest interests of human beings. In the Muslim mind, not only is beauty identified with truth and goodness, but ugliness is regarded as the opposite, that is, falsehood and evil. One could even say that inasmuch as in Arabic *al-Ḥaqq,* one of the Names of God, means at once Truth and Reality (which is therefore also beautiful), ugliness is, by the same token, unreality and separation from the One who is at once Reality, Truth, and Beauty. To speak of the functionality of architecture as separate from its beauty, which is then relegated to the trivial category of luxury, is to forget the most fundamental metaphysical teachings of the Quran and *Ḥadīth,* which repeatedly identify beauty with the source of all reality and truth as well as virtue.

The unity of beauty and functionality is also related to what one might call the already mentioned principle of "realism" in Islamic art and architecture.[7] In using "realism" here, I do not intend its modern philosophical meaning, but rather the point of view that considers the reality of each being on its own level and sees things "as they are" in an objective mode based on both the dicta of the Islamic revelation and the power of intelligence to be able to know and discern, the intelligence that Islam emphasizes so often in its definition of human beings and that is central to an understanding of the traditional *homo islamicus.*[8] In art, this realism means treating each material as it is, not as what it might be or be made to appear to be. Brick should be used as brick and should be experienced as brick, and stone as stone, and so forth. Even the physical forces and laws that govern the material with which architecture is concerned should be treated and respected in such a way as to bring out their character as parts of God's creation and therefore participants in that structuring of harmony and beauty that characterizes creation.

This view of the nature of materials and the manner of treating them is complemented by the emphasis upon mathematics in Islamic architecture, which always tends to accentuate purity of geometric forms and patterns. The Muslim mind sees in geometric forms and patterns not just quantities, but reflections of the archetypal and intelligible world;[9] one might in fact speak of a kind of "Abrahamic Pythagoreanism" that found a haven in the Islamic universe.[10] If Islamic sacred architecture is of a highly geometric character in both its definition of space and the treatment of its surfaces, it is because the intelligible world (or *'ālam al-ma'qūlāt*), with which traditional Islamic thought identifies the origin of geometric forms and patterns as well as mathematical rhythms, is none other than the spiritual and angelic world. Through this world of the Spirit, the sacred space created by this architecture leads to the sun of Unity, whose brilliance is too dazzling to be depicted directly, but to which allusion is made by all the regular geometrical forms and patterns that are generated by that Point, the symbol of Unity, that is everywhere and nowhere.

The emphasis in Islamic architecture upon the treatment of surfaces of buildings, especially mosques, Sufi centers, and the like, which are often covered with calligraphy, geometric patterns, and arabesque forms, must not be confused with mere decoration or cosmetics in the modern sense. This treatment might be called "cosmetic" only if one were to remember the original significance of this word as meaning "to make cosmic-like" or "to bring out the correspondence of something with the cosmos and cosmic harmony." Although apparently limited to the surface of an edifice, the patterns of Islamic architecture reflect the deepest structures of physical reality, bringing out the mathematical order and harmony that underlie the appearance of the corporeal world.

In accordance with the primordial character of the Islamic revelation and its reestablishment of harmony between human beings and nature, Islamic architecture and city planning have always emphasized the integration of architecture and the natural setting. Nature in a sense permeates and penetrates the traditional Islamic city and its buildings. The mosque itself is not a holy and supernatural space separated from natural space, but an extension into a man-made environment of the space of virgin nature, which, because it was created by God, is sacred in itself and still echoes its original paradisal perfection. Natural light and air enter easily into the spaces of the mosque and other buildings, and birds even fly around within religious edifices during the most solemn moments of a rite or ceremony. The countryside is always nearby, and the rhythms of desert and mountain penetrate into the city. The traditional edifices are what is called today "environmentally friendly."

Not only does one observe the absence of any opposition between the forces and elements of nature and the traditional Islamic urban ambience; but every attempt has been made in Islamic architecture to make maximum use of the forces of nature, of light, wind, shade, and so on. In short, architecture has never set itself up against the natural order or in defiance of the rhythms and harmony of nature. Even most materials used, such as mud walls or soft brick, have been treated in such a way as to allow a building to be reabsorbed into the bosom of nature once it is abandoned by its human inhabitants. Muslim towns and even large cities were built in such a way that, had they remained in their traditional form, they could in principle have survived indefinitely without bringing about the ecological catastrophes and environmental crises associated so much today with urban life, crises with which the modern world is only too familiar. Traditional Muslims, like other traditional peoples, saw themselves as the custodians of nature, whose laws and rhythms they respected, even if they built some of the largest towns and cities known to humanity before modern times.

In the building of monumental architecture in cities as well as in the construction of more humble units in small towns and villages, Muslims never distinguished between technology and the crafts or between the crafts and art. The arts, the crafts, and technology were in fact considered the same thing, and the same terms, such as the Arabic *ṣinā'ah,* were even used for them all. To make something was to make it beautifully, in conformity with the nature of the work and the material being used, and in accordance with one's vocation willed by God; the three were always intertwined.[11] The master architects were also well versed in the technology of the material with which they dealt, such as the baking of brick or the making of tiles. The people who performed the technological tasks, often of a remarkable nature even according to the standards of the modern world, which takes such great pride in its technology, the artists who designed patterns of great beauty, and the architects who created the buildings were often the same people or members of a group so closely knit that their work came out as if accomplished by one person. As a result of master-disciple relationships that made possible not only the teaching of architectural and artisanal techniques, but also the spiritual discipline transcending the individual, an anonymity was achieved that, far from destroying individual creativity, elevated this creativity to a level above and beyond individual idiosyncrasies. Unity permitted cooperation on such a scale and with such intimacy that works of universal significance with strong unity of form and function were produced as if created by a single architect. As for more humble and transient works of architecture, they were brought into being through the efforts of those who took great joy in working without having to assert their egotistical and individualistic tendencies. In fact, such traditional methods of creation themselves make possible the control of the ego, leading to a joy that can never be experienced within the confinement of the prison of individualistic passions, egotistical impulses, and impersonal modern technologies.

Islamic architecture and urban design facilitated the integration of the various facets of everyday life, such as work, worship, leisure, and so forth, while being itself the result of such an integrated view of life. As already mentioned earlier in this work, in the traditional Islamic pattern of life work is never separated from leisure, which is also integrated with worship or study. To this day, wherever such a pattern has survived, for example, in certain bazaar areas of traditional Islamic cities, one can observe craftsmen or shopkeepers spending some twelve to fourteen hours away from home in what would be called their place of work, which is usually nearby. But in that place of work during those long hours, they spend a good deal of time praying, eating, resting, talking to friends, or even going to a nearby mosque or traditional school (*madrasah*) for an hour or two of worship or study. When they come home in the evening, they are much less tired than workers who have spent eight hours in an office or a factory and who must seek leisure, rest, and culture as well as educational and religious activities elsewhere. Traditional Islamic architecture and city planning are based on such an integrated concept of life and also themselves make possible and facilitate such a pattern of life. They create spaces that, through their interconnection, proximity, and multifaceted use, enable people to experience this intertwining of work and leisure, of making a living and perfecting one's mind and soul through study and worship. In this as in so many other ways, Islamic architecture and city planning reflect the principle of unity and integration of life, which together are the primary factor responsible for the distinctive architecture and urban design characteristics of the world created by Islam.

The application of the principles of Islamic architecture and urban design, some of which have been described, to urban problems in the contemporary world depends not only upon the nature of these principles, but also upon the conditions prevailing in the world in which they are to be applied. Although some of the problems existing in urban environments today, such as overpopulation, pollution, and environmental decay, are worldwide, the question of applying these principles to the contemporary Islamic world may differ in form from what we see in the West or elsewhere. It has already been mentioned that most of the cities of the Islamic world are suffering from terrible urban upheaval and decay caused by overcrowding, excessively rapid growth, the intrusion of alien lifestyles, and inappropriate architecture. They are faced with social and economic problems complicated by cultural and religious dislocations. These cities are furthermore faced with the strange situation that, in numerous cases, most of the people now residing in them are from rural areas and are without experience of living in a traditional Islamic urban environment. Yet the population for the most part still follows the *Sharīʿah* in its everyday life, and if the inner dimensions of the Islamic tradition were to be revived and applied rather than suppressed or manipulated by those in power in the name of political reassertion,[12] the principles of Islamic art and architecture could be reapplied to solve many of the horrendous problems that many Muslim cities face today, solutions that can have a global significance beyond the borders of the Islamic world. For example, urban spaces could be created in which loci of religious, educational and cultural activities, commercial life, and housing for ordinary daily life could be intertwined and integrated, so that people could walk from one place to another rather than requiring cars and other mechanical means of transportation.

In the Western world, however, the social structure of society is very different from the one based on the Islamic *Sharīʿah;* so are the religious ethos and the secular ethos, which together, in a combination dominated mostly by the secular component, determine the value system of modern Westerners in both its ethical and aesthetic aspects. Nevertheless, given the nature of human beings, the comprehensive nature of the inner connection between Islam, Christianity, and Judaism, and the intensity of the crisis of the modern urban environment, the principles of Islamic architecture and urban design may have become worthy of serious consideration not only by some modernized Muslims who have abandoned them and adopted an alien worldview, but also by those Westerners concerned with the future of their own towns and cities.

The modern Western city, whose problems have now become also those of many Islamic cities, although often in more intense form, suffers from excessive segmentation; disequilibrium vis-à-vis the natural environment; unsound economical and ecological practices, particularly in its use of energy resources; and the spread of a blanket of ugliness in the name of economic necessity, with the result that beauty appears as luxury and is divorced from utility. The Islamic emphasis upon the unity of the facets of life as reflected in different architectural spaces, the harmony between human beings and the natural environment, and the wedding between beauty and utility as well as many other related principles, far from being of significance only for the Islamic world, cannot but be of interest to those in the West who are genuinely concerned with the future of urban life beyond the immediate desire for personal power and wealth. And this holds true despite obvious differences between Western and Islamic cities, even the more modern ones. Although Islam has over the centuries appeared as the "other" to the Christian and even "post-Christian" West, its architectural philosophy, based on its conception of humanity in its primordial harmony with the world of creation, can play a role in this dark hour of human history in the creation of an ambience, at once cultural and architectural, that can reflect human beings' true nature and remind them of who they are and why they are undertaking this earthly journey. Although these principles cannot bring about such a change without the transformation of human beings within themselves and in their society, their application in architecture and urban design can at least aid in that process.

Part IV

Postscript

Chapter Fifteen

THE ISLAMIC WORLD

Present Tendencies and Future Trends

The survival of traditional Islam in the modern world, the intrusion of modernism into *dār al-islām,* and the recent resurgence of forces associated in either name or reality with Islam, including what has come to be known as Islamic "fundamentalism"—added to the global significance of events that have occurred in the Middle East during the past few years, ranging from the Lebanese Civil War (1975–90) and the Islamic Revolution in Iran (1979) to terrorist acts committed in the name of Islam and the devastating wars in Iraq and Afghanistan, not to speak of events in East Africa—all of these have helped to create not a few, but a flood of works in European languages on Islam, its future, and its relation to the West. Some of these are by the very people who but a few years ago rejected the very possibility that Islam might be a force to be reckoned with in the future. The works produced by this veritable new industry, often based on either passing political currents or conclusions hastily drawn from incomplete data, have made many predictions for the Islamic world, ranging in style from melodrama to science fiction, with a few more balanced judgments thrown in between. The aim here is certainly not to add one more scenario for the future to the already existing ones, especially since, according to a belief strongly held by all Muslims, the future lies in God's Hands and He alone is aware of its content, as the Quran repeats in many of its verses. The goal, rather, is to delve beyond the surface in order to bring out the nature of some of the more profound issues, ideas, and forces at work within contemporary Islamic religious thought as well as in the Islamic world in general; also to cast an eye upon how these elements seem to be interacting with each other and with the world about them, especially with the West, and how they are likely to do so in the near future.

At the same time, we must remain fully aware of the unreliability of all deterministic futuristic projections and extrapolations based on present-day tendencies.

In carrying out this discussion, it is important to distinguish between Islam itself and the Islamic world, in which it remains the most powerful and determining force. There are today many currents of thought, movements, affirmations, and rejections within the world of Islamic religious thought. There are also, needless to say, very complex forces and movements of a political and social nature at play in the part of the world that is called Islamic. The two are by no means identical and should not be confused with each other for the purpose of any scholarly analysis. Nor should they be totally separated either. Despite the advent of modernism and the spread of secularism in certain sectors of the Islamic world, that part of the globe called Islamic is still Islamic in the most profound sense, in that, over the centuries, the laws, culture, social structures, and in fact the whole worldview of the people inhabiting it have been molded in depth by Islam. Moreover, after over a century of retreat and sometimes recapitulation before the West, many people in the Islamic world are now again seeking in various ways and modes to turn to Islam, so that there is without doubt a "revival" of one kind or another associated with Islam in many Muslim lands, although, as already discussed, the form and content of this "revival" are far from being the same everywhere. It is also essential to repeat that not all the movements using the name, symbols, and language of Islam are of an authentically Islamic character, least of all radical and violent forces that pretend to represent Islam and that distort the teachings of the religion for their own political ends.

There are, then, Islam as traditionally lived and understood and the present-day Islamic world to consider; and there is the link between the two in light of the pertinence of Islam, however it is understood and interpreted by different parties in that world. The future trends of the two, namely, Islam seen as a religion and the conditions of the Islamic world, will most likely not be the same in the future as they are now, but they cannot ever be unrelated either. To study the various current schools of thought and perspectives within Islam as put forth by current Muslim thinkers will therefore certainly cast some light upon what is likely to happen in the Islamic world itself. Moreover, in all likelihood different modes of Islamic thought, especially those of a traditional character, will continue to exercise great influence upon events within various Islamic countries in diverse domains beyond that of religion itself.

We must also remember that forces and events from outside the Islamic world are also likely to have a profound effect upon that world without being necessarily related to the internal religious and theological forces of Islam. Speculation about this type of future intrusion of alien elements into the Islamic world and the role of these external forces in changing the destinies of the Islamic peoples, as has been witnessed in many Islamic countries during the recent past, depends obviously on the transformation that will take place in the world beyond the boundaries of *dār al-islām,* especially in the West. The study of such forces belongs therefore to a separate field of inquiry beyond the subject of this book. Here, the task, rather, is to study the trends associated with Islamic thought itself as it might influence and affect the future of the Islamic world. The influence of a particular form of Islamic thought on this or that segment of Islamic society is one thing; possible invasions by foreign troops or less overt manipulation and interference quite another. Of necessity it is only with the former category that we can be concerned here.

To summarize what has been discussed extensively in previous chapters, within the Islamic religious universe one can discern a large number of forces and forms of activity that can be classafied into four categories, although within each category there is a wide spectrum of diversity, some of which overlaps. These general categories, as already stated, are modernism, messianism, "fundamentalism," and traditional Islam. Moreover, these categories are of such a nature that, despite their divergence and often inner opposition, they are likely to continue at least into the immediate future and also to react with each other.

Modernism, which is the most nebulous of these terms, continues itself to undergo a change of content from one decade to the next. The Muslim modernists of the late nineteenth century, or even of half a century ago, were not for the most part defending the same theses as those of today, because of the transient nature of the modern world itself. But they are all called modernists, because they place value on and some degree of trust in one aspect or another of that postmedieval development in the West that is called modernism and now postmodernism; and also because they have tried and continue to try to interpret Islam, or some of its features, according to the ideas, values, and norms drawn from the modern outlook, with its own wide range of diversity.

The modernist schools range from those that wish to reinterpret Islam in light of the humanistic and rationalistic trends of Western thought, allying themselves with the prevailing paradigm of liberalism in the West, to others that are drawn to the modern but antaliberalist currents associated until two decades ago with Marxism and now with its ideological successors. Islamic modernists range from serious scholars and thinkers, such as Fadl al-Raḥmān (Fazlur Rahman) and Muḥammad Arkūn (Arkoun), to journalistic popularizers, from those attracted to French existentialism and personalism, such as Muḥammad al-Ḥabābī (Lahbabi), to others who have been deeply influenced by Marxist thought, such as 'Alī Sharī'atī and 'Abd Allāh al-'Arawī (Laroui). This class of modernists has usually been deeply concerned at the same time with the social aspect of Islam and often a kind of "Third World philosophy" that was a hallmark of French intellectual circles after World War II and until recently, circles within which most of this type of Muslim "reformist" thinkers have been nurtured.

More recent years have been witness to a number of modernists of another kind and with other backgrounds, men (and also some women) who have sought to create a modernized or reformed Islamic theology. Such figures range from the Iranian 'Abd al-Karīm Surūsh to the Moroccan Muḥammad 'Ābid al-Jābirī. In some Islamic countries there is in fact talk of a *kalām al-jadīd,* or "new theology," but those who pursue such an idea are not necessarily all modernists. Some of them are traditionalists who want to add a new chapter to Islamic theology by applying traditional Islamic teachings to the solution of new challenges posed by modern science and technology, the environmental crisis, Western feminism, the idea of a civil society, the Western philosophy of law, and so on.

Altogether, the impact of the Islamic modernists of the older generations upon the Muslim intelligentsia has decreased in many Muslim countries. Often suffering from a sense of inferiority vis-à-vis the West and anxious to emulate everything Western, the earlier reformers were a strong force as long as the Western model itself seemed viable and, in fact, world-dominating. With the gradual weakening of the prevailing Western paradigm in the West itself, combined with the tragedies that continue to occur in the Islamic world in such a manner that they are associated in the eyes of the populace with the West, there has been a decrease in the impact of "liberal," Western-oriented Muslim thinkers. For example, the espousal of the cause of continuous material progress by "liberal" thinkers in the Islamic world does not appear as appealing today as before, in light of the consequences of such "progress" upon the health of the natural environment, whose degradation is now widely recognized in most Islamic societies. This trend is likely to continue as long as the forces at play, especially such political problems as the Arab-Israeli conflict and more generally the economic, cultural, and in some places military domination by the West of the Islamic world, continue to be what they are.

The second type of modernist, however, those who used to substitute Karl Marx for John Locke and some form of socialism for Western capitalism, and who tried to appear as heroes of the Third World and champions of the "downtrodden masses," might have been latecomers to the Islamic world, but their influence is far from being terminated. This force will diminish only if traditional Muslim thinkers confront the tenets of this kind of crypto-Marxism head on, as has happened once or twice (for example, by 'Allāmah S. M. Ḥ. Ṭabāṭabā'ī in his *Principles of the Philosophy of Realism*), rather than circumventing it and refusing to consider its implications, as has usually been the case with so many contemporary Muslim figures. Also the thrust of this "Third Worldism" will diminish only if the injustice inherent in the present-day process of globalization leading to ever greater economic inequality between the haves and the have-nots comes to an end or is at least diminished.

Messianism has always been present in Islam and has manifested itself whenever the Islamic community has felt an imminent danger to its world of value and meaning. The European invasion of the Islamic world in the nineteenth century was witness to one such wave of messianism, Mahdiism, ranging from West Africa to the Sudan, and from Persia to India. This wave took very different forms in contexts of diverse nature, producing the Mahdī in the Sudan as well as the Bāb in Persia. But the basis of the phenomenon was everywhere the same. It involved the appearance of a charismatic figure claiming to be the Mahdī or his representative in direct contact with God and/or His Agents in the universe and representing a Divine intervention in history with eschatological overtones. The last few decades have been witness to the revival of this type of religious phenomenon. The early stages of the upheavals in Iran in 1978 definitely had a messianic dimension, not to speak of the capturing of the Grand Mosque in Mecca in 1979, where, strangely enough, messianic tendencies were mixed with a brand of Wahhābism. In this context one can also mention the messianic movements that took place in northern Nigeria.

There is every reason to expect such forms of messianism to continue into the future. As a billion and a half people become ever more frustrated in failing to achieve the goals they believe themselves to be legitimately entitled to realize, one reaction is certainly some kind of a sociopolitical eruption or upheaval. Another possible reaction, however, is a messianism that promises victory with Divine help, but on the basis of the destruction of the existing order. Messianism cannot but posses a "revolutionary" character. That is why traditional Muslims believe that only the Mahdī himself, who will come before the end of history, will be able to carry out a veritable religious revolution signifying nothing less than the establishment of the Divine Order on earth; other revolutions can result in forms of subversion and further destruction of what remains of the religious tradition. To the extent that the world becomes a more dangerous place in which to live, especially while the Muslim peoples see themselves as confronted by alien forces on all sides that threaten their very existence, the wave of messianism is bound to increase in accordance, in fact, with some of the sayings of the Prophet of Islam about the signs of the latter days.

As far as "fundamentalism" is concerned, as pointed out in previous chapters, its use by journalists and even scholars in reference to a wide variety of phenomena in the Islamic world and to very diverse currents of Islamic thought is most unfortunate and misleading, because the term is drawn from the Protestant context, where it has quite a different connotation. "Fundamentalism" in Christian religious circles, especially in North America, refers to conservative forms of Protestantism, usually antimodernist, with a rather narrow and literalist interpretation of the Bible and a strong emphasis upon traditional Christian ethics on the personal level, but mostly an eye for an eye philosophy in political matters and foreign affairs. These characteristics have little to do with most of what is classified today under the name of "fundamentalism" in Islam, as discussed earlier in this book, although some of the excessively exoteric but traditional currents of Islamic thought also called "fundamentalist" do share a few common features with fundamentalism as generally understood in English in relation to Christianity. The differences, however, are much greater than the similarities, especially in the more aggressive anti-Western "revolutionary" and violent currents, which, despite their outward anti-Western attitude, now also refer to themselves as "fundamentalist"; to do so, they had to invent this word for their particular context, since such a term has not existed traditionally in the various Islamic languages (for example, *bunyādgarā'ī* in Persian, which is a recently coined term to translate "fundamentalism"). Despite phenomena such as the Oklahoma City bombing and some Christian militia, Christian fundamentalism is by and large not violent or militaristic, because it does not face continuous pressure by forces external to Western society. Islamic "fundamentalism" sees itself in a constant struggle against powerful forces coming from another civilization; it considers itself to be "at war" with these forces, and this "war" sometimes takes an actual militaristic and aggressive form.

The term *intégrisme,* used in French to describe the same set of phenomena as "fundamentalism" but in a Catholic context, might be more appropriate, because it refers to the views of those traditional Catholics who wish to integrate all of life into their religion and, conversely, their religion into all aspects of life. It might be said that traditional Islam is also *intégriste* in this sense and has never ceased to be so. But to use the term "fundamentalism" in the context of Islam is a subversion of its meaning and the destruction of the basic distinction that exists between much that is called "fundamentalism" in the West and traditional Islam, a distinction that has been insisted upon throughout this book. Be that as it may, the use of the terms *intégrisme* and "fundamentalism" and the classafication of a widely diverse set of phenomena and tendencies in the Islamic world under such names are a misleading feature of many of the current studies of Islam and help to hide the more profound realities involved, including the essential fact that some of what is called "fundamentalist Islam" is not traditional but in fact countertraditional and opposed to both the spirit and letter of the Islamic tradition as understood and practiced by Muslims over the centuries since the descent of the Quranic revelation. One need only compare the actions of al-Qā'idah with the teachings of the *Sharī'ah* concerning the killing of innocent people even during war.

It needs to be repeated that in the category of "fundamentalist" are included both organizations that hope to Islamicize society fully through the application of the *Sharī'ah,* but in a peaceful manner, and those that speak of "revolution," using all the ideologies and even techniques belonging to the revolutionary movements of modern European history, but with an Islamic coloring. They include movements based on the idea of the rule of the *'ulamā',* as in Iran, those that have established a military regime with an Islamic ideology, as in Sudan, and those that try to eliminate the influence of the *'ulamā'* and, for all practical purposes, their existence, as in Libya. They embrace organizations as different as the Jamā'at-i Islāmī of Pakistan and the Ikhwān al-Muslimīn in Egypt and governments as diametrically opposed in structure as those of Saudi Arabia and present-day Iran. The term is also applied to those who use terror and violence in the name of Islam, al-Qā'idah and the Taliban as well as the Shabāb movement in Somalia.

To gain a deeper understanding of the forces at play that are bound to determine trends in the near future, it is important to distinguish clearly between these diverse currents now all classafied as "fundamentalist Islam" by Western scholarship and the profound difference between these currents and traditional Islam. What the various movements described as "fundamentalist" have in common is a cultural and religious frustration before the onslaught of Western culture and Western economic and political forces and the desire to reassert themselves in the name of Islam. But their common ground stops at this point, because in trying to achieve their ends some have had recourse to revolutionary jargon drawn from the West, others to a puritanical and rationalistic interpretation of Islam, which would do away with the whole Islamic intellectual and spiritual tradition in the name of a primordial purity no longer attainable, and yet others to brute force, violence, and even terrorism. Some among the so-called Islamic fundamentalists, although limited in their understanding and appreciation of the Islamic tradition taken in its totality, at least accept a part of that tradition, namely, the *Sharī'ah,* and their defense of it is the part of their movement that is closest to traditional Islam. Others are antitraditional in both the ideas they espouse and the methods they have chosen for the implementation of those ideas, despite all appearances.

Also hatred, a sense of revenge, self-righteousness, constant agitation, blind fury, and a distorted understanding of *jihād* have come to characterize many of these movements, replacing the peace, tranquility, harmony, sense of justice based on objectivity, and the carrying out of combat, when necessary on the basis of honor and according to the Divine Law, that have characterized authentic manifestations of Islam from the beginning and that are found reflected in both the Quran and the personality and actions of the Prophet. In trying to render back to Islam its power on the stage of history and to overcome the effects of injustice, many of these movements have disfigured the nature of Islam itself. Rather than being a genuine revival of Islam, a revival that is in fact trying to take place in many quarters, they are in reality the other side of the coin of modernism, but of a much more dangerous kind than the earlier forms of puritanical reformism, because these new forms of "fundamentalism" make use of the language and certain popular symbols of the Islamic religion while adopting some of the most negative and spiritually devastating aspects of the modern West. Furthermore, in the name of religious fervor, they close the door to all intellectual efforts and logical deliberations about the problems and dangers that do confront the Islamic world, and they adopt an exclusivism opposed to other religions at a time when accord between religions is so much needed.

If the hopes and aspirations of the Islamic world continue to be shattered by the forces of current events, there is no doubt that the revolutionary type of "fundamentalist" movements and violent radicalism will continue to manifest themselves and even to spread. One must not forget the fact that many of these movements, such as that of the Taliban in Afghanistan, have been supported and aggrandized not only by internal forces, such as neo-Wahhābism, but also sometimes by external forces (in the case of the Taliban, elements of the Pakistani military and at the beginning of this movement even the United States), providing support in one form or another for the continuation of the life and growth of such movements. The truth of the matter is that once an ideology of this kind is tried, it cannot continue to survive for long unless it is able to achieve the goals it has promised. Islam is still strong enough in the Islamic world to be able to judge in the long run, if not the short run, the Islamicity of all the movements and ideologies that use its name. Most likely, with the passage of time, the rigor of this test by the religious conscience of the community will be felt more strongly by all movements, forces, and governments that speak of "Islamic ideology." Whatever the actual political implications of this sifting and testing of such forces by the Islamic population might be, there seems to be little doubt that on the level of religious thought, or of Islam itself considered as a religion, there is bound to be a greater discernment within Islamic society concerning all those movements that are dubbed "fundamentalist" today.

Ideology is a Western concept hardly translatable into Arabic and Persian. Once Islam itself is interpreted not as an all-embracing religion, or *al-dīn,* but as an ideology, or ideological prop, that serves a particular movement or regime, then the failure of that movement or regime reflects upon Islam itself. In this case, some of the people might lose their faith, but the majority most likely will begin to scrutinize and finally criticize the actual nature of the forces that have presented themselves as Islamic. Both of these tendencies are bound to occur in different degrees to the extent that the "fundamentalist" movements are able to wield actual power and to affect the everyday lives of human beings, but the vast majority of Muslims will continue to cling to their faith in Islam.

Finally, there is traditional Islam itself to consider, which, as stated, is often mistaken for "fundamentalism" as the term is currently used. Despite waves of modernism, puritanical reactions, messianism, and the violent and revolutionary or theologically limiting forms of "fundamentalism" that have appeared upon the scene, traditional Islam continues to survive. Most Muslims still follow it and still live in a world in which the equilibrium promulgated by the *Sharīʿah* and the serenity of Islamic spirituality are to be found to some extent, despite the experiences of European colonialism, a certain degree of decadence within the Islamic world (which became noticeable in the twelfth/eighteenth century and increased during the thirteenth/nineteenth century), the constant political turmoil, the numerous economic problems, and the pervasive invasion of Western cultural ideas and creations. Most of the interpreters of the *Sharīʿah* are still traditional *ʿulamāʾ*. The Sufi orders, far from being dead, still possess an inner vitality; one can also still find a few great spiritual masters within them. And the traditional intellectual and theological sciences are still alive and not by any means dead. Moreover, as already mentioned, during the past few decades a new class of scholars and thinkers has appeared in the Islamic world whose members are traditional in their adherence to and defense of the whole and integral Islamic tradition, but who also know the Western world in depth and are able to provide intellectual answers from the Islamic point of view to the philosophical, scientific, ideological, and social problems posed by the challenges of the modern world rather than having recourse to either blind faith, simple sloganeering and rhetoric, or mindless violence.

Traditional Islam is bound to survive in the future, especially since the very structure of the Islamic tradition, with its emphasis upon the direct link between human beings and God and lack of a central religious authority, contains the maximum protection for survival in a world such as that of today. Moreover, the newly created class of traditional Muslim scholars and thinkers, the new guardians of the tradition who are also fully cognizant of the nature of the modern world, its schools of thought, philosophies, and sciences, is bound to increase and is in fact doing so already. This trend is likely to continue, moreover, as various groups within the "fundamentalist" camp attempt to Islamicize society, knowledge, and education without the full support of the Islamic intellectual tradition and fail to deliver the results expected of them. The decay to some extent in the quality of traditional life is also likely to continue, but traditional Islam is bound to survive in its various dimensions and aspects and will ultimately be the criterion for judging exactly how Islamic are all those revivals and resurgent movements that claim an Islamic character.

For several centuries the predominant form of theology in the majority (Sunni) of the Islamic world has been Ash'arite, featuring an all-encompassing voluntarism based on the idea that the Divine Will itself defines what is good and what is evil and intelligence has no role to play in discernment between the two, resulting in a more or less fideist position, that is, relying on faith alone and making knowledge completely subservient to faith. Moreover, the rise of such movements as Wahhābism, the Salafiyyah, and the like has only helped strengthen this tendency, even though Ash'arism itself may be rejected. Even in the Shī'ite world, where the prevalent theology has been more conducive to the intellectual aspects of the Islamic tradition, the *akhbārī-uṣūlī* debates and the predominance of the exoteric element at the end of the Safavid period on led what are traditionally called the "intellectual sciences" (*al-'ulūm al-'aqliyyah*) to be eclipsed to a certain degree, although not by any means completely.

In any case, and despite the survival of centers of activity of the intellectual sciences in certain areas, especially in Persia and on the Indian subcontinent, when those Islamic thinkers affected by fideism and/or voluntarism confronted the West, they did so mostly from a perspective that was helpless before the specifically intellectual and rational challenges of the modern world and that had to have recourse to either an opposition based on fanaticism or refuge in the emotional aspect of faith alone without providing an intellectual response, which is only now appearing to some extent. The result of the earlier serious response to Western challenges, or perhaps one should say lack of response, could not have but been catastrophic, because the main challenge of the modem West to Islam, in contrast, let us say, to the Mongol invasion, is not primarily military, although the military dimension is certainly present even after the apparent end of the colonial period. Nor is it primarily religious in the narrower sense of the term, as it was in the encounter of Islam with Hinduism. The challenge, rather, concerns mainly the domain of the mind and requires a response suitable to its nature. During the contemporary period, the world of Islamic learning and thought has not produced its Ibn Sīnās, al-Bīrūnīs, or even its al-Ghazzālīs. The response of Islamic scholars has echoed for the most part the fideism and voluntarism that have dominated the religious centers of learning, with a few exceptions, to which I have already alluded.

During the past few years, Islamic thinkers have begun to confront this problem more fully and to come to terms with the necessity of responding to not only the social and political, but also the intellectual and cultural challenges of the West. Numerous authorities throughout the Islamic world have come to realize the importance of the re-Islamicization of the educational system and the integration of the modern sciences into the Islamic worldview. Many educational conferences dealing with these problems have been held and are being planned for the future. There is little doubt that this trend will continue to grow in coming years and not lose its momentum so easily. Attempts will most likely continue to be made to create a unified educational system in various Islamic countries to replace the two contending ones (the traditional Islamic and the modern) that dominate the scene at present. Likewise, efforts will continue to be expended to try to "Islamicize" various sciences, ranging from the humanities to the social and even the natural sciences, a process that is already attracting the attention of many leading Islamic thinkers. What is now being called "moderate Islam" will in fact most likely come from the success of such efforts and certainly not from some Western think tank.

The main question is whether, while making use of only one dimension of the Islamic tradition, namely, the *Sharī'ah,* and neglecting the other dimensions and the whole intellectual and spiritual tradition of Islam, it is possible to carry out such an enterprise. Is it in fact possible to integrate the sciences of nature into the Islamic perspective by limiting oneself only to the Islamic sciences of law and the literal meaning of the verses of the Quran? Or by replacing an intellectual response with piety, no matter how sincere that piety might be? At the present moment there are two forces at play in this endeavor to Islamicize education and the sciences. One is closely allied to certain segments of that spectrum called "fundamentalism" and thinks that the success of this process will result from nothing more than the reestablishment of the *Sharī'ah* in society. This group more or less follows the voluntarist-fideist theological position, to which it adds the rejection of the integral intellectual and spiritual tradition of Islam and a puritanical-rationalistic tendency going back to the so-called reform movements of the thirteenth/nineteenth century.

The second group, which is traditional rather than "fundamentalist," seeks to achieve the same goal of Islamicization, but through recourse to the complete Islamic intellectual tradition combined with an in-depth critique of the modern world itself based on traditional principles. While agreeing with the first group upon the importance of the implementation of the *Sharī'ah,* it believes that the intellectual challenges posed by the modern world can only be answered by, first of all, understanding the nature of these challenges in depth and, second, by applying the intellectual and spiritual principles of the Islamic tradition to counter these challenges and the premises of the modern worldview that oppose the sacred universe of Islam, not in this or that detail, but in principle. Furthermore, this latter group believes that the challenge of modernism cannot be answered until the Islamic intellectual and spiritual tradition is resuscitated and revived in its totality. It maintains that only the spiritual, inward, and esoteric aspects of religion are able to provide the remedy for certain cracks that have now appeared in the wall of exoteric religion in general as a result of the attacks of secularizing and antitraditional forces. The case of Islam cannot be an exception to this rule.

Both of these groups as well as their ideas and goals are bound to continue in the near future. Moreover, the degree of success that each school has will influence the course of Islamic theology and religious thought itself. Of course, the secularizing forces opposed to the educational and cultural aim of both groups are also alive and active in many lands and are bound to influence events in this domain to an appreciable degree, at least in some of the major Islamic countries. Their influence through educational channels upon Islamic thought itself is, however, in the long run bound to be less than that of the first two groups mentioned above. Where the secularists in educational theory and practice will wield their influence most visibly will be in helping to continue the existing dual system of education in the Islamic world, with the obvious results that such a system trains members of a single society who hold opposing views on crucial issues and who cannot unite with their fellow citizens in creating an integrated social and intellectual order.

In this realm, even those who wish to Islamicize the educational system often help unwittingly in its further secularization by their wish to sweep the already century-old "modern" educational institutions aside completely, in many of which generations of devout Muslims have sought to create some kind of bridge between the traditional schools and new ones and have even sought to mold the classical Islamic scientific vocabulary of such languages as Arabic and Persian to become suitable vehicles for the expression of contemporary scientific disciplines. In years to come, there will most likely be rivalry between those who wish to Islamicize the already existing educational institutions, thereby removing the present dichotomy that exists despite efforts by a number of dedicated Muslim teachers and thinkers over the past century, and those who would do away with the existing modern institutions completely in the name of model "new" institutions of an Islamic nature. Present-day efforts to create Islamic universities throughout the Muslim world and their minor successes outside the field of the specifically religious disciplines (such as Divine Law and hermeneutics), when set against the immense obstacles they face, reveal both the enormity of the task involved and the crucial role that the whole ongoing process of Islamicization in education and the sciences will have for the future of both Islamic thought and the Islamic world itself.

The increase in awareness of the Islamic world as a single entity, despite sectarian confrontations in certain areas, is itself one of the important trends to be observed in that world, a trend that is bound to continue with important political, economic, and cultural consequences. Both the traditionalists and the "fundamentalists" cherish the ideal of the unity of the Islamic world, although they envisage its realization in very different ways. Messianism has also always had the unification of the Islamic world as an intrinsic part of its goal and program. According to tradition, it is in fact the Mahdī who will finally reunify the Islamic world at the end of time. The rise of greater awareness of the Islamic ethos and reactions to the onslaught of the West have made the unity of the Islamic world a motto for political and religious forces of nearly every color and persuasion, save of course for secularists and nationalists. This strong Islamic sentiment has also been manipulated by some of the "fundamentalist" forces, and regimes have even been established, the immediate political ends of which are none other than the creation of this unity, but they usually have had no result save the further weakening of the bonds of the Islamic community, or *ummah*.

The desire to achieve this unity manifests itself also in a strong inclination in theological circles to have closer cooperation and better understanding between Sunnism and Shīʻism. This tendency, which is many decades old and which was highlighted by the declaration half a century ago by Shaykh al-Shalṭūt, then rector of al-Azhar University, that Twelve-Imam Shīʻite (Jaʻfarī) Law would be taught as one of the orthodox schools of law in that venerable institution, is bound to continue. Also intra-Islamic dialogue between Sunni and Shīʻite thinkers will most likely increase in the legal, theological, and philosophical arenas. Parallel with these religious developments, however, political use of Sunni-Shīʻite differences not only continues, but becomes aggravated to the extent that Islam is used as a political instrument by one group or regime against another or by the West. These differences provide an ideal opportunity for all the external forces to reap their own benefits from the weakening of the Islamic world and the creation of chaos and disorder—not to speak of open warfare—therein. Acute confrontation between Sunnis and Shīʻites, which we see especially in Iraq, but also in Lebanon, Saudi Arabia, the Persian Gulf region, Afghanistan, Pakistan, and India, constitutes one of the greatest problems of the Islamic world today, aggravated especially by events in Iraq. These disturbances, which escalated into wars and terrorist attacks of the past few years between Sunnis and Shīʻites, are unlikely to disappear in the presence of the political forces that are active particularly in the central areas of the Islamic world. Well-meaning Islamic thinkers and the traditional *ʻulamāʼ* in both camps must direct their full attention to this crucial issue and create, through dialogue with each other and rapprochement on theological and even legal matters, an ambience of accord opposed to extremism and radicalism in both camps. There is every indication that, barring unforeseen political obstacles, this cooperation will increase in the future. Certainly most Muslims are in favor of it.

Against this strong desire toward "unification" and the creation of greater awareness of the Islamic peoples as a single people, or *ummah,* as mentioned in the Quran, stands not only the force of nationalism in its secular sense, as derived from the French Revolution, and various forms of ethnic provincialism, but also the virulent forms of opposition to Shī'ism associated with many of the existing forms of "fundamentalism," such as Wahhābism, the Taliban, and al-Qā'idah. One can also see this opposition in a more moderate and sober form from Arab nationalism, which implicitly made Sunnism one of its bases and neglected Shī'ism, which now dominates one of the major Arab countries, that is, Iraq.

Since the thirteenth/nineteenth century, the forces of Arab nationalism, Turkish nationalism, Iranian nationalism, and the like have been very powerful in the Middle East region of the Islamic world. Now, there are also revolutionary pan-Islamic movements that oppose all such ideologies in the name of the political unity of the Islamic world. These two contending forces are bound to struggle against each other in the years ahead. It is difficult to imagine that the forces for the unification of Islam will succeed in achieving a goal that, according to Prophetic tradition (*Ḥadīth*), is to be accomplished only by the Mahdī himself, although greater cooperation, communication, and exchange are likely to take place among various Islamic nations and peoples in many fields, ranging from the economic and political to the cultural. Nor are the forces of nationalism likely to die out completely. In fact, additional manifestations of local nationalism are now occurring, which, if successful, would not only *not* lead to the unity of the Islamic world, but would increasingly isolate small and helpless states and put them at the mercy of outside forces, which could manipulate them more easily than if the Islamic world were united.

There is, however, another factor to consider, what one can call traditional "Islamic nationalism" in the sense of the famous *ḥadīth,* "The love of one's nation (*waṭan*) comes from faith." Long before the French Revolution, Arabs knew they were not Persians or Turks and vice versa, although Arabs could travel from Tangiers and settle in Delhi without any difficulty or Persians migrate to Istanbul or Hyderabad and make it a second home. Many analysts confuse this traditional awareness of ethnic identity with the more recent forms of the European type of nationalism. Between one extreme, the utopian idea of a single Islamic state covering the whole Islamic world, and the other, small warring states that continue to weaken internally as a result of constant enmity and rivalry, one can envisage the possibility of the rise, once again, of a kind of political thought that combines the ideal of Islamic unity based on culture, Divine Law, intellectual life, and so on, with separate but closely allied political units that would embrace the major peoples and cultural zones of the Islamic world, such as the Arabic, the Persian, the Turkish, and so forth. It is most difficult to predict trends in such a domain where, in a world in chaos, political factors are so diverse, where one stands on shifting sand. But certainly the combination of religion with patriotism in a more traditional sense is possible, especially among peoples already scorched by the fires of fanaticism and extremism forced upon them in the name of Islam and for the sake of an elusive and as yet nonexistent international Islamic order, which will not be able to replace people's natural love for their own immediate homeland, language, and culture. Claims of Islamic unity without its realization can even dangerously weaken their centuries-old love of matters Islamic, a love that has always been combined in their eyes with attachment to their homeland, seen as "their part" of *dār al-islām.*

There is little doubt that what has been called the "defiance of Islam" in the face of the modern world will continue in future years, but it is likely to take new forms in addition to already existing ones. Although political upheavals using the name of Islam are bound to continue in a world in which Islamic forces do not enjoy complete freedom of action, where instead external powers have access to and manipulate such forces, other reactions not based simply upon sentiments and fanaticism are also likely to occur. Some current forces working for revival use radio and television to attack the West; their representatives stand in buildings emulating Western architecture and drive through streets designed according to modern ideas of urbanization. Other forces, however, are already coming forward, and are likely to do so more in the future, to examine more critically Western science and technology, art and architecture, and social theories and ideas of development, which the Islamic world has been copying blindly, as if they had nothing to do with religion, while "attacking" Western civilization, of which they are the products. There is likely to be a greater battle within the Islamic world with modernism than ever before in the fields of the arts, architecture, literature, science, and philosophy. The recent interest in the revival of Islamic architecture and city planning as well as the arts and crafts is a sign of this important tendency, which only complements the revival of the intellectual and spiritual tradition of Islam. The battle is likely to be a bitter one, carried out directly with intellectual and cultural tools in fields ranging from historiography, the social sciences, language and literature, the arts and sciences to the study of other religions and indirectly through social and political battles. These intellectual battles will, moreover, affect the religious thought of Islam itself and the mentality of Muslims and therefore influence the whole course of future events in the Islamic world.

As various waves of Mahdiism and "fundamentalism" fail to solve the problems of the Islamic world until the Mahdī actually appears, and as the hitherto current types of modernism display their bankruptcy in a world in which the civilization that gave birth to them is itself facing its greatest crises, the central reality in the Islamic world will most likely become the battle not between traditional Islam and openly declared secularism and modernism, as was the case until recently, but between traditional Islam and various countertraditional ideologies parading as Islam. It is one of the characteristics of the life of the late twentieth and early twenty-first centuries, seen also fully in Christianity, that the forces opposed to religion no longer function only outside the citadel of religion, but try to destroy it from within by penetrating that citadel and masquerading as part of religion. There is a great difference between the time when Jamāl al-Dīn Astrābādī, known as Afghānī, wrote his *Refutation of the Materialists,* attacking the modern West as materialistic and agnostic, or the scholars of al-Azhar attacking Communism as godless, and the recent exchange between traditional Muslims and those who espouse all kinds of modern and secular ideologies, but who also call themselves Islamic. The main battle of the future in the Islamic world will most likely be between these two forces, and the central problem will be the subversion of Islam from within by forces claiming to speak in its name.

In years to come, likewise, the debate between those who would interpret Islam as religion in its traditional sense and those who speak of it as ideology is bound to continue, as are discussions between those who seek to revive ethics by reforming Islamic society from within and those for whom reform of ethics can only come by violent change of the norms and structures of a society from without. There will be those who will seek to blend Islam with every aspect of society; in the other camp will be those who are not necessarily irreligious (often quite the contrary), but who believe that, in order to preserve the purity of their religion, its sacred name should not be used in the politico-economic arena, where the very nature of the forces involved can only sully it. There will also be those who are not worried about the name of religion being sullied, but who wish to limit religion, against the teachings of Islam, to the private domain because of their own secularist views.

One will continue to see a strong opposition between those who have a triumphalistic and often sentimental view of Islam, according to which everything of value is "Islamic" and even the West is successful because of its heritage of Islamic science, and others who do not at all wish to identify Islam with the modern West and its triumphs, but who see Islam rather as an ally of the other traditional religions, including Christianity and Judaism, against modernism, which opposes not only Islam, but religion as such. They see the real battle of the future as not being between Islam and the West, but between tradition and modernism/postmodernism in both Islam and the West and in fact throughout the world. Finally, most likely there will continue to be contention between those who wish to revive the Islamic tradition in its wholeness and those who undermine the possibility of this revival by misusing the name of Islam to serve ideas of a completely different nature, as a result of their sense of inferiority toward the modern world, which is often veiled by an emotional triumphalism leading in many cases to "fundamentalism." In all these cases, there will be the desire, at least outwardly, to revive Islamic society and the ethical norms that govern it. This element will remain the common denominator, while all the differences here stated concerning not only the manner of implementing such a program of revival, but all the other factors of both an intellectual and political nature, will most likely continue.

It must be recalled that the four types of realities or movements present within the Islamic world today, namely, "fundamentalism," modernism, Mahdiism or messianism, and traditionalism, are not of course always exclusive of each other, although certain positions, such as that of the traditionalists, exclude others, such as that of the modernists. For example, in the various groups usually gathered together in the category of "fundamentalism," there are some who are attached to Sufism and close to the traditionalist perspective, others who share certain affinities with the antitraditional modernists, and yet others who are strongly attracted by Mahdiist sentiments. And of course there are the countertraditional elements that talk of Islam, but in fact represent the very antithesis of traditional Islam. Finally, some Mahdiists in a sense belong to the traditional world, while others have allied themselves with the "fundamentalists" of the countertraditional type.

If all the diverse forces present in the contemporary Islamic world have been divided here into these four categories, it has been for the purpose of facilitating discussion about the complex and yet basic types or attitudes discernible in the Islamic world today. Moreover, these four categories can be analyzed just as well in terms of the division between traditional, antitraditional, and countertraditional made earlier. Of course it is essential to remember that, in most parts of the Islamic world, the majority of Muslims continue their lives in the traditional manner and are not involved in any of the theological, religious, or political reactions to the modern world already mentioned. The vast number of Muslims, whose belonging to the Islamic tradition must be still defined in terms of traditional Islamic categories rather than of reactions to modern ideologies and thought patterns, must always be kept in mind.

Islam is still very much alive in the Islamic world today; but there are also so-called Islamic forces within that world that are often manipulated and altered in such a manner that, although they remain to be reckoned with, it is doubtful whether they are still Islamic. Not everything that happens in the Islamic world is Islamic, even if so called, nor does every birth in that part of the world herald an Islamic renaissance. After all, according to authentic Islamic traditions, the Antichrist is also to be born in the Islamic world. Close attention must be paid to the Islamic character of all that is called Islamic in a world in which the use and misuse of practically anything can take place, as long as it serves the aims of the powers that be. In any full discussion of Islam today, one must ask in every instance what is meant by "Islamic." Islam is not a vague idea. It is a religion with its Sacred Book, the traditions of its Blessed Prophet, Divine Law, social and economic structures, distinct ethical teachings, theology, philosophy, science, mystical paths, and a specific manner of looking at the world of nature and of creating art. There are certainly such things as Islamic orthodoxy and orthopraxy, and therefore their opposites exist as well. There are today traditional, antitraditional, and countertraditional forces, and such basic differences cannot be glossed over by the simple use of the term "Islamic."

Today we are witness to a vast religious community that is still very much alive and whose teachings on all levels, from the most esoteric to those concerned with daily laws, are kept to a large extent intact. But we are also now witnessing the destruction of certain elements of this religious world, not only through openly "fundamentalist" and modernistic forces alien to its genius, but also through the appearance of those forces that put on the guise of Islamicity to avoid appearing alien and to be able to enter within the citadel of Islam. It will serve the interests of neither the Islamic world, nor Christianity, nor even the secularized West to remain oblivious to fundamental differences between the forces at play here. Mass media dominated by a new version of triumphalism in the Islamic world itself and opportunism combined with ignorance in the West should not be allowed to blind people to the difference between Islamic forces seeking genuine intellectual, political, and social expression and totally anti-Islamic or at best non-Islamic forces using the guise of Islam to further their own ends. Nor is it wise to neglect the more hidden forms of inner revival and rejuvenation that have always been and will always be at the heart of every authentic religious regeneration.

It is the hope of every Muslim concerned with the future of Islam that the energy and vitality of Islam, along with those of other religions similarly faced with the withering effects of modern secularism, will be channeled in a constructive manner and not find expression in volcanic eruptions and violent reactions that will, in the long run, leave both the Islamic world and the world at large impoverished spiritually, whatever they might do in the short term to serve the immediate aims of present-day powers. Let us hope that Islamic movements and groups will channel and guide their activities in a manner that is worthy in the sight of God and not according to what might appear politically or economically opportune. Islamic history stands as witness to the fact that only those acts that have been performed in the light of eternity and according to the Will of the One, the surrender to whose Will is the raison d'être of Islam itself, have had an enduring effect upon the hearts and souls of Muslims and upon the Islamic world at large.

As the Quran states, the future is in God's Hands alone. All the tendencies mentioned above exist and can be projected into trends for the near future, but only in a provisional way, for, according to Islam, there is no determinism in history as seen from only the human point of view. A single unforeseen event or the appearance of a single figure could change the entire texture of forces and tendencies that are to be seen in the Islamic world. What can be said with certainty is that, despite becoming weakened, the Islamic tradition is still very much alive in both its outer and inner dimensions and that, at this point in its history, it has to react to a multiplicity of challenges from both without and within, some of which are openly opposed to it and others, though they bear its name, are in reality of quite another nature. In any case, the vitality of the Islamic tradition will continue to the end of days, as promised by God and the Prophet. As to which of the trends within the Islamic world cited above will gain the upper hand, what plans the outside world hides behind veils of secrecy as it conspires to manipulate these trends and tendencies, and how these forces will affect the Islamic world itself, it is not possible to say with certitude. In this domain more than in all others, one can best conclude with the traditional Islamic dictum that God knows best.

wa'Llāh^{u} a'lam
(and God knows best)

Appendices

Appendix I

THE TRADITIONAL TEXTS USED IN THE PERSIAN *MADRASAHS* AND THE QUESTION OF THE REVIVAL OF TRADITIONAL ISLAMIC EDUCATION

To understand the traditional Islamic educational system, it is necessary to consider not only the "philosophy of education" underlying the system, but also the actual curriculum of the *madrasahs,* or traditional schools. In many parts of the Islamic world, the curriculum became more and more limited in scope from about the eighth/fourteenth and ninth/fifteenth centuries on, until during the last two or three centuries there remained only subjects dealing with the transmitted sciences (*al-'ulūm al-naqliyyah*). The Persian *madrasahs,* however, reflected until more recently, more than the traditional schools of most other areas, almost the full spectrum of both the transmitted (*naqlī*) and the intellectual (*'aqlī*) sciences[1] that were taught in *madrasahs* as well as in private circles in various centers of Islamic learning during the full flowering of educational activity in earlier centuries of Islamic history.

In Persia and certain adjoining areas, such as Iraq, Afghanistan, Muslim India, and some of the republics of Central Asia, until a few generations ago there were many *madrasahs* that taught not only the Quran, *Ḥadīth,* law, and theology, but also the other disciplines included in the traditional curriculum, ranging from medicine to astronomy. It is only during the last hundred years that, even in this area, some of the subjects have been discontinued, while others have been changed or modified and new books of instruction introduced for their teaching.

Nearly seventy years ago the Persian scholar and statesman Seyyed Hasan Taqizadeh,[2] who had himself received his early education in one of the *madrasahs* and who was much interested in the Islamic sciences, asked one of the leading Islamic scholars of the day, Muḥammad Ṭāhir Ṭabarsī, known as Mīrzā Ṭāhir Tunikābunī, to write a treatise in which the works studied in the *madrasahs* would be described for posterity before this knowledge became forgotten. Mīrzā Ṭāhir, who was one of the leading traditional philosophers of Persia during the past century, set about this task and composed a treatise, which was finally published after a long period of neglect.[3] It remains one of the most authoritative and complete works on the subject, reflecting the educational curriculum in Persian *madrasahs* for the several centuries that preceded the composition of the treatise in 1938.

According to Mīrzā Ṭāhir, the texts used for teaching the various sciences in the *madrasahs* of Persia and adjacent regions were as follows:

THE TRANSMITTED (*NAQLIYYAH*) SCIENCES

I. The Science of Morphology (ṣarf)

1. *Ṣarf-i mīr:* A short treatise in Persian on the subject of the morphology of the Arabic language by Mīr Sayyid Sharīf Jurjānī, who lived in the eighth/fourteenth century.[4]
2. *Taṣrīf-i zanjānī* with commentary: A text written by ʿIzz al-Dīn Ibrāhīm Zanjānī, who lived in the seventh/thirteenth century, and commented on by Saʿd al-Dīn Masʿūd ibn ʿUmar Taftāzānī (eighth/fourteenth century).[5]
3. *Sharḥ-i niẓām:* The text of this work is the *Shāfiyah* of Jamāl al-Dīn Abū ʿUmar, known as Ibn Ḥājib al-Mālikī (seventh/thirteenth century), while the commentary is by Niẓām al-Dīn Ḥasan Nayshābūrī, whose commentary is favored over numerous others written on this celebrated work.

In older days, students also made use of *Marāḥ al-arwāḥ* by Aḥmad ibn ʿAlī ibn Masʿūd, but this work lost its popularity and gradually was dropped from the list of the main texts studied.

II. The Science of Syntax (Grammar; naḥw)

1. *al-ʿAwāmil* of Jurjānī: The work of the fifth/eleventh-century scholar ʿAbd al-Qāhir Jurjānī, on which many commentaries have been written, but it is the text itself that has remained popular throughout the centuries.

2. *al-'Awāmil* of Mullā Muḥsin: Although some consider this work to be by Mullā Muḥsin Fayḍ Kāshānī, the celebrated student of Mullā Ṣadrā, most likely it is by Mullā Muḥsin Muḥammad ibn Ṭāhir Qazwīnī, who lived in the late Safavid period and who also wrote a commentary on the *Alfiyyah* of Ibn Mālik.[6]
3. *al-Ṣamadiyyah:* A celebrated treatise by Shaykh Bahā' al-Dīn 'Āmilī[7] written for his nephew 'Abd al-Ṣamad. Numerous commentaries have been written on it, of which the most famous are the major and minor commentaries by Sayyid 'Alī Khān, who was his contemporary.
4. *al-Unmūdhaj:* A summary by the famous sixth/twelfth-century grammarian Jār Allāh Abū'l-Qāsim al-Zamakhsharī of his own extensive grammar, which is one of the best grammatical studies of Arabic.
5. *al-Kāfiyah:* Another of the important grammatical works of Ibn Ḥājib, on which numerous commentaries have been composed in Arabic and Persian, including those of Sayyid Sharīf Jurjānī and Sayyid Rukn al-Dīn Astrābādī, who was a student of Naṣīr al-Dīn Ṭūsī.
6. *al-Alfiyyah:* A popular work by the seventh/thirteenth-century Andalusian grammarian Ibn Mālik containing a thousand verses in which the principles of *naḥw* are outlined. Of the numerous commentaries written on it, that of Jalāl al-Dīn al-Suyūṭī is the most popular in Persia.
7. *Mughnī al-labīb:* A work by Jamāl al-Dīn ibn Yūsuf, known as Ibn Hishām, who lived in the eighth/fourteenth century. There are several well-known commentaries on this work, including those of Muḥammad ibn Abī Bakr al-Damāmīnī and Jalāl al-Dīn al-Suyūṭī.

III. The Literary Sciences (Rhetoric; ma'ānī and bayān) and (the Art of Metaphor; badī')

1. *Talkhīṣ-i miftāḥ:* The most popular work in this field has been this summary made by Jalāl al-Dīn 'Abd al-Raḥmān Qazwīnī (eighth/fourteenth century) of *Miftāḥ al-'ulūm* of Sirāj al-Dīn Yūsuf al-Sakkākī (seventh/thirteenth century), a work whose third section is devoted to the literary sciences. This summary is usually studied along with the two commentaries of Sa'd al-Dīn Taftāzānī, the long (*Muṭawwal*) and the short (*Mukhtaṣar*).
2. *Dalā'il al-i'jāz:* This work by the fifth/eleventh-century scholar 'Abd al-Qāhir Jurjānī has become popular only during the past century or two.
3. *Asrār al-balāghah:* Another fairly short work by Jurjānī.

IV. The Principles of Jurisprudence (uṣūl al-fiqh)

1. *al-Dharī'ah:* A famous work by 'Alī ibn Abī Aḥmad Ḥusayn, known as Sayyid Murtaḍā as well as 'Ālam al-Hudā (fifth/eleventh century).
2. *'Iddat al-uṣūl:* One of the most respected works on *uṣūl* by the famous fifth/eleventh-century Shī'ite scholar Shaykh al-Ṭā'ifah Muḥammad ibn 'Alī al-Ṭūsī, usually studied with the commentary of Mullā Khalīl ibn Ghāzī Qazwīnī.
3. *Minhaj al-wuṣūl ilā 'ilm al-uṣūl:* A work by the seventh/thirteenth-century scholar Najm al-Dīn Abū'l-Qāsim, known as Muḥaqqiq-i Ḥillī.
4. *Mabādi' al-wuṣūl ilā 'ilm al-uṣūl:* A work by the well-known 'Allāmah Ḥillī (seventh/thirteenth century), on which Miqdād ibn 'Abd Allāh al-Suyūrī al-Ḥillī has written a commentary.
5. *Tahdhīb al-uṣūl:* Another well-known work on the subject by 'Allāmah Ḥillī.
6. *Ma'ālim al-dīn:* This work by Ḥasan ibn Shaykh Zayn al-Dīn, known as Shahīd-i Thānī (tenth/sixteenth century), is very popular and has been commented on by numerous authors.
7. *Zubdat al-uṣūl:* This is one of the best-known religious works of Shaykh Bahā' al-Dīn 'Āmilī, on which his own student, Jawād ibn Sa'd Allāh al-Baghdādī, as well as Mawlā Ṣāliḥ ibn Aḥmad Sarawī have written widely studied commentaries.
8. *Kitāb al-wāfiyah:* A short but masterly treatise by Mullā 'Abd Allāh ibn Ḥajj Muḥammad Tūnī Bushrawī Khurāsānī (eleventh/seventeenth century). Several of the outstanding scholars of the past three centuries, including Sayyid al-Sanad Baḥr al-'Ulūm, have written commentaries on it.
9. *al-Qawānīn:* A work by the thirteenth/nineteenth-century jurisprudent Mīrzā Abū'l-Qāsim ibn Muḥammad Gīlānī.
10. *al-Fuṣūl fī 'ilm al-uṣūl:* This very popular work of Muḥammad Ḥusayn ibn 'Abd al-Raḥīm Ṭihrānī Rāzī (thirteenth/nineteenth century) gained almost immediate acceptance after its composition.
11. *Farā'iḍ al-uṣūl:* Also known as *Rasā'il*, a work composed a little over a century ago by the great master of *uṣūl,* Shaykh Murtaḍā ibn Aḥmad Amīn Anṣārī.

Most of these works belong to the later centuries of Islamic history. Several other works in *uṣūl,* written earlier (many by Sunni rather than Shī'ite scholars) and popular before the composition of these later works, continue to be studied, but not to the same extent as before.[8] Some of these works are the *al-Mustaṣfā* of Ghazzālī; the *Aḥkām fī uṣūl al-aḥkām* of Sayf al-Dīn al-Amīnī (seventh/thirteenth century); the *Mukhtaṣar al-uṣūl* of his student, Ibn Ḥājib, on which many commentaries have been written; the *Minhaj al-wuṣūl ilā ʿilm al-uṣūl* by Qāḍī Nāṣir al-Dīn Bayḍāwī (seventh/thirteenth century); the *Maḥṣūl* of Fakhr al-Dīn Rāzī (sixth/twelfth century) and its summary by Sirāj al-Dīn Urmawī (seventh/thirteenth century); and the *Jamʿ al-jawāmiʿ* of Tāj al-Dīn al-Subkī al-Shaftiʿī (eighth/fourteenth century).

V. Ḥadīth and Jurisprudence (fiqh)

Among the Shīʿites, the main source of *Ḥadīth*, which includes the sayings of both the Prophet and the Imams (although the clear distinction between them is preserved), and which serves, after the Noble Quran, as the fountainhead for the injunctions of the *Sharīʿah,* consists of four books, which are as follows:

1. *al-Kāfī:* The *Kitāb al-kāfī,* comprised of both *uṣūl* (principles) and *furūʿ* (branches), by Muḥammad ibn Yaʿqūb al-Kulaynī (fourth/tenth century), is the most authoritative of all these sources.[9] Numerous commentaries have been written on this work, especially on the *uṣūl,* including those of Mīr Dāmād (tenth/sixteenth century), Mullā Ṣadrā—his being one of the most important works of Islamic philosophy—Rafīʿ al-Dīn Muḥammad Ṭabāṭabāʾī (eleventh/seventeenth century), and Mullā Muḥammad Bāqir Majlisī (eleventh/seventeenth century).
2. *Man lā yaḥduruhu'l-faqīh:* A work by Ibn Bābūyah, known as Shaykh-i Ṣadūq, on which Mullā Muḥammad Taqī Majlisī (eleventh/seventeenth century) wrote two commentaries, one in Persian and the other in Arabic.
3. *al-Tahdhīb:* A major authoritative source by Shaykh at-Ṭāʾifah Muḥammad al-Ṭūsī (fifth/eleventh century).
4. *al-Istibṣār:* A second work of authority by Muḥammad al-Ṭūsī.

As for books on the science of jurisprudence itself and its basis in the Quran and *Ḥadīth,* numerous works have been written on it by both Sunni and Shīʿite authorities, of which the following became particularly popular during the past few centuries when Persia became predominately Shīʿite:

1. *Wasā'il al-shī'ah ilā aḥkām al-sharī'ah,* by Muḥammad ibn Ḥasan, known as Shaykh Ḥurr-i 'Āmilī (eleventh/seventeenth century).
2. *Kitāb al-wāfī,* by Mullā Muḥsin Fayḍ Kāshānī (eleventh/seventeenth century), concerned mostly with both the traditions upon which *fiqh* is based and the injunctions themselves.
3. *Biḥār al-anwār,* a voluminous religious encyclopedia by Muḥammad Bāqir Majlisī that includes nearly every branch of the religious sciences, from sacred history to jurisprudence. All parts of this work have been and still are popular in *madrasahs* throughout Persia.
4. *al-Nihāyah,* by Muḥammad al-Ṭūsī, with numerous commentaries by *mujtahids* of nearly every generation.
5. *al-Mabsūṭ,* also by Muḥammad al-Ṭūsī and commented on by numerous *mujtahids* over the ages.
6. *Sharā'i' al-islām,* by Muḥaqqiq-i Ḥillī and usually studied along with its summary called the *Mukhtaṣar-i nāfi'.*
7. *Masālik al-afhām ilā fahm sharā'i' al-islām,* by Shaykh Zayn al-Dīn, known as Shahīd-i Thānī.
8. *Madārik al-aḥkām,* by Shams al-Dīn Muḥammad ibn 'Alī 'Āmilī (tenth/sixteenth century) on which many commentaries have been written, the most famous being *Jawāhir al-kalām* of Muḥammad Ḥasan Najafī (thirteenth/nineteenth century).
9. *Irshād al-adhhān fī aḥkām al-īmān,* by Ḥasan ibn Yūsuf ibn Muṭahhar al-Ḥillī. Several well-known commentaries have been written on it, such as the *Ghāyat al-murād* of Jamāl al-Dīn Makkī, known as Shahīd-i Awwal (eighth/fourteenth century), and *Majma' al-fā'idah wa'l-burhān* of Aḥmad ibn Muḥammad Muqaddas-i Ardibīlī (tenth/sixteenth century).
10. *Qawā'id al-aḥkām,* also by Muḥaqqiq-i Ḥillī. Several important commentaries have been written on it, such as *Īḍāḥ al-qawā'id* by the author's son, *Kanz al-fawā'id* by his nephew Sayyid 'Amīd al-Dīn, *Jāmi' al-maqāṣid fī sharḥ al-qawā'id* by Muḥaqqiq-i Thānī Nūr al-Dīn 'Alī ibn 'Abd al-'Alī Karakī (tenth/sixteenth century), *Kashf al-lithām 'an mu'ḍalāt qawā'id al-aḥkām* by Bahā' al-Dīn Muḥammad Iṣfahānī, known as Fāḍil-i Hindī (twelfth/eighteenth century), and *Miftāḥ al-karāmah fī sharḥ qawā'id al-'Allāmah* by Sayyid Jawād 'Āmilī (twelfth/eighteenth century).
11. *Lum'a-yi dimashqiyyah,* by Shahīd-i Awwal with commentaries by Shahīd-i Thānī.

During the thirteenth/nineteenth century the *Makāsib* and *Ṭahārah* of Shaykh Murtaḍā Anṣārī, dealing with specific aspects of *fiqh,* have also become very popular and have been commented on by some of the most celebrated *mujtahids* of that era, such as Mullā Muḥammad Kāẓim Khurāsānī and Sayyid Muḥammad Kāẓim Yazdī.

VI. The Sciences Pertaining to Ḥadīth *and Its History ('ilm al-dirāyah)*

1. *Risālat al-bidāyah fī 'ilm al-dirāyah,* by Shahīd-i Thānī.
2. The *Wajīzah,* by Shaykh Bahā' al-Dīn 'Āmilī.
3. *Rawāshiḥ al-samāwiyyah,* by the great philosopher and founder of the School of Isfahan,[10] Mīr Dāmād, who before composing his commentary on the *Kāfī,* wrote the *Rawāshiḥ* on the science of *Ḥadīth.*
4. *Nuzhat al-naẓar fī sharḥ nukhbat al-fikar,* both text and commentary by Ḥāfiẓ Shihāb al-Dīn 'Asqalānī (ninth/fifteenth century). The work has many other commentaries, which, however, have not become popular in Persia.
5. The *Alfiyyah,* by Jalāl al-Dīn Abū Bakr al-Suyūṭī (ninth/fifteenth century).

VII. The Quranic Sciences (tafsīr)

Tafsīr is the crown of all the Islamic sciences and possesses many branches. As far as the science of the recitation of the Quran (*qirā'ah wa tajwīd*) is concerned, the popular treatise in Persia has been the long poem in rhyming couplets (*qaṣīdah*) *Ḥirz al-amānī wa wajh al-tahānī,* of Abū Muḥammad Qāsim al-Shāṭibī (sixth/twelfth century), among the many commentaries on which are *Sirāj al-qāri'* of Ibn Qāṣiḥ (eighth/fourteenth century), which is the best known, and the *Muqaddimah* of Muḥammad ibn Muḥammad al-Jazarī (ninth/fifteenth century).

Among the Quranic commentaries, composed by both Sunni and Shī'ite scholars, the most popular are the following:

1. The *Tafsīr* of 'Alī ibn Ibrāhīm al-Qummī (fourth/tenth century).
2. *Majma' al-bayān* of Abū 'Alī Faḍl ibn Ḥasan Ṭabarsī (sixth/twelfth century), summarized by the author himself as *Majma' al-jawāmi'.*
3. *Rawḥ al-jinān wa rūḥ al-janān* of Abū'l-Futūḥ Rāzī (sixth/ twelfth century), a vast Persian commentary that is also a masterpiece of Persian literature.

4. *Tafsīr-i ṣāfī* of Mullā Muḥsin Fayḍ Kāshānī, a commentary that is at once gnostic and theological.
5. The *Tafsīr* of al-Ṭabarī, the celebrated commentary by the fourth/tenth-century author Muḥammad ibn Jarīr al-Ṭabarī.
6. *al-Tafsīr al-kabīr,* one of the most extensive of all Quranic commentaries, by the sixth/twelfth-century theologian Fakhr al-Dīn Rāzī.
7. *al-Kashshāf* of Jār Allāh al-Zamakhsharī (sixth/twelfth century). Numerous commentaries have been written on it.
8. *Tafsīr anwār al-tanzīl wa asrār al-ta'wīl* of Qāḍī Nāṣir al-Dīn al-Bayḍāwī. Many commentaries have been written on this work.
9. *Kanz al-'irfān* of Miqdād ibn 'Abd Allāh al-Ḥillī (eighth/fourteenth century), dealing mostly with the Quranic basis of *Sharī'ite* injunctions (*aḥkām*).
10. *Zubdat al-bayān* of Aḥmad ibn Muḥammad (Muqaddas-i Ardibīlī), also dealing with the Quranic foundation of *Sharī'ite* injunctions.

THE INTELLECTUAL (*'AQLIYYAH*) SCIENCES

I. Logic (manṭiq)

1. *Risāla-yi kubrā:* A short treatise in Persian by Sayyid Sharīf Jurjānī.
2. *al-Ḥāshiyah* of Mullā 'Abd Allāh: One of the most popular works on logic, consisting of glosses on *Tahdhīb al-manṭiq* of Taftāzānī by Mullā 'Abd Allāh Yazdī (ninth/fifteenth century). The work has two parts, the first on logic and the second on theology (*kalām*). The first part alone became widely popular, while the second part is studied only among the religious students of Kurdistan.
3. *Sharḥ-i shamsiyyah:* The text is by Najm al-Dīn Dabīrān Kātibī Qazwīnī (seventh/thirteenth century),[11] while the commentary is by Quṭb al-Dīn Rāzī[12] (eighth/fourteenth century) and is one of the most popular works on logic.
4. *Sharḥ-i maṭāli' al-anwār:* The text is by Sirāj al-Dīn Urmawī (seventh/thirteenth century),[13] while the best-known commentary is by Sayyid Sharīf Jurjānī.
5. *Sharḥ-i manẓūmah:* Both the text and commentary are by the great Qajar philosopher and sage Ḥājjī Mullā Hādī Sabziwārī (thirteenth/nineteenth century). The work includes a complete cycle of traditional

philosophy starting with logic and ending with eschatology, prophetology, and ethics.[14]

6. *Sharḥ-i ishārāt:* The celebrated *al-Ishārāt wa'l-tanbīhāt* of Ibn Sīnā (fourth–fifth/tenth–eleventh century), with the commentaries of Fakhr al-Dīn Rāzī, Ṭūsī, and Quṭb al-Dīn Rāzī, has been over the centuries one of the mainstays of the programs of study in various branches of philosophy, including logic.
7. *Jawhar al-naḍīd fī sharḥ manṭiq al-tajrīd:* The *Tajrīd* is Naṣīr al-Dīn Ṭūsī's main theological work, but the first part is devoted to logic. With the commentary of his student, 'Allāmah Ḥasan ibn Yūsuf ibn al-Muṭahhar al-Ḥillī, this section on logic became known as a separate work and gained popularity during the thirteenth/nineteenth century.
8. *al-Baṣā'ir al-naṣīriyyah:* The work, by the seventh/twelfth-century philosopher Zayn al-Dīn 'Umar ibn Sahlān Sāwajī, was neglected until Muḥammad 'Abduh wrote a commentary on it and began to teach it at al-Azhar University in Cairo in the thirteenth/nineteenth century. It then gained popularity not only among Egyptian students, but among Persian ones as wel1.[15]
9. The logic of the *Ḥikmat al-ishrāq:* The whole of this masterpiece of *ishrāqī* theosophy by the founder of this school, Shaykh al-Ishrāq Shihāb al-Dīn Suhrawardī (sixth/twelfth century),[16] is extremely popular in Persia and is usually studied with the commentary of Quṭb al-Dīn Shīrāzī and the glosses of Mullā Ṣadrā. The logic, which is a departure from Peripatetic logic, is usually studied by students after they have completed the usual works on formal logic based on the *Organon* of Aristotle and the modifications made on it by Islamic logicians.
10. The logic of the *Shifā':* Because of its inaccessibility and difficult style, the logic of the *Shifā'* of Ibn Sīnā has never become a popular work. But being the most thorough and extensive treatment of formal logic in Islamic philosophy, it could not escape the attention of the most advanced students of the subject, who usually studied it with the glosses of Mullā Ṣadrā, Sayyid Aḥmad 'Alawī, and several other later *ḥakīms* of Persia.[17]

II. The Philosophical and Theological Sciences (falsafah and kalām)

1. *Sharḥ-i hidāyah:* The text of this celebrated work is by the seventh/thirteenth-century philosopher Athīr al-Dīn Abharī and consists of

three parts: logic, natural philosophy, and metaphysics. The section on logic was commented on by the ninth/fifteenth-century philosopher, Sufi, and jurisprudent Shams al-Dīn Fanārī, but, although this commentary has always been popular in Turkey, Syria, and Iraq, it has never become widely accepted in Persia. There are, however, numerous famous commentaries on the last two sections, of which those of Ḥusayn ibn Mu'īn al-Dīn Mībudī Yazdī and Mullā Ṣadrā are extremely well known in Persia and Afghanistan and in the Indian subcontinent.[18]

2. *al-Tajrīd:* This work of Naṣīr al-Dīn Ṭūsī is the main text for Shī'ite *kalām* and is usually studied with the following commentaries:[19]
   A. The commentary by 'Allāmah Ḥasan ibn Yūsuf al-Ḥillī.
   B. *Tasdīd al-qawā'id fī sharḥ tajrīd al-'aqā'id,* by the eighth/fourteenth-century theologian Shams al-Dīn Aḥmad Iṣfahānī, to which Mīr Sayyid Sharīf Jurjānī has written important glosses.
   C. The very popular commentary of the ninth/fifteenth-century scientist, philosopher, and theologian 'Alā' al-Dīn Qūshchī, which is famous throughout the Islamic world and on which over four hundred scholars have written glosses, including Dawānī and Khafrī.
   D. *Shawāriq al-ilhām fī sharḥ tajrīd al-kalām,* by 'Abd al-Razzāq Lāhījī (eleventh/seventeenth century), which, although incomplete, is widely read and considered one of the most important commentaries on the *Tajrīd.*[20]
3. *Sharḥ-i ishārāt:* As already mentioned in the section on logic, the whole of the *Ishārāt* of Ibn Sīnā, concerned not only with logic, but also with natural philosophy, metaphysics, and gnosis, as commented on by Fakhr al-Dīn Razī, Ṭūsī, and Quṭb al-Dīn Rāzī, has been over the centuries and continues to be one of the basic texts of Islamic philosophy in Persia.
4. *Ḥikmat al-ishrāq:* This work of Suhrawardī, along with the commentaries of Shams al-Dīn Shahrazūrī and Quṭb al-Dīn Shīrāzī and the glosses of Mullā Ṣadrā, constitutes the central work of the *ishrāqī* school and is studied by everyone who wishes to master the doctrines of this schoo1.[21]
5. *Sharḥ-i manẓūmah:* The already mentioned work of Sabziwārī is as popular in the general field of philosophy as it is in logic, and since the thirteenth/nineteenth century it has come to be taught in nearly all the *madrasahs* in Persia where philosophy forms part of the curriculum.

6. *al-Asfār al-arbaʿah:* The major opus of Mullā Ṣadrā consists of four "journeys" (*safar*) and deals, respectively, with metaphysics, theology (in its general sense, not as *kalām*), natural philosophy, psychology, and eschatology.[22] This vast work is considered the most advanced treatise on philosophy in Persia and is studied only after students have mastered all the other branches and schools of the "intellectual" and even "transmitted" sciences. Many commentaries have been written on it, including those of the thirteenth/nineteenth-century students of Mullā Ṣadrā's school, Mullā ʿAlī Nūrī, Ḥājjī Mullā Ḥādī Sabziwārī, and Āqā ʿAlī Mudarris (Zunūzī). (Commentaries on this work have continued into the contemporary period by such notable authorities as ʿAllāmah Sayyid Muḥammad Ḥusayn Ṭabāṭabā'ī.)

Several other works of Mullā Ṣadrā, such as *al-Mabda' wa'l-maʿād, al-Shawāhid al-rubūbiyyah, al-Mashāʿir, al-ʿArshiyyah, Mafātīḥ al-ghayb,* and *Asrār al-āyāt,* have also been popular among students of *madrasahs* since the beginning of the thirteenth/nineteenth century, when the teachings of Mullā Ṣadrā were revived throughout Persia, especially in the School of Tehran.

III. Sufism and Gnosis (taṣawwuf and ʿirfān)

1. *Kitāb al-tamhīd fī sharḥ qawāʿid al-tawḥīd:* Also called *Tawḥīd al-qawāʿid,* this important treatise on the Sufism of the school of Ibn ʿArabī by Ṣā'in al-Dīn ibn Turkah (ninth/fifteenth century)[23] deals with the two poles of all Sufi doctrine: the transcendent unity of being (*waḥdat al-wujūd*) and the universal man (*al-insān al-kāmil*). It has always been very popular as a treatise on gnosis (*ʿirfān*) and has been commented on by several masters, including Āqā Muḥammad Riḍā Qumsha'ī.[24]
2. *Sharḥ-i fuṣūṣ al-ḥikam:* The text of this most celebrated of all works on doctrinal Sufism is by Muḥyī al-Dīn ibn ʿArabī, and numerous commentaries have been written on it.[25] As far as Persia is concerned, the most popular commentaries over the centuries have been those of Dā'ūd Qayṣarī (eighth/fourteenth century), on which Āqā Muḥammad Riḍā Qumsha'ī has written extensive glosses; ʿAbd al-Razzāq Kāshānī (eighth/fourteenth century); ʿAbd al-Raḥmān Jāmī[26] (ninth/fifteenth century); and Bālī Afandī (tenth/sixteenth century). [There are also more recent commentaries and glosses, such as those

of Ayatollah Rūḥ Allāh Khomeini, Sayyid Ḥasan Jawādī Āmulī, and Ḥasan Ḥasanzādah Āmulī.] These commentaries all draw heavily from the commentary of Mu'ayyid al-Dīn Jandī, which, however, has itself never become popular.[27]

3. *Sharḥ-i miftāḥ al-ghayb*: The text of this advanced work on Sufi doctrine is by Ṣadr al-Dīn al-Qunyawī (seventh/thirteenth century), the foremost expositor of Ibn 'Arabī in the East, and the commentary by Shams al-Dīn Ḥamzah Fanārī.[28]

IV. Medicine (*ṭibb*)

1. *Sharḥ-i nafīsī:* The text of this popular medical treatise is the *Mūjaz* by 'Alā' al-Dīn 'Alī ibn Abi'l-Ḥazm Qarashī (seventh/thirteenth century), which is itself an epitome of the *Canon* of Ibn Sīnā. The most famous commentary, which has been printed with the *Mūjaz,* is by Nafīs ibn 'Iwaj Kimānī (ninth/fifteenth century). There are other commentaries on the *Mūjaz,* such as those of Jamāl al-Dīn Aqsarā'ī and Sadīd al-Dīn Kāzirūnī, which, however, have never reached the fame of *Sharḥ-i nafīsī.*[29]
2. *Sharḥ-i asbāb:* The text of this work is the *Asbāb wa 'alāmāt* of Najīb al-Dīn Samarqandī, the well-known seventh/thirteenth-century physician and pharmacologist, and the commentary by the same Nafīs ibn 'Iwaj Kimānī mentioned above.
3. The *Qānūn* (*Canon*): This magnum [medical] opus of Ibn Sīnā, consisting of five books, is the most important work in Islamic medicine.[30] It is usually studied in Persia with the commentaries of Fakhr al-Dīn Rāzī, Quṭb al-Dīn al-Miṣrī, 'Alā' al-Dīn Qarashī, and Muḥammad ibn Maḥmūd Āmulī. But the most thorough and respected commentary is that of Quṭb al-Dīn Shīrāzī, which stands as a major medical work of its own.
4. *Fuṣūl-i Buqrāṭ:* Many of the works of Hippocrates have been popular among medical students, perhaps the foremost being the *Fuṣūl,* which, in Persia, is usually studied with the commentaries of 'Abd al-Raḥmān ibn 'Alī (known as Ibn Abī Ṣādiq), Ibn Quff, and 'Alā' al-Dīn Qarashī.

V. The Mathematical Sciences (*riyāḍiyyāt*)

1. Geometry (*handasah*): The students of geometry have relied most of all upon the *Elements* (*Uṣūl*) of Euclid in the translations, recensions,

and commentaries of Ḥajjāj ibn Maṭar, Ḥunayn ibn Isḥāq, Thābit ibn Qurrah, and Abū 'Uthmān al-Dimashqī composed up to the seventh/thirteenth century. At that time, with the appearance of the *Taḥrīr* of Naṣīr al-Dīn Ṭūsī, this latter work became the main text for the study of geometry along with the glosses of Mīr Sayyid Sharīf Jurjānī. This in turn was translated into Persian and commented on by Mullā Mahdī Narāqī (twelfth/eighteenth century). Actually the section on geometry in the *Durrat al-tāj* of Quṭb al-Dīn Shīrāzī is also a Persian version of Naṣīr al-Dīn's recension.

2. Arithmetic (*ḥisāb*): In the older days the *Shamsiyyat al-ḥisāb* of Niẓām al-Dīn Ḥasan ibn Muḥammad Nayshābūrī (seventh/thirteenth century) and the *Miftāḥ al-ḥisāb* of Ghiyāth al-Dīn Jamshīd Kāshānī[31] were the most common works, but in the Safavid period they were replaced to some extent by the *Khulāṣat al-ḥisāb* of Shaykh Bahā' al-Dīn 'Āmilī (eleventh/seventeenth century) with the commentary of his student, Jawād ibn Sa'd Allāh Kāẓimaynī. In the Qajar period Mu'tamid al-Dawlah Farhād Mīrzā wrote another important commentary on it, which also became popular.
3. Astronomy (*hay'āt*):

   A. *Risāla-yi fārsī dar hay'at:* The text is by the already mentioned 'Alā' al-Dīn Qūshchī, and it is usually accompanied by the commentary of Muṣliḥ al-Dīn Lārī (eleventh/seventeenth century).
   B. *Sharḥ-i mulakhkhaṣ:* The *Mulakhkhaṣ* is by Maḥmūd Chagmīnī (eighth/fourteenth century) and was commented on by Mūsā ibn Maḥmūd, known as Qāḍīzāda-yi Rūmī (ninth/fifteenth century), who composed it for Ulugh Beg. 'Abd al-'Alī Bīrjandī and Mīr Sayyid Sharīf Jurjānī have written glosses on the commentary, which are usually studied with the text and the commentary, while many other existing glosses have been forgotten.
   C. *al-Tadhkirah:* This is the celebrated work of Naṣīr al-Dīn Ṭūsī on which many commentaries have been written, the most popular being that of Bīrjandī.[32]
   D. The "intermediate" works (*mutawassiṭāt*): These works stand between the *Elements* and the *Almagest* and were to be studied before undertaking the *Almagest.* They include the *Spherics* of

Theodosius, *On the Moving Sphere* of Autolycus, the *Spherics* of Menelaus, and the *Optics, Data,* and *Phenomena* of Euclid. All of these works came to be studied in the recensions of Naṣīr al-Dīn Ṭūsī.

E. The *Almagest:* Since the early Islamic period, the *Almagest* of Ptolemy has been popular in the Arabic translation of Ḥajjāj ibn Maṭar, Isḥāq ibn Ḥunayn, and Thābit ibn Qurrah. Later it came to be studied in the recension of Naṣīr al-Dīn Ṭūsī with the commentaries of Niẓām al-Dīn Nayshābūrī and 'Abd al-'Alī Bīrjandī.

F. Other branches of the mathematical sciences: An important branch of these sciences, which always attracted the interest of students, was the science of the astrolabe, on which many works exist, such as the *Kitāb al-usṭurlāb* of 'Abd al-Raḥmān Ṣūfī, whose *Ṣuwar al-kawākib,* dealing with stars and constellations, has also always been popular; the *Istī'āb fi'l-'amal bi'l-usṭurlāb* of Bīrūnī; the *Bīst bāb dar fann-i usṭurlāb* of Ṭūsī, on which 'Abd al-'Alī Bīrjandī has written a commentary; and two treatises by Shaykh Bahā' al-Dīn 'Āmilī, one in Arabic called *Ṣafīḥah* and the other in Persian entitled *Tuḥfa-yi ḥātamī.*

The description of the texts used in the *madrasahs* of Persia and adjacent areas until a couple of generations ago is an indication of the breadth of Islamic education when it was alive and embraced all the intellectual disciplines. It is true that this *madrasah* system did not come to terms with the modern scientific disciplines in the same way that Islamic thought confronted the Greco-Hellenistic heritage. The fault lies as much with the educational authorities, who sought to establish separate educational systems, as with the traditional scholars in the *madrasahs,* who refused to consider the challenge of modern science and learning. Consequently, today there reigns educational havoc nearly everywhere throughout the Islamic world, with contending and often contradictory educational systems vying for the minds, souls, and hearts of new generations of students.

In this critical situation, the *madrasah* system, as reflected in the breadth of the program outlined above and as seen in the classical period when this system was at the height of its vigor, must be seen not only as the precious repository of the traditional Islamic sciences, but also as the model from which any educational system claiming to be integrated within the various zones of Islamic culture, whether Persian, Arabic, Turkish, or other, can benefit in many basic ways. There is still a great deal that all contemporary Muslim educationalists can learn from the *madrasahs,* and these venerable institutions are of much greater importance to the future educational life of the various Islamic countries than the modern educationalists, who are enamored of the rapidly changing pedagogical theories of the West, are willing to admit. Not only is the content of the texts studied in *madrasahs* of significance, but their propaedeutic methods, based on the idea of the ultimate unity of knowledge, are also very pertinent for the creation of an authentic Islamic educational system today. Such a system can come into being only as an organic outgrowth from the tree of the traditional Islamic system, thereby preserving its heritage, and not through the blind imposition of alien educational philosophies and practices upon the Islamic world.

Appendix II

PHILOSOPHY IN THE PRESENT-DAY ISLAMIC WORLD

One of the arenas in which the confrontation between traditional Islam and modernism can be studied most directly is that of philosophy, understood in its most general sense. Here ideas encounter ideas, with consequences for nearly every other field of human thought and endeavor, from science to politics, from art to social activities. The philosophic and intellectual life of the Islamic world over the past century has been woven from many diverse strands and reflects all the tensions, contradictions, and conflicts that the encounter between tradition and modernism has brought about in all parts of the globe where tradition, Islamic or otherwise, still survives. To understand recent philosophic activity in various parts of the Islamic world, however, it is necessary to outline, albeit briefly, the underlying tradition and the general intellectual background within which, or occasionally in opposition to which, philosophical activity has and continues to take place among Muslims. However, because of the vastness of the Islamic world, stretching from the southern Philippines to the coast of the Atlantic, I am forced to concentrate in these remarks on the central lands of Islam; thus, although the vision will be extended in time, it has to be somewhat contracted spatially.

Islam was heir to the philosophical heritage of the Mediterranean world, Persia, and the Indian subcontinent. It transformed this heritage within the worldview of Islam, according to the spirit and letter of the Quran, and brought into being a vast array of intellectual and philosophical schools, only some of which may be technically termed "philosophy" (*falsafah*). But there are others, including several that did not bear the name of philosophy,[1] that have had the greatest philosophical importance, according to the most general meaning of the term in English. This tradition produced such renowned intellectual figures as al-Fārābī, Ibn Sīnā, al-Ghazzālī, Suhrawardī, Ibn Rushd, Ibn 'Arabī, Mīr Dāmād, and Mullā Ṣadrā, some of whom are well known in the West and others of whom are only now becoming known outside the Islamic world.[2] In the Arab world, philosophy as a distinct discipline known as *falsafah* disappeared, with a few exceptions such as Ibn Sab'īn and Ibn Khaldūn, after the sixth/twelfth century[3] and became drowned in the two seas of gnosis and theology. In Persia, the Turkish part of the Ottoman world, and the Indian subcontinent, however, in addition to theology and gnosis, philosophy as a distinct intellectual activity flourished, surviving in many of those regions to our own day.[4] When the Islamic world first encountered the West in the nineteenth century in such countries as Egypt, Persia, Turkey, and on the Indian subcontinent, the existing intellectual tradition in each land reacted according to local conditions, but within the general context of the universal intellectual tradition of Islam. Such figures as Sayyid Jamāl al-Dīn Astrābādī, usually known as al-Afghānī, Muḥammad 'Abduh, Rifā'ah Rāfi' Taḥṭāwī, Rashīd Riḍā—all associated with what is known as the Arab renaissance, or *al-nahḍah*—Malkam Khān, Sir Aḥmad Khān, Zia Gökalp, and Muḥammad Iqbāl,[5] just to name some of the more famous figures, set out to encounter Western thought in different ways and were influenced by it to varying degrees.

The influence of Western philosophy in each part of the Islamic world has depended upon the form of colonialism that happened to be dominant in a particular land.[6] Modernized circles on the Indian subcontinent, for instance, became dominated by the English philosophy of the Victorian period. In contrast, modernized groups in Iran, who were attracted to French language and culture in order to escape British and Russian influences from the north and south, became infatuated with Descartes and Cartesian philosophy and later with the Comtean positivism of the nineteenth century. Modernized Turks were attracted to a large extent to German philosophy and Westernized Egyptians to English, French, or German schools depending on the experience and philosophical proclivity of various individual philosophers and thinkers. North Africa and the French-speaking parts of Islamic Africa became dominated by French modes of thought in countries dominated by France and by English ones in areas controlled by Britain.

With the end of World War II, most Muslim countries gained political independence, but the philosophical scene, especially at the university level, continued for the most part to be dominated by Western thought. At this time, moreover, Marxism became a new element that attracted a number of thinkers, especially in lands where an intense struggle for independence had led certain people to join politically leftist causes. The sense of Islamic identity, however, continued to assert itself, and perhaps the most important philosophical concern of the majority of influential intellectuals remained the tension between Islam and modern Western civilization. Such themes as the spread of Western thought, including its Marxist version, and the interaction between science and philosophies of a positivistic nature, on the one hand, and religion and religious philosophies, on the other, became the main concern of most Muslims engaged in philosophical activity. During the past few decades, although the earlier schools of European philosophy, now out of fashion in the West, have continued to survive in a surprising fashion in certain Islamic countries,[7] newer modes of Western thought, such as logical positivism, analytical philosophy, existentialism, neo-Marxism, and even structuralism and deconstructionism, have also gained some attention. Also in more recent years much attention has been paid to Islamic political philosophy. In Iran such philosophical discussions have revolved around the theory of the "rule of the jurisprudent" (*wilāyat-i faqīh*), which was central to the political philosophy of Ayatollah Khomeini. In Pakistan and many other countries the debate has involved the nature of the "Islamic state."

During this same period, however, one can also observe another intellectual activity of the greatest importance, namely, the revival of Islamic thought in its various traditional forms, such as Sufism, theology, and philosophy itself in its technical sense of *falsafah*. A sense of disillusionment with modern Western civilization and thought, uncertainty about the future, and the need to return to the heart of religion have caused a rekindling of interest in Sufism and led many people, especially the educated, to reexamine its teaching, including its intellectual dimension. This change can be seen in the larger number of younger people, including many from the professional classes, drawn to this day to Sufi orders and Sufi doctrines in such countries as Egypt, Turkey, and Iran[8] and the extensive spread of the teachings of such outstanding recent Sufi masters as Shaykh Muḥammad al-Tādilī, Shaykh al-'Alawī,[9] and Shaykh Ḥabīb.

But one can also observe the spread of new versions of the earlier Wahhābī and Salafī movements, characterized by a moral puritanism, "return" to the norms of early Islam, and to a large extent disdain for philosophical discourse. Finally, these same forces have led many people to a rediscovery of Islamic philosophy itself and its subsequent revival, especially in Iran, while the study of Islamic philosophy has been spreading for the first time in Malaysia and Indonesia.[10] Therefore, it can be said that during the past few decades, at the same time that various forms of modern philosophical thought have penetrated farther into the intellectual life of the Islamic world, a revival of traditional Islamic thought, including not only philosophy in the technical sense (*falsafah*), but also Sufi metaphysics and gnosis (*'irfān*), philosophical theology as well as other modes and schools, has also been observable in many Islamic countries. Consequently at the present moment there is an intense battle being waged between these trends, on the one hand, and various currents of modern thought, on the other, for the minds and souls of educated Muslims.

In this brief survey, I can refer only to the most salient features of philosophical activity, seen in the more general sense of this term, especially in the intellectual center of that vast expanse of the earth's surface known as the Islamic world. It is only appropriate to begin with that heartland, namely, the Arabic, Persian, Turkish countries, which have nearly always provided the most widespread and enduring intellectual and spiritual impulses for the Islamic community as a whole. Today, the peoples in this area remain a numerical minority within the Islamic world taken as a whole, but this area must still be considered the intellectual center of that wider world whose life and thought are determined by the Islamic revelation.

Let us begin with the Arab world, especially its eastern part. In this region, Egypt and Syria were the greatest centers of cultural and philosophical activity in the earlier decades of the twentieth century and continued to hold this position after World War II, although Lebanon also came into prominence after its independence. In Egypt, the important institutions of philosophical activity of earlier days, such as Al-Azhar, Cairo, Ain Shams, and Alexandria Universities and the Arab Academy of Cairo, have continued to be dominant, and the heritage of earlier decades continues to have influences. In this context it is important to recall the seminal figure of the early twentieth century, Muṣṭafā 'Abd al-Rāziq, who sought to revive Islamic thought by turning to a more rationalistic philosophical *kalām,* which he called Islamic philosophy, in his most important work, *Tamhīd li-ta'rīkh al-falsafat al-islāmiyyah* ("Prolegomena to the History of Islamic Philosophy"). The influence of this work can be seen in many of the well-known Egyptian thinkers of the next two generations. One can mention among notable philosophical figures who came after him Ibrāhīm Madkūr (Madkour), who was devoted to and played a major role in the renewal of classical Islamic philosophy in its relation to Greek thought; 'Uthmān Amīn, who emphasized the importance of Sufism in the revival of Islamic thought; 'Alī Sāmī al-Nashshār, who, like 'Abd al-Rāziq, wanted to revive *kalām* as Islamic philosophy; and Zakī Najīb Maḥmūd, who was an empirical philosopher in the line of William James.

There also developed at this time in the Arab world a whole current of thought directly opposed to the Islamic heritage (*al-turāth*) usually combined with complete espousal of European philosophy. The group associated with this current includes 'Abd Allāh Laroui, who sought to erase even the memory of the *turāth* from the Arab mind; Luṭfī al-Sayyid, who submitted completely to European philosophy; Fu'ād Zakariyyā', who spent most of his intellectual energy combating Islamic philosophy; and Zakī Najīb, who was a logical positivist and spoke of the dynamism of reason while opposing the Islamic understanding of the intellect (*al-'aql*). This strong opposition to the *turāth* is also to be seen in other parts of the Arab world, for example, in the works of the contemporary Moroccan philosopher Muḥammad 'Ābid al-Jābirī.

Of course, in Egypt there were many other figures who opposed this current and who sought, on the contrary, to revive the *turāth* through the publication and study of classical Islamic philosophical texts. Among this group one can mention George C. Anawati, a Christian Egyptian devoted to Islamic philosophy, especially Ibn Sīnā; 'Abd al-Raḥmān Badawī, a very prolific scholar of Islamic philosophy and also a philosopher in his own right who sought to create a system of Islamic existentialism; and Aḥmad Fu'ād al-Ahwānī, Sulaymān Dunyā, and Muḥammad Abū Rayyān, all of whom edited and studied important texts of Islamic philosophy.

One sees also in Egypt in the period before and following World War II a number of notable scholars who were interested most of all in mystical philosophy and theoretical Sufism. This category included ʿAbd al-Ḥalīm Maḥmūd, a shaykh and later supreme head (of al-Azhar University) whose writings on Islamic philosophy are still popular in Egypt; Abū'l-ʿAlā' al-ʿAfīfī, known especially for his study of Ibn ʿArabī; and Abū'l-Wafā' al-Taftāzānī, himself a Sufi, like ʿAbd al- Ḥalīm Maḥmūd, and the author of the definitive work on the Andalusian mystical philosopher Ibn Sabʿīn.

There have, moreover, been major celebrations of the anniversaries of leading Islamic philosophers such as al-Kindī, al-Fārābī, Ibn Sīnā, al-Ghazzālī, Ibn Rushd, Suhrawardī, Ibn ʿArabī, and Ibn Khaldūn in Egypt and often in many other countries of the Islamic world. The recent extensive celebration of Ibn Rushd in many countries is a case in point. These activities have led to editions of texts, preparation of bibliographies, analytical monographs, and histories.[11]

Also since World War II, the aim of reviving Islamic thought has been combined with a major movement to translate Western philosophy into Arabic. Translations of European philosophy have included many of the best-known works of post-Renaissance philosophy, especially those of French and German philosophers such as Descartes, Voltaire, Kant, and Hegel. There have also been histories of Western philosophy, such as that of Luṭfī Jumaʿah. Unfortunately, a number of these translations into Arabic have been made by scholars not fully aware of the richness of classical philosophical Arabic; in quality many of them fall far short of the level of translations of Greek philosophical texts into Arabic of over a millennium ago.

Since the rise of the Palestinian problem, extreme Arab nationalism, and the spread of leftist ideologies in Egypt, Syria, and elsewhere in the region, numerous philosophical works in Arabic concerned with political and economic themes, rather than simply with theoretical philosophy, have appeared, and these were often influenced directly or indirectly by Marxism and more generally socialism. In this category perhaps the most famous are by ʿAbd Allāh Laroui and Ḥasan Ḥanafī. Some of the thinkers of Egypt, both Muslim and Christian, became followers of the fashionable Western leftist trend of the postwar era. This trend began to diminish after the downfall of the Soviet Union, but did not come completely to an end. One can cite as a more recent example the formation during the past few decades of an "Islamic left" (*al-yasār al-islāmī*) in Egypt and elsewhere, the best-known representative of which is Ḥasan Ḥanafī, currently the head of the philosophy department at the University of Cairo.

But many of the prominent thinkers of this kind, such as Anwar 'Abd al-Malik, soon lost their infatuation with Marxism and other leftist ideologies and turned either to some form of cultural nationalism or back to more traditional forms of Islamic thought. This trend has thus moved in a direction parallel with the revival of Islamic philosophical thought within the traditional Islamic quarters in Egypt, such as al-Azhar, although the development of various types of secular philosophy has continued among some of the Arab philosophers in general, such as Ṣādiq al-'Aẓm, who is, however, Lebanese and not Egyptian.

In most of the Arab East much of the revival of Islamic thought tends to be either in a puritanical vein following the Wahhābī-Salafī school[12] or concerned with Sufism, which has also been subject to an important rejuvenation over the past decades in Egypt and Syria. In this connection it is of some interest to mention the Muslim Brotherhood (Ikhwān al-Muslimīn), which, although intellectually akin to the Wahhābī-Salafī school and opposed to Sufism, was structured on the model of the Sufi orders. The leading intellectual figure of the Ikhwān, Sayyid Quṭb, although adamantly opposed to philosophy in its academic sense, himself produced a "philosophy" based upon the teachings of the Quran with which he sought to combat ideologies imported from the West.[13] In this context of confronting modernist ideologies with Islamic thought in its more specifically religious form, it is also necessary to mention Muḥammad Bāqir al-Ṣadr from Iraq, who, however, in contrast to Sayyid Quṭb, not only did not oppose Islamic philosophy, but belonged to that tradition, especially the school of Mullā Ṣadrā.

In Syria and Lebanon, a situation similar in many ways to that of Egypt is to be observed. Earlier figures such as Jamīl Ṣalībā, Khalīl Georr, and Ḥannā al-Fākhūrī were active for many decades. The Arab Academy of Damascus has continued its efforts to create a terminology to express modern philosophical thought. More traditional scholars, such as Sāmī al-Kiyālī and 'Ārif Tāmir, have been concerned with the revival of Islamic philosophy, while some of the Westernized intellectuals—mostly Christian, but also some Muslim—have continued their earlier fascination with European philosophy, and until recently especially with leftist politico-philosophical ideologies. Such men as Constantine Zurayk and Michel Aflaq, who wrote theoretical works on Arab nationalism and socialism, became fathers of political movements. Gradually, a form of

Arab socialism became dominant in the Fertile Crescent in the name of the Ba'th party, which still rules in Syria and has inspired many works of political philosophy based on the idea of Arab socialism and nationalism.

Parallel with this development there has also taken place the revival of interest in Sufism in Syria and to some extent Lebanon during the last few decades. Much of this revival is closely connected with the Shādhiliyyah Order and more specifically the great Algerian saint Shaykh al-'Alawī, who had many disciples in Syria.[14] The revival has also produced writings of intellectual quality, as can be seen in the case of the works of such Sufi masters as Shaykh 'Abd al-Qādir 'Īsā, Shaykh Muḥammad al-Hāshimī, Shaykh Muḥammad al-Burhānī, and Shaykh 'Abd al-Raḥman al-Shāghūrī. In the field of Sufi metaphysics, it is also necessary to mention the extensive works of the Syrian scholar 'Uthmān Yaḥyā, who resided in Paris and Cairo before his death. Besides editing and studying the works of major figures of Sufism, especially Ibn 'Arabī, he also wrote as a philosopher living within the tradition of Islamic philosophy, but concerned with contemporary problems, especially those of secularized modern people.

Lebanon has been the focus of a more modernized form of philosophical activity than either Syria or Egypt. In its universities, especially St. Joseph, most of the external philosophical influence has been French, as is also the case in Syria. Only in the American University of Beirut has Anglo-Saxon philosophy been substantially present. Until the civil war of the 1980s, Lebanon was the major center for the publication of Arabic books in the region, especially in the field of philosophy, Beirut vying with Cairo for the lead in the Arab world. The publishing activity in Lebanon especially in the field of philosophy became momentarily curtailed, but was revived after the end of the civil war, and today Beirut is again a major publishing center. Lebanon has also continued to seek to play the role of a bridge between the West and the rest of the Arab world, although it has been in reality more of a beachhead for the Western philosophical and cultural assault upon Islam than a bridge connecting two worlds.

In Lebanon, there have also appeared several eminent Christian Arabs. Perhaps the most famous among them was Charles Malik, who, while being immersed in the world of Western liberalism, remained deeply Christian. Constantine Zurayk, the most important political philosopher of the socialist Ba'thist movement, also belonged to the Lebanese scene.

One can also mention Archbishop Khodr, who is one of the leading Orthodox theologians and Christian philosophers of our day. In addition, during the past few decades, there have been such Lebanese scholars, both Muslim and Christian, as 'Umar Farrukh, Ḥasan Ṣa'b, Kamāl al-Yāzijī, Farīd Jabre, Albert Nader, Mājid Fakhrī, and 'Afīf 'Uṣayrān, who have been concerned with and produced many notable works on Islamic philosophy. Mention must also be made of Yusuf Ibish, who was an important contemporary student of Sufism and one of the leading exponents of the perennial philosophy in the Arab world. As far as Sufism is concerned, it is also important to mention Sayyidah Fāṭimah Yashruṭiyyah, who was perhaps the most eminent female figure in Sufism in the Arab East until her death a couple of decades ago; she produced some of the most notable works on Sufism in Arabic in recent years. She was also an important factor in the spread in Lebanon and Syria of the teachings of the Yashruṭiyyah Order, founded by her father. There has also been a great deal of scholarship in the field of doctrinal Sufism and philosophy in Lebanon by such figures as Su'ād al-Ḥakīm, who has made an in-depth study of the technical vocabulary of the school of Ibn 'Arabī.

As for Palestine, the traumatic events of partition and the war of 1948 have caused the intellectual community of this region to turn its attention almost completely to questions of a political nature, and the few Palestinians, such as 'Abd al-Latīf al-Ṭībāwī, who have been concerned with the philosophy of education and related fields have been active in other countries. In Jordan, interest in Islamic philosophy has been growing gradually, as such places as the University of Amman became interested in theological and philosophical studies; slowly Amman is becoming a center for the publication of works in Arabic dealing, among other subjects, with philosophy. There is also a notable interest in Jordan in traditional Islamic art and its philosophy. The Jordanian Royal Academy has played an important role in all these endeavors.

In Iraq, until World War II, the British style of education went hand in hand with the activity of major traditional Islamic centers of learning, especially the Shī'ite university in Najaf. One of the most notable activities during the earlier decades was the revival of scholarship in the field of Islamic philosophy, but as far as universities were concerned it was tempered with academic discipline derived mostly from Anglo-Saxon, but also from other European or continental forms of scholarship. Before the complete political domination and strong ideological indoctrination of the Ba'th, Iraq produced several scholars of note who combined both forms of discipline, namely, the Islamic and the European. These scholars include the already mentioned traditional scholar who had also studied Western thought Muḥammad Bāqir al-Ṣadr, Kāmil al-Shaybī, Ḥusayn 'Alī Maḥfūẓ, and especially Muḥsin Mahdī, who made noteworthy contributions to the study of al-Fārābī and Ibn Khaldūn while teaching in the West. There was also some effort in Iraq to study the philosophy of Islamic education, especially by Fāḍil al-Jamālī. Moreover, in that country, as in Syria, a number of philosophical works appeared that deal with various forms of Arab nationalism, socialism, and the like. Most of these works, however, are of a practical rather than a purely theoretical nature. Needless to say, the devastating events of the last few years in Iraq have shattered the Iraqi educational institutions. It remains to be seen how the study of intellectual disciplines will be revived in the country, which was known in the Arab world for its vibrant intellectual life.

The western region of the Arab world was a much more conservative and "conserving" region than the Arab East until fairly recently. In this western area, or the Maghrib, embracing the region from Libya and Tunisia to the Atlantic, until the independence movements arose, traditional Islamic thought in the fields of both Sufi metaphysics and theology was very strong. Several outstanding Sufi masters dominated the spiritual and intellectual climate of the Maghrib, foremost among whom was Shaykh al-'Alawī. His disciples have kept his presence alive in many regions, although the heart of his intellectual teachings, that part based on the pure metaphysics at the core of Sufism along with active interest in the truth of other religions, especially Christianity, was to travel to the Occident, where it has had a profound and incalculable impact. Other masters, such as Shaykh Muḥammad al-Tādilī and Shaykh Ḥabīb, have also contributed to the preservation in the Maghrib of the Sufi tradition, including its intellectual aspects.

Since World War II, at least two other notable tendencies have opposed Sufism in the Maghrib. The first is a crypto-Wahhābī and Salafī puritanism inspired by movements of a similar nature in Egypt and other eastern lands of Islam and modern antitraditional European philosophy. The puritanical rationalism of the Maghrib is little different from what is found among the Salafiyyah of Egypt and in the neo-Wahhābism of Arabia and elsewhere. It has been marked by an open opposition to both philosophy and Sufism, especially its popular form, which in the Maghrib is known as Maraboutism,[15] and a strong zeal for social reform as well as engagement in political action with the aim of reestablishing the rule of Islamic Divine Law (*Sharī'ah*). In this connection, it is important to mention the Istiqlal party of Morocco and its founder, 'Allāl al-Fāsī, who was one of the foremost thinkers of the Maghrib during the last century. He developed a political and social philosophy based on certain traditional Islamic theses with elements akin to those of certain Wahhābī-Salafī thinkers of the East who emphasized the primacy of the *Sharī'ah* and usually opposed existing political authority, but his had a distinct Maghribi color related to the central role of the Moroccan monarchy seen as a caliphate. He has also sometimes been called a "fundamentalist." If this appellation be accepted, however, then he represents a form of "fundamentalism" much closer to the traditional position than the violent "fundamentalism" of the countertraditional variety.

The second tendency, namely, espousal of European philosophy and opposition to both Sufism and traditional Islamic philosophy, is of a rather peculiar character in the Maghrib. In Egypt, the European philosophy that became influential was not limited to a single school. In the Maghrib, because of the predominantly French influence and the preponderance of Marxism and agnostic existentialism in French university circles after the war, these schools became nearly completely dominant as far as European philosophy was concerned. In no other region of the Islamic world have the Marxism and existentialism of the French school had such influence within university circles as in the Maghrib. It is also here that, over the past few decades, strange attempts have been made to wed leftist ideologies emanating from nineteenth-century European philosophy with Islam. The result was various forms of "Islamic socialism" and, until the fall of the Soviet Union, even "Islamic Marxism," which could be seen especially in Algeria and Libya. This type of thought, which is usually closely related to various political interests, was of course not limited to the Maghrib; it can also be found in other Muslim countries, especially Egypt and Syria, and even outside the Arab world, although its philosophical influence has been usually confined in most places to limited circles. In Iran such ideas reached a relatively wider audience until it was curtailed at least outwardly after the Islamic Revolution of 1979.

The Maghrib has also produced a small number of well-known thinkers who have attempted to chart a more distinct course and not simply followed Western fashions. Among this group is the Moroccan philosopher Muḥammad 'Azīz al-Ḥabābī (Lahbabi), who developed what he called "Islamic personalism," based on certain theses of Islamic thought and some of the predominant ideas of continental philosophy, especially existentialism. Lahbabi was also influenced by Hegelianism, and his thought followed a path from personalism to realism. He wanted to create a distinct Muslim contemporary philosophy, but he stood closer to modern thought than to the mainstream of Islamic philosophy. Another well-known figure from the Maghrib is the Algerian Muḥammad Arkoun, who, after a serious study of Western thought, including Marxism, turned to Islamic philosophy as a living reality, while criticizing it on the basis of ideas drawn from French philosophical thought. He has written both on traditional Islamic schools of philosophy and on the confrontation of Islamic thought with modernism. He is also one of the first contemporary Sunni thinkers to interest himself in a dialogue on the philosophical level with Shī'ism. One must also mention Ben Abboud, one of the leading thinkers of Morocco, who was much closer to traditional Islamic philosophy and Sufism, while interesting himself especially in the question of the nature of humanity. His interests were akin to those of the Tunisian Bin Mīlād, who also sought to apply Islamic philosophical teachings to the situation of human beings in the contemporary world with emphasis upon dynamism. Another significant Tunisian thinker, Hicham Djaït, has also tried to develop an Islamic form of contemporary philosophy, making use of Hegelianism and existentialism and trying to engage Western thought.[16]

During the last few decades a movement has begun to develop a rationalistic Islamic philosophy on the basis of the revival of the thought of Ibn Rushd and in conscious opposition to the post–Ibn Rushdian Islamic philosophical tradition. The most prominent member of this new group of "philosophical rationalists" is Muḥammad 'Ābid al-Jābirī, whose works, especially *Takwīn al-'aql al-'arabī* ("Formation of the Arab Mind"), are widely read.

As has already been stated, in Iran, Islamic philosophy did not cease to exist as a living tradition after the so-called Middle Ages, but has survived to the present day. In fact, there was a major revival of Islamic philosophy during the Safavid period with the appearance of such figures as Mīr Dāmād and Mullā Ṣadrā. A second revival took place during the thirteenth/nineteenth century, led by Mullā 'Alī Nūrī, Āqā 'Alī Mudarris, Ḥājjī Mullā Hādī Sabziwārī, and others,[17] which continued in the Islamic universities (*madrasahs*) and private circles into the Pahlavi period. After the end of World War I, European philosophy, especially that of the French school identified with such figures as Descartes and, more recently, Bergson, became influential among the Western-educated classes, in particular at the modern universities and colleges, although acquaintance with French philosophy goes back to the Qajar period, which covered the whole of the thirteenth/nineteenth and the early decades of the fourteenth/twentieth centuries.

During the past decades, the European influence has continued and in fact has been extended to include more contemporary trends, such as analytical philosophy, existentialism, and deconstructionism. At the same time, there has occurred a major revival of traditional Islamic philosophy among the class of *'ulamā'* and some of the modern educated classes. In its extent and breadth this marks a unique phenomenon in the contemporary Islamic world, inasmuch as this revival has not merely involved interest in scholarship in the field of Islamic philosophy. It has also signified that the tradition of Islamic philosophy, especially the school of Mullā Ṣadrā, has been taken seriously as a living and viable intellectual perspective capable of meeting the challenge of various schools of European thought.[18] The revival continues to this day through all the transformations that have taken place in Iran in recent decades, while paradoxically the study of European philosophy has also increased even in *madrasahs*. It is, moreover, interesting to note that during the last few years such famous Western philosophers as Michel Foucault, Emmanuel Levinas, Isaiah Berlin, Raymond Klibansky, Paul Ricoeur, and Richard Rorty have visited Iran, and that there are even many religious students in Qom who are familiar with and avidly studying the thought of Martin Heidegger, Michel Foucault, Ludwig Wittgenstein, Hans Georg Gadamer, Jürgen Habermas, and others.

One can do no more here than mention among the most active traditional figures in the revival of Islamic philosophy in Iran in the decades preceding the Islamic Revolution of 1979: Sayyid Abū'l-Ḥasan Qazwīnī, Sayyid Muḥammad Kāẓim 'Aṣṣār, Mahdī Ilāhī Qumsha'ī, 'Allāmah Sayyid

Muḥammad Ḥusayn Ṭabāṭabā'ī, Ayatollah Khomeini, Muḥammad Taqī Āmulī, Abū'l-Ḥasan Sha'rānī, and Maḥmūd Shahābī, all eminent philosophers and gnostics;[19] and belonging to the next generation, Murtaḍā Muṭahharī, Mahdī Ḥā'irī Yazdī,[20] Sayyid Jalāl al-Dīn Āshtiyānī, Jawād Muṣliḥ, Jawādī Āmulī, and Ḥasanzādah Āmulī. Many but not all of these figures have also tried to deal with modern philosophical questions and the challenges of Western thought from the point of view of Islamic metaphysics and philosophy, chief among them 'Allamah Ṭabāṭabā'ī, who was the foremost figure of his day in the revival of Islamic philosophy, and then Muṭahharī and Ḥā'irī Yazdī. Still others, although trained in modern universities, were and still are concerned mostly with editions and studies of Islamic philosophical texts. This last-named group includes such scholars as Muḥammad Khwansārī, Mahdī Muḥaqqiq, Jawād Falāṭūrī, Muḥammad Dānishpazhūh, Muḥammad Mu'īn, and Sayyid Ja'far Sajjādī.

Those who have been concerned mostly with European philosophy, its translation into Persian, and its exposition for the Persian world include Riḍā-zādah Shafaq, Ghulām-Ḥusayn Ṣadīghī, Yaḥyā Mahdawī, Karīm Mujtahidī, and Sharaf Khurāsānī, all of whom have made important studies and translations and helped in the development of a contemporary Persian philosophical vocabulary. Some of them have continued their activities into the decades following the revolution. Another group, including Manūchihr Buzurgmihr, Najaf Daryābandarī, and Muṣṭafā Raḥīmī, was concerned more with contemporary European philosophy, the first two with Anglo-Saxon philosophy and the third with French existentialism. There has also been much interest in Heidegger, whose ideas have often been expounded in comparison with traditional Islamic thought, especially by Aḥmad Fardīd and many of his colleagues and students. Likewise, some attention was paid until the 1990s to various neo-Marxist modes of thought. In this connection one must mention 'Alī Sharī'atī, who sought to combine a populist interpretation of Islam with certain Marxist theses and who had an important philosophical and political impact during the Islamic Revolution. His philosophical interpretations were, however, opposed by most of the traditional Islamic philosophers, especially Murtaḍā Muṭahharī.

After the beginning of the Islamic Revolution in 1979 with the wave of opposition to Western domination, one would have expected interest in

Western philosophy to be curtailed and attention paid almost exclusively to Islamic philosophy, in which Ayatollah Khomeini was such a recognized master. The former did happen, but not the latter. A vast wave of translation of Western philosophical texts into Persian has continued for the past three decades to a degree not seen in any other Islamic country with the possible exception of Turkey. This is the first time in Islamic history that we now have a large number of students of *madrasahs* who are clerics and recent graduates from seminaries, but are well versed in Western philosophical thought. This is true to such an extent that the Academy of Philosophy,[21] which I founded in 1973 for the comparative study of Islamic and non-Islamic schools of philosophy, has now become, more so than the traditional institutions of Qom, the major center in Iran for the study of Islamic philosophy itself.

As far as Islamic philosophy is concerned, the revival begun in the 1940s when 'Allāmah Ṭabāṭabā'ī' started teaching Ibn Sīnā and Mullā Ṣadrā in a *madrasah* in Qom and continuing into the 1970s, has become perpetuated since the Revolution. A number of his students, including the two Āmulīs, Miṣbāḥ Yazdī, and others continue to teach Islamic philosophy in Qom; another major authority, Ḥā'irī Yazdī, taught in Tehran before going to the United States and after his return until his death a few years ago. During these decades there have also appeared important new figures in the domain of Islamic philosophy such as Ayatollah Sayyid Muḥaqqiq Dāmād, Riḍā Dāwarī, Ibrāhīm Dīnānī, and Ghulām-Riḍā A'wānī, most of whom are associated with the Iranian Academy of Philosophy, along with Ayatollah Sayyid Raḍī Shīrāzī, Muḥsin Kadīwar, and Ghulām Riḍā Ḥaddād 'Ādil. One also needs to mention 'Abd al-Karīm Surūsh, at once philosopher and theologian, who has tried in his own way to modernize Islamic thought in both its philosophical and theological aspects.

Iran has also seen the formation of special organizations and other efforts to further the study of Islamic philosophy. One can mention as examples the Mullā Ṣadrā Foundation, founded by Ayatollah Sayyid Muḥammad Khāmini'ī, which has already held international conferences on Mullā Ṣadrā, brought out editions and translations of the master's works, and publishes a journal devoted to his thought. The Foundation, moreover, organizes international conferences on Islamic philosophy and is now bringing out for the first time in history the complete critically edited works of Ibn Sīnā under the editorship of Muḥsin Kadīwar. The British journal *Transcendent Philosophy,* published in London under the editorship of Qahrimān Ṣafawī, an Iranian philosopher of the younger generation, is devoted to the philosophy of Mullā Ṣadrā and also other schools of Islamic philosophy, all in interaction with Western philosophy.

The decades since the Islamic Revolution in Iran have also been witness to a great rise in the publication of Islamic philosophical texts, many hitherto unpublished. One can mention as an example the efforts of Mīrāth-i Maktūb, an organization responsible for the scholarly edition of a large number of philosophical texts. But there are also many university presses and foundations, not to speak of private publishers too numerous to name here devoted to this task. A whole new generation of very competent editors and translators of philosophical texts, such as Muḥammad Khwājawī, 'Alī Awjabī, and Inshā'a'Llāh Raḥmatī, have also appeared upon the scene. A separate study would be needed to do justice to the extensive philosophical activity going on in Iran today. Such a study would also need to consider a third category of works, those of Traditionalists such as Guénon, Schuon, Burckhardt and Lings, who have been translated extensively into Persian and whose ideas play an important role in the intellectual life of contemporary Iran.

One cannot foretell the results of the increased interest in Islamic philosophy combined with the ever growing attention paid to Western philosophy in Iran. But whatever the future brings in this domain, there is little doubt that what is taking place there is of great significance for the encounter of traditional Islamic thought with various modern Western philosophies. It is bound to also affect many other Islamic countries and have consequences for the intellectual encounter between Islam and the West in general.

As in other Islamic countries, so also in Iran the last decades have been witness to a major increase in interest in Sufism among the educated classes. Most of the important orders, such as the Ni'matullāhī and Dhahabī, were extremely active throughout the country until the events of 1979, producing many mystical works of great philosophical significance. In this context, the voluminous writings of Jawād Nūrbakhsh, the spiritual leader of the Ni'matullāhī Order, can be noted. Some of his shorter tracts on various aspects of Sufism have also been rendered into English and French. It is of interest to note in this context that, although elements within the Iranian regime are opposed to what is called *taṣawwuf-i khānqāhī,* that is, Sufism associated with the Sufi centers of various orders, and many have been suppressed, there has been an incredible recent surge of interest in the reading of classical Sufi texts, such as those of 'Aṭṭār and Rūmī. The new edition of the *Mathnawī* of Jalāl al-Dīn Rūmī, edited by Muḥammad Isti'lāmī in eight volumes and printed in thousands of copies, went into a second printing just a few months after its first publication. Works of non-Persian Sufis, especially Ibn 'Arabī, are also popular. Without doubt Iran remains one of the most important centers in the Islamic world for the study of the doctrinal, theoretical, and metaphysical aspects of Sufism.

Iran's neighboring country, Afghanistan, which shares the same philosophical tradition with it, was distinguished during the decades before the advent of various catastrophic wars mostly by activity in the domain of Sufism; and there such orders as the Naqshbandiyyah and Qādiriyyah flourished. Such scholars as G. Māyil Hirawī and Muḥammad I. Muballigh (both of whom later immigrated to Iran) have made important contributions to the study of Jāmī and the metaphysical school of Ibn 'Arabī in general. Scholars, such as A. G. Rawān Farhādī, have delved into the teachings and history of Sufism, taking into consideration the works of such European orientalists as Louis Massignon. Before the turmoil in Afghanistan, within university circles the philosophical scene resembled to some extent that of Iran with somewhat less diversity as regards the influence of Western schools of thought.

Despite a very different form of government, the philosophical situation in Turkey is similar in many ways to that of Iran; there has been a definite Islamic revival consisting of a marked rise of interest during recent years in the study of Islamic thought along with extensive translations of texts of Western philosophy, including numerous works of the Traditionalists. This revival, intellectually at least, is perhaps best exemplified by the publication of many texts of Islamic philosophy and also increase in interest in the thought of Badī' al-Zamān Sa'īd Nūrsī. The more secular atmosphere of Turkey has also allowed a wide range of modern philosophical works to be translated and studied in modern educated circles, often without any consideration of the Islamic intellectual tradition. In these circles, the influence of German schools of thought is more marked than in other Islamic countries.

As far as Islamic philosophy is concerned, much attention has been paid in Turkey to the works of al-Fārābī, Ibn Sīnā, and other Peripatetics as well as to the *ishrāqī* school, or the School of Illumination, and its spread into the Ottoman world. Moreover, during the past few decades, for the first time some attention has been paid to the philosophy of Mullā Ṣadrā, as can be seen in the works of younger scholars and philosophers such as Mahmut Kiliç, Ibrahim Kalin, and Alparslan Açikgenç, who has in fact written a comparative work on Mullā Ṣadrā and Heidegger. There is also some interest in recent philosophical developments in Iran and various philosophical activities there, in which many Turkish scholars have participated. It needs to be noted, however, that despite so much activity in the field of philosophy, there is still no thorough history of philosophy in the Ottoman world, which one would have expected following the pioneering work of Zia Ülken.

Perhaps the most notable contribution of Turkish scholars to philosophy in its wider sense over the past few decades has been in the domains of Sufism and the history of and philosophy of Ottoman science rather than in the more narrowly defined philosophical disciplines. In the field of Sufism, such scholars as 'Abd al-Bāqī Gölpinārlī, Aḥmad Āteš, Taḥsīn Yaziçi, Aḥmed Avni Konuk, and Ferīd Ram, have brought back the reality of the Sufi tradition to a contemporary Turkish society no longer familiar with the classical works of Sufism. Some of these scholars and philosophers also tried to respond to the challenges of modern philosophy with the help of the doctrinal and metaphysical Sufism of the school of Ibn 'Arabī, foremost among them Ismail Fenni Ertugrul, who, however, belongs to the earlier decades of the twentieth century. As for the history and philosophy of science, such figures as Aydin Sayili, Sevim Tekeli, Süheyl Unver, and Ekmeleddin Ihsanoğlu have made major contributions to the study of Islamic and more particularly Ottoman science and aspects of its philosophy. There have also been some notable Turkish contributions to the study of Islamic philosophy and theology proper, as shown in the work of Mubāḥat Türker, Ibrāhīm Āgāh Choboqchi, Hüseyin Atay, and others. In contemporary Turkey, there is a greater polarization in the domain of philosophy between traditional Islamic thought, on the one hand, and various forms of modern philosophy and ideology, on the other, than what one finds in most other Islamic countries. One can see this situation reflected especially within the universities.

Within this area of confrontation and often contention, the followers of traditionalist doctrines associated with Guénon, Schuon, and others play an important role. (We deal with Guénon, Schuon, and some other major figures of the Traditionalist School in Appendix IV.) Although I introduced traditionalist teachings in Iran in the late 1950s, they began to enter the Turkish scene a couple of decades later through translations of one work after another of this school by such scholars and philosophers as Mustafa Tahrali, Ilhan Kutluer, Yusaf Yazar, and Mahmut Kanik. Today among the Islamic languages one finds the largest number of traditionalist works in Turkish and Persian, and as in Iran, in Turkey the teachings of the Traditionalist School play a major role in the encounter between traditional Islamic thought and modern philosophies.

In the Indian subcontinent, in addition to the two Islamic countries, Pakistan and Bangladesh, there are over 150 million Muslims in India, Sri Lanka, and Nepal. The philosophical situation in this part of the world populated by so many Muslims is quite different from that of areas already described. As a result of British domination over the region, various schools of Anglo-Saxon philosophy became deeply entrenched in the philosophy departments of the major universities and continue to be dominant to this day. The earlier political and social "reformers" of the subcontinent, notably Sir Sayyid Aḥmad Khān and Muḥammad Iqbāl, were also much more concerned with philosophy in the Western sense of the term than were the "reformers" of the Arab world. This is especially true of Iqbāl, who was influenced by such European philosophers as Nietzsche while also being deeply drawn to Islamic philosophy. Philosophical institutions, such as the All-India Philosophical Congress, were carried over into the era of independence, and both the Indian and Pakistani Philosophical Congresses have been active ever since partition.[22] They have served as rallying points for philosophical activity, most of which is Western, specifically British and to some extent American. One can discern on the subcontinent, however, ever greater interest in Islamic thought in philosophy departments and among the educated Muslim public in general.

This new attention to Islamic philosophy in Pakistan began in earnest in the 1960s, as can be seen in the monumental *A History of Muslim Philosophy* edited by the late Mian Mohammad Sharif, one of the leading intellectual figures of Pakistan, and sponsored by the Pakistani government itself. In Pakistan, the older philosophers, including M. M. Aḥmad,

M. M. Sharīf, Chaudhry 'Abd al-Qādir, and Khalīfah 'Abd al-Ḥakīm, focused on issues arising from European philosophy, but they also sought to find some of the answers in the Islamic tradition, particularly Sufism, to which many of them, especially M. M. Aḥmad, were devoted. One must also mention Ẓafar al-Ḥasan, who provided a critique of Western philosophy from the perspective of Islamic philosophy. There were also a few figures during the early days of Pakistan, foremost among them being Muḥammad Ḥasan 'Askarī, who followed the traditional point of view and was completely opposed to modern European philosophy. He and his disciple Salīm Aḥmed translated many traditional writings into Urdu.

The most active students of this older generation of philosophers have pursued nearly the same combined interest in European philosophy and Islamic thought and have dealt with it in many ways like their predecessors. Bashīr Aḥmad Dār published numerous works on European philosophy, including those of Kant, while making comparisons with certain schools of Islamic thought. He thus exemplifies a trend that is strong among both Muslim and Hindu scholars on the subcontinent, namely, attempting to compare and often to synthesize Western and Eastern schools of thought.[23] Sa'īd Shaykh, another of the younger generation of philosophers, has been interested mostly in Islamic thought, as has M. S. H. Ma'ṣūmī, while Manzūr Aḥmad has turned to the study of the philosophy of art, education, and comparative religion. Some Pakistani thinkers, such as Ghulām Aḥmad Parwayz, have also followed Iqbāl in seeking to formulate a new *kalām,* or theology, in response to Western thought.

As for the younger generation attracted to tradition, those involved with the journal *Riwāyat,* which was completely dedicated to tradition, should be mentioned, especially its founder and editor, Suhayl 'Umar, the founder of the Suheyl Academy, who has brought out a whole library of the works of Guénon, Schuon, Burckhardt, Lings, myself, and others in local editions, making such names household words in intellectual circles in Pakistan. He is himself today the leading traditionalist thinker of the country and, as director of the Iqbal Academy also, a most influential philosophical voice in Pakistan. Other traditionalist thinkers concerned with various aspects of philosophy who are worthy of mention include Shahzād Qaysar and I'jāz Akram.

Pakistan has produced several notable philosophical thinkers who have been at the same time influential in the political life of the nation.

Perhaps foremost among them is Allāhbakhsh Bruhī (Brohi), an eminent political and legal figure who, after a long preoccupation with modern thought, returned to the bosom of Sufism and traditional metaphysics and expounded some of the deepest aspects of Islamic thought from a Sufi perspective. This group also includes Muḥammad Ajmal, a leading educationalist and psychologist. Ajmal was one of the first in the Islamic world to have sought to create a science of the soul based on the teachings of Sufism and Islamic philosophy rather than on the imitation of Western psychological and psychoanalytical techniques and theories. A word must also be said here about Fadl al-Raḥmān (Fazlur Rahman), who was concerned with both the revival of classical Islamic philosophy, including Mullā Ṣadrā, whom he discovered later in life through me, and a modernistic interpretation of Islam based on modern Western ideas. Finally, one must mention Mawlānā Abū'l-'Alā' Mawdūdī, the founder of the Jamā'at-i Islāmī of Pakistan who, although not strictly speaking a philosopher but a social reformer, is perhaps the most influential of all contemporary Pakistani thinkers as far as the question of the revival of the social and economic philosophy of Islam as reflected in the *Sharī'ah* is concerned. Mawdūdī himself was also interested in Islamic philosophy in his youth, and some among the followers of his thought, such as Khurshīd Aḥmad and Ẓafar Isḥāq Anṣārī, are important intellectual figures in Pakistan today. The Islamic University in Islamabad, with which Anṣārī is associated, has become a major center for the study of Islamic thought, with some notable professors, such as Muḥammad Ghazzālī, who are devoted to the study of Islamic philosophy.

As far as Sufism is concerned, as in so many other Islamic countries, in Pakistan there has been much interest in Sufism during the past decades, even in face of the rise of neo-Wahhābism and Salafism in many circles. Eminent Sufi masters such as Dhahīn Shah and Syed Barakat 'Alī have continued to appear upon the scene, and many Sufi orders, such as the Chishtiyyah, still flourish despite all the social and political havoc of this period. There are also many scholarly works on Sufism of an authentic nature published by such men as Ja'far Qāsimī and Suhayl 'Umar. There is, moreover, particular interest in Rūmī, inspired to a large extent by the dominating influence of Iqbāl, who had an ambivalent attitude toward Sufism. On the one hand, he criticized it and, on the other, was a great devotee of Rūmī and Shabistarī, writing in fact a work entitled *Gulshan-i rāz-i jadīd* ("The New Rose Garden of Divine Mysteries") in reference to Shabistarī's classical work and choosing Rūmī in the *Jāwīd-nāmah* ("The Treatise of the Eternal") as his guide in Paradise.

In India, nearly the same tendencies can be observed among Muslims over the past few decades. The major centers for Muslim intellectual activity during this period have been Delhi, Aligarh, Lucknow (especially the Deoband school, where traditional Islam was taught with some inclination toward reformism, but concentrated nevertheless on the main categories of Islamic thought), and Hyderabad, where some have devoted themselves to the revival of Islamic thought and others to the study of Western thought. In addition, there has been special interest in comparing the Islamic and Hindu traditions, an interest that is directly related to the particular situation of the Muslim community as a religious minority in modern India. This latter interest is reflected, for example, in the writings of M. H. 'Askarī and even of Muḥammed Mujīb. Such Muslim scholars as 'Abbās Rizwī, H. 'Ābidī, M. S. Khān, A. Ma'ṣūmī, and M. 'Abd al-Ḥaqq Anṣārī have been concerned with editions and analyses of classical works of Islamic philosophy, including the school of Mullā Ṣadrā. Some, such as Mīr Walī al-Dīn (Valiuddin), have sought to reformulate Sufism and make it better known. Others like Mīr Wahīd al-Dīn (Vahiduddin), 'Ābid Ḥusayn, and K. G. Sayyidayn (Sayidain) have been involved in studies based on the confrontation between Western trends of philosophy and Islam.

In India, as in Pakistan, there has been a great revival of interest in traditional Islamic medicine and its philosophy, as well as the ecological and philosophical issues involved in the confrontation between traditional and modern science. The activities of the Hamdard Institutes of Delhi and Karachi and of their founders, Ḥakīm 'Abd al-Ḥamīd and Ḥakīm Muḥammad Sa'īd, as well as those of the ancillary institutions they established, especially the Institute of Islamic Studies at Delhi and the Hamdard University outside of Karachi, are as important for the philosophy of nature as they are for science in general and medicine in particular.

As for Bangladesh, its philosophical life until recently was completely wedded to that of what became Pakistan and India. Since partition the same trend continued more or less, and Anglo-Saxon schools of philosophy remained strong in university circles. However, a more marked interest was shown in Islamic philosophy among later scholars, such as 'Abd al-Jalīl Miyā (Mia) and Muḥammad 'Abd al-Ḥaqq.

In the Malay-Indonesian world, which includes Singapore, the last decades have been witness to an attempt to rediscover a partially lost cultural identity. In Indonesia, numerous Islamic revivalist movements have emerged, most of which have a neo-Wahhābī color reflecting the close historical contact between that area and Arabia. There have also been attempts to revive Sufism, and certain modernistic movements appeared claiming a traditional mystical background, such as Subud, which gained some followers thirsty for spiritual experience at any cost, even in the West. Since the Iranian Revolution of 1979, one can also see a marked rise of interest in later Islamic philosophy and especially Mullā Ṣadrā, whose works are now taught in Jakarta by teachers such as Muḥammad Bāqir, who was trained in traditional Islamic philosophy in Iran. Perhaps the leading intellectual figure of Indonesia in recent decades, Nūr Khalis Majīd (Nurcholish Madjid), who died recently, was deeply immersed in the Islamic philosophical tradition. Interest in such classical Sufi figures as Ibn 'Arabī and Jāmī is also strong in Indonesia.

As for Malaysia, it has experienced a marked revival of interest in Sufism, but here the more intellectual school of Ibn 'Arabī and his followers, as it developed in that region, has received the greatest amount of attention. This particular slant in the study of Sufism is due most of all to Sayyid Naqīb al-'Aṭṭās, a notable philosopher himself and a leading Islamic thinker who has devoted numerous studies to this subject in addition to writings on Islamic metaphysics, especially the works of Fanṣūrī and his critic Rānirī, on the Islamic philosophy of education and on the confrontation with secularism. Another member of the same family, Sayyid Ḥusayn al-'Aṭṭās, who lived mostly in Singapore, charted a completely different course. He tried to create an authentic school of social science based on philosophical principles derived from the traditions of Asia rather than from nineteenth-century European philosophy.

As in Indonesia, in Malaysia there has also been a marked rise of interest in the later Islamic philosophical tradition. In Malaysia this phenomenon goes back to the 1980s, when some students who had studied Islamic philosophy with me in the United States, such as Usman Bakar, Baḥr al-Dīn Aḥmad (Baharuddin Ahmad), and somewhat later Zaylān Murīs (Zailan Moris), who has written a book on Mullā Ṣadrā, returned home. Also responsible are the efforts of Naquib al-'Aṭṭās, who instituted courses on later Islamic philosophy at ISTAC (International Institute of

Islamic Thought and Civilization), a major institution he founded in Kuala Lumpur, in which such scholars as Mahdi Muḥaqqiq from Iran and Alparslan Açikgenç from Turkey have taught Mullā Ṣadrā and other Islamic philosophers.

A further word needs to be said about 'Usman Bakar. Besides writing works on Sufism, especially in the Malay world, he has composed many important texts on the Islamic philosophy of science. He is well known internationally and is one of the leading Islamic philosophers of science. He must be considered along with Naquib al-'Aṭṭās the foremost Islamic thinker in Malaysia today. He is also the leading Traditionalist thinker in the Malay world.

Finally, a word must be said about various Muslim lands of Africa, which range from the Sudan in the east to Nigeria and Senegal in the west. In these lands, philosophical activity in the universities has for the most part followed English or French schools of thought, depending upon the colonial experience that each particular country has undergone. But there are also active Sufi movements in many areas, such as Senegal, as well as Islamic revivalist movements based on a rigorous application of the *Sharī'ah* in others. In Nigeria, the Islamic universities have shown some interest in the resuscitation of Islamic philosophy, while such thinkers as Ahmadu Bo have sought to establish a form of Islamic wisdom that is at the same time profoundly African.

Since World War II, nearly all Islamic countries have gained their political freedom, but they are now struggling with another form of domination, a cultural and philosophical one that ranges from positivism to postmodern deconstructionism. Parallel with the spread of such forms of thinking one sees a revival of interest in all aspects of the Islamic tradition, comprising the *Sharī'ah,* Sufism, theology, and traditional philosophy. Interest in these various aspects of Islamic thought is not the same everywhere, however. In this struggle between modern Western patterns of thought and the Islamic tradition, much remains to be done, including the achievement of a deeper understanding of the issues involved. Gradually, however, a few Muslim intellectuals have emerged who both possess a profoundly Islamic perspective and are well versed in modern thought, scholars and thinkers who are seeking to provide an Islamic answer to the challenges posed by modern philosophy and science ranging from existentialism and logical positivism, to deconstructionism in philosophy, to the exclusion of nonmaterial levels of reality in science, resulting in purely "mechanistic" cosmologies, evolutionism, reductionism, and so forth. Despite the anti-intellectual tendency of so many politically activist "fundamentalist" movements and the older opposition of some jurists and Ash'arite theologians to what they consider to be philosophical discourse, the activity of those devoted to Islamic philosophy continues to grow and to increase in influence. The work of this group represents perhaps the most notable feature of recent philosophical activity in the Islamic world. In its hands lies the intellectual defense of the citadel of the Islamic faith, at whose heart is to be found the purest form of *ḥikmah,* or *sophia,* with the appropriate means for its realization and teachings sufficient to answer all the intellectual challenges posed for Islam by the modern world.

Appendix III

WESTERN INTERPRETERS OF THE ISLAMIC TRADITION

Academic Scholars

The study of Islam in the modern West has not only molded the image of Islam there, but it has also influenced in numerous ways Islam's own interaction with the modern world and certain currents of thought within the Islamic world itself. On the foundations laid by medieval and Renaissance European studies of Islam, which began with the premise that Islam was a false religion and a Christian heresy, there developed, from the seventeenth century on, modern schools of the study of Islam that soon identified themselves with a "scientific" and "objective" methodology, combining rationalism, historicism, positivism, and many other Western ideas to produce a vast body of works on Islamic studies in nearly all the major European languages, chief among them German, French, and English. The discipline was called orientalism and was often supported by colonial powers to aid in the achievement of political goals. Nevertheless, many works of philological and historical value were composed and numerous Islamic texts critically edited and published by orientalists, but the religious and theological thrust of most of these works was, Islamically speaking, very negative and destructive. And parallel with those works of orientalism, based usually on a secularist worldview, there arose anti-Islamic tracts written by Christian missionaries; such works still appear today, in new guise.

After World War II, classical orientalism fell somewhat out of fashion in the West and was replaced to some extent, especially in North America, by methods drawn from the social sciences and based on prevalent theories and ideologies of the moment, ranging from positivistic sociology going back to August Comte or to Marxism, which was espoused especially by many European scholars and of course nearly all Soviet ones before the collapse of Communism in Russia and eastern Europe, and more recently to postmodernism and deconstructionism on both sides of the Atlantic. Yet amid a vast array of Western works on Islam that are ultimately anti-Islamic, sharing despite their many differences a common belief that either all religion is false or Islam is not an authentic revelation, there are some exceptions. There have appeared in the Western academic world a number of notable scholars who have been deeply sympathetic to traditional Islam and have made important contributions to its study. In this context one can name, among others, such outstanding figures as the British Islamicist Sir Hamilton Gibb, British scholar of religions Karen Armstrong, the Spanish Islamicist and Arabist Miguel Asín Palacios, followed as far as his field of study is concerned by the Puerto Rican Luce López Baralt, the Cuban Maria Rosa Menocal, the Canadian Wilfred Cantwell Smith, the Americans Marshall Hodgson and John A. Williams, and a number of German scholars, foremost among them Annemarie Schimmel.

The French world has been particularly rich in the cultivation of such scholars, producing such figures as Émile Dermenghem, Louis Gardet, Vincent Monteil, and Eric Geoffroy, the last two of whom are among a number of Western Islamicists who have themselves embraced Islam. France also produced two of the greatest Western orientalists and Islamicists, who were deeply devoted to various dimensions of traditional Islam and who made outstanding contributions to traditional Islamic thought. These two figures are Louis Massignon and his student Henry Corbin, both of whom have also exercised much influence within the Islamic world itself. It is therefore to them that I turn in this section, without wishing in any way to diminish the significance of other Western academic scholars who have devoted themselves with acumen, honesty, and empathy to the study of traditional Islam while using the methods of modern scholarship. Nor can one neglect the contribution of Muslim-born scholars writing in European languages. But here we are concerned with Western interpreters of the Islamic tradition and therefore have to forgo the very interesting discussion of the ever increasing contribution of Muslim-born scholars to Islamic studies in the West and the role they play in the confrontation between traditional Islam and modernism.

A. *In Commemoration Of Louis Massignon: Catholic Scholar, Islamicist, And Mystic*

Louis Massignon remains even today, decades since his death, a towering figure in the field of Islamic studies. I had the opportunity to encounter him for the first time in my student days, and our contact continued until his death.

Many consider Massignon to be perhaps the greatest academic scholar of Islam that the West has ever produced, and his works, especially on Sufism, continue to be a central part of the corpus of Western studies on the subject. It would therefore be appropriate to cite by way of prelude a poem by Rūmī, which in a sense recapitulates on a particular level the spiritual and intellectual destiny of Massignon:

> Regard the world as full of ecstasy.
> The dominion of the "Victorious."
> If thou wishest to be "victorious"
> Be impaled upon the gibbet.
> Be impaled upon the gibbet.

This poem, which was composed over three centuries after the death of the Sufi martyr Manṣūr al-Ḥallāj, echoes the singular significance of the martyrdom of the great saint; it is also the echo that dominated the life of Massignon. It is therefore quite significant that we view the life of Massignon through his unique experience of the spiritual reality of Ḥallāj, an experience that transformed him as a human being in his youth, that dominated the horizon of his life to its end, and that made possible the composition of his most important work, *The Passion of al-Ḥallāj*, which Herbert Mason spent twenty years translating into English, thus rendering a very major service to the cause of scholarship.[1]

The choice of Ḥallāj has a particular significance within the perspective adopted here, that is, the perspective of the Sufi tradition itself. I cannot do justice to Massignon otherwise; and here I write not only as a scholar, but as a person devoted to Sufism, for I wish to speak about certain subjects that are not merely scholarly, but that nevertheless need to be said.

The fact that Ḥallāj in a sense "visited" Massignon inwardly is not at all an academic question; rather, it is a providential event. Ḥallāj represents within Sufism the special grace of Christ as it manifests itself in the Islamic universe. He is a "Christic Sufi," if we can use such a term; that is, he manifests the Christic grace (*al-barakat al-'Īsawiyyah*) in his being. It is not that Ḥallāj was influenced by Christianity in a historical sense. This type of manifestation within the bosom of the Islamic tradition has nothing to do with the presence of historical Christianity as another religion. Rather, the structure of Islam is such that it is possible for the "spiritual light" of the prophets of other religions, especially Judaism and Christianity, to "shine forth" within the Islamic universe. It is possible to have an Islamic spirituality that is Abrahamic, Mosaic, or Christic and yet fully Islamic. That is why I use the word "Christic" and not "Christian."

Ḥallāj represents a Christic embodiment within the Muḥammadan universe of spirituality. And the fact that he, rather than another great early master such as Junayd, Abū Yazīd al-Basṭāmī, or another Sufi of Khurasan, happened to have been chosen by Massignon (or, more accurately, Massignon happened to have been chosen by Ḥallāj) is very far from being an accident from the point of view of the spiritual economy of the universe within which we live. The Ḥallājian perspective represents in fact perhaps the most accessible opening into Sufism for Westerners, the majority of whom are fundamentally Christian in their spiritual attitudes. Even if they try to leave their traditional religion behind, they nevertheless have a largely Christian perspective upon the reality of Sufism in general and, of course, that of Islam itself, of which Sufism is the heart. Therefore, the choice of Ḥallāj for Massignon or of Massignon for Ḥallāj, far from being an accident, represents in fact a providential event in the encounter between Islam and Christianity and by extension the West in the modern context.

Now, the man who was the vehicle of such a vision, namely, Massignon, whose hundredth anniversary was celebrated in both the Islamic world and the West a few years ago, needs to be studied at length precisely because of his significance as a bridge between the two religions. In fact, a number of biographies of him have been already written.[2] Here, it is important to recapitulate in a few words the main features of the contour of his life. He was a person who loved to speak of *le cours de la vie,* literally, "the course of one's life," that is, the moments whose traces delineate the significant features of a life. Let us briefly recall those moments. This question touches me personally, because Massignon was the first Western scholar about whom I ever heard from my very first teacher, my father, when I was only four or five years old.

Born in 1883 in the French town of Nogent-sur-Marne, Massignon entered the University of Paris in 1900. During the next year, he journeyed for the first time to the Islamic world, to Algeria, which was then part of France. In 1902, he finished his *licence* at the University of Paris. In 1904, he made his first journey to Morocco, which had an important effect on the whole future of that country, because it was he more than anyone else who advised Maréchal Lyautey not to destroy the old medinas of Morocco in order to build new quarters, but instead to build new cities next to the medinas. The consequences of that decision for Islamic architecture and urban design today are of course immense. The fact that the whole structure of the medinas in much of North Africa, especially in Fez, Meknes, and Salé, has been preserved to this day goes back to the role of Massignon in advising the powerful French official who ruled Morocco not to remodel the cities from within in modernizing them, as we see in many other cities in the Islamic world, but to build the *villes,* the French-style cities, outside of the old medinas and thereby preserve the structure of the traditional cities. This all-important choice is the result of the very first visit of the young Massignon to Morocco.

Then in 1907, a mysterious event took place in Massignon's life. Even his son and other members of his family considered it a mystical experience. The event was his discovery of Ḥallāj, a discovery that was not of a scholarly character, but of an inner and spiritual nature, one that in fact left an indelible mark upon the whole of his later life and brought him back to the fold of Catholic Christianity, which he had taken very lightly until then. From 1907 to 1909 he did archaeological work in Iraq, and from 1912 to 1913 he was a professor at the University of Cairo. With his exceptional command of Arabic, he was able to deliver his lectures there in that language. In 1914 he married, and in 1922, after World War I, he defended his great work on Ḥallāj entitled *La Passion d'al-Ḥallāj* as his principal thesis, while his auxiliary thesis, *Essai sur les origines du lexique de la mystique musulmane,*[3] was itself to become established as one of the major scholarly works on Sufism. These two works made him immediately famous and established him as one of the leading French Islamicists. As a result, he was chosen in 1926 as a professor at the Collège de France. From 1933 on, he also held the chair of

Islamic Studies at the École des Hautes Études. He held both positions until 1954, when he retired.

After World War II, more exactly in 1945–46, he was the envoy of France to various Arab countries, seeking to revive cultural relationships between France and the Arab world. In 1952, he came to the United States for the first time as a visiting professor and spent some time at Harvard. He retired in 1954 and in 1962 passed away, in the middle of the Algerian war of independence, when a very bitter struggle was going on between France and Algeria. In this battle, Massignon took the side of Algeria very strongly and therefore encountered much difficulty vis-à-vis the authorities in France.

It is of some interest to mention the following episode that demonstrates Massignon's concern with the Algerian question as it was playing out in Paris. The last time I met Massignon was a few months before his death at the beginning of 1962, when I was on my way from Tehran to Boston, where I was to be a visiting professor at Harvard. A night or two before, we had been at the house of Gaston Berger, the famous French author, with Henry Corbin. As we were coming out into the street, Corbin asked me, "Do you have your passport with you?"

"No," I said.

"Because of the Algerian War, the police are searching everyone," he said. "If you have no passport, you will have to spend the night in the police station. Then the following morning you can go to your hotel and fetch your passport."

So we retraced our steps to the building, and I made my way to a back alley and finally got safely back to my hotel. Later, when I went to Massignon's house, upon departure he accompanied me down to the first floor and asked, "Do you have your passport with you? If not, you are going to have trouble with the police."

"Well," I said, "you are very perceptive as to how foreigners, especially ones looking like me, are treated at the moment; but fortunately I have already had the experience of what this involves."

He laughed and said, "This is a very good thing, because we do not have any back alleys you can go through, and you would probably have to spend the night at the police station!"

Anyway, with regard to this brief contour of Massignon's life, it is essential to remember, first of all, that it was as a result of his encounter with the mysterious figure of the "Stranger," that is, Ḥallāj—in the spiritual world and not only through scholarship—that Massignon became a leading Catholic intellectual. It was this "converted" Massignon who became deeply involved with the religious life of the country, especially with the intellectual life of the Catholics of France, for a period of over fifty years, from 1910 to 1960, almost to the moment of his death. He knew such philosophers as Jacques Maritain and Étienne Gilson intimately. The latter was in fact his colleague at the Collège de France. Massignon was very close to the circle of French literary figures, such as Paul Claudel and François Mauriac, and he exchanged letters with many of them and other major intellectual and literary figures. He was also very close to certain Catholic spiritual figures who themselves were interested in rapprochement with Islam, the most important of whom was Charles de Foucauld.

Charles de Foucauld was a devout Catholic contemplative who founded a new religious order in North Africa and who actually lived in the Muslim world much of his life. But rather than try to convert Muslims, he sought to become a kind of Christian witness among them and to befriend them as people who followed another version of his religion with a message that also came from God. He had an important role to play not only for Catholicism, but for the whole of the Christian tradition in its relationship with Islam and the initiation of the first stages of serious dialogue between these two great religious traditions. Because he lived a life of simplicity and saintly piety, he was very close to the simple bedouin of the deserts of North Africa. Massignon's relationship with Foucauld is connected with one of the important functions that he, Massignon, had as a lay cardinal within Catholic circles in France and North Africa in the first decades of this century. When Foucauld died, Massignon composed a beautiful poem, which needs to be quoted here in the original French, because it recapitulates so poetically his sentiments toward Charles de Foucauld in relation to his own inner spiritual quest:

> Une consolation, je l'ai cherchée, à ma douleur;
> et ma douleur a fini par devenir pour moi cette consolation;
> Une preuve, je l'ai cherchée pour mon origine—et mon
> origine a fini par devenir pour moi cette preuve.
> A droite et à gauche, j'ai cherché a voir où était le visage de l'Ami;
> Mais j'étais au dehors, et Lui, c'est tout au fond de mon âme qu'Il est.[4]

This poem in itself reveals the profundity of Massignon's experience, not only as a scholar, but as a person of spiritual attainment.

Parallel with this concern with the Catholic/Christian world of France, Massignon began to enjoy a very wide circle of acquaintances in the Islamic world, in both Arab and non-Arab countries. In Iran, he had very close rapport with such scholars and statesmen as Mohammad Ali Foroughi, who also became prime minister; Badī' al-Zamān Furūzānfar, the great scholar of Jalāl al-Dīn Rūmī; and Reza-Zadeh Shafaq, a major scholar of history from Tabriz. He befriended especially the scholars of al-Azhar University in Egypt as well as those of Morocco and Algeria, which along with Iraq, which he knew particularly well because of his love for Ḥallāj, were the main centers of his contact in the Arab world. He also had a number of Arab students who later became famous scholars.

I recall clearly sensing Massignon's presence at the tomb of Ḥallāj the last time I was able to visit it in 1978. The tomb had been among a cluster of originally beautiful tombs of Sufis of the third and fourth Islamic centuries situated in an old cemetery that was, however, becoming part of an ugly urban development. Although that whole area had been taken over for the construction of a new quarter, Massignon put pressure upon Iraqi authorities, and one small room was built on the tomb of Ḥallāj to protect it. Although it is a pathetic sight, the fact that the tomb is still there is proof of Massignon's efforts and success in turning the attention of the authorities in Baghdad toward its preservation. Without his efforts, the very site of the tomb might have been lost or covered by an unmarked structure, as has happened to so many similar places in the Islamic world during past few decades.

As for Massignon's intellectual activity, at the center of it resides, of course, Ḥallāj, the remarkable Persian Sufi of the fourth/tenth century who was put to death in Baghdad in 922, because he was considered by his enemies as a heretic on the basis of his saying *ana'l-Ḥaqq* ("I am the Truth"). It was through him that his French "disciple" saw the whole of the Islamic tradition. Perhaps the greatest service that Massignon rendered to the cause of Islamic studies was his demonstration, as a result of the study of Ḥallāj, that Sufism has its roots in the Quran. Far from being a heretic, Ḥallāj was the epitome of orthodoxy, for only a saint is orthodox in the most universal sense of the term. He or she stands at the Center and, from the traditional perspective, everyone else is located at a point that is peripheral to that Center. Massignon realized that meditation upon verses of the Quran, emulation of the Prophet, and the grace issuing from the Quranic revelation constituted the origin and substance of Sufism. And at a time when everyone in orientalist circles considered Sufism to be a kind of alien tree planted in the soil of the Islamic world by extraneous forces—external influences that, like women's fashions, rotated every few years, from Indian to Christian to Neoplatonic and so forth—only Massignon, with great courage, came forward and defended the Islamic origin of Sufism. Fortunately, after nearly a century this truth has finally become accepted by many in scholarly circles in the West. Today, despite a few, such as Robert C. Zaehner, who have continued to write against this view, there are many serious scholars who defend the thesis of the Islamic origin of Sufism first presented in academic circles by Massignon and, later on, by David S. Margoliouth and several other well-known Islamicists in the early decades of the twentieth century.

Through the figure of Ḥallāj and by virtue of his inner "guidance," Massignon drew the attention of the Western audience for the first time to numerous other Sufis, such as Ibn 'Aṭā' Allāh, 'Alī Shushtarī, and Ibn Sab'īn. Ibn Sab'īn was the great Sufi/philosopher of Spain who journeyed to Mecca and there according to many accounts committed suicide, severing a vein before the House of God in order to die in ecstasy—quite a remarkable act considering the fact that suicide is forbidden by Islamic Law! The establishment in the West of the study of Sufism—its history as well as its doctrines, spiritual teaching, and language—as a major discipline within Islamic studies goes back to Massignon. Most later histories and technical studies of Sufism, of which in fact there are now a few, such as that of Louis Gardet and Georges C. Anawati[5] or Paul Nwyia's books on the Shādhiliyyah Order,[6] though not as yet definitive, mostly follow the path opened by Massignon and are extensions of his research. To this day, the substantial works being produced on the history of Sufism are still based to a large extent on his research, despite the numerous studies produced by those who have followed his lead during the past half century.

Massignon was also much interested in what he called "technical vocabulary," *la lexique technique,* the knowledge of which is so important for serious scholarship in Islamic studies. He was critical of the work of so many scholars, especially in North America, who are considered experts on matters Islamic, but who do not have complete command of technical texts in Arabic or Persian. Massignon insisted that, to be able to do serious scholarship in Islamic studies, one has to understand the technical language in depth; more particularly it is the technical language of Sufism that provides the key for the in-depth understanding of the teachings of Sufism. If one wishes to study the doctrines of Sufism or in fact any science in a traditional context, one must spend many years with a master studying texts pertaining to the discipline on the basis of the technical vocabulary involved. At the end, one becomes what we call in Persian *ahl-i iṣṭilāḥ,* that is, a person who knows the technical vocabulary. This is the end of the road of formal education, not its beginning. By mastering the language in depth one comes to know the subject itself. It is as it was in India in the old days, when one spent sixteen years studying Sanskrit, but after that did not need to study anything any more formally, because, having learned that language in depth, one had also learned the traditional sciences that are written in it. Massignon was really rendering an exceptional service when he opened the eyes of Western scholars to the significance of the actual technical vocabulary of Arabic texts. Otherwise the majority of scholars would have remained satisfied with "floating in the air," talking about great ideas without being able to relate them to a text, let alone being able to take an actual text and expand upon its various philosophical, mystical, or theological interpretations.

Massignon was very much interested in bibliographies, and he prepared three important ones, all of which would, from the point of view of Islamic studies, appear to concern far-fetched subjects. The first is on the Nuṣayrīs, who did not rule over Syria at the time considered by Massignon but were only one of the religious communities in that land and so did not attract much attention. The second is on the Qarāmiṭah, who created a violent and revolutionary movement in southern Arabia and the Persian Gulf area and whom few scholars considered to be of importance when Massignon wrote about them. The third, perhaps his most important bibliography, is concerned with Hermetic writings in Islam and was later published by André Festugière in his four-volume *La Révélation d'Hermès Trismégiste.*[7] This important research work introduced Western scholarship to the significance of Islamic writings, both Arabic and Persian, on Hermeticism.

Massignon was much concerned with the genius of the Arabic language, in which he was such a master and which he loved to the extent of attending Sunday mass in Arabic. He was not as great a scholar in Persian as he was in Arabic, although he was also much interested in things Persian. But what really corresponded to his own special destiny, the inner structure of his soul, was the understanding of the spiritual contribution of the Semitic people, both Jews and Arabs, through Judaism and Islam, and also Christianity, which is essentially a Semitic form of spirituality, as distinct from Greco-Hellenistic forms of spirituality as well as from other major religions of the world. What Massignon wrote on the genius of the Arabic language is, I think, among his most important contributions to scholarship.

Massignon also paid attention to Shī'ism. Although he wrote on Persian Shī'ism, his major contributions were to the study of Arab Shī'ism. In the world of Shī'ism, two figures always attracted his attention. One was Fāṭimah, the daughter of the Prophet. No one among Western scholars has written about her in the same sensitive manner as Massignon. In fact, this domain represents one of the incredible lacunae in the efforts of Western scholars, for there is no single full-fledged scholarly biography of her in any Western language. A number of books and articles have been devoted to so many minor figures, but there is no full study of spiritual depth by Western Islamicists of the person who plays such an important role in Islamic spirituality as it concerns women. If one wants to study Fāṭimah now in a European language, where does one go? One has to refer above all to the articles of Massignon. These studies also have a particular significance for comparative religious studies, for Massignon studied the relationship between Fāṭimah and the Virgin Mary; he pointed out that they really represent the same archetype, the same spiritual reality, on different levels, and that there is a kind of homologous relation between them, especially in those parts of the Islamic world, such as Syria, where Christianity and Islam live side by side. Many Arab women in Syria, for example, pray to God through both Fāṭimah and the Virgin for a sick child. In their minds, the sanctity of Mary and Fāṭimah are related and even identified.

The second figure in whom Massignon was especially interested was Salmān-i Fārsī, or Salmān-i Pāk, whose tomb near Ctesiphon he visited and whose significance for the Islamization of Persia and its culture he brought out in an unparalleled fashion. As far as Persia is concerned, perhaps the most important single work of Massignon is in fact that profound article entitled "Salmān Pāk et les prémices spirituelles de l'Islam iranien."[8] Here he unveils the symbolic and historic significance of Salmān, whose life marks the beginning of the attachment of the Iranian world to the new revelation. By adopting Salmān as a member of his family (*ahl al-bayt*), the Prophet of Islam in a sense adopted the Iranian people as an essential component of his "community," or *ummah.*

Outside of these intellectual and scholarly concerns, Massignon's main preoccupation in the world around him was on two levels. One concerned religious dialogue, to which many of his biographers have alluded. Massignon was without doubt the first of the major Catholic scholars and thinkers to open up religious dialogue with the Islamic world. Today it is often too easy to be "ecumenical," as this term is being currently understood in so many religious circles. When one does not have to believe in anything firmly, it is easy to open the doors to dialogue with other religions. Such was not the case of Massignon. In this context it is of some interest to mention an unforgettable lesson given by a great traditional teacher of mine in Persia. He said. "It is wonderful to have an open mind; it is like opening up the windows of a room. But it is good to have the windows of a room open only if the room has walls. If you take a couple of windows into the middle of the desert, it does not matter whether you keep them open or closed, since there are no walls!" Today everyone talks of ecumenism and openness in religious dialogue, but in most cases this exercise does little to produce better understanding among religions, because one is asked to sacrifice or dilute the principles and doctrines of each religion in order to carry out dialogue. There is, however, little value to dialogue when there are no principles to be defended. Such certainly was not the case with Massignon, who participated in dialogues with Muslims as a devout Catholic.

Massignon began his dialogue with Islam at a time when the Catholic Church was most serious in defending its traditional principles and exclusivist teachings. The atmosphere in which he had to speak was, therefore, to some extent different from that of today. He had to display exceptional courage and fortitude. But he persevered and, to achieve his goal of promoting better mutual understanding between Christianity and Islam, he propagated the cause of Charles de Foucauld, visited many Muslim centers, and wrote incessantly about Islamic-Christian relations. In fact, most of his Catholic followers, like Youakim Moubarak, Giulio Bassetti-Sani, and others, who have written works on him in French, Italian, and other languages, have also written on Muslim-Christian dialogue. Massignon was thus a sort of guiding light for a whole later generation of Catholics interested in Christian-Muslim relations. When, some forty years ago, I led a delegation of Persian Muslim scholars to the Vatican to meet the late Cardinal Pignedoli and discuss problems of mutual concern for Islam and Christianity with a group of Catholic scholars, the name and thought of Massignon often came up as the basis or setting for the debates that were to follow.

Massignon's second set of concerns involved contemporary social and political issues endowed with a religious dimension. He was deeply involved in the actual everyday world about him and was not at all a person who lived in an ivory tower. This saintly and aristocratic man was not only an outstanding scholar, but also a man of action who played a part in the world around him, especially in Islamic causes and events. He even attended the coronation of the Arab king of Syria in 1917 as a representative of France. He met Lawrence of Arabia and was deeply concerned with the partition of the Arab world and later with the cause of the Palestinians after their displacement from their homeland. He was keenly interested in the future of France's North African colonies, especially Morocco and Algeria. His concern with the social aspect of human life and the questions of war and peace are also to be seen in his espousal of the cause of Mahatma Gandhi, with whom he corresponded.

For the sake of honesty and truth, one must seize every opportunity possible to bring out this aspect of Massignon's activities over the decades, because it stands in stark contrast to what one often finds today in the West—a kind of occasional and intermittent interest in the question of human rights in the Islamic world. This interest resembles a kind of malarial fever; it comes once in a while and then, after a chill, goes away completely and only returns at a much later date when it is politically convenient. Meanwhile nations are turned upside down by the hypocritical and selective interest in human rights and periodic expressions of self-righteousness by a number of those who claim to be experts on the Islamic world. The study of Massignon's concern with the Islamic world reveals, by contrast, that he did not function in such a way. He did not change directions with the wind. Whether General de Gaulle was in power in France, or, before him, the socialist government, or the government after the armistice, Massignon's concern for the Islamic world and its problems was firm and unwavering. He had a passion for the lands of Islam that was based not upon opportunism or the desire to be invited to the next major conference or get a scholarship to go to a country regardless of its form of government, but rather upon certain principles and a love for Islamic culture.

I think that the disservice rendered in the last few years by a number of Western writers on Islamic subjects to the Islamic world, to the lives of over a billion people, indeed to the whole future relationship of the West with the Islamic world, and therefore to the West itself is great. Massignon's career and the way he went about dealing with the Islamic world stand as a great lesson in the present situation. They should be of interest to all those who are concerned with truth and justice, and not just expediency. It is interesting to note that those who have held the memory of Massignon dearest have been those who have been least culpable of this sin of hypocrisy. If one reads the list of scholars who one day shout about their love of humanity and the next day do not care about what is happening to the very people they were shouting about the day before, who then go back to their daily routines as if they had never concerned themselves with justice and human rights or been touched by love for humanity, one will see that the students of Massignon are not usually among them. That is a notable and positive moral feature of the influence that he imparted, either through his writings or through the imprint of his teachings and personality upon his students.

Now, who were the students whom Massignon influenced in this way? In France, the whole later generation of Islamicists, such as Regis Blachère, Roger Arnaldez, and similar scholars, were either directly the students of Massignon or were deeply influenced by him. In this latter category, one can mention a scholar of the stature of Louis Gardet. But among them is one person whom I must mention, whom I consider to be without doubt the greatest French student of Louis Massignon and his scholarly complement, namely, Henry Corbin, to whom I shall turn in the next section. Corbin did for Persia what Massignon essentially did for the Arab world; and the influence of Massignon on Corbin was immense. Corbin was one of my closest scholarly friends in France. In fact, the first time I lectured at the Sorbonne, I found that it was in the very chair in which for twenty years Massignon had taught at the École des Hautes Études. Corbin was then the chairman of the session, and we had a memorable afternoon during which I spoke of later Islamic philosophy.

As far as Massignon's influence upon Corbin's own formation is concerned, I must recount this story that I heard from Corbin himself. Having in mind the fact that no one has rendered greater service to the knowledge of Suhrawardī and later Islamic philosophy in the West than Corbin, I once asked him, "How did you become interested in Suhrawardī?"

He said, "For several years I was studying Martin Heidegger and the German *Existenz philosophie* and had gone several times to Freiburg to meet Heidegger, but his philosophy did not quite satisfy me. I knew that I was looking for something else. One day when I was a young student sitting in the front row of a class at the Sorbonne, Massignon came in with an old book, the cover of which was very tarnished [old Persian lithograph editions were like that], and he said, 'Take this book and read it. That is what you are looking for.' And that was the lithograph edition of the *Ḥikmat al-ishrāq,* published in Tehran in the late Qajar period, the old edition.

"I took that book home," Corbin added, "and read it. That event changed my whole life. Henceforth I put Heidegger 'aside, on the shelf' and became interested in 'serious philosophy.'"

In fact, he devoted the rest of his life to this "serious philosophy." This fact itself—I mean the possibility of training and influencing a man like Corbin, who produced an immense corpus in Islamic studies, especially philosophy—speaks of the great impact that Massignon had on the French intellectual world.

But this impact was not of course limited to French students. He also had many students from other countries and especially from the Arab world. In fact, some of the best-known intellectual figures in the Arab world, some of whom have already been mentioned in this book, were either directly his students or were influenced by him. I need mention only two names: 'Abd al-Raḥmān Badawī, perhaps the most famous Egyptian scholar of Islamic philosophy, and the late 'Abd al-Ḥalīm Maḥmūd, the Grand Shaykh of al-Azhar University and a major authority in both Sufism and Islamic philosophy. It might appear strange that the person who occupied the most important religious position in the Sunni world knew French well and, in fact, had been a student of Massignon. As for students from North America, one need only mention that in the United States several of the most competent Islamicists, such as George Makdisi, Herbert Mason, and James Kritzeck, were directly his students.

Despite these facts and despite his grandeur, Massignon did not, obviously, go uncriticized. He was, in fact, very severely criticized in many circles, and it would require another study to analyze all the criticisms that have been made of him. But there are a few points that must be mentioned. There are those who criticize Massignon for his overemphasis on the question of suffering in Islam. Now, this is a very complex question. There is no doubt that the Christian idea of redemption through participation in the suffering of the founder of the religion does not exist in Islam, especially in Sunnism. But it is also true that Muslims suffer, as all human beings do simply by virtue of being born into this world. One cannot live in this world without suffering, for this world is not Paradise. Therefore, suffering, like every other human experience, has a spiritual significance. To belittle the element of suffering in Islam as if it did not exist is to misunderstand a whole facet of this religion, including of course Twelve-Imam Shīʿism.

We live in a very strange world: on the one hand, one reads criticism of Massignon's overemphasis of the importance of suffering in Islam; on the other hand, one encounters articles in which supposed professors of Iranian and Islamic studies claim that all Persians want to suffer and be martyred, because Shīʿism is based on this idea. There seems to be little moderation, just two extremes, either denying any significance to the meaning of suffering in Islam or making it the central concern of Islam, at least in its Shīʿite form. In defense of Massignon's position, one can only point out that anyone who has had actual contact with Islamic piety, not only in the Shīʿite but also in the Sunni world, realizes that, although there is in Islam no central image of the cross on which Christ suffers and bleeds, the idea does exist of the unavoidable presence of suffering in human life and the importance of the spiritual transformation that suffering can bring about when combined with complete surrender to God. And that is the truth that Massignon wanted to bring out.

Another criticism made of Massignon by many scholars, including his student Corbin, who debated this issue with Massignon a great deal, is the latter's lack of interest in later Sufism. It has often been said that Massignon was interested only in early Sufism and that he did not pay attention to the significance of such figures as Ibn 'Arabī, 'Abd al-Karīm al-Jīlī, Maḥmūd Shabistarī, and other later Sufis of the school of *waḥdat al-wujūd,* or the "transcendent unity of Being." As a person who follows this school and is very sympathetic to this interpretation of Sufism, I believe that Massignon had every right not to be interested in this school. Sufism does not have only one dimension or one interpretation. There are many great Sufis who have not accepted this interpretation and who have not shown interest in the question of *waḥdat al-wujūd,* or at least have not spoken about it, choosing instead another language for the exposition of the teachings of Sufism. This is to be seen to some degree even in Jalāl al-Dīn Rūmī, who complements Ibn 'Arabī in many ways and who lived nearly at the same time. But in fact Rūmī's formulation of this doctrine is very different from that of Ibn 'Arabī. Massignon should therefore not be criticized on the ground that his sympathies lay with earlier interpretations of Sufism and that he did not devote much attention to the Ibn 'Arabian school. Moreover, later in life, in his second edition of *La Passion d'al-Ḥallāj,* which Massignon brought out a few years before his death, he displays a shift in his position and shows greater sympathy for the school of Ibn 'Arabī. That he loved Ḥallāj more than, let us say, Qunyawī or Jīlī cannot be criticized as a weakness or shortcoming on his part, even from the point of view of a person like myself, who has spent much of his life studying Ibn 'Arabī and his school and who was one of the first to write about him in the English language and defend him against his orientalist critics.

The third criticism leveled against Massignon that I wish to consider here is somewhat more problematic. It is the criticism made by those who could not accept the authenticity and seriousness of the concern for the spiritual and mystical aspects of Islam that Massignon showed. This type of criticism came first of all from the ranks of official orientalists in Europe and North America who were devoted to the study of Islamic thought and history, but strongly opposed Massignon's concern for Islam and Sufism as living spirituality. Massignon received a great deal of scathing criticism from those who did not want to accept this kind of "existential concern" with a tradition under study, especially if this tradition happened to be Islam. Massignon was a kind of pioneer in making Islamic studies serious from a religious and spiritual point of view, not merely as philology and history. Not that everyone accepted his view or that many people do so now. Nevertheless, he was a pioneer in the type of Islamic studies that combines religious and spiritual concerns with purely scholarly ones, a type that has many more followers now than when Massignon took up his study of Islam at the beginning of the twentieth century.

One group of Massignon's critics included those possessing a theological education and coming from a certain type of Protestant background opposed to the mystical dimension, which he emphasized so much, scholars such as Winfred Cantwell Smith and others who have been themselves deeply engaged in the theological implications of Islam, but who nevertheless have not been particularly interested in the mystical aspect of things. Their criticism, that Massignon exaggerated the spiritual and mystical aspects in his interpretation of Islamic history and thought, has become an unquestioned assumption even today in the work of many otherwise respected historians of Islam. Even the great historian of Islam Sir Hamilton Gibb, who was a close friend of Massignon, criticized him from time to time for jumping to certain conclusions, because of what Gibb considered to be Massignon's excessive emphasis upon the mystical elements in Islam. Needless to say, certain of Massignon's conclusions are inevitably open to criticism, for he was not omniscient; but his shortcomings as a historian of Islamic thought cannot be blamed upon his love and understanding of Islamic mysticism. On the contrary, it is this understanding of and sympathy for the inner dimension of Islam that enabled him to comprehend certain basic aspects of Islamic thought and history as well as their inner dynamics, which had been veiled from other scholars in the field before him and remained so to some extent even afterwards.

Massignon had a method of studying texts to which Corbin alluded in a facetious way as "the helicopter method of textual scholarship." What he meant by that characterization was that Massignon would "descend" from above upon a text, make a sort of reconnaissance study of it, and then take off again and go somewhere else. He did not go through most of the manuscript material with which he dealt in a step-by-step manner. There is no doubt an element of truth to this observation by Corbin and others. Massignon had a glimpse of many manuscripts, which he discovered in Istanbul or some other city, and wrote about them without fully knowing the whole text. As a result, there were certain misinterpretations on his part. For example, in his classafication of the works of

Suhrawardī, he made mistakes; nevertheless, he was the first to classify these writings, and that fact in itself is remarkable. Both Corbin and I have classafied the writings of the great Master of the School of *ishrāq* based on a long period of study of Suhrawardī's works; they are different from that of Massignon, yet we have been indebted to him.

The "helicopter method" of textual study carried out by Massignon, although open to criticism, nevertheless made many texts known that would otherwise not have become discovered. What is astounding is not the errors committed in this process, but the number of works discovered by Massignon during relatively short stays in Istanbul and other Islamic cities where major collections of Arabic and Persian manuscripts are to be found. It is certainly amazing that Massignon was able to discover, during a short period of time, the treatise of Ibn al-Nafīs, which changed the history of medicine, and many of the treatises of al-Kindī, a discovery that altered our conception of the early history of Islamic philosophy, not to speak of the significance of al-Kindī himself.

So much for the criticisms, which I wanted to answer before proceeding to evaluate Massignon's significance now that over a century has passed since his birth and some half a century since his death. How should we now characterize him? I suppose each scholar would do so in a different way, but if I were asked to summarize the salient features of Massignon, I would say that, first of all, he had a profound and universal appreciation of matters spiritual. He really was a spiritual being. In the modern intellectual and scholarly realms, that is certainly a very rare quality, especially for a scholar of the highest quality. The modern world is in fact characterized by its inability to combine intelligence with piety. People are so often intelligent, but not very pious, or else pious, but not very intelligent. But to combine deep piety with penetrating intelligence is a rare quality in our time, but one that Massignon possessed to an eminent degree. He was able to penetrate the spiritual significance of not only the Christian and Islamic worlds, which were his own, but also distant worlds, such as Shintoism, which he experienced on the island of Ise and about which he wrote the remarkable text known to the students of his writings.[9] One can also recall his great attachment to Gandhi and the Hindu spirituality that he represented.[10]

In addition to this quality, Massignon was a person who possessed great nobility of soul. He was a truly noble person, at once a saintly man and a genuine aristocrat in the traditional sense of the word. He was very shy, and it was difficult to photograph him. I remember in 1957 when I journeyed from the United States to Morocco for the first time to take part in a month-long seminar on Muslim-Christian relations with Massignon in the Atlas Mountains, I did everything possible to try to photograph him, but he would not allow it. I finally had to hide behind a wall and then managed to take some remarkable photos of him, but, alas, they were unfortunately lost during the revolutionary turmoil of 1979 in Iran. This quality of shyness in him came from a kind of spiritual concentration and inwardness. He did not want to overexpose himself, but when he did, his face was always intimate and directly personal.

As already mentioned, Massignon had a genuine concern for the rights of Muslims and, in fact, of all human beings, including of course the people of Europe itself. He also had a special role to play in the creation of Islamic-Christian dialogue. All these qualities make him, I think, as both a scholar and a human being, an example fully worthy of emulation by those in the modern world who pursue Islamic studies in more than just the academic sense, those who also aspire to act as bridges connecting the West with the Islamic world out of respect for the Islamic tradition as well as European Christianity.

Everything that Massignon did was carried out with great passion, in the positive sense of the term, and with great love. He was in fact totally involved in everything that he did. Once when he gave a lecture at Harvard University, a graduate student bent on quantifying everything asked, "How many Sufis are there in the Islamic world?"

Massignon smiled and replied, "How many lovers are there in Cambridge? Sufism is a matter of love. You tell me how many lovers there are in Cambridge, and I shall tell you how many Sufis there are in the Islamic world."

An excellent answer to such a question, an answer that could only come from an exceptional scholar.

Let me conclude by recounting an unforgettable moment that has always remained in my memory. It was actually late one morning in 1958 at the Benedictine monastery of Tioumliline at the top of the Atlas Mountains, which had been chosen as the site for an Islamic-Christian dialogue, a conference in which Gardet, Gibb, Filmer, S. C. Northrop, and many other distinguished scholars were taking part. Massignon was the last speaker, and he spoke about the permanence of Divine Love and its central role in the spiritual life. I could never forget the silhouette of this striking face with the small amount of white hair that he still had blowing gently in the breeze. He suddenly paused and quoted a poem in Persian. He recited it from memory and concluded his talk on that day in this abrupt manner. I also wish to conclude this brief discourse on Massignon with that poem, a poem that all those who have studied Persian literature know. The verses are those of Ḥāfiẓ, who says:

هرگز نمیرد آنکه دلش زنده شد به عشق
ثبت است در جریدهٔ عالم دوام ما

He whose heart is brought to life through love never dies.
Our perpetuity is recorded upon the pages of the cosmic book.

That is how Massignon will be remembered as long as there are men and women who study Islam, Christianity, and their intertwined destinies with perspicacity and empathy and who are also concerned with matters of the spirit.

B. *Henry Corbin: The Life and Works of the Occidental Exile in Quest of the Orient of Light*

Rarely has the West produced a figure who was at once a philosopher, in the traditional and still honored sense of the term, and a master of both the major Islamic languages and the intellectual sources written in these languages. Such a happy conjunction took place in the being of Henry Corbin. He was the foremost Occidental exponent of the integral tradition of Islamic philosophy and the leading hermeneutic interpreter to the contemporary world of the spiritual and intellectual aspects of the Islamic tradition, especially as they have blossomed in Persia. In order to achieve this task of interpreting the vast treasures of the Islamic, and more particularly the Iranian, world in a way that would be at once scholarly and spiritually, theologically, and philosophically significant, Corbin had to possess, from the earliest period of his intellectual life, both a love for detailed scholarly research in manuscripts and printed works of great philological complexity and difficulty and the ability to fly into the world of traditional philosophical and spiritual speculation and meditation, to have his feet firmly planted in a traditional metaphysical work associated with a particular historical figure or school and his eyes gazing away to the horizons of a transhistorical reality. The presence within him of these two often apparently contradictory characteristics made him attracted, from the beginning, to the disciplines of Islamic philology and philosophy. He in fact proudly considered himself an orientalist, but as he understood the term "Orient," not in the ordinary sense of the word. Referring to his own experience as a philologist, a connoisseur of Islamic books, and as a philosopher, Corbin writes:

> One can be an orientalist and at the same time a philosopher with a formation that is rigourously and technically philosophical. These are two disciplines that are only too rarely united in the same person, so rare at least as far as Islam is concerned, with the result that a whole domain of orientalism has for a long time been wasted. Moreover, philosophers have remained in ignorance of one of their most beautiful provinces.

Corbin then adds that for him there is "a complementarity of formation" between the two.[11]

The man in whom these two strains were to meet and to make possible the production of so many important works was born in Paris on April 14, 1903. After early religious studies, as a very young man he was drawn to mystical and gnostic doctrines that he identified at that time with some of the leading Protestant figures of the Renaissance and the seventeenth century, such as Jacob Böhme, for whom he continued to profess a special love to the end of his life. Corbin's particular intellectual and spiritual bent was to lead him to the Sorbonne, rather than to the strictly religious education of a seminary. He thus embarked upon a long period of formal university education in such institutions as the Sorbonne (*Licence des Lettres,* 1925; *diplôme d'études supérieures de l'École Pratique des Hautes Études, diplôme de la section des sciences religieuses,* 1928) and l'École Nationale des Langues Orientales (*diplôme,* 1929). The result was a mastery of not only the Western classical languages (Greek and Latin), but also of the two major intellectual languages of the Islamic world, namely, Arabic and Persian. Corbin was also deeply drawn to the German philosophical scene, spent considerable time in Germany, and was able to master philosophical as well as literary German perfectly.

Corbin entered the arena of intellectual life in France at a moment when several important currents dealing with traditional philosophy were coming to the fore, some in academic circles and others elsewhere. There were, first of all, the magisterial works of René Guénon, soon followed by those of Frithjof Schuon, which exposed the full range of traditional metaphysics for the first time in the modern West and mercilessly criticized the errors of what is called "philosophy" in Western languages today. Then there was the revival of medieval European philosophy, which, in the figure of Étienne Gilson, was in full sway in the 1920s and 1930s. Finally, certain aspects of Islamic esoterism were being presented in the West for the first time by a number of orientalists, especially Louis Massignon. Moreover, outside France and mostly in Germany, the school of phenomenology and *Existenz Philosophie* was attracting certain thinkers to a reexamination of the meaning of the relation between the outward and the inward, to the hermeneutic interpretation of the sacred texts of religion, and to that other grand book of theophanies that is nature itself.

Corbin was sensitive to all these currents and personally became closely associated with the last three. He studied directly with Gilson, who taught him the method of interpreting traditional philosophy on the basis of an established text, a method that Corbin was to apply to many of the major texts of Islamic philosophy, as Gilson has done for Latin works of Christian Patristic and Scholastic philosophy.

Corbin studied directly with Massignon, who opened new vistas into the worlds of Sufism and Shīʿism for the young student. It was in fact Massignon who acted as a major instrument of providence in charting the course of Corbin's destiny by turning his attention, through Suhrawardī, the sixth/twelfth-century founder of the School of Illumination, to that Orient that is not merely geographical, but that symbolizes the world of illumination, the world of the "Orient of Light," as Corbin himself would say.

After finishing his formal studies, he began to work at the Bibliothèque Nationale in Paris in the section for Oriental manuscripts and even spent 1935–36 in Berlin in order to continue his research in the rich collections of Arabic and Persian manuscripts in that city. But Corbin's relation with the German scene was mostly with the philosophical circles connected with the names of Edmund Husserl, Max Scheler, and especially Martin Heidegger, whose writings he studied avidly. In fact, it was Corbin who, in 1939, translated a major work of Heidegger, *Was ist Metaphysik?* (*Qu'est-ce que la métaphysique?*) for the first time into French and who in fact was instrumental in the rise of interest in Heidegger among such French philosophers as Jean-Paul Sartre. But, as he was to tell me when we visited St. Odile on the Franco-German border on the occasion of the first Western colloquium on Shīʿism ever held in Europe—at the University of Strasbourg in 1966—his discovery of Suhrawardī and the "Orient of Light" made it no longer necessary for him to cross this historic pass in order to seek knowledge at the feet of the *Existenz* philosophers. As he was to show later, in his masterly comparison of the ontology of Mullā Ṣadrā with that of Heidegger,[12] the discovery of an authentic metaphysics reveals how limited and truncated the discussions of being that were occupying the main currents of philosophy in Germany really were.

In any case, in 1939, Corbin left the Occident for Istanbul to gain closer knowledge of the manuscripts of Islamic philosophy, little aware that World War II would force him to remain nearly six years in the unique libraries of the old Ottoman capital, far from the intellectual and academic circles of Paris. During this period, Corbin acquired an unparalleled acquaintance with manuscripts on philosophy and Sufism in the almost inexhaustible libraries of that city. Moreover, he mastered the technique of editing and correcting Arabic and Persian manuscripts developed by Hellmut Ritter and used it in his edition of the metaphysical section of Suhrawardī's *Talwīḥāt* ("Intimations"), *Muqāwamāt* ("Apposites"), and *al-Mashāriʿ wa'l-Muṭāraḥāt* ("Paths and Havens"), which appeared in Istanbul in 1945 as the first volume of Suhrawardī's *Opera Metaphysica et Mystica*.[13] This first major work by Corbin on Islamic philosophy was to establish him immediately in the West as a notable scholar and was to lead, in 1954, to his appointment as director of Islamic studies in Paris (*directeur d'études islamiques, la section des sciences religieuses de l'École Pratique des Hautes Études*), occupying the chair of his former mentor, Massignon.

The plenary discovery of Suhrawardī made possible by his long stay in Istanbul attracted Corbin to Persia, where Suhrawardī was born and where his school is still alive. The "Master of Illumination" almost literally took the hands of his Occidental interpreter and guided him to the land to whose ancient culture Corbin had been attracted as a young man and whose rich intellectual life during the Islamic period he was to discover through his love for *Hikmat al-ishrāq,* which he translated as the "Theosophy of the Orient of Light." In 1945, Corbin made his first journey to Persia, where he immediately found his spiritual home. In 1946, he was appointed by the department of cultural relations of the French government to organize the department of Iranian studies at the newly created Institut Franco-iranien in Tehran and to begin the series of publications entitled *Bibliothèque iranienne* (continued later by the Imperial Iranian Academy of Philosophy until 1979), which has presented many major texts of Islamic philosophy and Sufism to the contemporary Islamic world as well as to the West. The enterprise was carried out indefatigably by Corbin with the collaboration of many Iranian scholars, such as Muḥammad Mu'īn, S. J. Āshtiyānī, Muḥammad Mukrī, S. H. Nasr, and Murtaḍā Ṣarrāf, as well as non-Persian scholars, such as Jean Aubin, Marijan Molé, and 'Usman Yahya.

From 1954 on, Corbin journeyed regularly to Iran until his death in 1978. He would spend the fall semester in Tehran, the winter one in Paris, and the summer also in France; for a period during the summer, however, he would be at Ascona in Switzerland, where he became one of the main figures at the annual meetings of some of the leading scholars of religion, philosophers, psychologists, and scientists of East and West, including C. G. Jung, Massignon, and G. Scholem, that came to be known as the Eranos gatherings. Upon retirement, he was able to preserve this rhythm of life lived between France and Persia by becoming an active scholar and teacher at the Imperial Iranian Academy of Philosophy, where he taught in the fall.

During his annual pilgrimage to Iran, Corbin became gradually acquainted with many of the leading traditional authorities of the country, with such theosophers and gnostics as 'Allāmah Sayyid Muḥammad Ḥusayn Ṭabāṭabā'ī and Sayyid Muḥammad Kāẓim 'Aṣṣār, and with some of their younger students, such as Murtaḍā Muṭahharī and Sayyid Jalāl al-Dīn Āshtiyānī; with Sufi masters, such as Jawād Nūrbakhsh, the master of the Ni'matallāhiyyah Order; with such eminent traditional scholars as Badī' al-Zamān Furūzānfar and Jalāl Humā'ī; and also with many younger scholars, some of whom, such as 'Īsā Sipahbudī, translated some of his works into Persian.

During this same period, his courses in Paris revolved completely around the spiritual and philosophical works of Persian Islamic masters such as Suhrawardī, Sayyid Ḥaydar Āmulī, Mīr Dāmād, and Mullā Ṣadrā as well as those of the great Andalusian gnostic Ibn ʿArabī. Students from many countries came to his courses, including Persians and Arabs, and he opened up a new dimension in Islamic studies in the West by unveiling fresh horizons in Islamic philosophy, Sufism, and Shīʿism.

Corbin also participated in numerous conferences in Western Europe and expounded teachings ranging from the study of Western esoterism to modern philosophy, from the doctrines of Zoroaster to those of the great Islamic sages. But the Eranos meetings at Ascona occupied a central position in Corbin's intellectual life in Europe. He was a continuous presence at these important meetings for three decades and, along with a few close friends, such as Mircea Eliade, Ernst Benz, and Gershom Scholem as well as Carl Gustav Jung, for whom the Eranos meetings were established, in a sense set the tone for these conferences. Much of Corbin's most important writings, which were discussed in Tehran and Paris with circles of friends and students, found their first expression in various volumes of the *Eranos-Jahrbuch* and only later appeared in more developed book form.[14]

Endowed with great physical stamina and mental energy, with a singular devotion to his subject and aided by a wife who was totally dedicated to him, Corbin was able for many years to continue a full schedule of teaching, research, and writing that took him annually from Paris to Tehran, back to Paris, and from there to Ascona. Throughout his life, from the time of his youth, he worked throughout the night and slept only with the appearance of the dawn. His teaching and research activities began at noon on days that were often spent, like the long nights, in both teaching and deciphering difficult Arabic and Persian manuscripts, interpreting the wisdom contained therein for the modern world. The result of his perseverance in this strenuous schedule over long years is the remarkably voluminous corpus of works that Corbin produced and that stands as one of the most impressive achievements of Western orientalism in the domains of traditional Islamic thought in general and of Islamic philosophy, Shīʿism, and Sufism in particular.

Corbin also taught in Tehran University, conducting advanced seminars with myself upon various themes of Islamic philosophy and examining them in confrontation with different problems posed by the West and various forces of modernization. Over the years there also took place in the fall regular sessions with 'Allāmah Ṭabāṭabā'ī and several leading Persian scholars, in which some of the most profound dialogues between East and West were carried out; the task of making the commentary and translation for these was usually left in my hands and sometimes in the hands of Sipahbudī and later Dāriūsh Shāyigān. Two widely popular volumes in Persian have resulted from this exchange between Corbin and 'Allāmah Ṭabāṭabā'ī, one of the foremost traditional authorities of Shī'ism and master of both the esoteric and exoteric sciences, who died a few years after Corbin.

The works of Corbin are so numerous and concern so many diverse fields that it is not possible to analyze them in any detail here. They would require a separate study to do justice to all the themes contained in them.[15] But they can be described in brief by considering them in several main categories. Let us begin by mentioning his essays dealing with esoteric currents in the Occident, with such figures as the *Fedeli d'amore,* Joachim of Flora, the Renaissance alchemists, Böhme, Georg Johann Hamann, Swedenborg, Goethe, and others, to whom Corbin was devoted both intellectually and spiritually. Moreover, he often compared the ideas and doctrines connected with this intellectual current with Islamic and occasionally Mazdaean themes, so that there is a greater concern with the Western esoteric schools as well as the spiritual and intellectual malaise of the modern West in the writings of Corbin than the titles of his writings might suggest.

From his early years as a student, Corbin was interested in ancient Persia and its religious traditions; in Zoroaster, whose teachings even influenced the Greeks; and in Mithraism and Manichaeism, whose "gnostic" cosmology and cosmogony he interpreted in a completely positive vein—not the way they were seen by early Christian theologians, who attacked them so bitterly because of their insistence on dualism, which is theologically unacceptable from the Christian point of view. Some of Corbin's earliest writings were on ancient Persia and translations from Pahlavi, which he had learned early in his student period. Later in life, he was to pursue his interests in this field through comparative studies, reflected in several of his discourses at Eranos; through his attraction to Suhrawardī, who saw both Plato and the ancient Persians as the source of true philosophy; by means of his appreciation of Gemisthos Plethon, who like Suhrawardī turned his gaze upon both Plato and Zoroaster; and by Corbin's attempt to trace the continuity of certain myths, symbols, and doctrines of ancient Persia into the Islamic period. As far as this last theme is concerned, although many of Corbin's works return to it again and again, it is his *Terre céleste et corps de résurrection*[16] that stands out as his most notable achievement in this domain.

The writings of Corbin on Shīʿism form another major category of his works, one that reflects his own inner life perhaps more than any other. Corbin was attracted early in his scholarly life to Shīʿism, especially Shīʿite esoterism, not only intellectually, but also in his heart and soul. When speaking of Shīʿism, he usually spoke of "us" and considered himself to be identified with Shīʿism in spirit as well as in mind. Whether it was in his pilgrimage to the mosque of the Twelfth Imam in Jāmkarān near Qom or in talks with Shīʿite spiritual and religious authorities, Corbin displayed an attachment to Shīʿism that went beyond that of the usual Western scholar engaged in his subject of research. It was participation in a spiritual world in which it can be said that he possessed faith.

It is of interest to note how Corbin even interpreted his own philosophical position from the Shīʿite perspective. Corbin called himself a phenomenologist. Yet when I once asked him how he would translate "phenomenology" into Persian, he told me that "phenomenology" means *kashf al-maḥjūb,* the "casting aside of the veil," which is a fundamental method of expounding the truth in Sufism and is also the title of one of the greatest classics of Sufism by ʿAlī ibn ʿUthmān Hujwīrī. For Corbin, the fundamental distinction made in Islamic esoterism in general and Shīʿism in particular was between the outward (*al-ẓāhir*) and the inward (*al-bāṭin*), and the process of relating the outward to the inward (*ta'wīl*), which, with an eye to the original sense of the word, he translated as "hermeneutics," was the *only* correct method of reaching the truth and the real meaning of phenomenology. He called himself a phenomenologist, ignoring the fact that there are other philosophers in the West who also call themselves phenomenologists, but who do not even accept the knowability of the noumenal world, much less the possibility of relating the phenomenal to the noumenal, the outward to the inward. It was characteristic of Corbin's immersion in the intellectual world of Shīʿism that he interpreted phenomenology itself from the Shīʿite point of view and considered himself a phenomenologist in the sense of one who "unveils" the hidden and esoteric truth, who participates in the process of *kashf al-maḥjūb.*

The contributions of Corbin to Shīʿite studies have been numerous and profound and have left an indelible mark upon Islamic studies in the West, precisely because they have revealed so much that was completely neglected before him. They are particularly precious now that strong political interests have, in one way or another, colored many of the more recent studies in Shīʿism. Corbin has shown how important the inner aspects of both Ismāʿīlī and Twelve-Imam Shīʿism are as integral parts of Islamic esoterism, and their philosophies and theologies as essential aspects of the intellectual life of the Islamic peoples. Corbin even had influence in the Shīʿite world itself and continues to do so to this day.[17]

As far as Ismāʿīlism is concerned, Corbin has made so many contributions to it that he has by himself completely changed the views that scholars had held before him about Ismāʿīlī intellectual history. His edition of the works of Nāṣir-i Khusraw, Abū Yaʿqūb al-Sijistānī, and other Ismāʿīlī theosophers and philosophers; his analysis of the teachings of the Fāṭimid as well as post-Fāṭimid schools of Ismāʿīlī thought; his discovery and publication of later Ismāʿīlī works belonging to the post-Alamut period in Persia and the very different school in the Yemen—all represent pioneering efforts in the field of Ismāʿīlī studies. Besides elucidating the teachings of the Ismāʿīlīs and showing their relation to various other schools of thought, Corbin has been able to establish Ismāʿīlī philosophy as one of the important schools of Islamic thought. Thanks most of all to his research, it is no longer possible to speak of early Islamic philosophy and neglect completely such figures as Abū Ḥātim al-Razī, Ḥamīd al-Dīn al-Kirmānī, and Nāṣir-i Khusraw as if they had not even existed.

As for Twelve-Imam Shīʿism, the contributions of Corbin have been of even more far-reaching consequence. In the field of Ismāʿīlism there had been at least some notable research carried out in European languages in earlier days, but before Corbin's writings appeared, the spiritual and intellectual aspects of Twelve-Imam Shīʿism were practically a closed book for those solely acquainted with Western courses. Corbin devoted numerous studies over the years to the Shīʿite Imams and the question of what he calls "*imamologie,*" to Shīʿite *Ḥadīth,* especially the *Uṣūl al-kāfī* ("Principles of 'The Sufficient' ") of Muḥammad ibn Yaʿqūb al-Kulaynī, to specifically Shīʿite gnosis (*ʿirfān-i shīʿī*) found in the works of such authors as Sayyid Ḥaydar Āmulī and Qāḍī Saʿīd Qummī, and to later schools that have grown out of Twelve-Imam Shīʿism, such as

Shaykhism. Moreover, certain themes of "Shī'ite gnosis" have affected many of his other studies, even those concerning Christology and certain esoteric movements in the medieval and Renaissance periods in the West.

Corbin's devotion to Shī'ism was paralleled by his interest in Sufism, the two comprising Islamic esoterism, which from the beginning was the main dimension of Islam that most attracted him. Unlike his teacher, Massignon, whose studies of Sufism concerned mostly early masters such as al-Ḥallāj, Corbin was especially interested in later manifestations of Sufism and the metaphysical and cosmological doctrines issuing from the school of Ibn 'Arabī and other later masters of Islamic gnosis. Besides numerous studies on various Sufi figures, some of whom, such as 'Alā' al-Dawlah Simnānī, he introduced to the West in a serious manner for the first time, Corbin produced several volumes on Sufism revolving around two major figures, Ibn 'Arabī, the sage of Andalusia, and Rūzbihān Baqlī, the master of the *Fedeli d'amore* of Persia. The *Bibliothèque iranienne,* directed by him, contains the first critical editions of the *'Abhar al-'āshiqīn* ("The Jasmin of Lovers") and *Sharḥ al-shaṭhiyyāt* ("Commentary on Words of Ecstasy") of Rūzbihān as well as two volumes of Sayyid Ḥaydar Āmulī, which are commentaries on and extensions of the works and teachings of Ibn 'Arabī, these last having been edited with the aid of 'Uthmān Yaḥyā. In fact, Corbin's contribution to the study of the Andalusian visionary and seer is based not only on his own works, which in this field are crowned by his celebrated *L'Imagination créatrice dans le soufisme d'Ibn 'Arabī,*[18] but also on his success in interesting the Syrian scholar 'Uthmān Yaḥyā in Ibn 'Arabī's works. The two-volume work on the classafication of the writings of Ibn 'Arabī by 'Uthmān Yaḥyā as well as the new edition of *al-Futūḥāt al-makkiyyah* ("The Meccan Illuminations"), most of which was brought out in Cairo in a critical edition before 'Uthmān Yaḥyā's death, owe a great deal to Corbin, both for their scholarly and intellectual inspiration and for their material realization.

It was in the nature of Corbin's definition of philosophy that he considered all the activities mentioned so far as belonging to the domain of his "philosophical" works, which meant that for him the term "philosophy" implied traditional wisdom, or *sophia,* rather than what passes these days for philosophy in modern European parlance. But even in the more strict sense of philosophy (*al-falsafah*) and theosophy (*al-ḥikmat al-ilāhiyyah*) as used in the Islamic tradition (namely, a particular branch of traditional wisdom distinct from, let us say, gnosis, *'irfān*, or theology, *kalām*), Corbin has made an enormous contribution and must in fact be considered the first European scholar and thinker who has written on Islamic philosophy with a knowledge of the main contours of its total history rather than according to the usual truncated version that ends with Ibn Rushd, a version that the West had accepted as unquestionable truth until recently.

Corbin's numerous studies of the more particularly philosophical dimension of the Islamic intellectual tradition during the past few centuries, a dimension that, as has been mentioned, has survived mostly in Persia, has opened new horizons and revealed that Islamic philosophy, far from being a short-lived activity among Muslims from al-Kindī to Ibn Rushd and endowed with the sole historical function of handing down the sciences and philosophy of antiquity to the Latin West, has had a continuous and independent existence to the present day. His *Histoire de la philosophie islamique* (vol. 1), written in collaboration with myself and O. Yahya, prepared the ground for a complete exposition of Islamic philosophy based not only upon the Peripatetic School and the first few centuries of Islamic history, but on all the different schools of traditional Islamic thought and covering the whole of Islamic history down to the present day. Although the other volumes of this history were never completed as first planned, Corbin himself produced a sequel in the *Encyclopédie de la Pléiade,* which completes this integral history of Islamic philosophy.[19]

Corbin's interest in Islamic philosophy began with Ibn Sīnā, and he wrote little on the earlier philosophers such as al-Kindī and al-Fārābī. But by means of a thorough reexamination of Ibn Sīnā and the brilliant reconstruction of his "Oriental philosophy" (*al-ḥikmat al-mashriqiyyah*) in his *Avicenne et le récit visionnaire,* Corbin was able to recreate the image of an Ibn Sīnā who has been alive in Persia for over a thousand years, an Ibn Sīnā who was meditated upon by such figures as Suhrawardī and Naṣīr al-Dīn Ṭūsī, an Ibn Sīnā who is very different from the exclusively Peripatetic master of the Scholastic texts. That is why Corbin's *Avicenna and the Visionary Recital* is a landmark in Avicennan studies in the West. This study also prepared the ground for Corbin's exposition of later Islamic philosophy, which depended, not only upon the Ibn Sīnā who wrote the *Shifā'* ("The Healing"), but also upon the Ibn Sīnā who was seeking the "Orient" of knowledge and to whom Suhrawardī was to refer a century and a half later in his recital concerning the "Story of the Occidental Exile" (*Qiṣṣat al-ghurbat al-gharbiyyah*).

Without doubt the figure who most occupied Corbin's attention and who may be considered his intellectual guide was, however, Shaykh al-Ishrāq Shihāb al-Dīn Suhrawardī. As has already been mentioned, he took Corbin by the hand and guided him from the libraries of Istanbul to his own spiritual homeland in Persia. Corbin's attachment to the doctrines of Suhrawardī, especially to his belief in the importance of both ratiocination and spiritual vision as "instruments" for attaining true knowledge, was something deeply personal; he felt a devotion to Suhrawardī that somehow embraced all his spiritual and intellectual interests and activities. Corbin was essentially the hermeneutic interpreter of the angelic world, and he saw in the "Theosophy of the Orient of Light" (*Hikmat al-ishrāq*) of Suhrawardī a complete science of the angelic world expressed in terms of the symbolism of light. I recall how once when going over certain pages of Suhrawardī with Corbin, he told me in a rather categorical fashion that all this discussion concerning existence and quiddity in classical texts of Islamic philosophy was not really of central interest to him; what excited him most of all in Suhrawardī and others was the study of angels, especially Suhrawardī's magisterial treatment of the longitudinal and latitudinal hierarchies of lights, or angels.

In recent times, Corbin has, without doubt, done more than anyone else, outside or even inside Persia, to revive the teachings of Suhrawardī and to make available critical editions of his works. His two-volume edition of Suhrawardī's *Opera Metaphysica et Mystica,* including the metaphysics of the *Talwīḥāt, Muqāwamāt,* and *Muṭāraḥāt,* several shorter Arabic treatises, and the all-important *Ḥikmat al-ishrāq,* and his encouraging me to prepare the edition of the Persian works of Suhrawardī as the third volume of the *Opera* have made it possible to have access to more writings of the master of *ishrāq* in a critically edited form than for any other major Islamic philosopher. Moreover, Corbin has written numerous monographs and articles on Suhrawardī, beginning with his still valuable *Sohrawardî, fondateur de la doctrine illuminative (ishrâqī)*[20] and culminating in his monumental treatment of the master in his *En Islam iranien.*[21] He also translated into elegant French the Persian treatises of Suhrawardī under the title of one of the most intriguing of the treatises, namely, *'Aql-i surkh*

(L'Archange empourpré)[22] and prepared a French translation of the *Ḥikmat al-ishrāq* with the commentaries of Quṭb al-Dīn Shīrāzī and Mullā Ṣadrā. This major opus was published by his wife, Stella, after his death.[23] His lifelong work on Suhrawardī, which also includes the editions of several of the still unpublished works, most important among which is a collection of sayings and prayers like the medieval European Book of Hours, a collection that was given the title *al-Wāridāt wa'l-taqdīsāt* ("Invocations and Prayers") by Shahrazūrī, have opened a new chapter in Islamic philosophy. This breakthrough is not only important for scholarship in general, but is of special concern in the revival of interest among the Persians themselves in their own intellectual and spiritual tradition, a revival that revolves most of all around the figures of Suhrawardī and Ṣadr al-Dīn Shīrāzī.

Corbin himself was led to the discovery of Mullā Ṣadrā through the works of Suhrawardī, the search for whose complete heritage was the reason Corbin had first come to Persia. Through the commentators on Suhrawardī, Corbin was led to such lesser-known but important figures as Ibn Turkah Iṣfahānī, whose works and ideas he made known to the West, and finally to the great revival of Islamic philosophy during the Safavid period. The study of the very rich intellectual life of this period led Corbin to the correct belief that a new school was born at this time, one that he (and I) named the School of Isfahan. During the last two decades of his life, Corbin dealt increasingly with this school, with such figures as Mīr Dāmād, who was its founder, and especially with Ṣadr al-Dīn Shīrāzī. Corbin did much to make Mullā Ṣadrā known to the West, and his edition and French translation of the Safavid sage's *Kitāb al-mashā'ir* as *Le Livre des pénétrations métaphysiques,* which, as already mentioned, contains an important introduction comparing the destiny of the study of being in both East and West, is without doubt one of his most important philosophical contributions.

The discovery of the intellectual richness of the Safavid period led Corbin to seek the aid of a Persian scholar to prepare an anthology of the works of this period and its heritage down to the present day. He was to find through my help an incomparable collaborator in Sayyid Jalāl al-Dīn Āshtiyānī who, with unbounded energy, combed through numerous public and private libraries and made many new discoveries that were startling even to Persian specialists of the period. The series *Anthologie des philosophes iraniens* has already altered our knowledge of the history of Islamic philosophy in Persia and has posed a major problem for those in the West who have thought until now that, since the end of the European Middle Ages, only in their own world has there been intellectual activity worthy of attention. It is hardly possible to study the wealth of material contained in these volumes and still think that Islamic intellectual activity stopped with Ibn Rushd or the Mongol invasion.

Besides philosophy, Corbin also showed much interest in the traditional Islamic sciences of a cosmological and even physical nature. He made a profound study of Jābirean alchemy and the doctrine of the balance, of cosmic cycles, sacred geography, the symbolism of geometric figures as reflected in the Holy Ka'bah, the symbolism of colors, and many other related themes. His contributions to the study of the Islamic sciences, especially their symbolic meaning, should not be underestimated, especially since Corbin always viewed these sciences in light of the general metaphysical and philosophical perspectives that were his central concern.

In many ways, Corbin's life's work is summarized by the monumental *En Islam iranien,* in which over forty years of research and meditation upon Shī'ism, Sufism, Islamic philosophy, the relation between Islamic esoteric tradition and esoterism in the West (as manifested in such teachings as the legend of the Holy Grail), and many other concerns are brought together. Without doubt this work is one of the most outstanding achievements of Western scholarship concerning the Islamic, and particularly the Persian, world, a study that has already exercised much influence and is bound to remain one of Corbin's most enduring achievements. Many of the themes discussed in his numerous earlier works found their most mature orchestration in this four-volume magnum opus.

If one were to summarize the contributions of Corbin to the world of scholarship, philosophy, and thought, one could say that he transformed Western scholarship in many fields of Islamic thought and in Persian studies in particular. Corbin made clear once and for all the significance of the non-Sufi mode of Islamic esoterism as contained in Twelve-Imam and Ismā'īlī Shī'ism; of the vast metaphysical and theosophical teachings of the school of Ibn 'Arabī; of the School of Illumination of Suhrawardī and its role in remolding the very concept of philosophy in Persia and other eastern lands of Islam; of the continuous and living nature of

Islamic philosophy stretching over the centuries after Ibn Rushd to the present day—and many other subjects of fundamental importance. He also remolded the concept of the intellectual and spiritual history of Persia, highlighting many salient features of pre-Islamic Persian culture, its fecundity and richness in the fields of metaphysics, cosmology, cosmogony, and so on, and the continuity of the life of many of the myths and symbols of pre-Islamic Persia into the Islamic period itself. Without doubt there have been very few Western scholars who have left such extensive influence upon so many fields of Islamic and Persian scholarship and contributed so much to traditional Islamic thought. All of these contributions are in addition to his influential studies of Western esoterism and certain aspects of modern German philosophy.

As far as philosophy is concerned, there is no doubt that the writings of Corbin have presented a "new" and, at the same time, ancient—even, in fact, perennial—world of wisdom in the contemporary language of Western thought for those concerned with the profoundest questions facing humanity today, just as they have faced people of all ages. Corbin's concern with "prophetology," "imamology," "gnoseology," and other themes that seem to be related to Islamic thought are actually as much connected with the deepest questions facing Westerners today as they are with Islam. The same may be said of Corbin's defense of the "cyclic" concept of time and his virulent attack against historicism, which he considered one of the most deadly maladies from which Western thought suffers today. Likewise, the repeated study and treatment by him of the "imaginal world" (*mundis imaginalis*) in the works of Suhrawardī Ibn 'Arabī, Mullā Ṣadrā, and others were carried out with one eye on the necessity of resuscitating the knowledge of this long-forgotten "world" in the West. His profound studies of the angelic world were achieved with the aim of bringing back the attention of mainstream Western philosophers, who since Leibniz had banished the angels from the cosmos, to the vital importance of the angelic domain in any serious cosmology and anthropology. Finally, it must be added that Corbin's often repeated concern with spiritual hermeneutics (*ta'wīl*) was as much related to his intention to revive spirituality and "interiority" in Western religious circles as it was to the understanding of the inner meaning of Islamic texts. Altogether, Corbin's concern with the living nature of this traditional philosophy and its application to the contemporary philosophical and spiritual predicament of

Westerners caused by the forgetting of perennial wisdom complements his profound study of Islamic philosophy as the last major crystallization of this wisdom in human history and the sole surviving repository of much of the wisdom of the ancient world. Corbin must be seen not only as an Islamicist, but also as a Western philosopher drawn toward tradition. Through him, for the first time since the Middle Ages, the Islamic philosophical tradition penetrated into certain European philosophical circles concerned with charting a new path and surmounting the debilitating obstacles by which modern Western thought is now beset.

The influence of Corbin has been extensive in both the Occident and the Islamic world, especially in Persia itself. In the West, Corbin trained numerous students in the field of Islamic thought and, as already mentioned, transformed many branches of Islamic studies. His writings have also affected the wider public interested in spiritual and intellectual matters. Figures with as widely different backgrounds as Gaston Berger and Jean Daniélou were attracted to Corbin's writings, and some of the philosophers who themselves gained eminence in France, such as Gilbert Durand and Antoine Faivre, have also been influenced by him, as have many of the new *philosophes,* such as Christian Jambet. Through the Eranos meetings, moreover, many well-known Western intellectual figures who had been concerned with other fields, such as the biologist Adolf Portmann and the outstanding scholar of Jewish mysticism Gershom Scholem, came face-to-face with some of the more profound aspects of the Islamic tradition. Corbin's poetic translations of Sufi and Islamic philosophical texts have also affected many of the younger French writers questing to rediscover the traditional cosmos and its resplendent symbolism.

As far as the Arab world is concerned, the influence of Corbin has been confined mostly to the training of a small but competent number of advanced students, who in fact hailed mostly from the French-speaking countries of North Africa and who are now mostly professors and teachers of Islamic philosophy. Some, such as Muḥammad Arkūn (Arkoun), who did not, however, at all follow Corbin philosophically, although he was influenced in some domains by him, are now themselves well-known scholars of Islamic thought.

In Persia, the influence of Corbin has been much more extensive. As a result of his regular visits there over the years, he was able to create numerous personal associations and have contact with groups far beyond the circle of professional scholars and students. Besides establishing close rapport with professors and students in various universities, religious scholars in Qom, Tehran, Mashhad, and elsewhere and Sufi masters in various cities, Corbin was able to draw the attention of a large number of Persians in other walks of life to their own traditions. For many Persians who had studied in the West and who were more at home in French than in their mother tongue, especially as far as intellectual matters were concerned, the writings of Corbin became the chief means of rediscovering a Suhrawardī or a Mullā Ṣadrā. Corbin's influence and aid in the recovery of awareness of the spiritual and intellectual traditions of Persia by modern Persians themselves can be seen in the imprint of his thought upon figures as different as the cinematographer Firaydūn Rahnimā, the miniaturist 'Alī Tajwīdī, and the designer M. Ibrāhīmiān, not to speak of many scholars in the field of Islamic and Persian thought, such as Dariush Shayegan. Corbin was also an important channel through which some in various positions of responsibility in Persia were drawn to the study of the writings of their own great sages and seers.

For forty years, Corbin worked with incredible energy and enthusiasm to interpret the spiritual and intellectual teachings of Persia, to which he referred symbolically as wisdom from the "Orient of Light," to an Occident that, during this same period, became geographically much more widespread and has now practically banished the "Orient," in Corbin's sense of the world of illumination, altogether from at least certain circles in all the seven climates, including not only the geographical Occident, but the geographical Orient as well. His work in Paris and Tehran, whether it was teaching or writing, was able to preserve its intensity and profundity for over four decades. This Occidental exile, who found his true home in the "Orient of Light," continued to strive to present to his contemporaries a whole intellectual universe that had been practically neglected before him. He accomplished a great deal, but the task he set himself was too vast, and therefore there is still much to be accomplished in presenting traditional wisdom to the contemporary world in all its fullness, depth, and breadth. In this crucial task of reinterpreting the intellectual patrimony of various traditions to the contemporary world, Corbin was one of the most productive and active figures and one of the foremost expositors of certain aspects of traditional wisdom, especially the Islamic.

In 1978, Corbin died after a short illness in Paris. It seems as if one of the angels to whose study he had devoted his life snatched him away from this earthly plane just in time to prevent him from witnessing the eruptions that transformed both Iran and the interpretation of Shīʿism that he had known—in at least certain circles—in such a drastic manner.

Appendix IV

ISLAM AND SOME OF THE MAJOR WESTERN TRADITIONALISTS

Many of those who have spoken of perennial philosophy and tradition in the West have played and continue to play an increasingly important role in the confrontation of traditional Islam with the modern world. It is they who have provided the most authentic presentations of the Islamic tradition expressed in contemporary language for the Western world and also for many modern educated Muslims, some of whom have in fact returned to the bosom of Islam through their works. These traditional authors have also led a number of Westerners in search of metaphysical truth and authentic means for its realization to Islam in its most universal and traditional form. It is also the traditional writings that have provided the most powerful intellectual means for the defense of tradition before the onslaught of modernist ideas within the Islamic world and that have revealed to many Muslims the real nature of modernism, its errors and follies. These authors have helped to create a new intellectual "elite" within that world that is at once traditional, rooted deeply in Islam, and fully aware of the challenges of modernism, the "elite" already referred to earlier in this work.

The class of traditional *'ulamā'* and Sufi teachers still survives, and the debates between them and those who espouse the cause of modernism and postmodernism in one form or another continue unabated in most Islamic countries and are of course at the center of the contentions between Islam and the modern West. Obviously this is a subject of great significance, but one that lies beyond our concern here. What is of special interest to us in the sections that follow is the significance of some of the seminal Western Traditionalists who have formally embraced Islam.[1]

Such figures, who are in fact growing in number, have produced a large corpus of works that, although at first neglected in academic circles, are now having an ever greater impact upon Islamic studies in the West as well as in certain circles within the Islamic world. The aim here is not to discuss their influence in the West itself, but primarily in the Islamic world. I have chosen four of the most significant of these figures, all of whom have exercised a profound influence in many Western countries as well as in a number of Islamic countries. These figures are René Guénon, Frithjof Schuon, Titus Burckhardt, and Martin Lings. And I begin by turning to the founder of what is called the Traditionalist or Perennialist School, René Guénon.

A. *René Guénon and His Influence in the Islamic World*

Numerous biographies have already been written of René Guénon, mostly in French,[2] and the aim in this chapter is not to deal in detail with the account of his life. For our purposes here it is sufficient to recall that he was born into a Catholic family in Blois in France in 1886. He was a very gifted student and turned to the study of mathematics and philosophy. But his real interest was in esoteric knowledge, and so he focused for a while on occultism, whose errors he came, however, to realize quickly. He then directed his attention to the Oriental traditions, especially Islam and Hinduism, and in the 1920s wrote his seminal work on tradition in general and Hinduism in particular entitled *Introduction to the Study of Hindu Doctrines,*[3] followed by his most important doctrinal work on Hinduism, *Man and His Becoming According to the Vedanta,*[4] both written originally, like most of his other works, in French and later translated into English and several other European and Islamic languages.[5] Parallel with such metaphysical works, he wrote a number of books and articles on the criticism of the modern world including *East and West,*[6] *The Crisis of the Modern World,*[7] which is still widely read, especially in France, and *The Reign of Quantity and the Signs of the Times,*[8] written after his immigration to Egypt. Numerous other works flowed from his prolific pen,[9] but he was singularly neglected and in fact dismissed in French academic circles until quite recently.

In 1930 after the death of his first wife, he came to Cairo seemingly for a temporary visit, but this was to be a one-way journey. He settled in that city, married an Egyptian woman, raised a family, and lived a life of a devout Muslim, while he continued to write extensively on various traditional subjects in articles and books that were published mostly in France. He also mastered Arabic to the extent that he wrote some articles in that language. He died after a short illness in 1951 in Cairo and was buried near the holy mosque of Sayyidunā al-Ḥusayn or Ra's al-Ḥusayn at the center of the city.

Although the impact of René Guénon's teachings upon the Occident as a whole has not been studied fully, at least there exist a number of studies concerning the far-reaching influence of his seminal writings in a number of European countries. Such is unfortunately not the case when one turns to the Islamic world. In fact, there are practically no studies that deal with this subject as far as the whole of the Islamic world is concerned, and many in fact believe that he is hardly known and has had no influence in Islamic countries. This conclusion is, however, totally false. Guénon has exercised profound influence in certain significant circles in a number of Islamic countries, and his impact is very much on the rise. In this first attempt to gauge the extent and significance of this influence, I shall deal not with the whole of the Islamic world, but with certain countries and areas where I believe his impact has been of particular significance.

Guénon's influence reached the Islamic world through three channels. The first is his works themselves, read by Muslims in the original French, translations into other European languages such as English, or renditions into various languages of the Islamic world. The second is the writings, in either their original language or translation, of other major Traditionalist authors who have shared basic principles with Guénon and who have alluded to his works and teachings. Among this group the most important is Frithjof Schuon, followed by Titus Burckhardt, Martin Lings, Gai Eaton, Jean-Louis Michon, Victor Danner, and Ananda K. Coomaraswamy, the last especially for Muslims of the Indo-Pakistani subcontinent and Iran, although he was not a Muslim. The third is the works of Muslim-born authors, such as Muḥammad Ḥasan 'Askarī and others, who have either written directly on Guénon or have discussed some of his basic expositions of metaphysics, the traditional sciences, criticism of the modern world, and so on in their own writings. I myself belong to this group. Such figures with various degrees of influence are to be found in several

Islamic countries, from Malaysia to Pakistan to the Arab world to Turkey and Bosnia.

Turning to specific regions of the Islamic world, it is logical to start with the Arab countries, especially the Arab East, because of the significance of Arabic throughout the Islamic world and since Guénon lived the last twenty years of his life in Cairo. Paradoxically, however, his influence in the Arab East has not been as great since his death as it has been in Persia, Turkey, Pakistan, Bosnia, and Southeast Asia for reasons having to do with the extensive change in the intellectual climate for many Arabs in the second half of the twentieth century. Guénon's influence in Egypt itself can in fact be divided into two distinct and very different phases: the first during his lifetime and the second after his death.

When Guénon arrived in Cairo in 1930, he first lived quietly near the mausoleum of Sayyidunā al-Ḥusayn and al-Azhar University, that is, at the center of both the religious and intellectual life of Cairo. It was only in 1937 that he moved to a villa in Duqqī near the banks of the Nile, where he lived until his death and where his library of over a thousand books remains intact today, just as it was on the day he left this earthly plane.[10] Known in Egypt primarily by his Muslim name, Shaykh 'Abd al-Wāḥid Yaḥyā, he had contact with many important Islamic intellectual and spiritual circles of the day. Several people have attested to the fact that he became the disciple of the famous Sufi shaykh Salāmah ibn Ḥasan al-Raḍī (1284/1867–1358/1939), the founder of the Ḥāmidiyyah branch of the Shādhiliyyah Sufi Order, into which he had become initiated much earlier in France.

During his stay in Cairo, Guénon was visited by many people from near and far, people who were in quest of authentic knowledge or wanted to have personal contact with the sage. Some of these visitors were from the West, others from the Islamic world, ranging from Frithjof Schuon to Najmuddin Bammate. As far as his influence in Egypt is concerned, however, none of these contacts were as significant as his association with Shaykh 'Abd al-Ḥalīm Maḥmūd, who, as already mentioned, was an authority in both the Divine Law and the Sufi path and who later became the shaykh al-Azhar. He wrote a small booklet entitled *al-Faylasūf al-muslim: 'Abd al-Wāḥid Yaḥyā aw René Guénon* immediately after Guénon's death and later on authored a major book in Arabic[11] in which a long section the size of an independent monograph was devoted to Guénon and the significance of his teachings for the preservation of the Islamic tradition. This widely read book made the traditional Islamic intelligentsia of Egypt aware of Guénon and the significance of his message. Shaykh 'Abd al-Ḥalīm Maḥmūd edited several of the classical Sufi texts, and while introducing the text to his readers he drew much of his material from Guénon's works.

Moreover, while residing in Cairo Guénon not only wrote essays in French, which were published in Paris and also read by a few francophone Arabs; he also wrote a number of essays in Arabic in the journal *al-Ma'rifah*[12] and participated in important intellectual discourses with a number of Egyptians. His criticism of the errors of the modern world, coming from a Western and not a traditional Muslim scholar, attracted the attention of a number of notable Egyptian intellectual figures. Yet with his death and the Nasserite revolution in Egypt, marked by the rise of nationalism and socialism, the milieu in which his influence was most felt became marginalized and to some extent destroyed. Few Egyptians today realize how significant the message of this remarkable Muslim and French expatriate is for the present-day intellectual crisis in their midst.

During the last decade, however, new attention has been paid to Guénon's message in the Arab world, as can be seen by the translation into Arabic of his *Crisis of the Modern World*[13] and a collection of essays[14] dealing mostly with esoterism in general and Sufism in particular. Although no influential Arab scholar has appeared upon the scene during the past few decades who could be called a Traditionalist in the Guénonian sense and whose writings are as widely known in the Arab world, as one finds in Persia, Turkey and Pakistan, a number of Arab writers now refer to him here and there. Moreover, the interest in recent years in Egypt, Jordan, and certain other Arab countries in the works of Schuon, Burckhardt, Lings, and myself has also caused the teachings of Guénon to become better known.

As far as the rest of the Arab world is concerned, the latter channel of influence is especially evident in Morocco and Algeria. In these lands the works of Schuon and Burckhardt are well known, as is the famous biography of Shaykh al-'Alawī by Martin Lings.[15] Moreover, Burckhardt's years in Morocco and his practical efforts to save Moroccan arts and crafts and the traditional character of the city of Fez have made him a well-known figure in that land. Let us recall that a major conference was devoted to his works in Marrakesh in 1998, the proceedings of which were published in Arabic, French, and English.[16] Considering the close connection between Burckhardt and Guénon, it is not surprising that many people have become interested in the latter through the works of the former. Even in traditional Sufi circles in both Morocco and Algeria many have come to know of Guénon through either personal contact with Schuon, Burckhardt, and others or their works, which, since they are mostly in French, have been readily accessible to the educated public of the Maghrib.

As a result of the introduction of modern ideologies, especially nationalism and socialism, into the Arab world and the eclipse of the more metaphysical and philosophical dimensions of the Islamic tradition in many traditional circles of learning, the Arab world has not shown the same degree of receptivity to the metaphysical doctrines expounded by Guénon as we find in Persia and a few other Islamic countries. That certainly does not mean, however, that the influence of Guénon in Egypt or the rest of the Arab world came to an end with his death. On the contrary, after being limited to a few individuals here and there, it has been growing during the past few years despite the dearth of good translations of his work into Arabic.

As far as Persia is concerned, Guénon was totally unknown there until my return from the United States to that county in 1958, when almost immediately I began to speak and write about traditional authors, particularly Guénon, Schuon, Coomaraswamy, Burckhardt, and Lings. It took a few years for the general intellectual milieu to become aware of the "school of Tradition." I even had to coin a Persian term for the French word *tradition* as Guénon understood it, *sunnat,* which has now gained wide acceptance in Persian, although it is sometimes used in the wrong sense. From the mid-1960s on the teachings of traditional authors became part of the general intellectual discourse in that land. In the late 1960s I commissioned the translation of two of his works, *La Crise du monde moderne* and *La Règne de la quantité,* into Persian.[17]

After the dust of the Islamic Revolution of 1979 in Persia settled down, interest in Guénon and other traditional authors began to manifest itself again in an even wider circle than before. Nowadays, a number of reputable Islamic scholars, especially in Qom and Tehran, have began to show serious interest in them. One of the major Islamic institutions of learning in Qom, Mufīd University, devoted two issues of its highly respected journal in 1998 and 1999 to the traditional perspective, and a number of essays appeared in them either dealing with Guénon or containing translations of some of his essays.[18] More recently, *Le Symbolisme de la croix* and *Aperçus sur l'ésotérisme islamique et le taoisme* have been translated into Persian, and *La Crise du monde moderne* has been retranslated.[19] Moreover, the keen interest in present-day Persia in tradition in general and Guénon in particular can be seen in the fact that early in 2002 a major conference was held in Tehran on Tradition and modernism, a section of which was devoted specifically to Guénon. A book entitled *Ḥikmat-i jāwīdān* ("Perennial Wisdom") has appeared containing both studies on Guénon's works rendered into Persian and his biography.[20]

The wide influence of Guénon, Schuon, and other major traditional authors in Persia did not, however, come only from the translation of their writings; it also came largely from works written by Persian authors who shared their perspective and alluded to their texts. In fact, it was this type of writing that led many people to the study of Guénon and Schuon. I started this genre of writing in Persian in the late 1950s, and only in the 1960s did I turn to the translation of some of the works of Schuon and Burckhardt and directed others to translate Guénon. Also gradually in the 1970s a number of Persian scholars, some my own direct students, adopted the traditional perspective and began to write about it. The Imperial Iranian Academy of Philosophy, which I founded in 1973 and of which I was the first president, was devoted openly to the presentation, study, and propagation of the perennial philosophy and traditional wisdom, and its journal, *Sophia Perennis,* which continued until 1979, contained articles by such masters of traditional doctrines as Schuon.

Today in Persia there are a number of well-known scholars and thinkers who are defenders of Tradition and linked closely with the teachings of Guénon. They include Hādī Sharīfī, Ghulām Riḍā A'wānī, Maḥmūd Bīnā Muṭlaq, Muṣṭafā Malikiān,[21] and a number of younger scholars, including many connected with the field of traditional art. There is probably no Islamic country, except perhaps Bosnia, where the influence of Guénon, Schuon, Burckhardt, and other traditional authors is as perceptible as Persia, where the traditional point of view plays a notable role in the intellectual life of many people among both the modern educated intelligentsia associated with various universities and those trained in the traditional religious schools or *madrasahs.*

In Turkey, interest in Guénon began somewhat later than it did in Persia, although there were a few solitary figures, such as Nuri Yarlasez, who had discovered the traditional writings many years before the appearance of traditional works in Turkish. By the early 1980s, a number of Turkish thinkers became attracted to both my works and those of Guénon, and the first translations of one of my books and one of Guénon's into Turkish appeared almost at the same time. Since then interest in traditional writings has grown remarkably, as a number of Turks with a Western-oriented education have become even more disillusioned with the advent of modernism and seek to understand the essence of their own religion as well as the real nature of modernism viewed from the perspective of traditional wisdom. Since the mid-1980s, besides some twenty of my own works, many books by Guénon, Schuon, Burckhardt, Lings, and Eaton have been rendered into Turkish. There are today, in addition to a number of articles, numerous books by Guénon available in Turkish,[22] while many articles have been written about him and other traditional authors or on various subjects from a traditional point of view.

The struggle between Tradition and modernism is of course to be found everywhere in the non-Western world, including the Islamic world, and is not unique to a particular country. But because of the extreme form of secularization that Ataturk tried to impose upon Turkey, the tension between Tradition and modernism is especially acute and felt in nearly every aspect of social and intellectual life in that country. Until two or three decades ago there were two types of thinkers in Turkey, as in other Islamic countries, although perhaps not with the same sharp contrast: the traditional scholars deeply rooted in the Islamic tradition but unaware of the real nature of the modern world and the modernized scholars uprooted from their own tradition with little or no serious interest in Islam, especially its intellectual and spiritual dimensions. Today there is the third group, to whom allusion has already been made, that is, those who are rooted in the Islamic tradition, usually with a universalist perspective, and at the same time are certainly as knowledgeable about the modern world as Muslim modernists are.

Like Persia, Turkey has now a class of gifted intellectual figures with a traditional perspective, a class that is bound to play a crucial role in the future of the country as far as religion and Tradition are concerned. Such a group also exists to a lesser extent in a number of other Islamic countries, such as Pakistan, Malaysia, Indonesia, Jordan, and particularly Bosnia, to which we shall turn soon. Now, in Turkey, as elsewhere in the Islamic world, the formation of this group, to which Guénon referred as *l'élite intellectuel,* owes a very great deal to the works of Guénon himself along with those of other traditional authorities. Moreover, in Turkey, as in several other Islamic countries, this *élite* plays a more central role in society in general than do those influenced by Guénon in the West.

When we turn to Pakistan, we have to consider both works in Urdu concerning Guénon and publication of English translations of his books, since the educated public there has a much greater knowledge of English than most Arabs, Persians, or Turks in general have of a European language (the knowledge of French in North African countries is an exception). As far as the availability of his work in English in Pakistan is concerned, the role of the Suheyl Academy, founded by Muḥammad Aslam Suhayl and directed by Muḥammad Suhayl 'umar (Suheyl Umar), who is himself a leading Pakistani scholar with a traditional perspective, is paramount. Since 1983 the Academy has brought out a number of Guénon's works in local editions, some in several printings,[23] and it is remarkable how widely disseminated the works of Guénon and other traditionalist authors have become in Pakistan thanks to the work of the Suheyl Academy. Furthermore, chapters of *East and West* were published over a period in *Iqbal Review* and a number of his essays appeared in *Studies in Tradition.*[24] The English works of Suheyl Umar himself as well as such well-known Pakistani authors as Allāhbakhsh Brohi, Muḥammad Ajmal, and Sirāj Munīr, all of whom have referred often to Guénon's teachings, have also played an important role in disseminating knowledge of Guénon in Pakistan and to some extent India.

As far as the Urdu language is concerned, no figure is as significant in making Guénon known through that language as Muḥammad Ḥasan 'Askarī. A report concerning his works in Urdu as well as those of later figures was sent to me specifically for this section by Muhammad Suheyl Umar, and I can do no better than to quote it in full:

> The name and words of René Guénon came to the notice of the Urdu readership in the late 1960s through the writings of the late professor Muḥammad Ḥasan 'Askarī. 'Askarī was a versatile genius, combining in his person the talents of a short-story writer, literary

critic, translator, educator, philosopher, and religious thinker. Apart from his native Urdu, in which he was the leading author of his times, 'Askarī had mastered English and its literature and was well versed in French as well as Persian and Arabic. His connections with Michel Valsân [a leading authority on Guénon in France] and his circle introduced him to the works of René Guénon, which brought about a total change in his previous views. A new 'Askarī was born who, having rediscovered the Tradition for himself, devoted the rest of his life to its exposition. . . . One can discern four ways his contributions influenced the Urdu readership, especially the literary and religious circles: through translations/adaptations, correspondence with his contemporaries, debates, and applications.

Translations/Adaptations: 'Askarī translated very few of Guénon's works into Urdu directly, though he did translate some into English that were all published in various periodicals.[25] However, one can find direct adaptations, translations of passages from Guénon, and abridgements of his view spread over all that 'Askarī wrote from 1969 till his death in 1978.[26] The most important work that 'Askarī produced in this regard was a brief but concise book entitled *Jadīdiyat yā Maghribī Gumrāhīyyōn kā Khāka* ("Modernism: An Outline of the Errors of the West"). Relying primarily on two of Guénon's works,[27] 'Askarī prepared a document in his inimitable Urdu prose that outlined the basic intellectual fallacies of the West in a lucid and concise manner. This document was first used as a manual of instruction for the students of one of the leading *madrasahs* of Pakistan, and it later appeared in print.[28]

Correspondence with His Contemporaries: 'Askarī maintained an extensive correspondence, and he was an untiring exponent of the traditional point of view. Several collections of his letters have appeared after his death, and all of these testify to the fact that he introduced, influenced, and convinced many of his contemporaries of the traditional point of view, some of whom later on emerged as excellent scholars in their own right.[29]

Debates: An important channel through which the works and views of René Guénon reached the Urdu readers is found in the debates that 'Askarī carried out with his contemporaries and the interviews/dialogues in which he was engaged.[30] One can also include in this category the close associates and students of 'Askarī whom he introduced to the works of Guénon and trained in their respective fields, so that they could carry on the task of spreading the traditional point of view.

Applications: By far 'Askarī's most important contribution, the one that was to become the most widely read and assimilated by Urdu readers, came in the form of those of his writings where he applied the point of view derived from the works of Guénon to art, metaphysics, symbolism, literature, religion, contemporary issues, and so forth.

Translations of Guénon's Works and Articles on Guénon: In 1979 a full section appeared in the leading Urdu journal, *Ma'āṣir,* under the title "Al-Shaykh 'Abd al-Wāḥid Yaḥyā (René Guénon)" introducing Guénon and his works. It contained: Muḥammad Suhayl 'Umar, "Shaykh kī Taṣānīf" ("Life and Works of Guénon"), Urdu;[31] 'Abd al-Ḥalīm Maḥmūd and Muhammad Suheyl Umar, trans., "Shaykh Ḥayāt wa Afkār" ("René Guénon: Life and Thought"), Urdu;[32] and Muhammad Suheyl Umar and A. Rauf, trans., "Infirādīyat Parastī" (a translation of chap. 5 of Guénon's famous work *The Crisis of the Modern World*), Urdu.[33]

In 1983 the first issue of *Riwāyat* appeared. It was an Urdu journal devoted to metaphysics, symbolism, tradition, religion, and philosophy. It contained: Tehsin Firaqi, "René Guénon: Exponent of Tradition" (a translation of the part of Gai Eaton's book *The Richest Vein* that deals with René Guénon), Urdu;[34] Jamal Panipati, trans., "Mashriqī Mā ba'd al-Ṭabī'īyāt (a translation of Guénon's *Oriental Metaphysics*), Urdu;[35] Ikram Chagatai, trans., "'Irfān-i Dhāt" (a translation of Guénon's "Connais-toi toi-même" ("Know Thyself"), Urdu;[36] and Muḥammad Suhayl 'Umar, trans., "Qadīm Aqwām kay darmiyān Rawābiṭ" (a translation of part of Guénon's *An Introduction to the Study of Hindu Doctrines*), Urdu.[37]

In 1985 the second issue of *Riwīyat* appeared. It contained: Jamal Panipati, trans., "Kaljug" (a translation of "Kali Yuga," a chapter from Guénon's *The Crisis of the Modern World*), Urdu;[38] "Dunyā-i Jadīd kā Buḥrān" (review article on *The Crisis of the Modern World*);[39] and "Kammiyat kī Salṭanat" (an article on *The Reign of Quantity*).[40]

Debates: In the wake of all this activity many debates took place addressing the issues of tradition and modernity, science and religion, metaphysics and philosophy, and so forth that reverberated for a long time in the literary, intellectual, and religious circles of Pakistan and India.[41]

It is clear from this long quotation from Muhammad Suheyl Umar how extensive the influence of Guénon and other traditionalist writers has been in Pakistan. Moreover, Guénon, through both the Urdu works and English translations of his writings, influenced a number of important Muslim figures in India as well. As in Persia and Turkey, in Pakistan an "intellectual elite" in the Guénonian sense has formed during the past few decades that is fully versed in the writings of Guénon, Schuon, and other master expositors of traditional doctrines while being deeply rooted in the Islamic tradition itself.

In other Muslim countries also, especially Malaysia and Indonesia, a whole new generation of younger scholars have discussed the writings of Guénon and other traditionalists, and some, like Osman Bakar of Malaysia, have already become well-known scholars. But I shall forgo dealing with these countries in detail here and conclude with an Islamic society at the heart of Europe, that is, Bosnia. Before the breakup of Yugoslavia, there was already keen interest among a group of Muslims, Orthodox Serbs, and some Croatian Catholics in Guénon, Schuon, and other traditionalist authors. Many in Bosnia believed that only the traditional perspective, based on respect for all traditional forms and what Schuon, with whom I shall deal in the next section, has called the "transcendent unity of religions," could provide the intellectual and spiritual matrix in which a multireligious society could live in peace. The horrendous tragedies of 1992–95, that led to the death of nearly a quarter million Muslim Bosnians and forced the migration of numerous people under the name of ethnic cleansing, have not diminished this hope in the hearts and minds of many leading Bosnian intellectuals. In fact, one could say that today perhaps there is no other place in the world where the reality of tradition and the perennial philosophy as understood by Guénon is so evident even in the public domain and where an attempt is being made to create a framework for the peaceful coexistence of Muslims, Orthodox, Catholics, and Jews on the basis of the unity of the inner meaning of traditional doctrines and practices as Bosnia.

A number of works by and about Guénon have appeared in Serbo-Croatian and Bosnian since the 1970s, and since Bosnian Muslim scholars read Serbo-Croatian as easily as Bosnian (they are in fact practically the same language, written in some cases in the Latin alphabet and in other cases Cyrillic, and historically even in other alphabets, including Arabic) mention must be made of works in both languages.[42] It is remarkable how alive works of traditionalist authors are in Bosnia, much more so than in other European countries. Many significant Bosnian Muslim thinkers consider Bosnia to be a bridge between the Islamic world and the West, and they find in these writings the perfect expression of that truth that belongs to both East and West and yet transcends all geographic determinations and limitations. While older scholars, such as Rusmir Mahmutćehajić, Enes Karić, and Reśid Hafizović, who are all well known in Bosnia, continue to write important works on the basis of traditional teachings, younger scholars, such as Hafiz Nevad Kahteran, have now arrived upon the scene. When one thinks of the influence of Guénon upon the Islamic world, one usually does not think of Bosnia, but it is here that the corpus of traditional writings has found some of its most staunch and intelligent admirers and defenders, who are also having a notable influence upon the general intellectual and spiritual life of the country.

One can hardly neglect the significance of the influence, both visible and invisible, of Guénon and other traditionalist figures upon the contemporary Islamic world and yet, as already mentioned, no thorough study has been made of this subject to this day. The influence of Guénon and other traditionalists can be seen in several domains. First of all, these writings have provided the traditional Islamic intelligentsia with an in-depth and thorough critique of the modern world and its hidden and manifest errors and deviations from the norm. Second, these works have been a major source for authentic knowledge of the Western tradition, including religion, philosophy, science, and the arts. It must be remembered that most ordinary educated Muslims do not possess a deep knowledge of the West. Although modernists do have some knowledge of the West, their knowledge is usually limited to the modern period. Traditionalist writings have led many a Muslim to an understanding of a St. Bernard, a Dante, or a St. Thomas and have made them aware of the significance of the European Middle Ages, which most Muslim modernists have erroneously called the "Dark Ages," following their Western models and counterparts, whom they seek to emulate in everything.

Third, these writings, which are themselves a continuation and reformulation of the metaphysics of religious diversity as expounded by such masters of old as Ibn 'Arabī and Rūmī, have provided in the contemporary context the framework necessary for the carrying out of religious dialogue in depth while making other religions, not only Judaism and Christianity, but Hinduism, Buddhism, and Shamanism as well, better known in traditional Islamic circles. Fourth, these writings have enabled those who are the guardians of Islamic esoteric teachings and gnosis to express these teachings in a contemporary language not only for Westerners, but also for modern educated Muslims themselves, enabling them to defend such teachings before the onslaught of secularist modernism.

Finally, the writings of Guénon, Schuon, and other traditionalist masters have aided traditional Islam to reformulate its teachings in a contemporary language. As mentioned earlier in this book, after the first shock of the intrusion of the modern world into the heartland of Islam with the Napoleonic invasion of Egypt in 1798, several reactions were created in the Islamic world, including puritanical "fundamentalism," messianism, and modernism. Traditional Muslims, who constituted and in fact still constitute the vast majority of Islamic society of the thirteenth/nineteenth century, opposed modernism, but did not react by reformulating traditional teachings in response to specific challenges presented at that time. Great Sufi masters and religious scholars of jurisprudence continued their teachings, intuitively aware of the deviations from the spiritual norm inherent in the militarily more powerful forces that were invading, colonizing, or influencing the Islamic world. But rarely did they seek to answer on the intellectual level the challenges of modernism, and few had the in-depth knowledge of the modern world necessary to carry out such a task.

As discussed earlier, after World War II, especially during the past few decades, a new set of responses has come from the Islamic world in reaction to the situation in which it has found itself as it seeks to reassert its independence. New forms of what is now widely known as "fundamentalism" as well as modernism (including postmodernism) and messianism have appeared on the scene and created currents that continue unabated, but in contrast to the early reactions of the nineteenth century, there has now appeared another reality, that of traditional Islam fully aware of the nature of the modern world and capable of explaining that world as well as expounding in a contemporary language the teachings of Islam in both its exoteric and esoteric aspects to both the West and the Islamic world itself. This newly formed group acts as the means for the older classes of traditional scholars to better understand the modern world. This group is also perfectly capable of defending the teachings of traditional Islam from the attacks of modernist and "fundamentalist" critics from both within and without. Certain members of this group have also succeeded in reformulating the principles and teachings of traditional Islamic philosophy, spirituality, the sciences, and the arts and enabling a whole younger generation of Muslims to study their own intellectual and spiritual tradition from within the traditional Islamic worldview. Now, all of these and certain other realities of great significance for the contemporary Islamic world owe a great deal to the works of Guénon, Schuon, Burckhardt and other traditionalist figures without whom the formation of this "traditional elite" in the Islamic world would not have been possible.

Of course above and beyond all these intellectual activities, there stands the central importance of traditional teachings in providing intellectual protection from deviations that take the mind and soul away from the path to God, from what constitutes the goal of human existence, and in making available expressions of the greatest lucidity of traditional metaphysics, the perennial philosophy, and sapiential esoterism. Many souls in the Islamic world, as in the West, have been brought back to the world of faith and received preparation to follow the path of spiritual realization, which is still a living possibility in the Islamic world, more so than in the West, through the works of Guénon and his illustrious company of traditionalist authors, especially Schuon.

The story of the influence of Guénon in the Islamic world is a long one that needs more extensive study. What is certain is that today the traditional writings continue to play an important role in many Islamic circles and are bound to have an even greater influence as the shortcomings and deviations of both modernism and "fundamentalism" become even more evident and it becomes even clearer to men and women of good faith and intelligence that the only abiding truth is to be found in the perennial wisdom residing at the heart of all the authentic religions. This wisdom manifested itself as light amid the intellectual and spiritual eclipse and darkness of early twentieth-century Europe through the remarkable works of René Guénon, who not only expressed the truths of

Tradition, but in his own life while in Egypt acted as a bridge between Islam and the Western tradition. He sought to create the mutual understanding between various religions and traditions that is so much needed today. Those influenced by him in the Islamic world are at the forefront in the task of seeking to further this mutual understanding upon which the human future depends. They are also most aware of the importance of preserving the truth at a time when subversion and perversion of perennial wisdom is to be seen everywhere. In this task they are aided, as are their counterparts in the West, by the teachings of Guénon and other traditionalists, teachings that are as alive and pertinent today as when they were written, being rooted as they are in the timeless reality of the Spirit.

B. *Frithjof Schuon and the Islamic Tradition*

Frithjof Schuon, one of the most remarkable metaphysicians and scholars of religion of recent times, lived a very private life away from the limelight, devoting himself to the exposition of the perennial philosophy and the verities of various religions as well as spiritually guiding many who were attracted to the realization of the truths revealed through Tradition. Born in 1907 in Basel, Switzerland, where he received his earliest schooling, Schuon was brought to Mulhouse by his mother after the death of his father. There he received a French education, in contrast to his earlier German education. Having become a French citizen, the young Schuon, already familiar with the works of Guénon, decided to go to Paris, where he worked, learned Arabic, and embraced Islam. In 1932 he traveled to Mostaghanem in Algeria, where he entered the Shādhiliyyah Order, one of the most universal and influential Sufi orders with a wide following in North Africa, the Arab East, and many other Islamic countries, becoming a disciple of Shaykh al-'Alawī. He went back to Europe after a few months and then returned to Algeria two years later. As representative and spiritual heir of Shaykh al-'Alawī, he established in Europe a branch of the Shādhiliyyah-'Alawiyyah Order, which he led for some sixty years.

During World War II, after being captured as prisoner of war by the Germans, he fled to Lausanne, Switzerland, where he was to live for the next forty years. In 1982 he immigrated permanently to the United States, where he settled amid a number of his disciples in Bloomington,

Indiana. He died there in 1998 and was buried in a forest near his house. He left behind not only numerous disciples all over the world and a remarkable body of writings on various aspects of traditional doctrines and the perennial philosophy in the areas of metaphysics, cosmology, religion, art, criticism of the modern world, the spiritual life, and many related subjects, but also works of art in the form of both poetry and painting. Although he lived away from the public eye, even during his lifetime his influence began to be felt in both the West and the Islamic world, although in the latter part of his life he did not emphasize his Islamic identity publicly.[43]

Now, however, that Frithjof Schuon has left this earthly plane and it has become public knowledge that his initiatic name was Shaykh 'Īsā Nūr al-Dīn Aḥmad al-Shādhilī al-'Alawī al-Maryamī, it is important to bring out into the open his relation to the Islamic tradition within which he functioned as the spiritual teacher of a branch of one of the most significant orders (*ṭuruq*) into which Sufism crystallized after the early centuries of Islamic history. It is particularly important to deal with this subject, because a misunderstanding can be created in the minds of certain people who have read of his constant reference to the *religio perennis* ("perennial religion") and the Primordial Tradition and who might therefore be unaware of his insistence on the necessity of following an orthodox tradition and of his own essential relation with Islam, a relation that he did not reveal publicly except in his earliest works. Schuon was of course the foremost expositor of esoterism and the *sophia perennis* ("perennial wisdom") of his day and always spoke publicly in the name of that universal and perennial wisdom that he also called *religio cordis* ("religion of the heart"). He wrote extensively about metaphysics, esoterism, spiritual ethics, traditional anthropology, art, and various religions. He taught that religions possessed an inner unity beyond the level of external forms, which he called the "transcendent unity of religions." If asked what his religion was by an outsider, he would say the "perennial religion" or the "religion of the heart," which is in fact the same answer that was given to this question by figures such as Ibn 'Arabī and Rūmī as well as many other classical Sufi figures.

Without doubt Schuon was deeply interested in pure esoterism and gnosis, whose veritable nature he unveiled in so many of his works. He also spoke of the subtle difference between Islamic esoterism and esoteric Islam, that is, pure esoterism as expressed in Islamic forms and the esoteric dimension of these forms, and his greater interest in the first over the second. But he also knew fully well that there was a place where the two met. Moreover, he wrote clearly that whereas esoterism issues from the Truth, which is the source of both esoterism and exoterism, and not from exoterism, to pursue an authentic spiritual path necessitates the acceptance and practice of the exoteric dimension, which alone forms the basis for embarking upon the esoteric path. In other words, in Islamic terminology, both the *Ṭarīqah,* or spiritual path, and the *Sharī'ah,* or Divine Law, issue from the *Ḥaqīqah,* or Truth, which is the source of both, and not from each other, but to enter a *ṭarīqah* one must first accept and practice the *Sharī'ah.* This is exactly what Schuon required of his disciples, while, like many Sufis of old, but with reference to a wider context, he spoke of the religion of the heart and pure esoterism. His discussions of pure esoterism should not, however, detract anyone for one moment from thinking that he was anything other than a Muslim in the deepest sense of the term and that he practiced the tenets of the Islamic tradition on the levels of both the Law and the Way, while always emphasizing the inner or esoteric meaning of the exoteric rites and practices in conformity with classical Sufism, especially that of figures such as Rūmī.

Besides speaking of the *religio cordis,* Schuon often expressed his attraction to the metaphysical formulations of the school of Śankara and the primordial ambience of the North American Native traditions. These assertions, added to the misinterpretation by many outsiders as well as some in his entourage of his understanding of the significance of the Indian forms, which he loved dearly and with which he concerned himself personally, have caused many to doubt the Islamic character of his teachings, especially at the end of his life. Yet he told me often that his love for such matters as Native American culture, art, and religion was a personal inclination having nothing to do with the *ṭarīqah* that he had founded and that was based on pure Islamic orthodoxy and orthopraxy. As a matter of fact, to his last days he remained deeply attached to the Islamic tradition, performed the Islamic rites, and read the Quran regularly. The invocation of God's Name as revealed in the Quran did not cease from his lips until the very moment of his death.

Schuon became attracted to Islam after beginning his studies of Arabic, which led to his formal entry into the religion in 1932 in Paris, where, as already mentioned, he was working at the time. He recounted the story that, one day in Paris while pondering what to do, he prayed to God and made the vow that if he were to receive a sign from Heaven on a particular day before noon, he would embrace whatever religion that sign indicated. On that day he left his apartment a quarter before twelve and walked toward a main thoroughfare. At five minutes before noon suddenly a whole group of North African soldiers on horseback in complete Islamic dress appeared in the street and marched by. The meaning of this unlikely sign in the middle of Paris was obvious; Schuon decided to fulfill his vow to God and embraced Islam immediately. Thereafter, he attended the Paris mosque often, but he told me that he learned the *Sūrat al-fātiḥah* (the opening chapter of the Quran), which is recited during the daily prayers, in Switzerland from the Persian scholar Sayyid Ḥasan Imāmī, who was later to become the Imām-jum'ah of Tehran.

From that period of his life on, Schuon adopted Islamic dress while at home. He wore that dress, especially in its *maghribī* (of the Maghrib) form[44] throughout his life, learned the *maghribī* style of calligraphy, which he wrote beautifully, being a gifted artist even at that young age, and spoke Arabic to those who knew the tongue. His journey to Algeria in 1932, where he spent several months and most important of all where he met Shaykh Aḥmad al-'Alawī, who initiated the young Schuon into Sufism, only strengthened his bond to the Islamic tradition in general and the traditional ambience of the Maghrib in particular.[45] He traveled to Algeria again in 1934 but this time he also went to Morocco, and to Egypt in 1938 to meet René Guénon. He visited Morocco again several times later in the 1960s and also journeyed in the same period to Turkey twice to visit the House of the Virgin, the Maryamana, in Kuçadasi. He never made the pilgrimage to Mecca, but was always joyous when his disciples made that sacred journey and would sometimes say that he participated in such pilgrimages inwardly. He therefore had personal experience and firsthand knowledge of some of the Islamic world—the Maghrib, Egypt, and Turkey.

Schuon's private life was in fact carried out in an atmosphere that recreated the traditional Islamic ambience in the heart of the West. The interior of his house was like the most beautiful traditional *maghribī* home, filled mostly with objects of Islamic art, and in it one hardly felt separated from the traditional atmosphere of the Islamic world. But it was not only his living space that resonated with things Islamic. His days were punctuated by the daily prayers, and when he was younger, he fasted not only during Ramaḍān, but also during many other days of the year, following the *Sunnah* of the Prophet. Almost every day he recited the Quran. I remember that when in the sixties he began to travel more extensively, he asked me to send him the thirty parts (*juz'*) of the Quran in separate bindings, so that he could take one or two along without having to carry the whole book, which in its larger editions is of course heavy. From the time of his conversion to Islam, he lived as a Muslim, practicing the tradition on its exoteric as well as most esoteric level. As already mentioned, that fact that he was the great spokesman for esoterism and universal metaphysics did not keep him from being a Muslim on the plane of forms. Although he wrote eloquently on Christianity, Hinduism, Buddhism, Shamanism, and other religions, his name for his followers remained Shaykh 'Īsā Nūr al-Dīn Aḥmad. And when he died, he was buried according to Islamic rites carried out strictly on the basis of traditional practices.

Those who were born in the Islamic world and who had had concrete experience of what the Sufis call "Muḥammadan grace," or *al-barakat al-muḥammadiyyah,* spoke unanimously of the fact that when they came to meet Schuon at his house, they immediately felt the presence of that *barakah* and smelled its unmistakable perfume. Such was also my own experience when I first met him in Lausanne in 1957, after a period of correspondence with him. Having met many saintly people in Persia, including several Sufi masters, and having visited many Islamic holy places, I was utterly astounded by the powerful presence of the Muḥammadan *barakah* emanating from him, when I first met him in his house in a narrow street overlooking Lake Leman in Pully outside of Lausanne. Clearly, despite the fact that his was a universal voice expressing the truth at the heart of all religions, Schuon himself was rooted in the Islamic tradition and more particularly in the soil of Sufism. Without this root he could have never established a *ṭarīqah* within which it was possible to practice and realize the truths about which he wrote so eloquently in his books and articles.

What Schuon loved most in Islam was its insistence upon the central reality of the Unity of the Divine Principle, which, while being One, is also Absolute, Infinite, and Perfection, this last Attribute being equated by him with the supreme Good of Plato. Schuon basked in the shining rays of the *shahādah* (testimony of Islam) and considered the first *shahādah, Lā ilāha illa'Llāh* ("There is no divinity but God") the most perfect formulation of integral metaphysics. He in fact composed some of the most profound commentaries ever written on the two *shahādahs,* relating the second *shahādah, Muḥammadun rasūl Allāh* ("Muḥammad is the messenger of God"), to the *illā* of the first *shahādah* and showing the deepest meaning of the former as formulation of the truth of the coming forth of all things from the Divine Principle.

Schuon's practice of Sufism revolved around the *shahādah* and the Supreme Name of God, which absorb and integrate all other Names and litanies into their principle and origin, while his theoretical exposition of Sufi metaphysics always came back to the central truth contained in the *shahādah.* He lived and breathed in its truth and in the Supreme Name, with which it terminates. Nevertheless, Schuon had also journeyed both "existentially" and metaphysically through the world of the Divine Names, which play such a major role in the Islamic universe. He wrote of the meaning and power of many of them and dealt with some of the difficult metaphysical and theological issues that arise from what appears to be the contradictory sense of some of the Divine Names when they are viewed in relation to each other outwardly. His masterly essay "Dimensions of the Universe in the Quranic Doctrine of the Divine Names," in which he deals with the deepest meaning of the Names *al-Awwal,* the First, *al-Ākhir,* the Last, *al-Ẓāhir,* the Outward, and *al-Bāṭin,* the Inward, bears testimony to the level of knowledge that he possessed of the "science of Divine Names."[46]

Schuon knew the Quran well and read it in the original Arabic, which he knew and loved. He was particularly attracted to the last *sūrahs,* or chapters, as well as some of the middle ones, especially the *Sūrat al-Wāqi'ah* (The Event), the first that he memorized after the *Fātiḥah.* In his daily discourse he often used certain well-known Quranic verses and spent a good deal of time in the study of the inner meaning of the Sacred Text, much of which would come to him through inner intuition rather than the reading of earlier inspired esoteric commentaries. He did, however, know some of those well, especially the one attributed to Ibn 'Arabī, but actually by 'Abd al-Razzāq al-Kāshānī, the seventh/thirteenth century master of the Ibn 'Arabian school, and those of al-Ghazzālī as well as the more general ones, such as those of al-Bayḍāwī and al-Ṭabarī, which are standard commentaries popular throughout the Islamic world. Schuon's chapter on the Quran in his *Understanding Islam* is itself a major esoteric commentary on the Sacred Text in the line of the greatest traditional Sufi commentaries.

As for the Prophet of Islam, Schuon knew well the traditional accounts of his life and the descriptions of his character as found in classical sources. But his knowledge of the inner reality of the Prophet was also direct and "existential," for he had "encountered" the transhistorical "Muḥammadan Reality" (*al-ḥaqīqat al-muḥammadiyyah*). He never wrote a book on the Prophet bringing out the esoteric significance of the episodes of his life, but he did write a number of works of the greatest importance on the inner reality of the Prophet and the significance of his virtues. More than anyone else in the West, he explained to a non-Muslim audience what the Prophet means to Muslims and why they love him so. He did so by making clear the spiritual dimension of the Prophet and his role as the supreme model for pious Muslims in their daily lives and in Islamic spirituality. Schuon's several studies of the Prophet culminated in his "The Mystery of the Prophetic Substance,"[47] which reveals a very rare intimacy with *al-ḥaqīqat al-muḥammadiyyah*. This essay is in fact one of the most important works ever written on the inner reality of the Prophet. Schuon of course also knew well the prophetic *Sunnah,* often quoting *ḥadīths* and writing on the meaning of the *Sunnah* of the Prophet in the life of Islam in general and of Sufism in particular.

Furthermore, Schuon was well acquainted with Islam's sacred and religious history. Besides the rightly guided caliphs, among whom he especially loved 'Alī, as had Shaykh al-'Alawī, Schuon also had studied and admired many of the great masters of *taṣawwuf,* including Junayd, Ḥallāj Niffarī, and of course Shaykh Abū'l Ḥasan al-Shādhilī. His favorite *maghribī* masters included Ibn Mashīsh, Abū Madyan, Ibn 'Arabī, and, needless to say, his own spiritual master, Shaykh al-'Alawī, to whom he would refer as a *surhomme* (superhuman) and whose works he continued to quote until the end of his own life. Schuon loved Ibn 'Arabī and translated some of his poems into French when he was young, but he refused to identify Ibn 'Arabī with the whole of Islamic esoterism and rejected the view of certain French Guénonians who did so. When, from the late 1950s on, I introduced him to the works of Persian Sufi masters, he became especially attracted to Rūmī, Shabistarī, and Jāmī and finally came to consider Rūmī the most universal saint of Islam.

There are few domains of the Islamic intellectual and spiritual tradition with which Schuon was not familiar. He knew the different formulations of Islamic metaphysics, to which he himself had made a great contribution.[48] He also wrote on angelology and cosmology in a manner that reveals his intimate knowledge of traditional sources, as can be seen in his extensive essay "*An-Nûr.*"[49] He furthermore dealt in many instances with Islamic doctrines of the afterlife, often comparing them to eschatological views of other religions, while at other times seeking to clarify some of the more difficult Islamic doctrines concerning the multiplicity of posthumous states.[50]

Schuon was also well aware of the distinctions between Sunnism and Shīʿism within Islam, and in contrast to Guénon, who showed no interest in Shīʿism, was attracted to the study of Shīʿism, especially its esoteric doctrines. The personalities of ʿAlī and Fāṭimah were of great interest to him, and he was in fact planning to write a book or long article on them in the 1960s and asked me to send him whatever references were available. It was because of the unavailability of easy-to-use sources that he finally abandoned the idea and settled for writing the very significant essay "Seeds of a Divergence,"[51] which contains some of the most profound statements on the relationship between Sunnism and Shīʿism in their understanding of God, His Names and Qualities, the nature of the Prophet, and the question of his successor as leader in the Islamic community. He also discusses how Sunnism and Shīʿism issue from two dimensions within the being of the Prophet and both belong to Islamic orthodoxy. In our private discussions over the years he would often bring up certain Shīʿite beliefs or practices and discuss their significance with me.

It is remarkable that being the metaphysician and esoterist that he was, Schuon should be so knowledgeable in the problems and discussions of *kalām,* usually rendered as Islamic scholastic theology. Like many North African Sufi shaykhs, his interest in *kalām* was mainly in the Ashʿarite school, whose "voluntarism" he discussed and also criticized often,[52] bringing out both the strengths and weaknesses of the theses of the Ashʿarites and their struggles with the Islamic philosophers over the question of the nature of the Divine Will, the relation between the Divine Will and human will, the created or "uncreated" nature of the world, the nature of causality, the relation between reason and revelation, and many other issues of central theological and philosophical importance. He showed that the problems discussed by the schools of Islamic theology and philosophy, such as free will, determinism, "createdness," or the "eternity" of the world, cannot be solved on the theological level itself, but only on the level of pure metaphysics. He also knew Islamic philosophy and often sided with the philosophers against the Ash'arites, saying that ultimately the Islamic philosophers belonged to the same family as the *'urafā'*, or gnostics. He certainly was not an antiphilosophical Sufi; on the contrary, he was in many ways more sympathetic to someone like Suhrawardī than to the "anti-intellectual" Sufis of the fifth/eleventh and sixth/twelfth centuries.[53]

Schuon also had the deepest knowledge of Islamic art in its various forms and wrote some of the most perceptive pages on its meaning. He was especially attracted to the art of the Maghrib, that is, the extreme western lands of Islam in North Africa, such as Morocco and Muslim Spain, with its purity, reflecting the ethos of the early centuries of Arab society in North Africa. But he also greatly admired Persian art as well as some of the outstanding architectural monuments of Muslim India. He loved both Arabic calligraphy, which, as already mentioned, he wrote in a beautiful hand, and Arabic poetry. Being a poet in not only his mother tongue, German, but also in English, he furthermore composed some Arabic poetry himself that always dealt with spiritual themes in the tradition of the Arabic Sufi poetry of old. He also enjoyed the music of the Islamic peoples, first and foremost the chanting of the Quran and the *adhān* (which are supreme forms of music, although never called "music" in Arabic), and then classical Arabic, Persian, and Turkish music, especially what was connected to the Mawlawī tradition.

As already mentioned, Schuon had traveled extensively in the western lands of Islam in North Africa. Being the extremely perceptive person that he was, he was able to pierce into and gain in-depth knowledge of the structure of Islamic society and the various classes of people who comprised it, especially in the Maghrib. He would often tell me that in the Islamic world he liked most of all the Sufis, then the class of *'ulamā'*, and then the pious artisans and merchants in the bazaars. He also had great love for the nomads wherever they might be and fully appreciated their great spiritual significance within Islamic civilization. Altogether there was little within Islam and classical Islamic civilization that Schuon had not come to know, study, and penetrate to its core meaning. His being, even more than his works, demonstrated his immersion in the universe of the Islamic tradition, while his heart dwelt in the Formless and his intellect spoke of the pure metaphysics and esoterism that lie at the heart of sacred revelations and yet transcend in their essence all that belongs to the formal plane.

If we consider all of Schuon's writings, including his published books and articles as well as unpublished texts, we will discover that he wrote more about the Islamic tradition than any other religion, although his perspective was always that of universal esoterism and the *sophia perennis.* In fact, the body of his writings contains not only an unparalleled exposition of traditional metaphysics and the inner study of religions, but also a peerless account of many facets and aspects of Islam and its main spiritual and intellectual currents seen from the most profound inward perspective. Schuon's first essay, published in *Le Voile d'Isis* in 1933, concerned Islam to a large extent and was entitled "L'aspect ternaire de la Tradition monothéiste." His first short book, which appeared two years later in 1935 in Paris, was also concerned with Islamic themes and bore the title *De Quelques aspects de l'Islam.* The fourth "book" of his profound meditations, which appeared in German as *Leitgedanken zur Urbesinnung* also in 1935,[54] was written in Mostaghanem and dedicated to Shaykh al-'Alawī, and his collection of German poems *Tage und Nächtebuch*[55] contains several poems with Arabic titles and Sufi themes.

This concern with Islamic themes continued in Schuon's major works, which began to see the light of day after World War II, starting with his first major doctrinal book, *The Transcendent Unity of Religions,*[56] in which Islam figures in a central fashion. His two next books, *The Eye of the Heart*[57] and *Spiritual Perspectives and Human Facts,*[58] likewise dealt largely with Islamic themes, with sections devoted specifically to Islam and Sufism. For books other than those dealing directly with Islam, such was to be the case in nearly all of Schuon's later books, such as the book that in many ways summarizes his teaching, *Esoterism as Principle and as Way,* which ends with a section entitled "Sufism," and *Approches du phenomène religieux,* whose longest section is devoted to Islam.[59]

Turning to works whose very titles include "Islam" or "Sufism," the most noteworthy is *Understanding Islam,* which, along with *The Transcendent Unity of Religions,* is Schuon's best-known work. No book of Schuon's has sold as many copies or become as globally disseminated as this remarkable book on Islam, and no work in a Western language has done as much to explain Islam to the Western audience and create a better bridge for in-depth understanding between Islam and Christianity. Furthermore, the influence of this work in the Islamic world itself, from Senegal to Malaysia, has been great, especially among Western-educated Muslims, who have come to learn so much about their own religion and have had the doubt created in their minds by Western attacks against Islam dispelled through this work. *Understanding Islam* has been translated into Arabic, Persian, Turkish, and some of the other Islamic languages,[60] while its French and English versions have also been very widely read in the Islamic world. It is hard to overestimate the spiritual and intellectual impact of this book in furthering understanding of Islam in both East and West, the East including not only the Islamic world, but also Hindu India, Japan, and other Asian countries.

Schuon's other works with specifically Islamic titles include his *Sufism: Veil and Quintessence,* which discusses the heart of Sufism and its teachings, and *Christianity/Islam: Essays on Esoteric Ecumenism,* which is a most masterly treatment of the subject, a subject to which he was to return in a schematic fashion in his *Roots of the Human Condition.*[61] There are also two collections of his essays in English dealing with Islam, namely, *Dimensions of Islam* and *Islam and the Perennial Philosophy,* which have no French original, but which have also been translated into some Islamic languages. When one considers all these works and the numerous passages concerning Islamic themes in other books and essays, one becomes more aware of the enormous amount of writing that Schuon devoted to the subject of Islam while presenting the *sophia perennis* and traditional doctrines in general.

The influence of these works in both the West and the Islamic world is much greater than what a cursory glance would reveal, and in fact only in-depth studies can make known the profundity and extent of his impact. Nevertheless, something can be said even now about his influence. If one considers not only Schuon's own writings, but also works of many other figures who were influenced in one way or another by his works, it becomes clear how extensive the impact of his work has been on various aspects of the study of Islam in Western languages.[62]

In the Islamic world itself, although Schuon had been more closely associated with North Africa than any other part of the Islamic world, it was in Persia where he first became well known to the general public starting in the late 1950s and early 1960s as a result of translations I made into Persian of some of his essays as well as extensive discussion of his writings in my own works. Gradually his writings as well as those of Guénon, Burckhardt, and Lings began to attract the attention of a number of perspicacious scholars among both Western-educated Persians and those trained in traditional *madrasahs*. This trend has continued to this day, with the result that his ideas, along with those of the figures already mentioned, are part of the current intellectual discourse in Persia, as the present-day public discussion in that land of "religious pluralism" reveals so clearly. There is a whole generation of younger Persian scholars who speak of *sunnat,* a word I used some fifty years ago as a translation for "tradition" as understood by Guénon and Schuon, and who consider their perspective *sunnatī,* or traditional, whether they are dealing with philosophy, religion, or art. This is due most of all to the impact upon such scholars of the thought of Guénon and Schuon encountered directly or through my writings and those of some of my students and colleagues writing in Persian.[63]

In Turkey likewise Schuon's writings, along with those of authors closely associated with him, began to become known from the late 1970s and early 1980s on, and by now there is, as already mentioned, a whole library of traditional works in Turkish, including several books by Schuon.[64] Moreover, in Turkey, as in Persia, Schuon's Islamic identity was well known even in his lifetime and people often spoke of him as a "gnostic," or an *al-'ārif bi'Llāh,* who was a disciple of Shaykh al-'Alawī, but who lived in the West. The "intellectual elite" in the Guénonian sense that has formed in Turkey as well as Persia, Pakistan, Malaysia, and certain other Islamic countries has been influenced as much by Schuon as it has by Guénon.

In Pakistan interest in the writings of Schuon and those closely associated with him began in the early 1960s through a number of lectures I gave and essays I published in that country. Figures mentioned already in connection with Guénon, such as A. H. Brohi, Muḥammad Ajmal, and Suheyl 'Umar, were also deeply influenced by Schuon, and a number of these in fact became his disciples. The Suheyl Academy continues to disseminate his works in English in Pakistan.

A fairly similar situation is to be found in the Malay world, although perhaps not with the same degree of amplitude and breadth. A number of scholars in Indonesia, and especially Malaysia, have been trained in the traditional perspective, and this point of view is well known in that part of the world. Moreover, a number of the works of the Traditionalist School, including those of Schuon, have been translated into both Bhasa Malay and Bhasa Indonesian. In the debate between tradition and modernism as well as the dialogue of civilizations going on in those countries today, the voice of Schuon can usually be heard in the background influencing what is being formulated in louder voice in the foreground.

It is strange that despite the centrality of the Arab world to the Islamic world and the fact that Schuon was more acquainted with that part of the Islamic world than any other, his influence is less perceptible in Arab countries than in the other parts of *dār al-islām* already cited. Although, as already mentioned, the Arabic translation of *Understanding Islam* was well received in the Arab world, Schuon has not found until now a group of competent translators who could render his works successfully into Arabic, both in translating those works and in writing in Arabic about the ideas and doctrines expounded in them.[65] In a country such as Egypt, which is the intellectual center of the Arab world, this lacuna is quite evident. As for North Africa, it is mostly through Schuon's French works that a number among the younger generation have come under the sway of his teachings. Meanwhile, in Morocco, Algeria, and Syria he continues to be remembered among older members of the Sufi orders as the Sidi 'Īsā who became the disciple of Shaykh al-'Alawī and later a shaykh of the Shādhiliyyah-'Alawiyyah Order.

Altogether the influence of Schuon's works and his followers in the Islamic world is more in the realm of presence than in external action. The ideas and doctrines he expounded are like a light that illuminates by its very presence without being the direct source of external action except in certain exceptional cases. One should not be fooled into belittling his universal influence by relying only on external actions and reactions that can be studied from the outside in a cursory fashion. The influence is there to be sure, powerful and immutable, yet transforming in ways that touch the deeper layers of the intellectual and spiritual life of many who themselves have great qualitative impact upon society.

Schuon's message has of course also had an impact upon a number of Christians, Jews, Buddhists, Hindus, and even those without a definite spiritual orientation, but who are in quest of the truth. This is especially true of Christianity, about which he wrote so many luminous pages.[66] But it would not be an exaggeration to state that, although he lived in the West and wrote in European languages, his greatest influence was in the Islamic world, as a comparison of the extent of intellectual concern for his ideas in North America and Britain, on the one hand, and Turkey and Persia, on the other, reveals. The reason for this phenomenon is to be sought in the inner reality of the man himself and the fact that he was nurtured by the Muḥammadan *barakah* that emanated from his being, as it does from his writings.

Without a doubt Frithjof Schuon was an exceptional person from childhood; he had already had profound metaphysical intuitions as an adolescent before embracing Islam. God had given him a "pneumatic" nature and an intellect that could perceive metaphysical truths from an early age. But as he himself wrote in reference to German Romanticism, a correct intellectual intuition remains inoperative, unless it is nurtured within the framework of a living tradition. In Schuon's case, God chose Islam as the tradition in which he and what he received from Heaven were to be nurtured and brought to fruition. It was Islam and the Muḥammadan *barakah* that allowed him to become a spiritual teacher and a shaykh of the Shādhiliyyah Order, to found a new branch of this *ṭarīqah,* the Shādhiliyyah-'Alawiyyah-Maryamiyyah, and to reach spiritual states and stations from whose perspective he was to write his remarkable and incomparable works. To be sure he had a providential function, beyond the specifically Islamic universe, in revealing the essential truths of other religions and their inner unity, which, lest we forget, is a major theme of the Quran itself,[67] in bringing out the true significance of esoterism and the *sophia perennis* in relation not only to theory, but also spiritual practice, in speaking with greatest profundity of the nature of the soul and the elements of an authentic spiritual life, in providing an in-depth criticism of the modern world, in reestablishing the correct mode of serious thinking and intellection, and in accepting non-Muslim disciples.[68] Yet there is no doubt that he was a Sufi shaykh, one, however, with an exceptional metaphysical vision and breadth of knowledge, who was a product of the Islamic esoteric tradition. Even his non-Islamic dimensions can be understood to a large extent in light of the fact that Sufism is the esoterism of the last major revelation of humanity, and that, like Islam, whose function it was to integrate all the revealed truths that came before it, Sufism contains within itself all the possibilities of esoterism.

No matter how much some might seek to aggrandize some of the deviant currents, eddies, and aberrations that surrounded him in his last years and try to present him as a figure that had gone "beyond" the Islamic norm, Schuon was and remained rooted in the Islamic tradition to the moment of his death and knew more than anyone else that one cannot live beyond the world or the level of forms while living in the world of forms, and that even one's journey to the "beyond" is determined by the tradition within which one has lived in this world. Only the Ultimate Beyond, beyond the beyond, is above all forms in the Supreme Unity that lies above all formal distinctions. Schuon was the great expositor of the doctrine of Unity and a spiritual teacher who led those qualified to reach that Unity, which manifests itself in all authentic religions. In his case the One (*al-Aḥad*), who manifested Himself in His fullness in Islam with its emphasis upon Unity (*al-tawḥīd*), chose him as the vehicle for a universal and synthetic expression of the truth that leads to the One, nurtured him to become a spiritual master, familiarized him with the "Breath of intimacy," revealed to him the spiritual reality of the Prophet, and made the Muḥammadan *barakah* to flow through his being.

C. *With Titus Burckhardt at the Tomb of Muḥyī al-Dīn ibn ʿArabī*

Titus Ibrāhīm Burckhardt, whose views on traditional Islamic art have already been discussed in chapter 12, was born in Florence in 1908 and, like Schuon, was schooled in Basel, where he was in fact his early classmate. The scion of the well-known Aristocratic family of Basel that has produced other well-known scholars, such as Jacob Burckhardt, Titus was born into a household in which art played a central role, as his father was an artist. Not satisfied with the secularized atmosphere of his homeland, Titus Burckhardt set out at an early age for Morocco, where he formally embraced Islam. He studied Arabic and the traditional Islamic sciences in Fez, a city he deeply loved all his life and in whose preservation he played such a central role. He also began to follow the path of Sufism under the direction of some of the outstanding Sufi masters of Morocco. Later he became a disciple of Schuon and returned to Switzerland, although he traveled often to North Africa. He became the director of Urs

Graf Verlag, centered in Basel and Lausanne, and supervised the series "Homesteads of the Spirit," in which his own incomparable works on Fez, Chartres, and Siena appeared. He also produced a number of seminal books and essays on Sufism, art, metaphysics, and the cosmological sciences,[69] writing in both German and French. Moreover, he was himself an artist, a remarkable photographer and drawer of designs, and many of his photos and sketches are to be found in his illustrated books. Most of his works were later rendered into English, other European languages, and several Islamic languages, especially Persian.[70]

To the end of his life Burckhardt continued his writing activities as well as acting as advisor to UNESCO in the project to preserve the traditional arts and crafts of Morocco and working himself to preserve the traditional character of Fez. He died in Lausanne in 1984 and was buried on the outskirts of the city.

Burckhardt wrote numerous books on sacred art, metaphysics, cosmology, and Sufism. His translation of the *Fuṣūṣ* of Ibn 'Arabī into French opened the door in the West for the appreciation of the singularly important ideas of this sage. And he was the first Westerner to explain fully the inner meaning of Islamic art. His works in this domain are so penetrating that they are now having a profound influence even in many Islamic countries among practicing artists and architects. The personal account that follows will reveal something of the person who produced so many pertinent works pertaining to the Islamic tradition and in fact traditional studies in general.

In the fall of 1966, on the occasion of the one hundredth anniversary of the founding of the American University of Beirut, I had the opportunity to meet Titus Burckhardt not on the soil of Europe, as had happened often before, but for the first time within the boundaries of the Arab world. Hearing the *adhān,* despite the din and noise of the modern Westernized city of Beirut, caused him to remark that the presence of Islam was to be felt even in this corner of the Islamic world, which had been the beachhead for the spread of modernization and Westernization in Arab lands. It was possible for us to visit together the few old mosques nearby and to read and contemplate, before the azure expanses of the Mediterranean and in the clear light of the Middle Eastern sky, certain Maryamian litanies by Schuon that had just been composed and sent to Burckhardt and to meditate over the role of the Virgin in the religious life of the whole Mediterranean world. Moreover, we were able to visit together the Yashruṭī Sufi woman saint Sayyidah Fāṭimah, who recounted to us how it was impossible for her to choose a title for her famous Arabic work on Sufism, *al-Riḥlah ila'l-Ḥaqq* ("Journey to the Truth"), until she saw Ibn 'Arabī in a dream and received the title from him. The daughter of the founder of the Yashruṭiyyah Order was in fact so impressed by Titus Burckhardt's spiritual presence and radiant character that she devoted a most beautiful page to him and to this encounter in her autobiography, *Masīratī ila'l-Ḥaqq* ("My Sojourn to the Truth").[71]

Burckhardt was, however, eager to visit the more traditional Islamic sites of the Arab Near East, sites that provided more of traditional Islamic life and art than it was possible to encounter in Beirut. Therefore, after some consultation, we decided to visit Damascus together. During the two-hour drive between Beirut and Damascus across the beautiful mountains and valleys, which at that time conveyed a wonderful sense of peace and tranquility, he commented upon many aspects of Islamic culture and tradition in general, upon such subjects as the ecological and geographical resemblance of the region to Andalusia and the Maghrib, which he knew so well, and the complementarity between the mountains and the deserts that surround so many Islamic cities, such as Damascus and Marrakesh. His comments brought joy and freshness to the experience of scenery that I had seen so often before and brought about an interiorization of the experience of the countryside that could result only from the spiritual effect of the companionship of a sage.

Upon arriving in Damascus, we decided to spend the day visiting the tomb, or "place of residence" (*maqām*),[72] of the granddaughter of the Blessed Prophet, Sayyidah Zaynab, the tomb of Ibn 'Arabī, and of course the Umayyad Mosque, in that order, for Burckhardt mentioned that traditional courtesy, or *adab,* required that we pay our respects first to the daughter of 'Alī and the granddaughter of the founder of Islam. Usually "Sit Zaynab," as Damascenes call it, is full of pilgrims, but, strangely enough, on that morning we were practically the only pilgrims present. The only other people there were a number of Persian craftsmen from Isfahan who were reconstructing the dome and placing tiles upon the walls of the edifice. After prayers and a long period of quiet meditation, we turned to the craftsmen, whose activity obviously attracted the author of the most outstanding works on Islamic art to appear in the contemporary world. Burckhardt commented upon the deep piety of the craftsmen and their attitude of humility in creating their work. We reminisced about Fez and discussed further plans we had made together for his writing a book on Isfahan in the collection of *Stätten des Geistes* ("Homesteads of the Spirit"), which, as already mentioned, he was then editing for Urs Graf Verlag. It was my intense wish to have a book like *Fes: Stadt des Islam*[73] written on the beautiful city of Isfahan, which he also wanted to visit. What a tragedy that this work was never realized and that the world could not benefit from seeing the delicate and almost ethereal edifices of the Safavid capital through the eyes of the master interpreter of Islamic art that Burckhardt was.

It was after this pilgrimage and brief encounter with Persian art in the persons and art of the Persian craftsmen working at Sayyidah Zaynab, that Titus Burckhardt and I set out from the southern fields of Damascus, where her *maqām* is located, for the slopes of the hills north of the city, where Ibn 'Arabī lies buried. We entered the sanctuary of the Andalusian master reverentially and, after offering prayers, sat down by the tomb of the great metaphysician and saint, which was surrounded by an atmosphere of contemplative tranquility and calm. The peace and serenity of this atmosphere were accentuated by the fact that, at that moment, Burckhardt and I again happened to be alone in that sacred space, which, like every veritable sacred space, is the echo of the Center and a reflection of Eternity upon the moving image of peripheral existence.

While meditating upon the verities or the *Ḥaqīqah* at the heart of Sufism, I occasionally glanced at the contemplative face of my companion, whose closed eyes seemed to gaze inwardly upon the heart and whose face reflected the light of the Intellect before which his mind and soul were so transparent. I thought at that time about Burckhardt's significance in making Ibn 'Arabī known to the Western world. I recalled his *La Sagesse des prophètes* ("The Wisdom of the Prophets"), *Von Sufitum,* written also in French as *Introduction aux doctrines ésotériques de l'Islam* ("An Introduction to Sufi Doctrine"), *Clé spirituel de l'astrologie musulmane* ("Mystical Astrology According to Ibn 'Arabī"), and *De l'homme universel* ("Universal Man") with its incomparable introduction, all of which I had read as a graduate student at Harvard. How *essential* these writings were in expounding the essence of the teachings of Ibn 'Arabī, al-Jīlī, and the Ibn 'Arabian (or Akbarian) School in a metaphysical language of great power and clarity, formulated first by Guénon, perfected in an amazing way by Schuon, and applied in an ingenious manner to the teachings of Shaykh al-Akbar by Burckhardt.

During the years, as I plunged further into the texts of Ibn 'Arabī and their numerous Arabic and Persian commentaries with traditional masters in Persia and discussed them extensively with Henry Corbin and Tashiko Izutsu (whose studies of Ibn 'Arabī were deeply appreciated by Burckhardt), I began to fully realize the significance of Burckhardt's achievement. He had succeeded in reaching the heart of Akbarian metaphysics and making it known in contemporary language without divorcing it from the *barakah* of Sufism or the rest of the Islamic tradition. His translations and commentaries, which are at once traditional and full of living wisdom and light, differ markedly from those pedantic and dry translations by some who also claim to adhere to the Traditionalist School. Some of these figures would reduce the whole of Sufism to Ibn 'Arabī alone, and Ibn 'Arabī himself to a cerebral presentation of theoretical metaphysics far removed from the living presence that emanates from his teachings and that can be seen both in the writings of Burckhardt and the traditional masters of Ibn 'Arabī's School, whom I had the privilege to meet and with whom I studied in Persia.

Later contacts with the School of Ibn 'Arabī have often brought back the memory of those moments when I sat with Titus Burckhardt at the tomb of the great master in Damascus. To have beheld Burckhardt there, lost in the contemplation of that Truth that lies at the heart of all traditional metaphysics and of course of Sufism itself; to have witnessed his humility before the Divine Presence and transparency before the Truth that manifests Itself in a mysterious fashion in certain loci determining and determined by sacred geography and usually identified with tombs, or *maqāms,* of great saints—to have done all of this was to realize fully the vast chasm that separates merely theoretical understanding of wisdom, or *al-ḥikmah,* from its realization. In contrast to many who write of Ibn 'Arabī and claim strict traditional orthodoxy without, however, having realized the truth of Sufism, Burckhardt lived the truth he wrote about. The exceptional light of intelligence that emanated from him pierced to the heart of the texts that he studied and illuminated their meaning in a manner that is possible only for a person in whom the Truth has descended from the plane of the mind to the center of the heart and become fully operative. At the tomb of Ibn 'Arabī, Burckhardt manifested the qualities of a saintly man possessing a penetrating intelligence of extraordinary lucidity, combined with virtue and a luminous soul transmuted by the presence of that Truth, whose doctrinal aspects he studied with such depth and understanding.

We left the tomb of the saint feeling a special proximity to the quintessential metaphysics of Sufism that Ibn 'Arabī had been destined to formulate and that he intertwined with many less central Sufi teachings in a vast tapestry that remains unique in the history of Sufism. Titus Burckhardt departed for Jerusalem with the aim of visiting not only the site of the Nocturnal Ascent (*al-mi'rāj*) of the Blessed Prophet, of which Ibn 'Arabī had written so eloquently, but also the tomb of the patriarch of monotheism, Abraham, after whom Burckhardt himself was named. He asked me to accompany him on this leg of the journey, but unfortunately other demands forced me to return to Tehran. Little did we know that in a few months the political status of both Jerusalem and al-Khalāl, or Hebron, would be changed so drastically. Later, he wrote me of the exceptional blessings of this pilgrimage and how they were a continuation of what we had received from Heaven during that incredible day in Damascus at the tombs of Sayyidah Zaynab and Ibn 'Arabī.

And again years later, as we circumambulated the Ka'bah, we discussed the reality of the connection between the *barakah* of the Center and the secondary centers that reflect and echo the Center, and the blessedness evoked by the visit to the tomb of the author of the *Meccan Illuminations*. Titus Ibrāhīm Burckhardt has now left this plane of ephemerality for the empyrean of the Spirit, but his works, which are the fruit of realized knowledge, continue in a unique fashion to illuminate the path of those seriously interested in Sufism in general and in the teachings of Ibn 'Arabī in particular. They are in fact among the most significant formulations of the essence of the teachings of traditional Islam in the modern world.

D. *Martin Lings and His Islamic Legacy*

Martin Lings, known by his students and associates and also so widely in the Islamic world as Shaykh Abū Bakr Sirāj al-Dīn, was born in Kent, England, in 1909. He grew up and studied in his country of birth and after graduating from Oxford spent some time teaching in Lithuania. As a result of the influence of the writings of Guénon and Schuon he embraced Islam and went to Egypt, where he taught English literature until

1952, when the Nasserite revolution forced him to return to England. There, he completed his doctorate, writing the now classic work *A Sufi Saint of the Twentieth Century* for his thesis, and became keeper of Arabic manuscripts at the British Library until his retirement. He retired to a humble house in Kent with a beautiful garden, which he cultivated with great love. He continued to travel extensively in the Islamic world, to nearly the end of his long life, journeying during the last two decades of his life annually to Egypt, where I would join him, but also often to Saudi Arabia, Jordan, Pakistan, and even all the way to Malaysia. Among the outstanding traditionalist authors discussed in previous chapters, he was the person who lived most openly and publicly as a Muslim scholar and thinker, lecturing often in Britain itself on Islamic themes and also in the Islamic world; his works are widely disseminated in different Islamic countries. His defense of traditional Islam and criticism of modernism became widely known in Islamic intellectual circles in the Islamic world, within the Islamic community in Britain, and even to some extent in North America. After an exceptionally long and fruitful life, he died in 2005 in his home in Kent and was buried in his own garden amid all the beautiful flowers that he had cultivated and nurtured with remarkable devotion and care over the years.

With his death the Traditionalist School lost one of its greatest expositors and the world as a whole one of its leading spiritual lights. His long life was gently extinguished, but not before his many works, lectures, and most of all spiritual presence and direction illuminated a whole world in both East and West. Highly gifted as a young man in language and literature and drawn deeply to religion, he became closely associated with C. S. Lewis at Oxford. It was his thirst for universal truth and his intelligence for understanding pure metaphysics, however, that caused him to leave the strong influence of Lewis for the pure expression of the perennial philosophy, which he discovered in the writings of René Guénon in the 1930s. C. S. Lewis was opposed to Guénon, as his collected letters reveal, and it is to the great credit of the young Lings and his sense of discernment that he was able to break the strong spell of the imposing figure of Lewis for what appeared at Oxford at that time to be the far away horizons of traditional doctrines. In the late 1980s when we were walking together at his invitation in a garden at Oxford University, Lings reminisced about his days at the university. He told me how disappointed Lewis was when the young Lings left Christianity for Islam and told Lings, "What a loss for Christianity!" As it was, Lings embraced Islam not to deny, but to reconfirm the deepest and often forgotten truths of Christianity, as his works amply reveal, and he, like the other traditionalist authorities discussed above, made great contributions to the study of that religion and the Western tradition in general.

The discovery of traditional writings was to lead him to the circle of Frithjof Schuon, to embracing Islam in Switzerland through Titus Burckhardt, and to entry into the path of Sufism. It was shortly before World War II that he set out for Egypt, where he met Guénon (Shaykh 'Abd al-Wāḥid Yaḥyā) and became closely associated with him, becoming in fact like a member of his household. But what was most important in Lings's life was that he became a disciple of Shaykh 'Īsā Nūr al-Dīn Aḥmad (Frithjof Schuon), to whom he remained extremely devoted and faithful even after Schuon's death.

Sidi Abū Bakr, as he was then called, did not only love Islam, the religion that God had chosen for him, but also the Arabic language, which he mastered, as well as traditional Arab culture. He was at once very English and deeply Arabized on a certain level, but his goal was to transcend all forms, those of his ethnic background and those of the religion whose forms he had adopted as the means to ascend to that Reality that is above all forms. He was planning to live in Cairo until the end of his life, but the Egyptian revolution of 1952 forced him against his will to return to England. With all his love for the English countryside and his lovely garden, which was in full bloom when he died in the month of May, he also always considered Egypt his home. During the more than twenty years that we visited Cairo together annually I always felt that he was as much at home there as he was in his home in Westerham, Kent. Once we were visiting the holy site of Ra's al-Ḥusayn in Cairo, which is the sacred center of the city. As we approached the grill surrounding the tomb of the grandson of the Prophet, he said, "When I am here, I feel that this is where I belong."

Shaykh Abū Bakr Sirāj al-Dīn spent over sixty years in actively following the spiritual path; his whole life was dedicated to God and the way that leads to Him. He traveled regularly in the old days to visit Shaykh 'Īsā in Lausanne and later in the United States. He would also journey extensively throughout much of the Islamic world on a regular basis from Morocco to Malaysia, but the anchor was always Egypt. Gradually his fame grew throughout the Islamic world, even more so than in England, and the perfume of his presence is to be sensed even now not only in certain circles in the West, but also in numerous Islamic countries where many tributes were made to him after his death. Now that he has left this lowly plane for the numinous abode, one might pause to weigh the significance of his writings within the Traditionalist School without forgetting the even more important significance of his spiritual legacy embedded in the hearts and minds of his many disciples, friends, and even unknown persons from near and far touched by his light. As a Persian poem says:

> Do not seek after our death our dust in the earth,
> Our tomb is in the breasts of the people of gnosis.

After the three founding figures of the Traditionalist School, that is, Guénon, Coomaraswamy, and Schuon, Lings is, along with Burckhardt, without doubt one of the most significant voices of the next circle of this assembly. Although initially drawn to the works of Guénon, one of which he translated into English after World War II,[74] Lings gravitated more toward the writings of Schuon, which he followed scrupulously and assiduously. In comparison to Burckhardt, who favored the cosmological sciences, Lings was more attracted to the field of literature, although both were metaphysicians and each made extremely important contributions to Sufi studies. Schuon and Burckhardt were both more interested in philosophy than was Lings, although all three were of course deeply immersed in the *sophia perennis*. Schuon did not mind being called a "Teutonic philosopher" in public. One can hardly imagine Lings allowing himself to be called an "English philosopher."

Like Schuon and Burckhardt, Lings was also very much interested in traditional art, but in a somewhat different way. Schuon and Burckhardt were both remarkable painters and designers, although in different media, while Lings, like Schuon, was a very gifted poet. And in contrast to the other two, Lings was more concerned with literary art, as seen in his masterly poetic translations of Sufi poetry and his unparalleled study of Shakespeare. One might say that the artistic genius of Lings oscillated between Quranic calligraphy and English literature, as seen in the titles of his two most important works on art: *Splendours of Qur'an Calligraphy and Illumination* (the title of the new edition of this unique work)[75] and *The Secret of Shakespeare*.[76] Furthermore, in the context of art one should not forget his splendid poetry contained not only in the *Collected Poems*,[77] but also in his translations of Sufi poetry assembled in his anthology of Sufi poetry,[78] one of the last of his works to appear before his death, and in his translation of some of the poems of Shaykh al-'Alawī in *A Sufi Saint of the Twentieth Century*.[79] Concerning the latter, Frithjof Schuon, who did not praise things easily, once told me, "This should be a model for the translation of Sufi poetry."

The other works of Shaykh Abū Bakr can be divided into two categories: one dealing with general traditional themes and the other more specifically with Islam.[80] The first category includes his brilliant and provocative work *Ancient Beliefs and Modern Superstitions*, which is a critique of many of the errors of the modern world following such books as *The Crisis of the Modern World* by Guénon, *Light on the Ancient Worlds* by Schuon, and many of their other writings; *Symbol and Archetype*,[81] which reveals his deep interest in symbolism and which summarizes in masterly fashion the traditional doctrine of symbols (he also played a major role in the English translation of Guénon's *Fundamental Symbols*); *The Eleventh Hour*,[82] in which he deals with eschatological questions, about which Schuon did not choose to write to any extent publicly; and his very last work, *A Return to the Spirit*,[83] which appeared after his death. All of these books, along with many articles on diverse traditional subjects, especially symbolism, are among the most precious writings in the traditionalist canon.

To the second category belong his first published book, *The Book of Certainty*,[84] a Sufi commentary on many verses of the Quran and certain *ḥadīths*, which is still widely read after over half a century since it was first published; his incomparable biography of the Prophet of Islam, *Muhammad: His Life Based on the Earliest Sources*,[85] which most Muslims consider to be the best biography of the Prophet in a European language and for which he is widely known in the Islamic world; *A Sufi Saint in the Twentieth Century*, which again is a unique masterpiece; *What is Sufism?* which is an eloquent and penetrating work dealing with the most profound aspects of the Sufi tradition; and his short personal and moving essay *Mecca from Before Genesis Until Now*,[86] which reveals the significance of some of the deepest meanings of the *ḥajj*, or pilgrimage, to what is for

Muslims the House of God. Except for the last work, which appeared fairly recently, all the other works in this category are not only known in the West, but are also widely appreciated in the Islamic world, where many of them have been translated into various Islamic languages.[87] Also again in this category one must mention many articles of the greatest intellectual and spiritual significance.

In the Islamic world Shaykh Abū Bakr was seen as one of the champions of authentic Islam in the West, as reflected in the many reports of his death in various Islamic countries. He brought many Muslims back to their own religion and opened their eyes to the spiritual grandeur of Sufism as well as the errors of modernism. In Turkey several of his books rendered into Turkish continue to be read by a large audience. In Iran he is practically a household name among scholars, and many of his books, which have been translated into Persian, remain very popular. A similar situation holds true for Pakistan, where the Suheyl Academy has made many of his works available in a local edition in English, which is widely read in that land, making translations into Urdu less necessary, although some of the titles have also been rendered into Urdu. In other Islamic countries the influence of Shaykh Abū Bakr's works is also to be seen, particularly Malaysia, Indonesia, and Bosnia.

One would expect that the Arabic zone of Islamic civilization would be where Shaykh Abū Bakr would be best known, considering his years of residence in Egypt and frequent later journeys to that country as well as his numerous visits to Jordan, Saudi Arabia, Morocco, and several other Arab countries. But as in the case of other traditionalist authors, less attention has been paid to him there than in other major Islamic countries, such as Turkey, Iran, and Pakistan, although again a few of Shaykh Abū Bakr's works have been rendered into Arabic, as mentioned above. This having been said, it is necessary to state that he was nevertheless well known and highly respected among major Egyptian Sufi masters, among the *'ulamā'* of al-Azhar, and within Sufi circles in other Arab lands, especially the Shādhiliyyah in the Maghrib.

In the West he had many readers among those in search of traditional truth in general and among the newer generation of Muslims living in the West, for many of whom he was the foremost exemplar of a Western Muslim with the virtues that the religion has sought to inculcate in its followers on the basis of the Prophetic model. Hamza Yusuf, perhaps the foremost and best-known American Muslim who writes and speaks about Islam, came to Islam when he was only seventeen years old through the writings of Shaykh Abū Bakr and went to visit him shortly before the latter's death. He was deeply impressed by Shaykh Abū Bakr's saintly presence and considered him the "prototype" of a truly Muslim Westerner.

Non-Muslim followers in the West, who constitute the majority of his readers in that area, are of diverse backgrounds and interests. Many are attracted to him as a member of the traditionalist circle and, having read Guénon, Schuon, Burckhardt, and others, have turned naturally to Lings's writings. Others are attracted particularly to his works on Islam and Sufism. It must not be forgotten that he played an important role in bringing many Westerners to the Sufi tradition and of course to Islam. There is no doubt that there is a distinct Muḥammadan *barakah* to his writings, which one can also see in the works of Schuon and Burckhardt. And yet others have been attracted to his poetry and concern for literature. Here his book on Shakespeare has played a unique role. Many people in England know him only through this work, which revealed the inner and esoteric meaning of the plays for the first time to many of the lovers of the Bard and even to some major Shakespearean actors.

Lings's long and fruitful association with the circle of Kathleen Raine and the Temenos Academy, of which he was a fellow, was mostly related to this aspect of his interest. He continued to give lectures at the Temenos Academy practically to the end of his life. They were in fact landmark events in the cultural calendar of London, some of them attended by the Prince of Wales, who was one of his great admirers.

Once I asked Shaykh Abū Bakr why he continued to be so concerned with Shakespeare. He said that since the English language was now becoming global, the time of Shakespeare "had arrived" and that it was most important to preserve this language at its peak and in expressions impregnated with the deepest wisdom and traditional teachings. In this way the spread of English would not contribute simply to the impoverishment of various cultures. Indeed, he himself sought to keep Shakespearean English alive, especially in his own poetry and Quranic translations as well as in translations of Sufi poetry, and he used the English language in its highest form throughout his writings.

The influence of Lings in the West is not confined to the English-speaking world. Many of his works, like those of Guénon, Schuon, and

Burckhardt, have been translated over the years into French, Italian, Spanish, German, Bosnian, and other European languages. He is in fact very well known in various European countries, both among those drawn to the study of tradition and within the European Muslim community in general. In recent years his works have played a widespread role in presenting an authentic and in-depth view of Islam for the general European public drawn to this subject and faced at the same time with whole libraries of works that are either shallow or based on ignorance, misinformation, or disinformation.

Few have been blessed with such a long life devoted to God and the spiritual life, one bearing so much fruit in the form of books, articles, and lectures from which the world could benefit both intellectually and spiritually, as Shaykh Abū Bakr. His life was totally dedicated to God, the spiritual path, and those who sought to walk upon that path. He was indeed what Rūmī called *mard-i khudā,* that is, a man of God. In him piety and intelligence, knowledge and love were combined. He was given the gift of speaking and writing eloquently. He left behind many works of unusual light and beauty combined with scholarly and intellectual rigor, works that will continue to emit grace. But his most beautiful work was the shaping of his own soul, on whose perfection he had worked so assiduously during a very long life. Finally he was able to present the fruit of this most important of his efforts to God. Quite justly some have called Lings himself a Sufi saint of the twentieth century and the first British Sufi saint.

wa'Llah[u] a'lam
(and God knows best)

CREDITS

page 207 View of the Mosque of the Prophet in Medina. Begun in the first/seventh century, with most recent renovations in the fourteenth/twentieth century.

page 208 The interior of the Mezquita, Cordoba, Spain, second/eighth century.

page 211 Imam (Shah) Mosque, Isfahan, Iran, tenth/sixteenth century. Photo by: N. Stone

page 212 Burūjirdī House, Kashan, Iran, thirteenth/nineteenth century.

page 215 Bādshāhi Mosque, Lahore, Pakistan, eleventh/seventeenth century.

page 216 Sultan Aḥmad Mosque, Istanbul, Turkey, eleventh/seventeenth century. Photo by: L. Pollack, Fieldscape Studio

page 219 The tomb of a saint in Kashan in Iran, thirteenth/nineteenth century

page 220 Miḥrāb (prayer niche) of the Jāmi' Mosque, Isfahan, eighth/fourteenth century.Photo by: S. Marín page 223 Contemporary mosque in traditional style: Qubā Mosque near Medina designed by Abdel-Wahid El-Wakil, fourteenth/twentieth century.

page 226 Beni Isquen and Ghardaia Oasis, Algeria.

page 229 General view of the town and mausoleum of Moulay Idrīs, Morocco, twelfth/eighteenth century.

page 230 General view of the city of San'a in Yemen.

page 231 View of old and new Cairo from the Citadel. Photo by: Wikimedia Commons

page 232 General view of the Kaẓimiyyah area of Baghdad, Iraq. Photo by: M. Hürlimann

page 233 General view of the city of Yazd, Iran.

page 234 Cairo minarets, many from the Mamlūk period, with TV dishes in foreground. Photo by: S. Marín

page 237 View of present-day Tehran. Photo by: Wikimedia Commons

page238 Present-day Dubai skyline. Photo by: Wikimedia Commons

page 245 Modern style mosque: Istiqlāl Mosque in Jakarta, Indonesia, fourteenth/twentieth century. Photo by: Wikimedia Commons

page 248 Modern style mosque: Faisal Mosque in Islamabad, Pakistan, fourteenth/twentieth century. Photo by: Wikimedia Commons

NOTES

Prologue

1. In Arabic *sunnah* also and in fact primarily refers to the actions and sayings of the Prophet of Islam.
2. This lacuna is now being filled gradually thanks to the pioneering works of such men as Martin Lings, whose *A Sufi Saint of the Twentieth Century* (Berkeley: University of California Press, 1973) has become a classic; and Michel Chodkiewicz, who has made several basic studies of Amīr ʻAbd al-Qādir, for example, *The Spiritual Writings of Amir ʻAbd al-Kader,* trans. James Chrestensen et al. (Albany: State University of New York Press, 1995).
3. There is now a fairly extensive literature in European languages, especially in English and French, devoted to traditional Islam or to aspects of the Islamic tradition, especially Sufism, written from the traditional point of view. These works include Frithjof Schuon, *Understanding Islam* (Bloomington, IN: World Wisdom, 1998); *Dimensions of Islam,* trans. P. N. Townsend (London: Allen & Unwin, 1970); *Islam and the Perennial Philosophy,* trans. P. Hobson (London: World of Islam Festival Publishing, 1976); Titus Burckhardt, *Introduction to Sufi Doctrine,* trans. D. M. Matheson (Bloomington, IN: World Wisdom, 2008); *Fez: City of Islam,* trans. W. Stoddart (Cambridge: Islamic Texts Society, 1992); *Moorish Culture in Spain,* trans. A. Jaffa (London: Allen & Unwin, 1972); Martin Lings, *What Is Sufism?* (Boston: Unwin Paperbacks, 1981); William Stoddart, *Sufism: The Mystical Doctrines and Methods of Islam* (Wellingborough, England): Thorsons, 1976); Roger Dupaquier, *Unveiling Islam,* trans. T. J. Winter (Cambridge: Islamic Texts Society, 1992); Gai Eaton, *Islam and the Destiny of Man* (Albany: State University of New York Press, 1985); Victor Danner, "Religious Revivalism in Islam: Past and Present," in Cyriac Pullapilly, *Islam in the Contemporary World* (Notre Dame, IN: Crossroads, 1980), pp. 21–43; *The Islamic Tradition: An Introduction* (Hillsdale, NY: Sophia Perennis, 2005); and Allāhbakhsh Brohi, *Islam in the Modern World* (Lahore: Publishers United, 1975). See furthermore John Herlihy, *Wisdom's Journey: Living the Spirit of Islam in the Modern World* (Bloomington, IN: World Wisdom, 2009); Jean-Louis Michon,

Introduction to Traditional Islam (Bloomington, IN: World Wisdom, 2008); Joseph E. B. Lumbard, ed., *Islam, Fundamentalism, and the Betrayal of Tradition* (Bloomington, IN: World Wisdom, 2004); Sachiko Murata and William C. Chittick, *The Vision of Islam* (New York: Paragon House, 1994); and Sachiko Murata, *The Tao of Islam* (Albany: State University of New York Press, 1992).

See also the following of my own works: *Ideals and Realities of Islam* (Chicago: ABC International Group, 2000; Cambridge: Islamic Texts Society, 2001); *Islam and the Plight of Modern Man* (Chicago: ABC International Group, 2001; Cambridge: Islamic Texts Society, 2002); *Islam: Religion, History and Civilization* (San Francisco: HarperSan Francisco, 2003); and *The Heart of Islam: Enduring Values for Humanity* (San Francisco: HarperSan Francisco, 2004).

There are a number of works by well-known traditional Muslim authorities such as Mawlānā Ashraf 'Alī Thānwī, Shaykh al-'Alawī, Shaykh 'Abd Ḥalīm Maḥmūd, and 'Allāmah Ṭabāṭabā'ī that have been translated into English. It is of interest to note that the writings of the famous author Maryam Jameelah, which have always been strongly antimodern, were close to the new "fundamentalist" perspective in many ways, but that more recently she came to embrace the traditional point of view as seen in some of her extensive book reviews of the past few years.

There is a great need in fact for a complete bibliography of works on Islam that are of a traditional character. Such a compilation would allow those who wish to pursue the subject to be guided through the maze of publications on Islam that have appeared during the past few decades.

4. On the meaning of tradition, see S. H. Nasr, *Knowledge and the Sacred* (Albany: State University of New York Press, 1989), pp. 65ff. Concerning tradition, Schuon writes: "Tradition is not a childish and outmoded mythology but a science that is terribly real" (*Understanding Islam,* foreword).
5. The vast commentary of 'Allāmah Ṭabāṭabā'ī, *al-Mīzān* ("The Balance"), is an outstanding example of a contemporary traditional commentary that can be clearly distinguished from those in which modern ideas appear either directly or in the guise of "Islamic ideology" with an outwardly anti-Western color, but with inward similarities to the antitraditional ideas that have emanated from the West since the Renaissance.
6. There have of course been differences among traditional authorities themselves concerning these principles, but these differences have always existed within the traditional worldview and not against it. These differences cannot therefore be used as a pretext for the rejection of this worldview, which embraces all these differences without identifying itself with only one school or denying the possibility of error and deviation in the traditional world. See Muḥammad Hāshim Kamālī, *Principles of Islamic Jurisprudence* (Cambridge: Islamic Texts Society, 1991).
7. On this crucial question as treated in a universal context, see Frithjof Schuon, *Esoterism as Principle and as Way,* trans. W. Stoddart (Bedfont, UK: Perennial,

1981); and *Sufism, Veil and Quintessence,* ed. James Cutsinger (Bloomington, IN: World Wisdom, 2006).

8. On this question see Titus Burckhardt, *The Art of Islam: Language and Meaning,* trans. J. Peter Hobson (Bloomington, IN: World Wisdom, 2009); and S. H. Nasr, *Islamic Art and Spirituality* (Albany: State University of New York Press, 1986).
9. It is remarkable how close the views of modernists and "fundamentalists" are concerning the rapid mechanization of means of production and the computerization of every section of the economy to the greatest extent possible without any concern for their religious and human implications.
10. As an example one can cite the case of women's dress and comportment. Traditional Islam insists that women dress modestly and usually wear some kind of veil or headdress that covers their hair. The result is an array of female clothing from Morocco to Malaysia, most of which possesses much beauty and reflects femininity in accordance with the ethos of Islam, which insists upon conformity to the nature of things and therefore the masculinity of the male and femininity of the female. Then came the modernist changes that caused many women to remove the veil, uncover their hair and certain parts of their bodies, and wear Western dress, at least in many parts of the Islamic world. This phase is now complemented by certain forms of "fundamentalism" or revivalism that in some areas has placed a scarf on women's heads and a machine gun in their hands with total disregard for the beauty of the rest of their dress as a reflection of their female nature as always envisaged by Islam. One wonders which is less pleasing to the eyes of God, the Western-clad Muslim woman who goes home and performs her prayers or a gun-wielding bomber whose Islamicity is summarized by a scarf that hides her hair while the fire of hatred burns within her, obscuring all the gentleness and generosity that Islam has traditionally identified with womanhood.
11. In this comparison attention is paid especially to recent forms of "fundamentalism," not those of the thirteenth/nineteenth and early fourteenth/twentieth centuries, which were a form of extreme exoterism and puritanism and therefore a truncated form of tradition, not properly speaking antitraditional or countertraditional, although, in impoverishing the intellectual, cultural, and artistic life of parts of the Islamic world, they played an important role in facilitating the advent of modernism and its aftermath in the form of countertraditional movements.
12. This is seen especially in Islamic penal codes, which traditionally have taken into account such factors, so that they have not been applied blindly and without consideration of all the moral factors involved.
13. See S. H. Nasr, *Science and Civilization in Islam* (Chicago: Kazi Publications, 2001); and *Knowledge and the Sacred,* pp. 130ff. See also Titus Burckhardt, *The Mirror of the Intellect,* trans. W. Stoddart (Albany: State University of New York Press, 1987), part I. Recently there has been greater attention paid among

a number of Muslim scholars to the problems of confronting the already secularized knowledge that emanates from the Western world and that has affected Muslims in many fields since the thirteenth/nineteenth century. See S. Muhammad Naquib al-Attas, *Islam and Secularism* (Kuala Lumpur: International Institute of Islamic Thought and Civilization, 1978).

14. No knowledge can be Islamically worthwhile unless it is related to a higher plane and ultimately to God, who, being *al-Ḥaqq,* or the Truth, is the source of all veritable knowledge.
15. See Titus Burckhardt, *The Art of Islam;* also his *Sacred Art in East and West,* trans. Lord Northbourne (Louisville, KY: Fons Vitae, 2001), pp. 135ff.
16. See Dariush Shayegan, *Qu'est-ce qu'une révolution religieuse?* (Paris: Presses d'aujourd'hui, 1982), which contains a profound analysis of this subject, although his treatment of the traditional point of view is not that of the traditionalists themselves.

Chapter 1: Islam in the Present-Day Islamic World

1. I have also dealt with certain aspects of this subject in S. H. Nasr, *Islam and the Plight of Modern Man* (Chicago: ABC International Group, 2001; Cambridge: Islamic Texts Society, 2002), chap. 7.
2. See Wilfred Cantwell Smith, *Islam in Modern History* (Princeton, NJ: Princeton University Press, 1957).
3. Some attention has been paid to the Sanūsiyyah in Western languages, but much more needs to be done in this field in general. On the Sanūsiyyah, see Nicola Ziadeh, *Sanusiya: A Study of a Revivalist Movement in Islam* (Leiden: Brill, 1983). As for a general treatment of various movements within the Islamic world, there exists a vast literature that, until a few years ago, possessed a general overemphasis on the modernists, but more recently it has focused on the "fundamentalists." For a general survey covering the whole Islamic world rather than just the Middle East, see J. Voll, *Islam: Continuity and Change in the Modern World* (Syracuse, NY: Syracuse University Press, 1994).
4. Again there were notable exceptions. For example, 'Abd al-Ḥalīm Maḥmūd, who was later to become Shaykh al-Azhar, was aware of the works of Guénon and other Western critics of the West and wrote a work on Guénon in Arabic. See his *al-Shaykh 'Abd al-Wāḥid Yaḥyā-Khamsūn 'āmman 'alā wafātihi,* with an introduction by S. H. Nasr (Cairo: Dār Idrīs, 2003). I deal with Guénon and his influence on the Islamic world in Appendix IV of this book.
5. See S. H. Nasr, *Knowledge and the Sacred* (Albany: State University of New York Press, 1989), chap. 3.
6. See the Prologue.
7. See S. H. Nasr, *The Garden of Truth* (San Francisco: HarperOne, 2008), p. 227.
8. See the works of John Esposito, especially his book written with John Voll, *Islam and Democracy* (New York: Oxford University Press, 1996).

9. See S. H. Nasr, *Science and Civilization in Islam*; *Islamic Science: An Illustrated Study* (Chicago: Kazi Publications, 2001); and *An Introduction to Islamic Cosmological Doctrines* (Albany: State University of New York Press, 1993); Osman Bakar, *The History and Philosophy of Islamic Science* (Cambridge: Islamic Texts Society, 1999); Muzaffar Iqbal, *Islam and Science* (Hampshire, UK: Ashgate, 2002); *Science and Islam* (Westport, CT: Greenwood Press, 2007); S. H. Nasr in conversation with M. Iqbal, *Islam, Science, Muslims and Technology* (Kuala Lumpur: Islamic Book Trust, 2007); and Leif Stenberg, *The Islamization of Science: Four Muslim Positions Developing an Islamic Modernity* (Lund: Lunds Universitet, 1996).
10. This group represents on the highest intellectual level the vast number of Muslims who remain traditional and who are neither modernist nor "fundamentalist." This circle is the articulated voice of traditional Islam and those traditional Muslims who remain more or less intellectually silent, but who live the traditional life of faith and share with this intellectual élite (*khawāṣṣ*), in the time-honored meaning of the term, the same traditional worldview.

Chapter 2: Jihād

1. On the traditional understanding of *jihād,* see Reza Shah-Kazemi, "Recollecting the Spirit of *Jihīd,*" in Joseph Lumbard, ed., *Islam, Fundamentalism, and the Betrayal of Tradition,* pp. 121–42. The author deals especially with the case of Amīr 'Abd al-Qādir, who in his life, thought, and actions exemplified fully the authentic meaning of *jihād.* On this remarkable figure, see the recent biography by John W. Kiser, *Commander of the Faithful: The Life and Times of Emir Abd el-Kader* (Rhinebeck, NY: Monkfish Book Publishing, 2008). The incredible life of Amīr 'Abd al-Qādir also continues to inspire works of fiction based on his biography. For a recent example, see the French novel of Waciny Laredj, *Le Livre d'Émire* (Paris: Babel, 2009). As for the Amīr's metaphysical teachings, see, in addition to the pioneering works of Michel Chodkiewicz, Émir Abd al-Kader, *Le Livre des haltes,* trans. with commentary by A. Penoit (Paris: Dervy, 2009).

Chapter 3: Islamic Work Ethics

1. By extension the term *ṣinā'ah* or *ṣan'ah,* related to *ṣun',* is now also used to mean "industry" and "technology" in the modern sense.
2. On the relation of Islamic art to the Islamic revelation, see Titus Burckhardt, *The Art of Islam: Language and Meaning,* trans. J. Peter Hobson; and S. H. Nasr, *Islamic Art and Spirituality.*
3. Muhammad Asad, *The Message of the Qur'ān* (Bristol, UK: The Book Foundation, 2003), p. 163, n. 1.

4. *'Amal al-ṣāliḥ,* that is, "righteous deed" or "good action," is interpreted by traditional commentators to mean, first of all, religious duties such as prayer and fasting and, by extension, work done with virtue and honesty.
5. For example, the verse, "And covet not that by which Allah has favored some of you above others—unto men a share of what they have earned, and unto women a share of what they have earned" (Quran IV: 32—this and other translations of the Quran are from *The Study Qur'ān,* to be published soon by HarperCollins).
6. The change of the rhythm of life of the community after migrating from Mecca to Medina and the development of the exceptionally spiritually gifted original nucleus of a new social order into the actual first Islamic society is described with great perspicacity in Martin Lings, *Muḥammad: His Life Based on the Earliest Sources* (London: Islamic Texts Society, 1991).
7. There are many *ḥadīths* that extol the virtue of agriculture, such as, "Whenever a Muslim plants, or cultivates a land, and if out of that men eat, or animals eat, or anything else eats, but that it becomes charity on his (the planter's) behalf" (*Ṣaḥīḥ Muslim,* trans. 'Abdul Ḥamīd Ṣiddīqī [New Delhi: Adam Publishers, 1996], vol. 3, p. 818).
8. On Islamic economics in relation to ethics, see Muhammad Abdul-Rauf, *A Muslim's Reflections on Democratic Capitalism* (Washington, DC: American Enterprise Institute, 1984); Muhammad Nejatullah Siddiqi, *Economics: An Islamic Approach* (Islamabad: Institute of Policy Studies, 2001); Yaseen Essid, *A Critique of the Origins of Islamic Economic Thought* (Leiden: Brill, 1995); Abbas Mirakhor, *A Note on Islamic Economics* (Jeddah: Islamic Development Bank, 2007); Umer M. Chapra, "Ethics and Economics in Islam and the West," paper presented at a seminar organized by the Goethe Institute, Munich, and the Dar al-Fikr, Damascus, in Damascus on June 21, 2007; Z. Iqbal and Abbas Mirakhor, "A Stakeholder's Model of Corporate Governance of Firms in Islamic Economic System," *Islamic Economic Studies* 11, no. 2 (March, 2004); Syed Nawab Haider Naqvi, *Perspectives on Morality and Human Well-Being: A Contribution to Islamic Economics* (Leicester: Islamic Foundation, 2003); Rodney Wilson, *Economics, Ethics, and Religion: Jewish, Christian, and Muslim Economic Thought* (London: Macmillan, in association with the University of Durham, 1997); and Syed Nawab Haider Naqvi, *Ethics and Economics: an Islamic Synthesis* (Leicester: Islamic Foundation, 1981).
9. See Seyyed Hossein Nasr, *Islamic Science: An Illustrated Study*; and *An Introduction to Islamic Cosmological Doctrines.*
10. See Burckhardt, *The Art of Islam.*
11. No human collectivity at this late stage of human history could be perfect or even nearly so according to the Islamic conception of history itself. Therefore, there were certainly shortcomings in traditional Islamic society in realizing and guaranteeing the ethical conditions of work in both a qualitative and quantitative manner. What is amazing, however, is the degree to which Islam

did succeed in bestowing an ethical dimension on all kinds of work and in extending the ethical to include even the quantitative aspect of any particular kind of work.

12. On these movements and their social, economic, and religious significance, see Bernard Lewis, "The Islamic Guilds," *Economic History Review* 8 (1937): 20–37; Yusuf Ibish, "Brotherhoods of the Bazaars," *UNESCO Courier* 30, no. 12 (1977): 12–17; and "Economic Institutions," in R. B. Serjeant, ed., *The Islamic City* (Paris: UNESCO, 1980), pp. 114–25.
13. This fact is of course as true for Hinduism, Christianity, or any other religion as it is for Islam. The works of the English artist Eric Gill, who sought to revive the crafts and bestow again a religious and ethical character upon work, is an example of the principle. See Eric Gill, *A Holy Tradition of Working* (Ipswich: Golgonooza, 1983); also the numerous works of Ananda K. Coomaraswamy, by whom Gill was deeply influenced, for example, Roger Lipsey, ed., *Coomaraswamy, 1: Selected Papers—Traditional Art and Symbolism* (Princeton, NJ: Princeton University Press, 1977), pp. 13ff. See also Brian Keeble, *God and Work* (Bloomington, IN: World Wisdom, 2009).
14. One must recall here that in Arabic *ḥusn* means at once "goodness" and "beauty" and *qubḥ* both "evil" and "ugliness."
15. On the traditional doctrine of art in which ethical and aesthetic elements are interrelated and in which art and work are inseparable see, in addition to the works of Coomaraswamy and T. Burckhardt, Frithjof Schuon's illuminating expositions, such as *Esoterism as Principle and as Way,* trans. W. Stoddart, pp. 177ff; see also S. H. Nasr, *Knowledge and the Sacred*, chap. 8.
16. *Ṣaḥāḥ Muslim,* trans. Ṣiddīqī, vol. 4, p. 1541.

Chapter 4: The Male and the Female in the Islamic Perspective

1. It is significant to note that the Quranic term for "man" is *insān,* which refers to the human state as such and not to only one of the sexes. The Arabic term is closer to the Latin *homo* or the German *das Mensch* than the English "man."
2. On the meaning of men and women as theomorphic beings, a doctrine that does not at all imply any kind of anthropomorphism, see Frithjof Schuon, *Understanding Islam*, pp. 13ff.
3. Schuon begins his well-known work *Understanding Islam* with the phrase, "Islam is the meeting between God as such and man as such. God as such: that is to say God envisaged not as He manifested Himself in a particular way at a particular time, but independently of history and inasmuch as He is what He is. . . . Man as such: that is to say, man envisaged, not as a fellow being needing a miracle to save him, but as man, a theomorphic being endowed with intelligence capable of conceiving of the Absolute and with a will capable of choosing what leads to the Absolute" (trans. D. M. Matheson [London: Unwin, 1981], p. 13).

4. According to Frithjof Schuon: "Loving each other, Adam and Eve loved God; they could neither love nor know outside God. After the fall, they loved each other outside God and for themselves, and they knew each other as separate phenomena and not as theophanies; this new kind of love was concupiscence and this new kind of knowing was profanity" (*Islam and the Perennial Philosophy,* trans. P. Hobson, p. 191).
5. This theme is particularly developed among certain Sufis who have been aptly called the *fedeli d'amore* (the faithful in love) of Islam. See Henry Corbin, *En Islam iranien,* vol. 3, *Les Fidèles d'amour* (Paris: Gallimard, 1972), esp. pp. 9–146, concerning Rūzbihān Baqlī, the patron saint of Shiraz.
6. Ibn 'Arabī devotes many pages of the last chapters of his *Fuṣūṣ al-ḥikam* to an exposition of the metaphysical significance of this *ḥadīth* of the Prophet and why in fact women, perfume, and prayer are mentioned in this order.
7. The beauty of woman is, for spiritual man, an unveiling of the beauty of the Paradise that he carries at the center of his being and to which the Quran alludes when it speaks of the houris of Paradise. Likewise, the goodness of man is for woman a confirmation and support of her inner goodness. According to an Arabic proverb, goodness is outward and beauty inward in man, while in woman beauty is outward and goodness inward. There is not only a complementarity between the sexes, but also an inversion of relationships. From a certain point of view, man symbolizes outwardness and woman inwardness. She is the theophany of esoterism, and in certain modes of spirituality Divine Wisdom (which, as *al-ḥikmah,* is feminine in Arabic) reveals itself to the gnostic as a beautiful woman.
8. See Muḥyī al-Dīn Ibn 'Arabī, *The Wisdom of the Prophets,* translated from the Arabic into French with notes by Titus Burckhardt, translated from the French by A. Culme-Seymour, (Gloucestershire: Beshara Publications, 1975), p. 120.
9. See Seyyed Hossein Nasr, *Ideals and Realities of Islam,* chaps. 1, 4, 5.
10. Titus Burckhardt deals with this subject in many of his penetrating studies of Islamic art. See especially his *The Art of Islam: Language and Meaning* and *Fez: City of Islam* trans. W. Stoddart.
11. On the metaphysical principles pertaining to sexuality and its character as found in sources drawn mostly from the Western traditions, see Julius Evola, *Metafisica del sesso* (Rome: Atanor, 1958).
12. Since sexuality is a double-edged sword, the other point of view, which is based on the monastic ideal, also has its metaphysical basis and has manifested itself in certain religions such as Buddhism and Christianity. Islam also recognizes the positive value of monasticism as separation from the world, although this state is realized inwardly, since there is no institution of monasticism in Islam. And despite the emphasis of Islam upon marriage and the positive role accorded to sexuality in Islamic spirituality, there have been many saintly men and women who have remained celibate or practiced sexual abstinence even within marriage. In fact, it would not be possible for most human beings to

experience the paradisal archetype of sexual union without the primary phase of asceticism that allows the soul to experience phenomena as symbols rather than facts. That is also why the experience of the spiritual aspect of sexuality remains inaccessible outside the cadre of tradition and sacred laws that regulate all human relations, including sexuality.

13. On this issue see Aisha Lemu, "Women in Islam," in Altaf Gauhar, ed., *The Challenge of Islam* (London: Islamic Council of Europe, 1978), pp. 249–67. The Quran also asserts: "Whosoever works righteousness—be it male or female—and he is a believer, We shall give him new life, and We shall surely recompense them their reward in accordance with the best of that which they used to do" (XVI: 97).

    On Islamic views concerning women and their rights and responsibilities from a religious as well as sociological and anthropological point of view, see Muhammad Abdul-Rauf, *The Islamic View of Women and the Family* (New York: Speller, 1977); Elizabeth W. Fernea and Basima Q. Bezirgan, eds., *Middle Eastern Women Speak* (Austin: University of Texas Press, 1977); and Daisy H. Dwyer, *Images and Self-Images: Male and Female in Morocco* (New York: Columbia University Press, 1978). There is, needless to say, a vast literature on the subject, but most of the works are written from the perspective of current prejudices in the West as well as from the profane point of view as far as the nature of the human state itself is concerned. There is also little that, by way of translation, would make accessible to English readers authentic writings by Muslim women of earlier ages on religious and spiritual themes, although there are now a few works on women Sufi saints.

14. The great master Ibn 'Arabī had some female spiritual guides (*shaykhah* in Arabic) while he was in Andalusia. On the female element in Sufism, see Annemarie Schimmel, *Mystical Dimensions of Islam* (Chapel Hill: University of North Carolina Press, 1975), "The Feminine Element in Sufism," pp. 426ff.; Laleh Bakhtiar, *Sufi Art and Imagination* (London: Thames and Hudson, 1976); Javad Nurbakhsh, *Sufi Women* (New York: Khaniqahi-Nimatullahi Publications, 1983); and Abū 'Abd al-Raḥmān al-Sulami, Rkia Cornell, ed. and trans., *Early Sufi Woman* (Louisville, KY: Fons Vitae, 1999).

Chapter 5: Traditional Twelve-Imam Shī'ism and the Reality of Shī'ism Today

1. Of course, if one remembers that much of present-day Afghanistan, Pakistan, Baluchistan, Caucasia, and Central Asia was part of Persia at that time, it becomes clear that all of Persia did not become Shī'ite and that the solidly Shī'ite part was located mostly within what comprises Iran and the Republic of Azerbaijan today.
2. See Michel Mazzaoui, "Shī'ism in the Medieval Safavid and Qajar Periods: A Study in *Ithnā 'asharī* Continuity," in Peter J. Chelkowski et al., eds., *Iran:*

Continuity and Variety (New York: Center for Near Eastern Studies, 1971), pp. 39ff.

3. See S. H. Nasr, "Spiritual Movements, Philosophy and Theology in the Safavid Period," first part, *Cambridge History of Iran,* vol. 6, ed. Peter Jackson (Cambridge: Cambridge University Press, 1985).
4. See Henry Corbin's prolegomena to Sayyid Ḥaydar Āmulī, *Jāmi' al-asrār wa manba' al-anwār,* ed. H. Corbin and Osman Yahya (Tehran-Paris: Andrien-Maisonneuve, 1969); also Peter Antes, *Zur theologie der Schi'a: Ein Untersuchung der Čāmi' al-asrār wa manba' al-anwār von Sayyid Ḥaydar Āmolī* (Freiburg: Schwarz, 1971).
5. See S. H. Nasr, "Shī'ism and Sufism," in *Sufi Essays* (Chicago: Kazi Publications, 1999); also Kāmil al-Shaybī, *Sufism and Shiism* (Surbiton, Surrey, UK: LAAM, 1991); also Henry Corbin, *En Islam iranien,* vol. 4 (Paris: Gallimard, 1972).
6. See Marian Molé, "Les Kubrawiya entre Sunnisme et Schiisme aux huitième et neuvième siècles de l'Hégire," *Revue des Études Islamiques,* 29 (1961): 61–142. There are certain scholars who deny the Shī'ite character of the Kubrawiyyah Order or its role in the spread of Shī'ism in pre-Safavid Iran. See the introduction by Hamid Algar to Najm al-Dīn Rāzī, *The Path of God's Bondsmen from Origin to Return* (North Haledon, NJ: Islamic Publication International, 2003) esp. pp. 6–7, where he argues for the Sunni character of the Kubrawiyyah Order. Even if the view of these scholars were accepted, however, one cannot deny the role of the spread of this order in creating a more congenial background for the later acceptance of Shī'ism, with the order's emphasis upon the *ahl al-bayt* and especially 'Alī.
7. On the background of the Safavid movement, see Erika Glassen, *Die frühen Safawiden nach Qāẓī Aḥmad Qummī* (Freiburg: Schwarz, 1970), pp. 86–96. On the exploits of Shaykh Ḥaydar, the rise of the Qizil-bāsh, and the religious wars leading to the establishment of Safavid rule, see Faḍl Allāh ibn Rūzbihān, *Persia in A.D. 1478–1490,* trans. Vladimir Minorsky (London: Royal Society of Great Britain, 1957), pp. 61ff. On the Safavids themselves, see also Roger Savory, *Iran under the Safavids* (Cambridge: Cambridge University Press, 2008).
8. See Michel Mazzaoui, *The Origins of the Safavids, Shī'ism, Ṣūfism and the Gulāt* (Wiesbaden: Harrassowitz, 1972), chap. 3.
9. On the spiritual significance of the art and architecture of this period, see Nader Ardalan and Laleh Bakhtiar, *The Sense of Unity: The Sufi Tradition in Persian Architecture* (Chicago: ABC International Group, 1999), including the introduction by S. H. Nasr.
10. This, for example, is the view of Sayyid Muḥammad Kāẓim 'Aṣṣār, one of the leading *mujtahids* (religious scholars with the authority to make new legal rulings) and *ḥakīms* (philosophers) of Persia during the fourteenth/twentieth century.
11. Arabic has, of course, always been the primary language of the Islamic sciences in Persia, as in the Arab world itself. But a relatively large number of works have also been composed in Persian in the fields of Quranic commentary, the-

ology, philosophy, and the like from the fourth Islamic century on. It is this type of writing that decreased in quantity during the Safavid period relative to the periods both before and after it. There is, for example, no major Quranic commentary in Persian at this time of the dimensions of *Kashf al-asrār* of Mībudī, and Mullā Ṣadrā wrote only one philosophical work in Persian compared with the many Persian writings of Suhrawardī, Afḍal al-Dīn Kāshānī, and Naṣīr al-Dīn Ṭūsī before him or many *ḥakīms* who succeeded him in the Qajar period.

12. Debates between Sunni and Shīʿite authorities became, in fact, much more pronounced than before as a result of the political identification of the first with the Ottomans and the second with the Safavids. See Elke Eberhard, *Osmanische Polemik gegen die Safawiden im 16. Jahrhundert nach arabischen Handschriften* (Freiburg: Schwarz, 1970).
13. *Rawḍah-khānī* deals in moving prose and poetry with the tragic events of early Shīʿite history, especially the martyrdom of the grandson of the Prophet, Ḥusayn ibn ʿAlī, and most of his entourage, most of whom also belonged to the "Household of the Prophet" (*ahl al-bayt*), by the army of the second Umayyad caliph, Yazīd ibn Muʿāwiyah. The commemoration of this event lies at the heart of Shīʿite religious ceremonies and is inseparable from Shīʿite piety.
14. For the meaning of various Shīʿite practices, see S. H. Nasr, "Islam in Persia, Yesterday and Today," in *Islam and the Plight of Modern Man*, pp. 101–21. As for Shīʿism in general, see ʿAllāmah Sayyid Muḥammad Ḥusayn Ṭabāṭabāʾī, *Shīʿite Islam,* trans. S. H. Nasr (Albany: State University of New York Press, 1975); Heintz Halm, *Shiʿism,* trans. J. Watson (Edinburgh: Edinburgh University Press, 1991); Maria M. Dakake, *The Charismatic Community: Shiʿite Identity in Early Islam* (Albany: State University of New York Press, 2007); Mohammad Ali Amir-Moezzi, *The Divine Guide in Early Shiʿism: The Sources of Esoterism in Islam*, trans. David Streight (Albany: State University of New York Press, 1994); and Said Amir Arjomand, *The Shadow of God and the Hidden Imām: Religion, Political Order and Societal Change in Shiʿite Iran from the Beginning to 1890* (Chicago: University of Chicago Press, 1984).
15. Concerning the *ʿulamāʾ* of this period, a valuable source is still Edward G. Browne, A *Literary History of Persia,* vol. 4 (Cambridge: Cambridge University Press, 1959), chap. 7, on *mujtahids* and *mullās.* As for firsthand sources of biographies of the *ʿulamāʾ* of this period, such works *as Rawḍāt al-jannāt, Majālis al-muʾminīn, Kashf al-ḥujub wa'l-asrār, Nujūm al-samāʾ,* and *Mustadrak al-wasāʾil* may be mentioned.

   As a result of current interest in Shīʿite political thought, many works have appeared during the past few years concerning the *ʿulamāʾ,* their relation to the present-day Iranian government, the religious policies of the Iranian state, and the question of the religious legitimacy of its political authority. There is, however, much difference of opinion concerning these politically crucial questions, not only among traditional and "revolutionary" Shīʿites, but also among Western scholars. See, for example, J. Eliash, "Some Misconceptions Regarding the Juridical Status of the Iranian *'ulamā'*," *International Journal of Middle East Studies* 10 (1979): 9–25; Hamid Enayat, *Modern Islamic Political Thought* (Kuala Lumpur: Islamic Book Trust, 2001); Said Amir Arjomand, *The Shadow of God and the Hidden Imām*; and Juan Cole, *The Ayatollahs and Democracy in Iraq* (Amsterdam: Amsterdam University Press, 2006). Norman Calder, in his "Accommodation and Revolution in Imami Shi'i Jurisprudence: Khumaynī and the Classical Tradition" (*Middle East Studies* 18, no. 1 1983.: 3–20), typifies the kind of scholarship that reads the present-day situation backwards into the classical period as far as the question of legitimacy is concerned, but fails to distinguish between traditional doctrines and the present-day "revivalist" or "fundamentalist" interpretations.

16. See *Tadhkirat al-mulūk,* part 1, ed. Muḥammad Dabīr-siyāqī (Tehran, 1332 [A.H. solar]), pp. 1–4.
17. Concerning this hierarchy of functions, see the perceptive description of the seventeenth-century traveler to Persia Engelbert Kaempfer, *Amoenitatem exoticarum, politico-physico medicarum fasciculi V, quibus continentur variae relationes, observationes & descriptiones rerum Persicarum ulterioris Asiae . . .* (Lemgoviae, 1712), pp. 98ff.; there is also a fine Persian translation of this work by Kaykāwūs Jahāndārī, *Safarnāma-yi Kimpfir* (Tehran: Khwārazmī Press, 1360 [1981]).
18. On the class of *mujtahids* and their importance in Shī'ite society, see Hamid Algar, *Religion and State in Iran 1785–1906* (Berkeley and Los Angeles: University of California Press, 1969); and Anne K. Lambton, "A Reconsideration of the Position of the *Marja' al-Taqlīd* and the Religious Institution," *Studia Islamica* 20 (1964): 115–35.
19. On the meaning of *marja'-i taqlīd,* see 'Allāmah Ṭabāṭabā'ī et al., *Marja'iyyat wa rūḥāniyyat* (Tehran: 1341 [A.H. solar]).
20. On Suhrawardī, see Henry Corbin, *En Islam iranien,* vol. 2 (Paris: Gallimard, 1971); S. H. Nasr, *Three Muslim Sages* (Delmar, NY: Caravan, 1976), chap. 2; S. H. Nasr, ed. Mehdi Aminrazavi, *The Islamic Intellectual Tradition in Persia* (London: Curzon, 1996), part 3, pp. 125ff; John Walbridge and Hossein Ziai, *Suhrawardī: The Philosophy of Illumination* (Provo, UT: Brigham Young University Press, 1999); Mehdi Aminrazavi, *Suhrawardi and the School of Illumination* (Richmond, Surrey, UK: Curzon, 1997); and John Walbridge, *The Wisdom of the Mystic East: Suhrawardī and Platonic Orientalism* (Albany: State University of New York Press, 2001). As for Ibn Turkah, see Henry Corbin, *En Islam iranien,* vol. 3 (Paris: Gallimard, 1972), pp. 233ff. On both figures see also S. H. Nasr, *Islamic Philosophy from Its Origin to the Present: Philosophy in the Land of Prophecy* (Albany: State Univ. of New York Press, 2006).
21. On the relation between *ḥikmat-i ilāhī* and Islamic theology, see "*al-Ḥikmat al-ilāhiyyah* and *Kalām,*" in S. H. Nasr, *Islamic Philosophy from Its Origin to the Present,* pp. 49ff.

22. For a bibliography of Mullā Ṣadrā, see my "*Ṣadr al-Dīn Shīrāzī*," in *The Islamic Intellectual Tradition in Persia,* chap. 2. See also Ibrahim Kalin, "An Annotated Bibliography of the Work of Mullā Ṣadrā with a Brief Account of His Life," *Islamic Studies* 42 (Spring 2003): 21–62.
23. The immense richness of the intellectual life of the Safavid period as far as *ḥikmat-i ilāhī* is concerned is beginning to reveal itself through current research and the appearance of printed editions of many important works of the period that were available only in manuscript form until recently. Of particular interest in this context is the anthology of the writings of the philosophers of this and later periods in Persia planned by Sayyid Jalāl al-Dīn Āshtiyānī and Henry Corbin, of whose seven projected volumes four have appeared. See S. J. Āshtiyānī and H. Corbin, *Anthologie des philosophes iraniens,* 4 vols. (Tehran: Département d'iranologie de l'Institut franco-iranien de recherche; Paris: Librarie d'Amérique et d'Orient Adrien Maisonneuve: 1972–78). Although as a result of the death of Corbin this major project was never completed, the volumes that did appear reveal the remarkably rich intellectual activity of the Safavid period. See also H. Corbin, *La Philosophie iranienne islamique aux XVIIe et XVIIIe siècles* (Paris: Buchet/Chastel, 1981). In the fifth volume of the *Anthology of Philosophy in Persia,* edited by S. H. Nasr and M. Aminrazavi (London: I. B. Taurus, forthcoming), we also deal with the major figures of the School of Isfahan.
24. See the introduction to *al-Tuḥfat al-'abbāsiyyah* (Shiraz, 1336 [A.H. solar]). There is now an English translation of this book by Mohammad Faghfoory. See *Tuḥfah-yi 'Abbāsī: The Golden Chain of Sufism in Shī'ite Islam* (New York: University Press of America, 2008).
25. It is remarkable that despite the very extensive activity of Sufism during the Safavid period, there are very few written sources to go by and one must rely to a large extent on oral traditions that have survived within the existing Sufi orders. On the Sufi orders in general, see S. H. Nasr, *The Garden of Truth* (San Francisco: HarperOne, 2007), appendix 1, pp. 163ff.
26. On the history of the Ni'matullāhī Order, see Javad Nurbakhsh, *Masters of the Path* (London: Khaniqah-i Nimatullahi Publications, 1993); and Nasrollah Pourjavady and Peter Wilson, *Kings of Love* (Tehran: Imperial Iranian Academy of Philosophy, 1978).
27. It is of great interest to note that Mullā Ṣadrā wrote his *Sih aṣl* (ed. S. H. Nasr [Tehran: Intishārāt-i Rawzanah, 1377, A.H. solar]), to refute exoteric authorities who did not understand esoterism and the *Kasr al-aṣnām al-jāhiliyyah* (ed. M. T. Daneshpazhuh [Tehran: Tehran University Press, 1340, A.H. solar]), to refute those who "pretended to be Sufis." A decayed form of Sufism or pseudo-Sufism often cut off from the *Sharī'ah* definitely existed at that time, which incited the rather violent and excessive reaction of exoteric authorities against organized Sufism at the end of the Safavid period.

28. See Morteza Sarraf, *Traités des compagnons-chevaliers, introduction analytique par H. Corbin* (Tehran-Paris: Andrien-Maisonneuve, 1973); also *Tuḥfat al-ikhwān,* ed. Muḥammad Dāmād (Tehran: Intishārāt-i ʿIlmī wa Farhangī, 1369 [A.H. solar]).
29. For a full treatment of the political dimension of the reality of Shīʿism today, see Vali Nasr, *The Shīʿa Revival* (New York: Norton, 2006).

Chapter 6: Islamic Spirituality

1. See especially S. H. Nasr, ed., *Islamic Spirituality Foundations* (New York: Crossroad, 1987), pp. xvi–xviii.
2. One needs to recall the saying of A. K. Coomaraswamy that God is meaning, echoing the language of Jalāl al-Dīn Rūmī, who referred to the world of the Spirit as *ʿālam-i maʿnā,* that is, the world of meaning. See S. H. Nasr, *Islamic Art and Spirituality,* pp. 128ff.
3. Traditional Christian spirituality has of course not only been associated with purely Christian elements; some Christian movements and persons were influenced historically by Islamic spirituality in the form of Sufism. They include groups as diverse as the *Fedeli d'amore* (*Fidèle d'amour*) and the Templars and figures as different as Dante, Raymond Lull, and Roger Bacon. Moreover, this contact was to continue into the Renaissance, especially in Spain, as one can see in the impact of Sufi symbolism upon St. Teresa of Avila and St. John of the Cross. See Luce López-Baralt, *Islam in Spanish Literature: From the Middle Ages to the Present,* trans. A. Hurley (Leiden: Brill, 1992); and *San Juan de la Cruz y el Islam* (Madrid: Hipérion, 1990).
4. See Jean Borella, "René Guénon and the Traditionalist School," in Antoine Faivre and Jacob Needleman, eds., *Modern Esoteric Spirituality,* vol. 21 of *World Spirituality: An Encyclopedic History of the Religious Quest* (New York: Crossroad, 1992), pp. 330–58; and S. H. Nasr, *Knowledge and the Sacred,* chap. 2.
5. See John Chryssavgis, *In the Heart of the Desert* (Bloomington, IN: World Wisdom, 2003); and James S. Cutsinger, ed., *Paths to the Heart* (Bloomington, IN: World Wisdom and Fons Vitae, 2002).
6. As examples, one needs only to point to Aelard Graham, *Zen Catholicism* (New York: Harcourt, Brace and World, 1963); and *Contemporary Christianity* (London: Mowbrays, 1975); Bede Griffith, *River of Compassion: A Christian Commentary on the Bhagavad-Gita* (New York: Continuum, 1995); and *Vedanta and Christian Faith* (Clearlake, CA: Dawn Horse Press, 1991). For a well documented general account, see Harry Oldmeadow, *Journeys East* (Bloomington, IN: World Wisdom, 2004).
7. The spiritual significance of the works of those like Massignon and Corbin cannot be separated from their intimate involvement with Islamic spiritual currents, and the masterly study of the Kabbala by Leo Schaya, *The Universal Meaning of the Kabbala* (trans. N. Pearson [London: Allen & Unwin, 1971]) was

abetted by his intimate knowledge of Islamic metaphysics. Numerous other examples of this kind could be cited in various European languages.

8. See S. H. Nasr, ed., *The Essential Frithjof Schuon* (Bloomington, IN: World Wisdom, 2005).
9. See especially Frithjof Schuon, *Esoterism as Principle and as Way,* trans. William Stoddart.
10. One of the most important of these scholars is Antoine Faivre, who, as already mentioned, is the co-editor of the volume in the series *World Spirituality: An Encyclopedic History of the Religious Quest* on modern esoteric spirituality as well as the editor of the journal *Aries,* whose issues bear witness to the works of the many scholars on both sides of the Atlantic devoted to the study of the Western esoteric tradition, including of course Hermeticism. See also Faivre, *Accès à l'ésotérisme occidentale* (Paris: Gallimard, 1986); and the more popular work of Pierre A. Riffard, *L'Ésotérisme* (Paris: Robert Laffont, 1990).
11. For such movements as well as eclecticism in North America, see Jacob Needleman, *The New Religions* (New York: Doubleday, 1970).
12. It is important to mention, along with the spread of the Sufi orders, the remarkable spread and increase in interest in Sufi metaphysics in both Europe and North America during the past few decades, as witnessed by the works of Michel Chodkiewicz, William Chittick, and others, and the large number of important doctrinal works translated into European languages, especially French. For an account of this activity, which has both an intellectual and a spiritual impact of much significance, see James Morris, "Ibn 'Arabī and His Interpreters," *Journal of the Muhyiddin Ibn 'Arabī Society* 106 (1986): 539–51, 733–76; 107 (1987): 101–19.
13. See René Guénon, *The Reign of Quantity and the Signs of the Times,* trans. Lord Northbourne (London: Luzac, 1953), chap. 38, "From Anti-tradition to Counter-tradition," pp. 313–20.
14. See, for example, Philip Sherrard, *Human Image: World Image* (Ipswich: Golgonooza Press, 1992); and *The Rape of Man and Nature* (Ipswich: Golgonooza Press, 1987). See also S. H. Nasr, *Man and Nature: The Spiritual Crisis in Modern Man* (Chicago: ABC International Group, 1997); and Stephen C. Rockefeller and John C. Elder, eds., *Spirit and Nature* (Boston: Beacon, 1992).
15. See Joseph Brown, *The Spiritual Legacy of the American Indians* (New York: Crossroad, 1982).
16. The various Sufi orders have been treated fairly extensively in *Islamic Spirituality II: Manifestations,* vol. 20 of *World Spirituality: An Encyclopedic History of the Religious Quest,* ed. S. H. Nasr (New York: Crossroad, 1991), where there is also to be found a bibliography of other major sources on this subject.
17. See S. H. Nasr, *The Islamic Intellectual Tradition in Persia*; also Henry Corbin, "The Force of Traditional Philosophy in Iran Today," *Studies in Comparative Religion,* Winter, 1968, pp. 12–26.
18. As an example one can cite the *Dīwān* of Shaykh Ḥabīb, the founder of the

Ḥabībiyyah branch of the Shādhiliyyah Order in Arabic and that of Javad Nurbakhsh in Persian. See Javad Nurbakhsh, *Divani Nurbakhsh: Sufi Poetry* (New York: Khaniqahi-Niʿmatullahi Publications, 1980).

19. One could cite as examples Asad ʿAlī (Assad Ali), an Arab, and Suhrāb Sipihrī (Sohrab Sepehri), a Persian. One could also mention notable examples from Turkey, Pakistan, Indonesia, and elsewhere. See Assad Ali, *Happiness Without Death,* trans. C. A. Helminski and I. Y. Shihabi (Putney, VT: Threshold, 1991); and Suhrāb Siphirī, *Les Pas de l'eau,* trans. with introduction by Darius Shayegan (Paris: Orphée/La Difference, 1991). A number of modern Arab poets such as Adonis have also shown much interest in the Sufi poetry of Ibn ʿArabī.
20. See Titus Burckhardt, *The Art of Islam,* and S. H. Nasr, *Islamic Art and Spirituality.*
21. On Shīʿism, its doctrines, and its spirituality, see ʿAllāmah Ṭabāṭabāʾī, *Shiʿite Islam,* trans. and ed. S. H. Nasr, esp. pp. 215ff.; and S. H. Nasr, H. Dabashi, and S. V. R. Nasr, eds., *Shiʿism: Doctrines, Thought and Spirituality* (Albany: State University of New York Press, 1988), pp. 244ff. For the spiritual significance of the mourning of Imam Ḥusayn, see Mahmud Ayoub, *Redemptive Suffering in Islam: A Study of the Devotional Aspects of ʿAshura in Twelver Shiʿism* (The Hague: Monton, 1978).
22. See William Chittick, *A Shiʿite Anthology* (Albany: State University of New York Press, 1981); and his translation of the fourth Imam's *The Psalm of Islam* (London: Muhammadi Trust, 1988). The esoteric character of Shīʿism and the particular flavor of its spirituality, including the intellectual dimension, has been treated amply by Henry Corbin in his numerous works on the subject. See especially his *En Islam iranien,* vol. 1.
23. On the Twelfth Imam and his spiritual and eschatological significance, see Henry Corbin, *En Islam iranien,* vol. 4, bk. 6, pp. 301ff.; and J. M. Hussain, *The Occultation of the Twelfth Imam* (London: Muhammadi Trust, 1982).
24. The Quran states concerning "the Companions of the Right Hand," understood traditionally to mean those who hold firm to the faith, "Many from those of old; and a few from those of later times" (Quran LVI: 13–14).
25. For this complicated doctrine, see Ṭabāṭabāʾī, *Shīʿite Islam,* pp. 210–11; Abdulaziz Sachedina, *Islamic Messianism: The Idea of the Mahdī in Twelver Shiʿism* (Albany: State University of New York Press, 1981), esp. pp. 78ff.; and Hussain, *The Occultation of the Twelfth Imam*, pp. 133ff.
26. Ḥājjī Mullā Hādī Sabziwārī, the thirteenth/nineteenth-century Persian metaphysician and sage, refers to eschatology as *fardā-shināsī,* literally the "knowledge of tomorrow," referring to the only tomorrow that really matters.
27. The image is developed profoundly and poetically by Martin Lings in his *The Eleventh Hour* (Cambridge: Quinta Essentia, 1987).
28. See Leo Schaya, "La Mission d' Élie," *Sophia Perennis* 3, no. 1 (Spring 1977): 16–28; also as "The Eliatic Function," *Studies in Comparative Religion* (Winter–Spring 1979): 31–40. There are also corresponding doctrines in Hinduism and other traditions.

29. A *ḥadīth* of the Prophet asserts, "The earth shall never be empty of a 'proof of God' [*ḥujjat Allāh*]."

Chapter 7: "Development" in the Contemporary Islamic World

1. It should be remembered that one of the most influential works written in the West at the beginning of the rise of awareness of the environmental crisis and calling for a reexamination of the idea of indefinite material development is Donella H. Meadows et al., *The Limits to Growth: A Report for the Club of Rome's Project on the Predicament of Mankind* (New York: Signet, 1974).

Chapter 8: Islamic Education, Philosophy, and Science

1. In the field of the Islamic sciences, despite thousands of articles and books in different languages, so many works, most still in manuscript form, remain to be studied and analyzed that practically every year there are major new discoveries. Although no exhaustive treatment of present-day knowledge of the Islamic sciences is available, as one would find for Western science or even Chinese science (thanks to the pioneering work of Joseph Needham and his collaborators), there are several works that provide a panoramic view of the field. As far as general works on the Islamic sciences are concerned, see Aldo Mieli, *La Science arabe et son rôle dans l'évolution scientifique mondiale* (Leiden: Brill, 1966); Manfred Ullmann, *Die Natur- und Geheimwissenschaften im Islam* (Leiden: Brill, 1972); Juan Vernet Ginés, *La Ciencia en al-Andalus* (Seville: Editoriales Unidas, 1976); Francis E. Peters, *Allah's Commonwealth* (New York: Simon and Schuster, 1973); José M. Millás Vallicrosa, *Estudios sobre historia de la ciencia española* (Madrid: Consejo Superior de Investigaciones Cientificas, 1987); Willy Hartner, *Oriens-Occidens* (Hildesheim: Olms, 1970); S. H. Nasr, *Science and Civilization in Islam;* and *Islamic Science: An Illustrated Study.*

   To these older and more "classical" works must be added such more recent writings as Ahmad Y. al-Hassan et al., eds., *The Different Aspects of Islamic Culture,* vol. 4, pts. 1–2, *Science and Technology in Islam* (Paris: UNESCO, 2001); Howard Turner, *Science in Medieval Islam* (Austin: University of Texas Press, 1997); Ahmed Djebbar, *Une Histoire de la science arabe* (Paris: Editions du Seuil, 2001); Roshdi Rashed, ed., *Encyclopedia of Arab Science,* 3 vols. (London: Routledge, 1996); and George Saliba, *Islamic Science and the Making of the European Renaissance* (Cambridge, MA: M.I.T. Press, 2007).

   As for works in particular fields, see Edward G. Browne, *Arabian Medicine* (Cambridge: Cambridge University Press, 1921); Donald E. H. Campbell, *Arabian Medicine and Its Influence on the Middle Ages,* 2 vols. (New York: ANS, 1973); Cyril Elgood, *A Medical History of Persia and the Eastern Caliphate* (Cambridge: Cambridge University Press, 1951); Marshall Clagett, *The Science of Mechanics in the Middle Ages* (Madison: University of Wisconsin Press, 1964);

Edward S. Kennedy, *A Survey of Islamic Astronomical Tables* (Philadelphia: American Philosophical Society, 1956); and *Astronomy and Astrology in the Medieval Islamic World* (Brookfield, VT: Ashgate, 1998); Carl A. Nallino, *Raccolta di scritti editi e inediti,* vol. 5 (Rome: Istituto per l'Oriente, 1948); David Pingree, *The Thousands of Abū Ma'shar* (London: Warburg Institute, 1968); Aydin M. Sayili, *The Observatory in Islam* (Ankara: Türk Tarih Kurumu Basimevi, 1960); Heinrich Suter, *Die Mathematiker und Astronomen der Araber und ihrer Werke* (Amsterdam: APA, Oriental Press, 1981); A. P. Juschkewitsch, *Geschichte der Mathematik im Mittelalter* (Basel: Pfalz, 1964); A. S. Saidan, *The Arithmetic of Al-Uqlīdisī* (Boston: Reidel, 1976); 'Alī Daffā', *The Muslim Contribution to Mathematics* (Atlantic Highlands, NJ: Humanities Press, 1977); David A. King, *Islamic Mathematical Astronomy* (Aldershot: Variorum, 1993); *World Maps for Finding the Direction and Distance of Mecca* (Leiden: Brill, 1999); Roshdi Rashed (Rāshid), *The Development of Arabic Mathematics,* trans. A. F. W. Armstrong (Boston: Kluwer Academic, 1994); *Geometry and Dioptrics in Classical Islam* (London: al-Furqān Islamic Heritage Foundation, 2005); and *Histoire des science arabes* (Paris: Editions du Seuil, 1997); Paul Kraus, *Jābir ibn Ḥayyān*, 2 vols. (Cairo, 1942–43); Julius Ruska, *Tabula Smaragdina* (Heidelberg, 1926); Saleh Beshara Omar, *Ibn al-Haytham's Optics* (Minneapolis: Bibliotheca Islamica, 1977); and Abd al-Hamid Sabra, *The Optics of Ibn Haytham*, 2 vols. (London: Warburg Institute, 1989).

Such general works on the history of science as George Sarton, *An Introduction to the History of Science,* 3 vols. (Baltimore: Carnegie Institution, 1927–48); and Charles Gillespie, ed., *Dictionary of Scientific Biography,* as well as studies on Arabic and Persian manuscripts, especially Fuad Sezgin, *Geschichte der arabischen Schrifttums* (Leiden: Brill, 1970), likewise contain a wealth of information on the Islamic sciences. The pioneering work of Sarton still remains of great value for general students of the subject and has in fact never been replaced, despite so much later research, by a more up-to-date work of the same scope.

As for education, there is even less available of a systematic nature that would consider the philosophy of education, its history, content of syllabi, etc., for the whole of the Islamic world. Among works that are available, see, besides the already cited works, Abd al-Latif Tibawi, *Islamic Education: Its Traditions and Modernization into the Arab National Systems* (London: Luzac, 1972); *Arabic and Islamic Garland* (London: Islamic Cultural Centre, 1977); Bayard Dodge, *Muslim Education in Medieval Times* (Washington, DC: Middle East Institute, 1962); and Burhān al-Dīn al-Zarnūjī, *Ta'līm al-muta'allim,* trans. Gustav E. von Grunebaum and Theodora M. Abel (Chicago: Starlatch, 2003). See also the series on Muslim education edited by Syed Ali Ashraf and printed in the United Kingdom, of which several volumes appeared from 1978 on.

For a more complete bibliography containing works in European languages on both science and education, see S. H. Nasr, *An Annotated Bibliography of Islamic Science* (Tehran: Cultural Studies and Research Institute, 1975–91), of which only three of seven projected volumes have been published so far.

2. The many names of the Quran, like those of the Prophet, contain in themselves a science that, if studied carefully, reveals the many facets of that reality to which the names refer.
3. See Franz Rosenthal, *Knowledge Triumphant: The Concept of Knowledge in Medieval Islam* (Leiden: Brill, 1970), where this veritable celebration of knowledge in Islam is recorded in detail.
4. See S. H. Nasr, *Knowledge and the Sacred*, where this theme has been treated extensively on a global scale and not limited to the case of the Islamic tradition.
5. See Frithjof Schuon, *From the Divine to the Human,* trans. G. Polit and D. Lambert (Bloomington, IN: World Wisdom, 1982); and *Logic and Transcendence,* trans. Peter Townsend (London: Perennial Books, 1984).
6. To this day education in official circles in most of the Arab world is called *al-ta'līm wa'l-tarbiyah,* while in Persia the Persian counterpart of this term, namely, *āmūzish wa parwarish*, continues to be used as the name for the ministry of education itself.
7. چو دزدی با چراغ آید گزیده تر برد کالا
8. The importance of this period in introducing the child to oral traditions existing within Islamic society is immense. Much of this oral tradition serves later in life as basis for the highest forms of metaphysical knowledge for those qualified to master such knowledge.
9. Before modern times this was true of most Islamic languages, the alphabets of which were drawn either from Arabic directly or from Persian, whose own alphabet is the same as that of Arabic, except for the addition of four letters.
10. Several miniatures of student scenes in famous medieval Islamic universities show female students, and there are also references to women in institutions of learning in the literature.
11. As mentioned by Ivan Illich in his many studies on education, including *De-Schooling Society* (New York: Penguin, 1976), which contains many ideas similar to the traditional Islamic philosophy of education. In traditional society a book was not confined only to the reader, but usually reached many people because, in most cases, books were read aloud while many listened. This practice is still to be seen in certain parts of the Islamic world, such as Persia, where many people who have never had a formal education know not only verses of the Quran, but also poems from Firdawsī's *Shāh-nāmah* ("The Book of Kings") or Sa'dī's *Gulistān* ("The Rose Garden") as a result of listening to traditional storytellers, who usually read and recite stories and poems from the greatest literary masterpieces of the language.
12. It has always been known that such academic terms as "chair" in English and *licence* in French are direct translations of Arabic terms (*al-kursī* and *ijāzah,* respectively), but in earlier works on the medieval European universities, such as the classical opus of Hastings Rashdall, *The Universities of Europe in the Middle*

Ages (London: Oxford University Press, 1969), this influence has usually been played down. The full import of this influence is traced with great care and scholarship by George Makdisi in his *The Rise of the Colleges: Institutions of Learning in Islam and the West* (Edinburgh: Edinburgh University Press, 1981).

13. See Bayard Dodge, *Al-Azhar: A Millennium of Muslim Learning* (Washington, DC: Middle East Institute, 1961), which provides a detailed study of the history and significance of this venerable institution.
14. On this important but little studied *madrasah,* see Fadil Jamali, "The Theological Colleges of Najaf," *Muslim World* 50 (1960): 15–22.
15. See Titus Burckhardt, "The Role of Fine Arts in Muslim Education," in S. H. Nasr, ed., *Philosophy, Literature and Fine Arts* (Sevenoaks, Kent: Hodder and Stoughton, 1982), pp. 41–48.
16. On this division, see Nasr, *Science and Civilization in Islam,* pp. 59–64. On the classafication of the sciences in Islam, see Osman Bakar, *Classafication of Knowledge in Islam* (Kuala Lumpur: Institute for Policy Research, 1992).
17. To this day, in fact, no *madrasah* in the Islamic world has been resuscitated successfully as far as Islamic responses to encounters with modern forms and modes of knowledge are concerned, despite many different types of experiments carried out in Morocco, Tunisia, Egypt, India, Iran, and other places. The traditional and modern educational systems became contending and competing forces in most of the Islamic world from the thirteenth/nineteenth century on and remain so to a large extent to this day.
18. See Abū Bakr al-Akhawaynī al-Bukhārī, *Hidāyat al-muta'allimīn fi'l-ṭibb,* ed. Jalāl Matīnī (Mashhad: Mashhad University Press, 1965), which concerns medical education, and the origin of whose ideas can be traced to Rāzī and the hospital educational system of the fourth/tenth century.
19. On the observatory as a scientific and educational institution, see the classical work of A. Sayili, *The Observatory in Islam* (New York: Arno Press, 1981).
20. See Nasr, *Knowledge and the Sacred,* chap. 4.
21. On Sufi training of the soul, see Javad Nurbakhsh, *What the Sufis Say* (New York: Khaniqahi-Nimatullahi Publications, 1980), pt. 1.
22. The arts and the crafts are the same in Islam and no distinction of a fundamental nature can be made in the context of Islamic civilization between what are called the major and minor or fine and industrial arts in the West.
23. This could in fact be said of all traditional art, but is especially evident in the mathematical clarity and harmony of Islamic art. See Ananda K. Coomaraswamy, *Christian and Oriental Philosophy of Art* (New York: Dover, 1956); and Titus Burckhardt, *The Art of Islam.* See also Nasr, *Knowledge and the Sacred,* chap. 8; and *Islamic Art and Spirituality.*
24. The reason for the spread of this learning eastward is itself a fascinating chapter of cultural history related to the separation of the Middle Eastern Christian churches from Constantinople. See the still valuable works of O. De Lacy O'Leary, *How Greek Science Passed to the Arabs* (London: Routledge and Kegan

Paul, 1949); and Max Meyerhof, *Von Alexandrien nach Baghdad* (Berlin: Walter de Gruyler, 1930).

25. On the significance of the school of Jundishapur built by the Sassanid king Shāpūr I on the model of the school of Antioch, see Mohammad Mohammadi, "The University of Jundishapur," *Regional Cultural Institute* (Tehran) 2 (1969): 152–66.
26. These Sabaeans are not to be confused with the present-day Sabaeans of Iraq and southern Iran. See J. Pedersen, "The Sabians," in *A Volume of Oriental Studies Presented to E. G. Browne,* ed. Thomas W. Arnold and Reynold A. Nicholson (Cambridge: Cambridge University Press, 1922), pp. 383–91; and C. Buck, "The Identity of the Ṣābi'ūn; An Historical Quest," *Muslim World* 74, nos. 3–4 (July–October 1984): 172–86, where the wide legal meaning of *Ṣābi'ūn* is emphasized. Buck writes: "Exactly because it was imprecise, the word *Ṣābi'ūn* functioned as a term of great legal importance by contributing to an attitude of toleration toward minority religions under Muslim rule" (p. 186).
27. On the "Islamic nature" of the Islamic sciences, see S. H. Nasr, *Science and Civilization in Islam,* introduction; also *An Introduction to Islamic Cosmological Doctrines* (Albany: State University of New York Press, 1993), prolegomena.
28. On Greek works in Arabic, see Moritz Steinschneider, *Die arabischen Übersetzungen aus dem Griechischen* (Graz: Akademische Druck, 1960); Franz Rosenthal, *The Classical Heritage in Islam,* trans. Émile and Jenny Marmonstein (London: Routledge and Kegan Paul, 1975); and Abd al-Rahman Badawi, *La Transmission de la philosophie grecque au monde arabe* (Paris: Vrin, 1987). See also Sezgin, *Geschichte,* where numerous references are made to Arabic translations of Greek texts.
29. It must be remembered that when the works of the Greek authorities, such as Aristotle, were being translated into Arabic, there was still a living oral tradition known to the translators; they made use of this "unwritten text" as well as the written one in their translations. Arabic translations of Greek texts, especially in philosophy, are therefore in a sense closer to the original than those made in modern European languages directly from the Greek but without the continuity of worldview and an oral tradition accompanying the written word. In any case, far from being less perfect renderings of the Greek originals, Arabic texts are precious documents providing knowledge of antiquity independent of that type of interpretation that in the modern world is colored by Renaissance humanism and seventeenth-century rationalism.
30. See S H. Nasr, "The Meaning and Role of Philosophy in Islam," in *Islamic Philosophy from Its Origin to the Present*, chap. 2, pp. 37ff.
31. On Ibn Sīnā and the philosopher-scientists in Islam, see S. H. Nasr, *Three Muslim Sages.*
32. Most Western works on Islamic philosophy include only this school and even then limit their discussions to the period up to and including Ibn Rushd, as if Islamic philosophy had ceased to exist after him. The histories of Islamic philosophy that do justice to the much richer intellectual life of Islam are Mian

Mohammad Sharif, ed., *A History of Muslim Philosophy,* 2 vols. (Wiesbaden: Otto Harrasowitz, 1963–66); and Henry Corbin (with the collaboration of S. H. Nasr and Osman Yahya), *Histoire de la philosophie islamique,* vol. 1 (Paris, 1964). This volume covers only the period up to the death of Ibn Rushd, but Corbin completed the later periods of this history in "Histoire de la philosophie," in *Encyclopédie de la Pléiade* (Paris: Gallimard, 1974). See also the other major studies of Corbin, such as *En Islam iranien*, 4 vols. (Paris: Gallimard, 1971–72); and *La Philosophie iranienne islamique.* Corbin's attempt to turn the attention of the Western world toward the integral tradition of Islamic philosophy has been followed by S. H. Nasr, T. Izutsu, M. Mohaghegh, and several other scholars. See S. H. Nasr and Oliver Leaman, eds., *History of Islamic Philosophy,* 2 vols. (London: Routledge, 1996); and Nasr, *Islamic Philosophy from Its Origin to the Present*. See also Majid Fakhry, *A History of Islamic Philosophy* (New York: Columbia University Press, 2004).

An extensive bibliography on Ibn Sīnā and general works on Islamic philosophy is found in Nasr, *An Introduction to Islamic Cosmological Doctrines*. See also the exhaustive works of Hans Daiber, especially his *Bibliography of Islamic Philosophy* (Leiden: Brill, 1999); and its supplement (Leiden: Brill, 2007).

33. The history of this school, like much of Islamic philosophy, remains full of unknown elements, and many texts remain to be studied and analyzed. For a summary of what is known of the history of this school, see Corbin, "Histoire de la philosophie," pp. 118–51. See also S. H. Nasr and Mehdi Aminrazavi, eds., *An Anthology of Philosophy in Persia,* vol. 2 (London: I.B. Tauris, 2008).

34. On Suhrawardī and the School of ILlumination, see Nasr, *Three Muslim Sages,* chap. 2; Corbin, *En Islam iranien*, vol. 2; and *Le Livre de la sagesse orientale* (Paris: Verdier, 1986); Hossein Ziai, *Knowledge and Illumination* (Atlanta: Scholars Press, 1990); Mehdi Aminrazavi, *Suhrawardī and the School of Illumination*; and Bilal Kuşpinar, *Ismāʿīl Anḳaravī on the Illuminative Philosophy* (Kuala Lumpur: International Institute of Islamic Thought and Civilization, 1996).

35. On these figures see Corbin, *En Islam iranien,* vol. 4; S. H. Nasr, *The Islamic Intellectual Tradition in Persia*; and *Ṣadr al-Dīn Shīrāzī and His Transcendent Theosophy* (Tehran: Institute for Humanities and Cultural Studies, 1997).

36. See S. H. Nasr, "The Influence of Traditional Islamic Thought Upon Contemporary Muslim Intellectual Life," in Raymond Klibansky, ed., *Contemporary Philosophy: A Survey*, (Florence: La Nuova Italia, 1968), pp. 578–83.

37. For a discussion in which a leading Catholic historian of Western philosophy looks upon the significance of this problem for Islamic thought in comparison with both Eastern traditions and Western thought, see Frederick Copleston, *Religion and the One* (New York: Crossroad, 1982), chap. 5.

38. For a general account of the contribution of Muslims to mathematics and astronomy, see, in addition to the works cited in n. 1, E.S. Kennedy, "The Arab Heritage in the Exact Sciences," *al-Abḥāth* 23 (1970): 327–44; and A. I.

Sabra, "The Scientific Enterprise," in Bernard Lewis, ed., *The World of Islam* (London: Thames and Hudson, 1976), pp. 181–200.

39. This model has been called the "Ṭūsī couple" by its modern discoverer, E. S. Kennedy. See his "Late Medieval Planetary Theory," *Isis* 57, pt. 3 (1966); 365–78.
40. On Islamic atomism, see the still valuable work of Shlomo Pines, *Beiträge zur islamischen Atomenlehre* (Berlin: A. Heine, 1936). See also Majid Fakhry, *Islamic Occasionalism: Its Critique by Averroes and Aquinas* (London: Taylor and Francis, 2008).
41. See Shlomo Pines, *Nouvelles études sur Awḥad al-Zamān Abū'l Barakāt al-Baghdādī* (Paris: Durlacher, 1955); and "What Was Original in Arabic Science?" in Alistair C. Crombie, ed., *Scientific Change* (London: Heinemann, 1963), pp. 181–205. See also Donald R. Hill, *The Book of Ingenious Devices by the Banū (Sons of) Mūsā bin Shākir* (Boston: Reidel, 1979), for an analysis of a major text on mechanics that, like al-Jazarī's better-known work (Al-Jazarī, *The Book of Knowledge of Ingenious Mechanical Devices,* trans. Donald R. Hill [Boston: Reidel, 1974]), touches upon certain problems of physics, although the discipline of mechanics (*'ilm al-ḥiyal*) belongs to a different category in the Islamic classafication of the sciences than physics.
42. For a more general account see Donald Hill, *Islamic Science and Engineering* (Edinburgh: Edinburgh University Press, 1993). On al-Jazarī, see his *Compendium on the Theory and Practice of the Mechanical Arts,* ed. Fuat Sezgin (Frankfurt-am-Main: Institute for the History of Arabic-Islamic Science at the Johann Wolfgang Goethe University, 2002); and *The Book of Knowledge of Ingenious Mechanical Devices.*
43. This work is probably the most influential single book in the global history of medicine.
44. For a general survey of Islamic medicine and pharmacology, see Manfred Ullmann, *Islamic Medicine* (Edinburgh: Edinburgh University Press, 1978).
45. For a historical account of the "occult sciences," see Manfred Ullmann, *Die Natur- und Geheimwissenschaften im Islam.* But the significance of these sciences, especially alchemy, cannot be discovered save in light of the metaphysical and cosmological principles of which alchemy is a particular application. See Titus Burckhardt, *Alchemy, Science of the Cosmos, Science of the Soul,* trans. W. Stoddart (Louisville, KY: Fons Vitae, 1997); Elémire Zolla, *Le meraviglie della natura: Introduzione all'alchimia* (Milan: Bompiani, 1975); and Mircea Eliade, *The Forge and the Crucible* (Chicago: University of Chicago Press, 1978).
46. See S. H. Nasr, "From the Alchemy of Jābir to the Chemistry of Rāzī," in *Islamic Life and Thought* (Albany: State University of New York Press, 1981), pp. 120–23.
47. In fact, no traditional civilization has ever sacrificed its vision of the Immutable for an ever changing and accumulative science of nature, as one sees today, at the expense of forgetting that *scientia sacra* that is rooted in the very substance of our intelligence.

Chapter 9: Islamic Philosophers' Views on Education

1. Trans. D. Gutas, in "Paul the Persian on the Classafication of the Parts of Aristotle's Philosophy: A Milestone between Alexandria and Baghdad," *Der Islam* 60 no. 2 (1983): 232.
2. As already mentioned, it is remarkable how the so-called fundamentalists share with the Islamic modernists their complete espousal of modern science and technology, indifference to Islamic sacred art, hatred of traditional wisdom and the peace and contemplation associated with the inner life, and many other aspects of traditional Islam. In many ways, Islamic "fundamentalism" and modernism are the two sides of the same coin and share much in common on many issues, including a stand against traditional Islam.
3. Those who claim otherwise are influenced either by Western interpretations of Islamic philosophy that see it merely as Greek thought masquerading in Arabic dress or by the criticism of those Islamic theological and juridical schools of thought that have traditionally opposed *falsafah*. On the Islamic character of Islamic philosophy, see Sayyed Muḥammad Ḥusayn Ṭabāṭabā'ī, *Uṣūl-i falsafah wa rawish-i ri'ālizm* (Qom: Ṣadrā Press, 1370 [A.H. solar]), vol. 1; and the already cited works of Corbin and myself on Islamic philosophy.
4. On the Islamic "philosopher-scientists," see S. H. Nasr, *Three Muslim Sages,* chap. 1.
5. This is the method I have developed in the study of Islamic philosophy, in Nasr, *Three Muslim Sages,* and cosmology, in S. H. Nasr, *An Introduction to Islamic Cosmological Doctrines.*
6. On the identity of the Ikhwān, see Nasr, *Introduction to Islamic Cosmological Doctrines,* pp. 25ff.; and Ian R. Netton, *Muslim Neoplatonists* (London: Routledge Curzon, 2002), chap. 1, where views of various scholars and the literature of the recent past on the subject are discussed.
7. See, for example, *Rasā'il* (Cairo: 'Arabiyyah Press, 1928), vol. 1, pp. 21, 347; vol. 2, pp. 129, 291, 348, 364, 380; vol. 3, p. 385.
8. See Louis Gardet, "Notions et principes de l'education dans la pensée arabo-musulmane," *La Revue des études islamique* 44 (1976): 1–13; also A. L. Tibawi, "Some Educational Terms in *Rasā'il* Ikhwān aṣ-Ṣafā'," *Islamic Quarterly* 5 (1959): 55–60.
9.

جوهَر روحانيّة سَماويّة نورانية حيّة عَلاّمة بالقوّة فعّالة بِالطبع.

Rasā'il, vol. 1 (Beirut: Dār Bayrūt, 1957), p. 260.

10.

" وَ نصف ايضا كيفية إخراج ما في قوة النفس مِن العلوم الى الفِعل الذي هوَ الفرَض الاقصى في التعاليم، و هُوَ إصلاح جَواهر النفس و تهذيب اخلاقها و تنميها و تَكميلها للبقاً في دار الآخرة التى هِيَ دار الحَيوان."

Rasī'il, vol. 1, p. 258.

11. See Tibawi, "Some Educational Terms in *Rasā'il* Ikhwān aṣ-Ṣafā'," p. 60.
12. On the Ismā'īlī understanding of these terms, see Henry Corbin, *Trilogie ismaélienne* (Tehran-Paris: Andrien-Maisonneuve, 1961), p. 138.
13. On Ibn Sīnā, see Nasr, *Three Muslim Sages,* chap. 1; Nasr, *An Introduction to Islamic Cosmological Doctrines,* pp. 177ff. (with an extensive bibliography on him at the end); Soheil Afnan, *Avicenna: His Life and Works* (Westport, CT: Greenwood, 1980); William E. Gohlman, *The Life of Ibn Sīnā* (Albany: State University of New York Press, 1974); Dimitri Gutas, *Avicenna and the Aristotelian Tradition* (Leiden: Brill, 1988); Jean R. Michot, *La Destinée de l'homme selon Avicenne* (Lovanii: Aedibus Peeters, 1986); Shams C. Inati, *Ibn Sīnā and Mysticism* (London: Kegan Paul International, 1996); and Corbin, *Avicenna and the Visionary Recital,* trans. Willard Trask (Irving, TX: Spring, 1980).
14. Ibn Sīnā writes: "Equality of states and proximity of measures concerning human beings lead to corruption and finally cause their annihilation and destruction," in Muḥammad Najmī Zanjānī, trans., *Ibn Sīnā wa tadbīr-i manzil* (Tehran: Majma'-i Nāshir-i Kitāb, 1319 [A.H. solar]), p. 6.
15. Ibn Sīnā, *A Treatise on the Canon of Medicine,* trans. O. Cameron Gruner (London: Luzac, 1930), p. 379.
16. Ibn Sīnā, *Treatise on the Canon of Medicine,* p. 379.
17. See Ibn Sīnā, *Fī tadbīr al-rajul li-manzilahi* (Tunisia: Nashr Mīdīyākūm, 1995).
18. For a summary of these views, see 'Īsā Ṣadīq, "Naẓariyyāt-i Ibn-i Sīnā dar bāb-i ta'līm wa tarbiyat," *Jashn-nāma-yi Ibn Sīnā,* vol. 2 (Tehran: Anjoman-i Āthār-i Millī, 1334 (A.H. solar)), pp. 149–58.
19. See *Avicenna's De Anima, Being the Psychological Part of Kitāb al-Shifā',* ed. Fazlur Rahman (London: Oxford University Press, 1959). See also Ibn Sīnā, *Psychologie v Jehe dile aš-Šifā',* 2 vols., ed. and trans. J. Bakoš (Prague: Ceskoslovenské Akademie, 1956).
20. See, for example, Herbert A. Davidson, "Alfarabi and Avicenna on the Active Intellect," *Viator* 3 (1972): 109–178; *Alfarabi, Avicenna and Averroes on Intellect* (New York: Oxford University Press, 1992); and N. Ushida, *Étude comparative de la psychologie d'Aristote, d'Avicenne et de St. Thomas d'Aquin* (Tokyo: Keio Institute of Cultural and Linguistic Studies, 1968), esp. chap. 5.
21. The category of "mind" as currently understood belongs to modern philosophy and is alien to Ibn Sīnā's worldview. The term *dhihn,* usually translated as "mind," is found in classical Islamic philosophical texts, but does not have the same meaning as the term "mind" as understood in Western philosophy since Descartes.
22. On the "Oriental Philosophy" of Ibn Sīnā, see Corbin, *Avicenna and the Visionary Recital,* trans. Willard Trask (Irving, TX: Spring, 1980), pp. 36ff; and Nasr, *Introduction to Islamic Cosmological Doctrines,* pp. 185ff.
23. One day the whole "Oriental Philosophy" and the cycle of "visionary recitals" should be studied in detail in light of Ibn Sīnā's philosophy of education.

24. On Suhrawardī, see Corbin, *En Islam iranien,* vol. 2; Nasr, *Three Muslim Sages,* chap. 2; and S. H. Nasr, "Shilhāb al-Dīn Suhrawardī," in *The Islamic Intellectual Tradition in Persia,* pp. 125ff.
25. Although the term *ṭālib* is used with a special meaning in *ishrāqī* philosophy or wisdom (*ḥikmah*), the term *ṭalabah,* closely related to it, has acquired in Arabic, Persian, and Urdu the general meaning of "student" (especially of the religious sciences). The term Taliban, now made famous through events in Afghanistan and Pakistan, comes from the same word and is simply the Persian plural of *ṭālib,* understood not in its *ishrāqī* sense, but as "student."
26. See Suhrawardī, *Ḥikmat al-ishrāq,* in H. Corbin, ed., *Oeuvres philosophiques et mystiques,* vol. 2 (Tehran: Institut d'Études et des Recherches Culturelles, 2001), pp. 10–12.
27. See Corbin, ed., *Oeuvres philosophiques et mystiques,* vol. 2, pp. 274–97; and Wheeler M. Thackston, trans., *The Mystical and Visionary Treatises of . . . Suhrawardī* (London: Octagon, 1982), pp. 100–108.
28. See Suhrawardī, in S. H. Nasr, ed., *Oeuvres philosophiques et mystiques,* vol. 3 (Tehran: Institut d'Études et des Recherches Culturelles, 2001), pp. 241–50; and Thackston, *Mystical and Visionary Treatises,* pp. 44–50.
29. Thackston, *Mystical and Visionary Treatises,* pp. 62–63.
30. As already mentioned, over the past few decades a fairly extensive literature has grown around the subject of Mullā Ṣadrā, and numerous studies have been devoted to him, especially by Persian scholars, but there does not exist as yet any independent work concerned with his educational philosophy. On Mullā Ṣadrā, see note 23 of chapter 5 and also James Morris, trans., *The Wisdom of the Throne: An Introduction to the Philosophy of Mullā Ṣadrī* (Princeton, NJ: Princeton University Press, 1981); Corbin, *En Islam iranien,* vol. 4 (Paris: Gallimard, 1972), pp. 54–122; Corbin, *La Philosophie iranienne islamique aux XVIIe et XVIIIe siècles* (Paris: Buchet/Chastel, 1981), pp. 49–83; Mullā Ṣadrā, *Spiritual Psychology: The Fourth Intellectual Journey in Transcendent Philosophy,* vols. 8 and 9 of the *Asfār,* trans. and annotated by Latimah-Parvin Peerwani (London: ICAS Press, 2008); and Mullā Ṣadrā, *The Elixir of the Gnostics,* trans. William C. Chittick (Provo, UT: Brigham Young University Press, 2003).
31. See Nasr, *Ṣadr al-Dīn Shīrāzī and His Transcendent Theosophy,* chap. 3; and Jawād Muṣliḥ, *'Ilm al-nafs yā rawānshināsī-yi Ṣadr al-Muta'allihīn* (Tehran: Tehran University Press, 1372 [1972]).
32. See Mullā Ṣadrā, *Tafsīr-i āya-yi nūr,* ed. Muḥammad Khājawī (Tehran, 1377 [1977]).
33. See Mullā Ṣadrā, *Asrār al-āyāt,* ed. Muḥammad Khājawī (Tehran: A.H. Solar, Iranian Academy of Philosophy, 1981), *al-mashhad al-thānā,* esp. pp. 126ff.
34. Mullā Ṣadrā explains the relation between knowing and being through two principles, the unity of the knower and the known (*ittiḥād al-'āqil wa'l-ma'qūl*) and transubstantial motion (*al-ḥarakat al-jawhariyyah*). On these principles, see S. H. Nasr, "Ṣadr al-Dīn Shīrāzī," in *The Islamic Intellectual Tradition in Persia,*

pp. 948ff.; and Ibrahim Kalin, *Knowledge in Late Islamic Philosophy: Mullā Ṣadrā on Existence, Intellect, and Intuition* (New York: Oxford University Press, 2010).

35. See S. H. Nasr, *Knowledge and the Sacred,* pp. 244–45.
36. *Qāb al-qawsayn.* See the Quran, LIII: 9.
37. See Mullā Ṣadrā, *al-Mabda' wa'l-ma'ād,* trans. Aḥmad Ardakānī, ed. 'Abd Allāh Nūrānī (Tehran: Markaz-i Nashr-i Dānishgāhī, 1362 [A.H. solar]), p. 304.
38. Mullā Ṣadrā, *al-Mabda' wa'l-ma'ād,* p. 306.
39.

"انّ اِدراک الحقّ تعالى بعلم مستأنف لا يمكن لاحدِ الاّ في مرآة قلب المؤمن المتّقي، و لِهذا العالم و خلق الكون وَ ابداع النِظام."

Mullā Ṣadrā, *Tafsīr-i āyah-i-nūr,* p. 168.

40.

" و كَذلکَ فى الانِسان الكامِل و المظهر الجامِع، يوجد جميع ما يوجَد فى العالَم الاسمأ وَ في مَظاهِرها الآفاقِيّه."

Mullā Ṣadrā, *Tafsīr-i āyah-i-nūr,* p. 168.

41.

"الإنسانَ الكامِل كِتاب جامِع الآيات رَبّه القدّوس و سجلّ مطوّى فِيه حَقايق العُقول وَ النُفوس، و كَلمةً كاملة مَملوة مِن فُنون اَلعلم و اَلشجون، و نسخةً مكتوُبة مِن مِثالِ كُن فيكُون. "

Mullā Ṣadrā, *Tafsīr-i āyah-i-nūr,* p. 175.

Chapter 10: Teaching Philosophy in Light of the Islamic Educational Ethos

1. *Yanba' al-ḥikmah min mishkāt al-nubuwwah.*
2. See S. H. Nasr, *Islamic Philosophy from Its Origin to the Present,* "Philosophy and Prophecy," pp. 1ff; and "The Meaning and Role of 'Philosophy' in Islam," pp. 31ff.
3. See Ibn Sīnā and al-Bīrūnī, *al-As'ilah wa'l-ajwibah,* ed. S. H. Nasr and Mehdi Mohaghegh (Tehran: Institute for Humanities and Cultural Studies, 1997), esp. the English introduction, which was also published as "al-Bīrūnī versus Avicenna in the Bout of the Century," *Courier* (June 1974): 27–29.
4. See Ibn Rushd, *Tahāfut al-tahāfut,* trans. S. van der Bergh (London: Gibb Memorial Trust, 1954).
5. See William Chittick, "Mysticism vs. Philosophy in Earlier Islamic History: The al-Ṭūsī, al-Qūnawī Correspondence," *Religious Studies* 17 (1981): 87–104.
6. It is very difficult to remove error once it becomes embedded in the generally accepted view of history. Despite all the works of Corbin, Izutsu, Nasr, and others about post-Ibn Rushd Islamic philosophy, the idea of the decadence of Islamic thought and philosophy after the Abbasid period continues to persist in many quarters.
7. Surprisingly enough, this is also true of many of the "fundamentalist" thinkers; their evaluation of Greek thought is based almost completely on modern

Western interpretations of this legacy rather than on the traditional Islamic view. Here again the modernist and "fundamentalist" camps meet, while they both stand opposed to the traditional perspective. The studies of Greek philosophy by someone like Peter Kingsley reveal how close an authentic study of Greek philosophy not influenced by the prejudices of the Renaissance and the Age of Enlightenment is to the traditional Islamic understanding of it. See his *Ancient Philosophy, Mystery and Magic* (Oxford: Clarendon, 1995); and *In the Dark Places of Wisdom* (Inverness, CA: Golden Sufi Center, 1999).

8. It is strange that there are as yet so few works on the history of European philosophy written in any Islamic language but from the Islamic point of view rather than being more or less translations from European sources.
9. Works by such scholars as Walter Pagel, Frances Yates, Allen Debus, and Antoine Faivre, among others, have cast new light on this subject and must be carefully studied by any Muslim scholar seriously interested in the appraisal of the philosophical and more generally intellectual history of the postmedieval West.
10. See S. H. Nasr, *Knowledge and the Sacred*, pp. 93ff.
11. See Roger Lipsey, *Coomaraswamy: His Life and Works*; and A. K. Saran, *Traditional Wisdom of Man* (Varanasi: Central Institute of Higher Tibetan Studies, 1998).
12. See also Schuon's *Light on the Ancient Worlds,* ed. Deborah Casey (Bloomington, IN: World Wisdom, 2006); and S. H. Nasr, ed., *The Essential Frithjof Schuon.*
13. Étienne Gilson's *The Unity of Philosophical Experience* (Westminster, MD: Christian Classics, 1982) is particularly important as far as this subject is concerned.
14. See S. H. Nasr, *An Introduction to Islamic Cosmological Doctrines,* and "Cosmology," in *The Different Aspects of Islamic Culture,* vol. 4, Science and Technology, ed. Ahmad Y. Hasan et al., pp. 361–404. See also Ian R. Netton, *Allāh Transcendent* (London: Routledge, 1989).
15. See S. H. Nasr, *Muḥammad: Man of Allah* (Chicago: Kazi Publications, 1995), pp. 14ff.
16. The valuable works of Roshdi Rashed are a rare exception.
17. Titus Burckhardt, who as already mentioned was the first contemporary Western scholar to formulate the principles of the Islamic philosophy of art, has dealt with this issue in many of his works, especially *Art of Islam,* and *Mirror of the Intellect,* trans. William Stoddart (Albany: State University of New York Press, 1987). See also S. H. Nasr, *Islamic Art and Spirituality.*
18. See chapters 12–14 of this work on Islamic art and architecture.
19. Fortunately, this is taking place to some extent in Iran and Malaysia today.
20. The Iranian Academy of Philosophy in Tehran and the International Institute of Islamic Thought and Civilization in Kuala Lumpur are viable examples of such institutions.
21. Mian Mohammad Sharif, ed., *A History of Muslim Philosophy,* 2 vols.; I have already referred several times to this still important reference source, which has also been translated into Persian. Attempts to write the history of Islamic philosophy on the basis of an authentic and inclusive Islamic methodology include:

Henry Corbin (with the collaboration of S. H. Nasr and Osman Yahya), *Histoire de la philosophie islamique,* vol. 1; S. H. Nasr and Oliver Leaman, eds., *History of Islamic Philosophy,* 2 vols.; and Nasr, *Islamic Philosophy from Its Origin to the Present.*

22. S. J. Āshtiyānī and H. Corbin, *Anthologie des philosophes iraniens,* 4 vols. (Tehran: Deìpartement d'iranologie de l'Institut franco-iranien de recherche; Paris: Librarie d'Ameìrique et d'Orient Adrien Maisonneuve: 1972–78). Unfortunately, after the death of Corbin, the publication of this magnum opus became interrupted. Only the first four volumes were printed, the last without the extensive French prolegomena of Corbin, which was such an important element of each of the first three volumes. The prolegomenas for the first three volumes were printed separately after Corbin's death as *La Philosophie iranienne islamique aux XVIIe et XVIIIe siècles.* During the past few years I have been preparing, with Mehdi Aminrazavi, a major five-volume *An Anthology of Philosophy in Persia* covering the period from Zoroaster to the beginning of the twentieth century. Three volumes have been already published by I. B. Tauris in London, and the last two are to appear soon.
23. An important step in this direction as far as Persian is concerned is Sayyid Ja'far Sajjādī, *Farhang-i ma'ārif-i islāmī,* 4 vols. (Tehran: Shirkat-i Mu'allifān wa Mutarjimān-i Īrān, 1357 [A.H. solar]). This work has been followed by several others in Persian. There are also some notable works on this subject in Arabic and Turkish.

Chapter 11: Traditional Islamic Science and Western Science

1. As far as technology, which will not be treated here, is concerned, see S. H. Nasr, "Islam, Muslims and Modern Technology," in Nasr with M. Iqbal, *Islam, Science, Muslims and Technology,* pp. 91–118.
2. For a detailed account of these responses, see Muzaffar Iqbal, *Islam and Science*; and *Science and Islam.* See also Ibrahim Kalin, "The Views of Science in the Islamic World," in Ted Peters et al., eds., *God, Life and the Cosmos* (Aldershot: Ashgate, 2002), pp. 47–76.
3. See, for example, S. H. Nasr, *An Introduction to Islamic Cosmological Doctrines,* and *Science and Civilization in Islam.*
4. On the meaning of traditional science and its contrast with modern science in general, see René Guénon, *Crisis of the Modern World,* trans. M. Pallis and R. Nicholson (Ghent. NY: Sophia Perennis, 2001), chap. 4; S. H. Nasr, *Knowledge and the Sacred,* esp. chaps. 4, 6; and *The Need for a Sacred Science* (Albany: State University of New York Press, 1993), "The Traditional Sciences," pp. 95ff.
5. Much of this tradition reached Muslims through the Ḥarraneans, who were also known as the Sabaeans in Islamic history. See J. Pedersen, "The Sabians," in *A Volume of Oriental Studies Presented to E. G. Browne* (Cambridge: Cambridge University Press, 1922), pp. 383–91; and Ethel Stefana Drower, *The Mandaeans of Iran and Iraq* (Leiden: Brill, 1962).

6. In traditional civilizations there has in fact never been a continuous "development" of science of the type that the modern world envisages as normal to civilization. Traditional civilizations display periods of interest and activity in the sciences of nature, interrupted by eras during which the intellectual energies of that civilization have turned to other domains without any signs of decadence of an intellectual or artistic nature. On the contrary, except for Islam, most other traditional civilizations seem to have turned more to the so-called exact sciences at the moment of their own decay and demise. Babylonian and Alexandrian sciences provide striking examples of this phenomenon.
7. See Theodore Roszak, *Where the Wasteland Ends* (Garden City, NY: Doubleday, 1973); Wolfgang Smith, *Cosmos and Transcendence* (La Salle, IL: Sherwood Sugden, 1984);and *The Wisdom of Ancient Cosmology* (Oakton, VA: Foundation for Traditional Studies, 2003); S. H. Nasr, *Man and Nature;* and *Religion and the Order of Nature* (New York: Oxford University Press, 1996).
8. See Nasr, *Introduction to Islamic Cosmological Doctrines.*
9. On the relation between science and metaphysics, see Fernand Brunner, *Science et réalité* (Paris: Aubier, 1954).
10. See Frithjof Schuon, *Light on the Ancient Worlds,* ed. Deborah Casey, chap. 2, "In the Wake of the Fall," pp. 28ff.
11. See Étienne Gilson, *The Unity of Philosophical Experience.*
12. Symbolic science is treated amply by contemporary traditional authors, because of the central role it plays in understanding both the languages and content of traditional writings. See René Guénon, *Fundamental Symbols: The Universal Language of Sacred Science,* trans. Alvin Moore (Cambridge: Quinta Essentia, 1995).
13. A symbol is always a symbol of some reality beyond itself, while a fact as seen scientifically cannot but be ontologically separated from higher realms of existence. To say "symbol," in the traditional sense of the word, is to mean beyond what is immediately perceived ordinarily. According to traditional metaphysics, only the Absolute Reality is totally Itself. Everything else in the universe is a symbol of a reality beyond the ontological level in which the being in question is perceived as a particular being.
14. Romans 1:20.
15. See Schuon, *Light on the Ancient Worlds,* chap. 3, "Dialogue Between Hellenists and Christians."
16. On Avicennan angelology, see Henry Corbin, *Avicenna and the Visionary Recital,* trans. W. Trask; and Nasr, *Introduction to Islamic Cosmological Doctrines,* chap. 15, pp. 263ff.
17. On alchemy as gynecology and the attempt to speed up the rhythm of nature in transmitting base metal into gold see Mircea Eliade, *The Forge and the Crucible,* trans. Stephen Corrin (Chicago: University of Chicago Press, 1978).
18. See Titus Burckhardt, *Alchemy: Science of the Cosmos, Science of the Soul.*

Chapter 12: Islamic Art and Its Spiritual Significance in the Contemporary World

1. It is strange that the most complete and penetrating exposition of the spiritual significance of Islamic art and architecture should come from a Western Muslim, the traditionalist scholar Titus Ibrāhīm Burckhardt. See especially his *The Art of Islam,* trans. J. Peter Hobson; *The Mirror of the Intellect,* trans. W. Stoddart; *Moorish Culture in Spain*, trans. Alisa Jaffa (London: Allen and Unwin, 1972); *Fez: City of Islam,* trans. William Stoddart (Cambridge: Islamic Texts Society, 1992); *Land am Rande der Zeit* (Basel: Urs Graf, 1941); *Marokko, Westlicher Orient: Ein Reiseführer* (Olten and Freiburg: Walter, 1972); and *Sacred Art in East and West,* trans. Lord Northbourne, chap. 4, pp. 135ff.
2. See S. H. Nasr, *Islamic Art and Spirituality.*
3. See Keith Critchlow, *Islamic Patterns: An Analytical and Cosmological Approach* (New York: Schocken, 1976); Issam El-Said and Ayse Parman, *Geometric Concepts in Islamic Art* (London: World of Islam Festival Publishing, 1976); and Lynette Singer, ed., *The Minbar of Saladin* (London: Thames and Hudson, 2008).
4. See Nader Ardalan and Laleh Bakhtiar, *The Sense of Unity* (Chicago: ABC International Group, 1999), pp. 11ff.
5. See the works of Burckhardt and myself cited above. See also Frithjof Schuon, "The Degrees of Art," in his *Esoterism as Principle and as Way,* trans. William Stoddart, pp. 183ff.
6. On the relation of Islamic architecture to Islamic cosmology, see Samer Akkach, *Cosmology and Architecture in Premodern Islam* (Albany: State University of New York Press, 2005).
7. On the Islamic garden and its spiritual significance, see Emma Clark, *The Art of the Islamic Garden* (Ramsbury, Wiltshire: Crowood, 2004).

Chapter 13: The Architectural Transformation of the Urban Environment in the Islamic World

1. The urban crisis is of course worldwide, and much that is taking place in the Islamic world is related to, and is a consequence of, this worldwide crisis. The fact that this is so indicates the passive nature of much of the Islamic world vis-à-vis the West and is itself an indication of this crisis. In any case, inasmuch as the main concern in this chapter is with the Islamic world, the discussion shall be limited to the architectural and urban problems of this region, although many comments stated here also apply elsewhere.
2. To some degree the principles of Islamic art in general that were dealt with in the last chapter will be reviewed as they apply more specifically to architecture later in this chapter and also in the following chapter. See also S. H. Nasr, *Islamic Art and Spirituality,* chap. 4.

3. See Frithjof Schuon, *Spiritual Perspectives and Human Facts,* trans. Peter Townsend (Bedfont: Perennial Books, 1987), pt. 1. A new translation was published by World Wisdom in 2001.
4. See S. H. Nasr, *An Introduction to Islamic Cosmological Doctrines,* pp. 58–59, 218–26.
5. During the past few decades some attempt has been made to rectify the situation, thanks mostly to the efforts of Hasan Fathy, the notable Egyptian architect, and some of his students. In recent years the Aga Khan program of Islamic architecture even began a degree program in Islamic architecture and urban planning at Harvard and M.I.T. This program does not, however, teach Islamic architecture itself as a living tradition, but rather what most of those involved in the administration of this program consider good contemporary architecture in the Islamic world. One wonders what criteria determine the meaning of "good" in such considerations. More recently, programs specifically concerned with authentic Islamic architecture have been established in Jordan and Pakistan following the model of the School of Traditional Art and Architecture founded in London under the patronage of the Prince of Wales, who is a true patron of traditional architecture. Because of his special love for Islamic architecture, Sultan Ḥasan of Morocco also established a school for the revival of traditional Islamic art and architecture in his country.
6. See Frithjof Schuon, *Understanding Islam*, chap. 2.
7. See Henry Corbin, *Creative Imagination in the Sufism of Ibn 'Arabī,* which has been published more recently under the new title *Alone with the Alone* (Princeton, NJ: Princeton University Press, 1997). See also Samer Akkach, *Cosmology and Architecture in Premodern Islam.*
8. See Henry Corbin, *En Islam iranien,* vol. 1, pp. 120ff.
9. Ibn Ḥanbal, *Musnad,* ed. Shu'ayb al-Arna'ūt and 'Ādil Murshid (Beirut: Mu'assasat al-Risālah, 2008), bk. 4, pp. 133–34.
10. See Schuon, *Understanding Islam,* chap. 1.
11. On a more external level, because inwardly the One shines like a never setting sun at the heart of all things and most of all of human beings, who are the complete and central receivers of the theophanies of the One in this world.
12. One must not forget that these schools must in turn be based on Islamic models that would allow long periods of apprenticeship, personal dedication to a teacher or master, and the possibility of training students morally and spiritually as well as technically.
13. A few such architects have in fact appeared in recent years in the Islamic world, such men as Abd al-Wahid El-Wakil and Umar Faruq from Egypt, Sami Angawi from Saudi Arabia, and Kamil Khan Mumtaz from Pakistan, and they, along with a few others, have already created an authentic contemporary Islamic architecture and urban design that can serve as a model and inspiration for others.

Chapter 14: The Principles of Islamic Architecture and Urban Design, and Contemporary Urban Problems

1. The methods and means of applying traditional principles of Islamic architecture and city planning to problems of contemporary Islamic society are therefore different from the methods needed for applying these principles to the situation of urban environments in the West. Concerning the contemporary Islamic world, see A. El-Wakil, "Identity, Tradition and Architecture," in *Arab Architecture: Past and Present* (Durham: Center for Middle Eastern and Islamic Studies, 1984), pp. 26–29.
2. Because of the inner or transcendent unity of religions, such actions and reactions can and often do take place across any religious frontier, but this possibility becomes stronger when the religions belong to the same family. In the case of Christianity and Islam, the family proximity has of course also caused the severest reactions and conflicts over the ages, especially from the side of Christian theology, which has until now repudiated for the most part the authenticity of the Islamic revelation. But this historical confrontation does not negate the possibility of positive interactions across religious frontiers today, as was the case in medieval Spain and Sicily. On the inner relation between Christianity and Islam and religions in general, see Frithjof Schuon, *The Transcendent Unity of Religions: Form and Substance in the Religions* (Bloomington, IN: World Wisdom, 2002); and *Christianity/Islam* (Bloomington, IN: World Wisdom, 1985).
3. See S. H. Nasr, *Ideals and Realities of Islam*, chap. 1, pp. 1ff.
4. On the levels of unity in Islamic architecture, see Nader Ardalan and Laleh Bakhtiar, *The Sense of Unity: The Sufi Tradition in Persian Architecture.*
5. The training of traditional Muslim architects reflected this principle clearly, for they were always taught to conceive of the whole and then descend to the parts rather than conceive or draw the parts of the building or complex of buildings and then weld them together as a whole, as is the case for most modern students of architecture.
6. For a unique study that relates the principle of unity to both the architecture and social, intellectual, and artistic life of a major Islamic city, see Titus Burckhardt, *Fez: City of Islam.*
7. These questions have been dealt with in a masterly fashion by Burckhardt in his many writings on Islamic art already cited. In this connection, see especially his "The Spirit of Islamic Art," *Islamic Quarterly* (December 1954): 212–18.
8. See Frithjof Schuon, *Understanding Islam*, pp. 13ff; also S. H. Nasr, *Knowledge and the Sacred,* chap. 5, pp. 160ff.
9. See Keith Critchlow, *Islamic Patterns.*
10. On the question of the Islamic conception of number and geometric form, see S. H. Nasr, *An Introduction to Islamic Cosmological Doctrines,* chap. 2, pp. 160ff. On the universal significance of numbers in their qualitative aspect, see Frithjof Schuon, *Esoterism as Principle and as Way,* pp.65–78.

11. Titus Burckhardt speaks of this matter in many of his writings, for example, *Fez: City of Islam,* pp. 76–77; see also Jean-Louis Michon, "Education in the Traditional Arts and Crafts and the Cultural Heritage of Islam," in S. H. Nasr, ed., *Philosophy, Literature and Fine Arts: Islamic Education Series*, pp. 49–62.
12. On the disregard of "fundamentalists" and modernists for the inner dimensions of Islam, from which the principles of Islamic art and architecture issue, and the spiritual consequences of such an attitude, subjects that have also been considered in earlier chapters, see also S. H. Nasr, *Islamic Art and Spirituality,* "Postscript," pp. 195ff.

Appendix I: The Traditional Texts Used in the Persian *Madrasahs* and the Question of the Revival of Traditional Islamic Education

1. On the "transmitted" and "intellectual" sciences, see S. H. Nasr, *Science and Civilization in Islam,* chap. 2; also *Islamic Science: An Illustrated Study*, pp. 14ff.
2. On the life of Taqizadeh, see the introduction of Īraj Afshār to his edition of *Maqālāt-i Ḥasan Taqīzādeh* (Tehran: Bist wa Panjum-i Shahrīwar Press, 1349 [A.H. solar]).
3. Mīrzā Ṭāhir Tunikābunī, *Kutub-i darsī-yi qadīm* ("Text Books of Old"), published by Īraj Afshār in *Farhang-i Īrānzamīn* 20 (1353/1975): 39–82. Throughout this chapter, the prevalent Persian pronunciation of the names of people and books has been preserved.
4. Mīr Sayyid Sharīf was at once theologian, philosopher, and Sufi and is best known for his "definitions" of the terminology of the Islamic spiritual sciences, the *Kitāb al-ta'rīfāt.*
5. Zanjānī's fame comes mostly from this treatise, whereas Taftāzānī, who was the chief *qāḍī* of Shiraz, is one of the leading exponents of late Ash'arism, and his theological works are read extensively to this day in Sunni *madrasahs* throughout the Islamic world.
6. This extensive and well-composed commentary is called *Zīnat al-sālik fī sharḥ alfiyyah ibn Mālik.*
7. Shaykh Bahā' al-Dīn 'Āmilī, who died in 1030/1621, was originally from the Jabal 'Āmil in Lebanon, but was brought to Persia when he was only twelve years old. He became a master of both the exoteric and esoteric sciences and was the leading religious authority of Isfahan, probably the greatest poet of the Persian language of the period, a fine Arabic poet, and a leading mathematician, architect, and city planner in addition to being one of the outstanding Sufis of the age. Many of his works in various fields have become authoritative throughout Persia; the *Ṣamadiyyah* on Arabic grammer is one of the most famous of all. On Bahā' al-Dīn al-'Āmilī, see Nasr, *Science and Civilization in Islam,* pp. 57–58; and *The Islamic Intellectual Tradition in Persia,* pp. 243ff.
8. The science of *uṣūl* has received a great deal of attention during the last few centuries in Shī'ism; in fact that time period might be considered its "golden

age," during which numerous essential treatises, very few of which have been studied in the outside world until now, have been written. In Sunnism, however, the most important treatises were written several centuries earlier. On Sunni *uṣūl,* see Bernard Weiss, "The Primacy of Revelation in Sayf al-Dīn al-Āmidī," *Studia Islamica* 59 (1984): 79–109.

9. On this major opus and Mullā Ṣadrā's commentary on it, see Henry Corbin, *En Islam iranien*, vol. 4, pp. 84ff.
10. On Mīr Dāmād, see Corbin, *En Islam iranien*, vol. 4, pp. 9ff.; also S. H. Nasr, "The School of Isfahan," in *The Islamic Intellectual Tradition in Persia,* pp.239ff. See also Hamid Dabashi, "Mīr Dāmād and the Founding of the 'School of Isfahan,'" in S. H. Nasr and Oliver Leaman, eds., *History of Islamic Philosophy,* 2 vols., chap. 34, pp. 597ff.; and S. H. Nasr, *Islamic Philosophy from Its Origin to the Present,* pp. 209ff.
11. Najm al-Dīn Dabīrān-i Kātibī Qazwīnī is one of the important philosophical figures in the circle of Naṣīr al-Dīn Ṭūsī, but is not well known in the outside world. In Persia itself, however, his writings have always been widely popular. See Nasr, *Islamic Philosophy from Its Origin to the Present,* pp. 191–92.
12. Quṭb al-Dīn Rāzī is best known for his *Muḥākamāt* ("Trials"), in which judgment is made between the commentaries of Fakhr al-Dīn Rāzī and Naṣīr al-Dīn Ṭūsī on the *Ishārāt* of Ibn Sīnā. But Quṭb al-Dīn Rāzī has also written other important works, which have been for the most part neglected by scholars so far.
13. Sirāj al-Dīn Urmawī, the author of numerous works, including the *Laṭā'if al-ḥikmah* in Persian, was one of the main intellectual figures of Konia during the lifetime of Mawlānā Jalāl al-Dīn Rūmī.
14. See Nasr, "Sabziwārī," in *The Islamic Intellectual Tradition in Persia,* pp. 304ff. The text of the section on metaphysics of this major work has been edited critically by Toshihiko Izutsu and Mehdi Mohaghegh, *Sharḥ-i ghurar al-farā'id ma'rūf bi-manẓūmah* (Tehran: Anjuman-i Āthār wa Mafākhir-i Farhangī, 2005). This work contains a long English introduction by Izutsu, but the text begins with the section on metaphysics and excludes logic.
15. The spread of the popularity of this work is a gauge of the intellectual relations that still existed between various *madrasahs* in the Islamic world in the thirteenth/nineteenth century.
16. On Suhrawardī's criticism of Aristotelian logic, see M. T. Sharī'atī, "Barrasi-yi manṭiq-i Suhrawardī wa muqāyasa-yi ān bā manṭiq-i arisṭū'ī," *Maqālāt wa barrasīhī* (*Journal of the Faculty of Theology of Tehran University*) 13–16 (1352): 318–29.
17. For these figures, see S. J. Āshtiyānī and H. Corbin, *Anthologie des philosophes iraniens,* 4 vols., vols. 1–2.
18. The commentary of Mullā Ṣadrā is so famous in India that to this day the work itself is referred to as "*Ṣadrā.*" In any case, it remains one of the four or five most popular works on Peripatetic philosophy.

19. The most recent major study of this work is the edition of the work with commentary by Abū'l-Ḥasan Sha'rānī, *Kashf al-murād: Sharḥ-i tajrīd al-i'tiqād* (Tehran: Islāmiyyah Press, 1351 [A.H. solar]).
20. Lāhījī is also the author of the popular Persian treatise on *kalām,* the *Gawhar-i murād.* See Nasr, "*Al-Ḥikmat al-ilāhiyyah* and *Kalām,*" in *Islamic Philosophy from Its Origin to the Present,* pp. 49ff; and Āshtiyānī and Corbin, *Anthologie des philosophes iraniens,* vol. 1, pp. 117ff.
21. The lithographed edition of the *Ḥikmat al-ishrāq* contains both the commentary of Quṭb al-Dīn and the glosses of Mullā Ṣadrā, while the critical edition of Corbin, *Oeuvres philosophiques et mystiques* vol. 1, includes the text of Suhrawardī and certain selections from Quṭb al-Dīn and Mullā Ṣadrā as well as the lesser-known but very important commentary of Shams al-Dīn Muḥammad Shahrazūrī. See Shams al-Dīn Shahrazūrī, *Sharḥ Hikmat al-ishrāq,* ed. Hossein Ziai (Tehran: Mu'assa-yi Muṭāla'āt wa Taḥqīqāt-i Farhangī, 1993).
22. On the *Asfār,* see S. H. Nasr, *Ṣadr al-Dīn Shīrāzī and His Transcendent Theosophy,* and Peerwani, op cit.
23. On Ibn Turkah, see Henry Corbin, *En Islam iranien,* vol. 3, chap. 3; also Nasr, *Islamic Philosophy from Its Origin to the Present,* pp. 209–10.
24. The first critical edition of this work, making use of the tradition emanating from Āqā Muḥammad Riḍā Qumsha'ī, has been edited by S. J. Āshtiyānī, with Persian and English introductions by S. H. Nasr (Qom: Būstān-i Kitāb, 2002).
25. On Ibn 'Arabī and the *Fuṣūṣ,* see Titus Burckhardt, *La Sagesse des prophètes* (Paris: Albin Michel, 1955; trans. into English from the French translation of Burckhardt by A. Culme-Seymour, *The Wisdom of the Prophets* [Gloucestershire, UK: Beshara, 1975]); Toshihiko Izutsu, *Sufism and Taoism* (Berkeley: University of California Press, 1983) Part I; Ibn al-'Arabī, trans. Ralph W. J. Austin, *The Bezels of Wisdom* (New York: Paulist, 1980); and Ibn al-'Arabī, trans. Caner Dagli, *The Ringstone of Wisdom (Fuṣūṣ al-ḥikam)* (Chicago: Kazi Publications, 2004). On the numerous commentaries on the *Fuṣūṣ,* see Osman Yahya, *Histoire et classafication de l'oeuvre d'Ibn 'Arabī,* 2 vols. (Damascus: Institut Français de Damas, 1964).
26. See William Chittick, ed., *Naqd al-nuṣūṣ fī sharḥ naqsh al-fuṣūṣ* of Jāmī (Tehran: Imperial Iranian Academy of Philosophy, 1977), in whose introduction Jāmī's direct commentary on the *Fuṣūṣ* is discussed. The *Naqd al-nuṣūṣ* itself contains what may be called an anthology of the major commentaries on the *Fuṣūṣ* composed until the time of the author.
27. The vast commentary of Jandī on the *Fuṣūṣ* has been edited for the first time by S. J. Āshtiyānī, as *Sharḥ fuṣūṣ al-ḥikam* (Mashhad: Mashhad University Press, 1982), with an English prolegomena by Toshihiko Izutsu.
28. The text of this difficult work has been partly translated and analyzed in a European language for the first time by Stéphane Ruspoli in his doctoral thesis at the Sorbonne, *La Clef du monde suprasensible.* See also the edition of Muḥammad Khwājawī (Tehran: Mawlā Press, 1996).

29. Mīrzā Ṭāhir Tunikābunī (*Kutub-i darsī-yi qadīm,* p. 54) complains of the lack of interest in the study of medicine in the *madrasahs* during his own day. The situation in fact deteriorated so rapidly afterwards in Persia that by the beginning of the twentieth century the teaching of traditional medicine in the *madrasahs* in Persia was discontinued completely. It has survived here and there in that land only through the private instruction of individual masters of the art, while it has survived fully in Pakistan and India in institutions created specifically for its teaching. See Nasr, *Islamic Science: An Illustrated Study,* chap. 8; and Cyril Elgood, *Safavid Medical Practice* (London: Luzac, 1970).
30. On the *Canon,* see Oscar C. Gruner, *A Treatise on the Canon of Medicine, Incorporating the Translation of the First Book*; Mazhar H. Shah, *The General Principles of Avicenna's Canon of Medicine* (Karachi: Naveed Clinic, 1966); and M. Ullmann, *Die Medizin in Islam* (Leiden: Brill, 1970), pp. 152–54.
31. *Miftāḥ al-ḥisāb* is probably the most important Islamic work on arithmetic and has drawn a great deal of attention during the past few decades. See Abū'l-Qāsim Qurbānī, *Kāshānī-nāmah* (Tehran: Markaz-i Nashr-i Dānishgāhī, 1368 [A.H. solar]), pt. 3.
32. This important work of Ṭūsī has been studied by many historians of astronomy, including E. S. Kennedy, and is now being translated by George Saliba. The commentary of Shams al-Dīn Khafrī on this work is also of particular significance for the history of astronomy as pointed out by Saliba.

Appendix II: Philosophy in the Present-Day Islamic World

1. Such schools as those of the principles of jurisprudence (*uṣūl*), theology (*kalām*), and gnosis (*'irfān* or *ma'rifah*).
2. On Islamic philosophy in general, see the already cited works of Corbin, Sharif, Fakhry and Nasr. For a synopsis of the intellectual background, see S. H. Nasr, *Islamic Life and Thought* (London: Routledge, 2008), chap. 6.
3. There are a few exceptions, such as Ibn Sab'īn and Ibn Khaldūn.
4. See H. Corbin, "The Force of Traditional Philosophy in Iran Today," *Studies in Comparative Religion* (Winter 1968): 12–26; S. H. Nasr, "Islamic Philosophy in Contemporary Persia: A Summary of Activity in the 50's and 60's" in *The Islamic Intellectual Tradition in Persia,* pp. 323ff.; and S. H. Nasr and Oliver Leaman, eds., *History of Islamic Philosophy,* 2 vol., pt. 9, "Islamic Philosophy in the Modern Islamic World."
5. On these so-called reformers, see the still valuable work of Albert Hourani, *Arabic Thought in the Liberal Age* (New York: Cambridge University Press, 1983); Kenneth Cragg, *Counsels in Contemporary Islam* (Edinburgh: Edinburgh University Press, 1965); Fazlur Rahman, *Islam and Modernity: Transformation of an Intellectual Tradition* (Chicago: Chicago University Press, 1983); Ibrāhīm Abū Rabī', "The Arab World," in Nasr and Leaman, eds., *History of Islamic Philosophy,* pp. 1082ff.; *Intellectual Origins of Islamic Resurgence in The Arab World*

(Albany: The State University of New York Press, 1996) and ed., *The Blackwell Companion to Contemporary Islamic Thought* (Oxford: Blackwell, 2006). A great deal of more genuine Islamic activity, mostly in the field of Sufism, took place, but it has received relatively little attention until now. On the orthodox and traditional criticism of these modernistic reformers, see Maryam Jameelah, *Islam and Modernism* (Lahore: Mohammad Yusuf Khan, 1966).

6. See S. H. Nasr, "The Pertinence of Studying Islamic Philosophy Today," in *Islamic Life and Thought,* chap. 12.
7. As mentioned, today late nineteenth-century British philosophy is still taken more seriously in the universities on the Indian subcontinent than in British universities themselves.
8. Morroe Berger detected this trend, which still continues, some forty years ago. See his *Islam in Egypt Today* (Cambridge: Cambridge University Press, 1970); and E. Bannerth, "Aspects de la Shadhiliyya," *Mélanges de l'Institut Dominicain des Études Orientales* (Cairo) 2 (1972): 248 ff.
9. See Valerie Hoffman, *Sufism, Mystics and Saints in Modern Egypt* (Columbia: University of South Carolina Press, 2009); Eric Geoffroy, *Introduction to Sufism: The Inner Path of Islam,* trans. Roger Gaetani (Bloomington, IN: World Wisdom Books, 2010), esp. "Conclusion," pp. 194ff; and Michel Chodkiewicz, "Le Soufisme au XXIe siècle," in *Les Voies d'Allah* (Paris: Fayard, 1996), pp. 532–43.
10. Gradually the works of the contemporary masters of traditional Islamic philosophy, such as 'Allāmah Ṭabāṭabā'ī, are becoming known even in the West. Meanwhile, in Iran the renaissance of interest in traditional Islamic philosophy, especially the school of Mullā Ṣadrā, continues and has spread to some degree to Pakistan, India, and many other Muslim lands as far away as Bosnia, Indonesia, and Malaysia, where there is now much interest in later Islamic philosophy.
11. Perhaps the most extensive celebrations were those held in 1952 and 1953 in Egypt, Iraq, Iran, India, and several other lands on the occasion of the millennium of Ibn Sīnā. These celebrations were responsible for the publication of hundreds of books and articles on this master of Muslim Peripatetics. As far as Iran and Iraq are concerned, see League of Arab States, *Millenaire d'Avicenne: Congrès de Bagdad* (Cairo: Maṭba'at Miṣr, 1952); and Dhabīh Allāh Ṣafā, ed., *Le Livre du millénaire d'Avicenne,* 4 vols. (Tehran: Tehran University Press, 1953). For accounts of these activities, especially in Egypt, see the numerous studies of Georges C. Anawati in the *Mélanges de l'Institute Dominicain.* On philosophical activity in the Arab world during the past century, see also ed., Khalāl al-Jurr et al., *al-Fikr al-falsafī fī mi'at 'āmm* (Beirut: American University of Beirut, 1962).
12. On the Wahhābī-Salafī line of thought and its background, see Louis Gardet and Georges C. Anawati, *Introduction à la théologie musulmane* (Paris: Vrin, 1948), esp. pp. 447ff., which deals with the theological aspects of this movement; and

the classical orientalist work of Henri Laoust, *Essai sur les doctrines sociales et politiques de Taqi-al-Din Aḥmad B. Taimiyah* (Cairo: Institut Français d'Archéologie Orientale, 1939). On later developments, see Muḥammad 'Imārah, *Ṭayarāt al-fikr al-islāmī* (Cairo: Dār al-Hilāl, 1984).

13. On the Muslim Brotherhood, see Isḥāq Mūsā Ḥusaynī, *The Muslim Brethren* (Beirut: Khayat's College Book Cooperative, 1956); Richard P. Mitchell, *The Society of the Muslim Brothers* (New York: Oxford University Press, 1993); and 'Alī 'Abd al-Raḥīm, *al-Ikhwān al-muslimūn* (Cairo: Markaz al-Maḥrūsah li'l-Nashr, 2004).
14. On this remarkable figure, see Martin Lings, *A Sufi Saint of the Twentieth Century*.
15. On Maraboutism in the Maghrib, see Octave Dupont and Xavier Copolani, *Les Confréries religieuses musulmanes* (Algiers: Jourdan, 1897); and Émile Dermenghem, *Le Culte des saints dans l'Islam maghrébin* (Paris: Gallimard, 1954). See also the thorough study of Maghribī Sufism by Vincent Cornell, *Realm of the Saint* (Austin: University of Texas Press, 1998).
16. It is interesting to note that thinkers in the Arab world (except for Iraq), especially in the Maghrib, were almost totally cut off from the later tradition of Islamic philosophy until quite recently. Finally, the efforts of Corbin, Izutsu, Nasr, and others are bearing fruit in directing the attention of not only Westerners but also other Muslims, including those of the Maghrib, to the significance of the later schools of Islamic philosophy.
17. In addition to the works cited in the previous chapter, see M. Mohaghegh and T. Izutsu, *The Metaphysics of Sabzavari* (Delmar, NY: Caravan, 1977).
18. See Nasr, "Islamic Philosophy in Contemporary Persia"; and S. H. Nasr, *Islamic Philosophy from Its Origin to the Present,* pp. 273ff.; also Corbin, "The Force of Traditional Philosophy."
19. See the introduction to S. M. H. Ṭabāṭabā'ī, *Shi'ite Islam,* trans. S. H. Nasr. See also Nasr, *Islamic Philosophy from Its Origin to the Present*, pp. 235ff.
20. Mahdī Ḥā'irī Yazdī was perhaps the only master of Islamic philosophy originally trained in a traditional school who was also completely familiar with Western philosophy. See his *Knowledge by Presence* (Albany: State University of New York Press, 1992). There are now a number of younger traditionally trained Islamic philosophers with such qualifications, but they have not yet gained his eminence.
21. The Imperial Iranian Academy of Philosophy, besides publishing numerous works on Islamic thought, comparative philosophy, and the like, also published the biannual *Sophia Perennis* and an annual bibliography of works on philosophy published in Iran. After the Iranian Revolution of 1979, the publication of the journal ceased, but was revived in 2008. Meanwhile a series of books on Islamic and contemporary philosophy has continued to appear under its auspices and under its new names, The Iranian Academy of Islamic Philosophy and The Iranian Institute of Philosophy.

22. See Richard V. De Smet, *Philosophical Activity in Pakistan* (Lahore: Pakistan Philosophical Congress, 1961).
23. Some of these attempts have been, to put it mildly, far from successful. See S. H. Nasr, "Metaphysics and Philosophy East and West," in *Islam and the Plight of Modern Man* (Chicago: ABC International Group, 2001; Cambridge: Islamic Texts Society, 2002), pp, 27–36. It is important to mention once again the writings of Maryam Jameelah who, although of American origin, belongs to the Pakistani scene. Her writings are among the most rigorous criticisms of the West to come out of the contemporary Islamic world. They stand diametrically opposed to the facile and superficial comparisons and so-called syntheses of Eastern and Western thought that do no more than create ambiguity and destroy rigor within the intellectual atmosphere of so much of the Islamic world. On Islamic philosophy in Pakistan, see also Suheyl Umar, "Pakistan," in Nasr and Leaman, eds., *History of Islamic Philosophy,* pp. 1076ff.

Appendix III: Western Interpreters of the Islamic Tradition

1. See Louis Massignon, *The Passion of al-Ḥallāj,* 4 vols., trans. Herbert Mason (Princeton, NJ: Princeton University Press, 1994).
2. See the important work of Patrick Laude, *Massignon intérior* (Lausanne: L'Age d'Homme, 2001); Mary L. Gude, *Louis Massignon: The Crucible of Compassion* (Notre Dame, IN: University of Notre Dame Press, 1996); Jacques Keryell, *Jardin donné: Louis Massignon à la recherche de l'Absolu* (Paris: Éditions St. Paul, 1993); Jean Moncelon, *Sous le signe d'Abraham: Louis Massignon l'ami de Dieu (Khalīl Allāh)* (Lille: A.N.R.T. Université de Lille III, 1990); Herbert Mason, *Memoir of a Friend: Louis Massignon* (Notre Dame, IN: University of Notre Dame Press, 1988); and Vincent Monteil, *Le Linceul de feu: Louis Massignon (1883–1962)* (Paris: Vega Press, 1987).
3. Louis Massignon, *Essai sur les origines du lexique de la mystique musulmane* (Paris: Vrin, 1968); trans. Benjamin Clark, *Essay on the Origins of the Technical Language of Islamic Mysticism* (Notre Dame, IN: University of Notre Dame Press, 1997).
4. Here is an English translation of my own:

   A consolation, I searched for it in my pain;
   and my pain finished by becoming for me this consolation;
   A proof, I searched for it for my origin—and my
   origin finished by becoming for me this proof.
   To the right and to the left, I searched to see where was the Face of the Friend;
   But I was outside, and He, it is at the very depth of my soul where He resides.
5. See Louis Gardet and Georges C. Anawati, *Mystique musulmane: Aspects et tendance, expériences et techniques* (Paris: Vrin, 1961). The major study of Annemarie

Schimmel, *Mystical Dimensions of Islam* (Chapel Hill: University of North Carolina Press, 1975), also owes much to Massignon in the chapters dealing with the history of Sufism.

6. Such works as Paul Nwyia, *Ibn 'Aṭā' Allāh (m. 709/1309) et la naissance de la confrérie šādilite* (Beirut: Dar el-Machreq, 1972). More recent works have also been influenced by him, for example, Eric Geoffroy, *Introduction to Sufism.*
7. André Festugière, *La Révélation d'Hermès Trismégiste* 4 vols. (Paris: Les Belles Letters, 1981).
8. Published in Youakim Moubarac, ed., *Opera Minora* (Beirut: Dar al-Maaref, 1963), vol. 1.
9. See his "Meditation d'un passant sur sa visite aux bois sacrée d'Isé," in Moubarac, ed., *Opera Minora,* vol. 3. See also Bernard Frank, "Louis Massignon et le Japon," in *Louis Massignon et le dialogue des cultures* (Paris: Cerf, 1996), pp. 357–64.
10. See, as an example, Massignon's "La Signification du dernier pilgrimage de Gandhi," in Moubarac, ed., *Opera Minora,* vol. 3.
11. Henry Corbin, "Humanisme actif," in *Mélanges d'art et de littérature offerts à Julien Cairn* (Paris: 1968), p. 310 (my translation). On the life and works of Corbin, see Mohammad Ali Amir, Moezzi, Christian Jambet, and Pierre Lory, eds., *Henry Corbin: Philosophies et sagesses des religions du livre* (Turnhout, Belgium: Brepols, 2005); Christian Jambet, ed., *L'Herne-Henry Corbin* (Paris: Éditions de l'Herne, 1981); Dariush Shayegan, *Henry Corbin: Le Topographie de l'Islam iranien* (Paris: Éditions de la Difference, 1990); and Tom Cheetham, *The World Turned Inside Out: Henry Corbin and Islamic Mysticism* (Woodstock, NY: Spring Journal, 2003).
12. In his *Le Livre des pénétrations métaphysiques.*
13. Suhrawardī, *Opera Metaphysica et Mystica,* vol. 2, ed. H. Corbin; vol. 3, ed. S. H. Nasr. All three volumes were reprinted by the Imperial Iranian Academy of Philosophy in 1976–77 and by the Institut d'Étude et des Recherches Culturelles in Tehran in 2001.
14. Some of these texts and many other manuscripts were published after his death thanks to the indefatigable efforts of his wife, Stella Corbin. For Corbin's extensive bibliography, see Jambet, ed., *L'Herne-Henry Corbin,* pp. 345ff.
15. Most of these themes are treated in Shayegan, *Henry Corbin.*
16. See Henry Corbin, *Spiritual Body and Celestial Earth,* trans. Nancy Pearson (London: I.B. Tauris, 1990).
17. Although after the Islamic Revolution of 1979 some Shī'ite scholars began to criticize Corbin, despite 'Allāmah Ṭabāṭabā'ī's defense of him, his ideas continue to occupy an important place in the intellectual life of Iran. Recently a whole volume of one of the most widely read journals on Islamic thought published in Persian has been devoted to him. See "Henry Corbin and Islamic Spirituality," *Ettela'at-Hekmat va Ma'refat* 17 (May 2009).

    In France Corbin has also hardly been forgotten. On the contrary, he remains very much alive.

18. See *Creative Imagination in the Sufism of Ibn 'Arabī,* which has been published more recently under the new title *Alone with the Alone.*
19. The English text of Corbin's *A History of Islamic Philosophy,* trans. Liadain Sherrard (London: Kegan Paul International, 1993) includes (without mentioning the collaboration of O. Yahya and myself) both the earlier *Histoire* and the later sequel in *Encyclopédie de la Pléiade.*
20. Henry Corbin, *Sohrawardī, fondateur de la doctrine illuminative (ishrāqī)* (Paris: Maisonneuve, 1939).
21. The whole of volume 1 of this work is devoted to this subject. It is subtitled *Sohrawardî et les Platoniciens de Perse.*
22. Henry Corbin, *L'Archange empourpré* (Paris: Fayard, 1976).
23. See *Le Livre de la sagesse orientale* (Paris: Verdier, 1986).

Appendix IV: Islam and Some of the Major Western Traditionalists

1. In this context, see Zachary Markwith, "Muslim Intellectuals and the Perennial Philosophy in the Twentieth Century," *Sophia* 13, no. 2 (Winter 2007–8): 87–140.
2. See, for example, Paul Chacornac, *La Vie simple de René Guénon* (Paris: Les Éditions Traditionelles, 1958). A list of such works is to be found in Pierre-Marie Sigaud, ed., *René Guénon: Les Dossiers H* (Paris: Éditions l'Age d'Homme, 1984).
3. *Introduction to the Study of Hindu Doctrine,* trans. Marco Pallis (Ghent, NY: Sophia Perennis, 2001).
4. *Man and His Becoming According to the Vedanta,* trans. Richard Nicholson (Ghent, NY: Sophia Perennis, 2001).
5. Sophia Perennis et Universalis, in Ghent, New York, has brought out the series of his books in English. See also John Herlihy, ed., *The Essential René Guénon: Metaphysics, Tradition, and the Crisis of Modernity* (Bloomington, IN: World Wisdom, 2009).
6. *East and West,* trans. William Massey (London: Luzac, 1941).
7. *The Crisis of the Modern World,* trans. Arthur Osborne, Marco Pallis, and Richard Nicholson (Ghent, NY: Sophia Perennis, 2001).
8. *The Reign of Quantity and the Signs of the Times,* trans. Lord Northbourne (Baltimore: Penguin, 1972).
9. For a bibliography, see Sigaud, ed., *René Guénon,* pp. 305ff.; and Jean-Pierre Laurant, ed., "Repères biographiques et bibliographiques," in *L'Herne-René Guénon* (Paris: Éditions de l'Herne, 1985), pp. 15ff.
10. On the life of Guénon in Cairo, see Xavier Accart, *L'Ermite de Duqqi: René Guénon en marge des milieux francophones égyptiens* (Milan: Archè, 2001).
11. Entitled *al-Madrasat al-shādhiliyyat al-ḥadīthah wa imāmuhā Abū'l-Ḥasan al-Shādhilī* (Cairo: Dār al-Kutub al-Ḥadīthah, n.d.). Pp. 229–341 are devoted to Guénon, his views of metaphysics, philosophy, and Sufism, his criticism of modern pseu-

dospiritual movements, and responses to Western misunderstandings of Islam. As already mentioned, this work was published later as *al-Shaykh 'Abd al-Wāḥid Yaḥyā*, with preface by S. H. Nasr. See also Muḥammad Nāshir al-Ni'am, *Min yanābi' al-tajdīd fi'l-fikr al-islāmī al-mu'āṣir* (Aleppo: Fuṣilat li'l-Dirāsāt wa'l-Tarjumah wa'l-Nashr, 2005).

12. These essays include "Know Thy Soul Through Thy Soul," vol. 1, no. 1 (1931): 61–71; "The Influence of Islamic Culture upon the West," vol. 1, no. 2 (1931): 177–82; and a number of essays on the errors of modern "spiritism" in vol. 1, no. 3 (1931): 355–60; vol. 1, no. 5 (1931): 593–97; and vol. 1, no. 7 (1931): 813–16.
13. See *Azmat al-'ālam al-mu'āṣir,* trans. with introduction by Sāmī Muḥammad 'Abd al-Ḥamīd (Cairo: al-Nahār, n.d.).
14. *Maqālāt min Rīnīh Jīnu al-Shaykh 'Abd al-Wāḥid Yaḥyā,* trans. with introduction by Zaynab 'Abd al-'Azīz (Cairo: Dār al-Anṣār, 1996); see also *Madkhal 'āmm ilā fahm al-naẓariyyāt al-turāthiyyah,* trans. 'Umar al-Fārūq (Cairo: al-Majlis al-A'lā li'l-Thiqāfah, 2003).
15. See Martin Lings, *A Sufi Saint of the Twentieth Century.*
16. See Ja'far Kansusi, ed., *Sagesse et splendeur des arts islamiques: Hommage à Titus Burckhardt* (Marrakesh: Les Éditions Al-Quobba Zarqua, 2000).
17. *La Crise du monde moderne* was translated by Ḍiā' al-Dīn Dihshīrī as *Buḥrān-i dunyā-yi mutajaddid* (Tehran: Mu'assīsi-yi Muṭālī'āt wa Taḥqīqāt-i Ijtimā'ī, 1970), and other editions; and *Le Règne de la quantité* by 'Alī Muḥammad Kārdān as *Sayṭara-yi kammiyat wa 'alā'im-i zamān* (Tehran: Sharif Technical University Press, 1982), and other editions. *La Crise du monde moderne* was the first book by Guénon to be translated into Persian. I therefore wrote an introduction to this Persian translation to introduce his whole corpus of writings and his significance to the Persian-speaking world.
18. These included the Persian translation of the essay of Martin Lings on Guénon, trans. M. Hidāyatī, *Naqd wa Naẓar* 4, nos. 3–4 (Summer and Fall, nos. 15–16, 1998): 68–79; "*Faqr*" by Guénon, trans. Muṣṭafā Malikiān (89–95); "Shell and Kernel" by Guénon, trans. Furūzān Rāsikhī, nos. 19–20 (1999): 396–97; Maḥmūd Bīnā Muṭlaq, "René Guénon and the Real Meaning of Tradition" (in Persian), nos. 15–16: 80–87.
19. *Ma'ānī-yi ramz-i ṣalīb,* trans. Bābak 'Alīkhānī (Tehran: Surūsh, 1995); *Islām wa tā'u'īsm,* trans. Dilārā Qahrimān (Tehran: Ābī, 2000); *Buḥrān-i dunyā-yi mutajaddid,* trans. Ḥasan 'Azīzī (Tehran: Ḥikmat Press, 1387 A. H. solar).
20. Ḥusayn Khandaqābādī, ed. (Tehran: Tawsi'a-yi Dānish wa Pajūhish-i Īrān, 2002), esp. pp. 12–17. See also the special edition of the journal *Ettlela'at Hekmat va Ma'refat* 3, no. 2 (May 2008), entitled *Sunnat-garāyān* ("Traditionalists").
21. Occasionally discussions and debates are held between such figures and opponents of the traditional perspective even on public television and radio or in various journals. See, for example, the long essay "Tradition" (in Persian) in *Naqd wa Naẓar,* nos. 15–16 (1998): 6–67, much of which deals directly with the views of Guénon.

22. The list of translations into Turkish of of Guénon's works, which has been prepared for this essay by Ibrahim Kalin and Harun Tan, is as follows: *Agarta Dünya Kralı*, trans. Haluk Özden (Istanbul: Ruh ve Madde Yayınları, 2008); *Alemin Hükümdarı*: Dinlerde Merkez Sembolizmi, trans. Ismail Taşpınar (Istanbul: İnsan Yayınları, 2004); *Büyük Üçlü*, trans. Veysel Sezigen (Istanbul: İz Yayıncılık, 2007); *Dante ve Ortaçağ'da Dini Sembolizm*, trans. Ismail Taşpınar (Istanbul: İnsan Yayınları, 2001). *Doğu Düşüncesi*, trans. Lütfi Fevzi Topaçoğlu (Istanbul: İz Yayıncılık, 1997); *Doğu ve Batı*, trans. Fahrettin Arslan (Istanbul: Yeryüzü Yayınları, 1980); *Geleneksel Formlar ve Kozmik Devirler*, trans. Lütfi Fevzi Topaçoğlu (Istanbul: İnsan Yayınları, 1997); *Hristiyan Mistik Düşüncesi*, trans. Ismail Taşpınar (Istanbul: İnsan Yayınları, 2005); *İnisiyasyona Toplu Bakişlar 1*, trans. Mahmut Kanık (Istanbul: Hece Yayınları, 2003); *İnisiyasyona Toplu Bakışlar 2*, trans. Mahmut Kanık (Istanbul: Hece Yayınları, 2003); *İslam Maneviyatı ve Taoculuğa Toplubakış*, trans. Mahmut Kanık (Istanbul: İnsan Yayınları, 1989); *Kadim Bilimler ve Bazı Modern Yanılgılar*, trans. Lütfi Fevzi Topaçoğlu (Istanbul: İnsan Yayınları, 2000); *Maddi İktidar Manevi Otorite*, trans. Birsel Uzma (Istanbul: İz Yayıncılık, 1997); *Manevi İlimlere Giriş*, trans. Lütfi Fevzi Topaçoğlu (Istanbul: İnsan Yayınları, 1997); *Metatron Dünya Kyarallıgı: Kiyamet Işçileri Ülkesi, Agarta'nın Öyküsü*, trans. Haluk Ozden (Istanbul: Ruh ve Madde Yayınları, 1992); *Metafizik Nedir?, Gabriel Marcel, René Guénon, Henri Bergson*, trans. Mustafa Tahralı (Istanbul: Birey Yayıncılık, 1999). *Modern Dünyanın Bunalımı*, trans. Nabi Avcı (Istanbul: Yeryüzü Yayınları, 1979); *Modern Dünyanın Bunalımı*, trans. Mahmut Kanık (Istanbul: Hece Yayınları, 2005); *Niceliğin Egemenliği ve Çağın Alâmetleri*, trans. Mahmut Kanık (Istanbul: İz Yayıncılık, 1996); *Ruhçu Yanılgı*, trans. Lütfi Fevzi Topaçoğlu (Istanbul: İz Yayıncılık, 1996); *Savaş Metafiziği ve Sembolik Silahlar*, Julius Evola, René Guénon, trans. Lütfi Fevzi Topaçoğlu (Istanbul: İnsan Yayınları, 2000); *Varlığın* Mertebeleri, trans. Vildan Yalsızuçanlar (Istanbul: Etkileşim Yayınları, 2008); *Vedanta'ya Göre İnsan ve Halleri*, trans. Atilla Ataman (Istanbul: Gelenek Yayınları, 2002); *Yatay ve Dikey Boyutların Sembolizmi*, trans. Lütfi Fevzi Topaçoğlu (Istanbul: İnsan Yayınları, 2001).
23. *The Reign of Quantity* and *The Crisis of the Modern World* were brought out first, followed by *The Multiple States of Being* and *Fundamental Symbols of Sacred Science*.
24. See vol. 2, nos. 1–4 (1993). This important journal devoted to the exposition of traditional teachings ceased publication after a few issues.
25. Later reprinted in the journal *Studies in Tradition:* "Namā Rūpa," vol. 1, no. 1 (1992); "Know Thyself," vol. 1, no. 2 (1992); "Anguish and Anxiety," vol. 1, no. 3 (1992); "Saif ul-Islam," vol. 1, no. 4 (1992).
26. For example, one can cite numerous articles that he wrote in Urdu and that appeared in various periodicals and later in his collected works, *Majmū'ah-i Muḥammad Ḥasan 'Askarī* (Lahore: Sang-i Mīl Publications, 2000). Most important of these were "Ibn 'Arabī and Kierkegaard," "Bāray Amoṇ kā Bayān ho Jā'ī," "Waqt ki Rāgnī," "Riwāyat kiyā nay," and "Urdū kī Adabī Riwāyat."

27. *L'Erreur spirite* and *Études sur l'hindouisme.*
28. Muḥammad Ḥasan 'Askarī, *Jadīdiyat* (Rawalpindi: 'Iffat Ḥasan, 1979).
29. Shams al-Raḥmān Fārūqī from India was among these people, and he later developed a remarkable acumen in literary criticism along traditional lines.
30. Published in various journals, including *Al-Bilāgh, Al-Rahīm, Shāh Khān, Civil and Military Gazette,* and *Oriental College Magazine.*
31. 'Aṭā' al-Ḥaqq Qāsimī and Sirāj Munīr, eds., *Ma'āṣir,* no. 1 (1979): 621–32.
32. *Ma'āṣir,* no. 1 (1979): 633–43.
33. *Ma'āṣir,* no. 1 (1979): 644–56.
34. Muhammad Suhayl 'Umar, ed., *Riwīyat* 1 (1983): 57–80.
35. *Riwāyat* 1 (1983): 189–207.
36. *Riwāyat* 1 (1983): 217–33.
37. *Riwāyat* 1 (1983): 217–33.
38. *Riwāyat* 2 (1985): 163–77.
39. *Riwāyat* 2 (1985): 404–10.
40. *Riwāyat* 2 (1985): 411–18.
41. This section on Urdu works devoted to Guénon is quoted from a private communication from Muḥammad Suhayl 'Umar. Used by permission.
42. The following list has been prepared by Hafiz Nehad Kahteran. The first translations of Guénon's writings were published in Serbia as follows: Gaetan Pikon, *Panorama suvremenih ideja* ("Panorama of Contemporary Ideas") (n.d.); "Ezoterija," a translation of a chapter from *L'Esotérisme de Dante* in the journal *Delo* (Aug.–Sept. 1976); "Beleske o angeologiji arapskog alfabeta," in *Sufizam,* ed. Darko Tanaskovic and Ivan Sop (Belgrade, 1981); *Bilten autora,* no. 12 (Lucani, December 1986); "Mracno doba" ("Dark Age"), trans. Dragos Kalajić, in *Alef* (Gradac, 1987); "Velika Trijda" ("La Grande Triade"), trans. Dragos Kalajić (n.d.); "Simbolika Krsta" ("The Symbolism of the Cross"), trans. Miodrag Marković (Gradać, 1998).

    In Bosnia and Herzegovina the following have appeared: Rusmir Mahmutćehajić, "Uciteljstvo René Guénona" ("Teaching Profession of René Guénon"), in *Dijalog,* no. 1 (Sarajevo, 1997): 68–84; René Guénon, "Osvrti na tesavuf i tao" ("Aperçus sur l'ésotérisme islamique et le taoisme"), trans. Rusmir Mahmutćehajić and Neira Baralić (Sarajevo, 1988); Hafiz Nevad Kahteran, "Utiranje puteva perenijalnoj filozofiji u Bosni i Hercegovini" ("Paving the Ways for Perennial Philosophy in Bosnia and Herzegovina"; text dedicated to Guénon, Schuon, and Nasr), in *Glasnik* 58, nos. 9–10 (Sarajevo, 2001): 879–900; Hafiz Nevad Kahteran, "Philosophia Perennis," in *Znakovi vremena* 4/5, no. 13/14 (Sarajevo, Autumn–Winter 2001–2): 10–34; and Hafiz Nevad Kahteran, *Perennial Philosophy in the Thought of René Guénon, Frithjof Schuon and Seyyed Hossein Nasr* (Sarajevo: El-Kalem, 2002).
43. On his life, thought, and writings, see *The Essential Frithjof Schuon,* ed. with introduction by S. H. Nasr; the special issue of the journal *Sophia* (vol. 4, no. 2, Winter 1998) dedicated to him; Jean-Baptiste Aymard and Patrick Laude,

Frithjof Schuon: His Life and Teachings (Albany: State University of New York Press, 2004); and José J. de Olañeta, ed., *Frithjof Schuon (1907–1998)* (Mallorca: Sophia Perennis, 2004). A complete new English edition of his works is now being published by World Wisdom Books under the editorship of James Cutsinger, who is an Orthodox Christian scholar and theologian.

44. In 1957 when I first met Schuon at his house near Lausanne, he was as usual in completely traditional *maghribī* dress. He told me that many wondered why we insisted on wearing traditional Islamic dress here in the middle of Europe. He added that it was because the *barakah* of the Prophet of Islam flows through such dress and can be experienced concretely in it. It therefore brings this *barakah* to one's being and facilitates prayers and invocation, while helping greatly in the creation of a traditional Islamic ambience, in which Schuon himself lived and which he insisted his disciples create to the extent possible in the intimate spaces of their lives, most of all in their homes and prayer rooms.

45. Schuon later recounted how he desperately wanted to find a spiritual master and how he had decided that if he were not to find such a person, he would retire into the desert to pass the rest of his life in solitude and seclusion. But the hands of destiny led him to the great Algerian Sufi master Shaykh al-'Alawī. In recent years certain detractors have sought to cast doubt upon Schuon's attachment to the Shādhiliyyah-'Alawiyyah Order and his belonging to a regular initiatic chain (*silsilah*), which alone guarantees traditional continuity in Sufism. Let it be said, first of all, that there is no proof whatsoever that Schuon was not initiated into Sufism by Shaykh al-'Alawī. On the contrary, over the years numerous Algerian and Moroccan *fuqarā'* (members of a Sufi order) have attested to his having received the initiation at the hands of the great Algerian shaykh. In the 1960s I met a number of members of the Syrian branch of the 'Alawiyyah Order who asked me about how Shaykh 'Īsā was faring and told me stories heard by older *fuqarā'* about his coming to Mostaghanem in 1932 and having been received into the *ṭarīqah* by Shaykh al-'Alawī, who put him in his first *khalwah,* or spiritual retreat. Only a few years ago in Morocco I again heard similar stories from older Shādhilīs who asked about him.

As for his being chosen a *muqaddam* (that is, an official spiritual representative of a shaykh and one who is given the function of both initiating and guiding disciples), even if this were to be cast into doubt by his detractors against the facts, this denial would not in itself destroy initiatic continuity. Many *fuqarā'* in various Sufi orders who were not designated as *muqaddams* (high-level representatives) or *khalīfahs* (vicegerents) later became shaykhs through the Will of Heaven. The history of classical Sufism is replete with such cases, especially in the earlier centuries when various functions prevalent in later Sufism did not as yet exist. In any case, the veritable nature of any *shaykh* or *murshid* can only be gauged by the quality of his disciples. A tree is judged by its fruits.

In this context it might also be added here that in 1938 when he was in Cairo, Schuon was also initiated into the Qādiriyyah Order and, like certain other Sufi masters, of whom Ibn 'Arabī is a well-known example, possessed more than one initiation. Schuon had also told me that early in his life, after entering the 'Alawiyyah Order, he had had an encounter with Khaḍir, the "Green Prophet," who corresponds to Elias (Elijah) in the Western tradition and who represents an ever-living initiatic function in the Islamic universe. This encounter could not have had nothing to do with the "Eliatic function" of Schuon himself. See Leo Schaya, "La mission d' Élie," *Sophia Perennis* 3, no. 1 (Spring 1977): 16–28; also as "The Mission of Elias," *Studies in Comparative Religion* (Summer–Autumn 1980): 159–67.

46. See Frithjof Schuon, *Dimensions of Islam,* trans. P. Townsend (London: Allen & Unwin, 1970), chap. 2, pp. 30–45.
47. See Frithjof Schuon, *In the Face of the Absolute* (Bloomington, IN: World Wisdom, 1989), pp. 209–34. This essay was originally written upon my request and published in *Islamic Spirituality: Foundations,* ed. S. H. Nasr (New York: Crossroad, 1989), chap. 4, pp. 48–63, under the title "The Spiritual Significance of the Substance of the Prophet."
48. A case in point is his essay "The Five Divine Presences," in *Dimensions of Islam,* chap. 11, pp. 142–58, which is a most profound discussion of the doctrine of *al-ḥadarāt al-ilāhiyyat al-khams* (the five Divine Presences), a doctrine that has been discussed over the past seven centuries by many eminent metaphysicians going back to Ibn 'Arabī and Ṣadr al-Dīn al-Qunyawī.
49. See his *L'Oeil du coeur* (Paris: L'age d'Homme, 1995). The essay "*An-Nûr*" was also published in English in *Dimensions of Islam,* pp. 102–20.
50. See, for example, his "Some Observations on a Problem of the Afterlife," in *Dimensions of Islam,* chap. 10, pp. 136–41; "The Two Paradises," in *In the Face of the Absolute,* pp. 235–49, which also contains references to classical Quranic commentaries; and "The Sufi Paradise," in *Islam and the Perennial Philosophy,* trans. J. Peter Hobson (London: World of Islam Festival Trust, 1976), chap. 10, pp. 181–87.
51. See Schuon, *Islam and the Perennial Philosophy,* chap. 5, pp. 91–110.
52. A good example is "Dilemmas Within Ash'arite Theology," in *Islam and the Perennial Philosophy,* chap. 7, pp. 118–51.
53. A seminal essay dealing with this subject is his "Tracing the Notion of Philosophy," in *Sufism: Veil and Quintessence,* trans. W. Stoddart (Bloomington, IN: World Wisdom, 1981), chap. 5, pp. 115–28.
54. This work was reprinted later as *Urbesinnung: Das Denken des Eigentlichen* (Freiburg im Breisgau: Autum, 1989).
55. *Tage und Nächtebuch* (Bern: Urs Graf, 1947).
56. *The Transcendent Unity of Religions.*
57. *The Eye of the Heart* (Bloomington, IN: World Wisdom, 1997).
58. *Spiritual Perspectives and Human Facts.*
59. This work, to which a number of other sections were added, appeared in English as *In the Face of the Absolute.* The English work therefore contains *Approaches du phenomène religieux,* but does not comprise only its translation.

60. Nothing is more difficult than translating Schuon's sentences into a Semitic language such as Arabic. It is a more daunting task than rendering them into Persian, not that the translation of his works into Persian is in any sense easy. As for Arabic, I spent three years with a leading Egyptian scholar, the late Ṣalāḥ al-Ṣāwī, translating *Understanding Islam* into an Arabic that would be classical and at the same time contemporary. The translation under the title *Hatta nafham al-islām* was published by Dār al-Muttaḥidah li'l-Nashr in Beirut in 1980 and is known in the Arab world by scholars in the field, as are the Turkish and Persian translations of this seminal work in Turkey and Iran.
61. *Roots of the Human Condition* (Bloomington, IN: World Wisdom, 2002).
62. One would also need to add to this list the names of Michel Valsân, who was Shaykh 'Īsā's disciple and his *muqaddam* in Paris. Some of Valsân's disciples such as Michel Chodkiewicz became themselves outstanding scholars of Sufism. There is moreover a whole younger generation of scholars writing mostly in French and English on various Islamic subjects who are influenced by Schuon's works.
63. It is also important to mention here the journal of the Imperial Iranian Academy of Philosophy, *Sophia Perennis,* in which several of Schuon's articles were published in the 1970s. Translations of Schuon's books into Persian include the following: *Gawhar wa ṣadaf,* trans. Mīnū Ḥujjat (Tehran: Suhrawardī, 1381 [A.H. solar]); *Islam wa ḥikmat-i khālidah,* trans. Furūzān Rāsikhī (Tehran: Hirmis Press, 2008); and *Manṭiq wa ta'ālī,* trans. Ḥusayn Khandaqābādī (Nigāh-i Mu'āṣir, 1387 [A.H. solar]).
64. Schuon's books that have been translated into Turkish include: *İslam ve Ezeli Hikmet,* trans. Şahabeddin Yalçın (Istanbul: İz Yayıncılık, 1998); *İslam'ı Anlamak,* trans. Mahmut Kanık (Istanbul: İz Yayıncılık, 1996); *İslam'ın Metafizik Boyutları,* trans. Mahmut Kanık (Istanbul: İz Yayıncılık, 1996); *Tasavvuf: Kabuk ve Öz,* trans. Veysel Sezigen (Istanbul: İz Yayıncılık, 2007); *Varlık Bilgi ve Din,* trans. ahabeddin Yalçın (Istanbul: İnsan Yayınları, 1997); and *Yansımalar,* trans. Nurullah Koltas (Istanbul: Hece Yayınları, 2006). (List of Turkish translations prepared by Harun Tan).
65. Besides the Arabic translation of his *Understanding Islam,* his works in Arabic include *al-Īmān wa'l-islām wa'l-ihṣān,* trans. Nihād Khayyāṭah (Beirut: Mu'assisat al-Jāmi'iyyah . . . , 1996).
66. See James Cutsinger, ed., *The Fullness of God: Frithjof Schuon on Christianity* (Bloomington, IN: World Wisdom, 2004).
67. The Quran presents a universalist doctrine of religion and revelation, but this has not been developed fully in Islamic history except in a few cases, such as those of Ibn 'Arabī and Rūmī. It was providential that this dimension of the Quranic revelation should receive its full elaboration in our times in the hands of the traditionalist writers, foremost among them Schuon. In this context, see the works of Reza Shahkazemi, who was one of his disciples.
68. It should not be forgotten that certain classical Sufi masters, such as Rūmī, had

Christian and Jewish disciples and that in India many Sufi masters accepted Hindu disciples.

69. For the bibliography of Burckhardt in European languages, see *The Essential Burckhardt,* ed. William Stoddart, with preface by S. H. Nasr (Bloomington, IN: World Wisdom, 2003), pp. 311ff.
70. The translation of his works into Persian includes *Hunar-i islāmī-zabān wa bayān,* trans. Mas'ūd Rajabniā (Tehran: Intishārāt-i Ṣidā wa Sīmā-yi Īrān, 1365 [A.H. solar]); *Hunar-i muqaddas-uṣūl wa rawishhā,* trans. Jalāl Sattārī (Tehran: Surūsh, 1990); *Darāmadī bar ā'īn-i taṣawwuf,* trans. Ya'qūb Āzhand (Tehran: Mawlā, 1374 [A.H. solar]); *Jahān shināsī-yi sunnatī wa 'ilm-i jadīd,* trans. Ḥasan Ādharkār (Tehran: Hikmat, 1388 [A.H. solar]); and *Kīmīyā: 'ilm-i jahān, 'ilm-i jān,* trans. Gulnāz Ra'dī and Parwīn Farāmarzī (Tehran: Hikmat, 1387 [A.H. solar]). One can hardly overemphasize the importance of his works on Islamic art, especially *The Art of Islam,* in present-day Iran.

    As for Arabic, a number of his essays are translated in *al-Ḥikmah wa'l-funūn al-islamiyyat al-'arīqah,* ed. Ja'far Kansūsī (already cited as *Sagesse et splendeur des arts islamiques*; also his essay on the teaching of Islamic art appears in S. H. Nasr, ed., *al-Falsafah wa'l-adab wa'l-funūn al-jamīlah* (Jeddah: King Abdulazziz University, 1984).

    Turkish translations include *Aklın Aynası: Geleneksel Bilim ve Kutsal Üzerine Denemeler,* trans. Volkan Ersoy (Istanbul: İnsan Yayınları, 1987); *Astroloji ve Simya,* trans. Mehmed Temelli (Istanbul: Verka Yayınları, 1999); Şeyh el-Arabi Ed-Darkavi, *Bir Mürşidin Mektupları,* ed. and trans. from Burckhardt's translation; Ibrahim Kalın (Istanbul: İnsan Yayınları, 1996); *İslam Sanatı Dil ve Anlam,* trans. Turan Koç (Istanbul: Klasik Yayınları, 2006); *İslam Tasavvuf Doktrinine Giriş,* trans. Fahreddin Arslan (Istanbul: Kitabevi Yayınları, 1995). (List of Turkish translations prepared by Harun Tan.)
71. On this remarkable saintly Sufi and her works, see *Two Who Attained,* trans. Leslie Cadavid (Louisville, KY: Fons Vitae, 2005).
72. There is some debate between scholars as to whether Sayyidah Zaynab is buried outside Damascus or in Cairo. In each of those cities there is in fact a tomb, or more strictly speaking *maqām,* identified with her, and both are sites of pilgrimage by vast multitudes coming from near and far. Whatever the historical reality, they are both her *maqāms,* where she resided, and are loci of the emanation of great *barakah* associated with the saint.
73. *Fez: City of Islam.*
74. He translated *Orient et occident* as *East and West* under the name of his maternal grandfather William Massey.
75. *Splendours of Qur'an Calligraphy and Illumination* (London: Thesaurus Islamicus Foundation, 2004), with stunning illustrations.
76. *The Secret of Shakespeare* (the title give to the new enlarged edition of the work; Cambridge: Quinta Essentia, 1996).
77. See Martin Lings, *The Elements and Other Poems* (London: Perennial, 1967); and *The Heralds and Other Poems* (London: Perennial Books, 1970).

78. Published as *Sufi Poems: A Mediaeval Anthology* (Cambridge: Islamic Texts Society, 2004). Lings was also an eloquent translator of the verses of the Quran, which he rendered over the years in a most poetic and elegant English. These verses have been collected in *The Holy Qur'ān: Translations of Selected Verses* (Cambridge: Islamic Texts Society, 2007).
79. *A Sufi Saint of the Twentieth Century,* pp. 214ff.
80. For a bibliography of his works in English, see *A Return to the Spirit* (Louisville, KY: Fons Vitae, 2005), p. 170.
81. *Symbol and Archetype: A Study of the Meaning of Existence* (Cambridge: Quinta Essentia, 1991).
82. *The Eleventh Hour: The Spiritual Crisis of the Modern World in the Light of Tradition and Prophecy* (Cambridge: Quinta Essentia, 1987).
83. *A Return to the Spirit.* Since this work was brought out after his death, it includes (pp. 83ff.) a long section entitled "In memoriam" consisting of numerous tributes that reflect his wide influence and impact.
84. First published in 1952 under his Muslim name and followed by many later editions, this work has also become a classic in Sufi studies.
85. This work has had several editions in both Britain and North America, for example, London, Islamic Texts Society, 1991. It has also been translated into several Islamic and European languages. It received a high award from the president of Pakistan soon after its publication.
86. *Mecca from Before Genesis Until Now* (Cambridge: Archetype, 2004).
87. Ling's works have been translated into Arabic, Persian, and Turkish as well as other Islamic languages, such as Malay, Urdu, and Bosnian. An Arabic example is *al-Shaykh Aḥmad al-'Alawī al-Ṣūfī al-Mustaghānimī al-Jazā'irī,* trans. Muḥammad al-Muwāfī (Beirut: Dār al-Kutūb al-Jadīd, 1973).

    Persian translations include *'Irfān-i islāmī chīst?* trans. Furūzān Rāsikhī (Tehran: Suhrawardī Press, 1378 [1978]); *'Ārifī az al-Jazā'ir,* trans. Naṣr Allāh Pūrjawādī (Tehran: Iranian Center for the Study of Civilizations, 1981); and *Hunar-i khaṭṭ wa tadhīb-i qur'ānī,* trans. Mihrdād Qayyūmī Bīdhindī (Tehran: Garrūs, 1998).

    Some Turkish translations are *Anitk İnançiar Modern Hurafeler,* trans. Nabi Avcı, Ufuk Uyan (Istanbul: Yeryüzü Yayınları, 1991); *Hz. Muhammed'in Hayatı,* trans. Nazife Şişman (Istanbul: Insan Yayınları, 1997); *Onbirinci Saat,* trans. Ufuk Uyan (Istanbul: Insan Yayınlaryı, 1998); *Shakespeare'in Kutsal Sanatı,* trans. Ihsan Durdu (Istanbul: Ayışığı Kitapları, 2001); *Simge ve Kökenörnek Oluşum Anlamı Üzerine,* trans. Süleyman Sahra (Istanbul: Hece Yayınları, 2003); *Tasavvuf Nedir?* trans. Harun Sencan (Istanbul: Akabe Yayınları, 1986); *Tasavvuf Nedir?* trans. Veysel Sezigen (Istanbul: Vural Yayıncılık, 2008). (List of Turkish translations prepared by Harun Tan.)

INDEX

Page references followed by *p* indicate a photograph.